THE ORIGINS OF MODERN GERMANY

THE ORIGINS

OF

MODERN GERMANY

BY

G. BARRACLOUGH

Fellow of St. John's College, Cambridge
and Sometime Fellow of Merton College, Oxford

BASIL BLACKWELL OXFORD

1962

FIRST PUBLISHED 1946
SECOND REVISED EDITION 1947
FOURTH IMPRESSION 1962

PRINTED IN GREAT BRITAIN FOR
BASIL BLACKWELL & MOTT LTD. BY
THE COMPTON PRINTING WORKS (LONDON) LTD. LONDON, N.1.
AND BOUND BY
THE KEMP HALL BINDERY, OXFORD

98911

CONTENTS

LIST OF MAPS

PREFACE TO FIRST EDITION

MANY books have been written in recent times on the history of modern Germany, beginning with the rise of Prussia in the eighteenth century or the redrawing of the map of Europe in 1815. The present volume covers wider ground. Its subject is the origin and rise of modern Germany; and the search for the original factors governing German history — which is essential matter for all who wish to understand the German question of to-day — carries us back into a remote past. No one is likely to underrate the importance for the rest of Europe — and, indeed, for world-history — of the German reaction, beginning in the days of Bismarck, to the crisis of modern industrial capitalism; but the peculiar character of that reaction is only comprehensible in the light of Germany's past. Factors deeply rooted in German history — both in the history of the German people in relation to their governments and in the history of the German states in relation to the other states of Europe — constituted an iron framework, a mould within which were cast all German efforts, from 1870 to 1939, to cope with the problems of modern capitalist society.

There cannot be too many analyses of capitalist society, both in its political and in its economic aspects, between 1870 and 1939. But there is a danger that the fierce light of publicity, which the present intense interest in the causes of international instability has thrown on the history of the period 1870-1939, may blind instead of illuminate. This danger will be real, unless awareness of immediate causes and contemporary events is counter-balanced by a deeper understanding of the continuity of history and of its underlying currents. In the seamless web of human history the years 1870-1939, which loom so large to us, are an episode; and we must beware of supposing that, because they lie nearest to us, they are more relevant than other phases of the past.

The present volume is therefore an attempt to establish the perspectives of German history, in the hope and belief that wider perspectives will cast a clearer light on present perplexities and problems. There has been a 'German problem' since at any rate the beginning of the sixteenth century; and although inevitably in a twentieth-century environment that problem has taken new shape, it is assuredly true that no attempt at a solution can succeed which, treating it in a purely modern context, ignores its long-standing causes and the enduring factors which have governed its history. It was because, as it seemed to me, there was a widespread tendency to devise remedies without a painstaking analysis of causes, that in 1944 (when the end of the war drew visibly near) I decided to write the pages which follow. Of their limitations no one is better aware than I; but a charitable reader will, I hope, account for some by the fact that the greater part of what follows was written under conditions of active service in the Royal Air Force. For this reason only a fraction of the literature I should have liked to have consulted was available to me. It was, however, less my intention to provide a work of scholarship, for which many more months of preparation would have been necessary, than to make available the conclusions and reflections springing from a study of German history which dates back now more than fifteen years to the time when I had the privilege of studying in the University of Munich. More than once, before the war ended, I was tempted to abandon the task; and I might have done so, had any other book covering the same ground been available in the English language. But the gap remained to be filled; and the importance of the subject demanded at least some attempt by an English historian to fill it.

Whatever disagreement in detail or even in principle the following pages may provoke, I therefore hope that they may provide that indispensable broad historical background without which no valid assessment of the 'German problem' of to-day and to-morrow, or of proposals for its solution, is possible.

January 1946   G. B.

PREFACE TO SECOND EDITION

THE friendly reception accorded to these pages has given me, sooner than I had anticipated, the opportunity to prepare a revised edition in the light of criticisms and suggestions offered privately and in the press. I am grateful particularly to Dr. H. Liebeschütz and Mr. P. Grierson for drawing my attention to erroneous or doubtful statements, and I have done my best with one exception to profit from all suggestions I have received. That exception is the widespread demand for substantial expansion of the sections dealing with the nineteenth and twentieth centuries. That there is still room for a full objective treatment of German history since 1815 by an expert on the period, I do not doubt; but apart from the fact that it would have been impossible within the limits of a single volume, any attempt to meet this demand would have completely altered the plan of the present book, which is concerned less with the history of modern Germany — the main facts of which are, after all, well known — than with historical analysis of its background, and which seeks, in its treatment of the period 1815-1939, only to demonstrate the underlying continuity. Even so, I hope the book may serve to explain certain aspects of German history which have not always been very well understood, for no one would suggest that understanding of German history is less vitally necessary to-day, in 1947, than it was two or more years ago when this book was first written.

March 1947   G. B.

PART ONE

THE FORMATION OF
MEDIAEVAL GERMANY
(800-1075)

CHAPTER I

THE GERMAN PEOPLES IN THE CAROLINGIAN EMPIRE AND THE RISE OF THE GERMAN DUCHIES
(800–918)

I

THE coronation of Charles the Great at the hands of Pope Leo III in St. Peter's in Rome on Christmas Day, 800, marks the birth of western European civilization. That civilization had been in gestation for many generations; thenceforward began its own independent existence. Merovingian civilization, an inglorious 'alliance of decrepitude and barbarism', looked back to a past which it could not emulate; Carolingian civilization, filled with a new breath of life, looked forward.

The reappearance of an Empire of the West in 800 has always appealed to the imagination of historians, the majority of whom have seen in the new empire the culmination of centuries of endeavour, the achievement of the conscious strivings of western intellects like Alcuin and of the movement of blind forces binding together the peoples of the west under the rule of the Frankish kings. For many it was a conscious revival of ancient Roman glory, symbolized in the erection at Aachen of a cathedral – originally the chapel of Charlemagne's own palace – the architectural inspiration of which was the Emperor Justinian's foundation, San Vitale in Ravenna. These two churches, the one completed in 547, the other consecrated in 805, seem to reveal graphically and symbolically the bonds uniting the last great emperor of Rome and the first great emperor of the west.

The actual chain of events leading to the consecration of Charlemagne as emperor was more modest. Without adopting the views of a distinguished French historian who, with scathing wit, described the coronation ceremony in St. Peter's as 'a comedy improvised by a handful of antiquarian-minded ecclesiastics', we shall do well to guard against attributing too weighty significance to Charlemagne's new title, which added nothing to his power and brought no accretion to his dominions. Perhaps the real importance of the imperial title, its value to Charles himself, lay in the sphere of foreign relations: it constituted a claim to independence from, even to equality with, the Empire in the East which still clung tenaciously to its legal title to lordship over all lands which the Roman emperors had ruled of old, in spite of the fact that its actual power had long been confined to the eastern shores of the Mediterranean. When, after protracted negotiations and even preparations for war, the ruler of the east, in 812, at length accepted Charles as emperor in the west — until then he had, in the eyes of strict Byzantine legitimists, been a mere usurper — one major achievement was secured: in place of the one undivided Roman empire with its capital in Constantinople, there were now two empires, an Empire of the East and an Empire of the West. This achievement — rendered durable by the rise of Islam, which won control of the Mediterranean sea-routes, thus severing for generations the life-line between Christian east and Christian west — left western Europe free to develop on its own, unencumbered by the oriental traditions of Byzantium.

• In this sense, the foundation of the Carolingian empire, marking the irrevocable breach between east and west, was undoubtedly a turning point in history. In any other sense we must not rate its importance too high. It did not constitute Charles ruler over western Europe: England, for example, and Spain owed him no allegiance, still less the Scandinavian north, which had not yet emerged from the obscurity of pre-history. Nor did it change the foundations of his power, which lay north of the Alps far from the imperial city of Rome. Charles became emperor because, as King of the Franks since 768 and King of the Lombards since 774, he alone could afford the Pope the protection the papacy needed amidst the turbulence of Rome in 800; but even after his coronation as emperor he remained first and foremost a Frankish king. It was from the lands of the Frankish kings that he drew his revenues; it was from among the vassals of the Frankish kings that he selected his ministers and servants. The seat of his power was still in the lands of his Frankish forbears between Rhine, Moselle and Meuse. His government moved from royal palace to royal palace without a fixed abode; but it is to Aachen or Ingelheim that we must look if we are seeking the centre of its wanderings, not to Rome. The strength and still more the stability of the new empire depended upon the strength and stability of the Frankish kingdom, and in a lesser degree upon the personality and abilities of the Frankish royal dynasty. If the Frankish kingdom remained strong and united, the empire would survive; but if the Frankish kingdom divided, the material foundation of the empire was gone, leaving only an empty title.

Three factors prevented the survival of the Frankish empire. The one was internal dissension and the deficiencies of Carolingian government; the second was the diversity, geographical and social, historical and cultural, of the lands incorporated within the empire; the third, and most important, was the impact of invasion from east, south and north, the incursions and ravages of Magyars, Saracens and Vikings, which acted as a solvent of Carolingian society, bringing in their trail devastation, economic retrogression, poverty, depopulation and a collapse of the new culture which had flourished in Carolingian monasteries and at the Frankish court. The strain of invasion and constant warfare reduced life to a struggle for existence, from which Europe as a whole scarcely recovered before the beginning of the eleventh century. When it recovered, it was a new Europe. Thrown back on local resources for withstanding the onslaught, subject to varying degrees of pressure from without, the different provinces of the Carolingian empire each reacted in its own way to the invaders; and the characteristic reactions of each, the different methods by which the threat of invasion was met in each part of Europe, modified the political and social structure, calling forth new and reawakening old forces. When, after more than a century, the barbarian threat was thrown off, the face of Europe had changed; not only were new states arising, but the new states had now each its own distinctive form and institutions.

Nevertheless, the new states of tenth-century Europe — France, Germany and Italy and the kingdoms of Lorraine, Burgundy and Provence, which arose from the decomposed body of the Carolingian empire — were not merely the accidental results of the upheavals of the ninth century. Beneath the superficial uniformity imposed by the Franks, each province of the Carolingian empire had its own life, its own history, its own problems and its own geographical peculiarities. These were the elements which went into

B

the crucible of war and invasion; and what emerged from the fire of rapine, want and brutal slaughter, was still composed of the same elements as before. These elements not only explained the different ways in which the different waves of invasion were met; they also determined the form of the new societies which emerged. The Carolingian empire was not a homogeneous state with a uniform political tradition. Already in Charles the Great's own day fundamental differences can be observed between the provinces which, after the wave of Barbarian invasions had passed, were to become France, and those which were to fall within the German kingdom. We must examine these differences because already in Carolingian times factors were at play, hidden by the superficial uniformity imposed by the Frankish kings on their wide domains, which were later to have a major part in determining the course of German history.

II

The Carolingian empire was not a homogeneous state with a uniform political tradition. Leaving aside the Kingdom of Lombardy, which was not conquered by the Franks until 774, and confining our attention solely to the lands north of the Alps, a number of fundamental differences are immediately evident between the eastern and the western halves of the Frankish lands. In the first place there are the basic geographical conditions: regional variations apart, there is no doubt that, compared with the west, the east as a whole was undeveloped, interspersed with large tracts of virgin forest and (particularly in Saxony) areas of marshy waste. But geography cannot be considered apart from human history; for geographical conditions were shaped by human settlement and cultivation. Here again the east was retrograde by comparison with Frankish Gaul which, by the end of the eighth century, had enjoyed generations of settled rural life and stable rural economy. Except in the Rhineland (and to a smaller degree in Bavaria) there was little municipal life in the east. Nor, on the eastern frontiers of the empire, was there the atmosphere of peace which accompanies settled rural and urban conditions. It is characteristic of the stability of the west that Charles the Great's successor, Louis the Pious, gave the Archbishop of Rheims permission to dismantle the Roman walls encircling his city and use the stone for rebuilding his cathedral, because (in the words of the chronicler) 'he was enjoying profound peace and, proud of the illustrious might of his empire, had no fear of barbarian incursions'. It is equally characteristic of the east that Charles the Great deliberately organized 'marches' on the borders of Saxony and Bavaria — the Saxon march and the Ostmark — for the express purpose of holding off incursions and ravages by such tribes as the Abodrites, the Sorbs, the Wends and the Avars, just as the Spanish march was established beyond the rampart of the Pyrenees to keep the Arab menace at a distance.

All these factors produced a diversity within the Carolingian empire which marked off one region from another. Their importance was, however, doubly emphasized by the fact that the different territories incorporated in the domains of the Frankish kings had been added at very different times and at very different levels of culture and social development. We must, in the first place, take account of the difference which five centuries and more of Roman provincial life made to the social and political environment of the western, as compared with the eastern parts of the later Frankish empire. Secondly, we must bear in mind the duration of Frankish control. Certain provinces, like Burgundy or Aquitaine, with an ancient culture of their own, had long been penetrated by Frankish civilization and Frankish institutions, although they had exploited successive weakenings of Frankish power under the successors of Clovis (486-511) to revert to a more autonomous position. Others, like Saxony and Lombardy, only came under Frankish control in the reign of Charlemagne himself, and hardly experienced more than a generation of unimpaired Frankish rule. In Lombardy the Franks found themselves face to face with a civilization in all material respects as advanced as their own: in Saxony, on the other hand, they had to deal with a people which had not yet reached the stage of monarchical government, which had never experienced the benefits of Roman administration and which had not yet been converted to Christianity. Bavaria which, unlike Saxony, had undergone Roman colonization and had a long history of contact with the Franks, retained a semi-independent position under its own dukes until as late as 788, when Charlemagne deposed duke Tassilo III and, instead of appointing a successor, divided the land up among Frankish counts, bringing it within the framework of the

Frankish county organization. Yet within a few months of Charlemagne's death, in the 'partition' of the empire which took place in 817, Bavaria reappeared as a subordinate kingdom, while by 833 Saxony was again leading a separate existence, with the other German lands, under the rule of Louis the German.

No people more tenaciously resisted Frankish conquest and incorporation in the Frankish empire than the Saxons under their famous leader, Widukind. Charles the Great's Saxon wars, which began in 772 and were not ended until 804, lasted a whole generation; and Saxon opposition to the Franks was only finally overcome after large numbers of the inhabitants with their families had been forced to leave their land and settle in Frankish territory, and the great annual assembly, in which the political life of the Saxon people had been incorporated, was brought to an end.

By measures such as these the Frankish conquerors, spreading out far and wide from their homeland between Meuse and Moselle, sought to obliterate the independence of the conquered peoples. Just as Charles the Great suppressed the Bavarian dukedom in 788, so Charles Martel had suppressed that of Swabia in 730, while Thuringia was brought under the direct rule of the crown in 741. In place of the native ruling classes Frankish counts were introduced to administer the land on behalf and for the profit of the Frankish king.

The question facing us is how successful these and similar administrative measures were. Were they effective and durable enough to obliterate long-standing provincial or 'tribal' cohesion, or did persistent regional divergencies, on the contrary, cut deep into administrative organization? Here again, we shall understand the position in the east, or German, parts of the empire better if we compare them with Frankish Gaul. In the west, the Franks inherited a Roman provincial organization of government — comprising *civitas, diœcesis, comes*, etc. — which was already functioning; and it was only necessary at the time of the invasion to introduce Frankish counts into the existing administrative machinery in order to direct government in accordance with the interests of the new Frankish ruling class. In the eastern or German provinces, on the other hand, there was no suitable administrative machinery in existence which could be taken over and adapted to Frankish needs and interests; here the Frankish counts were themselves the agents through whom a new framework of administration had for the first time to be established, organized and built up. For this task, however, they had incomparably less time than in the west, since the eastern provinces were (as we have already seen) only finally incorporated into the Frankish empire in the course of the eighth century. Moreover, the very circumstances in which they were appointed differentiated the Frankish counts in Saxony or Bavaria from their contemporaries in Gaul. In the east, the Frankish count was a royal commissioner appointed to enforce and maintain Frankish rule over a conquered people; his essential task was to watch over the interests of his master, the Frankish king, and his functions were primarily political.

In Merovingian Gaul, the functions of the *grafio*, or count, had originally been identical with those which the Carolingian counts, three centuries later, exercised in the German provinces of the east. There also a popular form of self-government, in which an elected *thunginus* (or 'thing-man') directed the affairs of the *Gau*, had persisted for some generations after the Frankish conquest; and the *grafio* or count was simply the King's local agent, the local administrator of the King's estates and his military representative. But this dualism of function between the popularly-elected *thunginus* and the royal *grafio* was of short duration in Gaul. By the end of the sixth century the count had supplanted the *thunginus*, and at the same time we find him appointing a delegate, his *vicarius* — who later takes the title of 'viscount' — through whom he controls and supervises the 'hundreds' within his county. The very fact that the words *vicaria* and *centena* (hundred) become interchangeable is evidence of the subordination of the older units of government to the count, of the replacement of the popularly-elected 'hundredman' by the count's deputy or 'vicar'. Thus in France the county organization gradually altered and absorbed the whole organization of local government. The old local institutions, which derived their strength from the communities which had settled the land as independent groups, waned and perished. The sense of local independence was lost; and France, partly as a result of the Roman traditions of government with which the Gallo-Roman population was imbued, but still more as a result of many generations of slow reconstruction, became under the Carolingians a state in which government was organized from top to bottom, in which authority was derived from above and penetrated down from the king through the counts to the subordinate localities.

This development was confined to Gaul, where Frankish settlement was longest and most enduring. In the eastern provinces the introduction of the county organization failed to produce parallel administrative changes or innovations. Few of Charlemagne's great judicial innovations penetrated into Saxony or other German provinces of the Frankish empire.[1] When the Franks conquered Lombardy, they succeeded to the work of Lombard kings like Luitprand and Aistulf; but in the German provinces there was no heritage of royal government to take over. The Saxons only elected a king, the Alemannians a duke, in time of war and then only for the duration of the war; hence royal institutions to which the popular hundred organization might have been subordinated, were lacking. The old popular judicial organization, which had been swept aside in Gaul, remained in existence; and the function of the count after the Frankish conquest was hardly more than to watch over it. He was the supervisor of a group of hundreds, and in the German east his authority was personal, not territorial. In Gaul, the counties take the names of cities or districts; east of the Rhine they are named after the count in possession. We must not, therefore, think of the Frankish county organization in Germany as a network of fixed and delimited territorial units. In spite of the Frankish conquest the old indigenous hundred organization remained the basis of local government.[2] In Frisia the doomsmen elected by the people of the hundreds, the *asegen*, were never replaced by the

[1] For example, the creation of bodies of sworn doomsmen or *Scabini* in every county, who were chosen by the count and appointed for life, and who had to swear an oath of office. This measure, which meant that the count chose his own colleagues in the execution of justice and had a permanent body on whose co-operation he could rely, was evidently a major contribution to the stability of the county organization; but there is no evidence of its assimilation in any of the Eastern provinces of Charles the Great's empire. Cf. Brunner-v. Schwerin, *Deutsche Rechtsgesch.* II, 301, A. Meister, *Deutsche Verfassungsgesch.* (1922), 184.

[2] Charles the Great's ordinance separating the competence of the county and hundred courts, and assigning to the former the more important, to the latter the minor causes, has been a great cause of confusion. What was at issue was simply the question of competence, not the territorial organization of the courts. The hundred courts were still the only courts, but they functioned in two distinct ways; first in major pleas under the count, and secondly in minor pleas under the hundredman. In both cases the court was the hundred court, and a county court as such did not exist. The county court was the hundred court sitting under the presidency of the count. Moreover, count and hundredman each had the same sphere of action: each acted within the hundred court, but the competence of each reached out beyond the hundred in which he was sitting to the whole group of hundreds which together formed a county. There was no special court, distinct from the hundred courts, for the whole county, since the county was not a distinct territorial unit but simply those hundreds over which a representative of the Frankish king, the count, exercised control. Cf. A. Gasser, *Die Entstehung und Ausbildung der Landeshoheit im Gebiet der Schweizer Eidgenossenschaft* (1930), 13 sqq.

Frankish *scabini*. In Saxony the *Gograf*, who is also elected, remains in existence with his court, the *Gogericht*; while in the south the *Zehntgericht* of Swabia had substantially the same importance as the *Gogericht* of Saxony. During the Carolingian and Ottonian periods the hundred courts, the original and really vital units of local life, were submerged for a time under the superimposed county organization; but their identity and vitality was not lost, and the re-emergence of the hundreds with an extending sphere of competence, which began in the twelfth century,[1] is conclusive evidence that government in Germany, as contrasted with France, had its roots in the local community. If in Gaul the county organization with three centuries of steady penetration behind it had become rooted in the soil, replacing popular local institutions, one or two generations of Frankish control were insufficient to achieve the same result in Germany. Frankish monarchy handed over — as we shall see — a substantial legacy to the later German kings; but by contrast with France, the inheritance of royal government was only one among many factors. Equally important for the future were the local communities with a deep sense of their own individuality and memories of recent independence.

III

After the death of Charlemagne (814) centrifugal forces within the empire soon got the upper hand. Charles himself, in 813, had sought to maintain the unity of his lands by associating his sole surviving son, Louis the Pious, with himself as emperor; but the notion of primogeniture was still weak and, consonant with the Frankish tradition of the division of the inheritance among all heirs, Charles conferred the kingship of Italy on his grandson, Bernard. Louis himself, after his succession, proceeded similarly, associating his own eldest son, Lothar, with him in the empire in 817, and allotting subordinate kingships in Aquitaine and Bavaria to his younger sons, Pepin and Louis. These schemes, although re-affirming the separate existence of outlying provinces like Bavaria, had the merit of maintaining the unity of the main core

---

[1] Cf. Meister, *Deutsche Verfassungsgesch.*, 185. See below, p. 145.

of the Frankish empire; but feuds among the sons of Louis the
Pious, revolts and civil wars which came to a head after Louis'
death in 840, soon led to further disintegration, culminating in the
famous Treaty of Verdun (843). This treaty, concluded as the result
of the intervention of the Frankish nobility to put an end to the

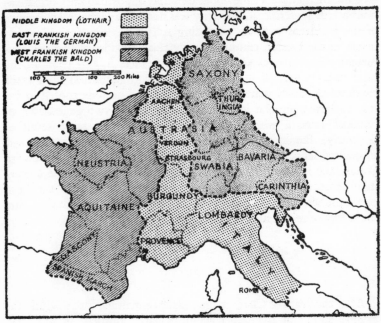

The Carolingian empire at the time of the Treaty of Verdun (843)

internecine warfare, was intended to strengthen the unity of the
empire by a peaceful division of government among Louis' three
sons: the west (Neustria, Aquitaine and the Spanish march) to
Charles the Bald; the central lands of the Middle kingdom including Frisia, Austrasia as far as the Rhine, Burgundy, Provence and
Italy, to Lothar; and Franconia east of the Rhine, Bavaria, Swabia,
Thuringia and Saxony to Louis the German. In fact, the division
marked the dissolution of the Frankish empire; for although Lothar
(with Rome and Aachen and the old homeland of the Carolingian
dynasty in his possession) kept the title of emperor, his brothers
were in practice independent sovereigns.

It is still usual to regard the Treaty of Verdun as reflecting the first emergence of the great monarchies of mediaeval and modern Europe, and to see in the division of the Carolingian empire the dawning of national sentiments and aspirations. This view is not easily reconciled with the facts. The division of the empire resulted not from racial or provincial differences, but from dynastic conflicts within the royal house.[1] In the civil wars between 832 and 840 only the Bavarians, whom he had ruled since 817, consistently supported Louis the German; the attitude of the other provinces east of the Rhine — Saxony, Thuringia, Franconia and Swabia — fluctuated, but on the whole they remained true to Louis' father, the Emperor Louis the Pious. In the wars of succession after Louis the Pious' death, the position remained the same, complicated in the case of Saxony by social divisions, the aristocracy supporting Louis the German because the mass of the freemen supported Lothar. There was, in short, no sign of German unity in the succession-wars leading up to the Treaty of Verdun.[2] Nor, after the succession of Louis the German as east Frankish king in 843, was there any unity of the German lands: Louis relied primarily on Bavaria, and after 852 neither he nor any subsequent east Frankish king set foot in Saxony.

The importance of the Treaty of Verdun lay primarily in its destructive effects on the foundations of royal power. The basis of Carolingian government was threefold: the royal estates which provided the material foundation of government, the personal obligations of the royal vassals who were the agents of royal government throughout the empire, and the Church. The dynastic struggles of Carolingian claimants and the division of the empire at Verdun adversely affected all three. The landed wealth of the Carolingian house was concentrated above all in the old homeland of the dynasty in the Middle kingdom (hence the further partitions of this territory and the repeated attempts of east and west Frankish kings to annex it): in the east, particularly in Saxony and Thuringia, royal estates were few and the material foundation of royal power correspondingly weak. No less significant were the effects of the

---

[1] Cf. Haller, *France and Germany. The History of One Thousand Years* (1932), 5. The idea that the unity of the Frankish realm was destroyed through the divergencies of the different nationalities was refuted by G. Monod in the *Annuaire de l'École des Hautes Études*, 1896.

[2] This important point was clearly established by G. Tellenbach, *Königtum und Stämme in der Werdezeit des deutschen Reiches* (1939), 24-28.

Treaty of Verdun on the higher clergy and the outstanding lay families, which, as servants of Charles the Great, had taken a major practical share in administering and welding together the empire. Both groups supported the policy of a united Empire. In particular, the great comital families, 'international' in character,[1] with possessions spreading throughout the empire, had every interest in maintaining imperial unity; but dissensions within the Carolingian house forced them to take sides. It was not, as historians have so often maintained, a question of a spirit of egotism and self-interest among the counts, of an inherent tendency to 'feudal anarchy' which only a strong hand from above could suppress. On the contrary, the bulk of the aristocracy clung to the legitimate Carolingian claimant. But it was a moot question which among many was the legitimate claimant. There was, in the Carolingian empire, no constitutional machinery for deciding such issues, except the clear designation of his successor by the ruling king. Once dissension arose within the ruling house, as it arose to the accompaniment of war and bloodshed after 832, the only answer was an appeal to armed power.

It is not difficult to see the effects of such a situation on a government so highly dependent on the bonds between king and vassals as that which Charles the Great had established. Carolingian government depended on the loyal services of the *vassi dominici* of the king, a small body of selected families, half of them related to or allied by marriage with the Carolingian dynasty.[2] The wars of succession broke up this class. Numbers alone were inadequate, if the *vassi dominici* were divided out between the different kingdoms emerging from the partitions. Furthermore, the constant flow of capable and trusted vassals from the centre, which had been a remarkable feature of Charlemagne's own reign, ceased when France and Italy and Germany and Burgundy and Lorraine all owed allegiance to different rulers. On the other hand, the character

[1] Cf. R. Poupardin, 'Les grandes familles comtales à l'époque Carolingienne', *Revue historique*, LXXII (1900), 72 sqq.

[2] The small numbers involved are remarkable. Tellenbach, who has compiled a comprehensive list of the great families active in Carolingian government, enumerates only 111 names from only 42 families. Of these 52 were allied with the dynasty. Omitting 3, whose origins are obscure, the list comprises 70 Franks (from 27 families) — mainly Ripuarian Franks springing, like the Carolingians themselves, from the lands between Meuse and Moselle — and 26 Swabians and Alsatians (from 8 families). The remainder is made up of 6 Bavarians (2 families) and 6 Saxons (2 families). Cf. *Königtum und Stämme*, 68.

of earlier Carolingian government meant that there was no immediate and obvious substitute. Relying on their own vassals, the
earlier Carolingians had not cultivated the loyalty of the local
nobility in the lands over which they extended their rule. This was
particularly true in the east Frankish kingdom, where the Carolingians placed little trust in the recently conquered Saxons and
Bavarians and gave all important offices to Franks and Swabians.
In Saxony only one local family was associated with government
until the second half of the ninth century, when a second family —
the famous Liudolfinger dynasty, from which sprang the later
Saxon kings of Germany — rose to prominence. In Bavaria it was
only under Arnulf of Carinthia (887-899), an illegitimate Carolingian whose mother was a Bavarian, that the 'Bavarian aristocracy
began to assume importance.

Thus between 840 and 887 the basis of Carolingian government
was gradually undermined. But there was as yet nothing durable
to take its place. The landed aristocracy, which alone exerted
political power, still gave its support to the Carolingian dynasty,
which — in spite of its maintenance of the old practice of partition
and its failure to develop a system of primogeniture — still drew
strength and lustre from the current belief in the almost super-
natural legitimacy of the line. In 884, profiting from the death of
his relatives, Charles the Fat reunited for a brief spell the whole
Carolingian empire with the exception of Provence. But a new factor
changed the situation, creating peremptory demands with which the
Carolingians could not cope. This factor was the growing peril
from without, the invasions of Danes and Magyars and Saracens.
Charles the Fat, unable to give protection and forced to pay tribute
to the Vikings besieging Paris, was deposed in 887. The only
surviving Carolingian was a child, still less able to cope with the
threatening situation. Thus a new solution was imposed by circumstances. In Germany the illegitimate Carolingian, Arnulf, succeeded
in imposing his rule; but it was rule imposed by the king on the
people. Arnulf forced his acceptance on the nobles; he was not
elected.[1] Moreover, Arnulf's aim was succession to the full
Carolingian inheritance, not the establishment of an independent
east Frankish or German kingdom; this was shown by his relations
with the *reguli* who sprang up after 887 in the other provinces of the

[1] Cf. Tellenbach, op. cit.. 36.

Carolingian empire, most of whom were glad to accept his suzerainty. Arnulf's state, weak though it was by comparison, was in true succession to the state of Charles the Great; his conception of his royal position and government was Carolingian through and through. Meanwhile the menace of invasion from east and west and south reached new intensity; and with it came changes which were to destroy the foundations of Carolingian government and establish in place of the empire the great states of mediaeval Europe. After Arnulf's death in 899, in the stress of invasion, devastation and plunder, the foundations of a separate German kingdom were laid.

IV

Viking raids had occurred in the reign of Charlemagne himself. A generation later the Northmen began wintering in the lands they were attacking: in Ireland in 835, in France in 843, in England in 851. From their stronghold on Walcheren, they became the scourge of Frisia until defeated by Arnulf at Louvain in 891. In the meantime in the east the Magyars, who were a more serious menace to the east Frankish kingdom than the Vikings, had appeared on the borders of Bavaria in 862. In 899 they swept through the Bavarian Ostmark into the Lombard plain; a few years later in 907 they defeated the Bavarians; then in 915 thrusting northwards, they sacked Bremen, and in 919 harried Saxony and penetrated as far as the old Middle kingdom.

The broad general effects of the invasions were everywhere the same. Everywhere there was what has been called a 'sinking of the demographic curve' – in plain terms, a marked and general decline in population. Parallel with this there was – in marked contrast with the earlier Carolingian period – a decline in the amount of land under cultivation, a grave economic setback. Old boundaries were lost, land returned to nature, cultivation ceased in wide areas. Everywhere also there were empty stomachs, persons seeking a patron who could give them a livelihood. And everywhere, finally, a need for protection was felt. At the same time Carolingian administration, based 'upon internal stability in the realm and upon the integrity and continuous functioning of the several devices of government', suffered dislocation and many Carolingian institutions proved

unable to 'maintain themselves in the face of adverse circumstances'. [1]
With its foundations crumbling and new problems arising, with
which it was ill-fitted to deal, it abdicated the onerous task of battling
with the invaders, providing protection and maintaining a semblance
of order, to other powers which rose by proving their capacity in the
anarchy of invasion and war.

These new powers took different shapes in the different parts of
the Frankish empire. In the west, where the Frankish county
organization spread in a solid network over the countryside, the
counts were the backbone of resistance. As such they increased their
political power, at the expense of the monarchy. They built castles
to give protection to the people of their countryside; and the persons
protected became their 'men'. In this way arose French feudalism.
At the same time the *vassi dominici*, on whom the Carolingians had
relied for the administration of government, died out as a class; [2] a
few rose in status and imposed themselves as lords over a wide
countryside, the majority sought the protection of the rising powers
and sank to the level of sub-vassals. Thus the anarchy due to invasion
led to another type of anarchy, in which one feudal lord imposed
his authority over others, and built himself a principality by absorbing counties and franchises; it produced a struggle of all against all,
in which certain families, relying on their own strength and persistence and intelligence, forced the smaller counts and barons to accept
their suzerainty. The result was that in France there were by the beginning of the tenth century some thirty distinct territorial divisions,
and that three generations later the number had risen to fifty-five.

The situation in the German lands in the east of the Frankish
Empire was far different. The historical preconditions for a development such as took place in the west were lacking, except in Lorraine
which had a large number of Frankish comital families and which
approximated in history and internal development to Frankish Gaul.
Elsewhere in the east, as we have seen, the county organization was
too rudimentary to provide a solid basis for resistance to the invaders;
nor had the German lands experienced to the full in Carolingian
times the progress towards vassalage and the decline in the status of
the free man, which was one reason·for the rapid progress of

---

[1] J. Goebel, *Felony and Misdemeanour*, I (1937), 131-133.
[2] Their last mention occurs in a charter of 943; cf. F. Lot, *Études sur le Règne de Hugues Capet*,
216.

feudalism in France. In the east, therefore, the stress of invasion necessarily produced a reaction different from that which led to the growth of French feudalism.

Instead of thirty or forty small territorial units, as in France, the period of Viking and Magyar invasion saw in Germany — excluding Lorraine — the rise of five great duchies: Franconia, Saxony, Thuringia, Swabia and Bavaria. These duchies represented in general shape and outline the German 'nations' which had been subjugated and brought within the Frankish empire generations earlier; and many historians, observing this fact, have seen in the rise of the duchies during the reigns of Arnulf (887-899), his son Ludwig the Child (899-911) and Conrad I (911-918) an 'instinctive and spontaneous rally of the German people, owing to the stress of the times around their natural and historical tribal representatives', 'a sort of resurrection of the ancient Germanic nations', which, 'not having been in the least degree affected by the partitions of their territory into counties, reconstituted themselves', since each had its own 'special customs and dialect' and therefore 'possessed a true moral personality'.[1]

This account of the rise of the German duchies, attractive though it is, does not altogether reflect the known facts.[2] The German 'nations' were not homogeneous racial or territorial units; they were not held together by a common language, local dialects being confined within far narrower bounds; nor were they united by legal institutions, which varied from class to class far more than from 'nation' to 'nation', or by political assemblies. More important, the families which rose to power in the German duchies at the end of the ninth century were in no case 'natural and historical tribal representatives'. Without exception they were Carolingian administrators, counts and margraves (*Markgrafen*), who increased their powers in time of war and invasion and assumed the title of 'duke'. The duchy was, in the words of one of the most famous of German historians, 'a revolutionary authority, whose only justification was the stress of the times'.[3] And the roots of this 'revolutionary authority' were military, not tribal or racial, military organization being

---

[1] L. Reynaud, *Les Origines de l'influence française en Allemagne* (1913), 118; J. W. Thompson, *Feudal Germany* (1928), 294.

[2] There is a critical review of the theories advanced in explanation of the rise of the German duchies in *Mediaeval Germany*, I, 26-35. The historical problems involved are also discussed at length by Tellenbach, *Königtum und Stämme*, whose views I have largely accepted.

[3] Giesebrecht, *Geschichte der deutschen Kaiserzeit*, I (1881), 806.

the only sphere in which racial or national differentiation was preserved. In the west, the Carolingians directed their summons to armed service indiscriminately to 'all inhabitants between Seine and Loire'. In Germany, on the other hand, the contingents were summoned 'nation' by 'nation', and in 869, for example, Louis the German divided his army, sending the Saxons and Thuringians to fight the Sorbs, the Bavarians against Moravia, and retaining the Franks and Swabians under his own command. The position of the Saxons is particularly significant: absorbed in the defence of their own land against the Slavs they were, as a people, freed by Louis the German from the obligation to take part in other campaigns, thus allowing them to devote all their energies to defence of the eastern frontiers.

The dukes who rose to power in Germany at the end of the ninth and the beginning of the tenth centuries were, in nearly every case, military leaders. In Saxony, the family of Liudolfinger, from whom sprang the later Saxon kings of Germany, began as *duces orientalium Saxonum*, i.e. military commanders on the eastern frontiers of Saxony. In Bavaria the ducal family sprang from Liutpold, the military leader in the Bohemian march, whose son Arnulf (907-937) assumed the title of duke of Bavaria. In Swabia, also, the ducal family first appears with the title *dux Raetianorum*, i.e. defenders of the Alpine passes of Switzerland. The pre-eminence won by these families was due partly to their services in defence of the frontiers, partly to the fact that, due to the small number of Carolingian crown vassals in the further provinces of the east, they had few competitors to face. In Franconia, where the Carolingian aristocracy was strongly entrenched, the situation was more complicated: here there was a long and bitter struggle — reminiscent of the feudal struggles in France — before one family secured predominance. But even here, and in Thuringia also, leadership of the army played a considerable rôle in the rise of the competing dynasties. It was the invasions from without, and the military necessities they created, which placed new power in the hands of the military leaders and the guardians of the frontiers, enabling — or perhaps compelling — them to extend their sway, until finally they assumed authority throughout the length and breadth of the province.

Such was not originally their position. The title or office of *dux orientalis Saxoniae* gave the Liudolfinger dynasty no rights over the Saxon people as a whole, particularly in time of peace. Nor, originally, was the title or office hereditary; kings such as Louis the German and Arnulf had no difficulty in dismissing *duces*, who enjoyed (so far as can be seen) little or no effective support from within their provinces against the monarchy. For long, however, the rising provincial leaders showed little inclination to exploit the disorders of the age with the object of establishing an independent position for themselves. So long as the Carolingian line remained in existence — even in the person of the illegitimate Carolingian, Arnulf — they were willing to take their place under the crown and serve the royal government.

This fidelity to the interests of the monarchy was proved when, on the death in 911 of Louis the Child, the son of Arnulf, the east Frankish branch of the Carolingian dynasty perished. True to Carolingian legitimist traditions, the Lotharingian nobility sought out Charles the Simple of France and placed themselves under his rule. For the other provinces of the east, on the other hand, the solution was not so easy. What they required above all else was help and leadership against Danes and Hungarians; and such help the west Frankish Carolingian, absorbed in the defence of France, could not be expected to provide. Apart therefore from Lorraine, which thus already showed signs of separateness, the east Frankish peoples were faced by the difficult problem of choosing a non-Carolingian king — a task which gave full scope for the interplay of provincial jealousy and personal interest. Yet few elections have in such circumstances proceeded with less friction than that of the Franconian duke, Conrad I. Far from seeking to exalt their own powers, the rising ducal families — particularly the Liudolfinger of Saxony, whose loyalty to the Frankish monarchy was proverbial — acting as leading members of the royal household rather than local territorial magnates, did their utmost to uphold royal interests by choosing a successor to Louis who could himself maintain the crown's rights and provide for the defence of the country. Conrad was chosen without opposition on the advice of the Saxon duke, Otto, and on Otto's advice was anointed king — unction at the hands of the episcopate serving to reinforce the position of a king who could not claim the divine right of Carolingian blood.[1]

---

[1] It was the first anointing of an east Frankish ruler, the cause almost certainly being the change of dynasty; cf. P. E. Schramm, 'Die Krönung in Deutschland', *Zeitschr. d. Savigny-Stiftung, Kanon. Abt.*, XXIV (1935), 195.

In spite of its auspicious beginning the reign of Conrad I (911-918) nevertheless soon witnessed far-reaching changes in the relations of crown and duchies. Whatever was done in 911 to strengthen Conrad's position, it remained radically different from that of his predecessors on the east Frankish throne. He was not a Carolingian and could not claim the same exalted position and loyal service as his Carolingian predecessors. In origin the strongest of the Franconian counts who — after long and bloody struggles with the almost equally powerful comital house of Babenberg — had wiped out his rivals, he had been set on the throne by men who were his equals and had risen in much the same way as he himself. If he had given a lead in war, he might have continued to command their loyalty and support. But his three campaigns to recover control of Lorraine were a failure, and he made no progress in the struggle against the Magyars. Instead, he set out to acquire the full powers of his Carolingian predecessors, seeking to establish his predominance throughout the east Frankish lands, as earlier he had established it in Franconia, at the expense of the other leading aristocratic families. In this policy he relied on alliance with the Church.[1] In the south Conrad based his rule on the support of Bishop Salomon III of Constance, in the north on that of Archbishop Hatto of Mainz, while in Bavaria the whole episcopate, led by Pilgrim of Salzburg, placed itself on Conrad's side when he attacked Arnulf of Bavaria in 916. In the same year the Synod of Hohenaltheim publicly proclaimed the alliance of crown and Church, threatening anathema against all of whatever rank or dignity who questioned the prerogative of the king.

The result of this policy was an immediate reaction on the part of the lay aristocracy, which for the first time came out in open opposition to the crown. Alienated from the monarchy by Conrad's intransigence, the leading magnates set about organizing their

---

[1] It has often been maintained that the east Frankish Carolingians also ruled through an alliance with the church against the dukes — a view reflecting the erroneous theory that the German duchies were already in existence in Carolingian times. Only in Swabia, however, is there evidence of an alliance between crown and Church in Arnulf's day; and this alliance had a concrete political basis, viz. the existence in Swabia of an extensive Carolingian aristocracy which had been the main support of the government of Arnulf's predecessor, Charles the Fat, and which was therefore opposed to Arnulf after Charles' deposition in 887. Elsewhere there was no alliance with the Church, because the lay aristocracy was in no sense antiroyal. With the accession of Conrad, however, the policy of alliance with the Church, which under Arnulf and his son had been confined to Swabia, was extended throughout the kingdom. Cf. Tellenbach, *Königtum und Stämme*, 38-39.

position and establishing duchies on a solid and permanent basis. The powers which they sought between 911 and 918 were regal or semi-regal in character; they were powers not under, but against the crown. Because of the changed political situation men such as Otto of Saxony, who had been a sponsor of Conrad's kingship, broke away from the monarchy and turned their energies to the rapid consolidation of a position of local autonomy. They sought to identify themselves with the peoples among whom they lived, to attract to themselves the loyalty of the inhabitants and to organize public life around their own persons, building up a new hierarchy of government at the head of which they stood. By 918 they were as powerful in their duchies as, a generation earlier, petty kings such as Boso of Vienne, Rudolf of Burgundy or Zwentibold of Lorraine, in their *regna*. Welding together loose provincial bonds, building on latent historical differences, they created duchies which were the equivalent of small kingdoms, at the same time laying claim to specifically ducal powers.

In the first place, they called the people around them in assemblies, thus assuring themselves of the support of the local nobility. Simultaneously they began to claim and exercise control over the churches in their land, nominating to bishoprics and abbeys and sharing in clerical income. Certain dukes, such as Arnulf of Bavaria and Burchard of Swabia, did not hesitate to pursue an independent foreign policy.[1] But the most significant innovation of all was the establishment of hereditary succession and popular election. In Bavaria, Arnulf succeeded his father, Liutpold, in 907, and was himself followed by his son Eberhard in 935; designated successor by his father, Eberhard subsequently received an oath of fealty from the Bavarian people, his succession thus in form resembling that of a king. The same holds true of the succession of Henry in Saxony in 912. As to Franconia, it is difficult to speak; for we do not know whether there was a duke in Franconia during Conrad's reign, nor do we know in what way Conrad's brother, Eberhard, became duke after Conrad I's death. Lorraine also stands apart, its development complicated by its intermediate position between France and Germany; but it is noteworthy that when, in 920, the nobility of the land turned away from the French king, to whom they had given allegiance in 911, they elected Giselbert as *princeps*. Swabia, on the

---

[1] We shall have to return to this aspect of ducal policy; cf. below, pp. 27, 48-49.

other hand, is a clearer case. Here the army raised their commander, Erchanger, to the dukedom in 915, after he had defeated Conrad I in battle. When he was killed in a subsequent campaign, another election followed; and even ten years later, in 926, in spite of the fact that the new duke was a royal nominee of non-Swabian origin, there is evidence of a meeting of the Swabian people and their assent to the nomination. Thus it is clear, in spite of the fragmentary nature of the evidence, that the dukes began after 911 not only to secure hereditary succession within their house, whenever possible, but also to obtain the assent and allegiance of the people of their duchies. Thus they set about creating bonds between duke and 'folk', which were affirmed in popular assemblies and strengthened by their growing hold over the churches within their lands.

The years 911-918 saw the creation in Germany of dukedoms with definite powers, and with a high, almost regal, conception of their rights. Partly due to the failure of Conrad I to deal with the Hungarian menace, partly owing to his alienation of the leading aristocracy, it looked as though the east Frankish kingdom was on the point of splitting, like the Lotharingian Middle kingdom, into a number of petty *regna*. This development was furthered by the persistence of deep-seated regional differences. It provided the setting in which the next century of German history was played out. When, in 918, Conrad I died and was succeeded by the Saxon, Henry I, the main internal problem facing the new king — a problem which engrossed the energies not only of Henry but also of his son Otto I — was to bring the duchies under the control of the monarchy and to ensure that they took their place within the framework of a united German kingdom.

CHAPTER 2

THE FIRST CENTURY OF THE GERMAN MONARCHY
(919-1024)

I

IN the last chapter we surveyed briefly the main factors, geographical as well as historical, which differentiated the German east from the other parts of the Carolingian empire in the ninth century. We saw how these factors, exploited and manipulated by astute and strong-willed men, were used, under the impact of political events, as a basis for the formation of the five great duchies: Franconia, Saxony, Bavaria, Swabia and Lorraine.[1] We must, however, be careful not to exaggerate the effects and durability of this development. There is no doubt that the fact of racial disunity — though hardly more serious than that of tenth-century England — favoured the pretensions of provincial magnates, which might, if left unchecked, have led to the break-up of the east Frankish or German kingdom. But the duchies were not, in 918, and never were to be, solid territorial blocks. Important political figures though the dukes were at the time when Henry I succeeded to the Frankish throne, it was still an open question whether the ducal office was destined to find a permanent place in German institutions. The political problems raised by the growth of the duchies were beyond doubt the most serious of the difficulties facing Henry I; but the rights which the dukes asserted were not yet firmly anchored in the constitution, they could still be moulded by a king with ability and political sense.

The future shape and constitution of Germany therefore depended, in 918, on the ability and material resources of the monarchy. It would be a serious error to suppose that the duchies held the field unchallenged in German politics at the beginning of the tenth century. When Henry I of Saxony succeeded Conrad in 919 less than a generation had passed since Arnulf had reconstituted a strong east

[1] The Thuringian duchy of pre-Carolingian times was not revived although some beginnings of Thuringian autonomy were evident at the end of the ninth century. The last mention of a *dux Thuringorum* occurred in 908; thereafter Thuringia tended increasingly to be absorbed into the sphere of Saxony.

Frankish kingdom. The tradition of Carolingian monarchy was not dead, nor was it a negligible political factor. Weak as were the foundations which the east Frankish rulers left for the German kings of the Saxon dynasty, they were strong in comparison with the basis on which the wielders of ducal power had to build. The inheritance of the dukes went back to the dark days of the dying ninth century: the inheritance of the German kings reached back to the heights of the Frankish monarchy.

This immediately became apparent when, in 919, the question arose of choosing a successor to Conrad I. Henry I of Saxony succeeded, not as a result of election by the German dukes or peoples, but because he had been nominated or 'designated' successor by the dying Conrad, who had called his brother, Eberhard, to his side and instructed him to hand over the royal insignia to Henry. Faithfully carrying out Conrad's orders, Eberhard went to Henry, handed over the insignia, and reaffirmed peace and friendship with the Saxon duke. Then, gathering together the leaders of the Frankish people, he 'designated' Henry king in the presence of the Frankish and Saxon peoples. Immediately afterwards Henry was offered consecration and coronation by the clergy, but this he refused, saying that it was sufficient if he were acclaimed and designated king before his magnates; whereupon the people, pleased with Henry's speech, raised their arms in acclamation and called aloud the new king's name.

Two facts stand out in these proceedings. First, the absence of Bavarians, Swabians and Lotharingians indicates that the transference of authority from Frank to Saxon, the accession of a new dynasty to the Frankish inheritance, was the work of the Franks alone, acting in the person of their leader, Eberhard. Secondly, the Saxons and Franks who were present did not elect Henry; they merely gave allegiance to the 'designated' king. The change of dynasty was not made the occasion for the assertion of novel electoral principles, but rather — like the election of 911 before it — was so contrived as to do the least possible injury to Frankish traditions of monarchy, in which the succession had always been a question of decision within the ruling house. Henry succeeded to the full inheritance of the east Frankish kingship. He ceased on his elevation to the throne to be a Saxon, gave up his native Saxon law for Frankish law, exchanged Saxon dress for the Frankish tunic, adopted the traditions and took over the powers of his Frankish predecessors. Despite the change of dynasty, there is in the documents emanating from Henry's chancery no sign of a repudiation of Carolingian traditions, just as Henry's political acts show no breach with Frankish precedent.

The proceedings at Fritzlar resulting in the elevation of Henry I to the throne, are thus evidence of the existence of an independent tradition of Frankish monarchy, which was a tangible counterweight to the power of the dukes. No one took the opportunity of Conrad's death to call in question the maintenance of the existing state; no one strove to introduce a revolutionary idea of 'elective' monarchy. The question in 919 was simply who was going to wield the existing royal authority. Besides Henry, there were two possible candidates: Burkhard of Swabia and Arnulf of Bavaria. The duke of Swabia, overawed by Saxon power, soon decided to submit to Henry, but Arnulf entertained ambitions of securing the German crown for himself with Bavarian support, and it needed a military campaign in 921 before he accepted the Saxon duke as king. Lorraine did not recognize Henry until 925. These facts clearly show the difficulty Henry had in asserting his position, and are an indication how far ducal independence had progressed between 911 and 918. On the other hand, even Arnulf of Bavaria, the most independent of the dukes, does not appear to have sought to break up German unity: his aim was to become German king, not the ruler of a separate Bavaria. Even in 919, therefore, the unity of the east Frankish or German lands was an accepted fact, and this unity was expressed in and through the monarchy, which could evoke against the stirrings of provincial autonomy and ducal ambition the traditions of the Frankish Church and the Carolingian kingship.

The question in 919 was whether the rights of the monarchy, already whittled away under Conrad I, would contract still further until they dissolved into a nebulous idea of monarchical overlordship over virtually autonomous duchies, or whether the new dynasty would succeed in giving new substance to the tradition of monarchy which it inherited from its Frankish predecessors. This question was decided in all essentials during the reigns of Henry I (919–936) and Otto I (936–973), but only after a hard struggle with the duchies. Otto I himself had three serious insurrections to face: in 937–8, 939 and 953–5. Otto II (973–983) had to fight four years before he finally overcame the opposition of Duke Henry of Bavaria; and even the last of the Saxon rulers, Henry II (1002–1024), met formidable internal opposition. The revolts of the tenth century, however, marked stages in the reassertion of royal power; they were the reaction of the aristocracy to a monarchy which was all the time placing itself more firmly in the saddle. Far from implying the persistence of strong provincial solidarity, they represented the inevitable hostility of ducal interests to the inexorable process of subjugation to the crown. That royal policy should have provoked bitter resistance, was only to be expected; but it was a resistance which, after the middle of the tenth century, expressed narrow interests more often than principles, reflected momentary opportunism, and had little if any prospect of enduring success.

The problem of the duchies was the key to the policy, both internal and external, of Henry I and Otto I. Three questions above all others called for solution. Were the royal estates going to be administered and controlled in each particular region by the duke? Were the counts — still the main vehicle of royal government — to become dependent not directly on the crown, but on the duke in the first place and only on the crown through a ducal intermediary? Was the duke to control the churches within his land, closing them to royal influence, and thus consolidating ecclesiastical as well as secular administration under his own control in furtherance of his own interests? In approaching these questions — with the solution of which the whole future organization of German government was bound up — Henry I's first care was Swabia, because Swabia, through its close connexion with Burgundy, Italy and the old Middle kingdom generally, was most likely to endanger the position of the German king and to break up the unity of the German people, of the *regnum Teutonicorum*, which was already a historical fact.[1] By 920 the king was again in control of the crown lands which lay within the Swabian duchy. By the end of Henry's reign Swabian bishops were once again attending German synods summoned by the king, whereas as late as 922 they had, with one exception, obeyed the Duke of Swabia's orders and remained away. Finally in 926 a new duke, nominated by the king, was appointed; a duke who was not a Swabian but a Frank by birth, and who was a representative and agent of the monarchy. The appointment of this royal nominee

---

[1] The phrase *regnum Teutonicorum* first occurs in 920; cf. *Monumenta Germ. hist., Scriptores,* XXX, 2, 1, p. 742. The most thorough examination of Henry I's policy is found in Lintzel, 'Heinrich I und das Herzogtum Schwaben', *Hist. Vierteljahrsschr.,* XXIV (1929).

shows that Henry, unlike Conrad I before him, was prepared to recognize the existence of the duchies; there was no question of abolition. But as a corollary to the recognition he gave, Henry was able, on the one hand, to set definite limits to the duke's competence (e.g. to reaffirm the direct connexion between crown and church) and on the other hand the new duke was a royal nominee closely bound to the monarchy and free from local ties.

The process which Henry I had started was continued by his son, Otto I. Already at Otto's coronation in 936, the monarchy's method of dealing with the duchies received striking symbolic expression. The dukes not only bound themselves to the king by ties of vassalage, thus giving him a handle by which to reduce them to dependence on the crown, but they also performed the ceremonial services at the coronation feast, recognizing in this way their position as royal servants. How effective these ties were, became evident only two years later. Arnulf of Bavaria had, as we have seen,[1] 'designated' his son, Eberhard, as his successor; and on Arnulf's death in 935, Eberhard received the allegiance of the Bavarian people. Relying on this twofold foundation of his power, the new duke refused to obey a royal summons to court. Otto's reply was to depose him, to set aside Arnulf's other sons and to confer the Bavarian duchy on their uncle, Berthold of Carinthia, who was forced to agree that he should nominate neither bishops nor counts. Furthermore, the crown lands in Bavaria were again brought directly under royal control, and by the side of the duke a count-palatine was appointed to watch over them and to safeguard royal interests within the duchy. The deposition of Eberhard, therefore, had a two-fold result: in the first place, it undermined the right, which had been asserted, for a duke to pass on his duchy in hereditary succession to his son and for a people to proclaim their own duke; in the second place, the king had once more regained control of the bishops and counts on whom the administration depended. As regards episcopal appointments and the control of the abbeys, Otto I's success was only temporary; ducal control over the Bavarian churches was not finally broken until the defeat of the Bavarian revolt of 975 by Otto II. But as regards the counts, Otto I's achievement was durable. Like other powerful lords, the dukes normally held a number of counties, which they administered through deputies or viscounts; but none of the ducal

[1] Above, p. 22.

families was able to assert control over all the counties within its province. The duke was not, in other words, the intermediary in the political hierarchy between the counts and the king. The counts were not appointed by him, but served under the crown. Even in Bavaria, where ducal power was strongest, it is now clear that the majority of counts were directly dependent on the king and free from intermediate ducal control.[1] If therefore we look, in the tenth century, for rights and functions which were specifically ducal, we shall not find them; if we seek to fit the dukes into the official hierarchy, we shall discover no vacant place. Henry I and Otto I gave the dukes personal recognition, but not a definite place in government; the duchy, as a potential administrative unit, had failed to obtain a fixed place in the constitutional order.

Swabia and Bavaria were the core of the problem facing Henry I and Otto I. In Saxony (which included Thuringia) and Franconia, where royal control was firm and the new dynasty had won support from the beginning, a solution was more easily found. When Henry I became king in 919 he appointed no successor to take his place as duke of Saxony; and although a new territorial power soon arose in Saxony, its basis was leadership in the east Saxon marches and not a duchy comprising the whole of the Saxon people. Hermann Billung, the founder of the new Saxon power, obtained lands and authority from Otto in eastern Saxony between the Weser and the Elbe, but Westphalia was retained by the king as crown land. Franconia, also, passed under the direct control of the crown after the death of Duke Eberhard, the brother of Conrad I, in the rebellion of 939, and was never again allowed to pass out of royal hands. From 939 onwards, therefore, Franconia became the special possession of the German monarchy: from whatever duchy the king originated, his own sphere of influence combined with Franconia, the land of the centre, formed a preponderant block, from the pressure of which no other duchy could permanently free itself. It dominated the routes from north to south and thus, apart from its strategic importance, allowed the king to keep his finger on the pulse of the country.

The policy of abolishing the dukedom and instituting in its place direct royal government through church and counts, which was applied in Franconia and Saxony, was not extended to Bavaria and

[1] This question has given rise to much controversy but appears to have been settled by M. Spindler, *Die Anfänge des bayerischen Landesfürstentums* (1937), 122.

Swabia, where the landed power of the Saxon kings was weaker. In the eleventh century, however, the position was different. Before succeeding to the throne Henry II (1002-1024) had been duke of Bavaria, and after his accession he kept the Bavarian ducal lands for the crown. Hence, for a period it seemed as though Bavaria also might come under the direct control of the monarchy; in the century between 995 and 1096 the Bavarian duchy was for no less than thirty-five years in the hands of the king himself, his consort or his son. But this was not to be. Nevertheless the power of the dukes in Bavaria, and also in Swabia and Lorraine, was progressively weakened. Bavaria, it has been said,[1] was treated like a geographical expression which could be divided at will. The Nordgau, comprising the lands north of the Danube between the Bohemian Forest and the Upper Main around Bamberg, was gradually separated from Bavaria between 938 and 976, and assimilated to Franconia, thus strengthening the very province where royal power was firmest. In the latter year Carinthia, with the marches south of the Alps, was separated from Bavaria and erected into a separate duchy, while the Bavarian Ostmark — later to be transformed into the duchy of Austria — received a regent of its own, who characteristically was a brother of the count in charge of the Bavarian Nordgau, thus creating on the two flanks of Bavaria a power which could counterbalance that of the duke. Lorraine, for a time under Otto I's brother, Archbishop Bruno of Cologne, was similarly divided during the same period. Swabia, which had lost Basel in 926 under Henry I, suffered no further territorial weakening, but the crown kept free disposition of the duchy; of the thirteen dukes between 926 and 1080 only one was a Swabian, the remainder Franks and Saxons.

II

By breaking up the territorial unity of the duchies, undermining ducal control of the church, securing royal nomination of the dukes and appointing at critical times members of the royal family, like Bruno of Cologne, the German kings of the Saxon dynasty gradually overcame the problem of provincial autonomy bequeathed by Conrad I. At the same time they preserved and consolidated the territorial cohesion of Germany. This achievement, which was the

[1] W. Sickel, *Hist. Zeitschrift*, LII (1884), 486.

precondition of further progress towards German unity under the German monarchy, was due to their success in building up the power, prestige and administration of the crown. As the duchies were weakened, the scope of royal government expanded; as royal government and the resources of the monarchy increased, the power of the dukes waned.

The Saxon dynasty triumphed over the inherent tendency to provincial autonomy and ducal ambition because it gave new substance to the tradition of monarchy which it inherited in 918. That legacy provided a foundation, but (as the reign of Conrad I had shown) it was in itself too weak to support a strong monarchy. Above all, the spoliation of the crown lands during the half-century between 870 and 918 had undermined the material basis of royal government. It has been calculated that, at the accession of the Saxon dynasty in 919, there remained, apart from 83 royal estates in Franconia, only 50 in Swabia, 21 in Bavaria, 12 in Thuringia and 5 each in Saxony and Frisia. In this respect, the change of dynasty brought an immediate change for the better. When Henry I became king in 919 the scattered royal estates were united with the family estates of the Liudolfinger dukes in Saxony, raising the total to about 600 properties, representing more than a threefold increase.[1] The material resources of the crown increased still further after 939, when the monarchy assumed direct control in Franconia. Nevertheless the importance of this increase in landed wealth, significant though it was, should not be exaggerated. Even at the end of the tenth century, the royal estates were still located almost exclusively in Saxony and Franconia, and therefore did not immediately strengthen the position of the monarchy in south Germany. In order to exercise royal control equally throughout the duchies, and particularly to strengthen its position in the south, the monarchy needed a less localized instrument. This it found in the Church.

There were solid practical reasons why the Saxon dynasty relied for local government on the Church, rather than on the secular hierarchy of counts. In the first place, there was not the danger of the establishment of hereditary succession, which weakened royal control over the counties and tended to turn the office of count into a property administered for the benefit of its occupant. In the second

[1] Cf. Thompson, *Feudal Germany*, 341; Seidlmayer, *Deutscher Nord und Süd im Hochmittelalter* (1928), 41.

place, the clergy was the educated class, trained to follow the ramifications of policy and competent to deal with the intricacies of legal
documents. Thirdly, local landed interests were scarcely as strong
among the clergy as among the laity, though with recruitment to
monasteries and cathedral chapters limited in the tenth and eleventh
centuries almost exclusively to members of the aristocratic classes,
this was not always the case. There was, moreover, without any
doubt a solidarity of interests between the monarchy and the Church,
which, in an age of lay oppression and exploitation, regarded direct
subjection to the monarchy as the surest guarantee of ecclesiastical
liberty. The alternative, in the age of violence which accompanied
and followed the Barbarian Invasions, was not between a Church free
from lay control and a Church under lay domination; it was between
a Church dominated and exploited by dukes and counts, and a
Church controlled, freed from oppression and utilized for the benefit
of the kingdom by the monarchy.[1]

This situation was fully understood by the clergy themselves. As
early as 916 the whole Bavarian episcopate had rallied to the side of
the monarchy against the duke, and just as control of the Church
gave the crown a *point d'appui* within the duchies, so dependence on
the crown gave the churches a *point d'appui* in their struggle to free
themselves from ducal exploitation. This alliance with the monarchy
had the approval and confirmation of the papacy; complaining in 921
that the duke of Lorraine had usurped the right of disposing of a
bishopric, Pope John X asserted that the king alone, according to the
ancient custom of the Church, had the right to appoint bishops.

The royal rights over the Church, recognized in this way by the
papacy, were not mere usurpation.[2] The king was, in the accepted

[1] 'Strong as Otto I was, the enormous wealth of the German Church still tempted some of
the great dukes in his reign to brave the might of the king. Henry of Bavaria blinded and
banished the Bishop of Salzburg and castrated the patriarch of Aquileia and divided the
episcopal estates among his vassals. Liudolf of Swabia seized the lands of the Bishop of Augsburg. The Lorrainer dukes Gilbert and Conrad often plundered the estates of the Archbishop
of Trier. The frequency with which such acts are mentioned implies the wide prevalence of
the practice. The bishops of Bremen, Metz, Liége, Hildesheim, Münster, Paderborn and
Cologne complain time and again of the greed of their feudal neighbours for their lands'
(Thompson, *Feudal Germany*, 29).

[2] John X's statement in the case of Giselbert does not stand alone. The chronicler Thietmar
of Merseburg, condemning the appointment of bishops by Duke Arnulf of Bavaria, writes:
'Rather our kings and emperors provide for such things, for they take the place of the highest
Lord in this earthly life, and rightly stand before all other pastors. For it would be entirely
unsuitable that the bishops, whom Christ has raised to be princes of this world, should be
subjected to any rule, save that of those who, after the example of the Lord, stand above all
mortals because of the nobility of their consecration and of the crown.'

view of the age, no ordinary layman; he had a mission from God, and in him God's ruling will was operative; set up and put down by God alone, his person was sacred. By his consecration — a mystery through which God conferred something of his power on the ruler — the king was constituted *rex et sacerdos*, and his sacerdotal position not only made him 'mediator' between clergy and people, a 'participant' in the ministry of the clergy, but also imposed on him the duty of 'ruling' the Church in his land. As representatives of Christ, acting in His name, kings were not merely servants and protectors but rulers of the Church. Indeed, the assertion was even made that, whereas the bishops were merely the representatives of Christ, the king was the Vicar of God the Father himself.

Because of his position as *rex et sacerdos*, the king could therefore use the Church, not as an uneasy ally or an unwilling tool diverted from its proper function, but as an instrument placed by God in royal hands for the work of civilization and social organization, regarding the objects of which Church and State were still as one. Already in the last few years of his reign, between 933 and 936, Henry I recognized the benefits to be gained from more direct contact with the ecclesiastical organization; but the transformation of the Church into a pillar of royal government in Germany was the work of Otto I (936-973), his son Otto II (973-983), and his grandson, Otto III (983-1002). These three reigns, and that of Henry II (1002-1024), saw royal control over churches and abbeys elevated into a principle of government.

The basis of Ottonian policy towards the Church was the withdrawal of bishoprics and abbeys and their lands from the ordinary ambit of secular administration, in which — due to the growing custom of hereditary countships — dukes and counts exercised local predominance, and their assimilation for administrative purposes to the crown lands over which, wherever they lay, the monarchy possessed direct administrative control. This was possible because, in view of its specially intimate relationship with the Church, the monarchy owed the Church protection and support;[1] and such protection was given by receiving churches and abbeys into the *mundeburdium* of the king — the *mundeburdium* being the special protection

---

[1] At his coronation the German king was addressed as 'protector of the Church of Christ in all adversities' ('strenuusque contra omnes adversitates ecclesiae Christi defensor'); cf. P. E. Schramm, 'Die Krönung in Deutschland', *Zeitschr. d. Savigny-Stiftung, Kanon. Abt.*, XXIV (1935), 319.

and authority exercised by a lord over his household and his household dependants. Singled out in this way as special objects of royal favour, churches and monasteries were 'exempted' from the ordinary jurisdiction of the counts, and erected into 'immunities' under special officers known as 'advocates', whose duty it was to provide protection and exercise administration within the Church estates on behalf of the king. Although frequently elected by the church or monastery which he was to serve, the 'advocate' was appointed by the king, received powers of office from the king, and was perhaps no more than a local agent or representative of the king, who was himself supreme advocate of all churches under his protection.[1] Hence the grant of 'immunity', far from loosening the bonds between the monarchy and the churches, created a new bond, stronger than the ordinary administrative connexion; it exempted churches from the ordinary county organization, but only in order to place them more directly under the control of the king. Thus, on the one hand, the power of the counts was diminished; on the other hand, the king assured himself of local resources throughout the land. Through the extension of 'immunity' the church became a mainspring of royal government in every part of Germany.

The grant of 'immunity' first became a general instrument of royal policy in Germany under Otto I (936-973). The first step was to ensure royal control of churches and monasteries founded and endowed by the king's predecessors and therefore *ipso facto* 'royal' foundations under royal protection. These had in many cases fallen under the power of dukes and other local magnates during the period of Barbarian Invasion; but by 951 Otto was strong enough to assert that all 'royal abbeys' — they numbered eighty-five by the end of the tenth century — were exempt from any secular authority save that of the crown and forbidden to enfief their lands without the consent of the king.[2] To these were added other foundations, which sought and received the benefits of royal protection, while in the course of the century it became the view, generally accepted by the time of Henry II (1002-1024), that the ancient bishoprics were royal foundations and as such subject to the same regime as the 'royal

---

[1] It is the merit of E. E. Stengel, *Die Immunität in Deutschland bis z. Ende d. 11. Jahrhunderts* (1910), A. Waas, *Vogtei u. Bede in der deutschen Kaiserzeit* (1919), and H. Hirsch, *Die Klosterimmunität seit dem Investiturstreit* (1913), to have elucidated the difficult and technical problem of 'immunity' and 'advocacy', which has been the source of much misunderstanding.

[2] Thompson, *Feudal Germany*, 37.

abbeys'. This was the position also of the new sees like Magdeburg, Brandenburg and Meissen founded in the colonial lands east of the Elbe after the first wave of German eastward expansion and conquest. By 1024 the sway of royal prerogative extended over all German bishoprics and the large majority of German abbeys.

As they broke the hold of the dukes over the churches and asserted their own ultimate control, the Saxon rulers increasingly gave the Church a share in secular government, at the same time endowing it, building up its landed wealth and favouring it with rights of toll and market, etc. Otto I distributed new immunities with a lavish hand, especially to the bishops, and confirmed many liberties which had formerly been conferred. After his death in 973 the privilege of immunity was so generally assumed that mention of it was frequently omitted in charters. Finally, Otto III (983-1002) in a decree of general application conferred the right of full justice upon all bishops within their domains, thus excluding the counts from all episcopal territories and diminishing their power.[1]

But ecclesiastical estates, built up from the gifts of the faithful, were usually scattered far and wide, and the immunity thus broke up the territorial cohesion of government. Hence, in order to strengthen the Church and make it a more effective instrument of government, the Saxon kings increasingly adopted the practice of investing bishops and abbots with the powers of counts, conferring whole counties on them, with all the rights and powers of the counts formerly in administrative control. Such grants were made by Otto I to the archbishops of Mainz, Cologne and Magdeburg and to the bishoprics of Speyer, Chur, Worms and Minden. But the culmination of the process was reached under Henry II when, following the rebellion of Count Henry of Schweinfurt, the Margrave of the Nordgau, in alliance with Bohemia and Poland, the king realized the necessity of erecting a safer defence for the heart of the country on both sides of the Main than Otto I and Otto II had succeeded in creating in the margraviate of the Nordgau. With this in view Henry II destroyed the power of the Schweinfurt family and, in 1007, set up in its place on the Upper Main the new bishopric of Bamberg, partitioning the counties of the old duchy of Franconia between his new foundation and the bishopric of Würzburg. Endowed in this way, Würzburg and Bamberg became the two great bulwarks of Germany on the

[1] Thompson, *Feudal Germany*, 41.

river Main: bulwarks of defence and outposts of Christianity against the pagan Slavs, and simultaneously bulwarks of royal government against the refractory nobility within the land.

The policy inaugurated by Otto I reached its culmination under Henry II (1002-1024), a man of deep religious conviction, who regarded it as his duty to exercise strictly and conscientiously the sacerdotal prerogatives of the monarch. Henry not only convoked synods and presided over their debates, regulating discipline, ritual and teaching; he also turned the royal chapel into a 'school' or training-ground for bishops, who were imbued with the same conscientious spirit as the king himself. Of the fifty episcopal nominees of his reign, Henry II himself personally invested forty-nine, and on these men he placed heavy responsibilities. Besides Würzburg and Bamberg, counties with their attendant rights and responsibilities were conferred by him on the bishoprics of Cambrai, Paderborn, Utrecht, Worms and Hildesheim, and the archbishop of Mainz was entrusted with the administration of the crown lands in Saxony. Bishops and abbots were rewarded with lands and privileges for the services they performed; but those services were real and onerous. In the council, in the chancery, on circuit in their dioceses, they attended to the king's business; they administered counties and acted as bailiffs of the king's estates. Moreover, apart from the work of administration, the churches had to bear out of their revenues the largest share in supporting the royal court, as it wandered from stopping-place to stopping-place through the land. The Church also provided the backbone of the army; 74 per cent of the forces for Otto II's Italian campaign of 981 were furnished by German abbeys and bishoprics, only 26 per cent by the laity. That ratio is eloquent of the part played by the Church in German government by the end of the tenth century, and of its importance for the political work of the monarchy. Less easily measured, but no less important, was its work of civilization and culture, which bound the provinces together around the king who was ruler of Church and State. The great bishops and abbots of Saxon times, travelling the country in the service of Christianity or king, broke down provincial boundaries, particularly the boundaries between south Germany and the Saxon north, thus contributing in large part to the consolidation of German unity.

III

The Church, which helped by its work of civilization in the consolidation of German unity, also had a major share in the first phase
of German eastward expansion and colonization, the main achievements of which fell between the years 929 and 983. These years
not only saw the defeat of the Hungarian menace, which had undermined German internal stability during the preceding half-century,
but also resulted in the annexation and settlement of a vast stretch of
territory extending from the mouth of the Elbe to Bohemia and
thence across the valley of the Danube east of Vienna to the mountains of Styria. Bohemia also became a tributary of Henry I in 929;
and although Czech resistance soon flamed up again in prolonged
warfare, Otto I compelled the Bohemian duke to accept German
overlordship and again to pay tribute in 950, although there was no
general influx of German colonists into Bohemia at this period.

There is no doubt that the defeat of the Hungarians, the subjection
of the Slav tribes along the Elbe and the creation of relatively settled
conditions on the eastern frontier contributed in a large way to
enhance the prestige of the Saxon dynasty, and to raise the Saxon
kings head and shoulders above the dukes, who had failed to solve
the problem of defence against the invaders. In this respect, Henry I's
policy was essentially a Saxon policy: for nine years, from 924 to
932, he bought off the Magyars, while he prepared the defence of
Saxony and Thuringia, building castles and fortified places as bases
for military defence and settling Frankish knights on Saxon lands, as
a professional element to stiffen the military levies of Saxon freemen,
who were no match for the Hungarian cavalry. Thus in a remarkably short space of time, an effective military organization was built
up, which proved its worth in the winter of 932-933 when the
Hungarians again made an appearance in Saxony. Henry's victory
over the Magyars in the battle of the Unstrut in 933 was a first check
to the Hungarian menace. It was not, however, until their defeat by
Otto I at Lechfeld in 955, that the Magyars ceased to be a serious
danger to Germany, and only in 1043, after Henry III had reorganized the marks which buttressed the south-eastern flank of the kingdom, were the German colonies in Austria finally secure.

It was, however, in the north that the greatest work of the Saxon
dynasty was performed. Here, in the winter of 928-929, Henry I

D

crossed the river Havel, captured Brunabor, the chief town of the 'Hevelli', and transformed it into a German garrison town (Brandenburg) on the model of the fortified places he had constructed in Saxony. Then, turning south, he advanced up the Elbe as far as Meissen, and defeated a great Slav coalition in a battle at Lenzen which shattered Wendish opposition. Finally, in 934, Henry turned north, defeated the Danish king, and set up the mark of Schleswig as a Saxon colony between the rivers Eider and Schlei.

These victories laid the foundations for German expansion across the Saale and the Elbe, but they were not exploited by Henry himself, who was content to exact tribute and exercise overlordship over the conquered tribes. Brandenburg and Meissen were isolated outposts without any supporting military organization. Nor was there any attempt at colonization or Christianization, Henry's attention still being concentrated on the development of Saxony and on the extension of the area of settled life up to the Saxon and Thuringian frontiers. It was Otto I who introduced Henry's system of fortified 'Burgwards' into the Sorb territories between the Saale and the Upper Elbe, thus firmly establishing German military control in the Thuringian march by the creation of a systematized network of strong-points controlling the rivers which divided up the territory. This important region covering the approaches to the Main and the heart of Germany, to the Weser and Saxony, was the object of Otto's special care: here the famous Gero, 'a great and powerful man', 'outstanding in our times', held office from 938 until his death in 965, but in spite of his eminence he was kept in strict subordination, and Otto I throughout treated the newly conquered land as a particular stronghold of the monarchy, the immediate territorial power of which was thus extended from Franconia far to the east. After Gero's death in 965, his territory was divided by Otto into several marks (the Ostmark, Lausitz or Lusatia, and the march of Meissen) partly perhaps for reasons of defence, but partly to prevent the rise of a great new territorial power which might oppose the crown.

In 936, two years before the appointment of Gero, Otto entrusted the defence of Lower Saxony to an equally famous figure, Hermann Billung, for whom a march was erected in the lands north of the Elbe as far as the Peene river. Here Hermann Billung enjoyed an independence far greater than that of Gero in the march of Thuringia. Otto never appears to have contemplated carving out another crown

DENMARK

ARKONA
I OF RUGEN
RANIANS

LUTIMINBURG •OLDENBURG
PLÖN
WAGRIANS

•ILOWE
•CUSCIN
SEGEBERG •LUBECK MECKLENBURG
SCHONBURG •RATZBURG
GADEBUSCH ABODRITES
HAMBURG •SCHWERIN •DOBBIN
DANNENBURG
•BREMEN BOIZENBURG
POLABII MALCHEW
PUTTLITZ
SMALDINGS •WITTSTOCK
WITTENBERG DOXANII

POMERANIANS

REDARII

R.Oder
LEUBUZZI

R.Weser
R.Aller
SAXONY
•HAVELBERG
HEVELLI
BRANDENBURG
R.Elbe
R.Havel LEBUS

MAGDEBURG PLAU
GERMANS MORTSANI

LUSIZZI

NIENBURG •WORLITZ
BERNBURG POUCH •MUHLBERG
WETTIN DUBEN •TORGAU
GIEBICHENSTEIN•
SCHKEUDITZ SORBS
MERSEBURG• EILENBURG •STREHLA TSCHELLN
SCHKOHLEN• TAUCHA •BICHEN KAMENZ BAUTZEN
•LEIPZIG •WURZEN BORITZ
SWENKAU •DOBER •LOMMATSCH •GOEDA
COLDITZ LISNIG •ZADEL
ZEITZ ROCHLITZ MEISSEN• •BREISSNITZ
GROITSCH• •DOBLIN •COSSEBAUDE
R.Saale DOHNA•
THURINGIA DALEMINZI
COLDIZZI R.Eger
CZECHS

POLES
R.Bober

The Elbe Frontier and the Slavonic Peoples East of the Elbe[1]

land in Nordalbingia as he did between the Saale and the Upper
Elbe; and Hermann Billung was left to maintain the peace and exact
tribute from the weak and small Slav tribes inhabiting the land.

Between them, Hermann and Gero pushed forward German
conquest with ferocious greed. During Otto I's reign there was
already a German settlement, protected by a 'Burgward', in Silesia,

[1] The German 'burgwards', established for the defence of the frontier, are underlined on
the map.

and in 979 an unsuccessful expedition was launched in the hope of compelling the Poles to pay tribute to Germany for the territory between the Oder and Warthe rivers. Less fantastic and over-reaching was Margrave Gero's extension of German conquest from the Sorben lands between Saale and Elbe eastward through Lusatia as far as the river Bober. In all these conquests the motive force was the hope of exacting tribute, the 'insatiable avarice' of the Saxons; the Germans came as conquerors, reducing the native Slav population to serfdom under the inexorable rule of the German lords. In the lands of Gero there was no Germanization and only insignificant German colonization; in the Billung march across the Lower Elbe the work of colonization may have begun but it left no permanent trace, and on the whole the Billung margraves were willing to leave the Wends their own religion, laws, leaders and way of life, provided they paid their tribute regularly.

For the stabilization, consolidation and extension of German rule in the east Otto I relied less on the two margraves than on the Church, founding and endowing a chain of new bishoprics beyond the Elbe, in order to subdue the Slavonic tribes under the weight of ecclesiastical administrative organization. Following the tradition of Charlemagne who had converted the Saxons by force of arms, Otto I followed up his military expeditions by compelling the vanquished Wends to worship the 'German God' and to pay tribute and tithe on pain of land and life. Tithe played as important a part in clerical expansion in the east as tribute in driving forward the Saxon aristocracy; it was ruled that all Slavs should pay tithe and even that increase of the tithes was a just motive for forcible conversion of the Slavs.[1] But tithe was not the only inducement to the Church to help in subjugating the heathen tribes across the Elbe: the new bishoprics were also endowed with immense grants of landed property, for the exploitation of which they exacted onerous services from the native peasants who were reduced to serfdom or even slavery upon the lands they had once cultivated as free proprietors.

Otto I's scheme of ecclesiastical organization was planned upon an ambitious scale and clearly looked forward to a steady expansion of German influence and political domination in the east, comprising both Bohemia and Poland. The foundation of the sees of Havelberg, Brandenburg and Oldenburg between 946 and 948 implied little

----

[1] Thompson, op. cit., 398.

more than the organization and safeguarding of the conquests made by Henry I in 929, just as the foundation of the Danish bishoprics of Schleswig, Ripen and Aarhus in the same year safeguarded Henry's victory of 934. But when, in 955, Otto began in Rome the negotiations which led to the foundation of the archbishopric of Magdeburg, he had evidently a more ambitious project in view.[1] Magdeburg was, in Otto's intention, to be the greatest ecclesiastical province of Germany. It had, according to the original charter of 962, no boundary on the east, but could be extended indefinitely by the creation of new suffragans, as need arose. The purpose of the foundation was to extend the frontiers of the Christian faith, and the province was therefore to include not only territories already conquered, but also all Slav lands conquered in future. When in 963, Margrave Gero again went over to the offensive, advancing rapidly east through the march of Lausitz, there is little reason to doubt that his campaign was a sequel to the charter authorizing the foundation of Magdeburg, and that Otto's plan was to subordinate the newly-founded church of Posen on the river Warthe, and its German bishop, to the see of Magdeburg.

Just as Hamburg (founded in 834) was the centre of German influence and expansion in the north, so Magdeburg was founded as a centre for the Germanization of the Slavonic east as far perhaps as the Warthe and the Vistula. But it seems equally probable that Otto's plans also embraced the south-eastern borderlands of Germany. Bishop Pilgrim of Passau, who played an important part in the colonization of Austria from the river Enns to the Wienerwald, was interested also in Hungary, and sent St. Wolfgang to convert the country in 972, while the Bishop of Regensburg was actively engaged in promoting the colonization of the Bohemian Forest across the Danube to the north. It was probably to co-ordinate and complete this work that Otto I in 973 erected the bishopric of Prague, which seems to have been intended to comprise the whole of Bohemia and Moravia (at that time under Magyar domination) and probably Hungary as well, as quickly as the conversion of that country proceeded.

Thus the keys to Otto's policy on his northern and eastern frontiers were Hamburg, Magdeburg and Prague; and of the three Magdeburg was outstanding. But the grandiose outlines of Otto I's

[1] Cf. A. Brackmann, 'Die Ostpolitik Ottos des Grossen', *Hist. Zeitschrift*, CXXXIV (1926).

policy were never filled in. In the Slav lands, the cruelty and oppression of the German conquerors, laymen and clerics, their massacres and rapacity, produced the inevitable reaction. The crushing defeat of Otto II at the hands of the Arabs in Calabria in 982 provided the opportunity, and in 983 the whole Slavonic world rose in an uproar. Brandenburg, Zeitz and Havelberg were destroyed; even Hamburg was plundered. Except in the far north, on the borders of Denmark, the whole German position east of the Elbe collapsed. Only the military administration with its network of 'Burgwards' established by Otto I in the Sorb lands, between the Saale and the Upper Elbe, held firm; elsewhere German power crumbled away and there was even danger lest the Slavs should penetrate into the heart of Saxony. Magdeburg itself survived, but half its province was lost and with it the ambitious prospect of further expansion into the still unconquered east; for the defeat of German arms, which halted German eastward expansion for a century and a half, was followed by a consolidation of the Slavonic states on Germany's eastern border. Bohemia had already emerged as a stable political unit under Boleslav I (929-967); under Boleslav Chobry (992-1025) Poland became a formidable power standing in the way of German eastward expansion, and Boleslav's policy put an end for ever to the project of subordinating the Polish to the German Church. Boleslav's father, Miesko I, had already in 990 handed over his lands to the successor of Peter in Rome and received them back as a vassal of the Church; Boleslav himself, with papal sanction, erected Gnesen into an archbishopric under which — to the indignation of the Archbishop of Magdeburg — were placed the sees of Breslau, Cracow and Kolberg. A similar process occurred in Hungary under Stephen I (997-1038), cutting off German expansion, political and ecclesiastical, in the south-east.

Thus along the whole frontier from Holstein to the Danube the policy inaugurated so successfully by Otto I was brought to a halt, and except in the Bavarian Ostmark (later to become the Duchy of Austria) the first phase of German colonization closed without permanent results. Across the Elbe the German settlements perished and disappeared; cultivated land returned to nature; churches and monasteries were left in ruins. In 1123 the linguistic frontier was still where it had been in the reign of Charlemagne. Even in the march of Thuringia the German lords lived with their men in the fortified garrisons, surrounded by a hostile Wendish peasantry; and the few churches in the land were also confined to the German townships, Christian islands in a pagan countryside. Within the old frontiers of Germany, eastern Franconia from Würzburg to Bohemia was still solidly Slav in population; when the bishopric of Bamberg was founded in 1007, the ostensible motive[1] was to root out paganism from among the Slavs inhabiting the region of the Upper Main. Unlike the later movement which got under way in the second half of the twelfth century, the German thrust to the east in the tenth century was a military occupation, exploited in their own interests by the higher clergy and lay aristocracy but unsupported by any substantial flow of colonization and settlement beyond the existing German frontiers.

Nevertheless the political significance of the eastern conquests of Henry I and Otto I must not be underrated, even though the great Slav rising of 983 undid their work beyond the Elbe. Its victories in the east played a great part in raising the prestige of the Saxon monarchy, and materially it profited both by the incorporation of the Thuringian march and by the creation of a new ecclesiastical organization reaching as far as the Elbe. Although the trans-Elbean suffragans of Magdeburg (Havelberg and Brandenburg) ceased to exist except in name after 983, the foundations between Saale and Elbe (Merseburg, Meissen and Zeitz) remained, while Würzburg and Bamberg contributed in great measure to the reclamation and colonization of the forests and wastes in eastern Franconia. In Saxony, Thuringia and Franconia, the area of colonization and settlement was extended; what had been frontier stations became centres of agriculture under the impetus of monasteries such as Fulda and Hersfeld. All this was, from the German point of view, a major gain; it increased the wealth and resources of the country, and denoted recovery from the devastation and depopulation which followed in the trail of Viking and Magyar incursions.

IV

The chronicler Widukind described Henry I, at the time of his death in 936, as 'the greatest king of Europe'. There is little doubt that this judgement was founded pre-eminently on Henry's victories

[1] For the political motive, cf. above, p. 35

in the east. Contrasted with the helplessness of France against the Vikings and of Italy against the Saracens and Magyars, this was what struck the imagination of contemporaries. Among contemporary kings Henry was singled out by the number of his tributaries, including Abodrites, Wilzi, Hevelli, Daleminzi, Bohemians and Danes. He was, in Widukind's words, 'emperor of many peoples'.[1] But the fame of Henry was small compared with the prestige won by Otto I through his victory over the Hungarians at Lechfeld in 955. Romans, Greeks and Saracens, it is said,[2] sent him embassies with gifts, and he became the object of both the fear and favour of many kings and peoples. According to Widukind, he was even proclaimed emperor in his hour of triumph by his victorious army.[3] This account can, it is true, hardly be accepted at its face value; but it is significant, nevertheless, as evidence that — more than six years before he was crowned emperor at the pope's hands in Rome — Otto I was the equal of an emperor, in the eyes of contemporaries, because of his victories over Magyars and Slavs and his services in protecting and extending the frontiers of Christendom. The use of the imperial title in 955 reflects the prestige won by the Saxon dynasty and the success of German arms on the eastern frontiers of Germany.

It was, however, not on the banks of the Lech in 955, but in Rome in 962 that Otto I received the title 'Imperator et Augustus', thus renewing, as heir of the east Frankish Carolingians, the tradition of Carolingian empire, which had been in abeyance since 924. This renewal of the empire, with which the whole fate of Germany was henceforth to be inextricably bound up, could hardly have occurred but for Henry I's and Otto I's success in restoring the power of the monarchy within Germany and in consolidating their position in the east; it reflected the emergence of the first stable political society on the continent of Europe after the collapse of European civilization in the second half of the ninth century. But the success of the Saxon dynasty on the eastern frontier and within Germany was only the background to the chain of events culminating in the foundation of the Ottonian empire in 962. If we are to gain an understanding of Otto I's motives in seeking and accepting the imperial title at the

---

[1] *Res gestae Saxonicae*, I, 25: 'imperator multorum populorum'. Widukind also describes Otto I as 'rex gentium' (op. cit., III, 76).

[2] Widukind, op. cit., III, 56.

[3] Op. cit., III, 49: 'triumpho celebri rex factus gloriosus ab exercitu pater patriae imperatoremque appellatus est'.

hands of John XII, we must turn from his eastern and domestic policy to his policy on his western and southern frontiers, and to the political environment in which that policy evolved. Thus we shall learn something of the meaning and import of the mediaeval empire, of the bearing of the imperial connexion on German history and internal progress, and of the motives which led to the revival of imperial traditions by the Saxon kings and their maintenance and development by their successors on the German throne. From 962 onwards, the relations of Germany and Italy and the close connexion with the papacy, which was a corollary, were of prime importance in German history, at any rate until the days of Louis of Bavaria (1314-1347), impinging on the political situation at every crisis in German affairs. This connexion of German affairs and Italian affairs, of empire and papacy, goes back to the coronation of Otto I as emperor in 962; having surveyed the progress of German history in the days of Otto I, our next concern must, therefore, be with the foundation and history of the Ottonian empire. Although their history carries us beyond the frontiers of Germany to Burgundy and Italy, and indeed to the Mohammedan south and the Byzantine east, the empire and imperial policy were closely entwined in the roots of German history, and their influence on German destiny was great and enduring. After 962 we cannot fully understand the course of German history unless we are conversant with the history and problems of the empire.

CHAPTER 3

THE FOUNDATION OF THE GERMAN EMPIRE

I

IN the history of the Carolingian empire, of which the Ottonian empire of the tenth century was the successor, the Treaty of Verdun (843)[1] marked an important stage. After the division of the imperial lands in 843, the theory and practice of the empire gradually underwent a far-reaching transformation – a transformation which was, indeed, resisted by the Frankish clergy and by such popes as Nicholas I (858-867), but which with the passage of time proved irresistible. The idea of the oecumenical character of the empire, which had waxed strong in the ecclesiastical circles around Charlemagne, waned under the impact of political reality and gave way to a more restricted and material conception of the imperial heritage.

This change reflected the changed political situation after 843 when the east and west Frankish kingdoms became virtually independent, and the effective authority of the Emperor Lothar I was confined to the lands of the Middle kingdom. From the days of Lothar (843-855) the imperial title came in practice to be increasingly bound up with rule over the Middle kingdom; and when, after Lothar's death in 855, the Middle kingdom itself was subdivided between his three sons – Italy and the imperial title to Louis II, the kingdom of Lorraine to Lothar II and Provence and imperial Burgundy to Charles – the significance of the imperial title contracted still further. In the dynastic struggles which followed the premature death of these three princes the imperial title came, for rulers like Charles the Bald, to signify little more than a claim to the disputed lands of the Middle kingdom. Charles himself, crowned emperor by the pope in Rome in 875, was reputed already to have had himself crowned emperor at Metz in 869, in order to strengthen his claim to Lorraine, which he had just occupied; the title of emperor, he believed, would establish his right to rule over two

---

[1] Cf. above, p. 12.

46

kingdoms.[1] So also he had his vassal, Boso, crowned king of Provence 'so that, like earlier emperors, he would be seen to rule over kings'.[2]

In the obscure and complicated political scene at the end of the ninth century the instability and disintegration of the lands which had formed the Middle kingdom was without doubt the governing factor. After the death of Charles the Fat in 888, the component lands — Italy, Burgundy, Provence and Lorraine — had gone their own way under independent *reguli*, too weak to hold their own against either their vassals at home or their rivals abroad. It was an age of sudden political upheaval, presenting countless possibilities of aggression and territorial conquest; for the disintegration and instability of the times provided the strong and unscrupulous with exceptional opportunities for 'reintegration'. In particular, there was always the possibility of a 'reintegration' of the Middle kingdom, threatening the stability and territorial cohesion of the French and German lands to west and east. Especially in the east, as we have seen, it was still far from a foregone conclusion that Swabians, Franks, Saxons, Bavarians and Thuringians would be welded together into one German nation. This depended on internal policy, on the resources and success of the monarchy at home; but it depended also on foreign relations and foreign policy.

In this world of crude power-politics and iron materialism, no rulers were perhaps more outstanding than the first two kings of Burgundy, Rudolf I (888-912) and Rudolf II (912-937), whose careers best illustrate the potentialities of the political situation of the period. Rudolf I's interests were concentrated on his northern frontier; leaving the west to Odo, Count of Paris, and Germany to Arnulf, he set out to annex Lorraine and was actually crowned King of Lorraine in 888. But this act provoked immediate reaction from Arnulf, and Rudolf was forced to surrender his claims to Lorraine, which passed under German control until 911, when it went over for a few years to France. When Rudolf II succeeded in 912, therefore, Lorraine was closed to Burgundian influence, and Rudolf consequently turned his energies to his eastern and southern frontiers. First he attempted aggression at the expense of Swabia, but,

---

[1] 'Se imperatorem et augustum quasi duo regna possessurus appellare praecepit'; cf. E. E. Stengel, 'Kaisertitel und Suveränitätsidee', *Archiv f. Gesch. d. Mittelalters*, III (1939), 7.
[2] Op. cit., 11.

defeated by the Swabians in 919, he turned to Italy and was crowned king at Pavia in 922. Nor was this the end of Rudolf's ambitions. He hoped, and around 930 contrived, to re-unite Provence and Upper Burgundy,[1] and when Duke Burchard of Swabia died in 926, Rudolf (who had married Burchard's daughter) was a serious candidate for succession to his father-in-law's duchy, hoping in this way to create a great new territorial power controlling the Great St. Bernard pass and the western routes to Italy. For a moment, it appeared as though in the turmoil of the post-Carolingian world Burgundy — grasping after new territories on all its frontiers — was the coming power.

It was in this atmosphere of intrigue and restless power-politics that the policy of the Saxon kings, Henry I and Otto I, was formulated. The unstable and often threatening political background was alone sufficient explanation and justification for the policy of the two kings in regard to Italy, Burgundy and Lorraine — a policy which, on account of the close historical and political connexion between the three lands in question, was too closely inter-related to be considered apart. Moreover, it must be remembered that the German dukes, particularly the Dukes of Swabia and Bavaria, were attempting to pursue an independent foreign policy,[2] which, if successful, would have produced radical alterations in the balance of power within Germany and might easily have resulted in dismemberment of the German kingdom and permanent separation between north and south Germany. Burchard of Swabia was killed in an expedition to Italy in 926; four years earlier he had made a formal alliance with Rudolf of Burgundy and supported Rudolf's invasion of Italy. Eight years later, in 934, Arnulf of Bavaria — acting directly contrary to Henry I's policy[3]— entered Lombardy with the idea of winning the crown for his son, whom he set up as anti-king in opposition to Hugh of Vienne. In the first half of the tenth century, with Italy utterly weak and disorganized, a prey to its neighbours, one expedition followed another from Swabia and Bavaria to the

[1] Whether Rudolf actually secured effective possession of Provence is another question; cf. Previté-Orton, 'Italy and Provence, 900-950', English Hist. Review, XXXII (1917), who has elucidated the obscure detail of Burgundian history in this period.

[2] The motives underlying German policy are convincingly set out by Fournier, Le royaume d'Arles et de Vienne (1891), xi-xiii; cf. also Grieser, Das Arelat in der europäischen Politik (1925), 6. 'Son propre intérêt', says Fournier, 'lui commandait d'empêcher, à tout prix, la formation d'un état puissant dont le chef, disposant des passages des Alpes, pourrait à son gré pénétrer dans les plaines du Nord de l'Italie.'

[3] Cf. above, pp. 22, 27.

western or eastern sector of the Po valley;[1] and there is much truth
in the view that 'a German king who wished to prevent the pursuit
of an independent Italian policy by Swabia or Bavaria, was of
necessity driven to pursue an Italian policy of his own'.[2]

There is, therefore, no question of innovation or change in policy,
when Otto I intervenes in Italy, and there is no need to go outside
the immediate framework of international power-politics, as they
had evolved since 888, to explain his intervention.[3] Apart from
Bavarian and Swabian precedents for intervention, Otto was only
continuing and carrying to a logical conclusion the policy of his
father, Henry I, whose attitude to foreign affairs was dominated by
the problems and dangers and opportunities created by the disintegration of the old Middle kingdom and by the ambitions of
Rudolf II of Burgundy.

This becomes clear from a brief recapitulation of the salient points
of Henry I's foreign policy. His first concern was Lorraine where
the Duke, Giselbert, was attempting to create an independent principality. Here Henry intervened decisively in 925, reconquered the
province, and so assured his western frontier. Thereafter he was
free to turn to Burgundy. In 926, just after Rudolf had been
defeated and driven out of Italy by his rival, Hugh of Provence,
Henry arranged a meeting with him, at which the German king
ceded the important city of Basel to Burgundy in exchange for the
Holy Lance. The latter was the symbol for the inheritance of
Constantine the Great (i.e. Italy and the 'Empire'),[4] and its acquisition by the German king was therefore a significant deal, justifying
the high price paid, for it implied at least the surrender of Burgundian claims over Italy, and probably their transfer to Henry.
Henry's decision, after a long period of hostilities, to reach a settlement with Rudolf is therefore most readily explained as preparation
for undertaking an Italian campaign.[5] But if such was the case,

---

[1] Cf. B. Schmeidler, in *Mediaeval Germany*, II, 75.

[2] H. Heimpel, *Bemerkungen zur Gesch. König Heinrichs I*, 45.

[3] This is doubtless what Ficker meant when he stated that the union of Germany, Italy and
Burgundy was not the result of 'a blind urge to conquer' or of an oecumenical theory of the
Empire derived from the Church, but was enforced by the international situation at
the period; cf. *Das deutsche Kaiserreich in seinen universalen u. nationalen Beziehungen* (1862), 76.

[4] Cf. A. Hofmeister, *Die Heilige Lanze* (1908); also *Deutschland u. Burgund im früheren
Mittelalter* (1914).

[5] When Arnulf invaded Italy in 894, Rudolf I of Burgundy had supported the Marquess of
Ivrea, thus compelling Arnulf to divert his forces to the west and invade the Valais. Henry I
can scarcely have been unaware of this precedent.

Henry's project was postponed, probably owing to the wars against the Slav tribes on the Elbe and the Hungarians. After the defeat of the Magyars in 933, however, Henry's Italian plans were once more revived. In 935 he again called a meeting with Rudolf and the king of France, at which agreement was secured between all parties, thus establishing in the west the settled peace which was prerequisite for any attack on Italy. The chronicler Widukind states that it was Henry's intention at this time to lead an expedition to Rome;[1] and there is no reason to doubt his testimony. But illness intervened and Henry's Italian plans came to nothing. Nevertheless the evidence of his political interest in Italy is important; it provides the link between the last east Frankish emperor, Arnulf (crowned in 896), and the first Saxon emperor, Otto I, and shows that German interest in Italy had not dropped in the interval. Just as Henry I was impelled by the unsettled state of affairs throughout the lands of the old Middle kingdom to active intervention, so his son, Otto I, could not remain an indifferent spectator of events on his southern and western frontiers.

The danger of the revival of a strong political power on his southern frontier faced Otto I within a few months of his succession in 936 as a result of the death, in 937, of Rudolf II of Burgundy. Rudolf had been called into Italy about 930 by the Italian nobles against Hugh of Arles, ruler of Provence, who had invaded and conquered Lombardy in 926; but unable to make headway, he subsequently came to an agreement with Hugh, by which he obtained Provence in exchange for an assurance that he would not intervene against Hugh in Italy. Thus the two provinces of the Burgundian kingdom, independent since 870, were reunited in Rudolf's hands. But Hugh of Italy was only waiting for Rudolf's death not only to regain Provence, but also to seize Upper Burgundy, thus creating for himself a new Middle kingdom almost equal in dimensions to that of Lothar I. This he sought to achieve in 937 by a dynastic alliance, he himself marrying Rudolf's widow, while his son Lothar was married to Rudolf's daughter, Adelaide. But against the threat involved in this alliance Otto I's reaction was immediate. Intervening as the protector of Rudolf's fifteen year old son, Conrad, Otto invaded Burgundy, 'received king and kingdom into his possession', and thus countered the threat of a union of Italy

[1] *Res gestae Saxonicae*, I, 40.

and the Burgundian lands. Conrad was removed to Germany, where he remained until 942, receiving his education in a German environment; and when he returned to Burgundy he proved a faithful vassal of the German king. Although it was not until 1034 that Burgundy was finally united with Germany, German control was assured from 938.

Thus, from the first months of his reign, Otto I had his western flank covered for the contingency of German intervention in Italy. It is also fairly evident that, after his intervention in Burgundy, he took over on his own account the Burgundian claim to the crown of Italy, regarding himself in relation to the Italian ruler, Hugh, as the successor of Rudolf II. From the time of his first intervention in 937, Otto was evidently determined to prevent a consolidation and extension of Hugh's power. Hence, when the latter, having secured the Lombard throne and north Italy, began to intrigue with a view to obtaining the imperial crown, Otto sought to hold a balance by giving his support in Italy to Hugh's rival, the Marquess Berengar of Ivrea, thus adopting in his southern policy the methods successfully employed in the west to nullify French plans for reconquering Lorraine.[1] Berengar became a vassal of the German king and, aided by German troops, took up arms in 945 against Hugh and his son, Lothar. But when Hugh and Lothar followed each other unexpectedly to the grave in 947 and 950 the balance of power so carefully established by Otto in Italy was destroyed. Berengar, who was left in control, immediately attempted to assume greater independence in his relations with Otto, hoping to secure for himself the vacant Italian throne. At the same time the confused situation in Italy awakened the rapacity of Swabia and Bavaria, whose dukes both saw in the weakness of Italy an opportunity for aggrandizement. In 949 the Duke of Bavaria seized the province of Aquileia; in 951 the Duke of Swabia crossed the Alps ostensibly to champion Adelaide (the Burgundian princess whom Lothar had married in 937) against Berengar.

[1] Otto's policy in relation to France cannot be considered in detail. It was based upon the maintenance of a balance of power between Louis IV and the leader of the nobility, Hugh the Great. For this purpose Otto repeatedly intervened in French affairs, and in this way he prevented a united French policy, comprising all parties, for the reconquest of Lorraine, which had been under nominal French rule for a brief period between 911 and 925, but was recovered in the latter year by Henry I. Cf. S. Kawerau, *Die Rivalität deutscher u. französischer Macht im 10. Jahrhundert* (1910), A. Cartellieri, *Die Weltstellung des deutschen Reiches, 911-1047* (1932), 26-27.

It was in these troubled circumstances that Otto led his first expedition to Italy in 951. Evidently he could not stand idle while the Bavarian and Swabian dukes contended over the spoils of Italy. Equally clearly, it was a negation of his previous policy to allow Berengar to consolidate his position in Italy. But more serious still was Berengar's project of marrying the widowed Adelaide, for this once again raised the possibility of a union between Burgundy and Italy, or at least a revival of Italian claims to Burgundy. In all these respects, Otto's intervention was a logical conclusion to the policy he had pursued since the beginning of his reign, and indeed to the policy of his father, Henry I; he could not have stood aside without jeopardizing his position and weakening the European standing of the German monarchy.

Otto's first Italian expedition resulted in immediate military success, and Otto secured the Lombard crown and himself married Adelaide. There is little doubt also that he contemplated an immediate assumption of the imperial title, and sent an embassy to Rome with this object in view. But the pope, who alone could crown the emperor, was the nominee of a Roman faction headed by the ambitious Alberic, who aspired to build up a secular principality in Rome on the basis of the papal patrimony. Under Alberic's influence, Otto's proposals were refused, and after some hesitation Otto decided, at least temporarily, to waive his claims. Probably the situation in Germany, where his Italian policy had brought about a sharp cleavage of interests among the nobility, was the immediate cause of his withdrawal. By intervening personally in Italy and marrying Adelaide, Otto had cut across the plans of his son, Liudolf, Duke of Swabia, who was further embittered by the preference accorded to Bavaria in Italian affairs.[1] Perhaps already in 951, certainly in 952, a conspiracy of discontented elements began to take shape, in which not only Liudolf was implicated but also Duke Conrad of Franconia, who had been left behind in Italy to carry on military operations against Berengar, but who instead came to terms with Berengar and probably brought him within the circle of conspirators. The result was the rebellion of 953 — the most serious of all the revolts and conspiracies which Otto I had to face. As far as Italy was concerned, the conspiracy upset all Otto's plans, and

[1] The north Italian provinces of Verona and Friuli were, with Aquileia, erected into Bavarian marches in 952.

forced a reconciliation with Berengar. Having renewed his promise of allegiance, Berengar was restored to favour and again received the Italian crown.

The civil wars, which lasted from 953 to 955, had serious repercussions on all aspects of German foreign relations. The Hungarians took the opportunity to renew their incursions. In Italy, Berengar again began to shake off German control, and reconquered the march of Verona. In 957 Liudolf was sent by Otto to contest his growing power; but death robbed Liudolf of the fruits of his victories and Berengar continued his policy of aggrandizement. In 959 he turned south and, conquering Spoleto, sought to extend his territory at the expense of the papacy, which had lost its lay protector and patron when Alberic died in 954. Finally Alberic's son, Octavian, who had become pope under the title John XII in 955, had no alternative save to call in Otto to defend Rome from Berengar. Papal legates left for Otto's court in 960; and in 961 Otto — who in the meantime had pacified Germany, defeated the Hungarians at the battle of the Lech, and thus settled the main problems confronting him north of the Alps — again appeared in Italy.

This time there was no hitch in Otto's plans. Descending upon Italy through Bavaria and Trent, he expelled Berengar, reassumed the Italian crown at Pavia, and then proceeded to Rome. Here in 962, amid the acclamations of the clergy and people of Rome, he was crowned emperor by the pope. Thus at length Otto secured the position to which he had aspired in 951, and to which his father, Henry, before him had looked forward in 935-936. The imperial title, so long the object of the ambitions of the princes of Italy and Burgundy, and the plaything of Roman factions, passed to the kings of Germany. The problems created in 843 by the Treaty of Verdun had at last found settlement.

II

We can only understand Otto I's Italian policy and his assumption of the imperial title in 962 if we understand its antecedents. The background to the policy explains the policy. Otto's empire has often been described as the linear descendant or heir of the Carolingian empire; but in fact it was not so much to Charlemagne that

E

Otto looked back,[1] as to Lothar I, who combined the imperial title with rule over the Middle kingdom. Otto's assumption of the imperial title in 962 solved, for the next three centuries, the problem of the Middle kingdom. Possession of the imperial crown meant possession of a title to the lands of the Middle kingdom, to Italy, Burgundy and Lorraine — a title which (like all legal titles) was an empty formula unless supported by political power, but which was not a meaningless formality because, from the time of the Treaty of Verdun onwards, every ruler who had tried to exercise authority in the Middle kingdom and to reunite Italy, Burgundy and Lorraine, had sought that title as a legal assurance and recognition of his hegemony. Hence the coronation of Otto as emperor meant less the beginning of a new epoch than the conclusion of a chapter of history: it looked to the past rather than to the future, and put an end to the international instability which had been the characteristic feature of the foregoing century. Conditioned by the circumstances of the post-Carolingian world, his imperial policy fitted in with and grew out of the policies of men like Rudolf of Burgundy and Hugh of Provence.

The imperial title was, therefore, important to Otto as the highest expression and legitimation of his right to rule not over Italy alone — for this was to all intents and purposes inherent in the crown of Lombardy — but over all the territories of the old Middle kingdom which had come into German hands after 925. It was the symbol of German hegemony, reflecting the success of Henry I and Otto I in preventing the restoration of the old realm of Lothar. In this sense, the assumption of the imperial title in 962 was undertaken in the interests of a purely German policy. Although circumstances forced Otto to reside in Italy for a large part of his later years, there was no radical change in his policy in 962. In particular there was no substitution of an 'imperial' for a purely German outlook. His newly acquired Italian dominions played a small part in Otto's plans and projects. Nor would it be easy to show that he sought to impress on his empire a universal, oecumenical character. The events of 963, when the pope — realizing that in Otto he had found not a momentary protector, but a ruler who was determined to make his power felt — swung over to Otto's opponents and

[1] The view that the Ottonian was a revival of the Carolingian empire is still often expressed. It was refuted by Ficker as long ago as 1862; cf. Ficker, *Das deutsche Kaiserreich*, 63, 76, 80.

attempted to reverse the decision of 962, forced Otto to intervene with a heavy hand in Church affairs, and call together a synod at which John XII was deposed; but this was a consequence of the political situation rather than a deliberate attempt to emphasize the theocratic character of the empire.

Just as many theories have been put forward to explain Charlemagne's political objectives when he assumed the imperial title in 800, so historians have disputed and discussed Otto I's motives in 962. Otto's great objective, the conquest and Germanization of the Slavonic east, could (it has been maintained) only be achieved after Otto, as emperor, had assured himself of papal backing, and the imperial title was invaluable to Otto because it conferred the moral right to pursue, and assured him of clerical support in pursuing, a policy of eastern expansion: conversion of the infidel was part of the imperial mission, a duty owed by the emperor to the Church.[1] But conversion of the infidel and propagation of the faith was a duty owed by every king to the Church, and there is no reason to suppose that his imperial title added to Otto's powers in this respect.[2] It is certainly true and significant that, ten days after Otto's coronation on February 2nd, 962, he persuaded the pope to authorize the foundation of the archbishopric of Magdeburg; but the fact that Otto used the occasion of his presence in Rome to secure papal authorization for his cherished foundation is no evidence that this was the reason, or even one main reason, why he went to Rome. Much the same is true of the older and more commonplace argument that Otto needed to secure control of the papacy because — having based his power in Germany on the Church — he needed the pope's support to maintain control over the German bishops.[3]

---

[1] This view was developed and vigorously maintained by A. Brackmann; cf. 'Die Ostpolitik Ottos des Grossen', Hist. Zeitschrift, CXXXIV (1926), 'Der römische Erneuerungsgedanke und seine Bedeutung für die Reichspolitik der deutschen Kaiserzeit', Sitz.-Berichte d. preuss. Akademie (1932), 346-374, and in summary 'Der Streit um die deutsche Kaiserpolitik des Mittelalters', Monatshefte, XLIII (1929), 443-449. Although Brackmann's main theses must, I believe, be rejected, his work has illuminated many aspects of the problem of German imperial policy, and is particularly valuable for the proof which it offers that there was no inherent contradiction between imperial (or Italian) and eastern policy in the Middle Ages.

[2] Cf. C. Erdmann, 'Der Heidenkrieg in der Liturgie u. die Kaiserkrönung Ottos I', Mitteilungen d. österr. Instituts für Geschichtsforschung, XLVI, 129-142.

[3] Cf. Haller, Epochs of German History (1930), 23: 'The German king, whose dominion rested on domination of the German Church, had an interest in commanding also in Rome, the see of the spiritual overlord of the German bishops.' Similarly Fisher, History of Europe, I (1943), 194: 'It was a means of securing for the service of the German monarchy the indispensable loyalty of the German Church.'

Against this view it must be argued that, so far as the immediate situation was concerned, the opposition to Otto within the German Church had died down after the death of Archbishop Frederick of Mainz in 954; that the influence of popes like John XII and Benedict V, the nominees of Roman factions, over the great ecclesiastics of Germany was a negligible political factor; that Otto's position as *rex et sacerdos*, the divinely appointed governor of the Church of his realm, was unchallenged; and finally that, where the interests of German bishops brought them into conflict in later years with the policy of the monarchy — over Merseburg, for example, or the foundation of Bamberg[1] — there is no sign that the imperial title or imperial control over the papacy acted as a curb on episcopal ambitions.

The significance of the empire and the imperial title changed from generation to generation and from emperor to emperor, reflecting the varying characters of the different rulers and the different *Zeitgeist* of succeeding ages. It was not an unvarying conception, a constant factor, meaning the same thing to all men at all times or even to all men at one time. For the great German monarch of the eleventh century, Henry III (1039-1056), the emperor's obligations to the Church, particularly his duty to purify and reinvigorate the papacy, were the keynote of imperial policy. Under Otto III (983-1002) Rome and Italy came into the foreground. But it would be an error to read back these later developments into the policy of Otto I. Many of the theories put forward to explain Otto's motives in seeking the empire are due to the mistaken belief that his imperial policy was a new departure, a breach with the immediate past, and therefore that it necessarily reflected a new outlook on affairs. Such, we have seen, was not the case. In foreign as in internal policy, Otto I was the direct successor of his father, Henry I: the antithesis between the two, which historians have sometimes sought to emphasize, is not borne out by the facts. If Henry did not go to Rome, the reasons were accidental; but when Otto finally went there in 962 his motives were little different from those which led Henry to contemplate winning the imperial crown in 935. Otto was not innovating; rather he was following to their

[1] The foundation of Bamberg provoked the opposition of the Bishop of Augsburg, who coveted for his own bishopric the lands given by Henry II to Bamberg. Merseburg (founded 967) was abolished again owing to the avarice of the Archbishop of Magdeburg, and only re-founded in 1004. Cf. Thompson, *Feudal Germany*, 51, 402.

natural conclusion the political tendencies of the past seventy-five years. The history of German relations with Italy and Burgundy and of Burgundian relations with Italy drove him south in search of the imperial title which expressed hegemony over the disputed lands on the southern and south-western borders of Germany. It was an obvious German interest to put an end to the instability within those lands, which was a potential source of political upheaval and dispute; and it was to this end above all others that Otto's imperialism was directed. With his keen sense of realities and keen appreciation of concrete results, Otto was pursuing the policy of a German national king, even when in 962 he left Germany to receive the imperial crown in Rome.

III

Once we understand Otto I's motives in seeking the Italian and imperial crowns, we have the key to his policy in Italy between 962 and his death in 973.[1] Out of the last twelve years of Otto's life ten were spent in Italy. But his lengthy stay was due above all to complications with Byzantium, which resisted the establishment of a new emperor in the west, just as it had resisted Charlemagne over a century and a half before, and only recognized Otto in 972. Otto was prepared to defend Rome against Byzantium; but, as he himself wrote back to Germany at the beginning of 968, he only intended to seize the Byzantine provinces of southern Italy, Calabria and Apulia, if Byzantium declared war on him. There was, in short, no plan for extending his dominion to the south, reuniting Italy and restoring the ancient Roman empire.

In north Italy, also, Otto's policy was conservative in character. He attempted no innovations in methods of government. He was emperor and king of the Lombards; but his power in Italy was largely indirect, and he was content that it should remain indirect. Confronted by a society which had been transformed from top to bottom by the anarchy, invasions and civil wars of the past seventy-

[1] For the following cf. S. Pivano, *Stato e Chiesa da Berengario I ad Arduino* (1908); P. E. Schramm, *Kaiser, Rom und Renovatio* (1929); P. E. Schramm, 'Kaiser, Basileus und Papst in der Zeit der Ottonen', *Hist. Zeitschrift*, CXXIX (1924); A. Brackmann, 'Der römische Erneuerungsgedanke u. seine Bedeutung für die Reichspolitik der deutschen Kaiserzeit', *Sitz-Berichte d. preuss. Akademie* (1932); M. Uhlirz, 'Die italienische Kirchenpolitik der Ottonen', *Mitteilungen d. österr. Instituts für Geschichtsforschung*, XLVIII (1934); K. Hampe, 'Kaiser Otto III und Rom', *Hist. Zeitschrift*, CXL (1929).

five years, Otto was satisfied to stabilize the new order, legitimizing by his confirmation the changes effected during the last two or three generations, and making permanent the results of the confused years between 888 and 962. In particular Otto confirmed the powers which the bishops had obtained in the cities at the expense of the counts. Except in cases of proved political unreliability or disloyalty, he was prepared to give recognition to all rights previously exercised, on condition that henceforward they would be exercised in subordination to the king. His task, as he saw it, was not to reconstruct royal government, which had suffered an eclipse under Hugh and Berengar, but, leaving intact the powers which confronted him on his appearance in Italy, to subject all to the overriding authority of the crown.

Otto I's policy in Italy was therefore simple in the extreme. Because of his limited objects in going to Italy, because his 'imperialism' was largely negative, he was content to exercise a loose hegemony, building up his own party among the Italian nobility and allowing them to rule in his name, but placing special reliance in Lombardy on the bishops who had invited and supported his intervention. His policy was concentrated on binding the most influential bishops of central Lombardy to his cause by grants and privileges. This was the policy of a man who wanted to open a road through a hostile country to Rome; and for the immediate purposes of a particular expedition it was adequate. But it is not surprising that, as soon as the new emperor withdrew, his party fell to pieces and revolts took place. As early as 965 it became obvious that even the bishops, in spite of the far-reaching concessions with which they were favoured, could not be relied on, once the king were absent. Furthermore, such a policy could not, in its very nature, be a long-term policy; it could not be pursued for long without ruinous consequences. The grants made to bishops, although they failed to win more than a transient loyalty, brought about a rapid decline in the extent of the crown lands, which in any case were small, for Berengar II had left little demesne for his German successors to take over. The main resource left to the monarchy was the monasteries which it owned, the royal *Eigenklöster*, in which the king exercised the rights of a protector. But Otto's policy — in this as in other respects no different from that of his predecessors, Berengar, Hugh and Lothar — necessarily tended to weaken royal control over the monasteries. Because Otto sought support for his government within the land, because he thought mainly of winning over the Lombard bishops by grants and privileges, the monasteries came under a regime of episcopal exploitation, which was gradually destroying the only solid asset left to the monarchy.

At the very end of his reign Otto I seems to have realized this, and privileges for the bishops decreased abruptly. Under Otto II (973-983), the incursions of the Saracens from their stronghold in Sicily into Apulia and Calabria and the principalities further north compelled the king to give increasing attention to the monasteries, on which he relied almost exclusively for the contingents of his army. But it was under Otto III (983-1002) that imperial policy in Italy was remodelled. Otto II's defeat by the Arabs at Cortone in 982 and its serious repercussions north of the Alps, the emperor's death in the succeeding year and the long period of regency between 984 and 995, all weakened the imperial position in Italy. Because Otto I and Otto II had created an imperial party in Italy, of which Marquess Hugh of Tuscany was the leader, the maintenance of German rule was assured; but Otto II's death was followed by risings against the foreigners he had introduced into the Italian Church, while the whole period between 983 and 995 witnessed a rapid strengthening of the position of the lesser Italian nobility, the 'vavasours' or *secundi milites*, whose feudal depredations were destroying both the monasteries' control of monastic lands and the crown's control over the monasteries, and thus weakening the resources of the monarchy.

By 996, when Otto III was solemnly crowned emperor in Rome, Italian affairs had therefore taken a turn for the worse. In Rome the imperial interregnum had seen a revival of factions recalling the days of Alberic, and the rise of John Crescentius who violently demonstrated his power after Otto's return to Germany by driving out Gregory V, the first German pope and Otto's own nominee, and setting up an anti-pope of his own appointment. In Lombardy the growing strength of feudalism was a less blatant but scarcely less insidious problem. Due to the general deterioration of the situation, a policy such as Otto I had pursued in Italy was no longer adequate, and Otto III and his advisers and ministers were faced by the necessity of devising a new policy. The loose hegemony over

Italian parties and factions on which Otto I had mainly relied, had
provided no sound foundation for his successors and was being more
and more undermined by the growing forces of feudalism: by the
end of the century the time had come when the construction of a
real imperial administration, independent of parties, could no longer
be postponed, if the Ottonian empire and German control in Italy
were to be maintained.

This was the situation which explained Otto III's policy after his
arrival in Italy on his second expedition in 998. Experience in 996
and 997 had shown that a policy similar to Otto I's was no longer
sufficient. But Otto III's government was in the hands of an exceptionally capable group of men — Gerbert of Aurillac and Bernward
of Hildesheim, Odilo of Cluny and the chancellor Heribert — and
they immediately began a systematic programme of governmental
reform, which was the mark of Otto III's reign. It was not — as so
often maintained — a programme of visionary imperialism seeking
to restore the lost glories of ancient Rome; rather it was a policy of
making German rule in Italy a reality by systematically extending
royal power southwards, at the same time broadening the basis of
power in the north.

One side of this policy — a policy systematically pursued by the
famous Gerbert when he was abbot of Bobbio and later archbishop
of Ravenna, and still continued when, in 999, he became pope with
the title Sylvester II — was to check the growth of feudalism by
putting German *ministeriales* on the Church lands to counter the
efforts of the lower feudality to expropriate those lands for their
own use; applied in the case of the abbey of Farfa, where the
Crescentii had usurped the monastic lands, this policy was part and
parcel of the measures for breaking Crescentian control over Rome
and the papacy. And from Farfa the same policy was transplanted to
Pavia and then to Lombardy as a whole, and reinforced in 998 by a
general constitution against the alienation of Church fees. The other
aspect of Otto III's policy was to build up, beginning in the north
and proceeding south to Rome, the demesnes of crown and Church,
but no longer of an Italian episcopate whose support was far from
certain. Throughout Otto's reign a non-Italian element was brought
into the highest ecclesiastical and secular positions in Italy. Vercelli
was given in 999 to Otto's German chaplain, Leo; and Vercelli
was a point of peculiar strategic importance in the north, essential

for the safety of Milan and Pavia. But equally essential, in central
Italy, was Ravenna; and here there was placed first the famous
Frenchman, Gerbert, and after Gerbert's promotion to the papacy,
the German, Frederick. In addition to the great possessions which
the Archbishop of Ravenna held as archbishop, Gerbert was also
given the administration of three counties; and when he became
pope as Sylvester II he received eight counties more, constituting an
unbroken connexion between Ravenna and Rome and dominating
central Italy. In Rome itself, where Sylvester II (999-1003) succeeded Otto III's cousin, Gregory V (996-999), secular control of
the city was taken out of the hands of the pro-Byzantine Roman
aristocracy, and placed in those of a Saxon count, Ziazo, who was
appointed 'patricius'.

Thus from Rome northwards through Lombardy to the German
frontier, Otto III had – what no emperor before him had possessed
– a firm line of communication, controlled by non-Italian administrators, guaranteed on the flank by an alliance with Venice, and
strategically so well placed that the whole country was dominated
and under control. Thanks to the statesmanship of the mature
advisers, French as well as German, who guided his policy, Otto III
was making German rule over Italy a reality, and lifting Italy out of
the anarchy in which there was no power strong enough to hold the
feuds and rivalries of the local magnates in check. Even the outer
forms of Otto's government, which have kindled the imagination
of posterity – the establishment of the imperial palace on the
Aventine, the innovations in court ceremonial and the revival of
ancient dignities – had a definite political purpose, namely to
provide a counter-attraction to win over the Roman nobility from
its Byzantine sympathies. After the crushing of the Crescentian
rebellion, new courtly dignities were bestowed in profusion on the
rivals of the Crescentii, the counts of Tusculum; but for the most
part they were empty titles. Otto had no intention of basing his
power in Rome on the Roman nobility, on whom the new ceremonial offices were conferred, and the politically important office
of Patrician was, as noted, given to a Saxon noble. Even if contemporary letters and writings prove that Otto and his court were
not unconscious of the glories of ancient Rome, such ideas did not
directly influence Italian policy or imperial policy, which were
dictated by events and circumstances calling for sober action.

It is therefore credible enough, without having recourse to a legend of 'Roma aurea', that Otto III should, in 998, have set on his seal the famous inscription: *Renovatio imperii Romanorum*, and that a year later, in 999, we should find in his charters reference to the *restitutio rei publicae*. *Restitutio rei publicae* was, in the policy of the Ottonian government, the practical means leading directly to *renovatio imperii*. But *renovatio imperii* was neither more nor less than a revival and reform of Italian government, where previously there had been the strife of factions and parties, only held in check on rare occasions by the intermittent presence of an emperor content with a loose and often nominal overlordship. The phrase *renovatio imperii Romanorum*, as used by Otto III, was doubtless programmatic; but the programme it represented was not to restore the lost glories of ancient Rome, but to make the rights and powers of the ruler real and effective. It was, indeed, no accident that the phrase first occurred under Otto III; for it expressed his policy and he was the first emperor from Charlemagne onwards whose policy it did express. He was the first emperor who set out to make his authority real and not merely a loose overlordship over the mighty dukes and marquesses.

There were, therefore, important differences between the imperial policy of Otto I and Otto III; but they were not, as has sometimes been argued, the difference between a 'Saxon' and a 'Roman' policy. They sprang less from differences of personality and blood and upbringing — whatever Byzantine traits Otto III may have inherited from his mother, the Empress Theophano — than from concrete changes in the political situation, calling for a new handling and a new policy. Otto III was only twenty-one years old when he died in 1002, and we must therefore beware of exaggerating his personal share in the policy of the imperial government during his reign. This government was in the hands of experienced and sober states-men like Odilo of Cluny, Bishop Bernward of Hildesheim, Notger of Liége and the Marquess Eggihard of Meissen, who were unlikely to be led astray by vain dreams of imperialism or to sacrifice German interests to Roman ambitions. During the six years between 995, when Otto began to play a personal part in government, and his death at the beginning of 1002, eastern policy claimed almost as great a share of his attention as Italy and Rome. In 997, despite the desperate position of Gregory V in Rome and the imploring letters of Gerbert begging the emperor to make his presence felt, Otto deliberately embarked on a campaign in the east against the Wends. In 1000, between his second and third expeditions to Rome, Otto journeyed to Gnesen which he raised into an archbishopric. His Polish policy, his Hungarian policy, his measures towards Bohemia, the embassy he sent to Russia and his Dalmatian projects, all indicate that Rome had no monopoly in his mind or in his political activity. His imperial policy was more active than that of Otto I, but it was no less subordinate to German interests, and no less realistic. If it had been pursued to its logical conclusion over a period of years, it might have stabilized German government in Italy, and provided a firm foundation for the future. But Otto's early death, and the tense situation resulting therefrom, prevented the completion of his programme, and his policy between 998 and 1002 remains as little more than a monument of what might have been achieved, if German policy in Italy had continued for one or two generations more on the lines laid down during his reign.

IV

On Otto III's death in 1002, the reaction in Italy to the systematic reform of government during the years 998-1001 was far more severe than that which overtook Otto II's less sustained efforts after his death in 983. The vavasours, or *secundi milites*, realizing the seriousness of the threat to their feudal independence, raised their leader, Arduin of Ivrea, to the Italian throne; but the factions and divisions within Italy prevented Arduin from consolidating his position. In fact, Arduin represented less a united Italian opposition to German rule, than simply that party within Italy the vested interests of which had suffered most from Otto III's policy. Consequently, once he had established his position in Germany and was free to turn to Italian affairs, Otto's successor, Henry II, had little difficulty in defeating Arduin and re-establishing imperial rule.

The reign of Henry II (1002-1024) was, however, taken up in large measure with the problems of the eastern frontier, where Poland under Boleslav Chobry had asserted independence and was engaged on a policy of territorial expansion. For Henry, Italy necessarily took second place. His appearances there were brief and infrequent, and the three expeditions which he undertook (1004,

1014, 1022) were mere episodes. By the time of his first expedition in 1004, moreover, the group of distinguished and able administrators who had directed policy under Otto III had been broken up, and — in no position to carry on a sustained administration on the model of his immediate predecessor — Henry II returned to the policy of Otto I, ruling by division and playing off one faction against the other. Thus in Rome he supported the counts of Tusculum against the Crescentii, in central Italy he relied on the well-recompensed loyalty of the Marquess of Tuscany, while in Lombardy he strengthened the position of the bishops on whom he relied against the feudality. But this policy — the inadequacy of which Otto III's advisers had perceived — only aggravated the Italian situation, widening the cleft between the episcopate and the nobility, and culminating (in 1035) in civil war. Nor, in the long run, was anything gained by the policy of Henry II's successor, Conrad II (1024-1039), who, completely changing tactics, in 1037 took up the cause of the lesser feudality, and sought to base his government on their support. It was no solution to switch from one party to another, the less so since Henry III (1039-1056) again reversed his policy, returning to the alliance with the bishops who again became the main prop of imperial government. But the blow which Conrad II's policy had struck at the unity and loyalty of the imperial party proved irreparable, while as the result of the strengthening of the position of the lesser nobility during his reign social and political antagonisms within Italy were heightened.

Imperial policy in Italy during the eleventh century thus proved that government through a party was no substitute for the direct imperial administration which Otto III's ministers had sought to create. The policy pursued under Otto III was, in the circumstances of the day, the only policy which might have settled the problems of Italian government. Because that policy was followed neither by Henry II nor by Conrad II nor by Henry III, deterioration of the Italian situation could not be checked, with consequences for the future of the empire which only became evident during and after the Investiture Contest.

V

A careful and judicious appreciation of the imperial policy of Otto III, particularly in contrast and comparison with that of his predecessors and successors, is very necessary if we are to attempt any estimate of the influence of what has frequently been described as the 'imperial entanglement' on the course of German history. Contrasted with the policy of Otto I, the imperial policy of Otto III has often been regarded as the beginning of an unhealthy preoccupation with Italian affairs, of 'chimerical ambitions' which conflicted root and branch with the native aspirations and fundamental interests of the German people. What has been said above has shown how little this was the case, and how mistaken it is to attribute to the Greek blood flowing in Otto III's veins the differences discernible between his policy and that of Otto I. Differences there were, but they arose from changing social and historical circumstances, necessitating a revision of policy; while the weakening of imperial control in Italy in the eleventh century was a consequence not of Otto III's policy but of the failure on the part of his successors to maintain that policy.

For almost a century the attempt to draw up a balance-sheet, for or against the imperial policy of the rulers of mediaeval Germany, has haunted the study of German history, giving rise to heated argument and bitter controversy.[1] There would be little profit in attempting to resume, still less in attempting to pursue further, that controversy in this place. But it may be suggested that nothing is gained, and many perspectives are lost, if the question is taken out of its strictly historical context and — as has so often occurred — reviewed as a general problem comprising many consecutive centuries, without regard to changing circumstances, changing environment, changing personalities, changing *Weltanschauung*, or even the changing content of the imperial idea.

There is no single answer, Yes or No, to the question of the

[1] The controversy (which began in 1859 with the publication of Sybel's *Ueber die neueren Darstellungen der deutschen Kaiserzeit* as a sequel to the appearance in 1855 of the first volume of Giesebrecht's epochal *Geschichte der deutschen Kaiserzeit*) has been briefly and usefully summarized by Schneider, *Neuere Anschauungen der deutschen Historiker zur Beurteilung der deutschen Kaiserpolitik des Mittelalters* (1934), and Hostenkamp, *Die mittelalterliche Kaiserpolitik in der deutschen Historiographie seit Sybel und Ficker* (1934).

expediency of the mediaeval empire. On the contrary, the different phases of imperial history must be considered independently and the answer at which we arrive in regard to the Hohenstaufen empire may well be different from our judgement on the achievements and liabilities of the Ottonian empire. We can attempt to assess the benefits and disadvantages for Germany both of possession of the imperial title and of the political connexion with Burgundy and Italy; but any such assessment must be related to the specific circumstances of a particular age. Before leaving the history of the Ottonian empire, it is necessary to attempt such an assessment because of the importance, for the subsequent history of Germany, of the union of the German kingship with the imperial crown and because of the oft-repeated assertion that the coronation of Otto I in 962 'diverted the national history of the German people out of its natural orbit, stimulated a false ambition in the minds of the German kings, and entailed the expenditure of an enormous amount of German blood and treasure beyond the Alps to no profitable use'.

Confining ourselves solely to the Ottonian empire during the century following Otto I's coronation in 962, we are now in a position to test the validity of this verdict in the light of the known facts. The following are, I believe, the main considerations on which any conclusion must be based:

1. Otto I's imperial policy was no innovation. He was not setting out on a new path, stirred by new ambitions. All his actions in Italy and Burgundy fell within the existing framework of late-Carolingian politics and reflected Carolingian traditions which he had inherited through his father, Henry I.

2. Intervention in Italy and the assumption of the imperial crown was not an 'adventure' which Otto was free to undertake or reject. If he had not intervened, others would have acted in his stead, including the Dukes of Swabia and Bavaria. In fact, Otto delayed direct intervention as long as he could control the situation by political and diplomatic means; only when events took a particularly threatening turn in 951, did he march into Italy at the head of an army.

3. Some solution of the political problems of the Middle kingdom, including Italy, was imperative and unavoidable in the circumstances of the time, since the dissolution of authority throughout this region left a void which was certain to be filled. Through historical

connexions going back a full century to 843, this question was inextricably bound up with the succession to the empire.

4. Otto's intervention in Italy was undertaken in the interests of a purely German policy. Far from standing in the way of German interests, the imperial title and position were used to further German interests. Particularly in the east, the early years of the empire were a period of German expansion and colonization, and it would be difficult to show that preoccupation with Italy hindered the pursuit of projects elsewhere.

5. The changes in policy which occurred under Otto III implied no sudden or fundamental break with the past. In attempting to impose a more regular and effective system of government on Italy, he was simply responding to conditions and needs which had gradually become manifest under his father and grandfather. His reforms were intended to make imperial rule more secure, not to change the character of the empire. For Otto III, as for Otto I, Germany came first: Aachen, Gnesen and Prague were the scenes of his activity as well as Rome; Charlemagne was his model and inspiration.

6. The union of the German kingship with the imperial crown and the pursuit of imperial policy evoked no opposition within Germany. To this generalization the revolt of Liudolf of Swabia in 953[1] may at first glance seem to be a pertinent exception; but Liudolf's revolt was the expression not of German hostility to intervention in Italy but rather of the resentment of a leader who had seen the spoils of intervention wrested from his hands. When, however, it is considered that Germany in the tenth and eleventh centuries was anything but a centralized state or an absolute monarchy, when the strength of provincial feeling and the difficulties of the monarchy in overcoming the inherent particularism of the duchies are taken into account, the lack of opposition to imperial policy is remarkable, indicating that, among contemporaries, royal intervention in Italy was not considered detrimental to German interests.

Once the above points have been established, it becomes clear that much of the criticism levelled at Otto I and at the Ottonian empire is wide of the mark. In particular, there has been a tendency to overlook the limited and concrete character of the empire and of

[1] Above, p. 5

imperial policy, and to suppose that it implied a claim to universal dominion or overlordship throughout the west. Whatever may have been true later, under the Hohenstaufen, there is little justification for such a view in the history of the empire in the tenth and eleventh centuries. Nothing would, to all appearances, have been easier for Otto I than to reduce the king of France to the position of a vassal;[1] but no such policy was pursued. In this sense there was not even an attempt to restore the empire of Charlemagne, let alone establish dominion over the west. For Otto, the extent and therefore the commitments of his empire were strictly limited to the lands over which he ruled or was overlord: Germany, Italy and Burgundy. And because his rule comprised three *regna*, his domains together formed an *imperium*. This *imperium* was, because of the traditional connexion of the imperial title with Italy, identified with the *imperium Romanum*; but, as one of the greatest historians of the mediaeval empire has truly emphasized, 'it was not identical with the *respublica Christiana* nor co-terminous with western Christendom'.[2] Neither Otto I nor any of his successors during the following century entertained ambitions of dominating the western world.

There is therefore much truth in the view that service, not dominion, was the keynote of the empire,[3] in the sense that the establishment of the empire brought a new breath of order and stability into a world racked with anarchy. And certainly we shall do well to look first at the benefits conferred rather than at the advantages derived. Italy itself benefited unquestionably from Ottonian government: after three generations in which it was torn by the anarchy of uncontrolled local powers and ravages from without, it passed under a superior authority capable of holding the local powers in check and establishing some form of political organization. Of even wider and more durable significance was the

---

[1] L. Halphen, *Peuples et Civilisations*, V (1930), 342-343, summarizes the evidence showing how completely dependent Louis IV of France was on Otto.

[2] Julius Ficker, *Vom Reichsfürstenstande*, II, ii (1921), 143: 'The mediaeval empire was not identical with the *respublica Christiana*, was not co-terminous with western Christendom. Nor did it include an idea of world domination. On the contrary, it was based on actual territorial power, on those lands which, because they were so long ruled by the German emperor, were conceived of as a German empire. And this empire had little in common, in its historical development, with the universal empire as conceived of by ecclesiastical thinkers.' Cf. also *Das deutsche Kaiserreich* (1862), 64, 98, and *Deutsches Königthum u. Kaiserthum* (1862), 50-51.

[3] 'Weltdienst, nicht Weltherrschaft'; H. Heimpel, *Deutschlands Mittelalter, Deutschlands Schicksal* (1933), 9.

service of the empire in rescuing the papacy from the decadence and subservience to Roman factions which seemed likely, in the first half of the tenth century, to destroy its moral power for all time: it was the emperors, supported by ecclesiastics of the calibre of Odilo of Cluny, who took in hand the reform of the papacy, who purged it of its narrow localism by securing the appointment of popes such as the Frenchman Sylvester II, the German Clement II, and the Alsatian Leo IX, and who thus raised the Roman see into a world-power strong enough to challenge the might of the empire itself. And what was done for the papacy was done for the empire also, which ceased to be a perquisite of petty Italian and Burgundian princes and rose again to European status: but for the work of the Ottonian dynasty, the empire could never have inspired the devotion and stimulated the minds of political thinkers from the time of the Investiture Contest to the days of Dante and Marsilius of Padua.

Nor can any reasonable person doubt that Germany itself derived concrete benefits as well as prestige from its association with Italy in the empire. Contact with the Mediterranean world brought on the one hand a richer culture, on the other a share in a less primitive economy. Through Italy and Burgundy, Germany secured contact with the main trade routes of the early Mediterranean world, which flowed from the east through Lombardy across the western Alps to the fairs of Champagne. Nor can it easily be maintained that these advantages were bought, during the first century of the empire, at too great a cost. There is little, if any, evidence to indicate that the effort entailed in establishing and maintaining German rule in Italy was in excess of German capacities or that its commitments south of the Alps prevented the German monarchy from exploiting its advantages in the north. But there were occasions when difficulties in the south reacted unfavourably on the situation in Germany: Otto II's defeat by the Saracens at Cortone in 982 was, for example, felt as a shattering blow on all the frontiers of the empire.

The real weakness of the imperial position was not that it placed too great a strain on imperial resources, or absorbed the energies of German kings at the expense of Germany itself, but on the contrary that no ruler after Otto III was willing or able to devote adequate time and energy to Italy. Consequently the hold established by Otto I and strengthened for a brief spell under Otto III was not consolidated. This, as we have seen, was due to the infrequency and short duration

F

of visits to Italy by Henry II and his successors and their return to
the expedient of ruling through an Italian party. But these facts hide
a more fundamental weakness of German rule in Italy: namely, the
failure to construct a permanent machinery of government through
which administration could be smoothly carried on in the king's
absence. Because such machinery was lacking, the effective power of
the emperor inevitably dwindled in the face of new and rising social
forces until, after the long minority following the death of Henry III
in 1056, the whole German position south of the Alps was undermined.

This lack of permanent administrative institutions was of course
in no way limited to Italy. Rather it was a characteristic feature of
early mediaeval monarchies, due in the last analysis to the primitive
forms of natural economy, which prevented systematic financing of
government and forced the king to rely in outlying provinces on the
co-operation of the landed aristocracy, voluntary or enforced by the
king's ability to punish disloyalty and rebellion. In this respect Italy
in the tenth century was little different from tenth-century Germany.
What is remarkable about Italian rule — and at the same time its
most serious weakness — was the failure during the eleventh century
to progress, on the foundations laid by Otto III, beyond this element-
ary form of political organization. This was not the result of Italian
resistance to German domination, the strength of which it is easy to
exaggerate, but was rather due to the failure of the eleventh-century
kings to recognize that, if they were to maintain their hold on Italy
and Burgundy, these two countries must have at least the same care
and attention as was given to Germany. Except under Otto III this
was not realized, and Italy remained a subordinate province of the
empire. Hence, during the eleventh century, imperial government
in Italy and Germany gradually drew apart. The Salian emperors
strove to introduce new principles and methods of government
north of the Alps; but, precisely because their attention was thereby
concentrated on Germany, and on the incipient opposition in
Germany which their administrative innovations bred, the southern
lands of the empire were neglected. We shall survey in the following
chapter the constitutional and administrative innovations introduced
into Germany by the Salian kings, and their attempt to place German government on a more stable foundation than anything which
tenth-century Europe had known: the important fact at this point is

that nothing similar was attempted south of the Alps. Thus, while in Germany new and progressive forms of political life were being evolved, government in Italy clung to forms and methods which reflected the conditions of an earlier century and were rapidly becoming obsolete, while the vital forces in Italian life were driven under the surface and into channels over which the empire had no control.

Hence, by imperceptible degrees the control of the emperors over Italy was weakened at the very period when it looked as though they were succeeding in welding Germany into a strong centralized monarchy. How powerfully this discrepancy in the growth of the two lands influenced the destinies of Germany was seen when, in 1075, the reformed papacy reached out from Rome to join hands with the German opposition, and struck at the foundations of the new German state which the kings of the eleventh century had struggled long and valiantly to build.

CHAPTER 4

GERMANY IN THE ELEVENTH CENTURY: THE ERA OF PROGRESS AND PROMISE
(1024-1075)

I

IT is only necessary to take our stand at the coronation of Henry III in 1028, eleven years before the death of his father, the emperor Conrad II (1024-1039), and to compare the state of Germany with that in 918, to measure the progress achieved under the Saxon dynasty. Compared with France under Robert II (996-1031), the second ruler of the new Capetian dynasty, it was a homogeneous land, held together by great and enduring traditions, ruled over by energetic and intelligent sovereigns, who had proved competent to resist and counteract the disintegration of society which accompanied the ravages of invasion from north and east. The leadership of Europe was firmly established in German hands. In Italy the inherent weaknesses in the German position were not yet visible; while the union of Germany and Burgundy in 1033 added new and important lands to the empire. The imperial title marked out the German king among the rulers of Europe; imperial rule brought stability to central Europe. In the east the attempt of Boleslav I (992-1025) to build up a greater Poland failed, and his successor, Miesko, was compelled to accept German overlordship; in the Hungary of St. Stephen (1000-1038) German influence was even stronger.

The establishment of German preponderance in Europe was the more remarkable in view of the problems facing the Saxon dynasty at home. In 918, the future of the new dynasty was anything but secure; even the maintenance of the precarious unity of the five German 'peoples' was in doubt. The elections of 911 and 919 and the double change of dynasty had necessarily weakened the principle of hereditary succession, which was a prerequisite of internal stability in the loosely organized states of mediaeval Europe. However, the Saxon rulers skilfully exploited the situation on their frontiers — defence against the Magyars, wars with the Slavs, expeditions into

Italy — not only to divert the energies of their people from internal strife, but also to unite them in a common cause, and to accustom them to the leadership of the monarchy. Gradually throughout the tenth century the predominance of the monarchy over the local powers was strengthened, and its strengthened position was reflected in the consolidation of its dynastic rights.

The consolidation of the position of the new dynasty began in 936, when Henry I, realizing that death was near, assembled princes and people at Erfurt and 'designated' his son Otto as successor, thus ensuring, so far as he was able,[1] the continuance of his line and the succession of his eldest legitimate son. After Henry's death, the choice of Otto as successor was confirmed by the election of the princes, the acclamation of the people, and the consecration of the clergy, while the dukes recognized their subordination to the crown by performing the ritual services in the coronation ceremony. Thus Otto I succeeded by his father's will, the electors' will and God's will, by hereditary right, election and divine right, receiving every symbolic and religious assurance which the century knew. Thereafter, the claims of heredity were gradually strengthened at the expense of the rights of election, the independence of the monarchy at the expense of the powers of the princes. Otto I himself went beyond the old, well-established right of 'designating' his successor and had his son Otto II raised to the throne as co-ruler in 961; even after Otto I's death in 973 it was from 961 that Otto II's regnal years ran. In the same way Henry III's regnal year began with the death of his father Conrad II, on June 4, 1039, and not with his own enthronement seven weeks later.

The principles of hereditary monarchy, which were established in Germany by the close of the tenth century, were carried over into the empire. From the time of Conrad II (1024-1039), it was an accepted fact that the German king was *ipso facto* ruler of Italy, and the electoral rights of the Lombards, passed over in silence, fell into disuse. From 1045 we find in use the title *Rex Romanorum in imperatorem promovendus*, a title which implies that the German king, although not yet invested with the imperial crown in Rome, is already 'King of the Romans' with an indefeasible right to succeed to the empire. Thus,

---

[1] 'Designation' was no formality. A party among the princes supported Otto's younger brother, Henry, because the latter was born in the purple, whereas Otto was born before his father succeeded to the throne. It was the old king, Henry I, who decided between the two claimants. Cf. F. Kern, *Gottesgnadentum u. Widerstandsrecht* (1914), 32.

already in the eleventh century the position was reached which was described by a later jurist in the words: 'He who is chosen by the election of the princes alone is the true emperor, even before he has been confirmed by the pope.' But in the eleventh century the election of the princes was little more than a formality: the right of the king's son to succeed, the right of the father to nominate a son as successor, was axiomatic. In this respect the facts regarding the succession of Henry III were typical: designated successor to the throne at the age of nine in 1026 by his father Conrad II (who had himself only succeeded in 1024), he was crowned king at Aachen in 1028, the year after his father's coronation as emperor in Rome. Thus king succeeded emperor and on reaching the imperial throne himself raised up a new king as successor: not only was continuity established and maintained, but at the same time the historically distinct rights of the monarchy were combined. Rome, Lombardy, Germany and Burgundy were welded into a single realm, the *imperium Romanum*, and the king who succeeded to the throne in Germany was also hereditary ruler throughout the Roman empire.

The situation was, of course, different when there was no direct successor from the reigning house and a new dynasty had to be chosen. This was the case after the death of Otto III in 1002 and again on the death of Henry II in 1024. Yet both these occasions only served to show the strength of hereditary principles, which was illustrated no less strikingly by the establishment of regencies during the minority rule of Otto III and of Henry IV. On the death of Otto III Henry II was chosen king because he was successor to the Saxon inheritance; the sole basis of his candidature was his hereditary right. In 1024 the only two candidates seriously considered both claimed the throne as descendants of Otto I's daughter, Liutgard, and Conrad II succeeded in part because Henry II's widow, Kunigunde, handed him the royal insignia and thus 'designated' him as the candidate best qualified to succeed. Thus we can measure the success of the Saxon dynasty in consolidating hereditary principles: even when election was unavoidable, respect was paid to the claims of royal blood. Far from the extinction of the ruling dynasty being a sign for a consolidation of electoral rights in opposition to the monarchy, nothing is more remarkable than the disinclination to use this opportunity for strengthening particularist claims and princely pretensions. Instead of attempting to build up a right of free choice, the princes revealed their acceptance of the monarchical idea and of the work of Otto I by genuinely discriminating between the reasonable claims of junior branches of the royal house. In the clash between the opposed principles of heredity and election, heredity had won the day.

The success of the monarchy was reflected in the breakdown of regionalism,[1] which could hardly have occurred had the dukes retained the powers and independence which they enjoyed in the first decades of the ninth century. Here the foundation was the success of Otto I in protecting the eastern frontiers of Saxony, thus allowing the growth of more settled life in the north-east of the kingdom. Already under Otto I a monk from Reichenau on Lake Constance became Abbot of St. Maurice in Magdeburg and subsequently Bishop of Hildesheim, while the Saxon Hildeward received at St. Gallen the education which he was later to turn to good account in Saxony as Bishop of Halberstadt. But it was during the following century, in particular as a result of the work of Henry II (1002-1024), that cultural interchanges began to alter the face of Germany, gradually breaking down the differences between north and south, and raising Saxony to the same level of civilization as Swabia and Bavaria. Southerners like St. Godehard of Niederaltaich in Bavaria, who was active at Hersfeld from 1005 to 1012 and at Hildesheim from 1022 to 1038, made a major contribution by the foundation of new monastic centres and the introduction of new standards, and St. Godehard's work was kept alive by his disciples.

Simultaneously new schools, like the monastic school of St. Emmeram in Regensburg and the episcopal school at Bamberg, became connecting links between north and south, collecting recruits and spreading culture in all regions of Germany. The same result was achieved by the Hirsau reform movement, which introduced a new spirit of centralization into the Benedictine order in Germany and thus formed a permanent link between widely dispersed monasteries: by the end of the eleventh century the political programme, religious outlook and even the artistic style of Hirsau had become the common property of north and south Germany. But the foundation of new monastic centres, particularly in the north, denoted economic as well as cultural progress, and here again the result was a further advance towards unity. In this regard two

[1] This aspect of the situation is admirably summarized in Seidlmayer, *Deutscher Nord und Süd im Hochmittelalter* (1929), on whose conclusions the following is based.

new groups of town settlements are particularly noteworthy, since
they contributed much to the establishment of commercial connexions: first, the group comprising Bamberg, Nürnberg and Neuburg
an der Donau, which provided a new route for commerce between
the Danube and the Main, and secondly the group reaching from
Ulm through Esslingen to Speyer, which connected the Upper
Danube valley with the central Rhineland. Thus the geographical
obstacles to unity, the Swabian and Franconian Jura, were gradually
overcome. As the eleventh century proceeded regional differences
fell into the background, and it was then that the collective name for
the German people, *Teutonici*, rapidly became usual. Even the
Saxons, who in 1073 rose in rebellion 'for their liberty, their laws
and their homeland', showed no inclination to resist the rule of the
first two kings of the new south German dynasty, Conrad II (1024-
1039) and Henry III (1039-1056), or to stand apart from the rest of
Germany.[1] By the middle of the eleventh century the realm was
firmly united under its ruling dynasty and all traces of particularism
seemed on the point of disappearance.

By the beginning of the eleventh century, the internal pacification
and the new stability achieved by the Saxon monarchy had also
brought about a sharp economic recovery. This was manifested
primarily in the spread of internal colonization and land reclamation,
itself probably the consequence of an expanding population. Settlement spread from the valleys into the foothills of the Bohemian and
Thuringian forests; and even in the heart of the Rhineland — for
example, in the Taunus — new settlements sprang up. On the whole,
this was the work of the peasantry themselves, who encroached on
woodlands and made new arable. In some cases already, the colon-
izers secured more advantageous conditions than their fellows in the
long-settled districts, paying rents in lieu of services, and securing
partial enfranchisement from manorial burdens. Hence economic
progress was accompanied by social change, which was further
stimulated by the first stirring of town life and a revival of commerce
due to the consolidation of the connexion between Germany and
Italy and German control of the Alpine passes. Local trade, the
necessary exchange (for example) between corn-growing and wine-
growing districts, and the wider needs of the new monastic centres,

---

[1] 'Der Sächsische Stamm ertrug die Herrschaft des zweiten Saliers ebenso willig wie die
des ersten' (Steindorff, *Jahrbücher Heinrichs des Dritten*, II, 366). However, cf. below, p. 93 sqq.

also played their part. Money, long a rare commodity, again began
to flow; land values began to rise, particularly as the growth of towns
provided outlets for surplus rural products.

None of these developments must be exaggerated. It was, in the
eleventh century, only the first stirring which made itself felt. But
the contrast with the previous century was marked enough, and
however small the immediate change, it implied the passing of a
turning-point and a movement which, unless circumstances altered,
could only gather momentum. In every respect the essential step
forward had been taken, as a result of the work of the Saxon
dynasty, and already a new breath of progress was in the air. The
only question was whether the crown, which had worked hard to
release the new forces in German life, would continue to control
and profit from the economic and social movements of the century.
If the monarchy retained its place at the head, the prospect for the
future was fair: for Germany had already far outstripped France and
England in the pace of its recovery and was already on the path
leading to a more modern form of government, based on the exploitation of new resources and the introduction of new political
conceptions.

II

It was the merit of the great Salian dynasty, which succeeded to the
Saxon inheritance on the death of Henry II in 1024, to have realized
the need for a new type of government more in harmony with the
changed social and economic conditions than that inherited from
Otto I.[1] The history of the Salian period from the accession of Conrad
II in 1024 to the outbreak of the revolutionary contest between
Henry IV and Pope Gregory VII in 1075 is the history of the attempt
by the German monarchy to adapt its machinery of government to
the new circumstances, to mobilize the new rising classes behind the
monarchy and to capitalize the new resources opening up. Historians
have seen behind these attempts a consistent Salian administrative
programme, consciously and systematically pursued. When we
consider the remarkable differences in character between the three

[1] The fullest appreciation of Salian policy is in Karl Wilhelm Nitzsch, *Geschichte des
deutschen Volkes*, vol. 2. The subject has also been carefully discussed in Thompson, *Feudal
Germany*, 185 sqq., 330 sqq., 346 sqq., 350 sqq., where all salient facts will be found with
ample documentation.

chief protagonists, the stern unlettered realist, Conrad II (1024-1039), Henry III (1039-1056) with his strong sense of divine mission and deep religious convictions, and the wilful, violent, shrewd but unstable Henry IV (1056-1106), such a view is hardly plausible. Yet each builds on the work of the other, and each moves forward beyond the forms of Ottonian government, revealing the constructive powers inherent in the monarchy and its determination to find a solution of the problems facing it.

These problems were partly the product of changes occurring in the course of the eleventh century, partly problems left over from the Ottonian age. For all its merits and achievements what is often (not altogether correctly) described as the 'Ottonian system of government' was not without its limitations. Otto I had governed less by system than by a shifting personal control; and Ottonian government had all the disadvantages inherent in this method. No lasting institutional check was established over the dukes; for the expedient of counts-palatine[1] was extremely short-lived. Instead Otto relied largely on the loyalty and self-interest of members of his own family whom he appointed to the duchies. And for all his reliance on the Church, his methods in Church policy were little different from those he adopted towards the lay aristocracy. His brother, Bruno, was raised to the archbishopric of Cologne, his son William to that of Mainz; but apart from these personal ties, the Church was not easily subordinated to the purposes of the State. That is seen in the ecclesiastical opposition to the foundation of the archbishopric of Magdeburg, and the similar resistance met by Henry II when in 1007 he founded Bamberg.[2] There is no doubt that the Ottonian Church was an effective counterpoise to the power of the dukes; but it was not organically incorporated in the scheme of government. Churchmen pursued objects of their own which conflicted with the objects of the government, and were not prepared to subordinate them to the interests of the state as a whole or to royal policy. Hence the same sort of 'juggling' with personnel was necessary to keep control over the great ecclesiastical sees as was necessary to control the great dukes. The whole functioning of government depended, in short, on an unstable balance, in which the decisive factor was the personal loyalty of individuals to (and often their family connexions with) the royal dynasty. About the whole

[1] Cf. above, p. 28.   [2] Above, pp. 35, 56.

political structure there was an element of instability; it worked well enough for the present, but there were no principles to provide guiding lines for the future.

Thus, from the very beginning of the eleventh century, there were very perceptible attempts by every German ruler of the period to cope with the problems Otto I had left unsolved and to reduce the tension in the political structure which his methods tended to create. Each ruler reacted in his own way, consonant with his character and circumstances. Henry II (1002-1024) sought to counteract the aristocratic leanings of the episcopacy and the great Benedictine abbots, whose ranks were still filled exclusively from the highest and most exclusive families in the land, by converting the royal chapel into a training-ground for bishops, thus making the episcopacy in a new sense an 'official class', its members at home in the court and conversant with royal policy. Perhaps an even more noteworthy feature of Henry II's policy, however, was his departure from the Ottonian attitude to the nobility. It is characteristic of Henry, who (by Ottonian standards) had few important family connexions, that he did not attempt a 'dynastic' policy, but deliberately ruled through the dukes and counts, compelling them to take a share in government and avoiding any taint of 'party' politics, such as had characterized Ottonian rule.

With Henry II's successor, Conrad II (1024-1039), there was a change of emphasis and a more distinct breach with the previous century. This was most graphically illustrated during the revolt of Duke Ernst of Swabia in 1027, when the king allied with the Swabian counts against the duke. Called upon by Ernst for support, the Swabians answered that their duty to him was limited by their duty to the king: 'We are free', they said, 'and the supreme protector of our liberty is our king and emperor. If we desert him, our liberty perishes.' But Conrad's policy of seeking support among the counts and rear-vassals — a 'feudal' policy, illustrated no less strikingly in the admission of hereditary succession to fiefs[1] — had serious limitations because, as we shall later see, the structure of German society was not yet genuinely feudal. Even on this notable occasion in 1027, what the Swabian counts emphasized was their 'liberty'; and they looked to the king not as the head of a feudal hierarchy (which did

[1] Wipo, *Vita Chuonradi*, cap. 6: 'Militum vero animos in hoc multum attraxit, quod antiqua beneficia parentum nemini posteriorum aufferri sustinuit.'

not exist), but as the defender of their freedom against the dukes who were seeking to bring them into dependence. Conrad's policy of reliance on the lesser against the higher nobility is interesting, because it reveals for the first time the new social antagonisms emerging in eleventh-century Germany; but it was not altogether practicable. The opposition between the Swabian duke and the Swabian counts in 1027 was a mere episode; normally all sections of the nobility stood united in defence of aristocratic liberties, and because few counts had to experience the burden of feudal bonds, few were normally willing to work with the crown against the princes. There were not, in short, the social conditions obtaining in eleventh-century Germany, which elsewhere made possible an enduring alliance between king and rear-vassals against the higher nobility.

Conrad II's 'feudal' policy was consequently not continued by his Salian successors.[1] Social conditions in Germany forced them to look outside the ranks of the free nobility for support and co-operation. Henry III still placed reliance on the Church and on his own theocratic position at the head of the Church; under him the imperial theocracy reached its apogee. But the very reforms which Henry sponsored produced a clerical reaction — clearly apparent from the days of Pope Leo IX (1048-1054) — against the idea of an imperial theocracy, while the new conception of simony as a heresy (warmly embraced by the emperor himself) made it difficult to exploit the revenues of the German Church for the purposes of the crown, as Conrad II had not hesitated to do. Moreover, it must not be forgotten that, down to the end of Henry III's reign, the German Church was aristocratic through and through. Hence, as the power of the aristocracy was consolidated in Germany, the churchmen became less dependable, more intent on their secular interests; and in Church as well as in secular administration the Salian kings had need of a new and more dependable class.

The support which the king looked for in vain from the free nobility, he found in the upper ranks of the dependent classes. In England and France a lord could look with assurance to his vassals for service in the administration of his honour. In Germany the lack of close feudal ties forced all lords, the king among them, to turn to the servile classes for such administrative officers and for armed

[1] We have already seen that the same was true in Italy; cf. above, p. 64.

knights; and so in Germany there rose a class of *ministeriales* different from any class in feudal society in western Europe. Like vassals, they were rewarded with land and honours; but they lacked the personal freedom of the feudal vassal and could not claim the same privileges of class. They seem to have been employed in the first place by the great churches, both as administrators of ecclesiastical estates and as armed knights performing the churches' military services, because bishops and abbots were loath to enfeoff their lands to free vassals, against the performance of such duties, for fear lest their property might be expropriated. Because of their traditions of obedience and dependence *ministeriales* were more tractable than vassals and less dangerous to entrust with power. Their holdings, moreover, were not true fiefs, but were servile tenures, the property still of their lords. But with the growing economic activity after the end of the period of invasions the *ministeriales* quickly rose in importance and became distinct from the main body of servile tenants. This was proved by their success in obtaining written confirmations of their rights, through which their social position was established on a firm basis of law. Most famous of these statements of ministerial law is that drawn up about 1023 by Bishop Burchard of Worms; but we possess many other statements of *Hof-* or *Dienstrecht* from about the same period, and all mark the growing importance in administration of the ministerial class.

What the ecclesiastics had done in promoting the growth of a ministerial class on Church estates, the Salian kings set about doing on the demesnes of the crown. Occasional instances of favourite *ministeriales* near the person of the king may be found in the Saxon period, but Conrad II was the first German ruler to favour the royal *ministeriales* as a class, and to organize them into an administrative staff. Werner, his chief *ministerialis*, was the earliest secular minister in the history of mediaeval Germany; in his capacity of supervisor of the fisc he was a kind of chief intendant or comptroller-general. Even more notable was Benno, who rose rapidly in Henry III's service, became mayor of the imperial palace at Goslar, chief administrator of the crown lands, and was selected for the bishopric of Osnabrück in 1054; his appointment to an episcopal see marked the first breach in the purely aristocratic constitution of the German Church. But it was under Henry IV (1056-1106) that the Salian policy of employing *ministeriales* as the backbone of the royal

administration was pushed to its logical conclusion: when the chroniclers of the period complain that Henry is surrounded by *vilissimi*
and *infimi homines*, that he listens only to low-born counsellors and
spurns the advice of high-born princes, they are voicing the complaints of the aristocracy against Henry IV's consistent and exclusive
use of *ministeriales*.

The development of a ministerial administrative class was only part,
though perhaps the keystone, of a greater programme of administrative reform which gradually took shape under the Salian kings and
which was perfected by Henry IV. When, under Henry II and
Conrad II, the lands of the royal abbeys were brought under the
same management as those of the royal demesne, when they were
'assimilated to the fisc', the object at least in part was to break the
power of the aristocratic 'advocates' and bring monastic estates
under the control of the more trustworthy and disciplined *ministeriales*. On the other hand, this reassertion of royal control over lands
it had placed in monastic and episcopal hands, was also part of a
general policy, inaugurated by Conrad II, of recovering crown-
lands and forest which had been encroached upon and expropriated.
At the time of Conrad's accession in 1024 the dilapidation of the
royal fisc had reached the extreme limit; the crown lands were
reduced to less than under the last of the Carolingians. Conrad's aim
was not only to recover such lands for the crown, but also to improve
their administration and increase their yield by putting them in the
hands of *ministeriales*, exchanging remote for adjacent estates, consolidating royal holdings, enforcing escheats and forfeitures, etc. In
all these aims he was outstandingly successful: by the time of his
death in 1039 the material wealth of the monarchy was greater than
ever before.

The policy inaugurated by Conrad II was carried further by his son,
Henry III, and then by Henry IV, who transformed Conrad's policy
of recuperation, revindication and reform into a concrete plan for a
centralized monarchy with a permanent capital at Goslar in the
Harz mountains. Already at the beginning of the century Henry II
had developed the importance of Goslar, just as — at the other
extremity of Saxony — he had built a royal citadel at Bremen. More
castles were built by Henry III, including the fortress of Goslar
itself; and Henry IV deliberately set out to cover the Saxon and
Thuringian countryside with a network of castles, garrisoned by

loyal Swabian *ministeriales* from the Salian estates in southern Germany. Of these the first and strongest was the Harzburg, described as the 'yoke of Saxony'. By about 1070 the mountains and even (as the chronicler, Lambert of Hersfeld, bitterly complained) all the little hills of Thuringia and the Harz country bristled with royal fortresses.

The heart of the new military system, dominating Saxony and giving the monarchy for the first time an entry into the colonial lands of the east, was Goslar. In the vicinity of Goslar were the famous Rammelsberg silver mines, discovered in the reign of Otto I, designed to provide the king with a supply of bullion and free him from the necessity of remunerating servants and adherents with grants of land. With increased economic resources and on the sure foundation of a money economy, it was Henry IV's intention to build up the royal demesne and subject it to systematic administration and exploitation. In 1064-5 an inventory of crown lands and of services owed was drawn up, reminiscent of the Domesday Survey in England some twenty years later. Inquests were held, and proprietors forced to produce their titles; royal rights and impositions, which had been exacted from freemen in Carolingian times but had since passed into desuetude, were revived; the royal monopoly over the forest was reaffirmed, the king not only laying claim to unappropriated forest and waste but also beginning to enclose them, while the inhabitants of the forests, who had settled the land as 'squatters' were subjected to the control of the king's officers. The forest villages, which had grown up through the clearance and colonization of the Harzwald and the Thüringerwald, were brought under the king's ban, while in the open countryside freemen were forced to pay over a proportion of farm produce and on royal manors predial services were increased.

It was, taking all in all, a ruthless and ambitious programme, bound to meet opposition. But it was also a statesmanlike project, revealing Henry IV's keen sense of the realities of the situation. Behind the whole programme was the energy and devoted service of the royal *ministeriales*, whose task it was to execute the king's plans. As its ultimate object there was the project of giving the monarchy a new and stronger foundation by building up the crown territories and securing a steady and permanent revenue. Henry IV's intention was, however, not so much to build his power on the old hereditary demesnes of the Salian family in south-west Germany as to set up a new crown territory in the colonized lands of the east. In this respect the way had already been pointed by Henry III, who after the death of Eckhard of Meissen in 1046, had retained Eckhard's allodial lands for the monarchy. With such a foundation the kingship would have nothing to fear from the aristocracy and no need to rely on aristocratic co-operation: with an improved organization of government, dependable servants, ample revenues and extensive demesnes the Salians could face the challenge of the aristocracy.

III

A challenge to Henry IV's policy was bound to come. It was bound to come not only because the Salian programme of constitutional and administrative innovation evidently impinged upon the vested interests of the free classes, particularly of the free nobility, but also because the economic and social developments of the eleventh century were not all favourable to the monarchy. Having surveyed the attempts of the Salian rulers to harness the new forces at play to the interests of the monarchy, it is therefore necessary for us to consider the factors weighing in the opposite direction.

Once again an analysis of the situation leads us back to the Ottonian period and to the Ottonian settlement. The Saxon kings, we saw, achieved two major successes: they defeated the strivings of the dukes after provincial autonomy, and they maintained royal control over the Church. Contrasted with the position in late Carolingian France, this was a great achievement. The great provincial magnates of France rose to power by subjecting all other lords of their region, clerical as well as lay; they enforced feudal dependence on themselves, creating beneath them a feudal hierarchy of subordinates. The long period of feudal struggle, in which this process took place, reduced France to something bordering on anarchy; but ultimately it created a firm foundation for government. In Germany the position was very different. Compared with the French principalities, the provinces over which the German dukes strove to rule were immense territories; but never — not even in the years before they had to face the challenge of the Ottonian monarchy — did the German dukes possess the same concentrated authority as was exercised by the feudal princes of France. We saw this in regard to the counts, who mainly escaped ducal control. We saw also that the German Church remained a royal or national Church, looking to the king as its supreme head and defender; except for a few years at the beginning of the tenth century, no German bishopric fell under ducal control. In other words the German Church in Ottonian and Salian times was not 'feudalized', any more than the administrative organization of counties was 'feudalized'. The essential difference between the German duke and the French prince is that the latter was, the former was not, a feudal lord; that the latter could consolidate his position by means of feudal law and in virtue of his position in the feudal hierarchy. To the position of the German duke before the period of the Investiture Contest, feudalism contributed little; that, in the last analysis, was why his power was never so concentrated as that of his equals in France.

The fundamental difference between German society in the tenth century and that of France was the lack, or at least the weakness, of feudalism. We cannot, indeed, in this respect speak of Germany as a whole. The duchy of Lorraine was as fully feudalized as France; but Lorraine stands apart, just as Burgundy, after its annexation by Conrad II in 1034, stands apart. Even in the heart of Germany, however, there were marked differences. Frankish feudalism had been introduced into Bavaria even before Charlemagne replaced Duke Tassilo by Frankish counts; hence it was a stronger force in Bavaria than anywhere else in Germany, and this is probably the explanation why, of all the German dukes, the Bavarian was the most powerful. But even in Bavaria there was no question (as occurred in France) of the extinction of all freemen who were not vassals. Nowhere in Germany did vassalage become the mark of a freeman; on the contrary it remained a sign of servitude, a bond which no free man would willingly accept. With the relatively rapid growth of feudalism in Bavaria, moreover, we have to contrast its failure to penetrate in this period into Saxony. Before the Investiture Contest, Saxony was practically untouched by feudalism. This was a fact of importance, since the German kings of the tenth century were Saxons and therefore in no way predisposed to employ feudal methods of government. Otto I's treatment of counties as offices, not as fiefs, his maintenance of Carolingian conceptions of a non-feudal organization of government and his reliance on administrative discipline, not on feudal sanctions, to secure the loyalty of his

G

servants, all reflect the state of Saxon society, in which the free man, working his own lands, is the typical figure.

What above all distinguished Germany from France was the survival of an extensive class of free men. This was not a homogeneous class. On the contrary, the abrupt cleft between different sections of the free population was characteristic of Saxon society, and there were similar class differences elsewhere. Throughout Germany we must distinguish between the peasant freeman, holding and working a single farmstead, and the noble freeman with wide estates, who regarded himself as a member of an hereditary ruling caste. But in one respect both sections of the free population stood on the same footing. Every freeman, great or small, was owner of his own lands. Even where (as in Bavaria) many of the free nobility might hold fiefs of the duke, they continued to hold their allodial lands as well, and allodial lands and fiefs were kept separate and governed — in regard to succession, for example — by different legal rules. In Germany, therefore, there was so much allodial land that the establishment throughout the kingdom of a network of feudal lordships was impossible. That is why, in the Saxon period, the feudal lordship did not in Germany become the unit of administration; and it was because they could not base their power on the solid foundation of feudalism that the German dukes, in the period after 899, sought to build up their position out of their functions as military leaders. In two ways at least, however, this was a weak foundation. In the first place, the duke's power extended only over persons and not over land; it was the authority of a military leader over his men. In the second place, it was not easy to extend to times of peace an authority justified only in time of war. The free classes were jealous of their liberty; they regarded vassalage as degrading; they considered it the mark of a free man to hold aloof from all ties which might be regarded as ties of subordination. Because they owned their own lands, they had a solid foundation on which to base this attitude of independence. There remained, therefore, in Germany a free class with a strong sense of its own liberty and of its own inherent rights, which was prepared to resist all inroads on its liberty, no matter whence they came.

Against this background it becomes evident that the successes of the Saxon monarchy in the tenth century, real though they were, hid more fundamental weaknesses. Ducal strivings for autonomy were defeated, but the wider problem of the free aristocracy was hardly touched. Its very preoccupation with the duchies prevented the monarchy from concentrating on other problems; and it is therefore no exaggeration to say that the tenth-century struggle between king and dukes left the way free for the development of the rights and privileges of the aristocracy. Negatively the defeat of the dukes itself contributed to this result. In France, a new political society was built up from the bottom by the feudal princes in Flanders, Anjou, Champagne or Aquitaine, as well as (and, indeed, far in advance of) the Capetian kings in the Ile-de-France. The constant weakening of the position of the dukes in tenth-century Germany prevented any similar subjection of the provincial aristocracy there, and the German dukes consequently left no inheritance of settled provincial government for the crown to take over, as the later Capetians were able to take over the local feudal governments which owed their origins to the abilities of the French princes. On the positive side, it is clear that the German nobility profited from the new impulses which began to reinvigorate German economic life after Otto I's victory over the Magyars in 955. Colonization, reclamation, the foundation of new villages, the growth of the dependent classes, improved their economic position, while their very achievements in the economic sphere — which were due solely to their own efforts and owed nothing to the government — both promoted their sense of independence and gave them the means whereby to enforce their rights.

Between 950 and 1050, therefore, the aristocracy strengthened its position. It could do this because there was no hierarchy, as in France, subordinating the small lord on his manor to the viscount, the viscount to the count, the count himself perhaps to another count or to the duke, and the feudal prince, whatever his title, to the crown. German society was not stratified in this way: normally the free classes knew no subordination, save to the king. But the king had not the means whereby to deal with the free aristocracy throughout the length and breadth of Germany. The county system was adequate as a means of exercising authority over the small peasant freemen, who remained numerous in Saxony. But the free nobility were socially the equals of the counts, the counts were chosen from among their numbers; and they were therefore loath to accept more than the loosest subordination under the counts. On the contrary, their whole effort was directed towards obtaining the same powers over their own lands as the counts exercised over the lands of the free peasantry on behalf of the crown. In this respect they were without doubt aided by their position as 'advocates' over ecclesiastical estates. The 'advocate', we saw,[1] exercised equivalent powers to the count within the bounds of his 'immunity'; like the count, he had authority over the small peasant freeman. Thus the free nobility, through its exercise of the 'advocacy', obtained powers over the free peasant population, while it had always possessed immediate authority over the servile population — now increasing in numbers as a result of colonization — resident on its own estates. In this way, the position of advocate was complementary to that of landed proprietor: together they gave the nobility control over the whole population, free and servile, on their estates and those of the churches which they administered. The count was excluded and the power of the aristocracy enhanced.

This process, which took place outside the law and was not accorded formal recognition until the twelfth century, implied, as it reached its completion, a far-reaching breach in the constitution of the Ottonian Church. As we saw, the parallel institutions of 'immunity' and 'advocacy' were introduced in order to strengthen royal control over the provincial churches at a time when they were threatened with subordination to the dukes. As a whole, this policy produced satisfactory results until the end of the tenth century. In the eleventh century things were different. Not only did the general pacification, due to the exertions of the monarchy, result in a spate of monastic foundations, but also the healthier state of society, due in the last analysis to the same cause, led to a demand for monastic reform. When Otto I died in 973 there were 108 monasteries in Germany, of which probably all — thanks to Otto's policy — were firmly attached to the crown. A century later, on the eve of the Investiture Contest, there were over 700, and these new foundations were nearly without exception 'reformed' houses founded by the aristocracy.

The flood of new monastic foundations during the second half of the eleventh century completely altered the relations between the German monarchy and the German Church, because the bulk of the new houses were dependent upon their monastic founders and not on

---

[1] Above, p. 34.

the crown. If it is surprising to find the nobility — against whose violence churchmen never ceased to protest — suddenly interested in monastic reform and expansion, it should be remembered that 'when a great layman restored or reformed or founded a religious establishment, it was because he owned it and profited from its revenues'.[1] The foundation of monasteries in eleventh-century Germany reflected the endeavours of the aristocracy to develop their economic position. Before the foundation of houses like St. Georgen, St. Blasien, St. Peter and Alpirsbach, for example, the Black Forest was practically uninhabited; the work of opening up and colonizing the land was performed by the monks. But the aristocratic owners of the monastic estates were unwilling to see the profits of this work booked by the monarchy. Inevitably they resisted the attempts of the Salian kings to bind all the churches of Germany, no matter by whom founded, into a national church under the supreme direction of the king, who was *rex et sacerdos*, the divinely appointed ruler of Church and State. 'Unless compelled, I am unwilling to make it a royal house', wrote Ulrich of Lenzburg of his family foundation, Beromünster, in 1036; but he was unable to withstand the dual pressure of the crown, striving to unite the German Church, and of the canons, seeking the liberty which the crown alone could give, and by 1045 Beromünster had become a royal priory.[2]

A few years later, with the accession of Pope Leo IX (1048-1054), an Alsatian closely linked with the south German nobility, a change set in. Against the 'liberty' guaranteed by subjection to the king, a new form of 'liberty', guaranteed by subjection to the pope, was set up. The new reformed houses which the aristocracy founded in hundreds during the eleventh century, were almost without exception made the legal property of the Holy See; the founders formally conveyed them into the proprietorship of St. Peter and his vicar in Rome. But the pope's control was rarely more than nominal. Unlike the king, the pope was distant. Unlike the king, who was seeking to control the temporalities of the churches through advocates responsible to him, the pope had no instruments through whom to exercise his proprietorship. By a tacit, perhaps even by an explicit, agreement the aristocratic founders or their descendants took over the position of 'advocate', exercising the powers which the papacy could

[1] F. Lot, *Etude sur le règne de Hugues Capet*, 225.
[2] Cf. H. Hirsch, *Klosterimmunität*, 7-8; Waas, *Vogtei und Bede*, I, 171.

not exercise: political control of monastic dependants, jurisdiction over tenants of monastic lands, governmental authority within the whole monastic territory. The surrender of proprietary rights to the papacy still left the aristocracy in actual control of their foundations; and the guarantee of their position was the 'advocacy' which they exercised not (like the older 'advocacy' over royal churches) on behalf of the king, but in the name of the pope. The arrangement between the aristocracy and the papacy was a trump card against the Salian monarchy.

The full effects of the changes in the constitution of the German Church did not become evident until the period 1075-1125. But the process was under way from 1048, and it was one means by which the aristocracy expressed its resistance to the centralizing policy of the crown. Opposed to the great German Church, the *Reichskirche*, which the Salians were seeking to bind together under their own authority, there was built up in Germany another union of churches, of which the pope was nominal head but the aristocracy the real masters. Thus the fissures in the German state, which were becoming evident as a result of the growing power of the aristocracy, were supplemented by a breach within the German Church. It is exceedingly difficult to trace the growing power of the aristocracy step by step through the period 950-1050; it was a process overshadowed by the achievements and projects of the monarchy. But it is evident that the free nobility was firmly in control of new *de facto* powers from the time of the death of Emperor Henry III in 1056, and in defence of these powers was prepared to fight the centralizing policy of the Salians, particularly as formulated by Henry IV. It was prepared to fight against royal control of the Church; it was prepared to fight against the new administrative system in which *ministeriales* and not the free nobility played the leading role; it was prepared to resist a revival of royal rights over water and forest, which threatened to check its own economic expansion; and finally it was prepared to fight against a monarchy which was becoming increasingly less dependent on aristocratic support and aristocratic good-will, and whose policy ultimately was directed against the aristocracy.

The resistance to the Salian programme of administrative reform, with its strong tendency towards centralization, was due not to deep-rooted provincial differences — these had largely disappeared owing to the spread of cultural interchange fostered by kings like Henry II — but to the very character of German society. It was not a society of lords and vassals, like contemporary France, but a society of freemen, stubbornly insistent on their freedom and resisting organization from above. Moreover, the very fact that the free classes were faced by a progressive monarchy forced issues to a head; there was no room for a period of slow adjustment. From the day on which Henry IV attained his majority and began to rule on his own account he set about the attempt to reorganize the government of his kingdom on more modern lines, in much the same way as Henry II of England was to do a century later. With the formation of the nucleus of a royal bureaucracy and the centralization of government in Goslar, he had his own constitutional programme, for which he was prepared to fight, and it was without doubt his energy in putting this programme into execution that awoke the aristocracy to opposition and led them to insist on recognition of the rights which they had slowly and silently been building up during the preceding century. Heightened royal claims provoked more vigorous aristocratic reaction, aristocratic intransigence confirmed the king in his diagnosis of the situation: the result was war.

IV

The Salian administrative programme, the outline of which we have sketched, was developed, from the time of Conrad II onwards, in response to specific political problems facing the monarchy. In the last analysis its purpose was political. Henry III and Henry IV were both determined to restore the authority of the monarchy in Saxony, where it was being undermined by the rising power of the house of Billung; the administrative policy of both had a specifically Saxon context. The policy of royal castle-building, the revindication of crown lands, the fixing of the capital at Goslar, were all measures for the coercion of Saxony. Had this policy succeeded, it would no doubt have been the preliminary, and was perhaps intended to be a preliminary, to a more general transformation of the German kingship and the German constitution; but the primary object was political, and this political object was to secure Saxony for the crown.

When Henry III succeeded his father, Conrad II, in 1039, the German monarchy was, to all appearances, at the height of its power. The new aristocratic opposition was as yet scarcely stirring; the power of the old tribal duchies, thanks to the efforts of the Ottonian dynasty, was broken. Of the six German duchies four — Franconia, Swabia, Bavaria and Carinthia — were, in 1039, in the king's own hands. Outstanding were only Saxony and Lorraine; and it was therefore round these that Henry III's policy inevitably pivoted.

In regard to Lorraine, Henry had recourse in the first place to the old Ottonian policy of division. On the death of Duke Gozilo in 1044, the duchy was divided between his two sons. But the geographical position of Lorraine between France and Germany made it difficult for any German king to secure lasting success; and within a few months of the division of the duchy the elder brother, Godfrey, entered into league with the French king and rose in rebellion. Godfrey of Lorraine is a portentous figure in the history of eleventh-century Europe, an ominous figure for the future of Germany. Deprived of his duchy in 1044, defeated and imprisoned in 1045, restored in 1046, he again rebelled in 1047 in league with the counts of Holland and Flanders, but was pardoned at the instance of Pope Leo IX. Expelled from his duchy again, he crossed the Alps into Italy in 1051, and there married the widowed marchioness of Tuscany, mother of the famous countess Matilda, thus acquiring a new and redoubtable sphere of influence with which to bolster up his position in Germany. At the same time he became a factor in European politics. On the death of Pope Leo IX in 1054, the bishop of Florence was appointed to the papal throne (Florence being the centre of Godfrey's Tuscan territory). The next pope, Stephen IX, who succeeded in 1057, was Godfrey's own brother. Thus a bond was formed between the papacy and the anti-imperial party in Lorraine, and the movement for freedom in the Church, which at this very moment was assuming first place in papal politics, was used to further particularist interests. The strength of the Lotharingian opposition to Henry III lay in the fact that it could rely on foreign complications to sustain it in the struggle. Exploiting his relations with France and the papacy, his position in Italy and the support of the princes of the Netherlands, Godfrey successfully resisted Henry III's attempts to assert royal control over Lorraine, and stood out at the end of the reign as a dominating figure in the political scene. He was the first prince in the history of Germany to use foreign politics as a means of achieving his political aims. Through him the opposition to the Salian empire in Lorraine, Italy and within the Church was formed into a united front.

The failure to break the power of Godfrey of Lorraine, significant though it was as an indication of the limitations of Henry III's power, was more fateful for the future than for the immediate present. A more direct threat to the monarchy than the particularism of Godfrey was the growing particularism in Saxony of the Billunger dukes, who had been left alone to develop their power in north Germany since the extinction of the Saxon royal dynasty in 1002. There is little reason to doubt that Henry III planned to abolish the Saxon dukedom and set in its place the archbishopric of Bremen—just as Henry II had raised up the dioceses of Bamberg and Würzburg in place of the duchy of Franconia—with the object of checking and ultimately of undermining the power of the Billunger family. With the appointment of the famous Archbishop Adalbert in 1043, a political conflict of first magnitude began, which lasted until Adalbert's death in 1071.

Because the archbishop of Bremen had the backing of the monarchy, of Henry IV no less than Henry III, the hostility between the Saxon dukes and Adalbert implied scarcely veiled opposition to the crown. Estates like Lesum (with 700 hides), which had once belonged to the Billunger but had been recovered for the monarchy by Conrad II in his great 'revindication' of crown lands, were conferred on Adalbert, who also acquired the vast county of Frisia at the expense of the Duchy of Lorraine; later Emsgau and Stade were added, and other estates as far south as Duisburg. Inevitably Adalbert's growing might provoked reaction. The first crisis came in 1047 when Thietmar, the brother of the Saxon duke, was accused of plotting against Adalbert's life. For the moment open rebellion was avoided, but Henry III realized the dangers of the situation and for the next five years he was almost uninterruptedly in Saxony, pushing forward the construction of royal fortifications and attempting to pacify the land.

The sudden death of Henry III in 1056 and the ten years of regency which followed brought matters to a head. The regency of the Empress Agnes allowed free play to all particularist interests, and nothing but the strength of Adalbert of Bremen saved the position of Henry IV in the north. Adalbert used his position and influence with the empress to build up the territorial power of his church, seeking to obtain control of all counties within his diocese. But his power was hotly contested by the Billung dukes, and the conflict between Adalbert and Duke Bernhard II reduced Saxony to a state of open warfare, until in the end Bremen was stripped of two-thirds of its lands. Simultaneously, princes and bishops laid hands on royal estates, and the regency government was powerless to resist, just as in Italy it abdicated its influence to Godfrey of Lorraine. The abduction of the young king by a gang of princely conspirators in 1062 showed clearly the way things were going. Still more symbolic of the new tendencies was the action of the princes in 1066 when, by the threat of deposition, they forced Henry to remove Adalbert from his counsels.

Such was the position at the beginning of Henry IV's personal rule. Even more than Conrad II, he was faced by the immediate necessity of recovering expropriated crown lands. Even more than Henry III he had to fear the powers of the Saxon dukes, whose position was strengthened and ambitions confirmed by their triumph over Adalbert of Bremen and their conquests during the regency of Agnes. Already during the regency the Saxon princes, learning a lesson from Henry III, had begun to construct castles to defend their properties; already the conflicts with Adalbert of Bremen had led to the introduction of professional soldiers, mounted knights, into the land. This, and the general atmosphere of unrest and hostility to the monarchy, was the background to Henry IV's policy of castle-building and recovery of royal rights and properties, which we have already surveyed, just as the egoistic, untrustworthy attitude of the nobility — only too well known to him from the days of his childhood — explains his reliance on his Swabian *ministeriales*. His reforms were primarily intended as a means of raising the monarchy from the depths into which it had fallen during the years of his minority.

Henry IV's personal rule began in 1065. In 1070 rebellion broke out in Saxony. Its origin lay in a private quarrel — which seems, however, to have expressed the hostility of the greater Saxon nobles to the ministerial parvenus surrounding the king — but Henry's policy in Saxony, the imposition of heavy taxes and the engrossing of common and waste, which had caused wide popular discontent, rallied the Saxon and Thuringian peasantry round the two leaders, Otto of Nordheim and Magnus Billung. As yet, however, there was no support from outside, and Henry — supported by the dukes of Bavaria and Swabia and Lower Lorraine and by the majority of the bishops — was soon in complete control. It appeared that his opportunity had come to assert his authority in the north once and for all time. The Saxon peasantry was crushed and Henry now began the systematic building of castles and fortifications on almost every hill in Thuringia. Otto of Nordheim, imprisoned until 1072, was released and given back his allodial lands. But the time seemed to have come to settle accounts with the Billunger. When in 1072 Duke Ordulf died, the king refused to recognize the succession of Magnus (who was still held a prisoner) and — apparently resolved to annex the Saxon duchy to the crown by forfeiture — seized the Billunger stronghold of Lüneburg.

In a sense, this act was a logical conclusion to royal policy since 1043, the key to all Salian endeavours. But in fact it crystallized the widespread resentment at royal policy throughout all classes of Saxon society, and fused the social and economic grievances of the Saxon peasantry with the political conflict between the Billunger and the monarchy. The new revolt which broke out in 1073 was as much a revolt of the free peasantry of Saxony as of the Saxon nobility; for the Salian programme of reorganization, although it ultimately threatened the aristocracy's hold over government, was an immediate threat to the freedom of the Saxon peasantry, who believed that the dues and services which the king was determined to exact would reduce them to the status of servile tenants. But the two wings of the insurgents had little in common, and their leader, Otto of Nordheim, failed to bridge the gap between them. The popular demand was mainly for relief from royal exactions; the nobility, on the other hand, had a typically aristocratic programme, in which the exclusion of *ministeriales* from the royal council loomed large. Neither group trusted the other; each was willing separately to temporize and to compromise with the king at the other's expense; and neither, finally, was a match for Henry IV either in political or in military strategy.

Thus, although the war went on from 1073 to 1075, Henry retained the master-hand, skilfully exploiting the divisions in the rebel ranks, and the issue was never seriously in doubt, in spite of temporary Saxon successes. In the negotiations at Gerstungen early in 1074, Henry came to terms with the nobility at the expense of the free peasantry. When the latter, enraged and embittered, sacked the Harzburg, the symbol of Salian power in Saxony, the breach between peasantry and nobility was widened, for the princes feared with reason that the incident would be used by the king as an excuse to go back on the terms of agreement. Henry's failure to fulfil the terms of the pact of Gerstungen was, in fact, the reason put forward for a renewal of the revolt in 1075 by Otto of Nordheim. But on this occasion, when the initiative was taken by the Saxon princes, the peasantry and smaller nobility held back, and besides freemen fighting on foot the Saxon army included serfs impressed into service by their lords. When finally the two armies came face to face at Langensalza on the river Unstrutt in June 1075, Henry won a decisive victory. The Saxon leaders, fighting on horseback, got away, but the free Saxon footmen were slaughtered in thousands. Nor did the king hesitate to press home his victory: Saxony and Thuringia were harried and pillaged, crops destroyed, the country reduced to starvation, and the population driven for refuge to the forests. In October, the Saxon leaders made formal surrender and were deprived of their fiefs. By now the mass of the people, who felt that they had been sacrificed uselessly by the nobility, were bitterly hostile to their aristocratic leaders. Broken and divided against itself, Saxony seemed this time to have been crushed. At a diet held at Goslar at Christmas 1075, Henry showed his willingness to introduce conciliatory measures with a view to a final settlement of the Saxon question, and Otto of Nordheim, released from prison and amnestied, was appointed royal viceroy in Saxony to execute the settlement. But the very appointment of a viceroy was evidence that Henry had no intention of restoring Saxony to its former position among the duchies. On the contrary, his plan without doubt was to abolish the duchy, govern Saxony directly through royal officials and make it, with Goslar as capital, the keystone of the strong monarchy he was intent on creating.

Thus by the end of 1075, Henry IV seemed to have brought to fulfilment the programme of the Salian house, and (in the words of a German historian) 'to have defeated continental Saxony in the same decade in which the Normans conquered the insular Saxons in England'. Indeed, in many respects his achievement was ahead of that of the Anglo-Norman dynasty, for his policy compares more easily with that of Henry II in the twelfth century than with the policy of his contemporary, William the Conqueror. Had the success of 1075 proved durable, it is scarcely to be doubted that Henry IV would have created a great German state coeval with Norman England and anticipating the French monarchy of Philip Augustus; from that era we should date the beginning of new forms of government in Germany and a new concentration of German national powers behind the monarchy.

But at the very moment of Henry's most sweeping success a new and mightier adversary took up arms. Under the leadership of Gregory VII, the papacy declared war on the German emperor and on the whole established system of German imperialism. The final submission of the defeated Saxon army took place on October 25th, 1075. Little more than a month later, on December 8th, 1075, Gregory threatened Henry with the loss of his throne.

The intervention of Gregory VII, reviving all the old animosities and tearing open the old wounds before they had time to heal, was a turning-point not only in the reign of Henry IV, but also in the whole history of Germany. Harsh as were the measures imposed by Henry IV to carry through his plans, we have seen what promise they held for the healthy development of the German constitution and of German political life. The struggle which began in 1076 and lasted in effect for the next fifty years, destroyed all Henry's early plans for the establishment of a stronger monarchy and irrevocably changed the forms of government and the social texture of Germany. The course of German development from 911 to 1075, whatever difficulties were encountered and setbacks suffered, was sound and progressive; already Germany was following the path which fifty years and more later the Norman rulers were to tread in England, and which the French Capetians were hardly to reach before the second half of the twelfth century. But the rising structure was ruined by the struggle with the Church, the social and political upheaval which we know as the 'Investiture Contest'.

When Gregory VII dispatched his letter of December 8th, 1075, he inaugurated a revolution which profoundly altered the whole course of German political development. A new chapter, a new period, in German history and in the history of Europe was opened. New forces directed politics, new and revolutionary ideas threw

Germany into turmoil, and from the fusion of new and old ideas a new *Weltanschauung* was born. Our next task must be to grasp the essentials of the Gregorian revolution, and to describe and assess its effects on German history. When, in 1122, the Concordat of Worms marked the end of the contest, a new Germany had arisen, as little like the Germany of Henry III as that Germany was like the Germany of Conrad I.

PART TWO

REVOLUTION AND REACTION
(1075-1152)

CHAPTER 5

THE INVESTITURE CONTEST AND THE GERMAN CONSTITUTION

I

THE remarkable recovery of Germany under the Saxon and Salian emperors, achieved in large measure through the willing co-operation of kings and churchmen, had rescued the Church from the heavy hand of the lay princes and built up its power and wealth and influence. Rulers like Henry II and Henry III had unhesitatingly turned from the immediate task of preserving royal authority to the further tasks of reform and the propagation of Christian culture which were incumbent on a 'just king'. They had willingly used their royal authority for the benefit of the Church, never doubting that such a use of authority was, in the Church's eyes, 'just' and 'righteous'. They had called on bishops and abbots to assist them in their task, and the clergy, impelled not merely by a sense of the solidarity of its own interests with those of the crown, but also and still more by a belief in the 'justice' of the king's control of Church and State, had willingly co-operated. They had accepted the king as the divinely appointed 'ruler' of the Church, as the *rex et sacerdos*, marked out by the sacred oil of unction as God's vicar on earth; and they looked to the monarch for leadership, and found in him a leader in the task of eradicating abuse and establishing a Christian society.

Suddenly, in 1073, with the election of Gregory VII to the Holy See, this whole conception of the relationship of Church and State, and with it the whole existing scheme of society, was challenged. It was challenged in the name of reform by a papacy which set out (in the words of an Italian bishop of the period) to champion lost laws which should be revived, against customs which had become corruptions.[1] Whether the needs of reform required a revolutionary

[1] G. Tellenbach, *Libertas. Kirche und Weltordnung im Zeitalter des Investiturstreits* (1936), trs. by R. F. Bennett under the title *Church, State and Christian Society at the time of the Investiture Contest* (1939), and J. P. Whitney, *Hildebrandine Essays* (1932), are, in the writer's opinion, the most lucid discussions of the questions at issue.

attack on the existing social and political order is one of the eternally debatable questions of history. There were, even among the most ardent reformers, many sincere and distinguished churchmen who were prepared to deny it and to oppose Gregory VII and his programme; they held that the Church's task was moral regeneration, not a re-ordering of the fundamental laws and principles of society, and on a lower and more practical plane they were unwilling to forgo the help which the monarchy could give to the reforming party. They appreciated the positive benefits of a strong monarchy in a corrupt, materialist society, and perceived that a major political conflict would compromise the true objects of reform. But the tide was against them, and when their leader, the great Peter Damiani, cardinal-bishop of Ostia, died in 1072, the Gregorian party won the upper hand. From the very beginning of his pontificate — indeed, from the remote days when he accompanied Pope Gregory VI into exile and when, under Alexander II (1061-1073), he became a more influential figure at the papal Curia than the pope himself — Gregory was a determined opponent of the German emperors, and seems to have made up his mind that the only way to bring the work of reform to completion was to overturn the old order, in which abuse and disorder had grown rife, and to remodel society on principles derived from a study of the old law and canons of the Church. Before he became pope, he urged Deusdedit and Damiani (and doubtless others) to search the libraries and bring together all decretals, canons and passages from historians setting forth the powers of the Holy See:[1] after he became pope he distilled what he considered the essence of this research into twenty-seven propositions, famous as the *Dictatus papae*. Like all revolutionaries he convinced himself that he was only restoring the old law; but the principles he enunciated fell like a bombshell on the traditional thought of the age, which they challenged at every turn. Every sentence of the *Dictatus papae*, drawn up by Gregory in 1075, implies a programme; but none is more astounding than the curt statement

[1] It is more than likely that one unexpected by-product of this search was the famous manuscript of Justinian's Digest, the *Codex Pisanus*, from which all later manuscripts are descended and without which, therefore, a revival of Roman law would have been unthinkable. It was discovered in Amalfi towards the end of the eleventh century. Hence it is probable that Gregory was ultimately responsible for the rise of the new Roman law of Bologna, which later kings and princes, beginning with Frederick Barbarossa, used as an answer to the arguments of the papalists.

that the pope may lawfully depose emperors. Gregory — 'the great innovator, who stood quite alone'[1]— was setting out on new and perilous paths.

After 1073, therefore, the political wing of the reform party assumed control. Many factors contributed to give it predominance, and thus to bring about open conflict with the empire. In the first place, we may recall the work of Henry III in freeing the papacy from the control of Roman factions and thus enabling it to resume its functions as the head of an oecumenical church. The popes introduced by Henry restored the prestige of the papacy in Europe, and his support enabled them to extend their field of action. He deliberately made the papacy a fit instrument for carrying out the work of reform to which he was devoted, and through the popes appointed with his support he brought it into contact with the main currents of reform, which had sprung up, independent of the papacy, in the western fastnesses of his empire, in Burgundy and Lorraine. Through Leo IX (1049-1054) the reform movement of Cluny found its way to Rome — a movement which was already pursuing objects less exclusively religious than the regeneration of monastic life. The Cluniac aim of freeing the churches, particularly monastic churches, from direct lay control — an aim expressed in the programme of 'free election' — was soon merged in a policy of raising the standards of lay society itself, because it was evident that the freedom of religious houses from aristocratic exploitation and control could never be assured unless lay society itself were purified and the worst excesses of feudalism eradicated. Hence it was through the action of Cluniac abbots and bishops that the Truce of God, the 'peace movement', was introduced at the end of the tenth century as a means of combatting feudal disorder which was particularly rampant in the old lands of the Middle kingdom, in Burgundy and Lorraine, where (in contrast with Germany) imperial rule was little more than nominal.[2] The object was to establish a new, more peaceful social order, in which the 'liberty' which the churches claimed would be secure; and in this sense there is at least an element of truth in the view that the Cluniac movement was,

[1] 'Der grosse Anfänger, der auf sich selbst allein steht': such is the judgement of E. Caspar, the editor of Gregory's register and therewith the most profound modern critic of the pope. Cf. *Hist. Zeitschr.*, CXXX (1924), 30.

[2] Cluny itself lay some fifteen miles outside the borders of the Burgundian kingdom in a remote part of the French duchy of Burgundy.

from its inception, a political movement.[1] But these political objectives did not involve hostility to the empire, or to the principles of imperial government, and it was only when Cluniac ideas and principles were adopted by the papacy and remoulded in combination with other elements of papal policy that the Cluniac movement and its off-shoots, of which the most important was Hirsau in southern Germany, became a formidable political power directed against the German monarchy. Under Gregory VII, although the leaders of the Cluniac movement still maintained a mediating position between pope and emperor, the monks and disciples of Cluny and Hirsau were the shock-troops of the papal army, the executants of papal orders, the protagonists of papal authority.

It was the pontificate of Leo IX (1049-1054) which saw the first rapid advance in the reconstruction of papal authority. Three times crossing the Alps to France and Germany, and holding synod after synod at which he legislated against abuse, Leo made the papal headship a reality. Already in 1049 at the synod of Reims he insisted on the requirement of canonical election to ecclesiastical offices. Everywhere he went he received the homage of bishops, thus demonstrating papal primacy in spite of the opposition of metropolitans, who refused to admit that the bishop of Rome had any right to interfere in the administration of their provinces. At the same time he gave the Roman Curia an international complexion corresponding to its oecumenic claims, by elevating non-Italians — chiefly his fellow-countrymen from Lorraine — to the cardinalate. Continuous control of the provinces was inaugurated by the frequent dispatch of cardinal-legates to inspect and reform, while bishops were pressed to visit the Holy See. Thus the foundations of the papal monarchy were laid. But it was the radical change in the political situation after Henry III's death in 1056 which enabled the papacy to consolidate its position. The succession of a minor and the regency of the Empress Agnes immediately resulted in a disastrous weakening of German power in Italy, and although the papacy still had to contend with the Roman factions, which again began to raise their heads, and with Duke Godfrey of Lorraine, who threatened to enthral it, it was quick to profit from the change of circum-

[1] The ablest and most recent exponent of this contention is A. Brackmann, 'Die politische Wirkung der kluniazensischen Bewegung', Hist. Zeitschr., CXXXIX (1929); for a reasoned statement to the contrary cf. L. M. Smith, 'Cluny and Gregory VII', Engl. Hist. Review, XXVI (1911).

stances. When the German pope, Victor II, the last of Henry III's candidates, died in 1057 and was replaced by Godfrey of Lorraine's brother, Stephen IX, the only acknowledgement of the old imperial right of confirmation was the dispatch to Germany of a belated embassy after the pope had already been consecrated. Two years later the procedure for papal elections was defined and remodelled, electoral rights being for practical purposes placed in the hands of the cardinals. This change was intended primarily to free the papacy from dependence on the Roman mob, which had intervened on the death of Stephen IX in 1058; but it could be, and was, used also against the emperor and the imperial government, whose rights were whittled away; for although a vague personal right of confirmation was reserved for Henry IV, it was rendered meaningless by a decision empowering the person elected to exercise all the prerogatives of pope from the moment of his election. Thus the choice of the pope was made the affair of the cardinals, who were already an international body with little sympathy for the German government. The danger was quickly perceived at the imperial court, and on the death of Pope Nicholas II in 1061 a last attempt was made to preserve imperial rights. Asked by the Roman nobles to nominate a successor, the empress designated Bishop Cadalus of Parma, who was elected by German and Lombard bishops at a synod at Basel; but in the meantime the reform party, without consulting the imperial government, had elected Bishop Anselm of Lucca, a protégé of Godfrey of Lorraine, as Alexander II. The result was a schism, which continued until Cadalus' death in 1072; but already by 1064 the course of events in Germany had broken imperial resistance. The abduction of Henry IV by the princes at Kaiserswert in 1062, and the collapse of the regency government brought new powers into the saddle: Anno of Cologne, the bitter opponent of Adalbert of Bremen and therefore of imperial policy, went over to the reform party and under his influence a synod held at Mantua in 1064 decided in favour of Alexander II.

Thus the minority of Henry IV and the weakness and embarrassments of the regency compromised German government to such a degree that the papacy was able to carry through a revolutionary reorganization almost without protest and to emancipate the Roman church from imperial and German influence. Deprived of effective imperial support the bishops of Germany and Lombardy were left to fight in isolation against the centralizing policy of the papacy which threatened to sweep away their privileges and independence. They saw themselves subjected to legates, who were sent out from Rome to enforce clerical celibacy and repress simony; and many of the most distinguished prelates, including Anno of Cologne himself, were summoned to Rome to answer for their actions. The Lateran Council of 1059 had attacked lay investiture, and the radical wing of the reform party already condemned all forms of lay investiture as simony, thus laying an axe at the roots of the established connexion between Church and State and at the system by which the monarchy, in Germany and in Lombardy, governed by entrusting counties and jurisdictions to carefully selected bishops. But conditions during Henry IV's minority were manifestly exceptional, and it was obvious that the papacy had to expect an imperial attempt to recover its lost rights as soon as Henry IV was firmly established in the saddle. To meet this contingency it needed allies, just as it needed allies within the Church against the bishops, whom a very evident community of interests drove into the royal camp. The earliest, as we have seen,[1] was Duke Godfrey of Lorraine, whose power in Tuscany was a constant though dangerous bulwark of the papacy, ever threatening to turn protection into domination. Equally dangerous was the alliance with the Normans, formed in 1059 at the very moment when Nicholas II's decree governing papal elections and the prohibition of lay investiture challenged the German monarchy. But both alliances helped the reform party to maintain its position, and it was the troops of Godfrey and the Normans which assured Alexander II's victory over his rival, Cadalus. In Germany, the papacy ever since the days of Leo IX had been in contact with the south German nobility, who saw in the reform programme — particularly in the demand for 'free election' — a useful vehicle for the assertion of their rights against the centralizing policy of the monarchy.[2] The German nobility, particularly in the west and in the south, quickly realized the advantages to be gained from support of the reform movement, and with their backing Cluniac influence spread with amazing rapidity during the decade following the introduction of Cluniac monks at St. Blasien in the Black Forest in 1060 and the reform of Hirsau about 1066. The result was the rapid propagation in Germany of a religious movement which owed its

[1] Above, p. 92.   [2] Above, pp. 89-90.

progress to the papacy and the princes, not to the empire, and which was organized with a maximum of cohesion since all new and reformed foundations received the status of priories, over which the abbot of Cluny retained control, without episcopal interference; for the papacy had granted Cluny exemption from the authority of any bishop save the bishop of Rome. This close-knit organization was of enormous advantage to the papacy. Dependent on papal prerogative for its autonomy, Cluny led the way in effective centralization in the western Church, and its monks were the best propagandists and champions of papal supremacy, particularly against the bishops who regarded the autonomy of the reformed monasteries as an encroachment on their canonical rights. Against the Lombard bishops, on the other hand, the papacy did not hesitate to ally with the social classes whose opposition to the episcopacy had introduced a new element of discord into Italian life during the past fifty or sixty years — an alliance with the 'mob' which provoked violent disapproval. In Milan, in particular, the so-called 'Patarini' stood out as champions of 'free election', hoping to obtain the chief see of the north for one of their own number, and thus to secure greater power for the feudatories in the administration of Milanese fiefs and territories.[1] Their alliance with and formal recognition by the papacy reached back to 1059, and the question of Milan, where a 'Patarine' and an imperial bishop faced each other in bitter hostility, was the major issue between Henry IV and Gregory VII, after the latter's election to the Holy See in 1073. It was the test case which led to the outbreak of the conflict between Church and State.

The pontificate of Alexander II (1061-1073) represented, on the whole, a phase in which the reformers marked time. Much of it was taken up by the struggle with the anti-pope, Honorius II. At its close, the pope's Norman allies, after overrunning Apulia and Calabria, launched an attack on the papal territories, which temporarily estranged the two powers. There were difficulties also in Tuscany, where the younger Godfrey of Lorraine, who had married

[1] The nickname 'Patarini' (i.e. rag-pickers) does not express the real social standing of the opponents of the Archbishop. They were the *secundi milites* or vavasours, led for example by influential men like Landulf, a member of the aristocratic family of Cotta, and their opposition was identical in part at least with the old opposition of the archiepiscopal vassals to their overlord. They wanted 'free election', because this was identical with election *ex gremio* by the *populus* and *clerus* of the Church, i.e. the choice of one of themselves by the local nobility and by the cathedral clergy which was recruited from the ranks of the local nobility. Thus they hoped to control the Archbishop and win freedom from archiepiscopal control.

his stepsister, Matilda, was at loggerheads with his wife, and prepared to accept Henry IV's aid in recovering from her the Tuscan lands. Hence the position of the papacy, when Gregory VII was elected pope in 1073, was no longer strong and there was some possibility of a compromise. Gregory appears to have proceeded cautiously over his election, the validity of which was disputed by the German episcopate,[1] and to have secured Henry's approbation by agreeing to postpone his ordination until royal confirmation had been received; and for some months longer he steered a moderate course, apparently seeking an understanding. Henry also, involved in the Saxon wars, was conciliatory, admitting that he had sold churches to unsuitable persons and laid hands on ecclesiastical property, and promising in future to observe the pope's precepts. He warmly received a papal embassy which appeared at Nürnberg in 1074, and agreed to dismiss five of his ministers who had been excommunicated by Alexander II for simony. Negotiations between pope and emperor continued through the summer and autumn of 1075, but gradually the complexion of affairs changed. Both sides appear to have been to blame for the deterioration which now set in. In December 1074, taking advantage of the disturbances in Saxony, Gregory forbade all married priests in Germany to perform the sacraments — a measure which stirred up wide unrest. In February 1075 he took the more decisive step of prohibiting lay investiture — a prohibition, the wording and implications of which were obscure, but which, issued at that juncture, was evidently a challenge to the monarchy.[2] The coincidence between the rebellion of the Saxons and the prohibition of lay investiture was not accidental; Gregory's action was deliberately timed.[3] On the other hand, Henry himself, once the Saxons had been defeated, threw off the mask, united his cause with that of the German bishops, whom the pope was threatening, and advanced to the defence of his position in Lombardy. Already before the death of Alexander II

[1] The election was violent and irregular in character, carried out largely by popular acclamation contrary both to the decree of 1059 and to the practice of Henry III; hence the German bishops urged that it should be quashed.

[2] It referred to the investiture of bishoprics, abbeys and ecclesiastical dignities, and hence technically excluded the secular appurtenances of these ecclesiastical offices; but in practice this fine distinction could not easily be maintained, and it is far from clear that Gregory intended to maintain it. Cf. Scharnagl, *Der Begriff der Investitur in den Quellen u. der Literatur des Investiturstreites* (1908), 30 sqq.

[3] Thompson, *Feudal Germany*, 136.

he had sought a solution of the Milan question by setting aside the two rival candidates and appointing and investing a third — much as Henry III had solved the Roman question in 1046 — but the new appointment was resisted by the 'Patarini' who, with the pope's approval, elected a new candidate. The failure of this attempt at a compromise solution led Henry to more extreme measures. Because the royal demesnes in Italy had shrunk to negligible proportions, royal authority there, when the king was not present with an army, depended chiefly on the bishops and became null if he could not appoint his own men. In 1075 Henry decided to support his candidate with armed forces, which quelled the riots of the Pataria. At the same time he entered into negotiations with the Normans and prepared to restore Godfrey of Lorraine to his position in Tuscany. Gregory's answer was the famous letter of December 8th, 1075, summoning the king to penance and due subjection, and threatening him with the loss of his throne. The formulation some time in 1075 of the theses of the *Dictatus papae* is the best evidence that, on Gregory's side, an open conflict was neither unforeseen nor unpremeditated. With the issue of the admonition of December 8th it became a fact.

Henry IV's reply to the pope's letter of December 8th, 1075, was to call together the synod of Worms on January 27th, 1076, where the king (in his capacity of *patricius urbis Romanae*) and the assembled bishops solemnly declared Gregory's election null and void, and called on him to abdicate.[1] Thus began the chain of events which led to civil war in Germany. At the Lenten synod in Rome, Gregory replied to the synod of Worms by excommunicating Henry and suspending him from government. Henry followed with the excommunication of the pope in an assembly of German bishops held at Mainz on the feast of St. Peter and St. Paul. Then came the first defections of German clergy and laity from Henry, the junction of the south German and Saxon oppositions, and the forging of a connexion between both and the papacy. In October 1076 the king came face to face with the united opposition at the Diet of

---

[1] A cardinal from Rome bore witness to the irregularities at Gregory's election, and it was after hearing him that the famous letter was drafted from Henry, 'king not by usurpation but by divine ordination', to Hildebrand, 'false monk', calling upon the latter to descend from his throne, because he had touched the king 'who according to the tradition of the Holy Fathers is answerable to God alone'. Cf. the full text of this characteristic document in Erdmann, *Die Briefe Heinrichs IV* (1937), 15-17.

Tribur, and was forced to accept its terms, namely to free himself from excommunication within four months on pain of loss of his crown, and meanwhile to accept his suspension and withdraw into private life until the pope's decision was made known. With this in view the princes invited the pope to Augsburg, and it was to avoid facing such an assembly of his enemies and opponents, which he fully realized would be fatal for his cause, that Henry decided to seek out the pope in Italy. There followed the famous journey to Canossa, the meeting with the pope, penance and absolution. But Henry's secret flight to Canossa, although a clever manœuvre to divide the papal and the German opposition, was in the eyes of the princes a breach of his undertakings at Tribur; and this breach and their consequent deep distrust of Henry decided the princes to proceed to the last step. On March 13th, 1077, they met at Forchheim, the traditional Frankish meeting-place for royal elections, and elected a new king, Rudolf of Swabia. Germany was divided into two camps, and a long generation was to pass before even the bare essentials of peace and settled conditions returned. But what was destroyed in these years could never be restored: the whole of subsequent German history bears on it the marks of the conflicts which raged through Germany between 1075 and Henry IV's death in 1106.

II

What were the issues in the war between Gregory VII and Henry IV which broke out at the end of 1075? The conflict is traditionally known as the Investiture Contest; but this is neither a very accurate nor a very adequate description. The question of lay investiture had been an element in the reform programme since the publication of Humbert of Moyenmoutier's treatise *adversus Simoniacos* in 1058; but it only became a central theme some years after Gregory VII's death when the conflict over greater issues had exhausted all parties, when both sides knew that their more sweeping claims could never be realized, and when detailed analysis of the questions at stake had fixed investitures as an issue the solution of which would permit compromise and peace.[1] Gregory VII himself, despite his pro-

[1] Cf. Z. N. Brooke, 'Lay Investiture and its relation to the conflict of Empire and Papacy' *Proceedings of the British Academy*, XXV (1939).

hibition of lay investiture in 1075, was scarcely irreconcilable in this respect;[1] what he was really concerned to enforce was his conception of free, canonical election, and provided this was assured there is every reason to suppose that he would — at any rate during the first phase of the conflict, prior to his recognition of Rudolf of Swabia in 1080 — have sanctioned the principle of lay investiture. But to secure such a solution, the king would have had to agree to limit investiture to bishops and abbots already canonically elected, and probably also not to refuse investiture to such candidates, whether or not he regarded them as politically suitable for their offices. The issue of canonical election was, however, a more difficult matter; for election by the clergy and people — which was the current meaning in reforming circles of 'free election'[2] — opened the door wide to local influence and particularist interests, which both in Germany and in Lombardy were all too apt to be directed against the crown and royal policy. In the twelfth century a solution was found, both in Germany and in England, by admitting the legitimacy of elections 'in the king's presence', thus allowing the king to bring influence to bear on the electors or their representatives; but this compromise was the result of long mediation, and for Henry IV, at the beginning of the conflict, to have accepted 'canonical election' in the sense of Gregory VII would have been tantamount to abandoning political control of the German and Lombard churches. Moreover, we must remember the atmosphere of suspicion engendered by reforming propaganda and by extreme elements, which were even more radical than the pope. The new and formidable connotation of the word 'simony', which stigmatized all forms of lay investiture as equivalent to traffic in the holy sacraments, was not calculated to appease the emperor; nor was the widely propagated view that there was no distinction between the church itself, the spiritualities, and its secular rights and properties.[3] The specious argument that what had once been given to the church

[1] Scharnagl, op. cit., 32.
[2] For an illuminating study of the theories of canonical election at this period, cf. P. Schmid, Der Begriff d. kanon. Wahl in d. Anfängen d. Investiturstreites (1926). The exclusive electoral rights of the chapters, cutting out the clergy and people of the diocese, were a later development; cf. v. Below, Die Entstehung des ausschliesslichenWahlrechts der Domkapitel (1883).
[3] Damiani argued convincingly for the moderate party that royal investiture was only for the church lands and not for the sacred office; but he was met by the retort that this was an artificial distinction. 'Artificiosi colore commenti simoniacae haereseos sibi machina menta configunt, asserentes se non spiritualia, sed terrena terrenis acquirere' (Gesta. Trev. cont., sect. 11).

had been given to Christ in perpetuity, and that the donor had no
further rights in his gift, was attractive; but it simply swept aside
the fact, of which moderate churchmen like Cardinal Damiani were
well aware, that apart from the gifts of the faithful most, if not all,
great churches held estates which were not gifts but territories
conceded for administration and political control. The churchmen
who regarded the counties they held as so much property belonging
to their churches, were deliberately or unconsciously confusing the
issue; the county was a secular office with lands attached, and as
such was properly conferred by lay investiture. Nor could the
crown afford to see its control of the counties broken. In Lombardy,
as we have seen, it was completely dependent on the bishops, who
had largely engrossed the county organization; in Germany, it has
been calculated that by 1073 no less than fifty-three counties were in
the possession of the episcopate.¹ In these circumstances Henry IV,
in any compromise, required specific assurances guaranteeing his just
interests, and no firm assurance was forthcoming: there was room
for a compromise to get rid of the undoubted abuses of the existing
system, but Henry could not throw the system over. Its maintenance was, for the German monarchy — which had only just begun to
construct new foundations for its power — a matter of life and death.

It was, however, against the current system, and not simply
against its abuse, that the Gregorian attack was launched. Henry was
unscrupulous and untrustworthy in political dealings, a born
tactician for whom the end justified the means; but it would be
unwarranted to assume that he was fundamentally hostile to reform.
There is no reason to doubt his sincerity when in 1082 he forswore
simony; and it is significant that his anti-pope, Clement III, stood out
in the cause of clerical celibacy in 1083 at the very moment when
Gregory VII, owing to the adverse situation in which he found
himself, had begun to waver. If the issue between Henry IV and
Gregory VII had been merely traffic in Church dignities and the
celibacy of the priesthood, the rupture between emperor and pope
would probably never have occurred.² The contest was not merely
a fight between zealous reformers and vested interests; on the
contrary one of the main arguments against Gregory was that he was
destroying the 'right order' of the Church, and the anti-Gregorians
were as insistent as Gregory on the 'justice' and rightness of their

¹ Thompson, *Feudal Germany*, 135.   ² Ibid., 127.

standpoint.[1] Nor were the twin problems of investiture and canonical election, important as they were in practical politics, more than side-issues, significant mainly as the expression of more fundamental divergencies. What was at issue was the whole accepted and time-hallowed position of the Salian monarchy. Gregory VII attacked root and branch the ideas of legitimacy, divine right and paramount overlordship, on which the claim of the Salians to rule the German Church was founded. The reformed papacy could compromise with the Capetian and Anglo-Norman monarchies, but the theocracy of the Salians had to be eradicated because it was so mighty that it endangered the supremacy of Rome over the other Churches of Christian Europe. It was because the German Church, as reformed by Henry II and Henry III, was the least undisciplined Church in eleventh-century Europe that it was attacked; reform which was directed by the crown and which, if successfully continued, would have strengthened the attachment of the German Church to the crown, did not suit the papacy. An attack on the Salian monarchy was necessary for the emancipation of the papacy from the imperial system built up by Henry III. It was necessary because of the connexion between Germany and Italy, which now became a funereal entanglement involving the German ruler in an out-and-out war which he might otherwise have escaped. And it was necessary, finally, if the papal headship of the Church, which was the ultimate object of Gregorian policy, was to be a reality. So long as the king was (as Henry III had been called) *caput ecclesiae*, standing above all mortals in virtue of the holy right of unction, the representative on earth of 'the highest Lord',[2] the allegiance of the bishops was likely to remain divided, particularly as most of them, rightly or wrongly, regarded the pope's monarchical pretensions as a revolutionary attack on the canonically ordained order of the Church. A kingship with sacerdotal qualities, a ruler who was *rex et sacerdos*, was a natural rallying-point for ecclesiastical resistance; and on the king's side was tradition and fervent conviction as well as political expediency.

[1] Cf. Tellenbach, *Church, State and Christian Society*, 144.
[2] Cf. the passage cited above, p. 32, n. 2.   Wido of Osnabrück (*Mon. Germ. hist., Lib. de lite*, I, 467) picks out the essence of the royal position: 'they say', he writes, 'that no layman was ever granted any power to dispose of anything ecclesiastical, but the king is rightly distinguished from the laity through the oil of consecration, which makes him a participant in the priestly office'. Cf. also Gregory of Catino (ibid. II, 538): 'Reges et imperatores propter sacram unctionem christi nuncupantur, et sic suorum ministerio vel officio sive prelatione sacramentis ecclesiae sunt uniti, ut in nullo debeant separari.'

Fundamentally, therefore, the contest between Gregory VII and Henry IV centred round the monarchy and its place in Christian society. It was an issue with the widest ramifications, reaching out into all spheres of social and political life, and in the struggle which ensued the monarchists were the conservative, the Gregorians the revolutionary party. Gregory took up arms against the very conception of monarchy by divine right. Turning its back on the old Gelasian theory of the harmonious co-operation of the two great powers, the Hildebrandine party sought a separation of Church and State, involving a complete change in the position of the king in Christian society. It did not necessarily mean his subordination to the pope, although Gregory soon drew this positive conclusion from his own arguments; but it did mean necessarily that the king's sacerdotal position and character were challenged. For Gregory, the king was a removable official. He had a divine duty on earth; but he only remained king so long as he performed this duty, and if he ceased to act righteously he became *ipso facto* a tyrant, to whom no obedience was owed. Furthermore, it rested with the pope, as successor of Peter and vicar of Christ, to determine when a ruler was acting as a *rex iustus*, when he was a tyrant who must be removed. Rejecting the ancient doctrine that kings were sent by God, either as leaders of the righteous or as a scourge for the wicked, Gregory turned his back on the Christian dogmas of passive obedience and non-resistance. One of the most penetrating of Gregory's critics picked out the essential novelty of the pope's position, when he wrote: 'Christ alone, in unison with God, can give or take away dominion, according to the scriptures; but Hildebrand teaches that he himself has authority over kings and kingdoms, and can do that which, according to the Psalmist, can be done by God alone, who abases the one and elevates the other.' And Henry IV himself laid his finger on the main point: 'You have dared', he wrote to Gregory, 'to touch me, who although unworthy have been singled out by unction to rule, and whom, according to the traditions of the Holy Fathers, God alone can judge.'[1] But Gregory denied that unction conferred on the king a sacred character, which

---

[1] Me quoque, qui licet indignus inter Christos ad regnum sum unctus, tetigisti, quem sanctorum patrum traditio soli Deo iudicandum docuit, nec pro aliquo crimine, nisi a fide, quod absit, exorbitaverim, deponendum asseruit; cur etiam Iulianum apostatam prudentia sanctorum patrum non sibi sed soli Deo iudicandum deponendumque commiserit' (*Mon. Germ. hist.*, Lib. de lite, II, 47).

marked him out above men as God's anointed. 'Aut rex est laicus, aut clericus', it was said; and thereby the whole earlier construction, in which the king's position was that of *rex et sacerdos*, priest as well as layman, was ridiculed. A good king could still serve the Church; but he was a subordinate serving a master, a warrior using his sword at the pope's behest. Moreover, because his position was that of an officer, he must be chosen as a lord would choose a bailiff. Not God's will, inscrutably manifest in the virtues of royal blood, was to decide who should rule, but practical tests of suitability. Suitability, *idoneitas*, was the test of kingship in Gregory's eyes; and it was the task of the lay princes to select and put forward for papal approval a candidate whose suitability was proven. The king's position in relation to the pope was, in short, to be the same as that which Gregory himself was striving to establish between pope and bishops. Like the bishops the king was to be freely elected, and the election was to be referred to the pope for confirmation. Like the bishops the king was to be chosen from below, he was to be the nominee of those over whom he was to rule, and not God's vicar, ruling by the grace of God and marked out for government by hereditary succession. For hereditary succession gave no guarantee of *idoneitas*; on the contrary, as Innocent III was later to affirm, it was a presumption against suitability. Gregory's theories of kingship therefore culminated in the political sphere, in a theory of election and of elective monarchy, which was the logical counterpart of his theory of monarchy as an office. The elective factor, which in Germany and the empire had retained only symbolic or formal significance, was thus revived and given new content. Hitherto the *electio* of which chroniclers speak had been the acclamation of an already designated king: henceforward it was to become election in the technical sense. Therewith it was implied that the real source of authority in the kingdom lay in the princes who elected the king. In the pope's view, the princes, not the king, were the representatives of the kingdom: king and kingdom were no longer (in the phrase of a seventeenth-century Englishman) 'one creature, not to be separate in their political capacity'. Clerical theory, as developed by the Hildebrandine party in the Investiture Contest, introduced an antagonism between king and kingdom, which in course of time found its culmination in the 'dualism' of the period of representative estates,[1]

[1] Cf. below, p. 332 sq.

and led to the establishment of a political order in which the king, with his royal rights, stood opposed to the princes, who represented – or claimed to represent – the interests of the kingdom against the king.

Contemporaries had no illusions about the revolutionary nature of Gregorian claims, the revolutionary character of the Gregorian movement, and the fact that Gregory himself often shrank abashed and hesitant from the practical consequences of his doctrines does not prove them wrong. The long period of hesitation before he recognized Rudolf of Swabia as king, the care with which for three whole years between 1077 and 1080 he addressed Henry as king and Rudolf only as pretendant, his denial that he had any share in Rudolf's election,[1] testify to his scruples and to his persistent hopes of a reconciliation, on his own terms, with Henry IV. The fact remains that he threw a flaming brand into Germany, and that his hesitation and scrupulousness, although certainly dictated by honourable motives, not only sowed dissension among his supporters but also prolonged the social upheavals and thus added to the horrors of a bitter civil war. On all sides there were denunciations of Gregory's monstrousness in dissolving the bonds which held society together, and in handing over Germany to violence and anarchy. His deposition of Henry IV in 1076 was attacked both as an unheard-of assumption of power, and for its disastrous political effects. In the eyes of many, Gregory was simply a *destructor regni*, a fomenter of civil strife, and even his supporters warned him that in deposing Henry he was placing an insuperable obstacle in the path of his own adherents.[2] 'It is a novelty, unknown in any past age', wrote Wenrich of Trier, 'for priests so easily to bring nations into civil strife, by a sudden act to shatter the name of king, which was discovered at the creation of the world and established by God, contemptuously to dismiss the Lord's anointed as if he were a mere bailiff, and to lay him under anathema if he does not instantly obey the command to abandon the kingdom of his fathers.'[3] Other writers condemned Gregory for 'resisting the ordinance of God', and

[1] As late as 1083 he called God to witness that Rudolf was elected neither on his orders nor with his advice (*Reg. Greg. VII*, VIII, 51).

[2] 'Illud vero reminisci pudet, literae vestrae domini regis depositionem continentes ... quomodo eis vestrae (ut dicitur) testimonium pertinaciae prolatis, nostrum et omnium pro parte vestra loqui volentium ora obstruuntur' (Martène, *Thesaurus Anecdotorum*, I, 219).

[3] *Mon. Germ. hist., Lib. de lite*, II, 289. In the next century Otto of Freising (*Chron.*, 35) said he had read and re-read the chronicles of the empire and never found that any ruler before Henry IV had ever been deprived of his realm by the Roman pontiff.

'destroying and bringing to naught the two powers by which the world is ruled'. Henry IV's own letters are full of the same charge. 'Contrary to God's ordinance', he writes, 'Gregory wishes to be king and priest at once; he wishes to discredit the king's sacred dignity, which derives from God and can only be taken away by God.' The 'Hildebrandine madness', he told the bishops in 1076, was confounding God's ordinance; he ruled by God's grace and not by the pope's grace, yet Gregory, who had no hand in raising him to the throne, was proposing to deprive him of his kingdom. God had set up two powers, but Gregory was attempting to reduce the two to one, and they who, as servants of God, ought to have no part in worldly business, were taking it upon themselves to rule and govern kingdoms.[1] Moreover, Gregory's inordinate ambitions were rending the body of Germany. Large parts of Saxony were uninhabited save for the beasts of the forests; civil strife was dividing families. Gregory, Henry said, was raising sons against fathers and arming brothers against brothers, and Berthold of Zwiefalten, described how 'no man knew when his own father or son or brother might not bring death or ruin upon him'. Right or wrong in principle, Gregory was doing irreparable damage.

The opponents of Gregory VII had at their backs the massive weight of conservative opinion; and it was to the traditional sentiments of the conservative masses that Henry IV again and again issued his stirring appeals. On the other hand, the Gregorian theories derived strength not only from their acceptance in reforming circles, but also from the fact that they fitted in with German political beliefs, which postulated that government was based on a pact, and that no king could continue to rule unless he observed the implicit conditions under which he was raised to the throne. Hence writers were not lacking who were prepared to argue that, even apart from the judgement of the Holy See, Henry had forfeited his title to the crown.[2] For those whose sentiments these writers

[1] Cf. Erdmann, *Die Briefe Heinrichs IV*, 16, 19, 25; *Mon. Germ. hist., Const.*, I, 112; ibid. *Lib. de lite*, II, 231, 248.
[2] Cf. Paul of Bernried, *Vita Greg. VII*, c. 97: 'Praeterea liberi homines Henricum eo pacto sibi praeposuerunt in regem, ut electores suos iuste iudicare et regali providentia gubernari satageret. Quod pactum ille postea praevaricari et contempnere non cessavit . . . Ergo et absque sedis apostolicae iudicio principes eum pro rege merito refutare possent, cum pactum adimplere contempserit, quod eis pro electione sua promiserat; quo non adimpleto, nec rex esse poterat. Nam rex nullatenus esse poterit, qui subditos suos non regere sed in errorem mittere studuerit.'

I

represented, Gregory was a welcome ally and Gregorian theories
were a useful supplement to their own political arguments; for,
where German political convictions justified revolt and self-help
against a king who failed to observe and maintain the rights of his
subjects, Gregorian theory provided a formal method of getting
rid of such a king by means of judicial proceedings which stripped
the king of his rights and released his subjects from allegiance. The
vigorous but inchoate right to resist an unjust king, to which free
German society was peculiarly sensitive because it had never
experienced the full rigour of subjection to a feudal monarchy, was
thus given a new lease of life and more precise political formulation
when it came into contact with the ecclesiastical theories represented by Gregory VII; it thereby became a dominant principle in
German political life at the very moment when elsewhere in western
Europe it was being slowly but surely eradicated by the assertion
of the king's prerogatives as feudal superior.[1] For Gregory, on the
other hand, the existence within Germany of a body of thought not
far removed in spirit from his own, was an essential factor in winning
popular support for his theories of monarchy and his attacks on the
Salian dynasty and its principles of government. Nevertheless, the
alliance between Gregory and the German opposition represented an
accommodation of interests and not an identity of views; and as
early as 1077, when the princes insisted on electing a new king, while
the pope looked forward to the restoration of a penitent Henry, it
became evident that the paths pursued by the princes and the
papacy did not run parallel. For Gregory, the object was to secure
Henry's adhesion to his own view of the place of the monarchy in
Christian society; for the princes it was a case of seizing, before it
was too late, the opportunity provided by the pope's suspension of
Henry to get rid of a king whose policy threatened their interests and
prerogatives.[2]

Behind all the resounding appeals to principle, therefore, we must
take into account the play and cross-currents of political interests.

[1] The points in this paragraph have been worked out in great detail by Kern, *Gottesgnadentum u. Widerstandsrecht* (1914); cf. the abridged translation by S. B. Chrimes, *Kingship, Law
and Constitution in the Middle Ages* (1939).
[2] Cf. Lambert of Hersfeld (*Annales*, 280): 'Nunc vero, cum ab ecclesiae corpore propter
flagitia sua apostolici anathematis mucrone precisus est, cum ei communicare sine commun-
ionis ecclesiasticae damno et fidei jactura non possimus ... extremae profecto dementiae
esset, divinitus oblatam salutis occasionem non obviis ... et quod diu premeditatum sit,
ut agatur, tam oportuno tempore non agere, cum leges humanae et ecclesiasticae sinant.'

The opponents of Henry were a motley crowd, pursuing divergent interests; and it required all the efforts of the pope and his legates to hold them together. Gregory was not fastidious in his choice of allies. Unlike the earlier reforming popes, from Leo IX to his own immediate predecessor, Alexander II, he was not by birth a member of the episcopal aristocracy, and this was probably one reason why he did not hesitate to enlist the people and stir up popular discontent both in Germany and Italy.[1] His alliance with the Pataria and the nascent communes in Lombardy brought him into disrepute; but he showed no hesitation in allying with forces which were seeking to revolutionize the existing order for secular ends. He appeared to throw over principle in favour of expediency when, in order to find a safe refuge at the moment of Henry IV's triumph, he came to terms with the Norman prince, Robert Guiscard, who had been excommunicated for occupying papal territory. His alliance with the German aristocracy was hard to justify save on political grounds; for its leaders were notorious despoilers of the Church,[2] and the civil war unleashed by the excommunication of Henry in 1076 resulted in unparalleled depredation, of which Gregory himself was well aware as early as 1078.[3] By his alliance with the German aristocracy Gregory sacrificed the prospect of lasting reform; for reform, in the eyes of the German princes, was little more than a pretext — as once again in the sixteenth century it was to be a pretext — to enable them to establish control over the Church. It is difficult to escape the conclusion that, for Gregory and his successors, the end justified the means, and that they were more intent on breaking the power of the crown within the Church than on purifying the Church from abuse. In this the Gregorian party was at loggerheads with the moderate party within the Church, the party led by Peter Damiani, which held that the movement against lay investiture was a false step which fatally distracted attention from the main task, the moral regeneration of the Church, and that

[1] E. Caspar, *Hist. Zeitschr.*, CXXX (1924), 10, describes his policy as that of a 'parvenu'.
[2] During Henry IV's minority Otto of Nordheim 'devoured' Niederaltaich, Rudolf of Swabia laid hands on Kempten; cf. Thompson, *Feudal Germany*, 129.
[3] 'Both sides pillaged wantonly. Probably there was not a bishopric or monastery in all Germany which was not despoiled at least once. When Adalberon became archbishop of Trier in 1131, the revenues of the see would hardly support him for a day. The condition of Metz and Verdun was similar. Augsburg was captured and pillaged twice. Salzburg fared no better. The losses of Mainz were huge. Of the abbeys, all were more or less plundered, and numbers of them completely destroyed, as Goseck, St. Gall, Schaffhausen, Prüm, Stablo, Lüttich, St. Trudo, St. Hubert and Corvey' (Thompson, op. cit., 164-165; cf. also ibid., 137-138).

co-operation with the monarchy was not impossible.[1] For the
Gregorians, on the other hand, the political struggle with the
German monarchy overshadowed all else; and in this struggle they
were willing to ally indiscriminately with princes, Saxons, Normans,
communes and Pataria. In this sense the Gregorian movement was a
truly revolutionary movement; just as its ultimate object was to
overturn the accepted order, so its instruments and methods and
alliances and associations were revolutionary in character. For the
attack on the Salian monarchy and its principles of government, the
papacy mobilized every revolutionary force within the empire:
hence the unparalleled fury when the cataclysm was, at last, let
loose.

III

The historical significance of Henry IV's reign lies in his resolute
defence of the traditional rights of the monarchy against the attack
led by Gregory VII. From his earliest manifesto at Worms in
January 1076, he stands out in defence of his inheritance, the hereditary monarchy, the monarchy by divine right, the monarchy which
is consecrated like the priestly office, the fate of which is beyond the
touch of man and confided to God alone.[2] 'He began his reign,' it
has been well said, 'as a revolutionary, attacking the old constitution:
he finished as its last and almost its sole defender.'[3] His object is
clear throughout, and he pursued it with amazing tenacity, turning
first one way, then the next, without scruple or hesitation to secure
any and every tactical advantage. He was quick to perceive and
adept at exploiting every favourable circumstance, and for this
reason it is not always easy to appreciate the logic of his policy.
On the whole it is safe to say that he sought, so far as he was able, to
come to terms with the Church in order to gain a free hand to deal
with the aristocracy, whose pretensions constituted in his eyes the
most serious threat to the monarchy; but this policy, forced on him by
circumstances, had strict limits, and he was never prepared, even at the
moments of greatest crisis, to accept the Gregorian programme, which

[1] Cf. Tellenbach, op. cit., ix, 82, 111.
[2] Cf. Erdmann, Briefe, 16: 'In ipsam regiam potestatem nobis a Deo concessam uxurgere
non timuisti, quam te nobis auferre ausus est minari; quasi nos a te regnum acceperimus, quasi
in tua et non in Dei manu sit regnum vel imperium.' Cf. ibid., 23, for a reference to Henry's
'debitam et hereditariam dignitatem'.
[3] Cf. P. Joachimsen in Mediaeval Germany, II, 110, who admirably summarizes the issues.

would have destroyed his political hold over the bishoprics of Germany and Lombardy and forfeited the support of the German episcopacy. What he saw, above all else, was that the only method of defending the traditional rights of the monarchy was to exploit to the full the divisions and divergencies of object and interests in the ranks of his opponents, and as time passed to profit from the general reaction against the excesses of the rebels; for the very arrogance of the coalition between pope and princes, and the anarchy into which it plunged Germany, had the unsought-for result of endowing the royalist cause with a new lease of popularity. In the measure in which Henry IV was successful, his success was due to the response his policy found in Germany, which was worn out by the long struggle and acutely perceived the situation to which the weakening of the monarchy was leading. Behind his conception of the kingship as something beyond the reach of the princes was a mighty force of ancient tradition, strongly rooted in German soil; and building on this strength Henry IV was at least able to maintain the old doctrine of hereditary monarchy. The principle of elective monarchy, enunciated at the election of the anti-king, Rudolf of Rheinfelden, in 1077, failed through Henry's efforts to find an immediate place in the constitution. He handed on the ancient theory of hereditary monarchy as an inheritance to his son, and the Hohenstaufen took it over from Henry V and defended it with new weapons. Only some two centuries after the election of Rudolf of Rheinfelden, in circumstances very different, did the view finally become prevalent that the German kingdom was an elective monarchy.

The Diet of Tribur, which met in October 1076 and sealed the alliance between the German princes and the papacy, first revealed the full dangers of Henry's position and the consolidation of the opposition to the Salian monarchy. Its prolonged deliberations appeared to spell the doom of the monarchy, but they also revealed the divergencies between the various elements which made up the opposition. Henry immediately used all his political skill to prise apart the united front.[1] He played on the fact that only one section

---

[1] A Brackmann, in two deservedly famous essays ('Heinrich IV u. der Fürstentag von Tribur', *Hist. Vierteljahrschr.*, XV, and 'Heinrich IV als Politiker beim Ausbruch des Investiturstreites', *Sitz.-Ber. der preuss. Akademie*, 1927) analysed Henry's policy at this period. His conclusions, which tend to exaggerate the extent of Henry's success, need modification in detail, but the general lines of his argument are beyond dispute; cf. C. Erdmann, 'Tribur und Rom. Zur Vorgeschichte der Canossafahrt', *Deutsches Archiv*, I (1937), and Brackmann's further article 'Tribur' (1939), now available with his earlier articles in *Gesammelte Aufsätze* (Weimar, 1941).

of the princes sought to depose him; the more moderate party, on the other hand, still hoped to retain him on the throne after he had purged himself and moderated his policy. He was well aware of the divergencies between the free peasantry and the nobility in Saxony, and the lukewarmness of the former who, after the failure of the revolt of 1073, came to realize that they were little more than pawns in the calculations of the princes.[1] Even in reforming circles, he had adherents — led by the great abbot, Hugh of Cluny, whose reputation and moral stature were equal to the pope's — who were radically opposed to the attempt to exploit his conflict with Gregory in order to abase the monarchy. But above all else he realized the extent of the divergence of aims between Gregory, whose first object was to secure acceptance of the programme of canonical election, and the princes who thought first and foremost of undermining the centralizing policy of the Salian dynasty. His first success, exploiting these differences, was to secure a postponement of any decision until after a second meeting had been held at Augsburg, at which Gregory was to preside. But he carefully refrained from any specific engagement to attend or accept the decisions of the proposed Augsburg meeting.[2] His second success was in avoiding any undertaking to surrender his rights over the Church. He promised Gregory due obedience and satisfaction; he accepted personal abasement and humiliation; but he surrendered nothing of the inherited rights of the monarchy. In brief, he only gave way to his enemies over those points on which the opposition was united.[3] The princes had little interest in investiture, and he was therefore able to refuse concessions on this point to the pope. The pope had no desire to stand in his way, if he was truly repentant, and could not refuse him absolution if he sought it before the meeting at Augsburg took place. This precisely is what happened. Immediately after the Diet of Tribur, he sent an embassy to Rome to secure his absolution. When this failed, he decided on a more dramatic move and shortly before Christmas, taking the princes by surprise, crossed the Alps and, meeting the pope at Canossa, obtained absolution at the pope's hand and was received back into communion with the Church.

[1] Thompson, *Feudal Germany*, 221-222, 226-227; cf. above, p. 96.
[2] Cf. Erdmann, *Deutsches Archiv*, I, 372-373. Instead he used the deliberately ambiguous phrase 'congruo tempore'; cf. the text of his *Promissio* in Erdmann, *Briefe*, 69.
[3] Erdmann, *Deutsches Archiv*, I, 382.

The dramatic scene at Canossa was a real act of personal humiliation, but it saved the cause of the German monarchy. Henry had to agree to accept the pope's judgement in his differences with the German princes; but the insertion of a clause *nisi impedimentum* into the agreement gave him a valid excuse for prevarication. Moreover, although Gregory maintained that Henry still remained suspended from the exercise of his royal rights, it was difficult to argue convincingly that whereas excommunication had deprived him of the right to rule, the raising of the ban did not restore him to the kingship. Finally, the reconciliation between Henry and the Church was a serious disillusionment for the German princes who were intent on deposition, and the breach between them and Gregory, for which Henry had worked since Tribur, was thus consummated. For them, Henry's secret flight to Italy was a deliberate breach of the Tribur agreement, and they forthwith decided to elect another ruler in Henry's place. For this purpose they met at Forchheim on March 13th, 1077, but they were now compelled to act without the pope. Not only did Henry bar the road from Italy, thus preventing the pope from travelling to Germany, but the papal legate who was present at Forchheim, acting on the pope's instructions, expressly requested them to postpone the election of an anti-king. When the princes elected Rudolf of Rheinfelden in 1077, they therefore no longer possessed the same power or standing as at Tribur in the preceding year. Gregory refused to recognize their nominee and attempted to adopt the role of mediator, calling on both parties to grant him safe-conduct and accept his judgement. But the Saxons were bent not on reconciliation, but on Henry's deposition, and Henry, seeing his star in the ascendant, was adamant. Meanwhile, the apparent hesitancy of the papacy, and its constant negotiations with both parties, lowered Gregory's prestige; soon his adherents were openly expressing doubts of his constancy. The great coalition against Henry was visibly disintegrating.

Canossa was thus a political victory for Henry IV. Now that he was again in communion with the Church, the loyalty of the German bishops, who had begun to waver in 1076, was restored. The effects of the excommunication were undone in the eyes of ordinary people. Rudolf of Rheinfelden, on the other hand, was too evidently the nominee of the princes to obtain wide popular support, and in the eyes of the Saxons he was suspect as a Swabian. Particularly significant was the support accorded to Henry by the rising towns, Mainz and Worms in the west, Regensburg, Augsburg and Würzburg in the south and east. The rebels experienced difficulty in keeping the Saxons in the field, for they were not interested in the cause either of the princes or of the papacy. Furthermore, Rudolf's resources were quickly exhausted through the rapacity of his aristocratic supporters, and when as a result he began to lay hands on Church lands he fell into disrepute. When at last in 1080 Gregory gave up hopes of mediation and declared himself for Rudolf, again placing Henry under the ban of the Church, his action misfired. Even Rudolf rebelled against the pope's presumptuous declaration that the new German king was a vassal of the Holy See. The renewed excommunication of Henry, on the other hand, was widely regarded as an act of persecution. In any case, the moment was unhappily chosen, for six months later, in October 1080, Rudolf fell mortally wounded on the field of battle.

Thereafter the civil war in Germany quickly lost every semblance of its original character, and became an open struggle for aggrandizement on the part of the princes. It was not easy to find a new anti-king, but eventually Hermann of Salm, a count from Luxemburg, was elected. He was an insignificant character, *inane portans nomen regis* (as one chronicler wrote), and it is characteristic that Henry felt strong enough to leave him to be dealt with by his adherents, under the leadership of the new royalist Duke of Swabia, Frederick of Hohenstaufen, to whom Henry had given the hand of his daughter, while he himself crossed the Alps to secure the imperial crown and deal the Gregorians a final blow. In Germany, the struggle was practically over. The mass of the people were avidly desirous of peace, and the divisions among his foes enabled Henry to gain the upper hand. Using every means of persuasion, and affirming that he had no wish to displant ancient Saxon privileges, he genuinely sought to reconcile the Saxon peasantry. By 1085, when Hermann was compelled to fly to Denmark for safety, Henry was again in control of almost every bishopric in the kingdom. Even in the ranks of the opposition, Hermann's uselessness was recognized, and a new candidate appeared in the person of Eckbert of Meissen. With the death of the former in 1088 and of the latter in 1090, the opposition collapsed. The Saxons made their peace, and in 1091 the last two leaders of the rebellion, Berthold of Carinthia and Welf of

Bavaria, submitted. With the death in 1091 of Abbot William of Hirsau, the protagonist of monastic reform, the last flame of opposition to Henry IV expired in Germany.

All now depended on the situation in Italy. Six years earlier, in 1085, Gregory VII had died in exile, after seeing all his hopes crumble. His declaration in favour of Rudolf in 1080 had immediately been answered by Henry who, at the head of the bishops and metropolitans of Germany and Lombardy, had declared him deposed for his crimes[1] and appointed a new pope, Clement III, in his place. Thus to the schism in the empire was added schism in the Church, and Gregory's position became so precarious that he was compelled to seek reconciliation with the Norman prince, Robert Guiscard, on the latter's terms. His whole position now depended on the military support of the Normans and of Matilda of Tuscany. But on the very day on which the German anti-king, Rudolf, fell in battle, Matilda's troops suffered a decisive reverse at Volta, near Mantua, while Robert Guiscard turned away from Italy, led eastward by the ambition of conquering the eastern empire. Thus the way was opened for Henry, and although the struggle was hard, he finally penetrated into Rome, where Gregory held out in the castle of St. Angelo, and was crowned emperor by Clement III in 1084. At this critical juncture, however, Guiscard came to the rescue with overwhelming forces, and Henry was forced to retreat northwards. The Normans captured and sacked Rome, leaving a third of the city in ashes, and then withdrew southwards. Clement III reoccupied the city, and Gregory, whom the Normans had taken with them, after a few months died in Salerno, an exile and a failure.

These reverses had serious repercussions within the Church, and for three years the reformers faltered. The college of cardinals was sharply divided, and Henry showed some astuteness in emphasizing his desire for peace and his regret for Gregory's misfortunes. But the anti-pope, Clement III, was the stumbling-block, and Henry himself, with his undoubted tendency to overplay his hand, was probably not willing to make real concessions, particularly as the

---

[1] The fruits of his pontificate, it was said, revealed its evil roots, his works showed the character of his intentions: he had subverted the ecclesiastical order, disturbed the government of the Christian empire, intended the death, physical and spiritual, of a catholic and peace-loving ruler, defended a perjured anti-king, sowed discord among the concordant, strife among the peaceful, scandal between brothers, divorce between spouses. Cf. the decree of the Synod of Brixen (1080) in Erdmann, *Die Briefe Heinrichs IV*, 69-73.

papacy was under Norman control and therefore scarcely free to come to terms, since Guiscard's policy, which was the decisive factor, was anti-imperial. Thus the most opportune moment for a settlement went by unused, and with the election of Urban II in 1088 the Gregorian party again resumed control. Supported by Matilda and the Normans, Urban's power proved unshakable. For seven years, from 1090 to 1097, Henry vainly waged war in Lombardy; but Matilda could not be subdued. Meanwhile Urban advanced the claims of the papacy, forbidding not only lay investiture but also fealty to laymen on the part of the episcopate; the bishops were henceforth only to be bound by oath to the papacy. The pope's part in the first crusade not only raised his standing in Europe, but placed him at the head of a *militia Christi*, which looked to him as its leader. It was not long before it became clear that the opportunity lost after Gregory's death in 1085 would not be repeated, that Henry had no chance of subduing the papacy, and that the continued struggle with the Church was defeating any hope of final pacification. All three successors of Gregory VII — Victor III (1086-1087), Urban II (1088-1099) and Paschal II (1099-1118) — confirmed and renewed the former's sentence of excommunication, thus casting doubt on the validity of all Henry's acts of government. Already in 1089, when the solidity of Henry's position in Germany had become manifest, the opposition had offered its mediation, if he would throw over the anti-pope; but he was unable to bring himself to the point of compromise, and thus the conviction gradually made itself felt that Henry alone stood between the realm and peace. In these circumstances, opposition arose even within his own family, where it was felt that his obstinacy was compromising the dynasty. Already in 1093, Urban had won over the king's son Conrad, whom Henry had had consecrated as his successor in 1087, and Conrad had gone to Italy, married the daughter of Roger of Sicily, placed himself at the head of a league of Lombard cities and received the Lombard crown, which he retained until his death in 1101. Henry himself, despairing of success in Italy, saw the need for settlement, and immediately on his return to Germany in 1097 summoned a meeting of the princes at Mainz to discuss terms of peace. But the more exalted claims set forth by Urban and maintained by his successor, Paschal II, offered little prospect of settlement. Henry was still unshakably determined to maintain his

rights of investiture, for which he had struggled so long. The over-
ture which he made to Rome in 1101 was repulsed, and even his
final offer to demonstrate his penance by going on crusade proved
unacceptable. Thus the issue with the Church was as far from
solution as ever, and so long as discord prevailed, there was little
hope of permanent betterment in Germany. Italy, on the other
hand, was completely out of control: after Henry withdrew in 1097,
and still more after the death of his son, the anti-king Conrad, in
1101, German influence collapsed, and Italy was left, in spite of
occasional brief imperial campaigns, to develop in independence on
its own lines for the next fifty years.

IV

It was in these circumstances that, in 1104, Henry's second son
who had been crowned king as his father's designated successor in
1099, rose in rebellion. Few acts in German history have been
more severely castigated than this betrayal of the father by the son,
at the very moment when the former seemed to have introduced a
new measure of peace and prosperity in Germany.[1] Contemporaries scornfully described his action as 'contrary to nature', and
Hermann of Tournai, who saw the letter of expostulation written
by Henry IV in his plight to the king of France, said that anyone
who read it and remained unmoved could only be described as
hard-hearted.[2] It was widely held, perhaps not without reason, that
the instigator was the pope, and it is far from certain that the plot
would have succeeded, in spite of the unscrupulous chicanery of the
insurgents, had Henry IV not died, in the midst of the struggle, at
Liége, whither he had withdrawn to prepare resistance. His death,
on August 7th, 1106, left his rebellious son, Henry V, unchallenged
master of the field.

The full story of Henry V's rebellion will never be known, and
there is no sure means of deciding what part personal ambition
played in his plans. But it is certain that there were substantial

[1] 'Undique terra satis quievit pace simul et fertilitate,' wrote Ekkehard in his chronicle for
the year 1104. A general peace had been decreed for four years in 1102, to the immediate
profit of the peasantry and the towns, but to the dissatisfaction of the nobility ('cum autem
domini cum satellitibus suis per aliquos annos hac lege stringerentur ... iterum adversus
imperatorem murmur movebant').
[2] For the text of Henry IV's letter, cf. Erdmann, Briefe, 52-58.

heads of disagreement between him and his father, and it seems likely that he was convinced that Henry IV's obduracy was mistaken and ultimately disastrous. Perhaps he realized that a continuation of the struggle with the Church would only undermine still further the power of the crown, and that, if the discord continued, the old emperor would bequeath to his heir, not a stable royal power, but weak and unsubstantiated claims.[1] Probably, also, Henry IV's policy of increasing reliance on and co-operation with the rising towns, and even with the peasantry,[2] was too revolutionary for his son, particularly as royal support of the towns was alienating the German bishops who saw their control of the episcopal cities thereby menaced. In contrast to his father, therefore, Henry V determined to come to terms with the aristocracy, intending thereby to secure the backing of a united Germany for the struggle with the papacy. In the long run his ultimate objects may have been little different from his father's; but there was a radical difference in his methods, which was the result of time and events. If, in 1076, Henry IV had perceived that his best prospect lay in reconciliation with the Church — hence Canossa — by 1105 it was apparent that the persistent discord with the Church was the main source of unrest. Hence, where Henry IV had fought above all to prevent the disruption of the work of the Salian monarchy by the princes, Henry V, when he broke away from his father, deliberately acknowledged the aristocratic character of the German constitution. 'The removal of a single person', he is reported to have said, shortly after the beginning of his revolt, 'even if he is the supreme head of the State, is a reparable injury to the realm; but the destruction of the princes is the destruction of the very kingdom.'[3] In these words he implicitly designated himself the representative of the princes, and in this respect the successor of the anti-kings, Rudolf of Rheinfelden and Hermann of Salm; and although he had, as legitimate heir of the royal dynasty, an independent power which neither Rudolf nor Hermann had ever possessed, the decline in the position of the monarchy was manifest. Henry V had not only to throw over the

---

[1] Thus Ranke, *Weltgesch.*, VII, 333 sq.

[2] The attempt to draw closer to the peasant class (implicit earlier in his conciliation of the Saxon peasantry) was a marked feature of the *Landfrieden* of 1102, which gave special attention to their protection; cf. H. Hirsch, *Die hohe Gerichtsbarkeit im deutschen Mittelalter* (1922), 138-139, 232-235.

[3] Cf. A. Degener's discussion in *Mitteil. d. ö. Instituts, Erg. -Bd.*, XIV (1939), 136.

Salian programme, which had originally provoked the opposition of the nobility to the crown and had created in Germany a party willing to ally with the papacy; he had also, ruling in co-operation with the princes, to accept and sanction the powers and privileges which the aristocracy had usurped during the thirty years in which Henry IV's energies had been diverted by the struggle with the Church. There was some tactical skill in winning the support of the aristocracy so as to oppose a united Germany to the claims of the papacy; but the longer such a policy was pursued the more difficult it became to shake off the control of the aristocracy; and there lay the real test.

Nevertheless, the short-term benefits of the change of ruler were immediately apparent, and within a few months of his father's death Henry V was able to take up the question of investiture with the full support and backing of the German bishops and princes. In face of the papacy Germany was at long last united. But negotiations were not easy, since the pope clung to the extreme demands he had formulated in 1102, and the moderate proposals put forward by Henry in 1107, in which — adopting the compromise views recently sponsored in France and England — he claimed only to confer the indisputably secular *regalia*, were rejected, although (as has been pointed out) these proposals would have satisfied earlier popes, including Gregory VII.[1] A further embassy, dispatched by Henry in 1109, received only the non-committal answer that the pope claimed only what was canonical and had no intention of diminishing the king's rights. In these circumstances, with the full support of Germany, Henry set out for Italy at the head of an army of 30,000 men, intent on restoring imperial rights and securing a final settlement with the papacy. Matilda of Tuscany, long the mainstay of the papal party, submitted to Henry, whom she made her heir, thus cancelling her earlier gift of her lands to the Holy See. Paschal realized that a decision could no longer be postponed and — still determined to avoid all forms of lay investiture — made the proposal which Henry accepted, that, in return for a renunciation of the royal right of investiture, the churches should restore to the crown all *regalia* and appurtenant lands acquired since the reign of Charles the Great.[2]

[1] Cf. Scharnagl, *Begriff d. Investitur*, 69.
[2] Ibid., 72-73. *Regalia* were defined by the pope as 'civitates, ducatus, marchias, comitatus, monetas, teloneum, mercatum, advocatias regni, iura centurionum et curtes quae regni erant, cum pertinentiis suis, militiam et castra.'

But when the pope published the treaty, which Henry had already confirmed, a tumult arose among both the prelates, who feared the loss of their fiefs, and the German nobility, who foresaw the loss of the fiefs they held from the churches. Paschal was compelled to denounce the agreement, which he was impotent to enforce, and was left to face the king, who took him and the cardinals prisoner and — using the threat of schism — compelled Paschal to issue a privilege, granting him rights of investiture. Once again all Henry demanded was recognition of his right to confer *regalia*, which would have been accepted without difficulty by reformers in the days of Gregory VII and Urban II; [1] but now a storm arose, the pope's action was condemned at a council in Vienne, and Paschal was faced by the threat of revolt among the French bishops. At a synod in Rome in March 1112 he was forced to retrace his steps, and in 1116 he finally issued an express revocation of his privilege.

These events had little effect on Henry V's position in Germany. The council of Vienne held him up to the obloquy of Christendom, but although the Archbishop of Vienne pressed for excommunication, he failed to secure papal assent, which alone would have given the sentence wide-reaching effect. As a result of cutting away from Henry IV's policy, the crown was evidently still too strong to fear a repetition of the events of 1076. But although the Church was no longer able to sow discord in Germany, the inherent weaknesses in Henry's position, due to his close dependence on the princes, now began to make themselves apparent. Despite his ruthlessness and energy, he was never able to restore peace in Germany or repress the plundering of feudal marauders. [2] Nor was he able to rehabilitate the crown lands, which had been wasted and pillaged during the civil wars, until nothing but scattered fragments remained. He was not slow in recognizing the necessity for a revival of the efficient administration which had been the mark of the earlier period of Henry IV's government, and was credited with the intention of instituting an inquest on the model of the English Domesday Survey, and on this basis of introducing a system of royal taxation. [3] But

[1] Scharnagl, op. cit., 75.
[2] The anarchy in Germany is vividly described in the chronicle of Ekkehard of Aura ('praedones quippe, qui sub nomine equitum undique superabundabant, villos et agros ecclesiarum invadebant, colonos domi forisque spoliabant'); summarizing the characteristics of the reign after Henry's death, he writes: 'iustitiis regni non multum invigilavit.'
[3] Cf. the authorities in Thompson, *Feudal Germany*, 355 n. 2. Henry was married to Matilda, daughter of Henry I of England, and was therefore well aware of Anglo-Norman practice.

these projects came to nothing; the opposition was too strong, and unlike his father Henry had neither the strong convictions nor the power to resist it. It was the same when he attempted, in 1112, to resume vacant fiefs in Saxony for the crown: this brought him face to face with the rising Supplinburg and Ascanian dynasties, while an attempt to reassert his rights in Frisia raised rebellion in the north-west of the kingdom. By the end of 1114 Saxony was in full revolt, and early in 1115 the Saxon leader, Lothar of Supplinburg, won a decisive victory at the battle of Welfesholz. Henry was still confident enough to leave German affairs in the hands of his nephews, Conrad and Frederick of Staufen, and himself go to Italy in order to secure possession of the lands of Matilda of Tuscany, who had died in 1115; but unrest continued during his absence and after his return. After the battle of Welfesholz, the sentence of excommunication proclaimed three years earlier at the synod of Vienne was promulgated in Germany. For a time it looked as though a junction of the feudal and reforming opposition would be effected, bringing with it a return to the evil conditions of Henry IV's reign.

In these circumstances Henry redoubled his efforts to come to terms with the Church, but for many months without positive results.[1] The pope, fearing a repetition of the violent measures of 1111, refused a conference, and when Henry appeared in Italy in 1116, fled to a safe refuge with the Normans. Paschal II's death in 1118, far from bringing about improved relations, resulted in a deterioration, for Henry, having failed in an attempt to lay hands on the new pontiff, Gelasius II, set up an anti-pope, and was promptly excommunicated; while Gelasius sought refuge first in southern Italy and then in France, where he died in 1119. He was succeeded by the Archbishop of Vienne who had first excommunicated Henry in 1112, and whose first act as pope, under the title Calixtus II, was to renew the excommunication. But an attempt, in a synod at Rheims in 1119 to renew the unqualified condemnation of lay investiture, failed in face of opposition from both clergy and laity,[2] and Calixtus was forced to the realization that some form of compromise was unavoidable. Henry also, by now fully conscious of the measure of his peril, was ready to make his peace with both princes and pope. The

---

[1] 'Non cessat legationes satisfactorias ad apostolicam sedem ... destinare, quas tamen constat minime profecisse,' says Ekkehard in his account of the events of 1117.
[2] Scharnagl, op. cit., 78-80.

papal sentence of excommunication had been proclaimed by legates at synods at Cologne and Fritzlar in May 1119, and there were rumours of an imminent meeting of the princes with the intention of deposing the king. This threat, recalling with all vividness the evil days of 1076, was decisive and Henry placed himself without reserve in the hands of the princes, promising to obey their decisions in matters both of Church and of State. In Germany he gave orders for each and every individual to be restored to his 'rights' and properties,[1] and in return he received an assurance from the princes that, in the settlement with the Church, they would firmly maintain the honour of the emperor.[2]

Thus the settlement between Church and State, when it came about, was the work of the princes, standing like a third power in an independent position between king and pope. A commission of twelve princes, chosen equally from both parties, was appointed to prepare the terms of settlement, and at the council of Würzburg in 1121 Henry had to agree to set aside his own wishes and abide by their decision. The princes, observing their earlier promise, gave solid support to the emperor's claims in the negotiations which now began with the Holy See; but the whole course of proceedings is evidence of the distance affairs in Germany had travelled since the beginning of Henry IV's reign. The princes, deciding high policy, were now manifestly the masters. Nevertheless, the evident unity of sentiment within Germany was impressive, and doubtless contributed towards producing a conciliatory attitude in Rome. Calixtus sent word to Henry that his intention was not to diminish but to enhance the honour of the empire, and a further council was held at Worms, at which, on September 23rd, 1122, agreement was reached. Henry agreed to renounce the traditional investiture with ring and staff — a form of investiture which through age-old tradition implied conferment of the ecclesiastical office — but in exchange the pope recognized his right to confer the *regalia* by investiture with the sceptre.[3] This latter investiture was to take place before consecra-

---

[1] 'Unicuique per totum regnum suis rebus spoliato propria concedi praecepit.' On the broader significance of this concession cf. below, p. 155.

[2] 'Hoc etiam, quod ecclesia adversus imperatorem et regnum de investituris causatur, principes sine dolo et sine simulatione elaborare intendunt, ut in hoc regnum honorem suum retineat' (*Mon. Germ. hist., Const.*, I, 158).

[3] No attempt was màde to define the *regalia*, probably deliberately in order to avoid further grounds of discord (Scharnagl, 128); but cf. Paschal II's earlier definition, above, p. 129, n. 2.

tion, thus ensuring that the elected prelate should not enter into his duties until he had sworn homage and fealty to the king. In addition, Henry obtained the valuable concession that elections in Germany should be carried out in his presence, thus enabling him to bring due influence to bear. Royal control over the German church was, therefore, substantially maintained. In Italy and Burgundy, on the contrary, Henry's concessions were more far-reaching. Here no form of election in the king's presence was granted, and the king agreed that the bishops should be consecrated (thus receiving full administrative control over their dioceses) before the grant of *regalia*, which were to be conferred within six months of consecration. This difference reflected the decline of royal power in Italy, where the civil wars had already *de facto* deprived the king of control over the Lombard episcopacy.[1] Even so, it is surprising that Henry was willing to grant formal recognition to this revolutionary change; but the explanation was in all probability his acquisition, in 1116, of the Matildine lands, which provided an alternative foundation for royal power in Italy. Here, if properly used, was a basis for royal power far more stable and assured than the doubtful loyalty of the Lombard bishops, whose position as instruments of the monarchy was assailed not only by the currents of ecclesiastical reform but also by the rise of the communes, which were already disputing episcopal control of the Lombard cities.

The Concordat of Worms was no final settlement of the conflict of Church and State; for no formal agreement could dispose of the insoluble problems arising from the two-fold loyalties of the bishops and prelates. Moreover, the papal concessions, which were admittedly far-reaching, were hotly criticized by reforming circles when the agreement was published at the Lateran Council in 1123, and were only accepted after it had been pointed out that there was no question of approving the disputed points, but only of tolerating them for the sake of peace. It was, furthermore, a fact that, whereas Henry V's concessions were granted to the Church in perpetuity, Calixtus' charter was addressed to Henry V alone; and whatever the reasons for this divergence may have been,[2] there is no doubt that it enabled the Church to maintain that the concession of election in

[1] It was already evident by 1112 that 'the old pro-imperial and German clergy in Italy had become wholly displaced during the long conflict'; cf. Thompson, op. cit., 154.
[2] They are discussed in *Mediaeval Germany*, I (1938), 98–101.

K

the king's presence — which was the main source of contention —
was only a personal concession to Henry, which did not extend to his
successors. Already as early as 1125, at the election of Henry V's
successor, Lothar II, this view emerged as a serious political argument. Nevertheless these facts should not blind us to the importance
of the Concordat of 1122, which — as contemporaries were well
aware[1] — did at long last introduce an atmosphere of peace and
concord. After fifty years of struggle, emperor and pope had at
length discovered a practical *modus vivendi*. Although many points
were held over for the future, a breathing-space had been secured in
which to review and repair the damage of half-a-century of civil
strife. The world-shaking issues over which Gregory VII and Henry
IV had fought intransigently were for the moment appeased. But
the cost in Germany and throughout the empire was immense. The
power of the monarchy had been shaken to its foundations. Peace
had been restored between *regnum* and *sacerdotium*; but to restore peace
and order and government in Germany was another question. Here,
in spite of Henry IV's life-long struggle for his inheritance, the old
order had passed beyond recall. In the welter of war and rapine and
confusion, Germany had passed over into a new age; it had undergone a revolution, which left its marks for all time on German
history.

---

[1] 'Annotare sufficiat', writes Ekkehard of Aura, 'pacem firmissimam et ab omnibus univer-
salem . . . institutam, regalia vel fiscalia regno, ecclesiastica ecclesiis . . . adiudicatam esse . . .'
'Incredibile memoratu est, quam . . . pro pace et concordia . . . certatum sit.'

CHAPTER 6

THE RESULTS OF THE INVESTITURE CONTEST

I

THE Investiture Contest resulted in a fundamental change in the balance of political power in Germany. The attempt of the Salian dynasty, relying on new methods and instruments of government, to establish a strong monarchy was wrecked. The aristocracy, whose power had seemed for a period to be waning, exploited the long struggle between Church and State to reaffirm its position. Hence the real victor was neither king nor pope, but rather the estate of princes. After the accession of Henry V in 1106, the princes were the preponderating power in Germany. Nor was this aristocratic predominance merely the temporary consequence of the shattering blows inflicted on the monarchy in the struggle with the Church. Not content with challenging and attacking the power of the Salian monarchy, the aristocracy exploited the anarchy and unrest of the period after 1076 to remodel German society and institutions on lines which ensured the maintenance of its own political prerogatives; the strength of its position lay in the fact that it was based not simply on a momentary shift in the balance of political forces, but was also rooted in profound social and constitutional changes. It took advantage of the stress of civil war and the dissolution of old social classes to strengthen its hold by reducing large elements of the population to dependence. It multiplied its clients and affirmed its control by deft exploitation of the bonds of feudalism. It used the pretext that for thirty years, from 1076 to 1106, there was no lawful, universally recognized German king as an excuse for exercising powers of government without royal assent and for extending the powers it was already exercising. In place of the Salian system of government, which it had wrecked, it built up on its own initiative a new administrative system in which the traditional rights of the monarchy were disregarded. By 1106 German society had undergone a revolutionary transformation: between the settlement of Worms in 1122 and the accession of

Frederick Barbarossa in 1152 a new social and political structure emerged and took shape.

The first fact on which we must insist is the transformation of German society. As a result of the Investiture Contest Germany advanced with remarkable speed along the path leading to feudalism. What the ninth century had done for France, transforming French society into a feudal society,[1] was accomplished in Germany by the civil wars during the reign of Henry IV. Castles sprang up everywhere, and political organization immediately began to evolve round the castle. The free society which had been characteristic, particularly of the Saxon north, passed away. Unsuccessful rebellion, following on the economic measures of the Salian kings, ruined the free peasantry who, at the beginning of Henry IV's reign, had still been numerically the predominant element in Saxon society.[2] In Frisia also and in Thuringia the same process went on, while throughout Germany, in the south as well as in the north, the land was wasted and insecurity, tyranny, poverty and famine undermined the social order. Under the stress of the times the weaker freemen, in particular the peasantry, went down to serfdom, while the stronger freemen became knights or *ministeriales* and were bound to higher lords by ties of vassalage and homage. The disintegrating effects of the civil wars drove small nobles to larger ones for protection, while others, owing to the collapse of royal authority, lost their direct relationship with and protection by the crown, and were reduced to dependence by the strong.

Simultaneously the campaigns of Henry IV revealed that militarily the peasants, who cultivated their own fields and fought lightly-armed on foot, were no match for the horsemen of Swabia, Alsace and Lorraine, who fought for the king and had already learned from France the principles of feudal warfare. Abbots of reformed monasteries, who feared attacks by royalists, or bishops supporting the king, who feared the aristocratic allies of the papacy, no longer dared to rely on their peasant tenants for military support and were driven to recruit trained warriors, whose profession was fighting and who were heavily armed. The same result was achieved by the spread of castles, and the need for professional troops for garrison and castle-guard. Moreover, the small, free landowner, faced with economic ruin as a result of the devastation of civil war, was no

[1] Cf. above, p. 17.   [2] Cf. above, p. 86.

longer able to bear the expense of military service. Hence bishops
and magnates turned increasingly to the *ministeriales*, who were
armed and maintained at the lord's expense and employed as knights.
On all sides there was a pressing demand for knightly *ministeriales*,
and many freemen, to escape bankruptcy and ruin, threw over their
liberty and entered the ministerial ranks, seeking in this way to
escape the rigours of serfdom. Thus the civil wars completed the
first phase in the rise and emancipation of the ministerial class.[1]
Every means was used by the magnates to make entry into the ranks
of the *ministeriales* attractive, and the ministerial class rapidly rose in
the social scale; its separation from the common body of servile
dependants, from whom it had sprung, was completed. The
ministeriales threw off personal bondage, adopting the slogan:
'Dienstmann ist nicht eigen', secured freedom to leave their lords
and succeeded in converting their servile tenures into fiefs which
they organized as manors and on which, as often as not, they built
themselves a castle. One of the most distinguished *ministeriales* of
Frederick I's reign, Werner of Bolland, rose so high that he possessed
seventeen castles and had 1,100 knights in his service.

   In this way the Investiture Contest reshaped German society.
The emancipation of the *ministeriales* constituted the addition of a
new class to German society, which, in spite of its servile origins,
was accounted part of the nobility; it was a knightly class with a
place in the feudal hierarchy. By the middle of the twelfth century
ministeriales were found allying by marriage with noble dynasties,
succeeding to aristocratic estates and franchises, and occupying high
places in church and state which had formerly been the prerogative
of the nobility. For the civil wars, which ruined the small freemen
and advanced the *ministeriales*, also broke up the unity of the old
German aristocracy of Saxon and Salian times. Many illustrious
names with a distinguished past disappeared: Otto of Nordheim,
the leader of the Saxon opposition to Henry IV, was the last of his
line, and with the death of Magnus Billung in 1106 the series of
Billung dukes of Saxony was extinguished. Other families went
down in the struggle, losing power and prestige. If one dynasty was
loyal to the crown and consequently sure of abundant reward,
family considerations and interests inevitably drove its rivals over
to the papacy and to the anti-king whom the pope recognized,

---

[1] Cf. above, pp. 81 sq. For the later history of the *ministeriales* cf. below, pp. 324-325.

while some families were divided among themselves.[1] Hence many noble families divided continuously, and soon, holding little more than a single castle, were scarcely distinguishable from the knights or *ministeriales* with whom eventually they amalgamated. But there were others which made their fortunes in the wars and from small beginnings rose to the front rank: among the most famous were the Hohenstaufen dynasty which first appeared in the limelight in 1079 when Frederick of Staufen was given the hand of Henry IV's daughter and made duke of Swabia; the house of Supplinburg from which sprang the emperor, Lothar II (1125-1137); the family of Zähringen which carved out a place for itself in the Black Forest and across the Rhine in modern Switzerland; and the Ascanian and Wettin dynasties which later made names on the eastern frontier. Such families gathered together lands and rights and tenures and political power and rose above their fellows, who were compelled to recognize their pre-eminence and frequently to become their vassals.

Thus the period of the Investiture Contest saw a rapid differentiation in the ranks of the aristocracy, and a great increase in the wealth and power of a few great lords. In a remarkably short space of time the relatively simple society of the Ottonian period gave way to a feudal society with many gradations from the princes, lay and ecclesiastical, through the counts to the *ministeriales* and simple knights. The subordination of man to man, of count to prince, was not accomplished at one stroke; down into the thirteenth century aristocratic families survived which had retained their independence, held aloof from feudal ties, and possessed allodial estates which were enclaves in a feudal society; but from the beginning of the twelfth century, in marked contrast to previous conditions, German society was predominantly feudal. At its head stood the princes whose pre-eminence was based no longer simply on great material wealth and vast allodial estates, but who represented the new society because they had subordinated nobles and freemen and knights by feudal ties, and so became political leaders with political powers over counts who hitherto had been direct representatives of the king. Throughout Germany, in lay and ecclesiastical territories, we can observe the extension of the network of feudal relationships, as the

[1] Two sons of Count Eberhard of Nellenburg, for example, died fighting for Henry IV at the battle of the Unstrut, while the third was one of the leading reformers in Swabia; cf. Hirsch in *Mediaeval Germany*, II, 153.

rising princes strove to bind the nobility to themselves by ties of vassalage and in particular to extend their control over the whole network of counties within their spheres of influence. This was the policy of the Welf dukes in Bavaria in the early years of the twelfth century. It was applied by the Zähringer to the advocacies in the Black Forest. It can be followed in western Germany, in Hesse, Guelders and Cleves. It was a policy no less characteristic of the ecclesiastical than of the lay princes. The bishop of Würzburg was the first to raise himself to a ducal position by subjecting all the counties in Eastern Franconia to his own authority; and we know on the authority of the chronicler, Adam of Bremen, that the famous archbishop Adalbert of Bremen, spurred on by the example of Würzburg, set out to do likewise in his own province,[1] striving at the same time to make the leading nobles his vassals.[2] Similar efforts can, over a period of time, be observed in Mainz and Cologne, at Utrecht and Halberstadt, at Münster and Trent and (with less success) at Bamberg and Brixen. There were setbacks and failures; but everywhere, from the beginning of the twelfth century, the same current was in motion; everywhere feudalism was exploited to secure the forfeiture of counties, the escheat of fiefs, the subjection of the nobility and the systematic consolidation of territorial control.[3]

The rapid spread of feudalism, which the civil wars of Henry IV's reign fostered, was thus one of the main sources of the new power of the princes; it enabled them to consolidate their position. But what the princes gained, the crown lost. The kingship of the Saxons and Salians had its foundations in an extensive class of freemen. The county organization, on which royal government was based, was essentially an organization of freemen acting at the king's behest on royal business under the representative of the crown, the count; legislation was legislation for a free class, and militarily the monarchy depended in large degree on the service of freemen in defence of the land. The depression of large sections of the old free population

---

[1] *Gesta Hammaburgen. eccl. pont.* (ed. Schmeidler), 188: 'Solus erat Wirceburgensis episcopus, qui dicitur in episcopatu suo neminem habere consortem; ipse cum teneat omnes comitatus suae parochiae, ducatum etiam provinciae gubernat episcopus. Cuius aemulatione permotus noster praesul statuit omnes comitatus, qui in sua dyocesi aliquam iurisdictionem habere videbantur, in potestatem ecclesiae redigere.'

[2] 'Omnes qui erant in Saxonia siue in aliis regionibus clari et magnifici viri adoptaret in milites,' says Adam (III, 35), 'multis dando quod habuit, ceteris pollicendo quod non habuit.'

[3] The territorial history is briefly recapitulated, with references to the more important literature, by H. Mitteis in *Mediaeval Germany*, II, 268-276.

and the spread of feudalism thus sapped the roots of royal power. Feudalism deprived the king, except on his own demesnes, of the means of direct government. So long as a numerous free class had existed, acknowledging no master save the king,[1] the monarchy had possessed the means of making its authority felt throughout the land; but the growth of feudalism and the decline of the free population meant that the king was excluded from direct interference, except where on the demesne-lands of the crown he himself was lord and master. The feudal dependants, great and small, free and servile, knew but one master: their immediate lord.

In this way the whole basis of Salian government was shaken to its foundations, and the county organization, which had been its framework, crumbled. It has already been seen that the county had never finally supplanted more ancient organs of local government, which still continued to function,[2] and that the upper ranks of free society, in possession of vast allodial estates, had succeeded in maintaining a privileged position outside the ambit of the ordinary county administration.[3] Furthermore, the spread of immunities and franchises, to which attention has been drawn, had already before the Investiture Contest broken up the territorial unity of counties, *Gaue* and hundreds, while the growth of hereditary succession, which can be noted from the reigns of Henry II and Conrad II, had weakened royal control of the county organization. All these were noteworthy trends, but none had progressed so far, by the time of the Investiture Contest, as to cause serious alarm to a firmly-established monarchy. After 1075, however, the position was different. The confusion, anarchy and lack of a universally recognized authority, which then prevailed, in conjunction with the decline of the free classes, reinforced the tendencies to disintegration, and in the space of a few years the old system of local government collapsed. Old administrative units and boundaries disappeared, and when after a generation peace was restored to the land, new units of government had taken their place. During the period when royal authority was weak and disputed, the aristocracy had, on its own initiative, taken charge and remodelled the administrative machine in accordance with its own interests and with the strengthened position which it had secured through the spread of feudalism.

---

[1] Cf. the statement of the Swabians under Conrad II quoted above, p. 79.
[2] Above, p. 10.   [3] Above, pp. 87-88.

A major factor in this process was the rapid spread of castle-building, which was a sign and outcome of the unquiet times. In contrast to France, where the feudal castles had dominated the land since the anarchy of the ninth century, this was a new feature of German life. Hitherto private castle-building had been rigorously repressed, and (as in England) any such structures put up in times of crisis were either destroyed or forfeited to the crown. Right down to the reign of Henry III even the German kings themselves had owned few castles, apart from citadels in towns like Goslar and Regensburg which were provincial headquarters, and nobles and kings alike lived in rambling unfortified manor-houses. With the outbreak of civil war the situation was changed, and a spate of castle-building set in, as all members of the nobility set about safeguarding their independence and their estates against their enemies in the hostile camp. These new castles, which each family raised on its hereditary estates, soon dominated the land, and even after the death of Henry IV and the formal end of the civil war Henry V was unable to suppress them; the process had gone too far. Of Frederick of Swabia, the arch-enemy of Lothar II, it was said that he dragged a castle at his horse's tail; he built castles from Basel to Mainz, while later, in the reign of Frederick I, Swabia was studded with the castles of the dukes of Zähringen.

From the beginning of the twelfth century the castle became not merely a strong-point of local defence but a centre of local administration; thenceforward the castellany or *Burgbezirk* spread throughout Germany. In the Saxon north and the Bavarian south, in ecclesiastical principalities and on the demesne-lands of the monarchy, the *Burg* became the middle-point of an administrative district, a centre from which powers of government were exercised.[1] The change was illustrated by the fact that the rising families now regularly named themselves after their castles,[2] assuming the title of count as an expression of the rank and power they had secured

[1] Many writers have observed this process locally; among the more recent and important cf. M. Spindler, *Anfänge des bayerischen Landesfürstentums* (1937), 143-144, R. Hildebrand, *Der Sächsische Staat Heinrichs des Löwen* (1937), 387, H. Niese, *Verwaltung des Reichsgutes*, 222 sqq., H. W. Klewitz, *Studien z. territorialen Entwicklung des Bistums Hildesheim* (1932), 29-37, and more generally J. Friedrichs, *Burg u. territoriale Grafschaften* (1907).

[2] Thus the Emperor Lothar (1125-1137) was the first of his family officially named after the Supplingenburg. Frederick of Büren built the castle of Staufen about 1077 and was thenceforward known as Frederick of Staufen. The family of Bertold began to call itself 'von Zähringen' about 1100. The examples can, of course, be multiplied; cf. *Mediaeval Germany*, I, 82 and II, 181.

during the troubled period of the civil war. It was from the castle that their authority was exerted, and in large degree the castle was the foundation on which their authority was constructed. Unlike the counts of the tenth and eleventh centuries, who were local representatives of the king, the new counts rose during the civil war in opposition to the crown, and their castles, built where possible on allodial land, were the symbol of their independent position. The backbone of their position was the allodial demesne, the *freies Eigen*, the rich allodial properties which they had possessed since time immemorial.[1] Here lay the main source of their strength and independence. In England, also, at the same period, during the reign of Stephen (1135-1154), there was a spate of castle-building and a marked increase in the independence of the baronage; but the English barons were feudal dependants, in possession only since the Conquest, when they had obtained their fiefs by grants from the crown, and Stephen's successor, Henry II, building on these facts, had little difficulty in course of time in reasserting his prerogatives as head of the feudal hierarchy. The German aristocracy, on the other hand, when they built their castles on their allodial lands, gave expression to the fact that the source of their local power was not the crown or governmental functions exercised on behalf of the crown. Behind their attitude of opposition there was not merely the traditional self-assertion and self-interest of a feudal baronage, but the consciousness of a position of authority not derived from the king but based on the ancient prerogatives of a privileged class. It was no accident that the German aristocracy entered whole-heartedly into alliance with the Gregorian church at a time when William II and Henry I of England could rely on the support of the English baronage against papal pretensions: they did so in defence of their inherited 'rights' and their ancient privileges. Hence the persistence into the twelfth century of a free and privileged aristocracy — so free that it was chary even of subordination to the crown[2] — was an important differentiating feature which, after 1075, became a dominant factor in German development. In France, the

---

[1] Cf. above, p. 86.

[2] Of Eticho, one of the founders of the famous Welf family, the characteristic story was told that he was a prince of 'such distinguished liberty' that he would never submit to anyone's authority, not even the emperor's, whatever inducement he was offered in return ('erat egregii libertatis princeps, qui nunquam alicui, nec ipsi imperatori, pro aliquo beneficio se subdidit dominio'; *Mon. Germ. Hist., Script.*, VI, 764).

growth of feudal relationships since the ninth century had set limits
to the independence of the aristocracy; in England the fact of the
Norman Conquest had assured the supreme overlordship of the
king over the whole land; in Germany alone a powerful aristocracy
persisted which had in large measure avoided the bonds of feudalism
and possessed immemorial rights deeply embedded in the social
structure. The feudalism which after 1076 spread through Germany
in a sudden wave from below, stopped short at the crown: in regard
to those they had subordinated the great noble families rigorously
enforced feudal subjection, but in regard to the crown they clung
to their ancient 'liberty' and profited from the unrest of the Investiture Contest to reject the tightening bonds of royal control which
Henry IV's early policy had foreshadowed.

The power amassed by the aristocracy between 1076 and 1106
was thus a combination of new and old, of feudal and pre-feudal
elements, and the immediate task which, exploiting the absence of
a universally recognized royal authority, the great noble families
and the ecclesiastical princes set themselves, was to weld together
all rights, fiefs, lands, powers and administrations in their hands,
regardless of their diverse origins. This, as has been indicated, was
achieved by attaching such rights and territories to their castles,
which became fixed points for the administration of territorial districts.[1] Such districts were still often denominated counties, and in
some instances were the linear descendants of old counties, but in
the main they were new units, thrown together from fiefs, fragments of old counties, allodial lands and advocacies over monastic
properties, all now administered regardless of their origins as
uniform parts of one territorial complex. The novelty of this
organization is attested by the fact that, from the very beginning of
the twelfth century, a new term was employed to denominate the

---

[1] Summarizing this process, Klewitz (op. cit., 31) writes: 'The castles were the centres from
which authority was exercised. From these centres a rigorous administration of the estates
was possible, and as simultaneously rights of government were attached to the castles, it was
possible to 'territorialize' such rights to such a degree that they became effective even over
districts with which originally they had nothing to do.' Cf. also Hirsch, *Mitteil. d. ö. Instituts*,
XXXV (1914), 76: 'From the beginning of the twelfth century mention of the old *Gaue*
gradually ceases, and instead the aristocratic dynasties name themselves after their family
castles, which now become focal points for their various rights of government (*Herrschafts-
gerechtsame*). The latter were, however, diverse in character, an agglomeration of count's
powers, advocacies, manorial rights and proprietary rights over Church properties. The first
task of the territorial powers was to replace these various titles and rights by a single, uniform
legal concept.'

great lords exercising power in this way: they were described as *domini terrae* and their properties were *terrae suae*. The new title, which was general in character, did not replace older ones, like count or duke, but it comprised them as the more general category. Its implication was that all the properties of one lord were now regarded as a unit; although of various origins, all together counted as his *terra*. And the corollary was that, very soon, the diverse origins of specific rights and properties fell into oblivion, and that the territorial lord began to assume new powers and duties needful for the better government and greater security of his *terra*. The earliest, called into existence by the turbulence of the times, was the guardianship of the public peace and. the issue of peace ordinances like that which Count Robert of Flanders proclaimed *per totam terram suam* in 1111; but others followed in due course, culminating in the right to impose taxation. On the other hand, the very fact that such powers were being exercised throughout the whole territory was a factor making for territorial cohesion and tending to bind together the segments from which the rising states were formed. Thus the whole process went on apace, the essential precondition being the impotence of the monarchy which, its hands tied by the struggle with the Church, could neither undertake the major tasks of government itself nor prevent the princes from undertaking them in their territories without its assent.

If we look to the origins of the territorial principalities which were being formed in this way, it is clear that they had no single root. Their birth was the result not of a slow, inexorable gestation of existing institutions, but of the convulsions of civil war. What was determinative was the precise constellation of political forces at a particular moment in historical development. For this reason it is misleading to search among institutions of the eleventh century for the sources of the powers the princes began to assume at the time of the Investiture Contest. The princes used all means at their hands, but pre-existing rights and institutions were simply raw material and the decisive factor was the will and ability to weld these heterogeneous elements into a single territorial unit. Among the aristocratic families which at this period began their rise to power in Germany a few — like the counts of Holland, Jülich, Hainault and Brabant — took their titles from old counties, indicating that the county was the most important source of their rights. But this, as

we have already seen, was exceptional: the bulk of the new and
rising families named themselves after their castles, which were the
seats of their power. Nevertheless, it is clear that landed wealth and
property, although a necessary substratum of power, was in itself
not enough, and that an essential element was the possession of
rights of jurisdiction which were used as a bond to hold the whole
territory together.[1] These were obtained in a variety of ways.
Some princes, as successors of counts, exercised county jurisdiction.
Others appear to have secured control of the old popular courts,
like the *Gogerichte* of Saxony, which had continued to exercise
powers of life and death in cases of flagrant crime, to have extended
their spheres of competence and to have raised them to an equality
with the higher courts.[2] But the most important source of jurisdiction was advocacy over monasteries and monastic lands. The power
of the Welfs in Swabia and of the Zähringen in the Black Forest
was largely built up from the advocacies in their possession; and
many other notable dynasties, including the families of Habsburg
and Hohenlohe, von der Lippe and von Wied, rose in the same way,
assuming the title of count at a later date.[3] The advocacy, as a source
of rights, was important because, during the period of Henry IV's
excommunication, it could be exercised on the basis of papal charters which, disregarding the established claim of the monarchy to
supervise and control the appointment of these officials, authorized
the advocate to exercise rights of government over the monastic
territory. Thus the period of the Investiture Contest saw a wide
extension of such rights,[4] and as advocacy was added to advocacy
the sphere of influence of their possessors grew. Advocacies over
the new monastic foundations of the eleventh century were therefore
a frequent starting-point for the secular princes' endeavours to
extend their authority and jurisdiction and build up their territorial

[1] Cf. the conclusive arguments of G. v. Below, *Territorium u. Stadt* (2nd ed., 1923) against
those historians, like Lamprecht and Seeliger, who maintained that richness in demesnes was
more important than rights, and that the sovereignty of the later princes sprang from
Grundherrschaft or landed proprietorship. Cf. also Th. Knapp's authoritative summary, 'Zur
Geschichte der Landeshoheit', *Württembergische Vierteljahrshefte für Landesgeschichte*, XXXVIII
(1932), 9–112.

[2] Cf. Meister, *Verf-Gesch.*, 185. The complicated question of the origins of the judicial
authority of the German princes was elucidated by H. Hirsch, *Die Hohe Gerichtsbarkeit im
deutschen Mittelalter* (1922).

[3] Other examples are the Counts of Berg and Tyrol; cf. v. Below, *Vom Mittelalter zur
Neuzeit*, 27–28.

[4] For a lucid analysis of the part played by the advocacy in the political struggles cf. Hirsch
in *Mediaeval Germany*, II, 131–173.

power. They were particularly important because the monastic communities were to the fore in the task of cultivating and colonizing barren lands, and opening up the countryside, which was taking place on a large scale; and thus the area under the advocates' control increased and expanded. Families like the Zähringen in the Black Forest derived their power almost exclusively from newly-colonized land over which, as advocates, they exercised political rights; for in the period of civil war the king's ancient monopoly of waste and forest land could be disregarded with impunity and land acquired by reclamation was treated as allodial property. Thus colonization contributed in marked degree to the strengthening of the position of the aristocracy,[1] particularly as — instead of being scattered and parcelled out, as in the older regions — landed property in the newly-settled areas tended to take the shape of great consolidated demesnes, easily subjected to uniform administration. A similar accession of power, and ultimately of wealth, was secured by the foundation of towns, like Freiburg-im-Breisgau, which Conrad of Zähringen founded in 1120 as a central point in the territorial principality his family had created through the exercise of advocate's rights over the monasteries and monastic settlements of the Black Forest.

In this way the period of the Investiture Contest saw the establishment throughout Germany of new territorial units, and these units were the nuclei from which were created the principalities of late mediaeval Germany. Hence the development which in the foregoing we have attempted to sketch constituted a momentous step forward in German history. Many generations were to pass before the principalities took shape and the princes established full territorial control, but already at the beginning of the twelfth century the great aristocratic families were mounting the path which led to territorial sovereignty. The powers asserted by the princes under Henry IV were the basis of their later *Landeshoheit*, and it was the Investiture Contest with its revolutionary social changes which gave them the opportunity to assert and consolidate these powers. This, in the final analysis, was the outstanding contribution of the Investiture Contest to Germany's future: in the civil wars which it loosed we have to seek the beginnings of the territorial disunity, of the

---

[1] Cf. Mayer, 'Die Ausbildung der Grundlagen des modernen deutschen Staates im hohen Mittelalter', *Hist. Zeitschr.*, CLIX (1939), 473-474, 477-478.

fantastic map of German particularism and of the unlimited sovereignty of the princes, which were the curses of German history from the fourteenth to the nineteenth centuries and which, indurated through long generations, have perhaps not been entirely obliterated even to-day.

II

The same process of the loosening of the bonds of royal government which took place in Germany between 1076 and 1122 occurred also in the other imperial territories, in Burgundy and Italy. In northern Burgundy, where imperial control had always been loose and intermittent, the favourable situation was exploited by the local princes to establish their territorial power, while in the south, in the counties of Provence and Forcalquier, the progressive weakening of government opened the way for the intervention of foreign powers, in the first place Aragon (from 1108) and then France and England.[1] This process marked a momentous change in the European political situation; for just as the acquisition of Burgundy by Germany had put an end to the instability of the ninth and tenth centuries,[2] so the gradual dissolution of imperial control in the borderlands overthrew the whole established European balance of power and ushered in a new period of international anarchy and wars of aggression.[3] This change, however, only gradually made itself felt; and it was in Italy, rather than in Burgundy, that the revolutionary consequences of the Investiture Contest were first apparent. Politically of first importance was the consolidation of Norman power in Sicily and southern Italy, which owed its rapid progress to exploitation of the needs of the papacy for allies against the empire. The rise of a great power, hostile and aggressive, on the southern flank of the empire was a second radical alteration in the international situation, as disturbing of the existing order as the beginnings of foreign intervention in Burgundy; it diverted imperial energies to the south, created a grave new preoccupation and betokened a permanent weakening of the imperial position in

[1] Cf. R. Grieser, *Das Arelat in der europäischen Politik* (1925), 15-18; P. Fournier, *Le royaume d'Arles et de Vienne* (1891), 1 sqq.
[2] Cf. above, p. 54.
[3] This cardinal point was finely perceived as early as 1862 by Ficker, *Das deutsche Kaisserreich in seinen universalen u. nationalen Beziehungen*, 75.

Europe.[1] But the rise of Norman Sicily was only one of the ways in which the period of the Investiture Contest reshaped the political system of Italy. In addition, it brought radical changes in the whole social and political structure of Lombardy and Tuscany. These changes must be briefly examined because, for a century after 1154, the destinies of Germany and Italy were so intricately interwoven that, without some knowledge of the Italian situation resulting from the Investiture Contest, it is impossible to understand the history of the Hohenstaufen empire, or the policy and endeavours, the difficulties and ultimately the failure of the Hohenstaufen emperors.

The revolutionary forces released by the Investiture Contest had freer play and greater scope in Italy than in Germany because the powers of the imperial government in Italy had already been weakened in the eleventh century, at the very time when in Germany the Salians were strengthening their administration.[2] But in Italy the social forces at play were different. Except for Conrad II, the emperors of the eleventh century had relied in the main on the support of the bishops — especially of the Lombard bishops — whose power was in the towns, and had helped them by privileges to extend their power into the neighbouring countryside. In Italy, therefore, the struggle centred round the powers of the bishops and their control of the cities. As early as 1035-1036 opposition to the bishops on the part of the lesser nobility led to open unrest and to the formation of *coniurationes* of knights and vavasours to withstand episcopal depredations and excesses by united action. These *coniurationes*, associations of knights to limit the powers of their episcopal overlords, or of peasants to control their commons and pastures, were the roots from which sprang the Italian communes. Thus the Italian communal movement, which was eventually to destroy feudal society in Italy, started from the heart of the old manorial and feudal organization. It was not a movement of the commercial middle classes, which were still at the turn of the eleventh and twelfth centuries militarily, politically and perhaps even economically insignificant, but a feudal and agrarian movement. There were rural as well as city communes, and the primary objects of the early *coniurationes* were defence of rural properties, free exercise of rights of ownership,

---

[1] Cf. Kienast, *Die Anfänge des europäischen Staatensystems im späteren Mittelalter* (1936), 2; Cartellieri, *Machtpolitik vor den Kreuzzügen* (1935).

[2] Cf. above, pp. 69-71.

freedom from feudal burdens and resistance to the greater nobles, whether lay or ecclesiastical, marquesses or bishops. But the struggle centred in the cities because in Italy the cities, the residences of counts and bishops, were the seats of government. Hence the feudal aristocracy began to enter the cities, although still retaining their castles and estates, some to enter into the political and religious movements which offered an opportunity for a strong man to make his fortune, some to influence the election of the bishop whose vassals in great part they were, some to exert a voice in the bishop's court and household. Thus in the first phase, during the century between Henry III's death in 1056 and the first appearance of Frederick Barbarossa in Italy in 1154, the struggle was an aristocratic struggle against the bishops, a struggle by the aristocracy to get control of the bishop's *curia*, and to exercise the powers of government in the bishop's place. It was for this purpose that most communes were formed, and the further question, what faction was to dominate within the commune — patriciate or *popolo*, feudal or commercial interests — only arose at a later stage. The first step was the establishment of a firm sworn association of episcopal vassals capable of taking over the actual exercise of powers nominally vested in the bishop.

The importance of the Investiture Contest in this process lay in the stimulus which it provided by weakening the bonds of government. After the withdrawal of Henry IV from Italy in 1097, imperial administration was virtually eliminated for half a century and Italy entered upon a period of spontaneous development. Earlier the cities had profited from the conflict of empire and papacy to wrest concessions and privileges from both parties. But the most important factor of all was Gregory VII's attack on the Lombard bishops and the recognition which, at Milan and elsewhere, he accorded to the feudal opposition. The papal attack on the Lombard bishops and on the German monarchy, which was their support, shook the bishops' control of the cities and favoured the demands of the vassals against their lords; by weakening the episcopacy, it created the preconditions for a sudden outburst of communal activity, which enabled the communes to take over the bishops' position within the cities and usurp the powers which hitherto the bishops had exercised. In Tuscany, where the ruling house of Canossa was pro-papal in politics, the communes sought — though

L

with markedly less success — to achieve the same result by opposite means. Unable, like the cities of Lombardy, to win greater freedom by allying with the papacy against their overlord, because that overlord was a main supporter of papal power, the Tuscan communities entered instead into alliance with the empire, obtaining by royal grant the very liberties which the Lombard communes were seeking by opposition to the crown. Thus Pisa, which had suffered oppression by viscounts appointed by the marquesses of Tuscany, sought and obtained wide privileges from Henry IV in 1081, and immediately afterwards, in 1085 and 1094, there is mention of 'consuls', the chosen representatives of the commune, who share in administration with the viscount who is now the nominee not of the house of Canossa but of the king. Further north, in Emilia, Bologna swung from one side to the other, securing charters and privileges from kings and popes as expediency dictated, but all the time increasing its liberties at the expense of its overlord, the patriarch of Ravenna. In Milan the long conflict between the archbishop and the pope resulted in a rapid extension of membership of the archiepiscopal *curia*. The archbishop, needing all the support he could get, called in representatives not only of the *capitanei* (or great nobles) but also of the *vassi* (or vavasours) and of the *negotiatores*; and for a period these concessions satisfied the citizens. The representatives of the three orders were content, for the moment, to share in archiepiscopal government, and the consuls were expressly described as archiepiscopal officials, *consules archiepiscopi*. But dependence on the archbishop was soon loosened. As early as 1097 there is mention of proceedings 'in consulatu Mediolensium civium', implying that the consuls are the representatives of the citizens, and already in the first part of the twelfth century they withdrew from the archiepiscopal household into an official residence of their own. A further sign that they were becoming the centre of gravity of the Milanese constitution was the increased complexity of organization. The number of consuls was doubled, and side by side with the College of Consuls of the Commune there appeared the College of Consuls of Justice, which later again split into two bodies. When the validity of any other courts than the communal courts was denied, the process was completed: the commune, which had originally been a voluntary sworn association, imposed its authority by force on all the inhabitants of the city and the surrounding district.

The three main steps in the rise of the communes were therefore the formation of a permanent association, the extension of its authority (by compelling outsiders to join or submit) to cover the whole city and adjacent territory, and the establishment of the responsibility of the consuls (who in the early stages had a dual position as representatives of the vassals and advisers of the bishop) to the community. In Genoa, for example, an oath was imposed on the consuls in 1143 to do nothing without the consent of the municipal council. But if the dual responsibility of the consuls was only gradually resolved into a single responsibility to the city, the establishment of consuls was nevertheless from the beginning a sign of the emergence of a communal organization and of the determination of the communes to settle the problem of their relations with their episcopal or secular overlords. It is, therefore, noteworthy that consuls appear everywhere during the period of the Investiture Contest, as a result of the shifting of power which the Investiture Contest brought about. We know of consuls at Milan by 1097, at Lucca by 1080, at Pisa by 1084, at Asti by 1093, at Pavia by 1105, at Genoa by 1099, at Arezzo by 1098, at Florence by 1138 (but probably already after the death of the countess Matilda in 1115), at Bologna by 1123, at Siena by 1125, at Brescia by 1127, at Cremona in the same year, while the commune of Venice is first mentioned in 1143. What is important is not the precise dates — these may, in many cases, be due to the fortuitous survival of evidence — but the widespread appearance of similar institutions within a brief period of time. It is this general similarity of development in cities of widely varied history and environment, and pursuing divergent interests and modes of life, which best indicates that all, whatever their previous history, were struck simultaneously by one great force: the force released by the Investiture Contest. After the death of Henry III Italy underwent a century of independent development which irretrievably altered the political balance. A new power had leapt into the saddle during the fifty years of conflict, which loosened the shackles which had hitherto held it back. The result of the Investiture Contest in Italy was the transfer of power from the bishops to the communes.

This change directly affected the German monarchy, which until and even after 1073 had looked to the bishops to bear the burden of government. There could, after the Investiture Contest, be no question of putting the clock back; the bishops' powers definitely could

not be reconstituted. On the other hand, a new balance of forces
had to be found, not least of all because the struggles of the communes for self-assertion, coupled with the long absence of effective
royal intervention, had reduced Italy to a state of chaos, in which
every local power was straining to secure independence and fighting
its neighbours. From end to end of Lombardy, there was rivalry,
violence, confusion, oppression of small communes by great and of
the countryside by the towns. According to Otto of Freising, the
marquess of Montferrat was almost the only nobleman in the north
who had succeeded in escaping the domination of the cities. There
were pitiful complaints from Como and Lodi, which had been
forced to accept Milanese rule and were being ruthlessly exploited
by Milan. 'Almost the whole country pertains to the cities', wrote
Otto of Freising, 'each of which forces the inhabitants of its territory
to submit to its sway, and there is hardly a man of rank or importance
who does not recognize his city's authority. They surpass all other
cities of the world in riches and power, and the long absence of the
ruler across the Alps has contributed to their independence.'[1] If such
was the position in Lombardy, it was no better in Tuscany. In the
days of Conrad III (1138-1152), who never set foot in Italy, the abbot
of Cluny, despairing of German help, implored Roger of Sicily to
incorporate the province in his kingdom and restore order. 'Cities,
townships, villages, roads and even churches', he wrote, 'are given
over to robbers and murderers; pilgrims and clergy, even archbishops and patriarchs, are robbed and plundered and left to die by
the roadside. Yet all these crimes and evils would cease, if only the
sword of royal justice were wielded. . . .'[2]

Such were the results of the Investiture Contest in Italy, as they
faced Frederick Barbarossa when he crossed the Alps for the first
time in 1154: on the one hand displacement of the bishops by the
communes, on the other the anarchy of rival powers. The communes
had exploited the period of anarchy, when royal government could
not intervene, to assume de facto powers, and a complete revolution
in the political conditions of north Italy had taken place with results
no less far-reaching than the simultaneous change in the balance of
political forces in Germany. In both countries, the Investiture Contest, by dissolving the old society, set the German monarchy a new

[1] Cf. Otto of Freising, Gesta Friderici, II, 13-15.
[2] Cf. the remarkable letter in Migne, Patrologia latina, CLXXXIX, l. iv, no. 37.

task: a task of reconstruction and reorganization. In Germany a new society, feudal and aristocratic, had arisen; in Italy a society of powerful urban communes. The task facing the monarchy, both north and south of the Alps, was to reduce the new society to order, to co-ordinate its many forces and to find a new balance. It was a difficult task for a monarchy whose foundations had been shaken, and little progress was achieved under Henry V's two successors, Lothar II (1125-1137) and Conrad III (1138-1152); but it was undertaken with courage and determination, both in Italy and in Germany, by the great emperor of the twelfth century, Frederick Barbarossa.

III

In Italy the consequences of the change in the political balance of power did not become fully evident until Frederick I intervened in 1154. In Germany, on the other hand, the results were seen from the moment when Henry V took over after his father's death in 1106, and during his reign and that of his two successors it looked as though the crown had become the plaything of the aristocracy. Henry V, Lothar II and Conrad III each tried in his own way to revive the power of the monarchy; but the hands of all three were tied by the circumstances in which they had secured possession of the crown, and the result of the long generation between 1106 and 1152 was to emphasize, rather than to weaken, the aristocratic character and aristocratic tendencies which the German constitution had assumed as a result of the Investiture Contest.

When Henry V broke away from his father and raised the standard of rebellion in 1105, he acknowledged the aristocratic character of the German constitution,[1] and throughout his reign he had to accommodate himself to the changed balance between monarchy and aristocracy which had resulted during the generation following the excommunication of Henry IV in 1076. He was only secure on his throne when he accepted aristocratic tutelage, placed himself at the head of the aristocracy and governed in accordance with aristocratic principles and interests, and all his efforts to assume an independent position came to nought. There is no doubt that he wished to revive the tried and tested administrative measures of his father,[2] and in spite of initial distrust and hostility he forged con-

[1] Cf. above, p. 128.   [2] Cf. above, p. 130.

nexions with the rising towns from which Henry IV had secured invaluable backing against the aristocratic opposition.[1] He attempted also, both before and after the Concordat of Worms, to restore the bonds between the monarchy and the *Reichskirche*;[2] but the clergy, who for generations had been a firm pillar of the monarchy, were divided and could no longer be relied upon for ungrudging support. Their loyalties were undermined by the current of novel ideas released by the Reform Movement, while material interests threw many bishops — now intent on building territorial principalities — on to the side of the feudatories. In particular, the archbishop of Mainz, who had long claimed and exercised the right to consecrate the king, sought to establish himself as kingmaker and to govern the destinies of the kingdom. In short, the legacy of independent rights and indefeasible prerogatives which the Saxon and Salian kings had inherited from their Carolingian precursors, had perished in the civil wars between 1076 and 1106, and Henry V failed to revive it. His kingship was based not on the ancient hereditary rights of the monarchy, but on a contract or engagement entered into with the princes, which left them the whiphand. This contractual basis of the monarchy was expressed by the archbishop of Mainz when, in 1106, he handed over the royal insignia to Henry V: 'If thou art not a just ruler and a protector of the church of God', he said, 'may that befall thee which befell thy father!'[3] In these circumstances the aristocracy was, after 1106, the predominant power in Germany; it seized the opportunity on Henry V's death in 1125 to demonstrate by a change of dynasty its predominance within the state, and both Lothar II (1125-1137) and Conrad III (1138-1152) ruled as nominees of aristocratic factions.

The elections of 1125 and 1138 revealed in a flash the new situation. The defeat on both occasions of the principle of hereditary succession, with all its implications, was a triumph for the principles enunciated against Henry IV and the Salian dynasty at the election of Rudolf of Rheinfelden in 1077 when the anti-king had been forced to forswear any claim to hereditary right or to the succession of his son.[4] The attack on hereditary monarchy was maintained

[1] Cf. Rörig, *Burgertum u. Staat* (1928), 9.
[2] Cf. below, p. 160.
[3] *Mon. Germ. Hist., Script.*, III, 110.
[4] 'Regnum non ut proprium, sed pro dispensatione sibi creditum reputans, omne haere-ditarium ius in eo repudiavit et vel filio suo se hoc adaptaturum fore penitus abnegavit; iustissime in arbitrio principum esse decernens, ut post mortem eius libere non magis filium eius quam alium eligerent.' Cf. P. Joachimsen in *Mediaeval Germany*, II (1938), 124.

when, after Rudolf's death in 1080, a proposal to set up Henry IV's son, Conrad, in his father's place was defeated by the ridicule of Otto of Nordheim.[1] But there was more involved in the proceedings of 1077 than the issue of hereditary or elective monarchy. By setting aside the principle of heredity the princes secured the opportunity to make election dependent on the fulfilling of conditions and the granting of pledges; and before they would recognize Rudolf as king a strong party demanded an undertaking to remedy their individual grievances.[2] This also was a precedent not forgotten in subsequent years. Henry V had to promise the Saxons, before they did homage in 1106, that every individual should receive justice at his hands;[3] and again in 1119 — bowing before the gathering storm — he renewed his promise in even more specific terms for the whole realm.[4] The corollary of election, in short, was recognition of the established rights of individual feudatories, and therewith a renunciation of the evolution of monarchical rights in the direction of strong administration, which was to be the foundation of English government in the twelfth century.

All the consequences of the acts and mentality of 1077 became evident after the death of Henry V without direct heirs in 1125. Henry's last act was to designate his nephew, Frederick of Swabia, the eldest son of his sister, Agnes, as his successor, making over to him his properties; but this designation was deliberately set aside in order to demonstrate once and for all the strength of the elective principles for which the Church had fought since Gregory VII's days. The leader of the opposition to the hereditary claims of the Salian house was Archbishop Adalbert of Mainz, who was resolved that the freedom of the Church and the integrity of the rights of the princes should prevail; and his first act, in the summons which he issued to the princes, clerical and secular, was to recall 'the oppressions under

[1] 'I have seen bad calves,' he said, 'bred from bad bulls; therefore I want neither the son nor the father' (Bruno, *De bello Saxonico*, cap. 125).
[2] Bruno, *De bello Saxonico*, cap. 91: 'cum singuli deberent eum regem laudare, quidam voluerunt aliquas conditiones interponere, ut hac lege eum super se levarent regem, quatinus sibi de suis iniuriis specialiter promitteret satisfactionem. Otto namque dux non prius volebat eum sibi regem constituere, nisi promitteret honorem sibi iniuste ablatum restituere. Sic et alii multi suas singulares causas interponunt, quas ut ille se correcturum promitteret volunt.' —They were checked by the papal legate who showed that for a candidate to make promises to individuals was equivalent to the sin of simony; but the attitude of mind persisted and coloured subsequent events.
[3] 'Ut omnibus iustum indicium faciat'; cf. Degener, *Mitt. d. österr. Instituts, Erg.-Bd.*, XIV (1939), 132-3, 136.
[4] Cf. above, p. 132, n. 1.

which the whole realm had laboured' and to urge the electors to substitute a king under whom there should be no such 'yoke of servitude'. That, in veiled language, was a call to set aside hereditary principles and to reject Frederick of Swabia who had been a loyal supporter and exponent of Salian policy; and after much bargaining and negotiation Adalbert achieved his object. Lothar of Saxony, the victor of Welfesholz and the leading opponent of Henry V, was elected. But that was only a first step. Having elected Lothar, who was in effect little more than the last of the anti-kings set up against the legitimate dynasty,[1] the princes went on to discuss 'what rights the crown ought to possess'; and the result of the whole negotiation was that Adalbert of Mainz, seconded by the papal legates, succeeded in whittling away the rights over the German church conceded to the German king only three years earlier in the Concordat of Worms.[2] The German princes, on the other hand, had every reason to be satisfied with the election of Lothar, whom they counted as one of themselves: his succession to the Saxon duchy on the extinction of the male line of the house of Billung in 1106 had been a triumph for the principle, dear to all feudatories, of collateral and female succession to fiefs,[3] and he himself could therefore be expected — as in fact he did[4] — to respect their feudal rights. Concessions to Church and nobles, although formally not conditions upon which Lothar was elected, were manifestly an integral part of the whole negotiation.

The whole of Lothar's reign was overcast by the shadow of its inauspicious beginnings. The open opposition of the Hohenstaufen, who set up an anti-king and took up arms in 1127, retaining the upper hand until 1130, threw him increasingly under the influence of the Church, whose support he was forced to buy by concessions. In particular, he was influenced by St. Norbert of Xanten, whom he

---

[1] H. Mitteis, *Lehnrecht u. Staatsgewalt* (1933), 422.

[2] The proceedings are described in the so-called *Narratio de electione Lotharii* (*Mon. Germ. Hist., Script.*, XII, 510 sqq.). Lothar's two main concessions were the surrender of the right to hold elections in the king's presence (election was to be free, 'nec regio metu extortam, nec praesentia ut antea coartatam'), and a waiver of homage from ecclesiastics ('a nullo tamen spiritualium, ut moris erat, hominium vel accepit vel coegit').—There has been much discussion of the implications of these concessions; but even Thompson, a strong partisan of Lothar, admits 'that Lothar by abandoning the old practice opened the door to papal usurpations—usurpations which he could not prevent owing to the fact that at his coronation as emperor he failed to demand the recognition of the former law' (*Feudal Germany*, 161).

[3] Cf. Thompson, op. cit., 236, 355.

[4] Cf. Mitteis, op. cit., 423.

made archbishop of Magdeburg in 1126. Consequently when, in 1132, he went to Rome in support of Pope Innocent II, he reversed the policy of Henry V and recognized the papal claim to the Tuscan lands of the Countess Matilda, accepting them from Innocent as a fief at an annual rent.[1] Thus it was possible to claim that the emperor was a vassal of the pope; and a picture to this effect, with an appropriate inscription, was set on the walls of the Lateran palace.[2] In Germany, Lothar's weakness in face of the Hohenstaufen forced him to build up a party among the princes, foremost among whom were the Zähringer (who were marked out to contest Hohenstaufen predominance in Swabia) and Henry the Proud, duke of Bavaria, whose influence had been the decisive factor in Lothar's favour in the election of 1125. The alliance between Lothar and Henry was cemented in 1127, when the Bavarian duke married Lothar's only daughter and heiress; and with the support of the Welfs, Lothar gradually managed to improve his position. In 1134 the opposition of the Hohenstaufen was finally broken, and in 1135 they made their peace. But as Lothar strengthened himself in Germany, he became more dangerous to the Church; and when he went to Italy for a second time in 1136 to aid Innocent II against the Normans, a number of serious clashes demonstrated that he was no longer the subservient ally of the papacy. There were clashes also between the pope and Henry the Proud of Bavaria, whom Lothar had made marquess of Tuscany, with control of the Matildine lands; and when, shortly afterwards, Lothar fell ill and died on his way back to Germany, the hostility of the Church soon became manifest.

Just as, in 1125, Frederick of Swabia had been the obvious successor to Henry V, so in 1138 Lothar's son-in-law, Henry the Proud, was the obvious candidate for the throne. One of Lothar's last acts had been to make him duke of Saxony, and on his deathbed he sent the royal insignia to Henry, who was thus designated for the succession. With Saxony and Bavaria in Germany, and Tuscany in Italy in his hands, he was beyond doubt the richest and strongest of the princes; through

---

[1] The pope's proprietary rights were fully and explicitly expressed in the charter he granted to Lothar (*Mon. Germ. Hist., Leges*, II, 82): 'allodium ... comitissae Mathildis, quod utique ab ea beato Petro constat esse collatum, vobis committimus ... atque per anulum investimus, ita videlicet ut 100 libras argenti singulis annis nobis et nostris successoribus exsolvas, et post tuum obitum proprietas ad ius et dominium s. Romanae ecclesiae ... revertatur.'

[2] Otto of Freising, *Gesta*, III, 10. It is well known that this claim culminated in the breach between Pope Hadrian IV and Frederick I in 1157.

Gertrude, his wife, he had inherited Lothar's private estates, which comprised the properties of the two greatest Saxon families of the past, while the wide domains of his own family in Upper Swabia were administered by his brother, Welf. Upon these foundations the government of Germany might have been stabilized and the superstructure of a new Germany erected. But as in 1125, so in 1138 the Church feared a strong king, and once again a clerical party, supported by the papal legate, secured a change of dynasty. Instead of Henry of Bavaria, Conrad of Swabia — the self-same Conrad who in 1127 had been raised as anti-king against Lothar — was elected; and although there was without doubt a party in Germany which had always favoured a return to the legitimate dynasty,[1] this legitimism was not the decisive factor. On the contrary, far from wishing to strengthen the monarchy by a return to hereditary and legitimist principles, the object of the personalities immediately concerned in Conrad III's election, headed by archbishop Adalbero of Trier, was to prevent the emergence of a strong king, who might have revoked the concessions wrung from Lothar.

In this object the clerical and feudal party was successful. Just as Lothar had been hampered from 1127 to 1135 by a crippling war with the Hohenstaufen, so Conrad III was faced from 1139 to 1142 — and indeed, at intervals until his death in 1152 — with the implacable hostility of the Welfs. Hence the rule of the first Hohenstaufen in no direction brought a change for the better; rather the country was plunged back into the anarchy from which it had, in the last four years of Lothar's reign, seemed gradually to be emerging.

Not least among the causes of Conrad's weakness was the fact that the twofold change of dynasty, following on the heels of a generation of civil war, had shattered the material basis of royal power. When seventeen years of civil war ended in 1092 the crown lands were reduced to shreds and patches, in particular in north Germany where in size and extent they were even more attenuated than at the end of the Carolingian period.[2] Henry IV himself, like Stephen in England, had been compelled to buy partisans by grants out of the

[1] Sigebert of Gembloux (Mon. Germ. Hist., Script., VI, 386) said that the princes elected Conrad, 'a man of royal stock', because they could not tolerate the dominion of a king without royal blood in his veins.
[2] Cf. above, p. 31.—For what follows cf. Thompson, Feudal Germany, 353 sqq., M. Stimming, Das deutsche Königsgut im 11. u 12. Jahrhundert (1922), 89 sqq., Seidlmayer, Deutscher Nord u. Süd im Hochmittelalter, 102 sq., Heusinger, Archiv f. Urkundenforschung, VIII (1923), 137 sqq., Schmeidler, Franken u. das deutsche Reich im Mittelalter (1930), 39, 62.

crown lands to clergy, nobles and *ministeriales*, thus ruining the whole programme of his early years, and Henry V was quickly forced to drop any idea of recovery and revindication.[1] The change of dynasty in 1125, carried further the disastrous setback. For two centuries crown lands and the king's private inheritance had remained uniformly administered, in the hands of one dynasty; and it was no easy problem, in 1125, to disentangle the crown lands, to which Lothar laid claim, from the private estates of the Salian family, which passed by ordinary laws of inheritance to the Hohenstaufen. The second change of dynasty in 1138 complicated the situation still further; for Lothar II had assimilated the crown lands which he took over from the Salians with his own family properties, and considerable portions of them, on his death, passed with his private inheritance to the Welfs, particularly to Henry the Proud who was so powerful that Conrad III, when he succeeded to the throne in 1138, was unable to obtain restitution. Moreover, Lothar and the Welfs had gone even further and sought not without success to lay hands on the family possessions of the Salians in Franconia and central Germany, the true heirs to which were the Hohenstaufen. Hence Conrad III found the material power of the monarchy seriously diminished; in particular, he had no secure foothold in the north which — engrossed in the conflict with the Slavs on the eastern border[2] — began to go its own way. The defeat of Henry V at Welfesholz in 1115, which allowed the Saxon duke to disregard the emperor in the conduct of Saxon affairs, and Henry V's subsequent failure in 1123 to enforce the appointment of his own nominee in the marches of Lausitz and Meissen,[3] were milestones along this path: thereafter the north enjoyed *de facto* autonomy and the power of the emperor in Saxony was undermined.

The weakening of the material foundations of the monarchy was, together with the strengthening of the electoral rights of the princes,

[1] Cf. above, p. 131. To restore his position in the north Henry V endeavoured to secure the ducal lands of Saxony on the death of Magnus Billung in 1106, and the estates of count Udalrich of Weimar in 1112. The latter attempt was the immediate cause of the unrest in Saxony leading to Henry's defeat at the battle of Welfesholz in 1115; cf. Schmeidler, op. cit., 16.

[2] Below, pp. 260 .qq.

[3] On the death of the margrave Henry of Eilenburg in 1123, Henry proposed to grant both marches, which were imperial fiefs, to Count Wiprecht of Groitzsch; but Lothar, as duke of Saxony, opposed this decision and by force of arms placed Conrad of Wettin in possession of Meissen and Albrecht of Ballenstedt in possession of Lausitz and the Ostmark. Henry V, unable to intervene, had to accept the fait accompli. Cf. Schmeidler, op. cit., 16.

a cardinal feature of the period 1106-1152. All three kings of the period sought, each in his own way, to pick up some of the threads which the Investiture Contest had broken and to re-establish royal power in face of the spread of feudal and aristocratic principles; but, hampered by material weakness and by the circumstances under which they had secured the throne, none achieved lasting success. Henry V's main concern was to restore royal control over the advocacy which (as we have observed) was one of the main sources of the territorial power of the princes; in particular, he sought to forge connexions with the reformed monasteries which had been founded without royal assent or participation during the Investiture Contest.[1] A similar policy was pursued by Conrad III who in 1149 secured a judgement of the imperial court making the exercise of advocate's rights dependent on royal authorization.[2] To his reign also can be traced the beginnings of the policy – pursued more consistently by Frederick Barbarossa – of claiming for the monarchy (to the exclusion of the nobles and princes) the advocacy over the lands of the rapidly increasing Cistercian foundations.[3] Lothar, on the other hand, who did not inherit the Salian tradition of close control over the German *Reichskirche*, concentrated his efforts on checking the power of the princes by reforms of local administration, creating the new office of *Landgraf* and the new district known as the *Landgrafschaft* for the exercise and consolidation of the rights of the crown. It is clear that the intention was to give the *Landgraf* a position equivalent to that of the dukes and princes, but without princely rank, and thus to counteract, by the creation of a new official class, the feudal and hereditary tendencies of the princes, as well as their attempts to engross and alienate the local exercise of royal rights.[4] But the dynastic changes in 1125 and 1138 prevented any continuity of policy, particularly as rulers of such widely different antecedents as Henry V, Lothar and Conrad found it impossible to work through the same personnel. Lothar in 1125 instantly dismissed all the existing chancery personnel, whose sympathies were doubtless with the legitimate heirs of the Salian dynasty; and an equally thorough-

---

[1] Cf. H. Hirsch, *Die Klosterimmunität seit dem Investiturstreit* (1913), 53-56.

[2] *Mon. Germ. Hist., Const.*, I, 181: 'quod nullus posset causas vel lites, que ad advocatorum ius pertinerent, audire vel terminare, vel placita advocatie tenere, nisi qui bannum de manu regia recepisset.'

[3] Hirsch, op. cit., 108 sqq.

[4] Cf. Mayer, 'Über Entstehung u. Bedeutung der älteren deutschen Landgrafschaften', *Zeitschr. d. Sav.-Stiftung für Rechtsgesch.*, Germ. Abt., LVIII (1938), 138 sqq.

going change of personnel occurred on Conrad's accession thirteen years later.[1] Thus the continuity of personnel which was a prerequisite for continuity of policy was lost, and the political antitheses of the time undermined the efficiency of the royal organs of government.

In these circumstances the attempts of the German rulers between 1106 and 1152 to reassert the positive functions of the monarchy — although of interest as indications of their awareness of the needs of the situation — lacked the consistency and vigour essential for success, and all attempts to re-establish the principles and framework of royal government floundered. Instead their power, such as it was, was built on the shifting foundation of an unstable balance among the great princes, which offered the king at best the prospect of asserting himself as *primus inter pares*. Henry V sought to maintain his position by playing off the south against the north German princes, the Hohenstaufen and the Welfs against Lothar of Saxony. The result was to strengthen the Welfs, who held the balance of power and for whose support both parties angled. The fact that Henry the Proud's support was the decisive factor in Lothar's favour in the election of 1125 strengthened the Welfs' position still further; and after his marriage with Lothar's daughter in 1127, Henry's was the decisive voice in the kingdom. Consequently the basis of Conrad III's policy was to build up an anti-Welf party and to break Welf predominance. Thus he sought to place Albrecht the Bear in possession of Saxony and his own half-brother, Leopold of Austria, in possession of Bavaria, and when this proved impossible attempted a balance of power by raising Brandenburg against Saxony and Austria against Bavaria. It was a hand-to-mouth policy, which showed how far the monarchy had sunk. From 1138 to 1152 Conrad III struggled on from expedient to expedient and from compromise to compromise, with difficulty keeping his head above water but achieving no substantial progress; the prestige and effectiveness of the monarchy continued to decline.[2] What was necessary was reconstruction from the very foundations, and at the same time, in place of Conrad's purely defensive attitude, a determination to give the monarchy a positive function and a distinctive mission in

---

[1] Cf. Erben, Schmitz-Kallenberg u. Redlich, *Urkundenlehre*, I (1907), 77 sqq.; Bresslau, *Urkundenlehre*, I (1889), 354 sqq.
[2] *Mon. Germ. Hist.*, *Script.*, XVII, 764: 'res publica sub eo labefactari coeperat.'

German society. It was a task which only a genius could attempt; but such a genius was found in Frederick Barbarossa (1152-1190). Under him Germany once again slowly rose from the depths into which it had been plunged by the Investiture Contest.

IV

The contrast between the position of Germany on Henry III's death in 1056 and Frederick Barbarossa's accession in 1152 was radical. The frequent changes of dynasty had undermined the prestige of the monarchy, and for Otto of Freising, the biographer of Barbarossa, the kingship which under the Salians had been in practice hereditary, was in 1152 an elective dignity, to be conferred at the will of the princes.[1] The old pillars of the Salian monarchy had gone. The Church was feudalized, the bishops no longer implicitly loyal to the crown; the imperial *ministeriales*, on whom so much of Henry IV's programme had depended, vacillated because of the lack of continuity of dynasty and policy. At the very moment when, throughout western Europe, other governments were beginning to create new organs of royal administration, the German monarchy was thrown back on retrograde administrative practices and unable to keep pace. Precisely when, with the rise of new social forces, monarchy throughout Europe was faced by new tasks, the German king's hands were tied; thus, for example, he failed to profit (as the Plantagenets profited) from the rising importance of the towns, and (lacking the organs of control) was unable to assert exclusive guardianship of the public peace. Long before Conrad III's death the princes had asserted control over public peace in their own regions, and were using the powers which it gave them to tighten their hold over the land.

Thus, where the tendency before the Investiture Contest had been towards consolidation of uniform royal control at the expense of regionalism and localism, the tendency from the outbreak of the struggle between Henry IV and Gregory VII was towards a rapid growth of local particularism. In part this tendency may have been reinforced by inherent differences between the main provinces of

---

[1] Otto of Freising, *Gesta Friderici*, II. 1: 'nam id iuris Romani imperii apex, videlicet non per sanguinis propaginem descendere, sed per principum electionem reges creare'.

Germany; particularly from the days of Lothar and Conrad III, when Saxon energies turned east against the Wends and Slavs, north Germany had interests and ambitions which south Germany did not share. But these differences should not be allowed to obscure the equally evident fact that the particularism which raised its head under Henry V, Lothar and Conrad III was a particularism not of the people but of the princes. The old duchy which, at the beginning of the tenth century, had for a period sought its roots in the people, had perished; and a new duchy, feudal, dynastic, territorial, had taken its place — a duchy which conformed neither in boundaries, nor in geographical formation, nor in racial composition to the old regional and 'tribal' divisions, and which differed only in size but not in character from the lesser principalities which the rising *domini terrae* were building. The structure of German government and administration, as the Investiture Contest left it, was — like the structure of German society — feudal, and the particularism which now became a dominant factor was feudal particularism. The Investiture Contest set the princes in the saddle.

This change, besides vitally affecting the relative positions of the aristocracy and the monarchy within Germany, inevitably had repercussions on Germany's standing in Europe. German predominance, which had been undoubted from the days of Otto I to those of Henry III, was shattered by the Investiture Contest, and under Lothar and Conrad the impotence of the monarchy lowered German prestige and influence still further. In Italy, where Lothar's renunciation of the Matildine lands had robbed the monarchy of its surest foundation, Conrad III was a nullity; indeed, he counted for less than Welf of Bavaria who, pursuing an independent foreign policy, entered into direct relations with the Normans of Sicily and accepted subsidies from the king's enemies to raise up unrest at home. The same policy — its earliest manifestations have been seen in the case of Godfrey of Lorraine[1] — was pursued by princes on the western frontier, who exploited their position between France and Germany to further their own objects and free themselves from royal control.[2] In these circumstances German foreign policy from 1106 to 1152 had scant success. Under Henry V, who was allied by marriage with Henry I of England, it was marked by the entangle-

[1] Above, p. 92.
[2] Cf. Kienast, *Die deutschen Fürsten im Dienste der Westmächte*, I (1924), 1-41.

ment of Germany for the first time in the perennial Anglo-French quarrel, ending in the failure of Henry V when in 1124 he attempted to lead an army into France in support of the English cause. Under Conrad III the outstanding event was German participation and leadership in the Second Crusade. But, unlike the First Crusade which contributed much to place the leadership of Christendom in French hands, the Crusade of 1147-1149 was an inglorious failure, and the German monarchy, far from winning new prestige, was implicated in and identified with its unsuccessful outcome. Torn by internal dissension, Germany had, from the time of the First Crusade, lost pride of place to France, which had forged close links with the papacy and was able to use the Church for the spread of French culture and French influence. In Germany itself the growing internal disunity and lack of a common German sentiment opened the door wide to foreign influence; and here also French chivalry, and the literature and culture of French chivalry, penetrated and made rapid advances.

Thus all facets of German life, its internal order and its external relations, were affected by the revolutionary upheavals of the Investiture Contest. The blows which had been struck at the roots of royal power were felt at home and abroad, in Burgundy and Italy as well as in Germany. What were the prospects for the future? The consolidation of the aristocracy was indisputable. But what of the monarchy? Was it capable of staging a revival, of reasserting control and coping with the new situation? Was the defeat it had assuredly suffered decisive and unalterable, or was it capable of restoring the balance in its favour? These were the questions confronting Frederick Barbarossa when he succeeded to the throne in 1152; they were the problems which filled his reign and that of his son, Henry VI. It is time to see what his answers were and how far they solved the problems which had come to a head since that day, seventy-seven years earlier, when Henry IV declared war on Pope Gregory VII: on his success or failure, at this critical juncture in German history, the whole future shape and character of German political organization depended.

PART THREE

THE RISE AND FALL OF THE HOHENSTAUFEN EMPIRE
(1152-1272)

CHAPTER 7

FREDERICK I AND THE NEW IMPERIALISM
(1152-1190)

I

WHEN Frederick I succeeded the weak and hapless Conrad in 1152, he was faced, as a result of developments reaching back to 1076, with the immeasurable task of bringing order and stability into government and society throughout the length and breadth of the empire. It was a new task, requiring new methods. By dissolving the old society, by loosening the old foundations, the Investiture Contest not only set the German monarchy new problems, but created a new environment which called imperatively for a radical change of outlook. The monarchy had to forge new links with the new powers which had arisen during the Investiture Contest in Italy and Burgundy and Germany; it had, above all else, to reconstruct and reorganize, to co-ordinate and to balance. In a new world with new horizons it had to establish a new hierarchy of government to replace the hierarchy of Ottonian and Salian times which had irretrievably perished.

It is against this background that the imperial policy of Frederick Barbarossa must be placed, if its purposes and what may be called its 'ideology' are to be judged aright. The task of reconstruction and re-organization, which was the bitter legacy of the troubled times of the Investiture Contest, was the keystone of Barbarossa's policy in Germany and in Italy alike. When he ascended the throne in 1152, every aspect of policy required redefinition. The old relationship of Church and State, of king and bishops, had broken down. A new foundation was also needed for the relations of empire and papacy; for the reformed papacy would never return to its position under Henry III, while no monarch conscious of his regality could accept the subordination Pope Innocent II had tried to impose on Lothar II. More important, the material foundations which the German monarchy had possessed before 1076 were shattered, and both in Germany and Burgundy, where the Investiture Contest had created an aggressive feudal aristocracy, and in Italy, where it had established the power of the communes, a new basis had to be sought for royal power, which took account of the new factors in the political situation, and yet gave the monarchy a chance to assert its position at the head of society. Hence the two main aspects of Barbarossa's policy were his attempts to come to terms with German feudalism and with the Italian communal movement; in the one case, to define the relations of the communes with the imperial government, in the other to subordinate to the purposes of government the inchoate feudalism which had sprung up in Germany between 1076 and 1152 and to create an organized and integrated feudal state. Neither of these objects, however, could be isolated politically from two other aspects of policy: Frederick's relations with foreign powers — particularly with the Normans in southern Italy but increasingly, as time passed, with France and England — and his relations with the papacy. It was the complications due to these factors that forced forward the evolution of his policy decade by decade. And yet, as we shall see, the basic principles with which he began his reign were adhered to through all fluctuations; only the methods by and the spheres in which they were applied, changed. For this reason we are justified in assuming that, from the beginning of his reign, he followed a deliberate plan or programme; and it is the existence of this programme, finely conceived and steadfastly maintained, which is Frederick's title to rank, equally with Henry II of England and Philip Augustus of France, among the great statesmen of his era. He understood the requirements of the situation and faced up to them; he assessed the potentialities and devised a remedy.

Although little was left, when Frederick took over in 1152, of the old material foundations of government, there were certain factors in his favour; and these he was adept at exploiting. In the first place, he profited by the almost universal reaction against the instability and violence of the two preceding generations. This reaction was seen when Conrad III named as successor, not his own infant son, whose succession would have opened the door to a long period of minority rule, but his nephew, Frederick; for the princes, instead of opposing gave unanimous approval to this last act of the dying king, and the intrigues of the archbishop of Mainz, who hoped by a long period of minority rule to perpetuate the evil precedents of 1125 and 1138, found no response. Frederick's accession was universally desired in Germany because, akin to the Welfs through his mother and known to have mediated between them and Conrad III, he alone was believed capable of putting an end to the discords which were ravaging the land.[1] In Italy, also, there was a strong reaction against the preceding anarchy, which hampered trade — already a mainstay of the cities — and left the weaker cities at the mercy of their more powerful neighbours.[2] There also — apart perhaps from Milan, which was trying 'bit by bit to reduce Lombardy to subjection' — the majority of cities realized that the benefits which Frederick had it in his power to confer on Italy were substantial, and welcomed the prospect of the intervention of a superior authority, capable of holding a balance between the contending parties. He was also favoured, at the very beginning of his reign, by a widespread reaction against the theocratic system of Gregory VII and the militant policy of the Hildebrandine party. Under the growing influence of the Cistercians, the ancient monastic ideal of withdrawal from the world gained ground and, by the pontificate of St. Bernard's pupil, Eugenius III (1145-1153), even secured a foothold within the Roman Curia. St. Bernard himself, in his treatise *De Consideratione*, not only exposed the abuses of the papal court, but also protested against the immersion of the papacy in secular affairs.

This new atmosphere was peculiarly favourable to a reassertion of the indefeasible rights of the empire; and it is a mark of the new spirit pervading Frederick's policy that when, after the untimely death of Pope Anastasius IV in 1154, a nominee of the more intransigent faction among the cardinals succeeded to the papal throne, he grasped his opportunity and boldly accepted the challenge which the new pope, Hadrian IV, threw down. When, at the Diet of Besançon in 1157, the pope's representative read out a letter from Hadrian insinuating — in terms reminiscent of the days of Lothar II[3] — that the imperial crown was a 'benefice' conferred by the pope, Frederick replied (in words reminiscent of Henry IV) that he held his kingdom and his empire from God alone.[4] But if Hadrian was hoping for a reaction such as had followed Gregory VII's attack on Henry IV in 1076, he was disappointed. Far from sowing discord,

---

[1] This desire for a settlement emerges very clearly from Otto of Freising's account of the election of 1152; cf. his *Gesta Friderici* (ed. Waitz and Simson, 1912), II. 2 (pp. 103-104).

[2] Cf. above, p. 152.

[3] Cf. above, p. 157.

[4] 'Cumque per electionem principum a solo Deo regnum et imperium nostrum sit . . . quicumque nos imperialem coronam pro beneficio a domino papa suscepisse dixerit, divinae institutioni et doctrinae Petri contrarius est'; *Gesta Friderici*, 179.

the pope's action united the German princes behind the king in
defence of imperial rights, and the bishops were equally wholehearted in Frederick's support.[1] But it was characteristic of Frederick, who was a true son of the twelfth century, nurtured in a new
environment, that he did not rest content to echo Henry IV's arguments. Every thesis provokes its antithesis; and the novel pretensions
of the papacy, asserted first by Gregory VII and developed by
Innocent II, gave rise, by a natural process of reaction, to a new and
heightened ideal of royal and imperial power.[2] Drawing ammuni-
tion from the arsenal provided by the revived study of Roman law,
Barbarossa defended the inalienable rights of the imperial monarchy
not only (as Henry IV had done) from the writings of the Christian
fathers but also from the theory and practice of pagan Rome.[3] Thus,
confronted by the theocratic pretensions of Hadrian IV, he sought to
establish a secular foundation for his imperial rights. It was no
accident that it was precisely in 1157 that the terms *sacrum* or
sacratissimum were first applied to the empire, with the evident
intention of contrasting the *sacrum imperium* with the *sancta ecclesia*
and thus affirming the independent equality of the imperial power.
A second step in the same direction was taken with the canonization
in 1165 of Charlemagne, whose virtues, sanctifying the imperial
cause, marked him out for the rôle of patron saint of the new
imperialism. But, although Carolingian traditions played a large
part in Frederick's ideology, it was no longer as the head of a
Christian *respublica*, as *rex et sacerdos*, that Charlemagne's name was
invoked. On the contrary, it was as a conqueror, who had won his
empire by force of arms, and not as a gift of the pope or of the
Roman senate. This standpoint Frederick developed forcefully and
at length against the Roman aristocracy, which in 1155 offered him
the imperial throne and therewith its support against the papacy.
The argument that it was the prerogative of the Roman people to
make the emperor, was resisted by Frederick with the same firmness
with which he opposed papal pretensions. Dismissing memories of
ancient Rome as empty words, long devoid of meaning, he attacked
the pretensions of the Senate and, in a powerful oration, traced the
origins of the mediaeval empire to the conquests of Charlemagne

[1] The whole incident is related at length in the *Gesta Friderici*, III, cap. 8-11. For the bishops'
reply to the pope's expostulations, cf. ibid., III. 17.
[2] Cf. Kern, *Kingship and Law in the Middle Ages* (1939), 110 sqq.
[3] Ibid., 66 sqq.

and Otto the Great. They had won Rome and Italy by the sword; conquest — first Frankish and then German conquest — and the right of conquest was the basis of imperial power; and it was on this realistic foundation that Frederick took his stand.[1]

The determination to establish new secular foundations for his imperial power, thus breaking away from the theocratic imperialism of the Salians, which was no longer powerful enough to withstand the counterblasts of the papacy, is a significant indication of the 'modernity' of Frederick's political outlook. But the practical importance of the new theories, except in relation to the doctrinal controversy with the Church, can easily be exaggerated. It was important for Frederick to establish his theoretical independence, and in this cause he was prepared to call in Roman law as a vehicle of imperialist ideas, useful for traversing the pretensions of the papacy. But, beyond this, the part played by Roman law in the formulation of Frederick's policy was negligible, and it would be a serious error to seek, as has sometimes been done, the key to Frederick's imperial policy in the revival of Roman jurisprudence and in the political theories which went with it.[2] Not the least interesting feature of Frederick's speech to the representatives of the Roman senate in 1155 is the scorn which he evinces for the vain, anachronistic romanticism which sought, in the twelfth century, a revival of an obsolete imperialism; and it is characteristic that the same realistic arguments he had used against the Romans in 1155 were used with equal force against the Milanese in 1158.[3] Frederick, who was fully aware of the havoc caused in Italy by the long absence and neglect

[1] 'You have related the ancient renown of your city,' he told the Romans, 'and have extolled the ancient state of your sacred republic. Agreed! Agreed! In the words of your celebrated author, "there was once virtue in this republic". "Once", I say. Would that we could truthfully say "now"! But Rome has experienced the vicissitudes of time ... First, as is known to all, the vigour of your nobility was transplanted to the royal city of the East ... Then came the Franks ... who took away by force the remnants of your freedom ... We have turned over in our minds the deeds of modern emperors, considered how our sacred predecessors, Charles and Otto, wrested your City with the lands of Italy from the Greeks and Lombards, and brought it within the frontiers of the Frankish realm, not as a gift from alien hands but as a conquest won by their own valour ... I am the lawful possessor ...' Cf. *Gesta Friderici*, 136-139.

[2] For the limited importance in Frederick's policy of Roman law and Roman lawyers—now a commonplace among historians—cf. the recent statement by H. Koeppler, *Engl. Hist. Review*, LIV (1939), 577-588. Even here, I believe, the Roman element is overstated; cf. Schneider, *Die Entstehung von Burg u. Landgemeinde in Italien* (1924), ix.

[3] The Milanese, he said, 'will not find us sluggish in preserving what our predecessors, Charles and Otto, added to the title-deeds of the empire, and in defending the annexations by which they—the former first among the West Franks, the latter first among the East Franks—extended the frontiers of the kingdom' (*Gesta Friderici*, 203-4).

of the emperors, was determined to restore imperial authority. From his earliest letter, in which he announces his election to Pope Eugenius III, reform and restoration, a revival of the empire, stand in the forefront of his programme.[1] But his aim was to revive, not the empire of Constantine and Justinian, but the rule of Charles the Great and Otto the Great, to restore the realities which had perished in the decades since the outbreak of the conflict between Henry IV and Gregory VII.

Nevertheless mere restoration was out of the question. Because of their limited interest in Italian and in imperial affairs, the Ottonian and Salian rulers had failed to create the prerequisites of a sound imperial administration, and the foundations they laid were already visibly crumbling in the eleventh century.[2] A restoration of the theocracy of Henry III, with its reliance on the episcopate, was unthinkable, and Frederick himself, breaking away from the outlook of earlier generations, rejected any such policy out of hand.[3] Instead, he adapted his policy to the environment created by the Investiture Contest. The controversies of the past generation, by singling out and emphasizing the conception of *regalia*,[4] had defined with new precision the essential prerogatives of monarchy; and it was the logical application of this and other new concepts, and not a vain attempt to restore obsolete and anachronistic forms, which was the hallmark of Frederick's policy. Just as his political ideas represented an advance on the theories of the eleventh century, so his practical measures of government reflected principles alien to the age which preceded the Investiture Contest. In a new environment he gave a new content to imperial policy.

There were other, more practical reasons why Frederick, instead of attempting to pick up the old threads which the Investiture Contest had broken, was forced to seek a new basis for government.

---

[1] His letter to Eugenius set out a programme of co-operation, by which the Church would be adorned with privileges, 'et Romani imperii celsitudo in pristinae suae excellentiae robur . . . reformatur' (*Mon. Germ. Hist., Leges*, II, 90). John of Salisbury, who was in Rome when Frederick's letter was received, confirms the impression it made ('Promittebat enim se totius orbis reformaturum imperium'; Migne, *Patr. lat.*, CXCIX, 39).

[2] Cf. above, pp. 70–71.

[3] This is apparent from his categorical statement in 1159: 'Episcoporum Italiae ego quidem non affecto hominium, si tamen et eos de nostris regalibus nichil delectat habere' (*Gesta Friderici*, 275).

[4] Cf. above, p. 129. The importance of the new doctrine of *regalia*, the development of which 'reflects the rise of the modern state and of a modern conception of the state', is rightly emphasized by Mayer, *Hist. Zeitschr.*, CLIX, 468 sqq.

When he succeeded Conrad III in 1152, he found the material power of the monarchy seriously diminished, and, furthermore, the main centre of royal power had changed. From Ottonian times the greater part of the royal demesnes had lain in Saxony and in middle Germany; but these demesnes had been lost and wasted in the civil wars,[1] and from 1138 Germany was ruled for the first time by a dynasty the possessions of which lay in the south-west corner of the kingdom. Outside of Swabia, where the Hohenstaufen demesnes were concentrated, Frederick lacked the territorial outposts, provided in an earlier age by the scattered royal estates, from which to supervise government and hold the aristocracy in check. This change in the territorial balance of power is a fact of fundamental importance for the evaluation of his policy. It meant in the first place, that the Hohenstaufen dynasty, unlike earlier German rulers, could not count on an adequate material basis for government within Germany itself. Hence from the very beginning of his reign Frederick's eye was on Italy and Burgundy. It was calculated in 1158 that a resumption of the usurped prerogatives of the crown in Italy would bring in approximately 30,000 talents annually.[2] How far Frederick was attracted by the fabulous wealth of Italy, which contrasted markedly with the backward economy of Germany, we do not know; but it is clear that the monarchy's losses in Germany during the Investiture Contest forced it to look elsewhere for a supplement to its resources. Furthermore, it was a natural policy for a Swabian dynasty to attempt to transform its position in south-west Germany—precariously isolated, if Germany were considered alone—into a central position within the empire as a whole. Geographically, Swabia was as close to Burgundy and Italy as it was to the rest of Germany; and it was an essential element in Frederick Barbarossa's policy to exploit the advantages of this central position, developing Swabian connexions to the south and south-west. For this policy his marriage with Beatrice of Burgundy in 1156 was programmatic; and the immediate result of the marriage was that Frederick took possession in his wife's name of Provence and Burgundy — 'lands long alienated from the empire' — and in the following year received homage from the archbishops of Lyon and Vienne and the other bishops and

[1] Cf. above, pp. 158-159.
[2] *Gesta Friderici*, 240. At the end of last century Lamprecht (*Deutsche Gesch.*, III, 134) calculated that this sum was the equivalent of 15,500,000 marks. Its present value may be set at approximately £1,500,000 per annum, its purchasing value at ten times that sum.

princes of the land. The famous Diet of Besançon in 1157 was, indeed, a culminating point in the policy of restoring imperial authority in the Burgundian provinces, while equally symptomatic of the direction of Frederick's thought was the development of the mountain passes into Burgundy and Italy. The Septimer, the Splügen and the St. Gotthard all received his attention and perhaps no single act was more expressive of policy than the transformation of Chiavenna, which lay at the head of Lake Como on the southern or Italian side of the Splügen pass, into a Swabian city. Holding Chiavenna, Frederick held the gateway to Lombardy. Switzerland was thus the strategic centre of Hohenstaufen power, joining together Swabia, Burgundy and Lombardy;[1] and joined in this way the three provinces offered Frederick an effective basis for government, giving him possession of a central stronghold, from which he could reach out and control Saxony in the north, Bavaria in the east, and Tuscany and central Italy in the south.

Such, in outline, was the scheme of government apparently envisaged by Frederick in the months immediately following his succession to the throne in 1152. It was a programme adapted to the new circumstances which faced him; and there is no doubt that, because it took into account the revolutionary changes in circumstances which had occurred, Frederick's imperial policy was radically different from that of any emperor of the past. It has sometimes been maintained that it placed too great emphasis on Italy and that, in the pursuit of his Italian policy, Frederick sacrificed the true interests of Germany, 'perverting her rightful destiny to wrong ends', and squandering German blood and treasure.[2] But a more measured judgement would insist rather that the novelty of his imperial policy lay in the equal subordination of all three constituent kingdoms to the interests of the whole empire. Under the Ottonians and Salians the empire had been little more than a personal union of three separate states, in which — except perhaps under Otto III — Italy and Bur-

[1] Hence the purchase from Welf VI in 1168 of the allodial possessions of the Welf family; hence also Barbarossa's conflict with the house of Zähringen which was seeking to establish its territorial power in Jurane Switzerland. To follow the details of this policy would take us too far; cf. Fournier, *Le royaume d'Arles et de Vienne* (1891), 21-23, 41, and Mayer, 'Die historisch-politischen Kräfte im Oberrheingebiet im Mittelalter', *Zeitschr. f. die Gesch. d. Oberrheins, Neue Folge*, LII (1938), 17 sqq.

[2] The most incisive statement of this point of view (subsequently taken over by Thompson, *Feudal Germany*, 288) is to be found in von Below, *Die italienische Kaiserpolitik des deutschen Mittelalters* (1927). Below's views have in general been rejected; cf. Schmeidler, *Hist. Zeitschr.*, CXL (1929), 386-392.

gundy had always played a subordinate part. Under Frederick the empire, for valid practical reasons, became for the first time a unit of government. In this sense it is fair to say that he was the first of the emperors of the west whose policy was truly 'Imperial'. It was an imperial policy in so far as it made equal demands on Germany and Italy and Burgundy, each of which was (in Frederick's plans) to contribute to the imperial territory which he intended to build up at the focal point where all three kingdoms met. Thus he hoped to use his control over what was the very core and centre of his empire in order to establish and maintain his predominance within the whole. Secure in the centre, with a great imperial territory stretching from Swabia to Lombardy, he set out to rule by holding elsewhere a balance of power between the princes, who were thus to take their place in the scheme of government under imperial suzerainty. This scheme was applied no less in Italy, where Welf VI in Tuscany and the pope in the Patrimonium were two great counter-poised powers, than in Germany, where the creation of the Austrian duchy in 1156 established a power counter-balancing that of Henry the Lion in Bavaria. In northern and eastern Germany where Frederick lacked the firm territorial basis requisite for the exercise of direct administrative control, the princes were left supreme; but here again the competing interests of Albrecht the Bear, Adolf of Holstein and Henry the Lion provided a balance[1] and allowed the emperor some measure of control. That this control was not merely nominal was proved in the case of Henry the Lion: in 1166, when Henry's rapacity and high-handedness provoked a league of Saxon nobles against him, he triumphed because he had Frederick's backing, but in 1178 when the emperor supported the Saxon nobility against the duke, Saxon opposition set in motion the chain of events which led, in 1180, to Henry's fall.

The scheme of government outlined above presupposed loyal co-operation with the princes, and the old thesis of a veiled conflict from the beginning of the reign between Frederick and Henry the Lion cannot be sustained.[2] Equally it would be rash to assume that the offers of co-operation made by Frederick to Pope Eugenius III were mere blandishments. The task of reconstruction facing the new

[1] For the conflict of interests aroused by the rapid spread of colonization in the north-east, cf. below, pp. 261, 263, 265.
[2] Cf. Güterbock, 'Barbarossa u. Heinrich der Löwe', *Vergangenheit u. Gegenwart*, XXIII (1933), 256-257.

ruler in 1152 required peace between Church and State; and it was also too big for one man to undertake alone. If, in particular, the German counts and nobles, who had risen high in the turbulence of civil war, were to be brought under control, Frederick needed the co-operation of the great princes, who alone had the means of reducing to order the turbulent nobility throughout the length and breadth of Germany. Hence the great privileges of 1156, 1168 and 1180 for the German duchies marked the establishment of intermediate authorities to help the monarchy to do what it could not achieve unaided. Provided that the princes recognized that their fiefs were held of the emperor, every reinforcement of government, whether due to Welfs or Wittelsbachs, to Zähringer or Babenberger, implied a reinforcement of the pivot around which government revolved. But the loyal acceptance of feudal bonds by the princes was a *sine qua non*; and it is characteristic that in the very charter in which Barbarossa granted Henry the Lion semi-regal rights over the bishoprics east of the Elbe, he expressly inserted a declaration that Henry's lands were held 'of our munificence'. On these terms Frederick was content to exercise, beyond the bounds of his immediate demesnes, a feudal suzerainty such as that exercised in France by his contemporaries, Louis VII and Philip Augustus; and so long as the princes accepted their position under the crown, they were sure of his support in their strivings to reduce the counts and 'advocates' of their regions to strict subordination.[1] A similar conception governed his relations, in a later phase, with the Lombard communes which (like the communes of France) were assigned the position of 'seigneuries collectives'.[2] Frederick's conception of his position, in short, was that of a feudal monarch, firmly ensconced on his own central demesnes, exercising feudal suzerainty in a state which was a federation of feudal principalities.

The organization of government which Frederick Barbarossa envisaged cannot, any more than the government of twelfth-century

[1] Hence the provision in the privilege of 1156 for Austria (there is a similar provision in the privilege of 1168 for Würzburg): 'statuimus quoque, ne aliqua magna vel parva persona in eiusdem ducatus regimine sine ducis consensu vel permissione aliquam iusticiam presumat exercere' (*Mon. Germ., Const.*, I, 222).—The essence of this provision was not, as is sometimes supposed, a transference of royal rights to the new duke or an undertaking by the crown to refrain from intervention in the jurisdiction of the duchy, but rather an authorization to subject the local aristocracy and the jurisdiction it had usurped during the previous half-century, to superior authority.

[2] Lenel, *Hist. Zeitschr.*, CXXVIII, 199-200, shows how in 1183 the Lombard League 'accepted the emperor's feudal point of view'.

England, be reduced to a simple formula: feudalism or anti-feudalism, centralization or decentralization. On his own demesnes, within his own immediate sphere of interests, both in Italy and in Germany and in Burgundy, Frederick pushed ahead with the organization of a new, non-feudal administration, and there was a very marked tendency to centralization, as there must always be where a process of rebuilding is at work. But there was also decentralization, in so far as much of the rebuilding was left to the princes, whom Frederick deliberately singled out from the rest of the aristocracy and endued with new powers, raising them high above the counts and other minor local authorities. As far as the relations of crown and princes were concerned, the empire was to be a state held together by feudal bonds; like twelfth-century France, it was to be a series of duchies grouped round the royal demesne. After the upheavals of the last fifty years, the dual task was to re-establish a hierarchy of government, and to assert the king's position at its head; and it was due to the social revolution which the Investiture Contest had inaugurated that this hierarchy — unlike the organization of government prior to the reign of Henry V — was feudal. In Germany, as in the rest of Europe, the monarchy still had important non-feudal attributes, the sovereign was still more than suzerain. But the reigns of Lothar and Conrad III had shown that, only if he were successful in establishing an undisputed position at the head of the feudal hierarchy, could the king make full use of his non-feudal rights; and it was this conviction that lay behind Frederick Barbarossa's work.

Frederick's feudal policy was nevertheless a carefully balanced and fully integrated policy. Although, after the Investiture Contest, the first necessity was to strengthen government whatever its form, to reanimate the principle of state authority, the consolidation of the position of the great princes requisite for this purpose was only one aspect of Frederick's plan for a feudal monarchy, and was balanced by a systematic attempt to build up, within the greater realm over which Frederick ruled as supreme overlord, a compact territory, administered through a well-organized bureaucracy, under his own immediate control. Without such a territory he could not hope to hold the balance or — dealing with princes of the calibre of Henry the Lion — to maintain royal predominance within the imperial federation. Hence much energy was devoted to building up the Hohenstaufen demesnes in Swabia, particularly towards the end of the 'sixties, when (the chronicler tells us) 'he acquired by gift or purchase the holdings of many nobles who were without heirs', including the immense family lands of Welf VI. But Swabia was only part of the territory selected by Frederick to provide a material foundation for the monarchy, and — divided between a number of competing families, including the powerful dukes of Zähringen — one which could only be consolidated slowly and gradually by acquisitions of estates and franchises as opportunity offered. More important in Frederick's plans from the beginning was Lombardy. On his success or failure in securing control over Lombardy the success or failure of his original scheme of government depended; and it is therefore round the question of Lombardy that the rest of his policy, both in Italy and in Germany, revolves. To see what Frederick achieved, and where he failed, we must first of all examine his policy in Italy; it is here that we have the key to the evolution of Hohenstaufen policy not only in his own reign but also in that of his son, Henry VI.

II

The first period of Frederick's reign[1] extends from his accession in 1152 to 1157, and includes his first expedition to Italy and his first conflict with Milan. But Lombard affairs played a subordinate part in this period, and Frederick was not ready to impose a settlement; his action against Milan was merely a response to the complaints of other cities, and not an essential feature of his business in Italy. In this period he was mainly concerned with Germany, Burgundy and central Italy. Profiting by the new spirit of reconciliation which marked papal policy under Eugenius III, Frederick's main aim in Italy was to win the goodwill of the pope and secure his own coronation in return for the destruction of the power of Arnold of Brescia and the restoration of papal authority in Rome. Both objects were achieved in 1155, and for a period it seemed as though

[1] Apart from standard authorities like Giesebrecht, *Geschichte der deutschen Kaiserzeit*, the following sketch owes much to W. Leriel, 'Der Konstanzer Frieden von 1183 u. die italienische Politik Friedrichs I', *Hist. Zeitschr.*, CXXVIII (1923); G. von Below, *Die italienische Kaiserpolitik des deutschen Mittelalters mit besonderem Hinblick auf die Politik Friedrich Barbarossas* (1927); H. Kauffmann, *Die italienische Politik Kaiser Friedrichs I. nach dem Frieden von Constanz* (1933); P. W. Finsterwalder, 'Die Gesetze des Reichstags von Roncaglia', *Zeitschr. d. Sav.-Stiftung für Rechtsgesch., Germ. Abt.*, LI (1931); G. Deibel, 'Die finanzielle Bedeutung Reichsitaliens für die staufischen Herrscher des 12. Jahrhunderts,' ibid., LIV (1934); K. Wenck, 'Die römischen Päpste zwischen Alexander III. u. Innocenz III', *Papsttum u. Kaisertum* (1926).

co-operation between empire and papacy had been secured, particularly as the pope was still in urgent need of Frederick's support against the Normans of Sicily. Thus Frederick was able to establish a workable balance in Italy: the hostile Norman power in the south was isolated as a result of the good relations between Frederick and the papacy; central Italy was divided into two spheres of influence, one under the pope, the other under Welf VI who had received the fiefs of Tuscany and Spoleto at the very beginning of the reign; and Lombardy, although not yet settled, was reserved as the emperor's own sphere of influence. The same period witnessed a similar settlement in Germany. Conrad III's son was given the duchy of Swabia, which only reverted to the crown in 1168. But more important was the settlement with the Welfs, the confirmation of Henry the Lion's position in Bavaria and the simultaneous separation of Bavaria and Austria in 1156. Finally, this was the period which saw the assertion of control over Burgundy and Arles: the Diet of Besançon, as already indicated, marked the culmination of the first phase of Frederick's reign.

Whether the work of this first period would provide a sufficient foundation for imperial government depended, however, on what sort of a settlement Frederick could secure in Lombardy. From the time of his first expedition to Italy in 1154-1155, Frederick clearly realized that a settlement of accounts with Milan was inevitable; and this beyond doubt was the purpose of his second expedition in 1158. He was determined to secure in Lombardy the same prerogatives as had previously been secured and confirmed by the Diet of Besançon in Burgundy;[1] and for this purpose — after Milan had made submission — a commission was set up at the famous Diet of Roncaglia to define the regalian rights of the crown which had lapsed during the period of weak government after the Investiture Contest. This decision to reassert the ancient rights of the crown meant inevitably a diminution of the powers actually being exercised by the communes; but it did not imply a frontal attack on the position of the communes, and even towards Milan Frederick showed, after its submission, an attitude of moderation and leniency, thus confirming

---

[1] The attempt by H. Koeppler (*Engl. Hist. Review*, LIV, 582 sqq.) to trace from 1158 a novel conception of imperial prerogative, associated with the rise of Rainald of Dassel to a leading place in the emperor's counsels, overlooks the inter-connexion of Burgundian and Italian policy. H. Hirsch, *Urkundenfälschungen aus dem regnum Arelatense. Die burgundische Politik Friedrichs I* (1937), has shown that the Roncaglian decrees were not a novel step but a direct continuation of the methods pursued in Burgundy.

in practice his expressed wish (in the speech in which he opened proceedings at Roncaglia) 'rather to exercise a legitimate authority than to transform our office of governing into arrogant domination'.[1] It never entered his head to restore the obsolete governmental system of the eleventh century; on the contrary, he was prepared to give full recognition to the position won by the communes in their struggle with the bishops. But many of the rights exercised by the communes were royal rights, which the Frankish kings had conferred on the counts to exercise in their name, which had then in the tenth and eleventh centuries passed into the hands of the bishops, and which the communes had wrested from the episcopate at the time of the Investiture Contest. These rights, defined in the *lex Regalia* of the Roncaglian decrees, included predominantly rights of jurisdiction — which was thus, as in the western monarchies, regarded as separate from feudal tenure, a power conferred independently by the crown — and certain profitable rights, of which the *fodrum* (a right to fodder for the royal army, and then to a payment in lieu of fodder) was the most important. But it was not Barbarossa's policy to resume these regalian rights wholesale. What he sought to establish was the principle — which Edward I later established in England by his *Quo Warranto* inquests — that they were held of the crown; and it was expressly stipulated that where a commune or feudatory could produce a charter conferring *regalia*, the rights conferred should be held perpetually as a benefice conferred by the emperor. Similarly in regard to city-government, Frederick's attitude was moderate. The *lex Regalia* claimed for the emperor the power of appointing magistrates to exercise justice; but the *lex Omnis*, proceeding from the principle that all jurisdiction pertains to the prince, simply stated that every magistrate should receive his jurisdiction from the prince's hands. Thus Frederick had two methods of proceeding. Where he could not trust the loyalty of a commune, he claimed for himself the right to appoint the magistrate; but where — as in the majority of cases — the loyalty of the city was assured, he was prepared to leave free election to the citizens, on condition that the freely elected magistrates sought royal authorization for the exercise of their judicial powers. How far he was prepared to go in applying the second of these methods was shown by the terms of the peace

---

[1] *Gesta Friderici*, 236: 'Nos tamen regium nomen habentes, desideramus potius legittimum tenere imperium...quam...imperandi officium in superbiam dominationemque convertere.'

he made with Milan in September 1158, in which he granted free election of the consuls by the people. Numerous privileges prove that this measure was not exceptional: in the year 1162 alone the same concession was made to Pisa, Genoa, Ravenna, Lucca, Ferrara, Cremona and Pavia.

For a time this system worked satisfactorily. There was trouble almost immediately with Milan, because the Milanese, misinterpreting the right of free election which the emperor had granted them, refused to allow Frederick's representatives to instal the consuls in office. But the majority of cities accepted the position and — in contrast with Milan — Pavia, Piacenza, Cremona and Lodi freely accepted the podestàs, chosen from within the city, whom Frederick installed. Encouraged by this success Frederick therefore set about applying the Roncaglian decrees in the adjoining territory of the march of Verona, just as, already at the end of 1258, he had sent officers to collect the *fodrum* in Tuscany and the Campagna. The imperial prerogatives, in short — the *regalia* which stood outside and above feudal law — were to be exercised throughout the whole land. But a protest was immediately made by the pope against the collection of *fodrum* in the papal demesnes; and this was accompanied by the ominous claim that imperial legates were not to visit Rome without papal permission, 'for every magistracy there belongs to St. Peter, together with all *regalia*'. Such a claim was a sure sign of the rising influence of the anti-imperial party among the cardinals, which favoured a return to the old Gregorian policy of alliance with Sicily against the emperor; and when on the death of Hadrian IV in 1159 Alexander III was elected pope in opposition to the pacific Victor IV, it was a triumph for the anti-imperial, pro-Sicilian party. It was also a triumph for Milan and its associates among the Lombard cities. The formation of an alliance between Sicily, the papacy and Milan destroyed the balance Frederick had established in Italy in 1154 and 1155, and the situation deteriorated further when, in 1162, Welf of Tuscany deserted the imperial cause. Frederick's party among the Lombard communes was weakened, and thereby his position in Lombardy was compromised. Hitherto, with the solid backing of a majority of the cities, it had been easy to hold the balance against the isolated group which supported Milan; but when Milan found allies outside Lombardy, the balance on which Frederick relied for the stability of his government was destroyed.

N

The inevitable result was an attempt to restore the old balance of power by destroying the Milanese party once and for all. Imperial government, initially moderate, became increasingly stringent. In 1161 the war against the Milanese cities was carried on with new vigour; and in 1162 Milan was captured and destroyed. Particularly after Frederick's return to Germany at the end of 1162, the whole character of Lombard administration changed. In the first place, the open hostility of Milan forced the emperor to strengthen his own party by ever wider privileges and concessions, so that his government became little better than a party government. In the second place, after Frederick's departure a new spirit of harshness and oppression entered German rule, not only in relation to Milan and the cities which had sided with Milan, but even in relation to the friendly communes; and the same harshness prevailed in the march of Verona. The Italians were treated, not like subjects permanently under imperial rule, but like enemies who were to be exploited as quickly as possible, while the army of occupation could maintain its hold.[1] There is no doubt that this oppressive administration was contrary not only to Frederick's own interests, but also to his intentions; and when in 1164 the League of Verona was formed to oppose the oppressive administrative measures of Rainald of Dassel, Frederick offered to compromise, promising justice where his officials had committed excesses, and offering to accept the arbitration of distinguished Lombards. But the rigour of the raw German knights had achieved what nothing else could have effected; it brought the communes of north Italy, long divided by conflicting interests, into unison and gave them a united purpose. In 1167 the Lombard League was formed and joined forces with the League of Verona; and Frederick, his army decimated by plague, had no choice save to withdraw to Germany. One by one his supporters were forced over into the hostile camp, and when in 1172 William of Montferrat joined the League the imperial party in Italy had ceased to exist.

Already as far back as 1162 Frederick had appreciated the change wrought by the intervention of Alexander III and his Sicilian allies; and although still at that time seeking a quick decision by force of

[1] Mon. Germ., Script., XVIII, 645: 'Cum imperator in Alemaniam profectus esset . . . procuratores . . . non solum huïus iura rationesque imperatoris, de quibus solummodo exactis nullum malum ac scandalum accidisset neque Longobardi inde maesti fuissent, exigebant, sed etiam plus de septuplo iniuste excutiebant.' Cf. also Engl. Hist. Review, LIV, 165.

arms, he was thereafter never unwilling to moderate his claims of 1158 and compromise with the communes in order to free his hands for the struggle with the Alexandrine papacy. After 1167 it was even more necessary to come to terms with one or other of his opponents; and from this time onwards he made offers first to one and then to the other, in the hope of breaking the hostile alliance. But neither party would negotiate without the other; and when his fifth expedition to Italy ended with the decisive defeat of Legnano in 1176, he realized that there was no alternative to a general pacification. At Venice in 1177 he made peace with the pope, a fifteen years' truce with the pope's Sicilian allies, and a six years' truce with the Lombards; and before the latter ran out, it was superseded by a definitive settlement, the Peace of Constance of 1183. At Constance the cities of the League received the right of electing their consuls and the *regalia* within the city walls; in short, their claim to self-government was in substance conceded. But Frederick did not emerge empty-handed. In the first place, comparison of the preliminary proposals and the final text of the treaty shows that the cities yielded on many important points, accepting in all essentials the feudal standpoint of the emperor. In the second place, they made a substantial payment of *l.*16,000 in return for the settlement. Thirdly, it was still necessary for the consuls to receive investiture from the imperial legates and to swear fealty to the emperor before entering into office. Finally, although the cities controlled the *regalia* within their walls, they paid an annual farm of *l.*2,000 for this privilege, and regalian rights in their territories beyond the city walls remained in royal hands. Even after the Peace of Constance, therefore, Frederick retained considerable revenues; he still had an independent position of some strength in Lombardy.[1]

It is, however, to central Italy that we must turn in order to appreciate what Frederick gained by his settlement with the Lombards. Neither the Peace of Venice with Alexander III nor the Peace of Constance was an end in itself. On the contrary, Frederick's object in both cases was to liquidate the two ruinous entanglements in order to exploit the possibilities opening out before him in Tuscany and the neighbouring regions. His first intervention in this latter area had occurred in 1162, after duke Welf had transferred his

---

[1] A measure is provided by the fact that in 1185 Milan agreed to pay *l.*300 per annum for the right to exercise *regalia* in its adjacent county.

support to the papacy. To counteract this move, German counts and vicars were sent to administer the land under Rainald of Dassel; and it soon became evident that Tuscany was a more favourable environment than Lombardy for the introduction of direct, bureaucratic administration. Compared with Lombardy, city autonomy had developed slowly in Tuscany, because throughout the period of the Investiture Contest Tuscany had been ruled by the powerful house of Canossa, which was well able to hold the cities in check. Hence, apart from the few great cities, Pisa and Lucca to the fore, communal development was retrograde, and in the countryside and smaller townships ducal rights were well preserved and effectively exploited. These rights passed, after Welf's defection from the imperial cause, into the hands of German agents who administered them, not as fiefs, but as dependent offices on Frederick's account. This administration was further developed in 1172 and 1173 under Christian of Mainz; and there is little doubt that Frederick's offer of favourable terms to the Lombards at Montebello in 1175, even before his defeat at Legnano, was due to his desire to free his hands to organize more thoroughly his control of central Italy. Equally significant is the fact that, although earlier he had been willing to cede the Matildine lands to the Church, in the negotiations at Venice he upheld the rights of the empire, and made no concessions in the Peace of Venice itself. From 1177 onwards, his Italian policy was based on the extension of direct imperial administration throughout central Italy; and it was this period which saw the completion of the new administrative system begun in 1162. This was not at first without setbacks, particularly during Frederick's absence in Germany between 1178 and 1183; but after the conclusion of the Peace of Constance with the Lombard cities in 1183, Frederick was able to organize the government of central Italy on a firm basis. What he had striven in vain to enforce in Lombardy during the earlier years of his reign, he achieved without difficulty in Tuscany and the neighbouring regions in the years 1184-1187. In this task, moreover, he secured at Constance the co-operation of the Lombard League which, as one of the terms of peace, agreed to help him recover lands and rights *extra societatem*, i.e. beyond the frontiers of the federation. When, in 1185, the good relations established in 1183 were transformed into a positive alliance with Milan, Frederick's position in the north was so secure that he could turn with assurance to Tuscany. The death of Alexander III in 1181 also favoured the emperor's policy, for it was followed by a strong reaction against political tendencies within the Church, and the pontificate of Lucius III (1181-1185) was marked by a conciliatory spirit. Finally, Frederick sought a settlement with Sicily and in 1184 — apparently through Lucius III's mediation[1] — terms of peace were arranged and confirmed by a union between Frederick's son, Henry, and Constance of Sicily.

Thus Frederick secured a free hand to complete the remodelling of the government of central Italy, the main lines of which had been drawn in the period preceding and following the Peace of Venice. In Tuscany alone of the central provinces was it necessary to come to terms with the cities; and here a satisfactory basis of agreement was found by conferring on Siena, Lucca, Florence and Pisa equivalent privileges to those granted in the north to the Lombard League. But the great Tuscan towns were few and constituted no more than enclaves within the uniformly administered imperial territory. Outside Tuscany — in Romagna, Spoleto, Ancona and the Matildine lands — the cities, small and retrograde, presented no difficulties. In Spoleto and the march of Ancona the towns were by and large granted self-government under consuls; but the consuls were not freely elected and their powers were confined within the city walls. Over each of the two provinces a German count had ruled since 1177; but he was an official and not a feudatory, and therefore held his province as an administrative district. To him the consuls were responsible; and his rule was based on solid foundations. The cities paid an annual hearth-tax; their officers swore fealty to him; and outside the walls of the towns he ruled the countryside through a well-ordered hierarchy of officials, who resided in the castles and administered the demesnes. This organization of uniform administrative districts, introduced into Spoleto and Ancona in 1177, was

---

[1] The evidence for Lucius' mediation was first set forth — in opposition to earlier historians, who believed that the marriage between Henry and Constance was aimed directly at the papacy — by Haller, 'Heinrich VI u. die römische Kirche', *Mitteil. d. ö. Inst. f. Geschichtsforschung*, XXXV (1914). He was supported on the basis of independent evidence by Wenck, op. cit., 424; but Lenel, op. cit., 248, and Hampe, *Wissenschaftliche Forschungsberichte*, VII (1922), 78, remained cautious and unconvinced. It is, however, reasonable to suppose with Haller that the object of the marriage was to consummate the peace, and not a first step towards linking Sicily with the empire and thus encircling the papacy, since in 1183, when negotiations started, William of Sicily had only been married three years and there was no reason to suppose that the marriage would remain childless and that William's aunt, Constance, would succeed her nephew.

carried into the Romagna, the Matildine lands and Tuscany in 1187, and financed in the same way by annual hearth-taxes, tolls and duties. Thus Frederick's last years saw in central Italy the construction of a solid administration with fixed revenues, divided into uniform districts: he had found at last the solid basis for a direct imperial administration which he had been seeking since the beginning of his reign.

Geographically, Frederick's government after 1183 was very differently ordered from that which he had set out to construct in 1152. Tuscany and central Italy were its basis, not Lombardy; and instead of direct rule in the north, his relations with the Lombard communes were governed by feudal principles. But, despite the shift in the geographical balance, the main principles of government remained the same. The foundation was still a solidly administered royal territory, and outside that territory a federation held together by feudal bonds and by a balance of groups and interests which left the emperor, at the head, in ultimate control. Few statesmen have emerged so successful from a struggle of two decades' duration ending in an overwhelming military defeat, as Frederick emerged from his struggle with the Lombard communes. Moreover, the period of peace inaugurated in 1177, besides allowing him to organize the government of central Italy, freed his hands also for a settlement of German affairs: here also the last years of the reign saw the establishment of a new balance highly favourable to the monarchy.

III

The long struggle with the Lombard communes and with Alexander III affected Frederick's policy in Germany no less than in Italy. It is true that the contest with Alexander III and the schism in the Church revealed the ecclesiastical princes — very different from their predecessors under Henry IV — in unison with the emperor;[1] but the strain imposed on the loyalty of many leading prelates was nevertheless great. More important, Frederick's preoccupation with Italian and papal affairs compelled him to make increasing concessions to the princes,.in particular to Henry the Lion. Thus, rights of

[1] A. Hauck, *Kirchengesch. Deutschlands*, IV (1913), 256-257. Alexander's plan 'to raise a revolution in Germany, like the earlier revolt against Henry IV' was (says Hauck, p. 262) a complete failure.

investiture over the eastern bishoprics of Oldenburg, Mecklenberg and Ratzeburg, which Frederick appears to have decided to withhold in 1154, were formally conferred on Henry in 1160;[1] and the need for Henry's support in expelling supporters of Alexander III and replacing them by adherents of Victor IV enabled him to tyrannize over the north German church and bring it under his own control. At the same period, Henry's conquests in the Slav lands east of the Elbe increased his territorial power.[2] His marriage in 1168 to the daughter of Henry II of England brought him into contact with the English court, and allowed him to pursue an independent foreign policy, which was extended to include Denmark. Already in 1164 he had been visited by envoys from the Greek emperor, Manuel, who was supporting Venice and the League of Verona against the German emperor;.and when in 1172 Henry on his way to the Holy Land paid a visit to Constantinople it was freely rumoured that he was intriguing with Manuel against Frederick.

Confronted with the growing might of Henry the Lion, Frederick gradually modified the policy of the early years of the reign. There was no open breach; indeed, at the Diet of Würzburg in 1168, Frederick mediated between Henry and the hostile Saxons with definite bias in favour of the former. But at the same time, he began to build up his own territorial power in Germany. To this decision, beyond doubt, the course of events in Italy contributed. The formation of the Lombard League and its amalgamation in 1167 with the League of Verona showed Frederick that he could no longer rely for his resources on Lombardy; and he therefore gave greater attention to his lands outside Italy. In 1168 Swabia, conferred at the beginning of the reign on Conrad III's son, escheated to the crown, and was thenceforward administered by imperial *ministeriales*; and it was from this period that the policy of strengthening Hohenstaufen power in Swabia by purchase and consolidation came to the fore. In 1169, furthermore, he restricted the power of the house of Zähringen in Burgundy. Thus within a few months of the formation of the Lombard League Frederick embarked on a reconstruction of his territorial position in Germany: as a result of the check to his plans in Italy, stricter control and wider resources in Germany had

---

[1] The charter of 1154 conferring such rights (*Mon. Germ., Const.*, I, 206) was not completed and was therefore invalid; cf. Giesebrecht, *Gesch. d. deutschen Kaiserzeit*, V (1880), 36 and 353.
[2] For Henry's share in German expansion to the east, cf. below, p. 261 sqq.

become necessary. Nor was this policy of consolidating the territorial power of the reigning dynasty confined to the south-west.
Eastern Franconia (or the duchy of Rotenburg), also in the hands
of Conrad III's son until 1167, reverted to the crown on his death,
while from the beginning of his reign Frederick had possessed the
neighbouring Vogtland, the territories of Pleissen and Eger;
together these carried his direct authority far to the east in a wide
belt running from the upper Rhine almost to the Elbe. Finally in
1168 he determined to regain a foothold in the north by resuming
control of Goslar — the Saxon citadel Henry IV had planned to
make his permanent capital — with which at the beginning of the
reign he had invested Henry the Lion.

Frederick's decision to take back Goslar into his own hands was a
clear sign of the growing strain in his relations with Henry the
Lion. For Frederick, Goslar was a vantage-point from which to
watch over Saxon affairs; for Henry its possession was essential for
his policy of consolidating Saxony into a united province under his
own full control. Its surrender was the price he was forced to pay
for Frederick's mediation and support at the Diet of Würzburg in
1168. But he never reconciled himself to its permanent loss; and
when in the winter of 1175-1176 — after the Lombards had suddenly
and unexpectedly rejected the peace proposals of Montebello —
Frederick found himself militarily in a very weak position in Italy
and sent to Germany for reinforcements, Henry the Lion sought to
strike a bargain, offering help if Goslar were restored. Such terms,
implying that the Saxon duke had no obligations to his sovereign
except in return for specific concessions, were unacceptable to
Frederick; and he fought on without Henry's help. But the result
was the defeat of the German forces at Legnano; and from 1176
onwards the breach between the two men widened. It was patent
that the reverses Frederick had suffered in Italy had weakened his
position in Germany also, and that the bonds on which he had relied
since 1152 were no longer effective. Probably the death in 1170
of Henry the Lion's rival, Albrecht the Bear, increased the former's
confidence, and encouraged him to take a more independent line
with Frederick; perhaps also he relied on English backing and hoped,
with papal support, to rally European opinion to his side against the
schismatic emperor. But, if such were his thoughts, Frederick's
action in 1177 in making peace with the Church, cut the ground

from under his feet. The terms of reconciliation between Frederick and Alexander III included the dismissal of Henry the Lion's nominees from the sees of Bremen and Halberstadt, and the restoration of Church lands in Saxony which he had seized. When Henry hesitated to fulfil these terms, the newly appointed prelates rallied the Saxon nobility against him; an appeal was made to Frederick to do justice; Henry was summoned to answer in the royal court; and when he failed to appear he was declared contumacious, outlawed and deprived of his two duchies and his numerous fiefs.[1]

The fall of Henry the Lion in 1180 gave Frederick an unparalleled opportunity to reorganize the structure of German government to the profit of the monarchy. Saxony was divided into two duchies: the lands west of the Weser were conferred, as the duchy of Westphalia, on the archbishop of Cologne, those east of the Weser passed to Bernard of Anhalt, the son of Albrecht the Bear. Bavaria, by judgement of the princes, was granted to Frederick's old and loyal supporter, Otto of Wittelsbach, the founder of a dynasty which lasted until 1918; but here also the opportunity was taken to reduce its extent and importance, by separating Styria which was made into a duchy held directly of the crown. Thus in north and south the great Welf territorial *bloc* was split up, and in place of one over-mighty vassal the king was left with a number of smaller princes, over whom he could more easily exercise predominance. Politically, the events of 1180 were an outstanding success for the monarchy, and at the Diet of Mainz in 1184 Frederick appeared at the height of his power. The proceedings of 1180 were also a striking justification for Frederick's policy; for it was as a contumacious vassal that Henry the Lion was tried and condemned by feudal law, and it was as a feudal penalty that he was deprived of his fiefs. In short, Frederick's reliance on the bonds of feudalism was not misplaced. He had already used them successfully as an instrument for reaffirming the close connexion between the monarchy and the German Church which the Investiture Contest had shattered; by treating the episcopal

[1] On the events leading up to the fall of Henry the Lion, cf. in addition to Güterbock's books (1909 and 1920) and his judicious summary, 'Barbarossa u. Heinrich der Löwe', *Vergangenheit u. Gegenwart*, XXIII (1933), the articles in the *Hist. Zeitschrift*, CIX and CXII (1914) by Hampe and Niese, and Haller's article in *Arch. f. Urkundenforschung*, III (1911). On Henry's foreign policy, on which he relied as a second line of defence, cf. R. Schmidt, *Hist. Zeitschr.*, CLIV (1936), 241-284. — In emphasizing the importance of Goslar I follow Güterbock, loc. cit., 263, and Niese: Goslar, it must be remembered, 'was not merely a rich city, but also the key to East Saxony' (Heigel and Riezler, *Das Herzogtum Bayern*, 28).

lands as feudal baronies he had succeeded in winning over the Church once again to the side of the monarchy. From 1180 the feudal basis of German government was even more clearly articulated.[1] The tenants-in-chief were singled out, and endowed with special privileges raising them up as *Reichsfürsten (principes imperii)* above the mass of counts and nobles, who took their place in the feudal hierarchy as their dependants. No doubt the new social hierarchy represented no more than the completion of a process which had been under way since the beginning of the century; but the definition in 1180 was nevertheless significant. It implied the re-establishment, on feudal lines, of social order after preceding anarchy; it set a term to the independence of the aristocracy, who now fell under the authority of the princes; and the fact that it was carried out as a deliberate act of the imperial court safeguarded the king's place at the head of society. Already in 1158 Frederick had asserted his special prerogatives as king in feudal society, reserving in every oath of fealty the fealty owed to the monarch;[2] and even earlier in 1157 he had enunciated the fundamental principle that all grants by the crown were feudal in character and, governed by the strict rules of feudal law, could not be further disposed of without the king's consent.[3] Manipulated in this way by a ruler with conscious purpose, feudalism revealed its value as a centralizing force, strengthening the king's position at the head of the feudal hierarchy.

If we remember the precarious position of the German monarchy under Conrad III, the progress achieved between 1152 and 1184 is astounding. It is, of course, true that Barbarossa profited from the widespread reaction not only against the external conditions but also against the whole outlook of the previous generation — a European reaction from which not only the Hohenstaufen but also the Capetian and Plantagenet dynasties derived immediate profit. It is true also that he only succeeded in restoring the power and prestige of the monarchy by according to Italy a place in his calculations far exceeding in importance anything it had attained earlier, even under Otto III. Few historians would deny that the new

---

[1] Cf. E. Rosenstock, *Königshaus u. Stämme* (1914), 109 sqq.; R. Moeller, 'Die Neuordnung d. Reichsfürstenstandes u. der Prozess Heinrichs des Löwen', *Zeitschr. d. Sav.-Stiftung, Germ. Abt.*, XXXIX (1918); H. Mitteis, *Politische Prozesse des früheren Mittelalters* (1927), 72–74; there is also a judicious summary by Mitteis in *Mediaeval Germany*, II, 249 sqq.

[2] *Mon. Germ., Const.*, I, 248: 'in omni sacramento fidelitatis nominatim imperator excipiatur.'

[3] *Ibid.*, 235: 'ea, quae ab imperio tenentur, iure feodali possidentur, nec ea sine domini consensu ad alterius possunt transferri dominium.'

preoccupation with Italy, although readily explained as a consequence of the weakened position of the monarchy in Germany, implied an ominous shift in imperial perspectives. If only because of Italian repugnance to German rule, there was an element of danger in relying, to the degree in which Frederick relied, on Italian resources. Through Italy, furthermore, Frederick incurred the risk of serious embroilments with the papacy, such as no ruler whose authority was confined to Germany need have feared. This danger was enhanced when Frederick transferred his attention from Lombardy to Tuscany, still more when he allied with the Normans of Sicily; and even the pacific Lucius III, a personal friend of the emperor, was reluctant to grant formal recognition to the new territorial settlement in central Italy. On the other hand, there was no feeling in Germany that Frederick was sacrificing German interests to the exigencies of Italy; and there is not a shadow of evidence to support the old hypothesis that Henry the Lion's refusal of aid in 1176 was inspired by dislike of the Italian 'entanglement' or reflected opposition between a 'German' and an 'Italian' policy. The success of Frederick's policy was due in no small degree to the fact that he carried the German princes with him; he worked deliberately through the princes who, as peers of his court, participated in all the major political decisions of his reign.

Nevertheless Frederick's personal share in the restoration of the German monarchy and the revival of the Empire was great. He had the benefit of outstanding ministers, like Rainald of Dassel, who probably brought from France (where he had studied) a deepened conception of the binding force of feudal ties, and Christian of Mainz who laid the foundations of imperial government in central Italy. But it was due first and foremost to Frederick's own mature political consciousness that, in the reconstruction of German government in the twelfth century, the monarchy asserted its place at the head of society. Throughout Germany the princes were engaged on the work of reconstruction, rounding off their territories, overcoming aristocratic opposition, and applying new methods and principles;[1] but none was in advance of Frederick, who

---

[1] Cf. for Saxony R. Hildebrand, *Der sächsische Staat Heinrichs des Löwen* (1937); for Bavaria M. Spindler, *Die Anfänge des bayerischen Landesfürstentums* (1937); for Swabia Th. Mayer, *Der Staat der Herzoge von Zähringen* (trs. *Med. Germany*, II, 175-202). For Hohenstaufen territorial policy Niese, *Die Verwaltung des Reichsgutes* (1905), has collected the basic facts. — The leadership of the Hohenstaufen in this field of policy is rightly emphasized by Spindler, pp. 15-16.

systematically extended and reorganized his territorial government in Swabia and Alsace, introducing uniform administrative districts and a new hierarchy of officials, and co-ordinating the new districts into provinces. In this way he ensured that the material foundations of the monarchy were such that the king could hold his own against even the most powerful of the princes. At the same time, he set about stabilizing the position of the new dynasty. Against the elective principles enunciated between 1076 and 1152 he revived the tradition of hereditary succession. His son, Henry, was 'designated' successor and raised to the kingship in 1167; in 1184 he was crowned king of Italy and made co-regent. Thus continuity of policy, essential if Frederick's works were to endure, was assured.

The assurance of continuity was an important point, perhaps the most important of all; for Frederick's work still needed consolidation. He had laid, in circumstances initially far from favourable, the foundation for a healthy development of German government; but his work still had to pass the test of time. Many of his measures were more than superficially similar to those of his contemporaries in France and England; but there was a fundamental difference in the material with which he had to work. Owing to the Investiture Contest, which had shaken Germany far more violently than the two western monarchies, he had to build up again from the very foundations; he could not afford, like the Capetians, to proceed slowly and progressively, but rather had to impose systematically a feudal framework adapted full grown from France. Hence the structure he built had still, by the time of his death in 1190, only weak roots; forty years could not create a durable system of government, capable of standing up to all the shocks to which government is exposed. Above all, a period of continuous tranquil rule was necessary to create an enduring tradition, and in particular to consolidate the territorial power of the monarchy in Germany which was based on scattered, heterogeneous lands with a constant tendency to break apart. The test of Frederick's work therefore came in the reign of his son, Henry VI (1190-1197), and still more in the critical years which followed Henry VI's premature death in 1197. After 1190 the Hohenstaufen empire advanced rapidly to its crisis.

CHAPTER 8

THE CRISIS OF THE HOHENSTAUFEN EMPIRE
(1190–1215)

I

FREDERICK BARBAROSSA had built well. His efforts and ability and firm grasp of realities had rescued the Empire from the set-backs of the Investiture Contest, which had retarded and perhaps even perverted German development by comparison with France and England. But there were still serious problems outstanding, both in Italy and in Germany, when he died in 1190.

In Italy the main weakness in the imperial situation, after the conclusion of peace with the Lombard communes, was the failure to settle outstanding territorial questions with the papacy. Although the imperial administration was running smoothly and efficiently, there had been no formal papal recognition of the new order in central Italy. Temporarily the pope was in no position to challenge imperial policy, but papal claims to the Matildine lands, to Spoleto, Ancona, the Romagna and Tuscany, had not been surrendered, and at any set-back to imperial control they might be revived. In the meantime they represented a useful counter for diplomatic bargaining. Already in 1184, for example, when Frederick requested the pope to crown his son, the counter-demand for a territorial settlement in central Italy was put forward, and it was Frederick's unwillingness to make concessions in this respect which was the pope's main reason for refusing coronation. In Germany the problems facing the monarchy arose from the settlement of 1180. The fall of Henry the Lion had materially strengthened the emperor's hand; but it had not been secured without tangible concessions on the part of the monarchy. In the first place, Frederick had been compelled to grant out Henry the Lion's escheated fiefs, instead of sequestrating and adding them to the crown demesnes; hence the material trophies of Frederick's victory, the confiscated territories, passed into the hands of the princes. The contrast with France is striking; for there, after the condemnation of John twenty years later, Philip Augustus added Normandy to the demesnes of the Capetian dynasty, which thus for the first time rose high above the princes. In Germany, on the other hand, the events of 1180 set a precedent which made it difficult for the king at any future date to retain escheated fiefs and use them (under the direct administration of royal officials) to build up the crown lands. The second factor limiting the king's freedom of action was the creation of a new and limited class of *Reichsfürsten*, which — conscious of its prerogatives — was unwilling to open its ranks to newcomers except under stringent conditions of its own making, and was thus able to restrict the king's freedom in filling positions of the highest political importance. Moreover, although the establishment of a new hierarchy gave much-needed stability to German feudal society, it also interposed between the monarchy and the counts a new rung in the feudal ladder, and thenceforward it was normal for the counts to receive their offices not directly from the king but at second hand from the local territorial princes. This was, indeed, only the culmination of a process leading back to the beginning of the century; but its legal formulation in 1180, as part of the price extorted by the princes for their co-operation in the proceedings against Henry the Lion, marked a stage in its development, as well as indicating the limits of Frederick Barbarossa's success. The fact was that the problems left over by the civil wars under Henry IV and Henry V inevitably involved the crown in inconsistencies. On the one side, it required to strengthen the princes in order to curb the aristocracy; on the other side, it shared the tendency of all monarchies to use the lesser baronage as a check on the magnates. Between these conflicting tendencies it was not easy to apply a uniform plan, and it was due to these factors that, in spite of all Barbarossa's efforts, the German monarchy had not, by 1190, achieved the same freedom of action as at the same date the monarchies of England and France.

At the same time the events of 1180 led to political complications which, although not serious, required careful handling. The archbishop of Cologne, on whom the duchy of Westphalia had been conferred after Henry the Lion's fall, proved less trustworthy than Frederick had anticipated; by 1187 he was openly hostile and in close touch with pope Urban III, who evidently saw in him a potential leader of princely opposition in Germany. At the same time he initiated intrigues in England, with which Cologne had growing commercial relations. Here, in exile at the English court, was Henry the Lion who had not given up hope of recovering his lands and position; in 1189, after Frederick had departed on crusade, he actually returned to Germany and sought to reoccupy Saxony by force. His intrigues created serious foreign complications; for the English king, alienated by Frederick's close relations with France and by the conclusion of a Franco-German treaty of friendship in 1187, gave Henry the Lion his backing and sought to nullify the effects of the Franco-German entente by interference in imperial affairs. Richard I's quarrel with Leopold of Austria at Acre in 1191 was not a gratuitous insult but an expression of the English king's hostility to an enemy of Henry the Lion.   More important was his interference in Sicily when, after the death of William II in 1189, he gave his support to the Sicilian claimant, Tancred, with whom he signed a treaty directed against the German king; for the papacy also in all probability encouraged Tancred, at least secretly. Thus, when Henry VI succeeded to the throne after Frederick's death in 1190, he was faced by all the elements of a major hostile coalition, implicating the papacy and reaching from Sicily to England, and the whole future of Barbarossa's work depended on his character and abilities and policy.

Few reigns have given rise to such diverse judgements as that of Henry VI.[1] His exploits and successes stirred the imaginations of contemporaries and created a lasting impression of power and purpose. The conquest of Sicily in 1194, the subsequent preparations for an attack on the Byzantine Empire, the dispatch of a crusading army to Palestine, the homage of Richard of England and of the kings of Cyprus and Armenia, all contributed to his renown. He was credited with the project of subjecting France to imperial overlordship, and when he died in 1197 many believed that he was on the point of establishing a universal dominion, such as men had

[1] For what follows cf. J. Haller, 'Heinrich VI. u. die römische Kirche', *Mitteil. d. österr. Inst. f. Geschichtsforschung,* XXXV (1914); id., 'Kaiser Heinrich VI', *Hist. Zeitschr.,* CXIII (1914); W. Cohn, *Das Zeitalter der Hohenstaufen in Sizilien* (1925); E. Perels, *Der Erbreichsplan Heinrichs VI* (1927); V. Pfaff, *Kaiser Heinrichs VI höchstes Angebot an die römische Kurie* (1927); E. Jordan, 'Henri VI a-t-il offert à Célestin III de lui faire hommage pour l'Empire', *Mélanges Lot* (1925); A. Cartellieri, *Heinrich VI u. der Höhepunkt der staufischen Kaiserpolitik* (1914); W. Norden, *Das Papsttum u. Byzanz* (1903), 114-133; W. Kienast, *Die deutschen Fürsten im Dienste der Westmächte* I (1924), 131-153.

dreamt of since the decline of Rome.[1] More than one modern
historian has shared this view, maintaining that Henry VI died with
the world at his feet, and that only a malignant fate, cutting short
his life at the age of thirty-two and leaving as his heir a mere child
less than three years old, prevented the completion of the work of
Frederick I, the stabilization of German government and the
establishment of a universal dominion in German hands.[2] Others
have taken a more sober view, pointing out that his policy exhausted
'the energies and political capital stored up by Barbarossa', and
maintaining that 'he was lucky to die young, before being overtaken
by the catastrophe which could scarcely have failed to strike at the
roots of the artificial, violent and detested régime which he
founded'.[3]

That Henry VI exhausted the political capital stored up by
Barbarossa is the gravamen of the charge against him. Those
historians who have seen in his ambitious schemes a plan to complete the work of his father have misunderstood the scope of
Barbarossa's policy and, indeed, the scope and objects of German
imperialism in the middle ages. Had that imperialism been in fact
an attempt to restore universal dominion on the pattern of ancient
Rome, then Henry VI might in truth be called its greatest protagonist; but such a conception of the nature of the mediaeval empire
overlooks the distinction between the theories and the ideals of a
universal Christian monarchy, propagated by philosophers and
churchmen, and the motives and actions of statesmen. None of the
German emperors from Otto the Great onwards, not even Otto III,
had turned aside from the interests of the constituent kingdoms of
the empire to pursue the chimerical aim of world-dominion; and in
this respect, Barbarossa's reign brought no change. *Renovatio
imperii* meant for him restoration of imperial authority in Germany,
Burgundy and Italy, and although his methods were new, his aims
were old. But the accession of Henry VI soon led to a break with the

[1] Otto of St. Blasien, *Chron.* (ed. Hofmeister), c. 45: 'Cuius mors genti Teutonicorum
omnibusque Germaniae populis lamentabilis sit in aeternum, quia aliarum terrarum divitiis
eos claros reddidit, terroremque eorum omnibus in circuitu nationibus per virtutem bellicam
incussit, eosque praestantiores aliis gentibus nimirum ostendit futuros, nisi morte praeventus
fuisset, cuius virtute et industria decus imperii in antiquae dignitatis statum refloruisset.'

[2] Thus A. L. Poole, *Cambr. Med. Hist.*, V (1929), 479: 'under him the idea of a universal
Empire, of world-domination, came nearest to realization during the Middle Ages'. Cf. also
Kienast, *Hist. Zeitschr.*, CLIII (1936), 232, and Haller, ibid., CXIII (1914), 494.

[3] C. W. Previté-Orton, *Outlines of Mediaeval History* (1929), 256; E. Jordan, *L'Allemagne et
l'Italie aux XIIe et XIIIe siècles* (1939), 150.

THE RISE AND FALL OF THE HOHENSTAUFEN EMPIRE 197

old conservative tradition. In Italy, where he had ruled since 1186, when he was crowned king at Milan, and in his relations with the church, Henry adhered to the lines of policy laid down at the time of the Peace of Constance; and in this respect his succession in 1190 marked no breach of continuity. But in other directions he pursued a policy different from anything Barbarossa had envisaged. In the affairs of western Europe he rejected Frederick's cautious attitude and sought to make capital out of the conflict between England and France.[1] But it was Henry's claim as husband of Constance to succeed to the Sicilian throne on the death of William II in 1189 that introduced a fundamental change in imperial policy. With Sicily Henry inherited the ambition of the Normans to dominion in the Mediterranean and the perennial hostility of the Normans towards Byzantium; it was his attempt to carry on Norman traditions which diverted imperial policy from its established paths. For this reason Ficker was assuredly right when, with unerring judgement, he singled out the connection of Germany and Sicily, the *unio regni ad imperium*, as the cause of the aberrations in imperial policy which prevented the consummation of Barbarossa's plans for imperial government.[2] The union of Sicily and the Empire, and the ensuing complications, introduced a strain, both internal and external, which the new structure of imperial government could not stand. From 1190 for sixty momentous years the attempt to incorporate Sicily into the Empire absorbed imperial energies, diverting attention increasingly from Germany, leading to ever new entanglements, until in the end it pulled down the structure Barbarossa had raised, destroyed the Hohenstaufen dynasty and enduringly crippled German government; from the strain of these years Germany never recovered.

The death of William II of Sicily without heirs of his body, in 1189, certainly opened up alluring prospects. The union of Sicily and the Empire meant an end of the Sicilian support for internal opponents of imperial policy which had thwarted imperial plans at

---

[1] The contrast between Henry's western policy and that of his father was evident already in 1185-1186, when the former attempted to support Flanders against France, but was checked by Frederick, who clung to his alliance with the Capetians. Cartellieri has suggested that Henry, 'the representative of the younger generation, who more clearly appreciated the situation and was intent on checking the rise of French power before it was too late', was right; but cf. Kienast, *Die deutschen Fürsten*, I, 119.

[2] Ficker, *Das deutsche Kaiserreich*, 117; cf. Kap-herr, 'Die unio regni ad imperium. Ein Beitrag zur Geschichte der staufischen Politik', *Deutsche Zeitschr. f. Geschichtswissenschaft*, I (1889).

o

many a critical juncture since the first alliance of the Normans and the papacy in 1059. Furthermore, it constituted an important new source of revenue exceeding even what Barbarossa had thought to obtain from Italy. Hence it is not surprising that Henry grasped the opportunity which William II's death presented. What is surprising is the lack of circumspection with which he asserted his claims. It will always remain an open question whether by a careful, measured policy Sicily could have been successfully absorbed into the Empire; but Henry VI's policy was not measured. On the contrary, it was marked by a restless activity and a rigorous logic which, in strong contrast to Barbarossa, closed all doors on compromise and led as though of necessity to acute crisis. This was a point in history where the personal character of the ruler could not fail to influence the course of events; and it was Henry's misfortune that he was incapable of resisting the allurements which Sicily held out, in particular the incitement to grandiose projects in the Mediterranean.[1] Moreover, it was characteristic of Henry's temperament that, unlike his Norman predecessors, he refused 'on account of the dignity of the empire' to do homage for Sicily to the pope. Thus on every side he went beyond precedent, exalting his imperial claims by reference to Sicily and supporting his Sicilian position by reference to the Empire, with the result that he forced the pope and the eastern emperor into at least tacit alliance and provoked acute papal suspicion of his designs in Italy and Germany. Through his forceful unconciliatory policy the prospect of durable agreement between church and state, which was an essential precondition of the stabilization of the work of Barbarossa, was destroyed: the papacy, which under Lucius III (1181-1185), Gregory VIII (1187) and Clement III (1187-1191) had been prepared to seek a working agreement, became under Celestine III (1191-1198) alive to its perils and began again to seek out allies in Sicily and Italy and Germany.

There is no doubt that Henry showed considerable tactical skill in dealing with this threatening situation, which was aggravated by unrest in Germany where Henry's attempt in 1191 to absorb

[1] It has been held that Henry VI's eastern policy was undertaken with a view to securing papal approbation and therewith papal support for his plans in Germany and Italy; but Perels and others have fully demonstrated the weakness of this argument. Rather it was a gratuitous and injudicious continuation of Norman policy, contrasting markedly with Barbarossa's scrupulous endeavours, when he went on crusade in 1189, to avoid provoking Byzantium; cf. Norden, op. cit., 118-120.

Thuringia into the royal demesne, after the death without direct heirs of the landgrave, quickly showed that the princes were prepared to go to extreme lengths in defence of the concessions wrested from the crown in 1180. In these circumstances he was fortunate in the capture of Richard I of England, who fell into the hands of duke Leopold of Austria in 1192 on his way back from the orient, and was handed over by Leopold to Henry. Here what counted was less the fact that Richard agreed to hold England as an imperial fief — a fact which has sometimes received undue prominence[1] — than the possibility of using Richard's influence to break up the hostile party in Germany, which looked to England for leadership, and of securing funds for the conquest of Sicily, which was financed largely from Richard's ransom. In both these respects Henry made the most of his opportunity, at last securing through Richard's mediation a settlement with the Welfs. But he showed his true character when, instead of resting content with the improvement in his position which ensued, he sought immediately to turn his new relations with Richard into a hostile alliance against France. Thus once again he involved himself in needless complications at the very moment when a slackening of tension was requisite in order to organize his government in Sicily. Already at this early date, moreover, the incompatibility of many of his aims and projects was apparent. The Sicilian undertaking was dependent on German support, and as early as 1190 his need to free his hands for the conquest of Sicily had compelled him to make concessions to Henry the Lion and the Welfs. The same motive, also, lay behind his renunciation of his project of taking over Thuringia; by conferring it instead on the brother of the late landgrave he created another dangerous precedent for the succession of collateral heirs. Equally significant was his decision in 1192 to confer Styria on duke Leopold of Austria, for this cumulation of duchies in the hands of a single prince implied a reversal of one of the main features of Frederick I's territorial settlement of 1180. If, however, Henry's Sicilian policy necessitated serious concessions in Germany, in Italy

---

[1] Taking all in all, the homage was probably more important to Richard than to Henry. In 1192, on the news of Richard's capture, John had immediately done homage to Philip Augustus, for England as well as for his continental lands, and John and Philip, in alliance with the Danes, had prepared an invasion of England for 1193. Richard's homage to Henry VI was thus a counterblast to John's homage to Philip Augustus; therein lay its political significance. Cf. Kienast, op. cit., I, 136.

it placed new difficulties in the way of a settlement with the pope. Without doubt Henry realized, like Frederick Barbarossa before him, the imperative need for such a settlement; but every step he took rendered a settlement less easy. Unable to perceive the wisdom of proceeding step by step and consolidating his position little by little, Henry conjured up an opposition which brought all his plans to nothing.

II

It was in 1195 that the critical turning-point arrived. By this time not only was Sicily occupied and brought under control, but also north and north-western Germany, which in 1192 and 1193 had been in almost open rebellion, were pacified. The year 1194 thus ended the first period of the reign, and another obstacle was removed by the death of Henry the Lion in 1195. Already, moreover, the emperor had turned to plans for conquest in the Near East and by 1195 was preparing for a crusade. Hence the moment had evidently come to consolidate his successes to date and to prepare for a lengthy absence from his lands. Could he so arrange government in Germany and Italy that he could safely leave Europe, in the knowledge that his dynasty was secure against conspiracy and revolt? Could he obtain loyal co-operation from the German princes, who as recently as 1193 had shown strong tendencies to resist his designs? Could he, above all else, solve outstanding questions with the papacy and secure a final peace with the church?

Such were the questions facing Henry at the end of 1195, and it is characteristic of the man that — after a first unsuccessful attempt in 1195 to get his two-year-old son elected king in the normal way — he boldly sought a radical solution. No single measure offered greater prospects than the final establishment of hereditary monarchy on the pattern of England and France, and it was through the acceptance of this fundamental reform that Henry sought both to overcome the immediate problems confronting him and to secure the requisite stability and continuity in imperial government. There is no doubt that, in envisaging this change, Henry unerringly picked out the most glaring weakness in his position and that of his dynasty. It was the irregularity of succession after the Investiture Contest, as contrasted with the strength of the hereditary principle before 1077, which had placed the monarchy at the mercy of whatever momentary political combinations happened to dominate on occasions when a new king was elected; and it is clear that Barbarossa had fully realized the necessity for re-affirming the principle of heredity. After 1194, however, the acquisition of Sicily made the question still more urgent. Henry claimed Sicily in virtue of his wife's hereditary right, and intended that it should pass by hereditary right to his son Frederick, born in 1194. Was the Hohenstaufen right of succession to the Empire, on the other hand, to be dependent on the election and assent of the princes? Were the latter to have, in theory at least, the power of electing another dynasty, and thus bringing about a separation between the imperial lands and Sicily? If the *unio regni ad imperium* were to be permanent, if Sicily were henceforth to be an integral part of the Empire, an abrogation of the electoral rights of the princes was essential and at the same time a regulation of the pope's rights and functions in imperial coronation.

In 1196, therefore, Henry began negotiations with the princes, and at Würzburg on March 31st secured the assent of fifty-two princes present to the principle of hereditary succession. But even here the contrast with the monarchies of the west is evident. What the Capetians and Plantagenets were able to enforce by steady insistence, from generation to generation, on ancient traditions, Henry was forced to buy by concessions. To the princes he offered full hereditary rights in their fiefs, extending to female and collateral heirs; to the prelates he offered the equivalent concession of testamentary disposition over their movable property.[1] But even these considerable concessions failed to secure the agreement of all parties, partly no doubt because a number of princes, including the duke of Austria and the margrave of Namur, had already secured hereditary rights by special privilege. Consequently opposition quickly came to a head; and a leader was found in the archbishop of Cologne, whose

[1] The exact parallel between what Henry asked and what he conceded, is noteworthy. In fact, it appears that the princes had in 1195 countered Henry's request for the election of his son Frederick, by making it dependent on the concession, on his part, of hereditary succession in their fiefs, and that it was because of Henry's refusal of this concession that negotiations broke down. Earlier in the year, he had taken Meissen (the margrave of which had died without direct heirs) into the direct administration of the crown, and his earlier desire to do the same in Thuringia (1191) was well known. The princes' demand for hereditary succession was thus part of a plan of resistance to Henry's centralizing policy. But he sought to turn the tables, and strike a bargain, by countering their demand with an equivalent demand of his own — 'ad suum refundens commodum', says Gervase of Tilbury, 'quod aliis impertitus est beneficium'.

preponderating influence, derived from his ancient right of crowning the elected king of Germany (and therewith of refusing coronation), was particularly threatened by Henry's project. But Henry's plans allowed for this contingency, and without attempting to overcome the German opposition, he left for Italy in the summer of 1196 to put the second phase of his project into effect. His object now was to gain papal support and co-operation, and thus to circumvent the opposition in Germany. In view of his forthcoming crusade, preparations for which were by this time advanced, he could with justice insist that further postponement of a settlement with the church was no longer opportune; he could also, in view of the perils of his undertaking, reasonably demand — Conrad III had obtained as much in 1147 prior to the second crusade — the coronation of his son. For his part, renewing and carrying further proposals which had formed the basis of negotiations between Frederick I and Lucius III, he offered the papacy a fixed and regular income from the churches of the empire in lieu of the disputed territories in central Italy to which the pope still laid claim.[1] In return Celestine was to baptize and crown the young Frederick, passing over the vested rights of the archbishop of Cologne. Papal co-operation, circumventing the opposition of the electoral princes of Germany, was thus the key to the whole project of hereditary monarchy.

But papal co-operation was not forthcoming. As long as Henry remained in the vicinity of Rome Celestine procrastinated with complaints and counter-claims. In view of the serious financial embarrassments of the papacy at this time, Henry's proposals were not unattractive; but they would clearly have meant an end of the temporal power of the papacy and a strict concentration on its spiritual headship. Even this was not impossible in the mood of the moment, which was seriously perturbed by the growth of heresy and the dangers to Christendom in the east. But Henry chose this very moment to create for his lieutenant, Markward of Anweiler, a great provincial administration, reaching along the Adriatic coast from Ravenna through Ancona to the Abruzzi; and although his object was probably only to safeguard communications between Sicily and the north, his action revealed graphically the dangers of encirclement facing the papacy in Rome. It has been argued with

---

[1] Haller's thesis, that Henry offered to become the pope's vassal and to hold the Empire as a papal fief, may be ignored; it is not plausible and has been rejected by all authorities.

much probability that Celestine refused a settlement except on condition that Henry resigned the Sicilian crown. In any case he was aware, and in his policy of procrastination took account, of the growing opposition in Germany. In October, 1196, the proposal for setting the German kingship on an hereditary basis was again before the princes, and this time it met determined opposition from a powerful group under the leadership of the landgrave of Thuringia, which used a new weapon in the form of opposition to the crusade. In the following month the pope negatived Henry's proposals. Thus all his plans seemed to be crumbling, and it only remained to save what he could. Withdrawing the plan of hereditary monarchy, he concentrated instead on bringing the preparations for the crusade to completion; and by his withdrawal he secured his immediate point. Not only did he obtain a united front for the crusade, but the princes, in return for his concession, agreed to the election of his son, Frederick, to the kingship, which actually took place at Christmas, 1196.

If the election of Frederick was far from the solution to which Henry had aspired, it was a partial success which provided a sufficient guarantee of continuity for the immediate future. Nevertheless the resistance of the German princes to his attempts to strengthen and stabilize the position of the monarchy was ominous, revealing how deeply embedded, even at this late date, were their rights. Ominous also was the formation of links between the German opposition and the papacy. But the widespread nature of the discontent only became evident in the spring of 1197 when revolt broke out in Sicily. This insurrection had local causes; but it was believed with some reason that the pope was implicated, and the insurgents had apparently also entered into relations with the Lombards and the Romans. Forewarned, Henry put down the revolt with un-exampled cruelty, influenced in all probability by the fact that his position, far away from his base, was dangerously insecure. But he was not vouchsafed the opportunity to exploit his success. Already in August he lay sick in Messina: on September 28th, 1197, death supervened. His reign had added Sicily to the lands over which the Hohenstaufen ruled; but it had also added complications unknown in the past, and it had still to be seen whether the new acquisition was a source of strength or a liability. On the other hand, he had made no contribution, for all his restless activity, to the chief problems which confronted him when he took over in 1190: a settlement with the papacy was still outstanding and there had been no progress towards defining the relations between the monarchy and the German princes. In both these respects deterioration rather than progress was the mark of Henry VI's reign.

Henry VI himself, on his deathbed, proved that he was fully conscious of the instability of his life's work. In his famous 'testament', never put into effect, he stipulated that Constance and Frederick, his heir, should do homage to the pope for Sicily, as earlier rulers of Sicily had done homage. Furthermore, Frederick was to obtain the pope's confirmation of the rights in the Empire which he had obtained as a result of his election in 1196. In return imperial forces were to evacuate the papal states, the Matildine lands were to be restored to the church, and papal suzerainty over the duchy of Ravenna and the march of Ancona was to be recognized. It is a cruel comment on Henry's statesmanship that, at any moment during his lifetime, he could have secured peace with the Roman curia on terms less rigorous than he was prepared to grant in his testament; and with peace would have come the opportunity to enforce a settlement with the German princes. But in 1198 it was too late. Henry had revealed his plans openly, and the papacy took heed; by grasping after too much he had thrown away his opportunities. Already under Celestine III the papacy saw its chance to recover what it had lost; but it was after the death of Celestine on January 8th, 1198, and the election of Innocent III that the reaction gathered speed. The new pope was the man to make the most of his opportunities; but it was Henry VI's failure to make the right concessions at the right time which ushered in the nemesis of 1198-1215. The responsibility for the catastrophe which followed Henry VI's premature death cannot be thrown on to a blind, malignant fate: it rests on Henry's own shoulders.

III

That Henry VI's death in 1197, leaving as heir a three-year-old child, ushered in a period of darkest crisis, was immediately manifest. Throughout Italy, from Sicily through Tuscany to Lombardy, a violent reaction broke out. In Sicily the empress Constance herself joined forces with the rebels, retaining her infant son, Frederick, with her until her death in 1198, when (theoretically under the pope's tutelage) he passed into the hands of one Sicilian faction after another. The situation in Germany, on the other hand, contrasted markedly with the collapse and anarchy in Sicily and Italy. No feature of the crisis was more remarkable than the initial unity of the German people in the face of the disaster which had overtaken them, their loyalty to the Hohenstaufen dynasty and its ideals, and their realization of the need for a common effort to uphold the proud structure which Barbarossa had built. It is this sense of responsibility, contrasting profoundly with the attitude of the princes in earlier generations, which is the outstanding fact in the first phase of the crisis of 1198. Many of the greatest princes were away in the east on crusade when the news of Henry's death was received; and the first act of the crusading army was to confirm the election of Frederick II carried out in 1196. In Sicily, Henry VI's great lieutenant, Markward of Anweiler, struggled manfully until his death in 1202 to maintain German rule, ultimately securing Sicilian support against the French adventurers whom the pope did not scruple to call in. Nearer home Henry's brother, Philip of Swabia, hurried from Tuscany back to Germany to rally forces on Frederick's behalf. His loyalty to the cause of his infant nephew was absolute, and he soon persuaded the leading princes, headed by the dukes of Bavaria and Saxony, to elect him 'guardian of the empire' until Frederick could be brought back to Germany.[1] Thus the hereditary rights of the Hohenstaufen dynasty, which the princes had rejected in theory in 1196, were approved in practice in 1198. It is, indeed, true that the old opposition to Henry VI, headed by the archbishop of Cologne, had immediately disavowed the earlier election of Frederick and initiated intrigues for the election of a new king; but their efforts were without success and their candidate, Bertold of Zähringen, withdrew. Instead, all the leading princes, from Saxony in the north to Styria and Carinthia in the south, urged Philip of Swabia to 'labour for the empire', and fearing the dangers of a long minority rule begged him to set aside all scruples and accept candi-

---

[1] Otto of St. Blasien, *Chronicon*, c. 46: 'Philippus ... satagebat omnimodis ut principes electionem, quam circa filium imperatoris fecerant, ratam haberent. Orientales itaque principes ... diem colloquii ... praefixerunt, quo veniente Philippo duce ... ipsum in defensorem imperii eligere decreverunt, quoad usque nepos suus, imperatoris filius, dudum electus, in Alamanniam deveniret.'

dature for the throne.[1] After long hesitation and a sincere effort to maintain Frederick's rights unimpaired, Philip gave way before their representations and was finally crowned at Mainz on September 8th, 1198. As the chronicler Arnold of Lübeck wrote, 'the whole strength of the empire adhered to Philip'.

For a moment, therefore, it appeared that Germany had surmounted the crisis unleashed by Henry VI's premature death; and there is no doubt that the responsible attitude adopted by the majority of the princes in 1198 was a tribute to the strength of Barbarossa's work and to the new sense of political maturity which it had engendered. If left to itself, there is every indication that Germany would have emerged unharmed from the test. But Germany was not left to itself to settle its own affairs. At the critical moment two outside factors, the one representing the culmination of old discords, the other the dawn of new complications, intervened with deadly effect. The first was the papacy, avidly desirous of regaining all the political power it had lost since the restoration of imperial authority after 1152; the second was the pressure of England and France, both anxious to foment dissension within Germany and to exploit it to their own advantage. It was the interplay of these factors, deliberately evoking the most retrograde and egotistic elements in German life, which destroyed the promise of a healthy outcome and threw Germany into a state of anarchy comparable to the worst phases of the Investiture Contest.

With the accession of Innocent III to the papal throne in 1198, it was immediately clear how unwise was the failure of Henry VI to grasp the opportunity of conciliation and a final settlement with the church, which had never been beyond the bounds of possibility since the death of Alexander III in 1181. The reaction after Alexander's death against a political papacy had been real and had offered real prospects of settlement; but the reaction in 1198 with the accession of a young, energetic, politically-minded pope was to the other extreme. There is no doubt that Innocent III's main object was to restore the temporal power of the papacy, assailed ever since Frederick Barbarossa had embarked on a policy of territorial reconstruction in central Italy after the peace of Con-

[1] There is a remarkably impressive and sincere narrative of the course of events, issued by Philip in 1206, in the *Registrum super negotio imperii*, no. 136; this includes the princes' request to Philip 'ut nos laborare vellemus pro imperio' — a statement characteristic of the high sense of duty and responsibility inspiring the Hohenstaufen cause.

stance, and doubly threatened since the consummation of the union of Sicily with the Empire. Hence from beginning to end, despite all pretence of standing above parties, and despite also the tergiversations forced on him by events, he was an unbending opponent of the Hohenstaufen dynasty, determined to destroy for all time the connection of Sicily and the Empire and the position in central Italy, for which the Hohenstaufen stood, at no matter what cost to Germany.[1] Two little-noted facts illustrate his ruthless determination. The one was the severe rebuke issued in 1200 to the great German patriot, archbishop Conrad of Mainz — once the staunchest supporter of Alexander III, now (in the twilight of his life) the altruistic sponsor of peace in Germany — because his attempts to reconcile the German factions threatened to create a common German front and thus to deprive the pope of the influence which German divisions gave him in imperial affairs.[2] The other, in the same year, was the instructions issued to the papal legate in the west, authorizing him to annul the peace concluded between England and France, because the withdrawal of English and French support from the contending parties was likely to put an end to German discords and leave the Hohenstaufen in control of a united people who would not brook papal interference.[3] To get his way, in short, to enforce his own conception of the relations of church and state, Innocent was prepared not only to destroy the internal peace of Germany, but also to set the states of Europe at war with one another. Against these facts it matters little that he protested — too often, perhaps, and too vehemently — that he had imperial interests at heart and had no intention of oppressing or destroying the empire.[4] His protests were doubtless sincere; but when he spoke of the empire, he meant an empire of his own conception and not the historical Empire which had been raised from the dust of the Investiture Contest by the genius of the Hohenstaufen. His praise of Lothar II,

---

[1] Innocent's policy towards Germany is laid bare in the famous *Registrum super negotio imperii* (ed. Baluze, 1682, reprinted in Migne, *Patr. latina*, CCXVI, publ. in facsimile by Peitz, 1927, German trans. by G. Tangl, 1923). For a sober judgement of Innocent's character and policy cf. E. Jordan, *L'Allemagne et l'Italie aux XIIe et XIIIe siècles*, 170, 183, 185.

[2] *Reg. sup. neg. imp.*, no. 22.

[3] Ibid., no. 25. Kienast, op. cit., 157, has failed to see that the pope, who in the previous year had been working for peace between England and France (*Epist.*, I, 355), abruptly reversed his policy when the furtherance of his interests in the Empire required it.

[4] *Reg. sup. neg. imp.*, no. 2: 'non, ut quidam pestilentes homines mentiuntur, ad imperii destructionem vel depressionem intendimus, sed ad conservationem et exaltationem ipsius potius aspiramus'; cf. also ibid., nos. 1, 15, 21.

the church's nominee, revealed the direction of his thoughts, which led back directly to the ideas of Gregory VII: an emperor selected by the free choice of the princes but unqualified to rule until, after due examination at the Holy See, he had secured the approval and confirmation of the pope.[1] Innocent's claims were, therefore, not new — new only was the rigorous logic with which he argued that the disposal of the German throne was *principaliter et finaliter* a prerogative of the Holy See — but they were claims which, after the revival of the principles of hereditary monarchy in the twelfth century, not one of the peoples of western Europe would willingly accept, and least of all the successors of Frederick Barbarossa. The clash of principles and ideas is nowhere more clearly revealed than in the letter, firm in tone and worthy in content, which Philip of Swabia's adherents dispatched to the pope from Speyer on May 28th, 1199.[2] Instead of asking for papal confirmation of Philip's election, they simply notified the pope in dignified words of the facts, announced that their election itself constituted an indefeasible right to the imperial throne, and, warning Innocent to attempt nothing against the honour of the empire, informed him that they would appear shortly in Rome to complete the formality of coronation. Here in the declaration of Speyer the age-old conception of the Empire, revived by Barbarossa, found its ultimate expression against the novel pretensions of the papacy: 'he who is chosen by the election of the princes alone is the true emperor, even before he has been confirmed by the pope'.[3]

Against this strengthened consciousness of an independent empire, backed in the manifesto by the signatures of the most notable princes in Germany, Innocent would have had little prospect of success, had it not been for the intervention of the western powers, of France and England. It was to England that the faction of German princes around the archbishop of Cologne turned when it became evident that they had no hope of raising an anti-Hohenstaufen candidate in Germany; and Richard I, who as early as 1194 had offered annual subsidies to all the important princes of north-west

---

[1] Cf. above, p. 115.
[2] *Reg. sup. neg. imp.*, no. 14.
[3] Cf. above, p. 74. — This formulation of the imperial case is found, surprisingly, in the standard commentary on the basic summary of church law, the *Decretum* of Gratian; cf. the glosses to *Dist.* XCIII, c. 24, and *Dist.* LXIII, c. 10. In his famous decretal *Venerabilem* (c. 34, X 1, 6) Innocent was therefore consciously reversing the common opinion of the church.

Germany for their support against France, grasped the opportunity of establishing an anti-French dynasty on the German throne. It was Richard's support alone, in particular his financial support, which was expended on a prodigious scale, that enabled the pitifully weak anti-Hohenstaufen party in Germany to embark on the struggle. They took up arms as clients of England. Their candidate was Richard's nephew, Otto, the youngest son of Henry the Lion. But in spite of the German blood in his veins, Otto had never seen the land of his fathers: he was a foreigner, born in Normandy, brought up at the Plantagenet court, created earl of York in 1190 and count of Poitou in 1196. Described by a chronicler as 'proud and stupid', he had scant respect for German interests and was a willing tool of his uncle on whose favour he depended; interested only in recovering the position his father had forfeited, he capitulated to Innocent, recognizing the 'recuperations' of the papacy in central Italy and promising obedience and honour to the pope.[1] Deliberately surrendering the independence of the empire and according full recognition to the electoral claims of the princes, he humbly requested Innocent to confirm his election and 'summon' him to Rome for coronation. Without scruple or principle, for the sake of papal support, he accepted the full implications of Innocent's papalist theories, hitherto resisted with unparalleled firmness — theories which made change of dynasty a principle of the constitution and foreshadowed the entire fate of Germany: to degenerate into a divided electoral state, instead of securing, like the monarchies of the west, the lasting benefits of a kingship stabilized in one dynasty.

The appearance on the German scene of Otto of Brunswick, who was crowned by his adherents at Aachen on July 12th, 1198, had other equally disastrous results. If the English king hoped, by supporting the Welf party, to win German support for a war on France, the French king was not slow in replying by according his support to his old allies, the Hohenstaufen. Thus each of the western powers vied with the other in buying support in Germany, both

---

[1] Cf. the notorious capitulation of Neuss (June 8th, 1201), *Reg. sup. neg. imp.*, no. 77. The exculpatory arguments of Haller, 'Innocenz III u. Otto IV', *Papsttum u. Kaisertum* (1926), are unconvincing. From the very first Otto and his supporters, including the king of England and the archbishop of Cologne, adopted an abject attitude towards the pope, in marked contrast to the dignified bearing of the Hohenstaufen; and their attitude became more and more abject as, after the death of Richard, the hopelessness of Otto's position became manifest; cf. *Reg. sup. neg. imp.*, nos. 3, 4, 5, 9, 19, 20.

fearing an overwhelming hostile coalition; and their efforts inaugurated the long and sordid struggle between the pound sterling
and the *livre tournois* which soon dominated German politics,
demoralizing the princes and turning them into mercenary pen-
sioners. French intervention also opened the door to French
expansion, which after the successful occupation of Normandy in
1202-4, turned east in search of a new outlet. Many contemporaries
believed that Philip Augustus aspired to wrest the imperial crown
from Otto of Brunswick – thus beginning the long series of French
attempts to bring the Empire into French hands and therewith to
stake out a claim to hegemony in Europe. What is more probable is
that he had designs on Lorraine, and it is certain that the treaty of
alliance, signed on June 29th, 1198, between Philip Augustus and
Philip of Swabia opened the door wide to French intervention in
imperial Flanders. But it would be erroneous to ascribe aggressive
intentions to Philip Augustus; his policy was defensive, aimed not at
Germany, but at Otto IV, the ally of England, and in spite of easy
opportunities there was during his reign no French expansion at
German expense. Nevertheless it was the weakening of the German
monarchy between 1198 and 1215, as a result of the unscrupulous
manœuvres of Otto of Brunswick, the divisions he introduced and
above all the precedent of foreign intervention, that prepared the
way for the French expansion into the western territories of the
empire, which set in under Louis VIII (1223-1226) and reached its
logical conclusion under Philip the Fair (1285-1314). More immediate, however, were the effects on the northern and eastern
frontiers. In the east, Ottokar of Bohemia, as the price of his support,
obtained from Philip the erection of his duchy into a kingdom, and
at the same time reduced Moravia to dependence.[1] In the north
Otto encouraged his Danish allies, Canute VI and Waldemar, to
attack and conquer Holstein, the land of his father's old adversary,
Adolf of Schauenburg, and to annex Nordalbingia and the important city of Lübeck. The struggle for the throne, fostered by
England and in a lesser degree by France, besides inaugurating a
new phase of chaos and retrogression within, thus weakened
Germany on all its frontiers.

[1] This implied the destruction in Bohemia of the work of Frederick Barbarossa, who – as
part of his policy of dividing the great duchies and constituting counter-balancing blocs (cf.
above p. 189) – had in 1182 separated Moravia from Bohemia and made it (on a par with
Bohemia itself) a fief held directly of the emperor; cf. Jordan, op. cit., 135, 186.

The civil wars, which began with the active support of Otto of Brunswick by Richard of England, persisted until the antagonism between England and France was halted by the overwhelming French victory in 1214 at the battle of Bouvines. Only a brief summary of events in Germany between July 12th, 1198, when Otto was crowned at Aachen, and 1214 is necessary, for at almost every turn it was the course of events in the west which dominated German affairs. With English support the Welf faction had some prospect of making headway; but with the death of Richard and the accession of John in 1199 English policy began to vacillate, and the loss of Normandy and the visible crumbling of English power in 1203 and 1204 sealed Otto's fate. In 1204 the dissident princes, headed by Otto's own brother and by the archbishop of Cologne, did homage to Philip; in 1206 the city of Cologne, the last bulwark of Otto's power, yielded and Otto himself withdrew to England. Innocent III, whose recognition of Otto in 1201 had failed to influence the course of events, was forced to seek an understanding with Philip, and a settlement between the two, under discussion since 1206, was within sight when, on June 21st, 1208, for reasons unconnected with the political situation Philip was assassinated. It was a cruel blow to German hopes; and yet once again when Germany was faced with a crisis as the result of the sudden death of the ruler, the course of events proved that it was not the proverbial self-interest and divisions among the princes which undermined the monarchy. Earlier during the Investiture Contest, and later after the extinction of the Hohenstaufen dynasty, these factors were important; but in 1208, as in 1197, the tradition of unity created by Frederick Barbarossa held firm. The attempt of Philip Augustus to perpetuate the civil war by putting forward the duke of Brabant as a candidate met no response; instead the princes unanimously re-elected Otto of Brunswick, who reconciled his earlier opponents by marrying Philip's daughter, and had no difficulty in securing general recognition. Innocent also gladly gave his approbation: in his negotiations with Philip he had been forced to renounce his claims to the provinces of Tuscany and Ancona and Spoleto, but Otto, renewing his promises of 1201, not only granted new and extensive liberties to the German church but also again conceded the disputed Italian provinces to the papacy.

But the peace was of short duration. Whether Otto ever intended to keep his promises to the church, will never be known. In form, at least, both his charter of 1201 and that of 1209 had manifest defects – in particular the omission of the consent of the princes, whose approbation was necessary for any alienation of imperial rights – and it is possible that these omissions were deliberately calculated in order to provide an excuse for non-fulfilment. Possibly also Otto was influenced by the patriarch Wolfger of Aquileia, who had been the leading figure in the negotiations between Philip of Swabia and the pope, and who now brought all his influence to bear on the new king to secure continuity of policy and the maintenance of Hohenstaufen traditions. More generally, it may be assumed that Otto, no longer the nominee of a faction but the duly elected and universally recognized German king, was forced, if he wished to maintain the support of all parties, to pursue a German policy. Whatever the reason, his arrival in Italy in 1109 saw a brusque change of attitude, an immediate and successful return to the territorial policy of Frederick I and Henry VI, which is of interest as showing how remote from the truth is the old contention that the Welfs, in their feud with the Hohenstaufen, were the figureheads of German opposition to the Italian 'entanglement'. When Otto IV went to Italy, he went as the exponent of Hohenstaufen imperial traditions. He offered to discuss with Innocent the question of the Matildine lands; but there was no question of the restitution of Ancona and Spoleto. Nevertheless Innocent, bending to necessity, crowned him Emperor on October 4th, 1209; but when Otto went on to plan the reconquest of Sicily, thus conjuring up again the prospect of an encirclement of Rome, the breach came. Innocent had threatened excommunication since February, 1210: on November 18th, when Otto had invaded Apulia and Calabria and was on the point of crossing over into the island of Sicily, the solemn sentence of excommunication was pronounced.

The breach with Otto was not entered into light-heartedly by the pope. Only by the election of an anti-king could Otto be effectively opposed, and there was only one candidate likely to win sufficient support: Frederick of Sicily, the son of Henry VI. But with the return of a Hohenstaufen to the German throne, the danger of a permanent union of Sicily and the Empire would again loom large; hence, no doubt, Innocent's long delay before finally excommunicating Otto. Probably it was Philip Augustus of France who won over the pope to agree to the candidature of Frederick. The death of Philip of Swabia in 1208 had been a serious blow to French policy, threatening an immediate combined Anglo-German attack on France; but Otto IV's decision in 1209 to restore his position in Italy afforded Philip Augustus an unexpected respite. Nevertheless it was clear that an attack on France was to be expected once Otto had completed the conquest of Sicily and already John of England was building up the necessary connections among the princes of the Netherlands. Hence Philip Augustus, at the end of 1210, immediately set to work to reconstitute, on Frederick's behalf, the Hohenstaufen party in Germany. This proved easier than might have been expected, because the ecclesiastical princes in particular, appalled at the prospect of a renewal of strife between the empire and the papacy, were alienated by Otto's attack on Sicily. When Frederick appeared in Germany in September, 1212, he immediately secured the adhesion of the Swabians and his party was rapidly rebuilt, though only by means of wholesale concessions to the princes and through the financial support of Philip Augustus who, renewing the old treaty of friendship on November 18th, 1212, at the same time lent Frederick 20,000 *l.* which the latter immediately employed to buy support. Soon only parts of Saxony and certain principalities on the lower Rhine whose loyalty was secured by English subsidies, remained on Otto's side. Before the end of the year Frederick, who had been elected *in imperatorem coronandus* in 1211 and re-elected at Frankfurt, was solemnly crowned *rex Romanorum*: the ceremony took place at Mainz on December 9th, 1212.

Nevertheless the decision did not depend on events in Germany. Otto's resources in Germany were small; but he still had the active support of his uncle, the king of England, and John, with the help of the counts of Flanders and Holland, planned to force a decision by a great encircling attack from the north and east and south on France. Early in 1214 he landed in Poitou, where he immediately scored notable successes, while a month later Otto began preparations in the Rhinelands, finally moving down to Valenciennes in the middle of July. But Otto's attempts to assemble an army were hampered by local discords and rivalries among the petty powers of the Netherlands, and the opportune moment for common action was lost. John, who had advanced across the Loire and taken Angers

P

on June 17th, fell back without a fight; and from that moment the plan of combined attack fell through. Without delay Philip Augustus swung his army round to the north, advanced into Flanders, and, meeting the German army at Bouvines, a hamlet between Lille and Tournai, on July 27th, 1214, inflicted a crushing defeat.

The battle of Bouvines was a turning-point not only in German but in European history. John and his allies had, it was freely reported, planned if successful to partition France; instead the Capetian monarchy was not merely saved but launched along the road leading to European hegemony. John, without thought of his allies in the Netherlands, immediately made a truce with France to last until 1220; but this move was insufficient to save him from the opposition in England which the financial measures necessary to support his policy of subsidized alliances had evoked, and in 1215 he capitulated to the barons and issued the Great Charter. For Otto also the French victory was a blow from which recovery was impossible. His last adherents in Germany came to terms with Frederick who had played no part in the decisive campaign, but who received from Philip Augustus the golden imperial eagle which Otto had left lying on the field of battle. When Otto's last remaining strong-points in the Rhinelands, Cologne and Aachen, capitulated in 1215, Frederick celebrated his victory by a renewal of his coronation in accordance with tradition in Aachen cathedral: he had ceased to be a pretendant struggling with a rival, and become the legitimate German king.

IV

After seventeen years of confusion the legitimate dynasty was once again in control in Germany. Unhappily this did not imply a return to normal; for the period between 1198 and 1215 was not simply an interregnum, which was closed when Frederick returned to the throne of his father, Henry VI. On the contrary, Germany had passed through a period of crisis. It was neither so long nor so bitter a crisis as that caused by the Investiture Contest; for unlike the Investiture Contest it was not a crisis of German seeking. Before the intervention of Richard of England and again after 1205, the country was willing to settle down peacefully under a Hohenstaufen ruler; after 1208 acceptance of Otto was general. Very different from the situation under Henry IV, there was no widespread opposition to the monarchy, and no conflict of constitutional ideas. Apart perhaps from a narrow circle round the archbishop of Cologne, which would have been impotent without English support, Otto's enunciation of electoral principles aroused no enthusiasm among the princes, who (although opposed to a strengthening of the monarchy, such as Henry VI had sought to bring about) were well-satisfied with the constitutional balance established by Frederick Barbarossa. The crisis was, therefore, one fomented from outside by the papacy and by the intrigues of the kings of France and England. But it was none the less real for that. Many of the least gratifying features of the Investiture Contest were again in evidence, in particular the dissipation of crown lands and therewith a weakening, difficult to make good, of the material basis of royal government. Inevitably, also, the situation incited the cupidity of many princes, who, demoralized (as we have seen) by offers of English and French gold, saw in the rivalries of Staufen and Welf a further opportunity for aggrandizement. Perhaps more important were the effects of the civil wars on the imperial *ministeriales*, who had been the backbone of imperial administration, in Germany and in Italy, under Frederick I and Henry VI; for their loyalty in administering the royal estates was, in the last analysis, the most effective instrument the Hohenstaufen possessed for transforming their royal position, with its roots in an Ottonian world which was dead and a feudal world which was dying, into a 'modern' kingship set above a 'modern' bureaucratic state. The murder of Philip of Swabia in 1208 left the Swabian *ministeriales*, who were the leading servants of the crown, in utter confusion with neither a master nor a directing policy to guide them; and immediately we see them pursuing their own individual interests, turning their offices into fiefs and adopting the class interests of the petty nobility.[1]

Much of the responsibility for the dissipation of the crown lands and for the failure to maintain the devotion of the imperial *ministeriales* rests upon Otto IV, who had inevitably only a limited

[1] Cf. Niese, *Verwaltung des Reichsgutes*, 197-198. Already in the letter in which Ugolino of Ostia reported the rumours of Philip's murder to the pope (*Reg. sup. neg. imp.*, no. 152), he repeats circumstantial stories of the usurpation of *regalia* by counts and burgraves.

interest in continuing the territorial policy of the Hohenstaufen in south Germany, and who in any case evinced only the slightest interest — except in Italy — in keeping alive the traditions of royal government established by Barbarossa.[1] But if Otto was, as we have seen, virtually a foreign adventurer for whom Germany was little more than a prize, the same was substantially true of Frederick II, when he first set foot in Germany in 1212. He also, like Otto, was born and bred in a foreign land under foreign influence; and like Otto he owed his following and his crown ultimately to papal support and foreign money and arms. The fact that he was a Hohenstaufen by birth did not mean an immediate return to Hohenstaufen traditions, either in internal affairs or in relations with the church. His hands were doubtless tied by his precarious beginnings; but the fact remains that no prince was more prodigal of damaging concessions than Frederick between 1212 and 1215. Apart from grants to individuals, which were issued on a lavish scale, he officially ceded Nordalbingia to Waldemar of Denmark in order to deprive Otto of Danish support, thus following exactly in Otto's footsteps. It was the same in regard to the church. To overcome Innocent III's hesitations, he renewed in 1213 Otto's promises of 1201, granting freedom of episcopal elections in Germany (and thus undermining royal control over the German church), and recognizing papal sovereignty over the lands of central Italy; but Innocent had learnt a lesson from Otto's chicanery, and this time the concessions were solemnly confirmed by the German princes, so that their authenticity was established beyond doubt. The profound contrast with Philip of Swabia, who as late as 1207 had succeeded in getting Innocent to renounce his territorial claims, reveals in all clarity the decline which had come about. Frederick acted as the spiritual heir not of his uncle, Philip, but of Otto of Brunswick; and it was evident that Philip, the loyal exponent throughout his life of the ideas of Barbarossa, carried with him into his grave the great traditions of Hohenstaufen policy.

Contemporaries were well aware of the change which had come over the Empire after Philip of Swabia's death. There was widespread resentment, reflected in the poetry of Walther von der

---

[1] In Burgundy also, unlike Philip, Otto made no attempt to maintain imperial authority; hence it was largely due to him that the Burgundian lands lost all sense of belonging to the Empire and fell increasingly under the influence of France; cf. Fournier, *Le royaume d'Arles et de Vienne*, 96–97.

Vogelweide, at the check to German unity caused by Innocent's intervention in German affairs; and Frederick II incurred some unpopularity as a puppet of papal politics. It was a more serious and more symptomatic consideration that he began his reign as a puppet of France. Philip Augustus' gesture in sending Frederick the damaged imperial insignia from the field of Bouvines was a truly symbolic act. 'From this time forward', a chronicler wrote after Bouvines, 'the fame of the Germans sank ever lower among foreigners.' The generation 1198-1215 had, in fact, witnessed a radical shift in the European balance of power to the detriment of Germany; and compared with the kings of England and France, who could already rely on ordered finances and efficient centralized institutions, the position of the German ruler was parlous. One main reason for this was that the Italian resources, particularly the financial resources, which had been an important element in Frederick Barbarossa's calculations, ceased entirely to count after the death of Henry VI. Hence the balance established by Barbarossa between the crown and the German princes again swung against the monarchy, while the ominous precedent was set for foreign powers to encourage German disunity and particularism as a means of crippling German foreign policy and preventing effective German intervention in international affairs. Politically, the decline since 1184, when Frederick Barbarossa stood at the height of his power, was indubitable; but it was not irrevocable. Certain important advantages weighed on Frederick II's side. Neither Philip Augustus nor his immediate successors, Louis VIII (1223-1226) and Louis IX (1226-1270), had any interest in weakening the position of the Hohenstaufen, the alliance with whom had, since 1187, served France well. The church, which had called Frederick to its aid against Otto of Brunswick, was not hostile to a reasonable settlement. The retrogression in Germany was of short duration; it had loosened but had not shattered the foundations of government. In short, when Frederick emerged victor in 1215 there were still infinite possibilities for a young and resourceful ruler. The achievements of Frederick Barbarossa had given a new impetus to German social development. German colonists were streaming east, new towns were springing up, chivalry was at its height, the German language was becoming the vehicle of poetry and of a common German civilization, German architecture was on the threshold of its greatest achievements at Cologne and Bamberg and

Naumburg. There was a fullness of life which demanded expression in appropriate political institutions, and which offered countless opportunities to a German king, conscious of his German heritage. Would Frederick II grasp the opportunities which lay so near at hand?

CHAPTER 9

THE REIGN OF FREDERICK II AND THE INTER-REGNUM: THE END OF THE IMPERIAL EPOCH (1215-1272)

I

FREDERICK II, a Sicilian on the German throne, let slip the opportunities which awaited a German king in 1215. His reign, often portrayed as the last great age of the German Empire,[1] was really its epilogue. Under him the contradictions and conflicts which had been felt as soon as Henry VI laid hands on Sicily in 1194, became a dominant theme. It was not that there was any opposition, either in Germany or in Italy, to imperial government as such; nor was there any glimmering, on the part of the Italians, of radical hostility to foreign rule. Frederick's problem lay rather in the conflicting requirements of the constituent kingdoms of the Empire which, heightened by rapid independent development between 1198 and 1215, had reached a point at which they could no longer be reconciled. Frederick I, in order to restore his power and authority after the Investiture Contest, had developed his Italian resources and assigned Italy an important place in his calculations; Henry VI had strained every nerve to absorb Sicily. But neither had in the process knowingly sacrificed German interests, and under Barbarossa the balance between Germany, Italy and Burgundy was firmly held. Throughout Frederick II's reign, on the other hand, Sicily and Italy came first; for the first time, and on a grand scale, the Italian elements in imperial government were developed at the expense of the German. This change of emphasis

[1] E. Kantorowicz, *Frederick the Second* (trs. E. O. Lorimer, 1931), describes Frederick (p. 3) as 'the last and greatest Christian Emperor of the German Roman Imperium'. — This well-known biography is, however, of literary interest rather than of historical merit, and should be used with caution; cf. the trenchant criticism of A. Brackmann, 'Kaiser Friedrich II in mythischer Schau', *Hist. Zeitschr.*, CXL (1929), and K. Hampe, 'Das neueste Lebensbild Kaiser Friedrichs II', ibid., CXLVI (1932). For a more sober approach cf. K. Hampe, *Deutsche Kaisergeschichte in der Zeit der Salier u. Staufer* (3rd. ed., 1916); E. Jordan, *Les origines de la domination angevine en Italie* (1909); G. Blondel, *Étude sur la politique de l'empereur Frédéric II en Allemagne* (1892); M. Stimming, 'Kaiser Friedrich II u. der Abfall der deutschen Fürsten', *Hist. Zeitschr.*, CXX (1919); F. Schneider, *Kaiser Friedrich II u. der Staat* (1930); F. Schneider, 'Kaiser Friedrich II u. seine Bedeutung für das Elsass', *Elsass-Lothringisches Jahrbuch*, IX (1930), 128-155.

was doubtless due in part to the decline in royal power in Germany
between 1198 and 1215, to which Frederick's own policy between
1212 and 1215 had materially contributed; by the time he was in
undisputed possession of the throne in 1215 the situation was such
as to deter him from the formidable task of attempting to restore
royal authority to the level reached under Barbarossa. But it was
due also to his own prepossessions, to his Sicilian upbringing and to
the Sicilian blood in his veins. Frederick considered himself a
Sicilian, spoke of Sicily and its provinces as 'his own land' and of
Italy as his 'inheritance'; he had a horror of Germany with its 'long
winters' and 'sombre forests', its 'muddy towns' and its 'rugged
castles'. In the whole duration of his reign, from 1212 to 1250, little
more than nine years in all were spent in Germany, and of these
over seven fell in the period of his first intervention against Otto of
Brunswick. Immediately after Otto's death in 1218 Frederick began
preparations to cross the Alps and to carry out the projects which
really interested him: the restoration of royal government in Sicily,
the crusade and the conquest of Jerusalem, and finally the re-
establishment of imperial authority in Italy. When in August, 1220,
he marched southwards across the Brenner, he was not to see Germany again for fifteen years.

This revolutionary change in the direction of imperial interests,
combined with an equally revolutionary change in the seat of
imperial power, had been foreshadowed under Henry VI; but it had
no parallel in the acts or policy of any earlier ruler, and was only
possible after the conquest of Sicily in 1194. His Sicilian inheritance,
the effective centralized government established by the Norman
kings, was the basis which Frederick deliberately chose for his
administration; it was the ideal of the dominion which he desired
to exercise throughout the Empire.[1] It was to Sicily that he immediately turned, when he could safely leave Germany; and his
first task, occupying him from 1220 to 1224, was to restore the
Norman system of government as it existed at the death of William
II in 1189. This completed, he turned to Lombardy (1225-1226) and
to the crusade (1227-1229); but on his return it was again Sicily, where
papal attacks during his absence had caused disorders and retrogression, that claimed his first attention. As soon as relations with

---

[1] Blondel, op. cit., 385; 'au fond, avec lui', says Jordan (op. cit., 606), 'ce fut la Sicile qui
essaya de conquérir l'Italie'.

the papacy had been restored by the peace of San Germano (1230), he began again the task of reorganizing Sicilian government; but the reorganization now undertaken, unlike that begun in 1220, went far beyond Norman precedent; and it was in the years after 1230 that he created the system of government — reflected in the famous constitutions of Melfi (1231) — which was later extended to other parts of the Empire. If Frederick was (as many historians have maintained) in advance of his age in spirit and policy, it was here, in the legislation of Melfi and the routine of Sicilian government, and not in his propaganda and the manifestos by which he vainly sought to rally lay society against papal theocracy, that his 'modernity' made itself felt.

The key role which Sicily played in Frederick's plans reacted inevitably on his attitude to Germany, which sank under him to the level of a subordinate province, almost a colony, of the Empire under a regency government exercised in the name of his sons, Henry and Conrad. The same change of perspective also coloured Frederick's attitude to the Empire, which he saw less through German than through Sicilian or Italian eyes. Consequently any similarities between his policy and that of Frederick I or Henry VI are largely superficial, and his imperialism is explained less by the continuation of Hohenstaufen traditions than by the circumstances which led to his first intervention in imperial affairs. It was Otto IV's attempt, immediately after he was crowned emperor in Rome in 1209, to conquer Sicily in the name of the Empire that convinced Frederick that the imperial title was necessary in order to safeguard his Sicilian crown against attacks from the north. In the same way it was requisite as a means of freeing the way for the spread of Sicilian domination in Italy. But the imperial crown could still only be acquired through election by the German princes, who alone had the power of making the *Rex Romanorum*. Hence it was for the protection of his position in Sicily and for the furtherance of his policy in Italy that Frederick turned to Germany. What he wanted above all else from Germany was the imperial title, legitimizing his rule in Italy and excluding the threat of a competing dynasty. In this sense his policy recalls the policy of Otto I;[1] but it was Otto's policy in reverse, for whereas Otto assumed the imperial title in the interests of Germany to prevent the formation of a potentially

[1] Cf. above, p. 54.

anti-German power in the south and south-west, Frederick acted in the interests of Sicily to prevent the formation of an anti-Sicilian power in the north. In these circumstances, it was inevitable that Germany took a subordinate place in his policy, and that he was prepared to pay almost any price to the German princes to secure the imperial title for himself and his sons. It was inevitable, also, that the Empire became less and less a German empire in character. This change was reflected — as Frederick's reign progressed and the German auxiliaries who had governed Italy through all vicissitudes since the twelfth century, one by one died out — in the increased reliance placed on Sicilian officials for discharging all the more important functions of government south of the Alps; here again his policy contrasted markedly with that of Barbarossa and Henry VI who had relied almost exclusively on the services of German *ministeriales* for the government of Italy and Sicily. Under Frederick, therefore, the sense of unity and cohesion between the constituent lands of the Empire, hitherto supported by powerful historical associations, was gradually lost; in particular a distinction was drawn between Germany, or the *regnum*, and the *imperium*, and when in 1240, after Frederick's second excommunication, the pope threatened to transfer the *imperium* to another nation, opinion in Germany was already largely indifferent.[1] Now that imperial policy was no longer a German policy, it was no longer felt that German interests were directly affected by events in Italy or by the contest between Frederick and the papacy. Left to the princes, who profited from Frederick's need of support to wring concessions from him, Germany went its own way, following a course of development which differentiated it with great rapidity from Italy and Sicily, where Frederick worked hard to make imperial government a reality.

The main scene of Frederick's activities lay south of the Alps; the fate of Sicily and Italy, not the fate of Germany, was the foremost object of his political calculations, and it was in Sicily and Italy that the great, world-resounding events of his reign were played out. He could not, indeed, be indifferent to Germany because discontent or rebellion on the part of the German princes, particularly in combination with the papacy, might endanger his imperial position; but

---

[1] Cf. the correspondence of Albert Beham, an active papal agent in Germany, ed. Höfler *Bibl. d. lit. Vereins in Stuttgart*, XVI (1847), 16.

his method of forestalling or counteracting this danger was to make concessions which undermined the position of the monarchy in Germany. It has, indeed, been argued that Frederick intended, if the Lombard struggle had ended quickly, to carry through a reorganization of German government parallel to his reorganization of Sicilian and Italian government; and the beginnings of this process have been seen in the activities of the Diet of Mainz in 1235.[1] This suggestion, probable enough in itself, can be supported by the fact that, in the last years of his reign, the Sicilian system of government was carried across the Alps and applied in Austria and Styria, which were administered after 1246 by captains-general with extensive powers parallel to those of the vicars-general of Hohenstaufen Italy;[2] moreover, this system of direct administration was foreshadowed ten years earlier, at the very period of the Diet of Mainz, after the rebellion of the last Babenberg duke of Austria in 1236. But, if Frederick had such plans, it is noteworthy that they took second place to his Italian projects, and that he never found time for the prolonged stay in Germany which would have been requisite if any serious constitutional reform were to be put into effect. Nor is it easy to see how, at this late date, he could have revoked or stultified the privileges conceded earlier in his reign to the German princes in order to secure their adhesion to his imperial policy. However reasonable it may be to suppose that Frederick had 'some uniform method of administration' in mind, 'which would have guided the princely governments into definite lines', it is difficult, after Frederick's concessions of 1213, 1220 and 1232, to picture the precise form which such an administration would have taken. Moreover, his own words in 1236, when he was preparing to break the resistance of the Lombard League, indicate clearly enough that he was well satisfied with the existing situation in Germany.[3] Nor can we forget his refusal of support in 1232 to his son, Henry, who was seeking to maintain the freedom of action of the monarchy in Germany in face of the princes — a conflict of policy which was the clearest

---

[1] Cf. Kantorowicz, op. cit., 382-384, 409-411; Blondel, op. cit., 19-20, 129-130; Stimming, op. cit., 247.

[2] Cf. Niese, *Verwaltung des Reichsgutes*, 287.

[3] *Mon. Germ. hist.*, Leg., II, 320: 'Nec enim ob aliud credimus quod providentia Salvatoris sic magnifice, immo mirifice dirigit gressus nostros, dum ab orientali zona regnum Ierosolimitanum ... ac deinde regnum Siciliae ... et praepotens Germaniae principatus ... sub devotione nostri nominis perseverant, nisi ut illud Italiae medium, quod nostris viribus undique circumdatur, ad nostrae serenitatis obsequia et imperii redeat unitatem.'

indication of his unwillingness to sacrifice any part of his Italian plans to the exigencies of the deteriorating situation in Germany.[1] It is particularly significant that the breach between Frederick and Henry occurred in a period of peace with the papacy, when the emperor could, had he so wished, safely have devoted attention to German affairs; but in line with his earlier policy he had already determined to use this opportunity to re-establish his authority in Lombardy and could therefore not risk the possibility of unrest in Germany. Hence he gave the German princes his wholehearted support against Henry, addressing them (in words characteristic of his attitude) as 'the glory and acme of the Empire', the columns on which his throne rested. It is this attitude of compliance towards the princes that is the mark of Frederick's German policy. But his attempt to base his rule on co-operation with the princes was very different from that of Frederick Barbarossa; for where the latter sought by this means to restore equilibrium in Germany, the former thought only of freeing his hands to pursue his Italian policy. Indeed, it can fairly be said that Frederick II's choice had already been made in 1220 when, going back on his engagements of 1216, he persuaded pope Honorius III to leave Sicily under his control. That, as Ficker finely perceived,[2] was the turning-point. If he had intended seriously to take the government of Germany in hand with a view to restoring the position of the monarchy after its decline between 1198 and 1215 — as Frederick I restored it after the upheavals of 1076-1152 — the first step was a frank abandonment of his Sicilian ambitions. When he showed himself unable to take this decisive step, the die was cast; engrossed in the affairs of Sicily and Italy, he left Germany to the princes and consumed his energies in the contest with the papacy which any essentially Italian policy involved.

II

Apart from the reorganization of Sicilian government, the great questions which filled Frederick's mind, stirred his ambitions and dominated his political activities were summed up in the words: Italy, Lombardy, the papacy. Except in so far as they reacted upon Germany these complicated and heated issues hardly concern us

[1] Cf. below, pp. 237-238.   [2] Ficker, *Das deutsche Kaiserreich*, 112-114.

here; for Frederick II's imperial policy was only in the smallest degree a continuation of the imperial policy of Frederick Barbarossa and Henry VI, which was still a German policy carried out by a German ruler anxious to strengthen his position in Germany. Frederick II's imperial policy, on the other hand, was so little a German policy that it has plausibly been maintained that, whatever else it might have resulted in, had it been successful, the one thing its success would not have brought about was a reconstitution of the German Empire as it existed down to 1197.[1] Hence it is less correct to attribute (as has often been done) the collapse of the German monarchy and the destruction of German unity to the failure of Frederick II's imperial policy, than to lay the responsibility for these results on the policy itself and its author. It is assuredly true that the triumph of pope Innocent IV (1243-1254) hastened these results and set the seal of irrevocability on the unpropitious developments which took place in Germany after 1212; but the developments themselves, and their rapid progress, were already a fact by Innocent IV's time, due to the line of policy which Frederick deliberately adopted from the beginning of his reign.

In the atmosphere of suspicion and distrust which had prevailed ever since Henry VI occupied Sicily, Frederick's imperial policy was bound to lead to misunderstanding and even to open conflict with the papacy. It was not, indeed, that he saw himself as heir and executor of his father, called upon to complete what Henry VI had failed to put into effect; he made no attempt, for example — and this again is a fact which casts a clear light on his indifference to German affairs — to resurrect the projects of hereditary monarchy which had a key place in Henry's plans, and his Lombard policy marked a complete breach with that pursued so successfully between 1183 and 1197. Furthermore, whereas Henry had not scrupled to occupy the papal states in 1186 when open conflict with pope Urban III seemed imminent, Frederick was throughout conciliatory; in 1229, for example, after decisively defeating the papal army which had invaded Sicily during his absence on crusade, instead of following up his victory by an invasion of papal territory, he disbanded his army without delay and sent ambassadors to treat with the pope for peace. Indeed, throughout his reign nothing is more evident than his willingness to make wide concessions for the sake of a settlement.

[1] Ficker, *Deutsches Königthum u. Kaiserthum*, 58.

As late as 1244, in the hope of securing peace with the new pope, Innocent IV, he offered to accept the pope's mediation in his conflict with the Lombard League, to renounce all rights over Rome and the patrimony, to depart for three years to the Holy Land, not to return earlier without the pope's express permission, to forfeit all his territories if he broke his vow, and to appoint kings and princes as his sureties.[1] This sweeping offer was, of course, made with an eye to his own interests; for he was fully aware at this stage, when he had been five years under the church's ban, of the pressing need for peace and of the strain on his resources. But his conciliatoriness was not simply the opportunism of a politician who had failed to get his way by force. His loyal surrender in 1220 of the central Italian provinces which he had renounced in favour of the papacy in 1213 in the golden bull of Eger, establishing pope Honorious III in much firmer control than Innocent III had ever been, was the surest proof that he had no set intention of continuing the territorial policy of Henry VI, which had stood in the way of a settlement with the church.[2] To suppose that he embarked from the beginning on an inevitable struggle with the papacy for dominion, using guile and chicanery to find loopholes in his solemn engagements, would be to show complete misunderstanding of his attitude. He realized, as Frederick Barbarossa had discovered before him, that there was more than one possible solution to the Italian problem, without sacrificing the ultimate object of a settled, organized government; and it may be taken for granted that there was room, in Frederick II's plans, for an independent papacy with dominions of its own, such as he recognized — not simply as an expedient to gain time, but as a fair and durable settlement — in the Treaty of Hagenau in 1219. If Frederick was forced into the position of a radical opponent of papal pretensions, seeking to rally secular thought and interests against the church, it was against his own will and never without the hope of securing, by substantial concessions and a full protestation of orthodoxy, a lasting *modus vivendi*.

What, then, stood in the way of such a settlement, which would

---

[1] Kantorowicz, op. cit., 591; cf. Brackmann, op. cit., 547, and Hampe, *Hist. Zeitschr.*, CXLVI, 473-474. For further detail, cf. below, p. 231.

[2] Honorius III's encyclical of February 18th, 1221 (Potthast, *Reg. Pont. Rom.*, n. 6567) is the best evidence of the good impression made by Frederick's renunciation; he went so far as to use his authority to compel the Tuscan nobility to do homage to the pope for fiefs in the Matildine lands. Cf. Jordan, op. cit., c-ci.

have been to the lasting benefit of both parties? We may discount the question of the crusade which Frederick had sworn in 1215 to undertake; for although viewed by the church as a test of good faith, its significance to both sides was mainly tactical. The decisive factor was Frederick's inability to reconcile himself to the surrender of Sicily — a surrender which would, indeed, have necessitated a complete reorientation of his policy — in spite of his solemn engagement in 1211, renewed at Strassburg in 1216, and at Hagenau in 1220, to renounce the Sicilian throne in favour of his son, Henry, as soon as he himself had received the imperial crown. Inevitably this radical change of attitude, the ultimate explanation of which was probably psychological rather than political, raised again the spectre of the *unio regni ad imperium* against which Innocent III had struggled so hard; and papal suspicion was increased when in 1220 the young Henry, who had been crowned king of Sicily in 1212, was elected king of the Romans by the German princes, and therewith implicitly designated successor to the imperial throne. Yet the pope's suspicions, comprehensible though they were, were probably unwarranted. It was not in Frederick's interest to renew, in face of his explicit engagements, the imperial policy of Henry VI. After his son's election, Frederick protested vehemently that he was not pursuing the union of *regnum* and *imperium*;[1] and in spite of suggestions that he was playing with the nice legal distinction between 'real' and 'personal' union, his protestation was probably sincere.[2]

[1] Cf. Huillard-Bréholles, *Historia diplomatica Friderici secundi*, I (1852), 803: 'Absit enim quod imperium commune aliquid habere debeat cum regno, aut occasione filii nostri de electione sua ipsa ad invicem uniamus; immo eorum unioni ne possit esse temporibus aliquorum, totis nisibus obviamus.'

[2] For Kantorowicz (op. cit., 100), the election of Henry in 1220 was 'Frederick's first great victory over curial diplomacy'. 'Frederick had won the game ... Sicily had, of course, not been legally incorporated in the Empire, the feudal overlordship of the church over Sicily still stood, but that personal union of the two crowns which Frederick had had to renounce on his coronation as Emperor became suddenly an accomplished fact ... without any breach of all the treaties with the pope, for they were all made in the name of Frederick II, and contained not a syllable about Henry. All the rights and powers which Frederick was debarred by treaty and agreement from claiming for himself he had now passed on boldly to his son. The one flaw in the treaties had been exploited.' And this was apparently but a first step; for Frederick (Kantorowicz adds) was only acknowledging papal overlordship over Sicily 'for the moment'. The argument is, of course, specious. The 'personal union' renounced by Frederick was the union of the imperial and Sicilian crowns; it did not become 'an accomplished fact' when Henry was elected king of the Romans. And what rights and powers did Frederick 'boldly' pass on to his son? If he had renounced the imperial and Sicilian crowns in favour of Henry, the situation described by Kantorowicz would, in fact, have come about; but there was no question of renunciation — on the contrary, all Frederick's efforts were concentrated (cf. Huillard-Bréholles, op. cit., I, 742) on securing the pope's agreement to his retaining Sicily in his own hands. It seems possible that the election of Henry as king of the Romans in

His tergiversations, which in the end aroused incurable suspicions, were not (as some modern apologists have sought to prove) the outcome of Machiavellian scheming and Bismarckian logic, but rather the result of confusion, opportunism and unclarity of aim, and of the wellnigh insoluble difficulties inherent in his situation.[1] He was quite frank with the pope about his own desire to retain Sicily,[2] and careful, until the breach came, to keep Germany and Sicily separate. In fact, there was no 'personal union' under his son, Henry, who remained exclusively in Germany; from 1220 to 1232 Frederick governed Italy and Sicily and Henry ruled in Germany, and the separation of functions was real. Hence in spite of papal anxiety over the consequences of Henry's election in 1220 and in spite of the lack of scruple in the methods by which it was brought about, the question of the union of Sicily and the Empire did not result in a breach between Frederick and the papacy. The breach came when, in addition to Sicily, it became clear that Frederick had plans for Lombardy. Here again fear and suspicion were at the root of the trouble. Frederick had respected the pope's position in central Italy; but the latter feared lest the papacy might again be crushed between the upper and the nether millstones, if Frederick succeeded in reaffirming his authority both in Sicily and in Lombardy. There is no evidence that such an oblique attack on the church was really part of Frederick's plan; but it is easy to comprehend the growing suspicion and anxiety in the Roman curia, and not surprising that the papacy felt that it was bound to the cities of the Lombard League by a substantial community of interests. The pope did not take sides immediately; but when in 1226 war between Frederick and the League became imminent, he took up a mediating position with the obvious intention of maintaining the

1220 may even have been carried through as a means of putting pressure on the pope to this effect. Frederick had sworn to surrender Sicily to his son after his own coronation; but would the pope wish this oath to be implemented, if Henry were already *Rex Romanorum*? Finally, does Kantorowicz really wish us to understand that Frederick was so naive as to suppose that a mere piece of legal sharp-practice really affected the political issue? Politics are based on power, not on 'parchments', and even if the treaties with the church had a 'flaw' in them, exploitation of that 'flaw' was merely a theoretical success; it did not alter the political facts — except perhaps by making lasting reconciliation between Frederick and the papacy more remote and difficult than ever.

[1] Hampe has collected examples of Frederick's political instability; cf. *Hist. Zeitschr.*, CXLVI, 463-464.

[2] When he renewed his renunciation of the Sicilian crown at Hagenau in 1220, he told the pope he had done so 'sub spe obtinendi a vestra paternitate ipsius regni in vita nostra dominium' (Huillard-Bréholles, op. cit. I, 742).

status quo, the solution which above all others best suited the church's interests.

The struggle with the Lombard League, which Frederick was, from 1225, clearly intent on fighting to a finish, looks at first sight like a deliberate reversal of the policy adopted so successfully by Frederick Barbarossa and Henry VI after 1183. In fact, the situation was more complicated. The Constance settlement, which was the sheet-anchor of Barbarossa's and Henry's policy, had ceased to function when effective imperial government collapsed in 1198, and the period 1198-1225 was used by the communes to extend their power far beyond the limits agreed at Constance.[1] Furthermore the League, led by Milan, had strenuously supported Otto of Brunswick, even after his defeat at Bouvines; and although Frederick as a result had gained the support of the group of cities which, under Cremona, was violently opposed to Milan, the result was only to embroil him in the intricacies of Italian politics. It is probably true that Frederick would have been wiser to seek a new *modus vivendi* with Milan, rather than to break its hostility by force; but it is undeniable that a settlement of Lombard affairs was imperative by 1225. The reason why Frederick proceeded as he did, revoking the peace of Constance and subordinating the cities to a highly integrated administrative system, which destroyed the autonomy created in 1183, is probably to be found in the changed situation in central Italy. Frederick I was able to compromise in northern Italy because he had secured direct administrative control of central Italy; Frederick II, having restored central Italy to the church, felt the need for a restoration of imperial power in the north. Such a restoration played a key part in his policy after 1225: the suzerainty established in 1183 was no longer effective in view of the radical changes in the distribution of power which had occurred after 1198, and Frederick was determined to replace it by a more effective system of direct control. Yet what brought him into open conflict with Milan was less rooted Milanese opposition to a revival of imperial power in Lombardy, than fear that such power would be exercised through and for the benefit of Cremona and its allies: it was this local conflict and Frederick's inability or unwillingness to take a stand above and independent of

---

[1] The best and most detailed description of the development of the communes after 1198 is in the lengthy introduction to Jordan's *Origines*. Previté-Orton (*Outlines of Mediaeval History*, 311) sums up the attitude of the Lombards in 1226 when he says: 'even the conditions of the Peace of Constance were now unwelcome to them.'

the conflicting parties, which accounts for the intransigence of Milan's hostility, and this intransigence, visible from the first announcement of Frederick's impending arrival in Lombardy, provoked on Frederick's side an inveterate hostility to Milan, which far outstepped what was politically desirable. When early in 1226 Milan renewed the Lombard League for a period of twenty-five years and closed the Alpine passes to the army approaching Italy from Germany, refusing to open them except on inacceptable terms, open conflict became inevitable.

The conflict which seemed on the point of breaking out in 1226 was, in fact, postponed for a decade. The detail of the diplomacy of these years can be passed over in silence. In 1226 Frederick, with the organization of the Crusade on his hands, was not prepared to intervene with force in Lombardy, and both parties accepted a *modus vivendi* negotiated by the pope which left the real grounds of dispute untouched. But neither side was prepared for peace. The towns, at the first breach between Frederick and the new pope, Gregory IX (1227-1241), did all they could to keep the quarrel alive. Frederick, although after his reconciliation with the papacy in 1230 he continued to negotiate under papal mediation, refused throughout to compromise over the main question at issue: recognition of the legitimacy of the Lombard League. This refusal aroused, with good reason, the suspicions of the Lombards, and when Frederick appeared again in north Italy in 1231 and held a diet at Ravenna, the League was renewed and once again a confederate army barred the Alpine passes. The hostile attitude of the Lombards was confirmed in 1234 when they allied with the young king Henry, who had risen in rebellion in Germany, and once this revolt was put down, Frederick determined to deal once and for all with Lombardy. At a diet held in Mainz in 1235 he secured the support of the German princes for his policy, and in 1236 the war against the Lombards began.

Frederick's success was immediate. Militarily the Lombards suffered a crushing defeat at Cortenuova in 1237, while politically town after town went over to the imperial side. Milan offered to dissolve the League, which after Cortenuova comprised only six towns, and to recognize imperial rights; but Frederick, under the influence of Cremona and Pavia, insisted on unconditional surrender, and therewith lost the chance of a favourable settlement. A few months later, in 1238, the imperial army failed to take Brescia, and this failure proved a turning-point. The papacy which from the beginning had warned Frederick of the dangers implicit in his policy and had tried to save the Lombards by mediation, now came out into the open, dispatching a legate to Lombardy who quickly became a focus for all anti-imperial elements; and in 1238 Frederick was excommunicated. By securing the support of the three naval powers, Genoa, Venice and Pisa, the pope sought to undermine the foundations of Frederick's strength by a concerted attack on Sicily; but the defeat of the Genoese fleet in 1241 ruined this plan, while in central Italy Frederick carried all before him, occupying Spoleto and Ancona in 1240 as a preliminary to an attack on the papal states. Such an attack was certainly not desired by Frederick. Negotiations were continuous with Gregory IX until his death in 1241, and were renewed without delay with Innocent IV, when he succeeded to the papacy in 1243. But they broke down every time over one key point: the pope would not make peace unless the decision of the issues between Frederick and the Lombards were left entirely in his hands, and Frederick, although willing to make every conceivable concession in ecclesiastical affairs, and to accept papal mediation, was not prepared to allow the pope to define the scope of imperial rights in Lombardy.[1] Under these circumstances the breach became irrevocable. At the very moment when a settlement was expected — and had, indeed, been announced by Frederick — Innocent IV, in the midst of negotiations, fled secretly from Italy.

With Innocent's flight to Lyons in 1244 all hope of a negotiated settlement was ended. The general council of the church which met at Lyons in 1245 was used to vilify Frederick, and to propagate the papal case far and wide, and repeated offers of mediation by the kings of France and England were rejected. For good or for ill, Innocent's mind was made up; he was no longer prepared to negotiate. His one object henceforward was the destruction of Frederick, and his attitude left no loophole for compromise. Hence

[1] Frederick agreed to overlook all acts of hostility committed by the Lombards since the beginning of his discord with the church, and to accept the ruling of the pope and cardinals regarding earlier acts of insubordination ('de offensis commissis ante ortam discordiam stabimus provisioni et ordinationi domini papae et fratrum'; cf. Huillard-Bréholles, op. cit., VI, 204). This formula was evidently not equivalent to authorizing the pope to decide the question of principle involved in the conflict with the Lombard League; but this was the interpretation put upon it by Innocent, and it was this difference which led to rupture. Frederick was ready to observe all the terms of the treaty which had been negotiated, but the pope, 'quia nolebamus in eum super negotio Lombardorum de iuribus scilicet et regalibus nostris compromittere', refused at the last moment to grant absolution (ibid., 210).

after 1245 he went to work systematically to undermine Frederick's power, and it is this systematic attack on the imperial position, maintained with extraordinary vigour and unflinching disregard of consequences, which is the mark of Innocent's pontificate. He is distinguished from his predecessors, Honorius III and Gregory IX, not only by his inflexibility, but also by the cool realism of his methods, by his cynical appeal to egoism and selfish interests, and by the careful attention which he gave to Germany. The object of his struggle with Frederick was Italy; it was to prevent the establishment of unbroken imperial control stretching from Germany in the north through Lombardy to Sicily, which would have been fatal to the independence of the papacy. But Innocent realized, after Frederick's successes in Italy between 1236 and 1244, that there was little hope of successfully fighting the battle for Italy on Italian soil. Hence after 1245 his main effort was transferred to Germany. It was in Germany that Innocent sought a decision, for the attitude of Germany was the decisive factor. So long as Frederick could rely on Germany for military and financial support, he could continue the attack on the Lombards with good prospects of final success. What was necessary, therefore, was to foster and organize the elements of opposition in Germany; and it is no accident that by far the largest proportion of papal instructions, dispatches and directives in the years 1245 and 1246 are concerned with Germany. It was through Innocent IV's systematic organization and direction that the anti-imperial forces in Germany, which had remained a negligible factor in the first phase of the conflict with the church, from 1239 to 1244, were in the end a serious menace to Frederick's position.

The course of events in Germany between 1245 and Frederick's death in 1250, the gradual emergence and consolidation of a strong anti-imperial party, provides the best comment on the policy pursued in Germany during the first thirty years of Frederick's reign. As late as 1235, when the princes rallied round the emperor and supported his decision to wage war on the Lombards, it looked as though his German policy was paying dividends; but the last five years of the reign, from 1245 to 1250, revealed its bankruptcy. By concentrating his energies throughout on Italy and continuously weakening the royal position in Germany, Frederick gave full rein to the growing pretensions of the princes. So long as their power and independence could be increased by concessions from the monarchy, they remained loyal; but after 1245 their interests were best served by neutrality, by using the conflict to extort concessions from either side, or by profiting from the lack of governance to build up and strengthen their territorial power. Between 1212 and 1235 Frederick helped the princes into the saddle; after 1245 they took control of the horse. The conflict to the death between Frederick and the papacy, which was unleashed at the Council of Lyons in 1245, gave them their opportunity, and they made the most of it. The powers which passed into their hands during Frederick II's reign remained in their hands for six centuries, surviving the dissolution of the Empire in 1806 and the creation of a new Empire in 1871; only in 1918 were the last vestiges swept away. The reign of Frederick II was thus a turning-point in German history: the resources which the crown had hitherto possessed, dissipated in the interests of Frederick's Italian policy, withered to a mere simulacrum of monarchy, and the reality of power was vested in the princes. The future lay with them and with the principalities.

III

The reign of Frederick II was a turning-point in German history. When he replaced Otto IV in 1215 nothing was irretrievably lost; when he died in 1250 the political structure of Germany was irrevocably changed. There was, indeed, for a century after 1250 still the ever-recurrent possibility of the creation of an effective royal government in Germany, and it was only after the death of Charles IV in 1378 that this possibility ceased to count. But the efforts of the German rulers after 1272 were based on new principles and new foundations; their starting-point was the consolidated princely territory, and their power and influence in the land was directly proportionate to their power as territorial princes. Between 1212, when Frederick first appeared in Germany, and 1250 the old foundations of royal government perished, and with them the ancient traditions and loyalties which were a potent force on the side of the monarchy; and the long interregnum, which followed Frederick's death in 1250, only consolidated the changes in sentiment and in the actual distribution of political power which were the direct result of Frederick's German policy.

It is, of course, true that Frederick II succeeded to a difficult heritage in Germany, and there is no sure means of deciding what prospects of success a systematic policy of reviving the powers of the monarchy would have carried with it after the events of 1198–1215. Already at the end of Frederick I's reign and under Henry VI there were ominous signs of the strength and solidarity of the princes. But the important fact is that Frederick II never tried to put such a policy into effect. Barbarossa had shown what could be achieved in an apparently hopeless position, and the situation in Germany was scarcely more difficult when Frederick II intervened in 1212 than when Frederick I succeeded in 1152. The dissipation of crown lands in the time of Philip of Swabia and Otto of Brunswick, though serious, has certainly been exaggerated,[1] and in any case the duration of the unrest was not so lengthy that recuperation was out of the question. The imperial *ministeriales*, who rallied to Frederick's support in 1212, were still a useful instrument of royal policy, and Frederick himself proved in his early work in Alsace that the construction, with the aid of the *ministeriales*, of an efficient administration was not impossible.[2] It is hard to believe that this administration was not capable of extension. The great German law-book, the *Sachsenspiegel*, which was put together by Eike von Repgau in the very middle of Frederick's reign, is indication enough of the existence of a workable constitution, culminating in the monarchy; it portrays a kingdom still, in spite of the principalities, forming a single unit beneath the crown, and shows that the royal position, when Frederick succeeded, was far from being merely a concatenation of empty rights.[3] There was, in short, still a substantial foundation, if Frederick had devoted his energies to consolidation and reconstruction. Nor were economic developments unfavourable. It was a period of agricultural prosperity and of rapid urban expansion, which offered the monarchy sources of revenue still virtually untapped; the tax-returns for 1241, which show that approximately two-thirds of the German revenues of the crown were derived,

---

[1] Cf. Schneider, *Elsass-Lothringisches Jahrbuch*, IX, 144; Niese, *Verwaltung des Reichsgutes*, 56; H. W. Klewitz, *Gesch. d. Ministerialität im Elsass* (1929), 60; H. Eberhardt, *Die Anfänge des Territorialfürstentums in Nordthuringen* (1932), 40.

[2] For the organization of Alsace as a *procuratio* or province, with a single provincial court (*Landgericht*) and a central administration with its seat in Hagenau, cf. Niese, op. cit., 273 sqq., and Schneider, op. cit., 142 sqq.

[3] Cf. H. Fehr, 'Die Staatsauffassung Eikes von Repgau', *Zeitschr. f. Rechtsgesch., Germ. Abt.*, XXXVII (1916).

largely by direct taxation, from urban sources, are an indication of the possibilities awaiting a ruler conscious of his task and prepared to devote his energies to the laborious business of administration.[1]

Frederick II deliberately sacrificed these possibilities. Indifferent to Germany, except as a source of supply for his Italian campaigns, he made no attempt to oppose the existing tendencies to decentralization or to reaffirm the rights of the crown. Unwilling to compromise his Italian plans by provoking the opposition of the German princes, he deliberately sought to identify the interests of crown and princes by implicit acceptance of the princely point of view. Provided that he secured acquiescence and support for his Italian policy, no concession was too great. In Sicily, he treated the powers acquired by the baronage between 1198 and 1220 as illegitimate usurpations, and after 1220 put into effect a strict policy of recuperation; in Germany, on the contrary, he accepted the abnormal conditions of 1212 as the *status quo*, and far from attempting to return to the position of 1197, confirmed the princes, lay and ecclesiastical, in their acquisitions. This confirmation was contained in the three famous privileges, the Golden Bull of Eger (1213), the *Confoederatio cum principibus ecclesiasticis* (1220), and the *Statutum in favorem principum* (1232), but it also took the form of concessions to individuals, of which the outstanding example was the creation of the new duchy of Brunswick for Otto of Lüneburg, the heir of Henry the Lion, which took place in 1235 with the intention of settling old discords in Germany as a preliminary to the Lombard war.

These concessions cut away the ground from under the feet of the monarchy. The privileges granted in 1213 and 1220 to the German church severed the old administrative bonds between the monarchy and the episcopate which had survived the Concordat of Worms and had been reaffirmed by Barbarossa; they destroyed royal control over episcopal elections and removed the last vestiges of the bishops' official character. From the beginning of the twelfth century there had been a growing tendency for the latter to identify themselves with the lay princes. After 1220 this tendency became dominant, and the bishops, who under Barbarossa had been leading exponents

---

[1] The tax-returns were discovered by J. Schwalm in 1896; cf. *Neues Archiv*, XXIII (1898), 517-553; also K. Zeumer, 'Zur Geschichte der Reichssteuern', *Hist. Zeitschr.*, LXXXI (1898), 24-45, and Niese, op. cit., 114-118.

of royal traditions and imperial policy, concentrated their efforts on their own territories. This territorial policy was favoured by Frederick's great privilege of 1220. By renouncing the right to levy new taxes in ecclesiastical territories, to build castles or cities on episcopal lands, and by granting the bishops free disposition of the fees of their vassals, Frederick virtually renounced his right to interfere in the internal administration of ecclesiastical principalities. In 1232 these concessions were confirmed and extended to all princes, lay and ecclesiastical. In addition, the princes were guaranteed full control of all courts and jurisdictions within their territories, which meant that they had the power to remodel the administrative machinery in the way best suited to their interests; the local courts were expressly placed in their hands and their rights of coinage were safeguarded. The constitution of 1232 was a Magna Carta of princely liberties; but it was significant also in two other ways. It revealed the growth of a community of interests between the lay and ecclesiastical princes, and was the first occasion on which the whole princely aristocracy, clerical and temporal, acted as a body against the crown, compelling it to respect their common territorial interests. In the second place, it was the first occasion on which the monarchy openly threw over the forces in Germany which were prepared to support the crown against the princes. The *Statutum in favorem principum* was directed first and foremost against the rising towns which, with the backing of royal agents, were threatening to disrupt the organization and destroy the unity of the princely territories;[1] they were grasping out, like the Italian communes before them, into the countryside, but at the same time they were prepared to take their place in a royal scheme of bureau-

---

[1] Of the 23 clauses of the *Statutum*, thirteen refer expressly to towns and markets; cf. the text in *Mon. Germ., Const.*, II, 211-213 (trs. Thatcher and McNeal, *Source-Book*, 238-240). — The king promised (§.1) to build no more castles or walled towns in princely territories. No new (in other words, royal) markets were to compete with the older markets in the princes' hands (§§.2, 3); travellers must not be compelled to take the new roads, and thus pay toll to the king instead of the princes (§.4). Royal jurisdiction in the cities, which had been extended to the detriment of the princely courts, was to be limited to the 'ban-mile' of the cities (§§.5, 18); the location of hundred courts (which had been moved into royal towns) was not to be changed without the lord's consent (§.8); lands and fiefs of princes and nobles, which had been absorbed by the cities, were to be restored (§.13). The cities were not to admit dependants of lords and princes (§.12), and royal officials in the cities were not to prevent any such persons returning to their lords (§.23); in particular the so-called 'phalburgers' — i.e. persons residing outside the cities, but enjoying the privileges of citizens — were to return to their former status (§.10). Finally, just as Frederick surrendered the independent rights of the cities, so he agreed to surrender the dues paid him by the 'free peasants' in token of their direct connection with the royal courts and their independence from feudal jurisdiction (§.11).

cratic government in order to emancipate themselves from the princes. When Frederick in 1232 rejected the support of the towns and in characteristic phrases sided with the princes against the urban communes,[1] he struck down one of the few remaining pillars of monarchical government. The policy of 1220 and 1232 was abdication pure and simple: it destroyed all hope of a monarchy with independent powers strong enough to assert superiority over the princes.

The consequences of Frederick's attitude were soon clear to his son, Henry, who began to pursue an independent policy about 1228; and there is no doubt that the conflict between the two, which came to a head during the next six years and culminated in open rebellion on Henry's part, expressed a real conflict of principle, in which the whole future of German government was at stake.[2] Henry, who had grown to manhood in Germany, stood for the traditions of Hohenstaufen policy, which he had learnt from the ministerial servants of the monarchy who surrounded him in his early days: he stood for the policy of consolidating and extending the royal demesnes pursued by Barbarossa after 1168, of efficient administration conducted by the *ministeriales*, and of reliance on the towns against the princes. He sought to make the towns centres for the government of the countryside, developing Bern and Ulm, Frankfurt, Hagenau and Rotenburg as seats of provincial administration. It is scarcely to be doubted that he envisaged, like Barbarossa,[3] a gradual extension of this system of government throughout south Germany, from Alsace in the west through Baden and Swabia and Franconia to Bavaria, and that his alliance with the Lombard cities in 1234 was part of this plan. But his territorial policy brought him into conflict with many leading powers, including the landgrave of Baden, the bishop of Würzburg and the duke of Bavaria, while his implicit reliance on the *ministeriales* aroused general hostility among the princes, who saw in his policy

[1] The communal movement, he said, detracted from the rights of the princes and therefore weakened imperial authority ('et principum imperii iuri detrahitur et honori, et imperialis per consequens auctoritas enervatur'); he wished to put 'the broadest possible interpretation' on the 'liberties and concessions' which the princes enjoyed and therefore revoked and annulled all communes, municipal councils and elected magistrates in every city and town of Germany; cf. the *Edictum contra communa civitatum* of January 1232 (Blondel, op. cit., 405-406).
[2] Cf. E. Franzel's interesting study, *König Heinrich VII. von Hohenstaufen. Studien zur Geschichte des Staates in Deutschland* (1929); also E. Rosenstock, 'Ueber Reich, Staat u. Stadt in Deutschland von 1230-1235', *Mitt. d. Inst. f. österr. Geschichtsforschung*, XLIV (1930).
[3] Cf. above, p. 187 sq.

an attempt to exclude them, as a class, from a voice in government. The decisive factor, however, was Frederick's attitude. He could not afford a breach with the princes, through whose mediation he had secured peace with the papacy in 1230, and he threw the full weight of his support on to their side. Henry was forced to give way in 1231, and in 1232 the concessions wrung from Henry in the previous year were confirmed in the famous *Statutum in favorem principum*. But Henry's surrender was only tactical, and within a few months he resumed his support of the towns and ordered his officials to ignore the privilege of 1232. Finally, again opposed by Frederick, he raised the standard of rebellion; but with the princes united in opposition, his resistance collapsed, and he was deposed and imprisoned in 1235.

In the circumstances in which he found himself, it is hard to see what other course Frederick could have taken between 1231 and 1235. Henry showed neither tact nor moderation in the execution of his policy, and by provoking a united opposition created a threatening situation in which Frederick had no practical alternative to withdrawal. But the objects which Henry pursued were sound in themselves, and the error lay in the diametrically opposed policy Frederick had introduced in his early years, and in his subsequent neglect of Germany, which was left in the hands of the princes from 1220 until Henry took control in 1228. Henry's determination to resist the growing encroachments of the princes was worse than useless, unless he were assured in advance of the emperor's support; but he showed real political acumen in his realization that Germany's strength and hope lay in the towns and knights and in his attempt to mobilize these forces under the monarchy. After his second excommunication in 1239, when a number of bishops began to waver in their loyalty, Frederick attempted haltingly to renew the bonds between the cities and the crown; but it was too late and he was never in Germany long enough to provide effective support. Instead the cities relied against princely encroachments on leagues for mutual defence, while the knightly families were, with few exceptions, reduced to dependence on the princes and forced to adapt themselves to life within the framework of the principalities. The towns and the *ministeriales*, which might have provided a solid foundation for royal government, became instead the backbone of the rising principalities.

After 1232 the main energies of the princes were devoted to the exploitation of the concessions wrung from Frederick, to the rounding-off and building-up of their territorial power. Frederick's breach with the church in 1239, and still more the vicious attack on the monarchy opened by Innocent IV after the Council of Lyons in 1245, created conditions peculiarly favourable to such a policy. Once again, as in the days of Henry IV, papal excommunication and the election of a papal nominee as anti-king, gave the princes the opportunity to pursue their own interests at the expense of the crown; but unlike Henry IV, Frederick II had already surrendered all his strong-points, while his indifference was demonstrated by the fact that he left the government of Germany in the hands of his son Conrad, and never once, during all the long years of struggle, appeared personally to rally Germany to the imperial cause. Thus the Hohenstaufen case went by default. The princes watched the progress of events with indifference, and neither Conrad nor the anti-king, Henry Raspe, who was elected by an insignificant faction in May 1246, received serious backing. The princes, who had nothing to gain by using their strength to bring the conflict to an end, intervened only when their own immediate interests were involved, and what drove them into one camp or the other was the prospect of territorial gain. Archbishop Conrad of Cologne deserted Frederick in 1240 out of hostility to his competitors in the Rhinelands and the Netherlands, the Count-Palatine, the dukes of Brabant and Limburg, and the counts of Berg and Jülich, who had the support of the royal government. He was joined by Siegfried of Mainz because of the territorial rivalry between Siegfried and the duke of Bavaria, who supported Frederick in the hope of being rewarded by the grant of Austria when the heirless duke of Austria died. On neither side was any question of principle or loyalty involved; tangible concessions alone secured adherents, and the pope only persuaded the landgrave of Thuringia, Henry Raspe, to lead the opposition by making secret territorial concessions at the expense of the church of Mainz. But, although the civil wars in Germany after 1245 resulted only in an indecisive contest, from which the princes alone profited, this result was not unsatisfactory to the pope. The material resources of the monarchy were dissipated, and above all else the forces which earlier had been available for employment in Italy were tied down in Germany. In the last years of his reign Frederick was hard pressed to maintain his position in north Italy; defeated at Parma in 1248 and at Bologna in 1249, the imperial forces were thrown on to the defensive, and imperial successes in 1250 were insufficient to retrieve the situation. By intervening in Germany, Innocent struck Frederick where he was weakest; it was a skilful tactical move, decisively altering the balance of power in favour of the papacy. But it was more than that. Innocent's intervention, giving rein to the interplay of territorial interests, set the seal on the process of emancipating the principalities from royal control, which Frederick's policy had called into existence. When Frederick died in 1250 the bonds created in time past by the monarchy to weld Germany together, had already sprung apart, and the position of the monarchy itself was irretrievably compromised. Between 1212 and 1250, sacrificed by Frederick to the exigencies of Italy, Germany took a road which differentiated its history for centuries to come, if not for all time, from that of England and France: its destinies passed out of the hands of the monarchy into the control of a princely aristocracy, whose horizons rarely extended beyond the boundaries of their own territories, and whose policy showed scant respect for the common interests and traditions of the German people.

IV

The reign of Frederick II thus marked the end of an epoch. Had he once secured his objects in Italy, it is possible that he would have sought to go back on his early policy in Germany and take a stand against the encroachments of the princes; and in that sense the issue remained open, the fate of Germany undecided, until his death intervened in 1250. But the failure to secure a decision in Italy, after the favourable opportunity in 1238 had been let slip, and the subsequent deterioration of the situation in Germany prevented any such developments; and the long interregnum, which followed Frederick's death in 1250, confirmed for all time the evil results of his policy.

The bankruptcy of Frederick's policy made itself evident immediately on his death. From 1250 it was clear that he had left no system capable of standing fast once his personality was removed. Throughout the Empire every unwholesome development of the previous half-century was immediately accentuated. Sicily, merci-lessly exploited to furnish resources for Frederick's Italian wars, rose in rebellion. In Italy the local magnates, on whom Frederick had increasingly relied in his later years, stood out as the actual repositories of political power and, unflinchingly pursuing their own interests, began to lay the foundations of the *signorie* or tyran-nies, which soon became the dominant factor in Italian politics. The papacy, unappeased and irreconcilable, converted the anathema on Frederick into an anathema on the whole Hohenstaufen dynasty, every member of which, it maintained, must 'beyond all doubt be an oppressor of the church'; and Innocent IV immediately forbade the German princes to elect Frederick's son, Conrad IV, in his father's place. Conrad himself was not slow to abandon Germany. Asserting that his 'hereditary realm of Sicily' was dear to him above all others, he hastened south across the Alps in 1251, thus proclaiming himself the true political heir of his father; but his early death in 1254 destroyed the last flickering hope of a continuation of Frederick's policy. Manfred, Frederick's illegitimate son, who assumed the leadership of the imperial cause after 1254, pursued an exclusively Italian policy seeking — like Frederick before him — to dominate Italy with the resources of Sicily, but he made no attempt to renew connexions with Germany. Finally Manfred's very success drove the pope to call in Charles of Anjou, and Charles's victories over Manfred in 1266 and over Conradin in 1268 decided the issue. The connexion between Germany and Sicily, forged by Henry VI in 1194, ceased for all time, and with it went the basis of imperial policy as pursued by Frederick II since 1220. Italy, where the actual exercise of power was in the hands of local despots, could no longer be dominated without a firm foothold in Sicily; and Ger-many, which as late as 1219 might still have been the heart of a substantial empire, was thrown back on itself. This result, so often treated as the inevitable consequence of German imperialism as it had developed since 962, was in reality the consequence of Frederick II's policy, which was never a German policy; it was the consequence of Frederick II's refusal to execute the terms of his treaties with the papacy, to surrender Sicily when he received the imperial crown in 1220, and to base his policy in accordance with tradition on Ger-many. The tendency to move the seat of the empire from Germany to Italy was, without doubt, much older; it can be seen under

Henry VI and its origins can be traced back to Barbarossa. But no irretrievable step had been taken before Frederick II ascended the throne, and in that respect responsibility falls on his shoulders. It is difficult to judge Henry VI's policy, which, cut short by his early death, remains a torso; but down to 1190 German imperial policy had all the elements of a sane and practical policy, and it was only after the union of the empire with Sicily, and after the accession of a ruler who viewed the empire through Sicilian eyes, that disastrous consequences intervened. In this development there was nothing inevitable; nor was it inevitable that Frederick II should neglect Germany and treat his German inheritance with indifference. His attitude to the empire, far from being the culmination of mediaeval imperialism, was a complete breach with the past. He abandoned the traditions on which his German predecessors had built, and substituted a Mediterranean tradition compounded of Norman lust of conquest, Italian tyranny and cynical *raison d'état*, in which the dawn of a new — and scarcely better — age was heralded. In Italy, where he helped the tyrants and *condottieri* into power, and in Germany he destroyed the old foundations of government, without setting anything durable in their place; he sacrificed Germany to an imperialism which was not German, but Sicilian or Italian. If we survey the course of German affairs from the first outbreak of conflict between Henry IV and Gregory VII in 1076, no single event had more disastrous consequences than Innocent III's act in summoning Frederick II to the imperial throne in 1212. It was an act dictated not by German but by papal and French interests; and it set in charge of Germany a ruler who, in spite of his Hohenstaufen blood, was Sicilian in outlook and policy, a foreigner in the land of his fathers. Under his rule the work of generations was shattered.

This sudden collapse would not have been possible, had there not already been an inner canker at the roots of the German constitution; and we have in fact seen already how, from the early days of the twelfth century, the distribution of power had changed steadily to the detriment of the monarchy.[1] The rise of the principalities had proceeded far by the time Frederick II set foot on German soil in 1212. But Frederick Barbarossa had found the means of bringing the principalities into harmony with the interests of the monarchy; and down to the thirteenth century the development of the princi-

[1] Cf. above, p. 135 sqq.

palities had taken place under the crown within the framework of German unity, while the monarchy had retained sufficient independent power of its own to hold the princes in check. It was Frederick II's unwillingness to devote himself to the tasks of a German monarch, which was the turning-point. His continued absence from Germany dissociated the princes from the emperor; it removed from Germany the royal court which was the very heart of aristocratic society and left an unfilled void, for which the household of neither of his sons was a substitute. Personal association with the king, participation in the business of government, in legislation and in judgement, the traditional duty of attendance and service, all these ceased and therewith ceased the main concrete demonstrations of the existence of a unity towering above the princes, of an organization of which the princes were only members. Frederick's neglect of his royal duties turned the princes into egoists; dissociated from the empire, which was now Italian or Sicilian in character, they concentrated their energies inevitably on their own territories and territorial interests, and viewed the ruler and the realm thenceforward as they affected their own territorial policy. There was no visible opposition in Germany to Frederick's Italian policy; but, except on the part of the knights and *ministeriales* of Alsace and Swabia, traditionally loyal to the Hohenstaufen dynasty, who made up the German contingents for the Lombard wars, there was a comprehensible attitude of indifference to a cause which was no longer a German cause. In their very mediation between Frederick and the pope, for example in 1230, the princes took up an independent attitude; and both Frederick and the popes, Innocent IV in particular, paid them for their services. But the pope's concessions, apart from money collected in England and France, which flowed into the coffers of Henry Raspe, were at the expense of the German church, while Frederick's were at the expense of the German monarchy and of the lands on which the monarchy depended in order to maintain an independent position over the princes. So long as Henry VII remained in control, the Hohenstaufen territories had found an active protector; but after 1235 their history becomes a process of rapid decline. Frederick himself alienated the former properties of the Salian dynasty in the central Rhinelands — a complex of territories from which the later principality of the Palatinate arose — to the duke of Bavaria to secure his support. Under Conrad IV, between 1237 and 1251, the process of alienation became general, as the need to secure adherents became more pressing, and the crown lands fell into ruin. Thus the monarchy lost the solid and independent territorial basis which alone could make the king's prerogatives a reality; without a strongly organized territory and adequate material resources, the monarchy was unable to exploit its rights, and the result was atrophy, loss and powerlessness.

This result was confirmed between 1250 and 1272. There is little to be gained from a detailed examination of the political history of the interregnum; its lasting result lay rather in the administrative field, in the collapse of royal authority, the wholesale transfer of royal rights and properties, and the practical consummation of the tendencies licensed by the *Statutum in favorem principum* of 1232. But these results, and the régime of anarchy and violence which set in, were the corollary of the failure to unite on a successor to Frederick II, of the conflict between Conrad IV and William of Holland, who had been set up as nominee of the papal party on the death of Henry Raspe in 1247, and of the double election of Richard of Cornwall and Alfonso of Castile in 1257. For the first time in German history there was no solid body of support, among either princes or episcopate, for the legitimate dynasty; at the court which Conrad summoned to Augsburg at midsummer 1251, practically no one of importance appeared. Nor was there any party, outside the towns, which seriously sought to put an end to the discord and secure a unanimous election. William of Holland might, had he lived, have won general acceptance; but his death in 1256 dashed this prospect. In any case he was not sufficiently powerful to establish effective government, and his rule is significant not least because he was the first German king who was not even of princely rank. Thus his election marks the emergence of the tendency to elect weak kings, incapable for lack of territorial power of checking the territorial ambitions of the princes. The alternative, as in 1257, was to choose a ruler from outside; but this opened wide the door to foreign intervention, and fatally involved Germany in the hostility of England and France, and Italy in the rivalry of France and Spain. In fact neither Richard nor Alfonso played any part in German affairs; the latter never set foot in Germany, and the former, on his few brief visits, remained in the Rhinelands, which were allied with

England by close commercial relationships, and therefore favourable to his cause. But the very existence of rival candidates played into the princes' hands, and from the moment of Frederick's death they were able to wring major concessions from the conflicting parties. Thus William of Holland handed over the imperial city of Lübeck to the margraves of Brandenburg, thereby resigning a foothold on the Baltic, and at the same time subjected the bishoprics of Lübeck, Schwerin and Ratzeburg to the duke of Saxony. In the west he placed the administration of Alsace in the hands of the bishop of Strassburg, but the bishop's authority was challenged by count Rudolf of Habsburg, who received his rights from Conrad IV. Everywhere the rival kings surrendered royal territories, and by their concessions gave rise to rival territorial claims. None was more prodigal in his grants than Richard of Cornwall, but few princes or nobles waited for formal grants to seize fiefs and tenements necessary to round off their territories.[1] It is highly significant that these usurpations were not confined to the great princes, but now occurred on the part of the *ministeriales* who had risen in the service of the Hohenstaufen.[2] With the extinction of the Hohenstaufen dynasty the whole organization of government built up by the dynasty collapsed.

The result of the period 1215-1272 was thus to throw Germany back, to check its development by comparison with England and France. The functions carried out elsewhere by a strong monarchy, the protection (for example) of public peace and the suppression of crime, were in Germany either carried out by private associations within limited areas for limited purposes, or were not carried out at all. The centralized machinery of administration and law enforcement, which in England was in formation in the days of Henry II, had no parallel in Germany, and it was only later and haltingly that a similar organization was formed in the principalities. In 1250 the whole organization of German government was extraordinarily retrograde, and for this the growing tendency to rely on Italian

---

[1] Cf. the chronicle of Colmar (*Mon. Germ., Script.,* XVII, 241): 'Post mortem imperatoris Friderici imperii res quas quilibet dominorum poterat, confiscabat.'

[2] A case among many is the *ministerialis*, Gerhard of Sinzig, placed by Frederick II in charge of the royal stronghold of Landskrone. By 1248 he was calling himself *dominus de Landscrone*; during the Interregnum he ceased altogether to use his family name, and in the next generation the former *ministerialis* had become a lord with an independent lordship. The same process is evident throughout the royal demesnes, at Kaiserswerth or Dortmund or Aachen for example; cf. Niese, op. cit., 166-167, 256.

R

resources must be blamed. Frederick II, in particular, made little attempt to develop his resources in Germany; at the very time when he was reorganizing Sicilian and Italian government on bureaucratic lines, he allowed the organs of German government to atrophy, and what development there was towards more modern forms of administration was due to the princes and worked for the benefit of the princes. The result was to place political power in the princes' hands. It has been calculated that the demesnes of the crown at the end of the Hohenstaufen period amounted in the aggregate to the equivalent of only three-quarters of the margraviate of Brandenburg; but they were scattered fragments, a weak basis for political power, which could not compare with the resources of the greater princes.[1] Hence the allegiance of the princes was based no longer on respect for a monarch who was powerful enough to make his supreme authority felt, but rather on compromises, capitulations and promises. The king became the puppet of the princes; and after 1250 the electoral principle, combated until the very end of Hohenstaufen times, became a tenet of constitutional law. Within a few years the destinies of Germany fell into the hands of the electoral college, and the electoral college represented the principalities. Thus the defection of the monarchy, the abdication by Frederick II of his German tasks, involved disruption. The extraordinary vigour which was developed precisely at this time by German town life and commerce, the rich bloom of German civilization, were canalized into sectional channels. Without the unity provided by the crown, the principalities of north and east Germany went their own way, fulfilling a destiny which was provincial rather than national. Germany was condemned for centuries to decentralization and disunion and to the evils which went with decentralization and the unchecked conflicts of competing interests.

[1] Cf. Thompson, *Feudal Germany*, 359.

PART FOUR

THE AGE OF THE PRINCES
(1272-1519)

CHAPTER 10

THE EXPANSION OF GERMANY: COLONIZATION AND CONQUEST IN THE EAST

I

THE years 1250-1272, the years of the great Interregnum, marked a transition in German history equal in importance to the period of the Investiture Contest. Between 1250 and 1272 Germany crossed the threshold of a new age. The ruthless determination of the papacy to eradicate the whole Hohenstaufen dynasty, to extirpate the 'nest of vipers', which found its consummation in the execution of the young Conradin in 1268, loosed upon the empire a generation of anarchy, which brought to nothing the constructive work of the Hohenstaufen. In Italy the basis of imperial government collapsed; the very links between Italy and Germany were shattered. In Germany the Interregnum enabled the princes to consolidate at the expense of the monarchy all they had won in the preceding fifty years. When, in 1273, Rudolf of Habsburg succeeded to the pillaged inheritance of the Hohenstaufen, the age of princes succeeded the age of the emperors.

Fundamentally it was the alliance between the German opposition and the papacy which defeated all attempts by the Hohenstaufen dynasty to set imperial government in Germany and Italy on a durable foundation. This alliance had its roots in the past, reaching back (as we have seen) through the turmoil and revolution of the Investiture Contest to the days of Pope Leo IX (1048-1054); and there is no need to recapitulate the factors, political and constitutional, from which it drew strength. From the time when the Investiture Contest undermined the old constitution and threw the whole social organization of Germany into the melting pot, it had been an open question whether the necessary process of social and political reconstruction would be controlled by the crown and provide a new foundation for royal power, or whether it would establish the princes firmly in the saddle. Down to 1198 the course of events seemed to indicate that the monarchy was succeeding; and in spite of the setbacks between 1198 and 1208 and of the resultant concessions which Frederick II was forced to make, the question remained open so long as Frederick's genius dominated the scene. Only the war of extermination waged against Conrad IV, Manfred and the young Conradin after Frederick II's death in 1250 sealed the issue.

Nevertheless we have seen in the Hohenstaufen period many symptoms of the progress of the princes towards independence. Even the dramatic events of 1180, which seemingly marked the triumph of Frederick Barbarossa over his most dangerous adversary, Henry the Lion, constituted (we saw) a compromise between the monarchy and the greatest princes of the realm, which defined and strengthened the rights and privileges of the latter. The two great concessions of Frederick II, the *Confoederatio cum principibus ecclesiasticis* of 1220 and the *Statutum in favorem principum* of 1232, were further milestones along the same road. In the meantime great territorial changes, transforming the face of Germany by new settlement and colonization, had already by 1250 brought about a major shift in the balance of power within Germany which resulted in an irrevocable weakening of the old foundations of government. By the end of the Hohenstaufen period the political geography of Germany was revolutionized. The old duchies, which had so long provided a broad framework for political life, were broken up and replaced by new territorial units; Saxony disappeared in 1180 and was succeeded by Westphalia, Anhalt and Brunswick; Bavaria lost its identity through the separation of Austria, Styria and the Tyrol. Simultaneously the older regions round Rhine and Main gradually lost the leading role they had formerly played in German politics. During the second half of the twelfth and the first half of the thirteenth centuries the seat of political power moved from west to east. As a result of colonization and settlement new territories arose east of the old Reich frontiers, where the king had no entry and no direct influence. It is a significant indication of the change which had taken place in the political balance of power in Germany by the end of the twelfth century that of the sixteen lay princes constituted in 1180 no less than half drew their title from lands which lay east of the German boundaries of 919.[1]

[1] They were the Dukes of Bohemia, Austria, Styria and Carinthia, the Margraves of Brandenburg, Meissen and Lausitz and the Count of Anhalt. The Margrave of Moravia was added to their number in 1182.

The great wave of German colonization, carrying the frontiers of the Reich forward from the Elbe to the Vistula and along the Baltic to the Gulf of Finland was — alongside the failure and downfall of the Hohenstaufen dynasty — the second factor ushering in a new era in German history. It changed not only the whole political balance but also the economic and social substructure of German life; it gave for all time a new direction to German aspirations, a new outlet for German energies; it added to Germany an area equivalent in dimensions to two-thirds of its original territories. The Elbe, hitherto Germany's eastern frontier, henceforward ran through the heart of the land, taking the place of the Rhine as the centre of German life; Breslau replaced Magdeburg or Brandenburg as a frontier city. In little over two centuries, between 1125 and 1346, two-fifths of modern Germany was conquered, colonized and absorbed.

This immense achievement was accomplished, after the death of Lothar II in 1137, virtually without support or help from the imperial government, and often in direct opposition to imperial policy. Indirectly Frederick I eased the progress of colonization when, in 1157, he forced the Poles once again to accept imperial overlordship, and when in 1163 he separated Silesia from Poland and brought it, under Germanophile princes, into close contact with the Reich. The conferment of a royal crown on the Bohemian duke, in 1158, was also useful in securing his support for imperial policy. But after 1198 even this indirect assistance ceased. Otto IV recognized the conquests of the great Danish king, Waldemar II, who laid hands on Holstein, Mecklenburg and Pomerania in 1203, in order to secure his support against Philip of Swabia; and in 1214 Frederick II, to deprive Otto of Danish support, had to confirm the Danish conquests. Later, in 1244, his conflict with the papacy compelled him to renew his concession in part, bestowing on Denmark all the lands beyond the rivers Elbe and Elde. The defeat of the Danes, which finally freed the Baltic coast for German expansion and colonization, was the work of a local coalition between Holstein, Mecklenburg, Lübeck, Hamburg and Bremen; their victory at Bornhöved in 1227 and the first naval victory won by Lübeck in 1234 restored access to the Baltic. In this the empire played no part. Deeply embroiled in Italy, Frederick II could not afford to incur the hostility of his northern neighbours and could only passively watch the course of German expansion in the north-east. In 1207 and 1225, after the conquest of Livonia, the bishops of Livonia were made princes of the empire and in 1226 East Prussia was granted by Frederick II to the Master of the Teutonic Order, who also was made an imperial prince. But these acts were little more than a formal registration of conquests in which the empire had no share. Conquest, settlement, the foundation of cities and the opening of trade routes were all the independent work of generations of princes, monastic leaders, peasants and traders, who relied on their own capital and energy and power, and who laboured without any co-ordination of effort or direction by the central government.

This situation was not merely an accidental result of the pre-occupation of the Hohenstaufen with Italy, or of the weakness of the later rulers after the Interregnum. It also reflected the character of German eastward expansion in the Middle Ages, which was only in limited degree inspired by political motives. The whole character of the movement would be obscured if, under the influence of modern ideologies, it were depicted as a phase in an eternal conflict between Germans and Slavs. Racial antagonism played a part, as we shall see, just as did the crude antagonism between paganism and Christianity; but its scope can easily be exaggerated. Taking all in all, it can safely be said that the more we know of German eastern colonization in the Middle Ages, the less it has the appearance of a racial or nationalist movement, directed from above. Only in two areas was there anything approaching a war of extermination or the deliberate subjection and depression of the native population: in Prussia in the thirteenth century, and in the twelfth century in Nordalbingia, where the situation was aggravated by a legacy of bitter hostility between the Saxons and the Wagrians and Abodrites reaching back, as we have seen,[1] to the tenth century. This antagonism was unhappily fanned by the crude intolerance of the Church which — whipped to a high pitch of fanaticism by Bernard of Clairvaux — deliberately unleashed the bloody Wendish crusade of 1147 with the hateful slogan 'baptism or extermination'. But if Holstein and western Mecklenburg were mercilessly conquered by the sword, and the way was cleared for colonization by the decimation and expulsion of the Wendish population, further east settle-

[1] Above, p. 42.

ment proceeded more peacefully and the sword gave way to the plough. In Brandenburg, Pomerania and Silesia German settlement and the establishment of German political control took place without serious friction or bloodshed: it was a peaceful penetration, carried through without racial or national antagonism and only completed after generations — in some regions, centuries — of interaction.

If such, briefly, was the position on the German side, still less was there any question in the twelfth and thirteenth centuries of an opposing spirit of Slav racialism or nationalism. After generations of bloody border warfare the Wendish or Baltic Slavs were bitterly hostile to the Saxons; but they were scarcely less hostile to the Slavs of the Warthe and Vistula, particularly after the conversion of Poland to Christianity. Their independence and the survival of their traditional way of life were as much menaced in the east by Poland, which embarked under Boleslav III (1102-1139) on a policy of territorial expansion, as by the Germans in the west; indeed, both Pomerania and Brandenburg preferred, and deliberately chose, German domination to the 'hated overlordship' of Poland.[1] The smaller Slav states, isolated and curiously averse to the development of strong and durable political systems, had little chance against their greater neighbours, Poland, Bohemia and Lithuania, once the latter had been consolidated under grasping, aggressive dynasties and an oppressive nobility. How little common Slav sentiment there was is shown by the fact that it was their Slav neighbours who, after Henry the Lion's final conquest of Mecklenburg in 1177, sold the survivors of the defeated Abodrites into slavery among the Poles and Bohemians.[2] Religious differences were a further source of division. As early as 1113-1114 a Christian Abodrite prince joined forces with the Saxons to attack the stronghold and temple of the pagan Slavs on the island of Rügen,[3] while it was Boleslav III of Poland who, after conquering Pomerania, called in Otto of Bamberg and his German helpers to convert the native population. Nor should it be forgotten that it was the Polish Duke of Masovia who summoned the Teutonic Order in 1226 to help him subdue the independent Prussians, and that it was a Slav prince and a feudatory of Denmark, Wizlaw of Rügen, who in 1221 exclaimed: 'God forbid

[1] Cf. Thompson, *Feudal Germany*, 433, 446.　　　[2] Op. cit., 508.
[3] For the date, cf. Thompson, op. cit., 424.

that the land should ever relapse into its former state, that the Slavs should drive out the German settlers and again undertake its cultivation!'[1]

The fact was that the loosely-knit Slav peoples were not only disunited among themselves and in no way fundamentally opposed to the influx of German colonists, but that the German colonization of the east was as much the work of Slav as of German lords and princes. Urged on by the prospects of economic advantage, by the hope of profit from lands which had hitherto given no yield, all parties competed for the services of German settlers, and the work of colonization went on in much the same way whether the landlord was a German or a Slav. This was true not only of lands, like Pomerania and Silesia, which were later fully absorbed into Germany, but also of Poland and Hungary and Bohemia, where progressive princes realized the advantages which would be derived from German immigrants and encouraged peasant and urban settlement even in face of the opposition of the native nobility which feared the loss of its own privileged position and of the monopoly of exploitation. The advantages sought were principally but not exclusively economic; dynasties like the Przemyslids of Bohemia saw also the possibility of offsetting the power of the unruly native nobility and Ottokar II (1253-1278), under whom Germanization reached its peak, deliberately called German knights and *ministeriales*, as well as urban settlers, into Bohemia in order to free himself from dependence on the Slav nobility.

It was only in the latter part of the fourteenth and in the fifteenth centuries, after the main work of German colonization had been completed, that political antagonism became a serious factor on Germany's eastern frontiers. This was the result of the rise of greater states already imbued with the germs of incipient nationalism and strengthened politically by the introduction of more modern institutions: Hungary under Louis the Great (1342-1382), Bohemia under Charles IV (1346-1378), and Poland under Casimir the Great (1333-1370). Of these events none was fraught with greater significance than the rise of Poland which had already embarked on aggression in the east in 1340, when the Russian kingdom of Galicia was annexed, and which became a great power after its union with Lithuania in 1386. From the time of Wladislav II (1386-1434)

---

[1] K. Hampe, *Der Zug nach dem Osten*, 35.

Poland aspired to the leadership of eastern Europe. Already in 1308 it had sought unsuccessfully to annex Pomerelia after the extinction of the native Pomerelian dynasty, hoping thus to secure by conquest an outlet to the Baltic and the port of Danzig. Under Wladislav it renewed the same project in opposition to the Teutonic Order, sedulously propagating the myth that Prussia and Pomerelia were former territories of the Polish crown and holding out to the Prussian nobility the prospect of that despotic liberty at the expense of towns and peasantry which was the notorious perquisite of the Polish and Lithuanian aristocracy. The results are well known: the great victory over the Teutonic Order at Tannenberg in 1410, the successive treaties ending with the Peace of Thorn in 1466 which broke the power of the Teutonic knights, the downfall of the Ordensland and the establishment of Polish sovereignty on the shores of the Baltic.

Against this surge of Polish nationalism, directed against lands populated alike by Germans and by alien Slavs who had never submitted to the yoke of Polish tyranny, there was no corresponding German reaction. From the first the Teutonic Order was left to fight alone its battle against Poland. The emperor Sigismund (1410-1438) regarded the dispute between the Order and the Poles simply as a pretext to pursue his own dynastic interests, and appeals for succour went unheeded. It was the same at the end of the century when, with the conquest of Novgorod by Ivan the Great (1462-1505), Russia appeared as a great power in the Baltic, menacing the Teutonic Order's hold in Livonia. Like Sigismund, Maximilian I (1493-1519) was eager to compromise with Bohemia and Hungary at the expense of Prussia. Nothing, indeed, is more remarkable than the lack of awareness throughout Germany at this period of the political implications of the decline of Germanism in the north and east. Frederick II of Brandenburg may have had some idea of the issues involved; but elsewhere there appears to have been no consciousness that vital German interests were at stake. Throughout Maximilian's reign there was intense awareness of the deterioration of Germany's external situation, and a growing national consciousness; but dissatisfaction was focused on the problems of the western frontier, particularly the French threat to Alsace, and the fate of the eastern frontier was viewed by all classes with indifference.[1] A

[1] Andreas, *Deutschland vor der Reformation*, 216-217.

sense of common German interests in the east, an idea that Germany's political destiny was involved in the Germanization of the Slav lands, only arose centuries later under the stimulus of Hohenzollern policy.

The anti-German reaction which gathered strength in Bohemia and Poland in the last decades of the fourteenth century, coming after the stream of German colonists had sunk to a mere trickle, set a definite term to German eastwards expansion. What had not been Germanized by 1350 was not Germanized later; and where — for example, in the Baltic lands between the Gulfs of Riga and Finland — conquest was unaccompanied by a broad wave of German peasant settlement, territorial gains proved ephemeral. What gave German eastern expansion the character of a sweeping, irrevocable movement of peoples, changing for all time the ethnographical and political map of eastern Europe, was the ungrudging labour of thousands of peasant and urban settlers, above all of the peasantry. Their work transformed the economic system of eastern Europe; and very soon the German agrarian system began to spread beyond the strict limits of German colonization. Because of their manifold advantages, German methods of colonization were used as a model for the settlement of non-German colonists on virgin land; this was particularly the case in Poland among settlers who were predominantly Poles. The result was that, in addition to areas of pure German colonization, there were others of colonization 'under German law'. Nothing is more difficult — since in later centuries non-Germans have been extensively Germanized, and *vice versa* — than to draw a clear line of division between these areas, but it is certain that there were many areas 'under German law' where there was no considerable immigration of German peasants. In these circumstances it is futile and dangerous to attempt to draw any precise territorial divisions between the races. What is important is to realize the widespread character of German influence. 'Economic Germanization' extended to wide areas which underwent neither linguistic nor political Germanization; and the influence of 'economic Germanization' should not be underrated because it did not always lead to territorial acquisition. For the bulk of the Slav population, German colonization and colonization according to German law meant a definite rise in social and economic conditions. Among the agents of German colonization the Teutonic Order has a bad name; the repression of the Prussian peasantry is notorious. Yet it has rightly been pointed out that we have only to contrast the position of the peasantry in Livonia and Esthonia to see all that Old Prussia gained by being Germanized, and it is notorious that after the defeat of the Order there was serious deterioration in the conditions of the peasants in those parts of Prussia annexed by Poland.[1] Even in Poland, however, in spite of a strongly-entrenched reactionary aristocracy, the example of German colonization and the introduction of German standards brought about improved social conditions. Throughout the east German settlement resulted in a tendency to assimilation of the native with the favoured German peasantry, limitation and fixing of burdens, an improved legal status amounting (where German influence was strong) to personal freedom, and individual ownership and cultivation. To the work of German urban settlers the Slavonic east owed a complete permanent market-controlled economy and an export trade in which grain was the staple commodity.

These were major benefits, widely shared by thousands of nameless workers from the Baltic to the Carpathians; but the greatest achievement of the German colonizing movement lay in the immense tracts of virgin country, hitherto waste and forest, which it opened to cultivation and exploitation. Only in relatively few regions did the German settlers compete for land already under cultivation (though with their improved technique they introduced more intensive cultivation of lands opened up by Slav peasants); their main work was the clearance of forest and the draining of marshlands. Here the Germans, with their heavy ploughs and their knowledge (won in Holland and on the Ems and Weser) of the art of diking performed a task which the native population had neither tools nor skill nor incentive to undertake. Not only was the country, before the arrival of German immigrants, too thinly populated to warrant intensive cultivation; economic and social conditions were also against it. The bulk of the population lived in oppressive serfdom without either fixed standards of dues and services or protection against arbitrary ejection, and had no incentive to undertake work which could only benefit their lords. Hence the German colonists found cultivable land to spare, when they

[1] Cf. H. v. Treitschke, *Origins of Prussianism*, 57-58, 150. Cf. also p. 77: 'maltreated serfs fled from Lithuania to enjoy the milder rule of the Order.'

moved across the Elbe, apart from the devastations caused by war; in particular there were the vast frontier forests which the Slavs had left untouched for strategic reasons. These and the marsh-lands, which the natives did not know how to dike and drain, provided huge reserves of potential arable capable of sustaining a large population.

It was the achievement of the German colonists to win these wastes for culture, to plant villages in hundreds where previously humans had never trod, to open communications and establish the flourishing urban communities which, like a backbone for the land, often served to hold together the peasant settlements. No overall figures can be given, but it has been computed that in Silesia alone between 1200 and 1350 about 1200 villages were founded and that in a comparable period in east Prussia the knights and bishops established about 1400 rent-paying villages.[1] Taken together these settlements would require a peasant population in the region of 300,000. Such figures, extended to cover the other centres of colonization, Mecklenburg and Pomerania, Holstein and Meissen, give the best idea of the magnitude of the work and the flow of population involved. A new land, almost unknown, was opened up and populated; new states with a great future were formed. Not without reason has the colonization of the east been called the 'greatest deed of the German people during the Middle Ages'.[2]

II

Many factors contributed to the great movement of German colonization across the Elbe in the early years of the twelfth century. Conditions on the Slav side of the border played their part. As we

---

[1] Cf. H. Aubin, *Cambridge Econ. Hist.*, I (1941), 396-397.
[2] K. Lamprecht, *Deutsche Geschichte*, III, 363: 'es ist die Grosstat unseres Volkes während des Mittelalters'. — What follows is based primarily on R. Kötzschke, *Quellen z. Gesch. d. Ostdeutschen Kolonisierung im 12-14. Jahrhundert* (1912), E. O. Schulze, *Die Kolonisierung u. Germanisierung der Gebiete zwischen Saale und Elbe* (1896), K. Hampe, *Der Zug nach dem Osten* (1921), H. v. Treitschke, *Das deutsche Ordensland Preussen* (*Hist. u. polit. Aufsätze*. Bd. 2, 1862, trans. E. and C. Paul under the title *Origins of Prussianism*, 1942), E. Caspar, *Hermann von Salza u. die Gründung des deutschen Ordensstaats in Preussen* (1924); in addition the detailed chapters (XII-XVII) in Thompson's *Feudal Germany*, 387-658 — a most comprehensive treatment, far ahead of any other work in English — and the invaluable contribution by H. Aubin, 'The lands east of the Elbe and German colonization eastwards', in *Cambridge Economic History*, I (1941), 361-397. Cf. also the brief but pregnant survey by R. Koebner, 'The Settlement and Colonization of Europe', *Cambr. Econ. Hist.*, I, 1-88 (particularly 56 sqq., 80 sqq.).

have seen, the Baltic Slavs were divided by Christianity; more important, the great Slav revolts had depleted their powers of resistance. The great rebellion of 983[1] had been followed by others, no less formidable, in 1018 and 1066, which although successful used up the energies of the Slav peoples, which were worn down still further in almost incessant border warfare with the Saxons. The appearance of a hostile Poland on their eastern flank was another factor reducing their ability to resist. Nevertheless none of these factors was as important as the changes in Germany itself during the preceding century, where new social and economic and political forces created a pressure which found outlet in eastward expansion.

First among the changes in Germany was the rapid expansion of economic activity during the eleventh century, accompanied by a growing population.[2] Engrossing of the commons and clearing and expropriation of the forest made it more difficult for the poor man to gain his livelihood; land became scarcer and land values rose. The older peasant holdings were split, and the result was a deteriorating standard of living for their occupants in a period of increasing plenty. By the end of the century land-hunger and the struggle for possession of the soil were rife in the areas of old cultivation. But these factors alone, working steadily but slowly to produce a shift of population, would hardly have sufficed without the upheavals of the Investiture Contest to inaugurate a mass movement. The Investiture Contest accentuated all the problems. Stimulating (as we have seen) the rapid growth of feudalism, it led to an onerous extension of manorial dues and burdens; it resulted also in the depression of the free Saxon peasantry to unfree status. Emerging from their struggle with Henry IV with all the material fruits of victory, the nobility lost no time in exploiting their success, and fastening new and heavy burdens on the land. The ravages of civil war reduced many a valley to waste and many a village to ruin; they left a trail of dispossessed. The great rebellion of Saxony, which Henry IV ruthlessly suppressed, left in its train large numbers of broken and impoverished freemen, who welcomed the opportunity to begin life over again beyond the Elbe.

That such an opportunity awaited the surplus population of Germany was the result of changes in the political situation in the north. The death in 1106 of Magnus Billung, the last of his house,

[1] Cf. above, p. 42.   [2] Cf. above, p. 76.

and the succession to the Billung inheritance of Lothar of Supplinburg, brought about a new constellation of forces in Saxony. The
old crippling feud between the dukes and the Church for political
control, which had dominated and enervated Saxon politics throughout almost the whole of the eleventh century, was replaced under
Lothar by a sincere policy of co-operation. Unlike the Billungs,
Lothar was an ardent supporter of the Church, in no way averse to
the spread of Christianity among the Slavs.[1] After 1106, therefore,
church and state in Saxony were united in a common purpose:
the sword of the duke was employed in support of the clergy in a
series of attacks upon the neighbouring Slavs which were at once
military expeditions and missionary campaigns. From about 1110
Saxon incursions into Wendish territory became more frequent and
more intense. In 1114 the titular bishop of Brandenburg invaded his
see and returned boasting that he had destroyed many pagan idols.
In 1115 Count Otto of Ballenstädt, father of the famous Albrecht
the Bear, won a crushing victory over the Wends at Köthen. In
the winter of 1124-1125 Lothar himself invaded the Slav lands. But
it was Lothar's election to the German throne in 1125 which opened
wider prospects. The Salians, hereditary enemies of the Saxon
dukes, had with rare exceptions maintained friendly relations with
the Slav tribes on the borders of Saxony, regarding them as a
valuable counterpoise to the power of the Billunger. Lothar's
attitude as king and emperor was naturally different. The very
situation of his duchy and of his own dynastic lands compelled
him, more than his predecessors on the throne, to keep his eye
steadily on the east. He began his reign — in spite of opposition
and dissension at home — with an expedition to Bohemia, where
the duke paid him homage. This was followed in 1131 by an
expedition to Denmark, which also acknowledged German overlordship. Four years later Boleslav III of Poland was forced to
recognize imperial suzerainty. The tribute received from the Poles
was used by Lothar to further the missionary work of Otto of Bamberg, which contributed more than any other factor to the Germanization of Pomerania; similarly in eastern Holstein the emperor
gave his support to the missionary work of Vicelin of Neumünster.

[1] For the Billunger, on the contrary, Christianization meant the extension of the Church's
tithe at the expense of the tribute which they levied from the heathen tribes; hence they did
all they could to resist it; cf. Thompson, *Feudal Germany*, 410-415.

Of wider interest were his claims, on behalf of the archbishopric of Magdeburg, to metropolitan rights over the Polish church. All in all, it looked like a revival of the traditions of Otto the Great and the beginning of a new period of active imperial policy in the east.

This prospect was dashed by the change of dynasty after Lothar's death in 1137; as we have seen, the Hohenstaufen contributed little to German eastern expansion. But the traditions of Lothar's reign survived, and it was after his death that they were most effectively applied by the lieutenants he had set up in the marches of Saxony: the Ascanians and the houses of Wettin and Schauenburg. It was to these dynasties, supported by the Archbishop of Magdeburg,[1] and to Henry the Lion, that the direction of eastern policy passed after Lothar's death. The rise of Conrad the Great of Wettin, Margrave of Meissen (1124-1156), of Adolf of Schauenburg, Count of Holstein (1130-1164), of Albrecht the Bear, Margrave of Brandenburg (1134-1170), and of Henry the Lion, Duke of Saxony (1139-1195) — all infused with a new spirit of territorial expansion and with a new attitude to the problems of the eastern frontier — set going a movement which, gathering pace and weight, continued throughout the thirteenth century and only came to a standstill two centuries after their deaths.

It was in the turmoil following the death of Lothar II and the change of dynasty in 1138 that the movement across the Elbe was launched. The revolt of Henry the Proud and the struggle between Albrecht the Bear and the Welfs for control of Saxony soon involved the whole border in uproar, and the Slavs — as was their wont — exploited the occasion to attack the Saxons. In retaliation Henry the Proud, in the winter of 1138-1139, led an expedition into the land of the Abodrites and laid it waste. Albrecht the Bear and Adolf of Holstein, seeking to extend their territorial power to the detriment of their German rivals, were not slow to follow; Henry the Lion, who succeeded his father, Henry the Proud, in 1139, was a third competitor. By 1143 the first definitive conquests had been made, and the scheme of things to come was visible. Albrecht the Bear, with an ample field of activity opening before him further east on the river Havel, withdrew from Saxony to concentrate on his

---

[1] It is noteworthy that Archbishop Wichmann of Magdeburg, the most famous of the colonizing prelates, was descended on his father's side from the Billunger dukes of Saxony and on his mother's side from the Margraves of Lausitz and Meissen.

S

marchlands; Adolf of Holstein and Henry the Lion divided the field between them. The latter took as his share the Abodrite country of Mecklenburg, east of the river Trave; to the former fell the lands of Wagria, the lake country of eastern Holstein between Lübeck and Kiel. Here in 1143 he founded the city of Lübeck, which by opening the door to the Baltic became a key point in the extension of German influence in the east.

What made Adolf of Holstein's conquest of Wagria, completed by 1143, a turning-point in the history of German eastern expansion, was his decision to follow it up by thorough colonization. From the beginning he gave his support to the missionary activities of Vicelin of Neumünster. More important he called in settlers. Even to-day the appeal which he sent out far and wide to attract colonists, preserved for us in Helmold's vivid chronicle, can scarcely fail to stir the imagination:

> Inasmuch as the land was without inhabitants, Count Adolf sent messengers into all the regions roundabout, to Flanders and Holland, to Utrecht, Westphalia and Frisia, proclaiming that all who were oppressed by want of land should go thither with their families; there they would receive the best of soils, rich in fruits and abounding in fish and flesh, and blessed with fine pastures. And to the Holsteiners and Sturmarians he said: 'Did ye not invade the land of the Slavs and purchase it with the blood of your fathers and brethren? Wherefore then are ye the last to come and take possession thereof? Be ye rather the first to enter into the delectable land, and till and enjoy your portion of the precious fruits thereof; for the best portion is yours, seeing ye have delivered it out of the hands of the enemies.' And when he had said this there arose a countless multitude from many regions with their families and all that they possessed, and they came into the territory of the Wagrians to Count Adolf to receive the lands he had promised them.

Such was the beginning of German colonization in the north-east. It was a modest beginning, extending only to the smallest and most westerly province of the neighbouring Slavs. But it was a model for the future, showing for the first time how, with determination and systematic planning, an area of some two to three hundred square miles could be covered with new villages. Nor were there wanting, among Adolf's contemporaries, princes who appreciated the significance of his achievement and the prospects which it opened out.

Foremost among them was Henry the Lion, less conciliatory than Adolf, grasping, unscrupulous, cruel and ever on the watch for opportunities to extend his power over Germans and Slavs alike. He it was who engineered the Wendish crusade of 1147 and carried it through to its cynical conclusion, in deliberate opposition to the conciliatory policy of Adolf, who had made a treaty of peace and friendship with the Abodrite prince, Niklot, in 1143, induced the Abodrite nobles to open their lands to German settlers, and secured a welcome for the missionary, Vicelin of Neumünster. All this peaceful work was brought to nothing by the Wendish crusade of 1147. Mecklenburg and Pomerania were subjected to a regime of devastation and slaughter, of violence and brutality, from which Henry the Lion alone profited. 'In all his various expeditions', wrote Helmold, 'there was no mention of Christianity, but only of money.'

The Wendish crusade, with its attendant devastation and depopulation, created the opportunity for organized, systematic colonization and ushered in a period of intensive settlement, the effects of which were felt all along the line of the Elbe as far as the borders of Bohemia. Here, before 1162, the Margrave of Meissen at his own expense colonized 800 hides (*Hufen*) in the frontier forests of the Erzgebirge — land which had been in German hands since the tenth century, but which had to wait until the age of great colonizing enterprises before it was developed. Of all the great figures active as promoters of colonization, however, none was more energetic than Wichmann who, as Bishop of Naumburg from 1148 and Archbishop of Magdeburg from 1152, introduced Dutch and Flemish settlers in large numbers into the unoccupied and uncultivated marshlands bordering the river Havel. He it was who opened up the barren plateau separating the Elbe from the Havel in the region just east of Magdeburg — a region still known on account of the origin of its settlers as the Fläming. Here and at Jüterbog, another famous Flemish settlement, Wichmann took the initiative in developing land which had fallen into the hands of Albrecht the Bear in 1147. It was, indeed, characteristic of Albrecht, unlike Henry the Lion, that he worked hand in hand with the Church, to which he handed over vast areas for colonization, just as, contrasted with Henry, he avoided the worst excesses of racial animosity and sought to develop his land peaceably, curbing clerical attempts to impose a heavier tithe on the Slavs than on the German settlers.

Above all else he warded off the crusade of 1147 from his lands, and when the Christian prince of Brandenburg, dying without heirs in 1150, left his territory to Albrecht, most of the inhabitants accepted the new order without opposition. What opposition there was came from Poland, which hoped to acquire the vacant lands, but by 1157 the issue was decided and Albrecht in undisputed control. But though less violent and juster than Henry the Lion, Albrecht was no less thorough in his colonization. Summing up Albrecht's work about 1157, Helmold writes:

> He subjugated all the territory of the Brizani and Stoderani and many other tribes that dwelt along the Havel and the Elbe, overcoming those of them in rebellion. Then, as the Slavs gradually disappeared, he sent to Utrecht and the land about the Rhine, and also to those peoples living near the coast, who suffered from the irruptions of the seas, namely the Dutch and the Zealanders and the Flemings, and brought a great multitude of them to dwell in the towns and villages of the Slavs. He greatly furthered the immigration of settlers into the bishoprics of Brandenburg and Havelberg; whereat the churches multiplied there and the value of the tithe increased exceedingly. Dutch settlers began to occupy the east bank of the Elbe, settling all the marshland and meadow from the city of Salzwedel as far as the frontier of Bohemia. Formerly, it is said, the Saxons inhabited these lands . . . But afterwards, when the Slavs prevailed, the Saxons were killed and the land was possessed by the Slavs. But now, because God has generously given health and victory to the duke and other princes, the Slavs everywhere have been worn down and expelled, and peoples strong and without number have arrived from the shores of the sea, and have taken possession of the fields and built towns and churches and increased in wealth beyond all expectation.

A similar policy was pursued further north by Henry the Lion In 1160, after he had again attacked and defeated the Abodrite prince, Niklot, Helmold reports that he divided the conquered land among his knights, who brought large numbers of Flemish colonists into the country around Mecklenburg. Compared, however, with Adolf of Holstein and Albrecht the Bear, Henry's policy was retrograde: he was more interested in levying tribute from the subjugated Wends than in the patient work of colonization. Helmold describes the whole of Nordalbingia, from the river Eider on the frontier of Denmark to Schwerin, as a great Saxon colony by 1171; 'the Slavs', he says, 'little by little failed in the land, and the Saxons

came in and dwelt there'. But this account is exaggerated, and until
the thirteenth century the German settlers were certainly a minority
of the population in this region. In particular, Henry the Lion's
attempts to lay hands on the whole of the province of Mecklenburg
were checked by the reaction which his over-reaching policy provoked in Saxony. In 1166 the opposition of the Saxon nobles, led
by Archbishop Wichmann of Magdeburg, came to a head, and
Henry found himself faced by a strong coalition. In these circumstances — in order to cover his rear — he was forced in 1167 to give
back the greater part of Mecklenburg to Pribislav, the son of Niklot,
retaining for himself only the county of Schwerin with the newly-
founded town of the same name. Thus any policy of immediate
Germanization was confined to the western part of Henry's
conquests.

What was novel and important in Henry the Lion's work was his
interest in commerce and his support of commercial relations,
particularly in connexion with the northern powers: here, rather
than in his relations with the Slav lands of the east, we can see the
elements of a far-sighted policy looking beyond mere territorial
expansion to the later objectives of the Hanseatic League. This
policy took shape after 1158 when Henry forced Adolf of Holstein
to hand over the flourishing city of Lübeck, founded in 1143, and
immediately took steps to develop its importance. 'He sent out
embassies to the cities and kingdoms of the north', writes Helmold,
'to Denmark and Sweden, to Norway and Russia, offering them
peace on condition that they would trade freely with his city of
Lübeck. And he established there a mint and a customs-house, and
conferred the most extensive privileges on the citizens; whereupon
the city prospered and the number of its inhabitants multiplied.'
That this prosperity outlasted the fall of Henry in 1180 and the subsequent period of Danish hegemony over the Baltic, and continued
until by 1350 the city numbered some 18,000 inhabitants, was due
to the incomparable situation of Lübeck at the gateway between
east and west; particularly in the first century of its existence, before
the sea route between the Baltic and the North Sea through the
Skaggerak was opened up, it enjoyed almost a monopoly. It was
the starting-point from the west for the Baltic coast, and here arose
a series of daughter-cities, all endowed with Lübeck law: Wismar,
Rostock, Stralsund, Greifswald, Kammin and Kolberg.

The spread of German commerce and the foundation of German cities along the Baltic coast not only strengthened and supplemented peasant colonization, which was stimulated both by urban markets near at hand and by the possibility of exporting surplus products,[1] but also created the environment in which the Hanseatic League rose to power. Furthermore, it determined the next phase in German expansion. This, unlike all that had gone before, was the work not of peasants but of merchants, desirous of exploiting the great eastern trade route to Novgorod and on through Smolensk to Kiev. Before the end of the twelfth century German merchants were settled in Novgorod, which later took its place with London, Bruges and Bergen as one of the four main establishments of the Hanse, and other warehouses were set up at Pleskau and Smolensk. But these far-distant branches remained trading-stations, and never led to German settlement. It was otherwise on the Gulfs of Riga and Finland. Here a definite colonizing movement, initiated by the merchants of Lübeck, began about 1184, when a German priest, Meinhard, was sent on a mission to Livonia with results described by the chronicler, Arnold of Lübeck, in the following words:

> In the year of the incarnation 1186 the episcopal see of Livonia was founded in a place called Riga. And because the region abounded in good things, Christian settlers and planters of the new church never failed there. For the land was one of fertile fields and abundant pasture, well watered by rivers full of fish and well covered with trees ... Moved by the impassioned preaching of Abbot Berthold of Loccum not a few rich people and gentry migrated to break the strength of the heathen and establish the religion of Christ ... Prelates and priests, soldiers and merchants, rich and poor, came from Saxony, from Westphalia and from Frisia unto the city of Lübeck, where vessels were laden with arms and foodstuffs; and from there they went to Livonia.

But the venture was beset by difficulties. The distance involved and the lack of a land route prevented colonization on an adequate scale, and it proved impossible to secure a flow of peasants from Germany sufficient to occupy the country. The Livonians resisted

---

[1] 'The shipping of corn from Brandenburg to Flanders and England is demonstrable from about 1250. In 1287 we have the first documentary mention of corn from the *Oesterlande* on the Flemish market. After that its export remained a regular thing, of first-rate importance both for the Baltic lands and for the consuming centres, far beyond the Middle Ages' (*Cambr. Econ. Hist.*, I, 397).

the Christian missionaries by force; Meinhard's successor was killed
in 1198. Only when the next bishop, Albrecht of Appeldern,
decided on a policy of conquest was any progress made. Albrecht
re-founded Riga in 1201 as a military stronghold, and the following
year he founded a military order, the Brethren of the Sword — more
dependable than the irregular flow of crusaders — for the conquest of
the land. By 1207 this was completed, and Albrecht received Livonia

The Germans in the Baltic (thirteenth and fourteenth centuries), showing the lands
of the Teutonic Knights

from the hands of Philip of Swabia as an imperial fief. Even then,
however, the German position was only secure in the towns — Riga,
Dorpat and Reval — while in the countryside a cowed but recalcitrant native population had to be held down by the new lords. This
was possible so long as there was no external intervention; but in
1236 the Brethren of the Sword suffered a serious reverse at the
hands of the Lithuanians. At this moment of crisis, when the
collapse of the German colony in the north seemed imminent, a new
solution was found, and in 1237 the Brethren of the Sword, weakened
by defeat, amalgamated with the Teutonic Order, which in the
meantime had begun the conquest of Prussia. With the intervention
of the Teutonic knights German political control of Livonia was

secured for another three centuries, although there was never any appreciable colonization or Germanization of the Baltic lands.

Like the conquest of Livonia, the conquest of Prussia was a military undertaking carried out with ruthless tenacity by a military order which regarded baptism simply as a token of subjection. But, unlike Livonia, Prussia — which was accessible for settlers by land — was in course of time colonized and Germanized; indeed, no province was subjected to a more thorough and systematic process of Germanization than Prussia, where the German settlers were forbidden to use the native language and the native Prussians were ruthlessly uprooted and transplanted in order to create an irrevocable breach with the past. This policy, however, did not get under way until a relatively late stage. In the first place the Teutonic Knights, who (we have already seen) were called in as auxiliaries by the Polish duke of Masovia in 1226, appeared to have contemplated a policy similar to that employed in Livonia, and, indeed, in Asia Minor where the military orders originated: a rapid penetration of the province, the establishment of a network of towns as military strongpoints in strategic positions, and the exploitation of the native population for labour on the land. After 1231, when Hermann Balke, the provincial appointed by Hermann of Salza, crossed the Vistula at the head of a crusading army, the conquest proceeded rapidly. The first fortified centre, Thorn, was founded in 1231, followed the next year by Kulm and Marienwerder. From these points the conquest was carried systematically forward, and a first Prussian insurrection in 1240 was pitilessly repressed. After the Frisches Haff and the channel of the Vistula had been won and safeguarded by the fortress of Elbing, the order prepared for the conquest of Samland, the core of the heathen territory. Here Königsberg was founded in 1255. But the ambitions of the new militarist state, after the amalgamation with the Livonian Brethren of the Sword in 1237, were even more expansive: by securing control of the Kurische Nehrung, the Order gained contact with the north, founded Memel in 1252 and won the coastline from Memel to Polangen. It even sent its army in the direction of Novgorod, but its defeat at the hands of Alexander Nevsky, prince of Novgorod, on the ice of Lake Peipus in 1242, put an end to any further idea of expansion in that direction.

Meanwhile renewed rebellions occurred in Prussia itself, enforcing a radical change of policy. The revolt of 1240 was followed by an even

more serious insurrection, which lasted from 1261 to 1273, and it was
not until 1283 that the last native Prussian chieftain laid waste his lands
and migrated to heathen Lithuania. 'The region he forsook', writes
Treitschke,[1] 'bears to-day the traces of the devastation he wrought,

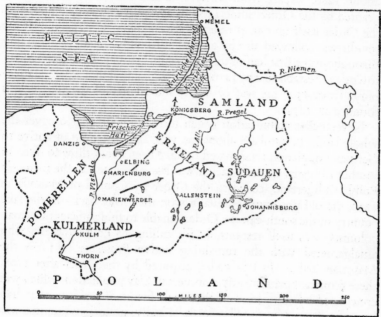

The Conquest of Prussia by the Teutonic Knights

for the great wilderness of Johannisburg now extends where the com-
fortable villages of the pagans were once abundant.' At the same
time, the German knights inaugurated their policy of transplantation
and the rigorous suppression of all connexion with previous conditions; in this way 'the last of the Sudauers were forced to deforest
the sacred grove of Romove in Samland, which no Samlander dared
touch, and its original site is now known as the Sudauen Nook.'[2]
    More important was the start of German peasant colonization. So
long as there had been any prospect of cultivating the land with
native labour, immigration had been on a small scale, particularly as
at first only the sea route was open. But a radical change of policy

[1] Treitschke, *Origins*, 46.   [2] Op. cit., 47.

followed the great revolts. The Prussians, who at first had been granted personal freedom, were now for the most part reduced to the level of serfs, and the best of the land was handed over to German settlers, who started to arrive in appreciable numbers after about 1280. Apart from villages founded by knights on lands granted by the Order, some 1400 villages were by 1410 founded by the Order itself on estates reserved for its own use. The end of the revolts was followed also by a spate of town foundations extending throughout the first half of the fourteenth century: in all 93 German towns were established by 1410 within the lands of the Order. Marienburg, from 1309 the seat of the Grand Master of the Order, was founded in 1274.

Nevertheless colonization began too late in Prussia to cover the whole land. In Samland about the year 1400 the ratio of native to German population is estimated to have been about three to five. In southern Prussia, Germanization was less complete. In the formerly Polish Kulmerland, ceded to the Order by Conrad of Masovia in 1230, the old possessors gradually won their way back. In the lake country of the south-east the Order, unable to find sufficient German colonists, was itself responsible for calling in Polish settlers, who amalgamated with the remaining native Prussians to form the Masurian 'tribe'. In Pomerelia, acquired by the Order after 1308, there remained permanently a numerous Slav population, which was conciliated by mitigation of the harsh forms of serfdom that had been maintained by the Slav lords. Finally, no serious attempt was made to colonize the territory of Samaiten, between Prussia and Courland, which was only under the Order for a few years after 1398. Hence, although 'amid the encircling abundance of German life, the last vestiges of the old Prussian language and Prussian manners and customs were effaced', the lands of the Teutonic Order, threatened always by Polish and Lithuanian irredentism, were never as a whole so securely Germanized as the provinces further west. Only by comparison with Courland, Livonia and Estonia, where there was no more than a thin German stratum superimposed upon the masses of native inhabitants, and where even among the towns only Riga, Dorpat and Reval developed a healthy German burgher life, was Prussia secure. What held it together was the unique, quasi-modern form of territorial authority exercised by the Order, which reached its heyday under the greatest of the Grand Masters, Winrich of Kniprode (1351-1382). When this government, rigid and un-alterable, proved unable to adapt itself to changing circumstances, a period of decline began: after the defeat of the Order at Tannen-berg in 1410 'the last traces of greatness vanished from the degenerate state'.[1]

III

Apart from Prussia and the Baltic States, military conquest did not play an appreciable part in the movement of east German coloni-zation. It is, indeed, true that the wars of the first half of the twelfth century, culminating in the Crusade of 1147, unleashed the move-ment; but this military and predatory phase was soon over, and the areas it affected were limited. As we have seen, Henry the Lion's conquests extended only to the western part of Mecklenburg, while in Brandenburg — although small risings had to be suppressed — Albrecht the Bear succeeded by peaceful inheritance, and not by force of arms. Except in the country immediately bordering the rivers Saale and Elbe, moreover, the main phase of colonization did not begin until after the conclusion of the period of military con-quest, and then it was largely carried out by native princes and the Slav nobility.

This was true, in particular, of Pomerania, eastern Mecklenburg and Silesia. Niklot and Henry Borwin, the princes who succeeded Pribislav in Mecklenburg in 1178, were both well disposed to the Germans from the outset, and soon found means to stimulate coloni-zation. Already by 1189 several German nobles were found at the court of Niklot in Rostock, while a decade earlier Henry Borwin granted half the district of Marlow in north-eastern Mecklenburg, near the frontiers of Pomerania, to a German knight for the purpose of colonization; as early as 1210 there were eight places in this neigh-bourhood with German names. It was Henry Borwin, also, who (some time before 1210) settled German colonists on the island of Poel, near Wismar, 'because of the poverty and small number of Slavs in that neighbourhood, who were insufficient for the cultivation of the land'.[2] The main agents of colonization and cultivation em-ployed by the Christian Slav princes were, however, the monasteries, particularly the Cistercians. From about 1170 monastic foundations

<hr>

[1] Treitschke, op. cit., 126.   [2] Thompson, *Feudal Germany*, 515.

began to receive large stretches of territory in Slav lands for cultivation: among the wealthier and more famous were Oliva near Danzig in Pomerelia, Doberan in Mecklenburg, Kolbatz and Eldena in Pomerania, Leubus and Heinrichau in Silesia. One case illustrating how much land might be entrusted to a single monastery for settlement, is provided by the Cistercian house of Leubus, founded in 1175: partly in association with daughter houses, it received 500 *Hufen* from the Duke of Silesia in 1216-1218, 400 more in 1225 in the see of Lebus on the Oder, 2000 *Hufen* on the Netze in the same year from the Duke of Poland, and 3000 more on the lower reaches of the same river in 1233.[1] For this land, which was too extensive to be farmed by the old system of lay brethren on dependent monastic granges, the monasteries required tenants; and even before the Ordinance of 1208 permitting them to lease remote estates instead of cultivating them by monastic labour, they called in immigrants from Germany and Flanders.

It was, however, in the early part of the thirteenth century, approximately in the period 1210-1230, that the greatest wave of colonization took place. How little this movement was dependent on German military or political pressure is indicated by the fact that it occurred precisely during the period of Danish predominance, when Waldemar the Victorious (1202-1241) was master of Holstein, Mecklenburg and Pomerania. It was at this time that German emigrants entered parts of eastern Mecklenburg and eastern Brandenburg, Pomerania, Silesia, northern Moravia and Poland. By the thirties they were across the new territory of the Teutonic knights on the Lower Vistula, by Kulm and Thorn. Further south, in Brandenburg, the line of the Oder was reached by 1240, and after 1242 the Neumark was formed east of the Oder with Frankfurt (founded in 1253) as a centre of communications, a crossing-place and an entry to the east. At Lebus, in the same region, where the population was still predominantly Slav (it was the ancient land of the Leubuzzi), the native princes were very active even earlier in attracting colonists from Flanders and Eastphalia, from Hesse and Thuringia: in the thirty-five years between 1204 and 1239 they are said to have recovered over 160,000 acres of waste or marshland. In

---

[1] *Cambr. Econ. Hist.*, I, 372. The *Hufe* (or hide), which may be defined approximately as the land of one family, varied in size according (among other things) to the quality of the land. Standard measurements in the east were 42 and 60 acres.

Silesia the main phase of colonization occurred under Duke Henry I
(1201-1238), the son of a German mother and the husband of St.
Hedwig, who laboured hard to win the people for Christianity
and German culture. This settlement was carried out by 'undertakers' and peasants from the Elbe-Saale region, and the majority of
Silesian towns followed the law of Magdeburg. Finally, eastern
Mecklenburg was also colonized in the early years of the thirteenth
century, first along the coast, and then (from about 1230) further
inland: the first two German towns, Friedland and Neubranden-
burg, were founded in the fourth decade of the century.

Thoughout this period of intensive colonization the competition
for settlers was so great among Slav and German lords, and between
bishops and monasteries, that the demand for a time far outran
supply. For all who could undertake it, colonization was of all
investments the most attractive; a thirteenth-century Polish chronicler
tells, for example, of a bishop of Gnesen who, by laying out villages,
raised the money yield of a certain district from 1 to 800 marks.
In these circumstances recruiting agents were sent off to Germany
to collect emigrants. But the areas involved were so vast, the capital
expenditure so heavy, and the task of management and organization
so complicated and specialized that from an early date a regular body
of entrepreneurs or contractors arose who organized colonization
to profit by it. This professional class, known as 'undertakers' or
'promoters' or 'locators', was found on the Middle and Lower Elbe
from about 1150, and from that time forward locators were the
indispensable agents of village and town foundation throughout the
whole north-eastern colonial area. In general, they undertook single
settlements or 'locations' at their own risk on behalf of particular
lords, and were paid by the assignment of a holding in the village
free of rent and tithe and usually twice the size of a normal peasant
holding, as well as the post of village magistrate (*Schultheiss*) with
two-thirds of the profits of justice and certain monopolies. But,
in addition, there were locators of bigger standing, with considerable capital of their own, who purchased land outright with a view
to speculation and to re-sale to the peasant settlers. This was the
rule, for example, in Silesia from about 1250, and it is clear that
many of these wealthy locators, willing to invest capital in land,
were burgesses. Thus it is clear that urban and rural settlement
were very closely interconnected. Many people came to the new

colonial towns with their eyes fixed from the start on the acquisition of landed property. The laws of Kulm, in the lands of the Teutonic Order, assumed that substantial burgesses would hold forty *Hufen* or more, and in many regions there was definitely a planned relationship between towns and countryside. Archbishop Wichmann of Magdeburg, in his charter of 1174 for Jüterbog, already conceived of the whole region (*provincia*) as a unity when he explained that the foundation of the town, as *exordium et caput provinciae*, was important *ad edificandam provinciam*. This systematic association of towns and countryside, of peasant and urban settlement, soon spread far and wide. In Silesia, from about 1220, the duke and the locators began to establish groups of villages, each of which had as its centre of trade and justice a colonial town, and existing Slav villages lying between the groups of new colonial settlements gradually adjusted their lay-out and economic life and law to those of the Germans. The system was carried by the Bishop of Breslau to the episcopal lands on the river Neisse; the Polish duke used it in the valleys of the Warthe and the Netze; a little later it passed into northern Moravia and eastern Bohemia. The Teutonic knights, commencing later and profiting from the experience in the older colonial regions, adopted a uniform system of town and country groups, which was the main instrument in the process of opening up the Prussian land.[1]

This association of urban and peasant settlement was one among many factors illustrating the orderly and systematic process of colonization. The towns provided a framework within which the whole scheme of settlement was articulated: their markets were a stabilizing factor in the economic sphere, their walls a protection, and their legal system a means of cohesion. Through their connexion with the towns, the isolation of the German villages in a strange land was broken down. Moreover, the very uniformity was necessary in order to carry out the immense tasks facing the immigrants. Not only were single villages carefully planned; where possible, several neighbouring villages or groups of villages were established at the same time, and the planning was completed organically by coupling rural settlement with the foundation of towns. The necessity for collaboration, for acting together (for example) in fixing boundaries, was one factor explaining the success of the movement. The immigrants were not isolated, but took their

[1] Cf. *Cambr. Econ. Hist.* I, 84-85, 87, 384-385.

place in a comprehensive scheme, and were strengthened by a sense of solidarity in a communal undertaking.

This uniformity, so necessary for rapid expansion, was due primarily to the leading part played by the professional locators, who naturally worked upon lines tried and tested by experience. Where numerous new or remodelled settlements were made in a short time, it was a natural tendency for the same procedure to be reproduced. That such a procedure was available was due to the fact that, already generations earlier, internal colonization within Germany had established a few well-tested types of settlement, which had already been tried out in the Danube valley and the eastern Alps during the German expansion into Austria and the south-east. This was true both of villages and towns. The municipal law which Conrad of Zähringen gave to his newly-founded town of Freiburg im Breisgau in 1120 was used as a model not only for many other new urban foundations in the region of the Upper Rhine, but also for Henry the Lion's foundations (e.g. Brunswick and Munich) in the duchies of Saxony and Bavaria. Urban life within Germany had, by the second half of the twelfth century, developed to a point at which the main lines of town planning and town law were established and could henceforth be imitated on fresh sites; hence the recurrence throughout the east colonial region of a few basic plans and of municipal codes like the laws of Lübeck and Magdeburg and Halle. Village types show a similar uniformity. In Silesia and adjacent regions, where there was plenty of forest land to settle, 50 *Hufen* was the standard size; in Prussia where the Master of the Teutonic Order directed most of the work himself and where an outstandingly strong and efficient authority stamped uniformity on the whole process, a village of 60 *Hufen* was favoured.

This is not the place for a detailed description of the structure of the eastern colonial villages. Characteristic was the *Waldhufen* type with the *Hufen* stretching in long narrow strips side by side up the sides of the valley, usually terminating on the village street where the homesteads stood in a row, each separated from the next by a *Hufe*'s breadth. This type originated in forest clearings in mountain districts and was most suitable for such land: as more land was reclaimed, it was easy to add single-strip *Hufen* to the existing plots. But in the wide plains beyond the Elbe the traditional *Gewanndorf*, with an indeterminate number of *Gewanne* (furlongs) in the open fields and strips for every *Hufe* in each *Gewann*, was common enough. Whatever the type, there was a general tendency to discard the traditions and practices of the old manorial system of the west. Even in the traditional *Gewann* village there was, in the east, more rational consolidation of each cultivator's shares in the fields; the *Gewanne* were fewer and more uniform, the strips more regularly laid out. But the main consideration was the freedom from the burdens of manorialism. The landlord in the east lived from rents, not from the services of dependent tenants obliged to cultivate the lord's demesne. From the first colonists under German law had no work to do for their lords, unlike the greater part of the peasants in old west Germany and the Slav peasants in the east. Instead they received for moderate fixed rents holdings which were heritable and freely alienable. Instead of the manorial rights of the lord and the corresponding dependence of unfree tenants, emphasis lay on the exact contractual relationship of an hereditary tenure. Thus the settler in the east was not part of a 'manor', and although his place in the village community necessarily placed certain limitations on his economic freedom, here again the more rational system of the east compared favourably with conditions in the west. In the *Waldhufen* type of village, in particular, the peasant was free to farm his own long strip of land as he wished.

It was the prospect of these favourable conditions, of a fixed tenure and legal security, and of personal freedom, which irresistibly appealed to the Germans from the west, and which assured the flow of recruits and the rapid success of the whole colonizing movement. Exemption from the exasperating and multiple manorial obligations which burdened them in the homeland was a primary inducement to colonists. In addition, there were special inducements to secure the development of virgin soil. Both in towns and in countryside, a number of 'free years' were granted during which the settlers were free of all liabilities. In many parts, the clergy was induced to remit payment of tithe in whole or in part. Thus the settlers were enabled to get on to their feet and tide over the initial unproductive years. But these temporary concessions were not so important as the prospect of a permanently improved status: personal freedom and liberty of movement was the most precious acquisition of the colonist. In Silesia, all German immigrants enjoyed the duke's protection of their freedom, if the native nobility or others sought to interfere. Personal freedom and an excellent economic position were the characteristics of the German settlers in the east until the end of the Middle Ages — advantages soon passed on to the native population which, as it was assimilated and Germanized, threw off the burdens of dependence and in most parts came to enjoy the personal freedom which the German immigrants had introduced.

Such were the factors and methods and processes which, following the initial period of military conquest, made possible the rapid spread of German colonization in the east and the peaceful establishment of German settlements, rural and urban. The benefits conferred were immeasurable. A sparsely populated land of negligible economic value was rendered productive. In Silesia and Brandenburg, in Pomerania and Mecklenburg, even in Prussia, the lot of the considerable Slav population remaining was improved, as progressively German law and custom were introduced. Town life for the first time became a factor of importance, and German burgess colonists promoted trade and industry and mining (the latter particularly in Meissen where silver, copper and zinc were exploited after 1165). Above all else, a new agrarian system was established, supported by a healthy, vigorous, economically sound and free peasant class. The improved status of this peasant class resulted in a breach with the old social structure, and the appearance of a new social structure with manifold advantages over that prevalent in western Germany. It was a progressive society, unimpeded by old traditions and entrenched interests, inhabited by people accustomed to independence and responsibility, to hard work and foresight. That these factors and qualities made for rapid economic development is self-evident; they were also fraught with political consequences, which were not long in making their influence felt.

IV

From the very beginning of the colonizing movement, early in the twelfth century, the princes who were its chief promoters showed themselves fully aware of its political implications. They realized that the colonial east, with its freedom from traditional rights and its material potentialities, offered a basis for a territorial power stronger and more independent than anything which could

T

easily be created in the west. In this calculation they were undoubtedly right. In particular the lack of intermediate authorities played
into the hands of the prince. It was only towards the close of the
fourteenth century, in circumstances which we shall later examine,[1]
that changing conditions compelled the princes to transfer many of
their rights to the local aristocracy, thus creating a starting-point for
developments which led later to the assertion of aristocratic privilege,
the depression of the peasantry and the development of the *Rittergut*.
To begin with, and thereafter for many generations, the settlers
came directly under the prince, even when established on private
land. In general, moreover, the number of villages founded by the
territorial princes on demesnes which remained under their control
was everywhere high; in Prussia they were predominant. And in
other villages the lord never, in the Middle Ages, crept in as an
intermediate political authority between settler and prince. The
princes were not, of course, oblivious of the need for building up a
knight class for the purposes of defence; in Brandenburg, in particular, the endowment of a 'castle-owning nobility' to protect the
frontier against the Poles was on an extensive scale. But the knight
class in the east failed to secure that manorial control over rural
economy and rural society, which was the main foundation of its
power in the west. The knight's estate was generally small, varying
from the size of a big peasant holding to twice or four times that
extent, and the mediaeval knight was (in a famous phrase) 'the
peasant's neighbour' rather than his lord. Neither economically nor
politically was he in control.

The eastern colonial lands were thus particularly well suited,
economically and socially, for that attempt to construct a more
modern form of territorial government, untrammelled by early
mediaeval theories and practices, which was one of the main objects
of all rulers, great and small, after the Investiture Contest. From the
beginning the princes set out to make the most of their position in
the colonial east. Henry the Lion, in particular, saw here the
opportunity for exercising semi-regal powers. Thus he forced both
pope and emperor, for example, to concede him the royal right of
investing the bishops in the colonial dioceses of Oldenburg, Mecklenburg and Ratzeburg; the famous missionary, Vicelin of Neumünster, ordained Bishop of Oldenburg by the Archbishop of

[1] Below, pp. 331, 392 sq.

Bremen in 1149, was refused recognition until he had accepted investiture at Henry's hands. Whether or not Henry claimed to rule the conquered lands by divine right is an open question;[1] but Helmold attests the freedom with which Henry was able to act east of the Elbe when he writes that 'in this land the duke's authority alone was heeded'. Above all else there was the opportunity of introducing, under the most favourable conditions, a systematic quasi-modern administration, organized on rational territorial principles, manned by *ministeriales* and run on bureaucratic, non-feudal lines. That Henry over-reached himself, alienated the lay and clerical nobility of Saxony, and came to grief when, after 1176, the emperor lent his support to the Saxon nobility, only proves his inability to use to good purpose the solid advantages of his position. It was otherwise in the case of Albrecht the Bear who, from as early as 1150, treated all his lands on both sides of the Elbe as one coherent territory. Albrecht, it has been said, 'was the freest and most untrammelled prince in Europe in the twelfth century'. Since there were few traditional rights and no antiquated feudal interests burdening the soil of Brandenburg when he acquired it, he could build a state and establish a society almost *de novo*. His political authority was simple and complete: every person from peasant to baron and bishop was a subject of the margrave.[2]

These facts sufficiently explain the rapidly growing importance of the eastern principalities in German politics after the middle of the twelfth century. Throughout Germany the period after the Investiture Contest saw an attempt, in a new political environment, to create new foundations for the political structure; but it was in the newly colonized lands, where the opposition of established interests was least intense, that this process went ahead most rapidly, most easily and most systematically. Hence the rising territories of east colonial Germany rapidly outstripped the politically disjointed west in political development; they provided a more solid foundation for princely power, with consolidated estates, uniform administration and a population who were free subjects and not feudal dependants. Here government could act more freely along more modern lines.

---

[1] F. Güterbock, 'Barbarossa u. Heinrich der Löwe', *Vergangenheit und Gegenwart*, XXIII (1933), 254, denies this view citing Barbarossa's statement that Henry's lands beyond the Elbe were held of his imperial bounty. But, as Güterbock points out, only the course of events could determine whether this statement was theory or reality.

[2] Cf. Thompson, *Feudal Germany*, 519.

Hence anyone seeking to exercise political power sought for a foothold in the colonial lands. Frederick Barbarossa himself, in his efforts to create new foundations for his royal power, early secured the Pleissnerland – a consolidated province on the borders of the march of Meissen, centred round the town of Altenburg – and the adjacent Egerland. His son, Henry VI, undoubtedly intended to secure direct and permanent control of the march of Meissen on the death of the margrave in 1195. These efforts of the imperial administration, whose chief territorial interests were in south Germany, to establish a dominion of its own near the upper reaches of the Elbe, were in spite of their failure a clear indication of the trend of the times. But it was in the struggle for power after the extinction of the Hohenstaufen dynasty in 1268 that the east colonial lands definitely came to the fore as the seat of political leadership. First in point of time was Austria, where colonization had proceeded steadily since the tenth century, and which was already an effective state at the time when the colonization of the north-east began. Next was Bohemia, from 1311 the territorial basis without which the Luxemburg dynasty could not have maintained its predominance in the fourteenth century. After the accession of Rudolf of Habsburg in 1273 all German rulers save three derived their power from their lands in the east; and of these three the reigns of two, Adolf of Nassau (1291-1298) and Rupert of the Rhine (1400-1410), were little more than an illustration of the impossibility of ruling successfully without a firm territorial basis in the east. Ludwig of Bavaria (1314-1347) stood apart; but he governed in the early part of his reign through the co-operation and support of the mighty Luxemburg dynasty, and (like the Luxemburgers before him) he sought to stabilize his dynasty by the acquisition of the march of Brandenburg when the last Ascanian margrave died in 1319. Lands and power in the east were a prerequisite of kingship.

From the time of the Interregnum onwards, therefore, the new dynasties of the east, the Wettiner of Meissen, the Habsburger of Austria, the Luxemburger of Bohemia and later the Hohenzollern of Brandenburg, exerted decisive influence in German politics. Perhaps it was the need for military preparedness, for energy and for co-operative effort in developing the newly colonized territories, which produced a degree of efficiency and practicability increasingly lacking in the west; in part it was certainly the free play accorded to

new forms of political organization. In any case it was in the territories of the north-east and south-east, inhabited by a mixed
German and Slav population, that the more concentrated powers
came into existence which offset the late mediaeval decay of government in central and southern Germany. Under the leadership of the
dynasties enumerated above new territorial states began to develop
which, as the axis of German history moved from Rhine to Elbe
and from Elbe to Oder, secured an increasing voice in German
affairs. At times there was even an open cleavage of interests
between east and west, just as the immense eastward expansion of
north Germany brought with it — at least momentarily, in the
conflict between Henry the Lion and Frederick Barbarossa, between
Welf and Hohenstaufen — the danger of a split between north and
south. That nothing of the sort occurred, that unity was unques-
tioningly maintained even after the death of Frederick II and the
eclipse of the Hohenstaufen monarchy, was the result of the work
of the emperors during the three centuries beginning with Otto the
Great. They established a sense of German unity, which persisted
even when the empire had ceased to be a political reality. Nevertheless the predominance of the colonial lands of the east created new
problems and a new attitude to German affairs when, after the
Interregnum, the task had to be faced of establishing a new foundation for German political life in a Germany transformed geographically and ethnographically, politically and socially, by the great
colonizing movement.

CHAPTER 11

GOVERNMENT AND POLITICS FROM THE INTER-REGNUM TO THE GOLDEN BULL
(1272–1356)

I

THE traditional framework of German political life, already dislocated by the policy of Frederick II, was shattered by the long interregnum between 1250 and 1272. What was to take its place? This was the question facing the next generation; and it was a question of vital importance in German history, for the solution worked out in the years after 1272 determined the conditions under which Germany made the transition from mediaeval to modern times. The possibilities of a reorientation of German political organization, bringing it into the current of national development which was strong in Europe at the end of the thirteenth century, were far from negligible; the basic principles of a united, national organization of government had been preserved through the Interregnum by the League of Rhenish Cities, founded in 1254 for the 'salvation of the people and of the country', and here and in the crown estates and vacant fiefs to which he immediately laid claim, the new king, Rudolf of Habsburg (1273–1291), had a reasonable foundation for the construction of a revived monarchy.[1] It would be a mistake to suppose that this attempt was doomed to failure or that the future character of German government was already determined at the time of Frederick II's death. The principalities were only in the early stages of formation, their organization and boundaries still fluid; there was still a long struggle ahead before the princes were strong enough to assume the full exercise of sovereign powers within their territories.[2] Nor was the college of electoral princes yet dominant over the monarchy and its traditions of hereditary succession and independent prerogatives; although its

[1] Cf. E. Bielfeldt, *Der Rheinische Bund von 1254. Ein erster Versuch einer Reichsreform* (1937); O. Redlich, *Rudolf von Habsburg. Das deutsche Reich nach dem Untergange des alten Kaisertums* (1903).
[2] Cf. below, p. 322 sqq.

origins are dimly discernible as far back as 1198, it only took shape in 1252 and 1257, and it was not until 1290 that its composition was finally defined.[1] Hence there was no direct transfer of existing political rights from the crown to the principalities and the electoral princes after the disappearance of the Hohenstaufen dynasty. The sovereignty of the princes was built up not on the old but on new foundations during the fourteenth and fifteenth centuries; and the preceding period, between 1250 and 1356, was a period in which there was no clearly defined and generally accepted framework of government and political life. It was a period of transition, a period of conflicting tendencies and radical instability, marked by an inexorable struggle for a new political order; and until the conflicting tendencies had, under the pressure of political events, crystallized out, Germany's future hung in the balance.

In this period of transition two stark necessities overshadowed all else: the one was to define the framework of German political organization, to determine once and for all the direction of German political development; the other was to liquidate the past. Hohenstaufen imperialism had left many unsolved problems which required to be wound up before Germany could embark on a new course; it had left strong traditions and, above all in relations with the papacy, difficult complications and a legacy of bitterness and suspicion. Could this legacy be liquidated, so that Germany was free to face the future unimpeded by the imperial entanglement, which particularly under Frederick II had so catastrophically retarded German political development? The time was past when, as under the Hohenstaufen, the resources of Italy could be used to bolster up the position of the German crown; but the connexion with Italy and with the imperial lands of Burgundy and Arles still remained. What was to become of that connexion, now that the foundations of a direct imperial administration had perished? The question of Italy continued to play an important part in German politics, and all the rulers of Germany from Rudolf of Habsburg (1273-1291) to Charles IV (1347-1378), with the exception of Adolf of Nassau (1291-1298), pursued an active Italian policy; but Germany was, in fact, thrown back after 1250 on its own resources. From the time

[1] Cf. H. Mitteis, *Die deutsche Königswahl. Ihre Rechtsgrundlagen bis zur goldenen Bulle* (1938). There is a summary of the earlier literature on the rise of the electoral college in Meister, *Verf.-Gesch.* (1922), 150-163. For the texts cf. M. Krammer, *Quellen z. Gesch. d. deutschen Königswahl u. des Kurfürstenkollegs* (1918).

of the victory of Charles of Anjou over Manfred in 1266, until the death of his grandson, Robert of Naples, in 1343, the Angevin dynasty was the dominant power in Italy, and the German king could only intervene south of the Alps as a foreign ally of Italian factions hostile to Naples; that was true even of Henry VII of Luxemburg (1308-1313) who, attempting for the last time to link up across the chasm carved by the Interregnum with Hohenstaufen traditions, sought for a brief moment to establish an imperial authority standing above party. Moreover, the papacy, supported by France and the Angevins, maintained with a large measure of success that only a duly crowned emperor was authorized to intervene in Italian affairs; and since, after the death of Frederick II, there was no emperor until 1312, and again no emperor recognized by the church between Henry VII's death in 1313 and 1355, Italy was in fact left to develop on its own lines. Except for the nominal connexion, vested in the imperial title which was almost permanently in abeyance, all direct links between Germany and Italy had ceased, between 1250 and 1268, to exist; and the position of Burgundy and Provence and the other provinces of the 'middle kingdom' was little different. In fact, if not in name, Germany ceased after 1250 to be the centre of an empire; the very factors which destroyed the reality of royal power in Germany, destroyed the unity of the Empire and undermined the position of Germany in Europe. Hegemony, visibly within French grasp in 1215, passed definitely into French hands after 1250.

It was against this background that German history between 1272 and 1356 was played out. The winding-up of the old order after the Hohenstaufen bankruptcy, the rise of France to European predominance, were the basic factors in European politics, and their repercussions in Germany were profound. Once again as after the death of Henry VI, the political development of Germany came to depend upon the policy of the European powers; and this time the results of their intervention, spread over many generations, were enduring. With the death of St. Louis (1226-1270) a new spirit, which had already made itself felt in the person of Charles of Anjou, the conqueror of Sicily, pervaded French policy. Abandoning the caution of the earlier Capetians, the French monarchy under Philip the Bold (1270-1285) and Philip the Fair (1285-1314) embarked on a policy of aggressive nationalism and imperialism, designed to carry the French frontiers forward into the territories of the Empire and ultimately to win for France the imperial title vacated by the Hohenstaufen. Hence the fall of the Hohenstaufen, far from eliminating the question of empire, placed it in the forefront of European politics; it ushered in an attempt to bring about a territorial redistribution which took place primarily at the expense of Germany for the benefit of France. Inevitably this policy led to intervention in Germany, in order by pressure and negotiations to secure the desired changes. But just as France intervened, in order to secure the predominance of those elements in Germany which it believed favourable to its pretensions, so England intervened in order to support the anti-French forces; and so Germany was thrown open to the interplay of international diplomacy, which stimulated German political divisions for national ends. The results were disastrous. The internal problems which divided Germany throughout the period after 1250 became inextricably involved in the complicated ramifications of foreign politics; and foreign intervention, rubbing salt into old wounds, fatally hindered the solid reconstruction of German political society which was imperatively necessary after the extinction of the Hohenstaufen dynasty.

During the period 1272-1356, the long transition during which Germany struggled to escape from the anarchy into which it had been plunged between 1245 and 1272, three problems awaited solution, each of which was of major importance for Germany's future shape and development. The first was the question of Germany's constitution: would monarchy or oligarchy carry the day, unity or territorial division? The second was the question of Germany's frontiers: would it be possible, following the revolutionary changes which had occurred in the balance of international power, to maintain within the old boundaries the unity established of old by the monarchy? The third was the definition of the relations between Germany and the Empire, between *regnum* and *imperium*, now that the unified imperial government created by the Hohenstaufen had collapsed. It was in the solution of these three problems that the period 1272-1356 made its lasting contribution to the evolution of modern Germany, which began on new foundations after the end of the Hohenstaufen period. But the solution was only in limited degree a German solution. In all three problems foreign powers were implicated and foreign interests involved; and it was only through the slow and complicated interplay of internal and external factors, with all the obstructions, delays and compromises inherent in such a situation, that there was finally established the imperfect framework in which German life was destined to be confined from 1356 to 1871.

II

The first theme, setting the tone for all else, was the process of steady French encroachment on the frontiers of Germany and the Empire, which went on, year in, year out, as the background accompaniment of more resounding events. It does not fall within our province to trace the ideological background of French policy, the legends of Charlemagne and of Gaul with its frontiers on Rhine, Alps and Pyrenees, which were the smokescreen behind which the officers and lawyers of the French crown, often more relentless than the king himself, carried on a niggling warfare of parchments and precedents, of litigation and blackmail, pressing forward systematically step by step into neighbouring territory.[1] The first innocuous beginnings had taken place under Louis VIII (1223-1226) and Louis IX (1226-1270), when French officials began to interfere in imperial territory at Avignon and St. André, in the bishopric of Viviers and the county of Valentinois; and French influence in the south increased when, in 1246, Charles of Anjou became count of Provence and Forcalquier without doing homage to the emperor. Further north the prestige and influence of St. Louis himself was an important factor; according to Joinville, the Burgundian and Lotharingian princes brought their disputes to be settled by him in Paris. But it was after St. Louis' death in 1270, when Germany had no ruler strong enough to withstand French pressure, that the process, which St. Louis himself had held in check, gathered speed. The reigns of Philip III (1270-1285) and Philip IV (1285-1314) are the turning-point: they established the enduring framework of Franco-German relations, and it is essential to the understanding of the broader issues to

[1] For the ideological background, cf. F. Kern, *Die Anfänge der französischen Ausdehnungspolitik* (1910); A. Sorel, *L'Europe et la révolution française* I (*Les mœurs politiques et les traditions*), 244 sqq.; H. Kämpf, *Pierre Dubois u. die geistigen Grundlagen des französischen Nationalbewusstseins um 1300* (1935). For the background of Franco-German relations in the immediately preceding period, cf. W. Kienast, *Deutschland und Frankreich in der Kaiserzeit: 900-1270* (1943).

pick out the salient points and dates in the steady French advance.[1]

It was a piecemeal process, in which French statesmen often turned back to pick up threads, and continually reiterated and strengthened old claims. It began with intervention at single points, interference in local rivalries, the offer and often the imposition of French protection, the introduction of a French *gardiator* or the issue of a summons to appear before a French official across the border; and only gradually were the single points of French penetration linked together, after French control had been consolidated, and a general advance inaugurated along the whole line. Thus the advance into Lorraine, which began under Philip the Bold within a few months of his accession in 1270, was only consolidated in 1299. The first broad objective, without doubt, was the line of the rivers Scheldt-Meuse-Saône-Rhône, all of which formed for part of their course the Franco-imperial frontier; but it did not stop there. Having laid hands on territories west of these rivers because they were on the western bank, French policy went on to claim associated territories on the east bank — Lyons and the county of Bar are cases in point — because they were politically connected with the lands on the opposite bank. It was a policy without limits or final objectives, unless perhaps in the north the ultimate object was the Rhine frontier. As early as 1299 a first unsuccessful scheme to advance the French frontier to the Rhine was broached when negotiations were opened envisaging, as part of a marriage settlement between Philip of France's sister and Albrecht of Austria's son, the transfer as dowry of territories including the whole province of Alsace. But more effective than such far-reaching diplomatic negotiations, which rarely produced tangible results, was steady French pressure which established France in actual control of strategic vantage-points long before any attempt was made to secure legal sovereignty. French policy was more concerned with facts than with theory, since France knew full well that, so long as the political consolidation of Germany could be impeded and delayed, *de facto* exercise of power

---

[1] In addition to Kern, who covers the period to 1308 in masterly fashion, the basic facts are clearly summarized by A. Longnon, *La formation de l'unité française* (1922). Cf. also R. Grieser, *Das Arelat in der europäischen Politik* (1925), Pirenne, *Histoire de Belgique* I-II (1922–1929), H. Weiss, *Frankreichs Politik in den Rheinlanden am Vorabend des hundertjährigen Krieges* (1927). For a brief factual summary, such as must suffice here, no reference is possible to the literature dealing with local points of conflict, e.g. L. Hüttebräuker, 'Cambrai, Deutschland u. Frankreich, 1308-1378. Untersuchungen zum Kampf um die deutsche Westgrenze', *Zeitschr. d. Sav.-Stift. f. Rechtsgesch., Germ. Abt.*, LIX (1939).

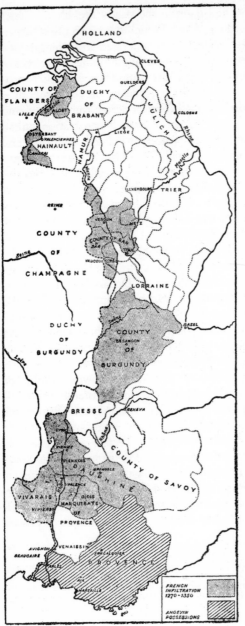

The Franco-German and Franco-Imperial Frontiers (*c.* 1270-1350)

would in time create prescriptions leading to *de iure* sovereignty. This policy inevitably resulted in occasional local set-backs, and not all annexations proved permanent; at Cambrai, for example, which was on the point of annexation in 1306 and under effective French protection in 1337, Charles IV succeeded after French defeats in the Hundred Years War in restoring German authority, and it was only under Louis XIV that France finally acquired the city. But such failures were few, and the net result of the period 1272-1356 was a substantial French infiltration into the imperial territories along the whole frontier from the North Sea to the Mediterranean, and lasting annexations which provided a springboard for French expansion in later centuries. Down to the time of Richelieu, for example, the parts of Bar west of the Meuse — the so-called *Barrois mou-*

vant—ceded by Albrecht to France in 1299, were to be a corner-stone of French policy and French penetration in Lorraine.

Under Philip III (1270-1285) French expansion was directed towards the rivers Meuse and Rhône. In the north, after 1273, a French official was placed in the territory of Montfaucon, near to Verdun; a few years later, in 1281, the bishopric of Toul came under French protection. In the south Avignon, Lyons and the Vivarais were the scenes of French pressure; at Viviers, in particular, the seneschal of Beaucaire vigorously enforced French authority. In both areas pressure was intensified under Philip IV (1285-1314); but the mark of his reign was its extension to the regions of Scheldt and Saône, and therewith the subjection of Germany for the first time to a consistent attack along the whole frontier. In the north the attack was launched in 1290 against the county of Osterbant (that part of the duchy of Hennegau or Hainault lying west of the Scheldt) and was carried forward against the city of Valenciennes, which became French in 1292; at the same time the boundaries of the French city of Tournai were advanced into Hainault territory and the town of Quesnoy, a strong-point in the south of Hainault, was lost to France. In the region of the Saône the stakes were bigger. In 1291 the first steps were taken which, confirmed in 1295, led in 1307 to the establishment of effective French authority in the extensive and important county of Burgundy (the *Freigrafschaft* or *Franche-Comté*). Further south the process of French penetration already begun under Philip III was consolidated, the results were booked and credited. In 1305 the bishop of Viviers, who had been subjected to renewed pressure by the seneschal of Beaucaire after 1286, was forced to recognize French sovereignty over his lands between France and the Rhône. In 1310 Lyons was occupied by French troops and two years later the Archbishop resigned himself to acceptance of the new *status quo*; thus was completed the incorporation of the Lyonnais, which had its origins in 1267 and which had proceeded step by step, beginning with the lands west of the Saône in 1272, more extended occupation in 1294, further intervention in 1305 and 1307, and ending in 1310 with an energetic protest to the German emperor against German intervention in the city 'which has always belonged and with God's help always will belong to the kingdom of France!'[1] A similar policy of pressure,

[1] *Mon. Germ., Const.*, IV. ii, no. 811.

threats and encroachment was pursued in Lorraine. In 1291 the lands of the bishopric of Toul west of the Meuse became French; in 1297 the bishopric of Metz came under French officials. In 1287 the abbey of Beaulieu, appealing to Philip against the count of Bar, was declared French by the parliament of Paris, and in 1290 Theobald of Bar was constrained to accept its decision. But this was only a beginning, and it was after the failure of the Anglo-German coalition against France in 1297 that Philip IV drove home his advantages. The main support along the eastern frontier for the English alliance had come from Flanders, Hainault and Bar, and all three were made to pay the penalty by Philip the Fair. Henry of Bar was forced in 1301 to do homage to the French king and to hold the *Barrois mouvant* of France. At the same time a parallel partition of the duchy of Lorraine took place. The duke had to do service to the French king with sixty knights, and just as there was henceforward a German Bar and a French Barrois, so there was a German Lothringen and a French Lorraine. It was in vain that Pope Boniface VIII, awakening too late to the dangers for the papacy in the rapid establishment of French hegemony, sought to check French penetration, issuing in 1303 an injunction to all subjects of the Empire to throw off allegiance to France. The only result was the violent French attempt to take him captive which, although it failed in its immediate objective, hurried on his death and the collapse of his policy. When death removed Boniface VIII from the scene on October 12th, 1303 — less than a month after the *attentat* at Anagni and less than five months after he had sought to rally Germany against France — the anti-French prelates he had appointed to the three key bishoprics along the frontier, Liége, Verdun and Lyons, were left to make the best terms they could with the French king. Philip IV's success, already assured by Edward I's withdrawal from the Anglo-German alliance in 1298, was complete.

The most intensive phase of French expansion, including the acquisition of the Scheldt-Meuse-Saône-Rhône frontier, was completed under Philip IV. But the subsequent period saw little relaxation of French pressure, and although French gains were less extensive and less spectacular Germany was never free from danger. Under Louis X (1314-1316) the counties of Valentinois and Diois on the east bank of the Rhône came under French suzerainty, and Louis was the first French monarch to accord royal protection to the city of Verdun. Thus in spite of the internal crisis which supervened in France after Philip IV's death in 1314, the main lines of French policy were upheld; but it was not until the accession of Philip VI (1328-1350) that a revival of the aggressive traditions of Philip the Fair came about, with far-reaching plans for further French expansion. From about 1333 Philip VI had his eye on two important areas. In the north it was the Cambrésis where, about 1337, he acquired certain castellanies, followed in 1339 by de facto control of the city of Cambrai which was garrisoned with French troops. In the south his efforts were set on securing for France the succession to the kingdom of Arles, for which local French encroachments along and beyond the Rhône, culminating in the occupation of the bridge-head over the Rhône at Vienne in 1335, had already paved the way.[1] From 1333 to 1339, in spite of the outbreak of the Hundred Years War, the kingdom of Arles remained a focal point in French diplomacy; and it was only after the first major French reverse in the war with England, the battle of Sluys in 1340, that Philip VI modified his plans. Yet even so the French advance went on, and Philip grasped the substance while letting go the shadow. When in 1343 a succession treaty was negotiated with the Dauphin of Vienne, a central province of the kingdom of Arles was brought within French reach, and on the abdication of the Dauphin in 1349 the Dauphiné passed effectively under French rule. It was an acquisition worthy of comparison with the annexations of Philip the Fair, important enough to 'compensate in large measure for the funereal consequences of the defeat inflicted on France at Crécy'.[2]

The Dauphiné was the last great French annexation of imperial territory before the reverses of the Hundred Years War set a halt to French expansion. At the same time the rise of Burgundy under Philip the Bold (1363-1404), John the Fearless (1404-1419) and Philip the Good (1419-1467) created an entirely new situation, with a formidable state interposed between France and Germany encroaching on both. But between 1270 and 1350 — and in particular between 1285

---

[1] Having occupied the bridgehead, which was situated at Sainte-Colombe, a suburb of Vienne, the French forces immediately built a tower dominating the bridge and the course of the river. The implications of the incident were fully realized at the time. 'Ayez à cœur l'affaire de Sainte-Colombe,' a councillor wrote to the Dauphin, Humbert II, 'car elle vous cause un notable préjudice: en effet, les gens du roi étendent leurs ailes sur toute la cité de Vienne et au delà, en même temps qu'ils se sont emparés de la garde du pont du Rhône' (Fournier, Royaume d'Arles, 413).
[2] Longnon, op. cit., 205.

and 1314 — the foundations of French policy on its eastern frontier had been laid; and even before the Burgundian menace had been overcome the traditions of the reign of Philip the Fair were revived. When in 1444 Charles VII entered Lorraine and summoned the cities between the Meuse and the Vosges to accept his authority, while at the same time the Dauphin advanced on Alsace, it was to 're-assert the rights of the kingdom of Gaul, which extended to the Rhine', and to put an end to usurpations damaging to the French crown in 'provinces, lordships, cities and towns which, being situated on this side of the Rhine, ought by ancient right to appertain to the kings of France'.[1] Already, in short, France was setting out along the dubious path leading towards the Rhine frontier, the object of French policy through all succeeding centuries. That it was able to entertain this ambition — the most potent cause of war and international instability throughout modern times — was the result of the successes achieved under Philip the Fair and in the fourteenth century, which carried the French frontiers forward towards the Rhine and gave France a substantial foothold in imperial territory.

German territorial losses in the west between 1270 and 1350 were severe; but the decline in German powers of resistance was revealed not merely by the extent of actual French encroachments, but also by the manner and method of the French attack. The reduction of German princes to servile dependence on France, flagrant interference by officers of the French crown in German territory, the specious arguments of French jurists, alliances with German cities against German princes and German princes against German cities, the use of the papacy to establish pro-French prelates in German sees, all these were the day-to-day devices of French policy, pursued relentlessly year after year, from reign to reign. The result was disastrous. Apart from the territories which passed from Germany to France, the whole life of western Germany was subject to constant French pressure, and throughout wide regions which escaped French annexation the voice of the French king was the decisive factor in politics. Behind French territorial encroachments was a deeper plan still, a plan drawn in clumsy outline in the days of Philip the Fair by Pierre Dubois, moulded and refined at the beginning of the

---

[1] At the same time Aeneas Sylvius (the future Pope Pius II) reported rumours in the French court 'qu'il fallait profiter des circonstances pour revendiquer les anciens droits de la couronne de France sur tous les pays situés en deçà du Rhin'. Cf. Sorel, op. cit., I, 255-256.

seventeenth century by Sully and reformulated in the revolutionary
period by Sieyès: a plan for the creation, based upon the ruin of
Germany and the dismemberment of the Empire, of a 'monarchie
occidentale', a new French Empire expressing in practical form
French cultural predominance and political hegemony.[1] At the
time when Pierre Dubois first formulated it, this plan seemed on the
point of realization: 'the king of France', said a Spanish observer in
the spring of 1308, 'is pope and emperor. All the world knows that
the pope counts for nothing and that the king does whatever he wills
with him and with the church. And — what is more wonderful still —
kings, princes and lords obey him as emperor'. There is an element
of exaggeration in this statement; but it reveals the trend of French
policy. French demands on Germany did not stop short at territorial
cessions: in addition France, laying claim in manifestos and propaganda to the imperial title, sought to wrest the Empire from
German hands. The advance into the borderlands, into Lorraine
and Burgundy and Arles, extending the frontiers of France and
increasing French political influence, was also important as a preparation for the transfer of the imperial territories and the imperial
title from Germany to France: this was the ultimate object of French
policy.

III

The second major complication running through German history
from 1272 to 1356, inextricably involved with the problem of the
western frontier and French aggression, was thus the question of the
Empire.[2] Whether to save what could be saved of the imperial
connexion and the imperial territories or to cut away from the
imperial tradition and concentrate on national development, was a
dominant theme of German politics, a major source of internal
division; but it was also a major source of international complications. French writers like Pierre Dubois and Jean of Jandun main-

[1] Cf. Sorel, op. cit., I, 269-270.
[2] Apart from more general works (Kern, Fournier, Grieser, Kämpf, etc.) cf. Busson, 'Die
Idee des deutschen Erbreiches und die ersten Habsburger', Sitz.-Ber. d. k. k. Akademie zu
Wien, Phil.-hist. Kl., LXXXVIII (1877); Rodenberg, 'Zur Geschichte der Idee eines deutschen
Erbreiches', Mitt. d. österr. Inst., XVI (1895); Zeller, 'Les rois de France candidats à l'Empire',
Revue hist., CLXXIII (1934); Baethgen, 'Der Anspruch des Papsttums auf das Reichsvikariat',
Zeitschr. d. Sav.-Stiftung, kanon. Abt., XLI (1920); Bock, 'Kaisertum, Kurie u. Nationalstaat im
Beginn des 14. Jahrhunderts', Röm. Quartalschrift, XLIV; Stengel, Avignon und Rhens.- For-
schungen zur Geschichte des Kampfes um das Recht am Reich in der ersten Hälfte des 14. Jahrhun-
derts (1930).

U

tained that the French king was the natural successor to the imperial dignity of the Hohenstaufen, that France alone was strong enough effectively to exercise imperial powers, and that a transfer of the empire into French hands was the only solution compatible with the interests of Christendom.[1] But the question was not only one between France and Germany. The papacy also, which claimed to exercise imperial rights whenever the imperial throne was vacant, was deeply interested; so was the Angevin dynasty in Naples, which desired no imperial competitors to challenge its predominance in Italy; so also were the Italian factions; and so finally were the leading opponents of the Capetians and Angevins, the kings of England and Aragon and the Aragonese ruler, Frederick II (1296-1337), in Sicily. The distribution of the spoils which had fallen from the hands of the Hohenstaufen, the division of the corpse of the Hohenstaufen empire, was a European question of first magnitude.

This problem, which divided Europe, also divided Germany. The project of separating Germany, under a German king, from the Empire and dividing the latter into three or more counter-balancing kingdoms, emerged as a matter of practical politics in the days of Pope Urban IV (1261-1264); it was revived at the time of the council of Lyons (1274) by the influential general of the Dominican order, Humbert de Romanis; and it was again brought into the forefront of politics by Pope Nicholas III (1277-1280). As formulated, it was devised in the interests of the papacy, which hoped in this way not merely to avert the revival of Hohenstaufen imperialism, but also to prevent any other power — the danger came from France and the junior branch of the Capetian house in Naples — stepping into the imperial legacy and dominating Italy. But it offered also certain evident advantages to Germany. As compensation for the cession of Italy and Arles, where independent kingdoms were to be set up, the pope was prepared to work for a restoration of stable conditions in Germany, and in particular to countenance the substitution of hereditary, for elective, monarchy; in this way he hoped to create in Germany an effective counterweight to France and the house of Anjou. Such a policy could only be of advantage to the house of Habsburg, which succeeded to the German throne in 1273, and Rudolf of Habsburg (1273-1291) therefore worked in close alliance with the pope. Provided that continuity of succession were main-

[1] Cf. Kämpf, op. cit., 97-99, 106.

tained, and at the same time the friendship of the other European powers, particularly France and the papacy, were assured, the Habsburgs had a reasonable prospect of establishing sound rule in Germany; and they were therefore willing to negotiate for a re-drawing of the map of Europe which would enable them to ex-change their imperial burdens for greater control within Germany. On the other hand, they were opposed by the electoral princes, particularly the archbishops of Mainz, Trier and Cologne, who saw in the project of hereditary monarchy a threat to the electoral privi-leges they had asserted with increased emphasis at the double election of 1257. This antithesis was strengthened when, after the defeat of Ottokar of Bohemia in 1278, the seat of Habsburg power was trans-ferred to the south-east, to Austria and Styria. Engrossed in the consolidation of a strong territorial power in eastern Germany, Rudolf's interest in western Germany and still more in the non-German lands of the Empire declined; and this growing indifference — more marked under Rudolf's son, Albrecht, than in his own reign — was due not least to the fact that western Germany was the seat of the power of the ecclesiastical electors, who were the leaders of the opposition to hereditary monarchy.

Thus the imperial question divided Germany into two factions. The one was represented by the Habsburgs, who were prepared to surrender imperial pretensions in return for the reality of hereditary monarchy; the other was represented by the electoral college under the predominating influence of the archbishops of the west, whose interests not only brought them into opposition to any reorganiza-tion which would eliminate electoral rights, but also made them the natural opponents of French infiltration into the Low Countries and Lorraine. They were the guardians of the western frontier, and therewith the upholders of established imperial traditions, since the maintenance of the Empire was the only means of safeguard-ing their flank by assuring the continuance of German rule in Burgundy and Arles; they looked to the king above all else to take the lead in maintaining the integrity of the western frontiers. The Habsburgs, on the other hand, were prepared to make sub-stantial territorial concessions in the west in order to secure French and papal support for the creation of an hereditary monarchy. Rudolf was on the point of transferring the kingdom of Arles to Charles of Anjou's son in 1280, when the death of Pope Nicholas III brought the project to an end; Albrecht made over the lands west of the Meuse to France in 1299. Right down to 1330 the Habsburgs maintained their connexions with France and their policy of hereditary monarchy; but throughout the same period they were confronted by the opposition of the ecclesiastical electors. It was due to their influence that, instead of a Habsburg, Adolf of Nassau was elected to succeed Rudolf I in 1291; and although Rudolf's son, Albrecht I, succeeded Adolf by force of arms in 1298, the election of Henry of Luxemburg in 1308 was another blow to Habsburg aspirations. A double current runs through German history after 1272; an antithesis between heredity and election, between the new colonial east and the old western lands, between alliance with, and opposition to, France. The Habsburgs, seeking to introduce revolutionary changes in both the German and the imperial constitution, necessarily proceeded by understanding with France and the papacy; for only with French and papal diplomatic support was there any possibility of overcoming the resistance of the electors. The German kings elected in opposition to the Habsburgs, on the other hand, were forced almost of necessity into opposition to France; that was the case under Adolf of Nassau (1292-1298), under Henry of Luxemburg (1308-1314), and under Louis of Bavaria (1314-1347), and in the case of Adolf and Louis opposition to France led directly to alliance with England.

The radical conflict of interests and ideals which the question of the Empire and its destinies fostered in Germany was a cardinal weakness in German history between 1272 and 1356. Above all else, it undermined the possibility of a united, national resistance to French encroachments. In the last years of Rudolf I's reign, shortly before 1291, all the elements of a national anti-French movement were in existence, goaded into life by French encroachments at Lyons and Valenciennes, in the Franche-Comté and Bar, and by the pontificate of the most pro-French of all popes, Martin IV (1281-1285). But by exploiting the division of interests within Germany, France was able to cripple German policy, and to maintain steady pressure. It is indicative of the part that France played in German affairs that six times in sixty years, in 1273, 1308, 1313, 1324, 1328 and 1333, a French candidate was put forward for the imperial throne. But French policy, although for ever toying with the idea of a French empire, to be secured either by inducing the German electors to set a

French prince on the imperial throne, or by putting pressure on the pope to transfer the empire away from Germany, was pliable and resourceful; it was willing at all times to barter imperial pretensions in exchange for tangible territorial concessions in the German Netherlands and in Lorraine, in Burgundy or the kingdom of Arles. Its primary object was to prevent such a consolidation of German power as would raise a barrier against French aggression; but if French expansion were assured, it was prepared to support any German ruler who would guarantee French territorial gains. In the meantime, it could scarcely fail to profit by the *status quo*. According to a theory widely propagated after 1250, although the king of the Romans ruled in Germany from the day of his election, only a duly crowned emperor possessed rights of government in Italy, Arles and Burgundy; and thus, so long as the Empire was in abeyance, the door was left wide open for French expansion. France was therefore in no hurry to bring about a settlement of the imperial question, unless it was assured of a settlement which would be to its own advantage. But in view of the conflicting interests of the powers, such a settlement was difficult to obtain. Both the Capetians in Paris and the Angevins in Naples hoped, for example, to secure succession to the kingdom of Arles, and neither party was prepared to see the other installed in power; French opposition prevented the cession of Arles to Robert of Naples in 1310, while in 1333 Robert joined forces with Louis of Bavaria in order to prevent the transfer of Arles to France. In Italy also, Capetian and Angevin interests were in conflict; the appearance in Italy of French armies under Charles of Valois in 1302 and under Philip of Valois in 1320 raised the spectre of a French kingdom in Tuscany or Lombardy, limiting the powers and prospects of the king of Naples. Hence Neapolitan interests were in the fourteenth century as opposed to a French as to a German empire; and it was Robert of Naples who formally proposed, in 1313, that the pope should, on principle, leave the imperial throne vacant. This was a solution which, in normal circumstances, well suited papal interests. The papacy had not broken the power of the Hohenstaufen in order to fall under the dominion of the Angevins or of the Capetians; and the efforts of most popes were directed to establishing an equilibrium so balanced that neither Italy nor the Holy See ran the risk of falling under the control of a single power. With this end in view popes like Gregory X, Nicholas III and Boniface VIII were prepared to strengthen Germany as a counter-weight to France; but after the collapse of Boniface VIII's policy in 1303, and the transfer of the papacy to Avignon in 1309, no pope dared to stand out openly for a restoration of stable government in Germany for fear of provoking violent French reactions. On the other hand, they were averse to a radical solution of the imperial question, fearing that this could only mean a further strengthening of France. Hence papal policy inclined to a maintenance of the *status quo*; aware of the evils of the situation, but frightened of the reactions any attempt to tackle it must provoke, the papacy – in spite of the lead given by certain outstanding popes – tended to temporize, to postpone decision, and to wait on events, leaving the situation to work itself out. This was a policy pursued under French pressure; and so long as France remained strong, it worked to French advantage. From 1270 to 1348 – and particularly during the reign of Philip VI (1328-1350) – French intervention, direct or through the papacy, was a determinative factor in German history; and it was only through the English victories over French arms, beginning at Crécy in 1346, that a new situation was created in which French power was so reduced as to leave Germany free, at long last, to settle its own destinies.

The failure, between 1250 and 1356, to secure any solution of the imperial question inevitably had adverse repercussions within Germany. Gradually all parties awakened to the realization that the country's well-being and internal stability were being sacrificed to the exigencies of hostile powers, particularly of France; and the result was the reaffirmation of national solidarity which found expression, in 1338, at the Diet of Rhens. Already a year earlier Benedict XII had pointed out to Philip VI of France the way the wind was blowing, emphasizing the calamitous state of Germany, the revulsion which delays in settlement caused by France were bound to produce, and the risk of throwing Germany, out of opposition to France and the papacy, into the arms of England.[1] From 1272 to 1338, on the other hand, the intervention of foreign powers, seeking a share in the imperial inheritance, divided and crippled Germany, deflecting attention and activity from the pressing needs of reorganization at home to the wider issues of imperial policy, and fatally impeding any revival of the German monarchy.

[1] *Registres de Benoît XII* (ed. Daumet), no. 280 (April 4th, 1337).

Thus, due to foreign complications, Germany missed the opportunity for national development which the failure of Hohenstaufen imperialism created; driven by French encroachments and papal pretensions to defence of its imperial legacy, it hovered hesitant and undecided between the old and the new, between the imperial traditions of the past which were not yet liquidated and the territorial system of the future which was not yet consolidated. The Interregnum, formally over in 1272, really continued until 1356, when at long last a new balance was provisionally struck.

The situation between 1272 and 1356 was faithfully reflected in German political thought of the period, which revealed unambiguously the adverse effects of the imperial complication. Germany had nothing to offer comparable to the political thought of France, which was busy laying the foundations – on the basis of a new philosophy with its home in the schools of Paris – for the nation-state and for the national policy of the nation-state, and which supported the policy of Philip the Fair with a barrage of propaganda, of manifestos and memoranda, in which the imperial tradition was virulently attacked.[1] Divided politically, and rooted to the imperial traditions of the past, German propaganda, as reflected in the writings of Jordan of Osnabrück and Alexander of Roes, of Englebert of Admont and Lupold of Bebenberg, failed to generate a decided or united attitude towards the aggressor. Jordan feared the *sublatio* of the Empire, its abrogation by the pope; Alexander feared its *translatio*, its transfer into French hands. The arguments of both were therefore essentially defensive and negative; they sought to traverse the claims of French propaganda, but developed no new arguments of their own; they were intent on proving the right of the German king to Burgundy and Arles, but brought forward no practical proposals for making his rights a reality. Only in the time of Philip of Leyden, writing after 1355, does a breath of actuality enter; he was the first to admit that the empire had ceased to count and that the future lay with the principalities.[2] But by

[1] The best survey of the new political outlook, superseding earlier summaries such as Rivière, *Le problème de l'église et de l'état au temps de Philippe le Bel* (1926), is now to be found in G. de Lagarde, *La naissance de l'esprit laïque au déclin du moyen âge* (1934-1942). For Germany cf. Kämpf, op. cit., 82 sqq., and W. Berges, *Die Fürstenspiegel des hohen u. späten Mittelalters* (1938), 101 sqq.

[2] 'Scissum est imperium'; cf. Berges, op. cit., 254. The penetration into Germany of the spirit and realistic outlook of the French jurists in the days of Charles IV (1347-1378) probably owes something to the connexions between the Luxemburg dynasty and France; cf. below, pp. 341-342.

then it was too late; under the impact of political events territorial divisions had taken root, preventing the uniform development of a national outlook concentrated round the reigning dynasty. The weakness of dynastic feeling, in contrast to the sense of unity which bound together the destinies of the Capetians and France, is well illustrated in the case of Englebert of Admont; in spite of his close connexions with the Habsburg dynasty he remained under the ban of imperial ideas, and in this he was representative of his contemporaries. Their concern was the Empire, not Germany, and even in approaching the imperial problem they adopted a universal rather than a national point of view; Alexander of Roes' arguments, for example, hinged round the assertion that, if the Empire were destroyed, world order would collapse. Hence German political thought had nothing on a practical plane to counteract the concrete plans of Dubois or Nogaret or Pierre Flote; it was still anchored in the realm of natural law while contemporaries in France were elaborating the theory of the state; it had no new principle to expound, no positive plans or will for the future, no sense of the need for a new 'ideology'.

The question of the Empire thus played a cardinal part in German politics between 1272 and 1356. It caused political division and ideological confusion. At a time when England and France were moving by rapid steps towards national unity, it prevented the completion of a corresponding national concentration in Germany, although all the elements of incipient nationalism were visible. The division of interests it created goes far to explain the ineffectiveness of German opposition to France. The cleft within Germany between the new colonial east and the old western lands, the east dominated by the princes, the west by the archbishops, was itself sufficient to cripple German policy in this respect; but the concentration on the Empire was still another check on the formation of an opposition capable of withstanding France. There was in Germany no national opposition, because the nation was divided by the imperial question; and the long contest over the Empire, opening the door wide to French and papal interference, blighted the prospects of a national revival in Germany which was within the bounds of possibility when the house of Habsburg succeeded to the German throne in 1273. Gradually, between 1272 and 1356, the political structure of Germany was reshaped, under the impact of political

events, in such a way as to postpone for centuries the hope of
national unity. It remains to survey, in the briefest of outlines, the
course of events which produced this result; to see how the conflict
of imperial and national interests and the intervention of foreign
powers, reacting on German development, created the political
system under which the German people was destined to live from
the fourteenth to the nineteenth centuries.

IV

Already in 1272 and 1273 the interplay of foreign interests was
the dominant factor in the German political situation.[1] It was the
new pope, Gregory X (1271-1276), threatened by the overmighty
power of Charles of Anjou in Italy, who decided to bring the
Interregnum to an end, in order to secure a counterweight in
Germany which he could use to resist Angevin pressure. It was
Gregory who resisted and defeated the proposal for the candidature
of Philip III of France, through which Charles of Anjou hoped to
secure recognition of his territorial position in Italy and the kingdom
of Arles. It was Gregory, finally, who by admonitions and the
threat to use his power of provision to fill the vacant throne, at
length obtained the unanimous election of Rudolf of Habsburg.
Rudolf was not, indeed, a papal nominee: except for opposing the
candidature of Frederick of Meissen, the nearest heir of Frederick II,
the pope left the choice of the new ruler in the hands of the electors,
and it is clear that he would willingly have accepted Ottokar of
Bohemia who, through his acquisitions during the Interregnum,
was by far the strongest of the princes. It was the hostility of the
electors to Ottokar, much of whose territorial power rested on
force without legal title, and their fear of a strong king, which

---

[1] Cf. H. Otto, *Die Beziehungen Rudolfs von Habsburg zu Papst Gregor X* (1895). No
attempt can be made to refer to the voluminous literature on which the following sketch
draws for fact and interpretation. The surveys in Loserth, *Gesch. d. späteren Mittelalters* (1903),
and Ranke, *Das Zeitalter der Kreuzzüge u. das späte Mittelalter* (vols. 8 and 9 of the *Welt-
geschichte*, new ed. 1935), are still useful and there is a brief but clear outline from 1308 in
Mollat, *Les papes d'Avignon* (1930), 192-228; cf. also W. Kienast, *Die Anfänge des europäischen
Staatensystems im späteren Mittelalter* (1936). For the period down to 1308 Kern, *Ausdehnungspolitik* (1910), is still fullest and best, requiring only minor modification. For Adolf of Nassau
cf. *Cambr. Hist. Journal*, VI (1940); for Henry VII cf. Wenck, *Clemens V u. Heinrich VII* (1882);
for the period of Louis of Bavaria, Stengel, *Avignon und Rhens* (1930), is the most recent and
suggestive survey, with full references to the earlier literature. For Charles IV the biography
by Werunsky (1880 sqq.) is still basic; cf. also K. Zeumer, *Die goldene Bulle* (1908).

resulted in the choice of Rudolf, who, like William of Holland, was a simple count, not even a prince of the empire. Nevertheless Rudolf had substantial possessions, reaching from the Alpine passes of Switzerland, from the lake of Lucerne and the river Aare, to the gates of Colmar and Alsace; and he soon revealed his determination to create, on the basis of territorial power, a new foundation for the monarchy.[1] Already before his election, agreement had been reached on the recuperation of crown lands and fiefs and jurisdictions usurped during the Interregnum; and one of the earliest acts of the new reign was the proclamation, at the Diet of Speyer in December 1273, that all illegally acquired crown lands were to be surrendered. This proclamation was directed above all against Ottokar of Bohemia, who refused to recognize Rudolf's title; and when Ottokar rose in rebellion and was defeated and killed in battle in 1278, Rudolf's position was assured. Not only was the most dangerous opponent of the new dynasty removed, but through the acquisition of Austria and Styria (1282) the Habsburgs became at one stroke the strongest dynasty in Germany. From this moment Rudolf could, with good prospects, plan the establishment of an hereditary monarchy and the stabilization of German government in Habsburg hands.

Such a policy was bound to arouse the opposition of the electoral princes, particularly of the archbishops of Mainz, Cologne and Trier. To strengthen his hands against the latter, Rudolf drew close to the main opponents of the archbishops in the Rhinelands, the duke of Brabant and the counts of Cleves and Guelders. But more than this was needed. Without doubt Rudolf planned to secure his own coronation as emperor in order, following Hohenstaufen traditions, to get his son crowned king during his own lifetime; thus continuity would be assured, and the foundation laid for transforming hereditary succession, established in fact, into the rule of law. For such a policy papal co-operation was requisite, and the opportunity to put it into effect seemed to have occurred with the election of Pope Nicholas III (1277-1280), who revived, after a short break, the ideas and policy of Gregory X. To secure Nicholas' approbation Rudolf not only dropped his plans for an

---

[1] In the words of von Below, 'he was on the way to overcoming the territorial states through the territorial state' ('er war auf dem Wege, die Territorien vor allem durch das Territorium zu überwinden'); cf. von Below, *Vom Mittelalter zur Neuzeit* (1924), 31.

alliance with England to resist French and Angevin designs on
Arles, but also made over the Romagna to the papacy and accepted
a draft treaty, dated June 7th, 1279, for a settlement by which the
kingdom of Arles was to pass into the hands of the house of Anjou
as compensation for its withdrawal from central Italy. But the
death of Nicholas III in 1280 brought the project to nothing.
Determined to secure a pro-French pope, servile to his interests,
Charles of Anjou terrorized the cardinals into electing his partisan,
Martin IV (1281-1285), a bitter enemy of Germany. With Martin's
accession all hope of imperial coronation vanished, and Rudolf
postponed the completion of a plan which no longer offered him
any benefits. Charles of Anjou still hoped to seize Arles by force;
but in March 1282, when the Sicilian fleet was already anchored in
the Rhône, the Sicilian Vespers — an outbreak of popular hatred of
the French which swept Sicily from end to end — shattered all his
schemes. Arles still remained German.

The radical change in papal policy under Angevin pressure after
the death of Nicholas III in 1280 was a decisive set-back to Rudolf of
Habsburg's plans, depriving him of the external support on which
he had relied to overcome the opposition of the ecclesiastical electors.
Even after Martin IV's death in 1285, his successors, engrossed in the
struggle for Sicily, were opposed to a revival of the empire, fearing
that, after the crumbling of Angevin might, they would have no
counterweight to oppose to Rudolf. Thrown back on his own
resources, Rudolf redoubled his efforts, making concessions to
Ottokar of Bohemia's son, Wenzel, in order to secure support for
the election of his own son to the throne. But his efforts were in
vain. At a diet held at Frankfurt in 1291 a few weeks before his
death, he failed to secure the adhesion of the princes to his proposals
to make his son, Albrecht, his successor; and when he died on July
15th, 1291, the opposition of Cologne and Bohemia led to the election
of Adolf of Nassau. Thus the project of hereditary monarchy fell
through, the electors even proclaiming the principle that it was not
right that the son should immediately follow the father on the throne.

Fear of Austrian power, opposition to hereditary succession,
Bohemian hopes of regaining some of the territories lost in 1278,
these were all major reasons for the reaction against the Habsburg
dynasty in 1291 and the election of Adolf; but they were not the
only ones. In 1291 Rudolf had again entered into negotiations with

the house of Anjou, doubtless as part of his final efforts to secure the succession of his son. He had also neglected, in order to secure French good-will, to oppose the French penetration into imperial territory which had begun on a major scale after the accession of Philip IV in 1285. Already in 1290 there was bitter criticism in Germany of Rudolf's indifference to French aggression, and there was no reason to think that Rudolf's son, Albrecht, would reverse Habsburg policy in this respect. These considerations also played a part in the rejection of the Habsburgs in 1292. The election of Adolf of Nassau, closely connected with the archbishop of Cologne and through Cologne with England, was a reaction against the pro-French policy of the Habsburgs, against French encroachments which Habsburg policy connived at, and against the papacy which, under French and Angevin influence, refused to come to any decision in the imperial question and thereby sacrificed Germany's well-being to extrinsic considerations. Adolf at the time of his election was territorially weak, and his choice was undoubtedly a set-back to the prospect of an effective monarchy; but he was not a nullity. At home, following the precedent set by Rudolf of Habsburg, he immediately began an effective policy of territorial expansion, securing Thuringia and Meissen for the crown in 1295. Abroad, he stood out from the beginning of his reign against French encroachments. In 1294 he entered into alliance with Edward I of England, and a combined Anglo-German attack on France was planned for 1295. But long-drawn-out diplomatic preparations, complications in Scotland, and Boniface VIII's intervention on behalf of France led to postponement of the campaign; and this gave Philip the Fair the opportunity for energetic intervention in Germany. As early as 1295 negotiations were in progress between France and Austria; and in June 1297, a conspiracy against Adolf, led by Albrecht of Austria, took shape. At the same time opposition to the war and to the expenses it entailed came to a head in England, and after a brief campaign Edward, fearing for the stability of his crown, made an armistice with France. Adolf also sought to save his position by negotiation with Philip the Fair; but it was too late. At the beginning of 1298 the Austrian party came out in open rebellion; in June the electors deposed Adolf and set up Albrecht in his place; and a few weeks later, on July 2nd, 1298, Adolf fell in battle.

In the fall of Adolf both internal and external factors were at play. Elected primarily to lead the opposition to France, he failed to safeguard Germany's frontiers, and instead used his position to build up the territorial power of the monarchy. His successes in Thuringia and Meissen injured the territorial interests of the archbishop of Mainz, and of Wenzel of Bohemia, to whose efforts he had largely owed the throne; his contacts with the estates of Austria, restive under Albrecht's arbitrary and oppressive rule, alienated the Habsburgs, who feared that he intended to dispossess them; his relations with the cities of Germany and Flanders, all of which with the exception of Strassburg were solidly behind him, alienated the princes as a body. But the decisive factor was foreign relations. A successful outcome of the Anglo-German alliance would have strengthened his position immeasurably, and destroyed all hope of successful rebellion; failure ruined his chances. By ample use of subsidies, France had built up a strong pro-French party, including Hainault, Luxemburg, the duke of Lorraine, the count-palatine of Burgundy, the dauphin of Vienne and the duke of Austria, and the existence of this party crippled Adolf's plans. Nor was the French king disposed to make serious concessions to Adolf, when in 1297 direct negotiations began between the two rulers; he manœuvred in order to lull Adolf into inaction, but he had more to gain through support of the Habsburg party. Albrecht, continuing Habsburg traditions, had no repugnance to sacrificing western German interests to France, if thereby he could neutralize European opposition to the plan of hereditary monarchy. Within a few months of Adolf's death the community of Franco-Austrian interests was revealed. Meeting Philip the Fair at Quatrevaux (near Toul) in 1299, Albrecht not only entered into a close alliance with France, but also ceded the territories in French occupation west of the Meuse and dropped all opposition to French penetration in the Franche-Comté.

After the failure of the Anglo-German coalition of 1294-1297 the question was not whether, but how, Burgundy and the lands west of the Meuse would become French. Albrecht's surrender of them in 1299 showed a hard streak of realism. By his cessions to France he set out to gain French support, both at Rome and in Germany, for the old plan of an hereditary monarchy with powerful demesnes in the east. The terms of the Franco-Austrian treaty of alliance show that Philip was prepared to recognize the succession of Albrecht's son, Rudolf. But once again, as in the days of Rudolf I, this plan struck at the interests of the electors, and the Franco-German alliance was also a blow to the pope who, already involved in conflict with Philip the Fair, feared the pressure of an overwhelming coalition. Against the electors of western Germany, Albrecht struck hard and quickly. Between 1300 and 1302, with the aid of French troops and the support of the German cities, he subdued the archbishops of Mainz, Cologne and Trier, and the Elector-Palatine. Towards the pope a more diplomatic policy was necessary. Although he had been a bitter opponent of Adolf, Boniface VIII refused from the beginning to recognize Albrecht, calling on him to answer the charge of murdering Adolf; and with the conclusion of the Franco-German alliance his hostility became even more extreme. But it was in the pope's interest to divide the coalition, and when in 1302 Albrecht offered to come to terms, Boniface quickly agreed. In 1303, an Austro-papal alliance was sealed. Albrecht agreed to swear an oath of fealty and obedience to the pope, hoping in return to secure the imperial crown, abrogation of the rights of the electors and the succession of his son. But both Boniface and Albrecht underestimated the strength and ruthlessness of French opposition. Philip the Fair immediately set in motion plans to capture and depose the pope, while against Albrecht he entered into alliance with Bohemia. The death of Boniface VIII on October 12th, 1303, and the collapse of the anti-French coalition which followed immediately, forestalled the armed attack on Albrecht, which was the object of the Franco-Bohemian alliance. But Albrecht's position was already compromised. Realizing that there was no longer any hope of papal support, he concentrated his efforts on building up Habsburg territorial power in the east, securing Meissen and the Egerland in 1305 and Moravia and Bohemia in the following year. His policy was to build up the territorial power of his dynasty as a foundation for the monarchy; and it seemed, in spite of the opposition of the princes, as though he was near his goal. When in 1306 he sought, like Adolf of Nassau before him, to incorporate Thuringia in the crown lands, he encountered strong resistance, followed by unrest in Bohemia; but still more significant was the opposition of France. After the death of Boniface VIII, Philip the Fair devoted his efforts to establishing French control of the bishoprics of western Germany, and between 1303 and 1308, by subsidies, treaties and nominations which Clement V was unable to resist, pro-French bishops were installed at Cambrai, Liége, Cologne, Verdun, Mainz, Basel and Constance.

The effects of this policy were seen on Albrecht's death in 1308. In spite of its hereditary tendencies, the lay electors were in no way fundamentally opposed to the house of Habsburg, and they were ready to raise Albrecht's son to the throne, if he could secure the support of two out of the three ecclesiastical electors. But the ecclesiastical electors, already alienated by Albrecht's policy in 1301 and 1302, and fearful for their privileges, were now tied to France and assured of French support; and the chances of the election of a Habsburg were therefore negligible. Thus the scheme of an hereditary German kingship died with Albrecht I. Instead the year 1308 saw a determined effort to set a French prince on the German throne. But this scheme, which would have extended French influence to Italy, Germany and Hungary, encountered papal opposition; and the outcome was a compromise solution. Both the French and the Habsburg candidates were rejected, and instead Henry of Luxemburg, a minor count from the western borderlands, was elected. But the election was far from being a French defeat. Henry of Luxemburg was French in speech and upbringing, a vassal of the French king, and his family had risen through its close connexion with France; his brother, Baldwin, owed the archbishopric of Trier to French influence. There was therefore no risk of a renewal of the policy of Adolf of Nassau, of an attempt in alliance with England to build up the territorial power of the German monarchy so as to put it in a position to resist French encroachments. On the contrary, Henry VII definitely chose to rule as an instrument of the electors, and made no attempt to throw off their influence; under him the attempt to reassert the independent rights of the crown, which every ruler from 1273 to 1308 had pursued, was thrown over. Exploiting the confused and unsettled situation in the east after Albrecht's death, he firmly established his dynasty in Bohemia and Moravia in 1311. But this was a dynastic success, not a success for the monarchy. To secure Bohemia, he confirmed the rights of the Habsburgs in Austria, Styria and Carniola, and gave up the royal claims, for which both Adolf and Albrecht had struggled hard, to Thuringia, Meissen and the Pleissnerland. Likewise in the west he restored the electors to the rights of which Albrecht had stripped them in 1301 and 1302. Hence his reign marked a decisive step forward in the consolidation of German territorial divisions and in the rise of particularism, which left Germany more than ever a prey to foreign intervention.

The radical change in the relations between the king and the princes which Henry inaugurated, determined the lines of his policy. Unwilling or unable to oppose the electors in Germany, he attempted to revert to Hohenstaufen traditions and — apart from Bohemia — to seek in Italy the basis of power which he had surrendered in Germany. New factors in the general European situation favoured this policy, above all else the attitude of the papacy which, to escape the pressure of Philip the Fair and the threat of captivity at Avignon, desired a restoration of order in Italy which would make possible its return. Hence Clement V hastened in 1309 to recognize Henry's election, and at the same time promised the imperial crown in 1312. Thus it was with the pope's full approbation that, in 1310, Henry crossed the Alps. But events soon proved that it was less easy than Henry or Clement had imagined, to still Italian factions. Furthermore, under pressure from France papal policy soon veered round, and there were complications with Robert of Anjou. It was obvious to all concerned that an arrangement with the house of Naples was necessary, if there were to be any stabilization in Italy; and once again, as in the thirteenth century, there was an attempt to secure Angevin co-operation by the offer of the crown of Arles. But in 1311, at the instance of Philip the Fair, the pope vetoed this plan, which conflicted with French hopes of territorial gains east of the Rhône; and deprived of the prospect of compensation, Robert of Anjou, with the secret backing of the pope, soon came out into open opposition in Italy. Disillusioned, Henry began to adopt a more independent attitude, which increased Clement's fears of a revival of Hohenstaufen imperialism. These fears became a dominant factor after Henry's sudden illness and death in 1313. Once again a French candidate was put forward, and this time he secured the pope's backing. But the death of Clement V shortly afterwards, and the long vacancy in the papal see which followed, relieved the German electors at the decisive moment of papal pressure; the French candidature again fell through, and for the first time for many years the electors were left free to decide without serious external complications.

What policy in these circumstances would the German electors pursue? The election which followed in 1314 reveals faithfully the situation in Germany. Henry VII's reign had strengthened the position of those who favoured an aristocratic form of government with control vested in the estate of princes working through the electoral college; yet the political forces in Germany were still evenly balanced, and a strong party still supported the house of Habsburg and the contrary tendencies which it represented. A further factor was that the western electors, whose joint action had secured Henry's election in 1308, were now divided. Mainz and Trier, both closely connected with the Luxemburg dynasty, maintained their allegiance, but the archbishop of Cologne and the Elector-Palatine went over to the Habsburg party. But Henry VII's heir, John of Bohemia, was not only too young but also unlikely (in view of the conflict which had come to a head between his father and Clement V) to secure papal approbation, and so the vote of the Luxemburg party was transferred to Louis of Bavaria. The outcome was the double election of Louis and Frederick of Austria — a double election which reflected not merely the momentary balance of parties, but also the deeper currents and political tendencies which divided Germany and were still struggling for predominance.

Left to itself, Germany might still, after 1314, have found a way out among these conflicting tendencies; but it was not left to itself. The new pope, John XXII (1316-1334), although unwilling to accept Neapolitan plans for a separation of Italy and Germany, which would have placed Italy under the domination of Robert of Naples, had plans of his own for a restoration of papal authority in Italy and these were favoured by a vacancy in the empire, during which the pope himself claimed as imperial vicar to exercise the emperor's rights. The double election in Germany therefore played into John XXII's hands, and he carefully refrained from taking positive steps to bring it to an end. But in 1322 events forced his hand; Louis of Bavaria defeated Frederick of Austria at the battle of Mühldorf, quickly consolidated his power, and requested the pope's approbation. John XXII's answer was in substance negative. He refused to agree that the victory at Mühldorf had decided the issue, and in October 1323, admonished Louis to lay down his powers of government within three months, to appear within the same period before the papal court at Avignon, and not to resume royal authority until

x

he had secured papal confirmation; he also cast doubt on the rights of the electors, and claimed not only the right to confirm but also to reject their candidate. Louis rejoined with a vehement protest against the pope's pretensions, against his theory that the throne was still vacant, his claim to administer the empire, and above all against his asserted right to examine the election. The result was to widen the breach; and finally, on March 23rd, 1324, Louis of Bavaria was excommunicated.

Thus began the long conflict, only settled after Louis' death in 1347, which prolonged for a generation the anarchy, uncertainty and instability under which Germany was labouring, at the very moment when Louis' victory in the battle of Mühldorf seemed to portend a settlement. From a German point of view John XXII's intervention was a gratuitous blow, by which the pope sacrificed the country's future to the dubious exigencies of his own halting and vacillating Italian policy, and precipitated a major European crisis. For present purposes only an outline of the salient developments, as they affected Germany, is requisite, and we must ignore the complications which arose through the linking of Louis of Bavaria's cause with the opposition of the spiritual Franciscans to the secularized papacy and with the Roman people. These factors, and Louis' expedition to Italy (1327-1330), were scarcely more than incidental. Unlike Henry VII, Louis of Bavaria was not concerned primarily to establish his position in Italy; as has been well said,[1] he was fighting — even in Italy — for the independence of the German crown, for the freedom of Germany to set its own house in order, against a pope who fomented German discords as the easiest means of securing a free hand in Italy. The outstanding fact is that the conflict with Louis of Bavaria threw the pope, far more decidedly than his predecessor, Clement V, into the arms of France. Instead of throwing his support on to the side of Frederick of Habsburg, John XXII used all his influence to secure a French candidature, and once again there began a series of complicated negotiations in which the kingdom of Arles assumed major importance as an object of compensation. First, in 1323-1324, was a project to raise up John of Bohemia against Louis, securing French support by the cession of Arles to Charles of Valois; but this plan fell through owing to the opposition of Robert of Naples. It was followed almost imme-

[1] E. Jordan, L'Allemagne et l'Italie aux XIIe et XIIIe siècles (1939), 420.

diately by an attempt to revive the old Franco-Austrian alliance, to confer the imperial throne on Charles IV of France on condition that the position of imperial vicar, with the exercise of royal powers in Germany, was left to the Habsburgs, who were also to be helped to restore their territorial power in Switzerland. But the electors refused to countenance this plan, and Louis overcame the danger by reaching agreement with the Habsburgs and establishing a scheme of joint-rule with Frederick of Austria (1325).

Already at this early stage it was evident that the overbearing attitude of the pope, the exaggerated nature of his claims, his refusal to compromise, and above all his close alliance with France, far from dividing the princes from Louis was closing the German ranks in resistance and rousing a national opposition in Germany. It was characteristic that a further project, in 1328, to substitute Frederick of Austria for Louis collapsed because Frederick, as firmly as Louis before him, refused to submit the election of 1314 to the pope's scrutiny. European complications, on the other hand, ruined a Franco-Bohemian project of 1332-1333, in which French support was guaranteed to the Luxemburg candidate, in return for the cession of Arles and the Cambrésis; once again Robert of Anjou successfully opposed any extension of French influence in the kingdom of Arles. But it was after the death of Frederick of Austria in 1330 and of John XXII in 1334 that the issues became clear. In 1330 determined efforts were made in the cause of internal peace and order to break down John XXII's intransigence; the king of Denmark, the count of Holland, the duke of Austria, Archbishop Baldwin of Trier, even John of Bohemia, all intervened with the pope, but without success. The question in 1334 was whether the death of John XXII would create the possibility of a reorientation in papal policy. The new pope, Benedict XII (1334-1342), conciliatory by nature and genuinely desirous of breaking with John XXII's precedent, realized that Germany was solidly on Louis' side, and was ready in 1335 to reach a settlement. But he counted without France and Naples. Robert of Anjou had no desire for a settlement which would destroy the advantages he enjoyed as vicar of the church in Italy; Philip VI of France was opposed to a reconciliation, unless he could use it to secure territorial cessions across the Rhône or in the Rhinelands. Their joint pressure was too much for Benedict, who dared not risk a breach with France, and after repeated delays the pope obeyed·

Philip VI's injunctions, and in April 1337 negotiations with Louis were dropped. The pope himself laid the blame on the French king;[1] he would, he was reported to have told the German ambassadors, gladly have come to terms, had he not feared he might suffer a worse fate than Boniface VIII. The impossibility of a solution, except by taking positive steps to break French predominance, was evident; and with this in view in July 1337, Louis entered into alliance with Edward III of England.

Thus French intractability and intervention provoked at length the inevitable reaction. Louis, who in two years had sent three embassies to the papal curia to sue for peace, could fairly claim to have made every effort and concession to the pope, and German opinion was solidly on his side. The German episcopate, hoping to succeed where the king had failed, made one further appeal to the pope early in 1338; when this was ignored, the revulsion of feeling was immense. At the Diet of Rhens on July 16th, 1338, the estates of the realm — led, in spite of the opposition of the houses of Luxemburg and Wittelsbach, by the Luxemburg prince, Archbishop Baldwin of Trier — swore to defend the rights and liberties and customs of the empire, proclaimed that the imperial dignity was held directly of God, and that a king elected by the majority was the legitimate ruler, entitled from the day of his election to exercise his functions without papal consent or confirmation. Louis himself who, after the conclusion of the Anglo-German alliance, had waited in the hope that, in the new circumstances, Benedict would break loose from France, now took steps to make the alliance a reality. On August 6th, in the edict *Licet iuris*, he confirmed the Rhens decrees; on September 5th, he formally invested Edward III with the dignity and powers of a vicar of the empire.

Thus, once again, as in the days of Edward I and Adolf of Nassau, the issue with France was brought to the arbitrament of arms; and once again, as in 1297, the Anglo-German alliance failed. Once again, complications with Scotland and a financial and constitutional crisis at home ruined the English king's continental policy; once again, the limited resources of the German ruler prevented effective military measures. In September 1340, Edward made a truce with France; in January 1341, Louis of Bavaria, fearing to be left to face France in isolation, followed suit. The fact was that his interest in

[1] Cf. above, p. 298.

the Anglo-French struggle had always been subsidiary; he had
entered the lists less to engage in a decisive campaign against France,
than to bring pressure on the pope to grant him the recognition
necessary to stabilize his position in Germany. This result could be
obtained as readily through French support as by the threat implicit
in an Anglo-German coalition; and, in fact, it was one of the
conditions of the peace with France negotiated in 1341 that Philip
VI should give Louis diplomatic support at the papal curia. But
once again, as in 1337, Philip VI deliberately broke his promise, while
the new pope, Clement VI (1342-1352), who had held an important
post in Philip VI's administration, was pro-French in sentiment, and
returned to the intransigent policy of John XXII. In the meantime
Louis, by his failure to throw all his efforts, side by side with England, into the war against France, had lost the enthusiastic support
which had been his at the time of the Diet of Rhens, and from about
1341 his cause began to weaken. The princes began to feel that only
his person stood between Germany and peace; and from 1343 they
were prepared to proceed to another election. In these circumstances
Louis made one further effort to appease the pope; but no concession
was enough. Pressure from France and Naples, supported now by
John of Bohemia, overcame Clement's scruples. More significant
of the trend of events, the German estates rebelled against the abject
surrender to the papacy which Louis was now prepared to make;
but Clement VI pursued his objectives systematically and finally in
1346, Charles of Moravia, the son of John of Bohemia, was elected in
Louis' place. Even at this late date, however, the election was far
from popular. Charles, who had made far-reaching promises to the
pope, was scorned as an instrument of the papacy, and Louis still
retained the allegiance of the greater part of Germany, in particular
the solid support of the cities. The prospects of the anti-king were,
therefore, not good; but he was saved by events. Louis died in
1347. To have elected his son in his place would have meant a
continuation of the struggle with the papacy, and such a course was
not entertained. The other branches of the Wittelsbach family were
so subdivided among co-heirs that they were unable to play a leading
part.[1] The opposition therefore offered the crown to Edward III of
England, but met with cautious refusal. Then it turned to Frederick
of Meissen and thereafter to Günther of Schwarzburg; but on the

[1] Cf. below, pp. 326-327.

death of the latter in 1349 opposition died down, and Charles was duly crowned at Aachen on July 25th, 1349; from that date he was the universally accepted German king.

V

From 1272 to 1349 foreign intervention, particularly the intervention of France and of the papacy normally dependent on France, had decisively prevented Germany from setting its house in order. There were problems enough in Germany, conflicting tendencies which could not have been solved without a struggle; but what made these problems so serious was their interlacing with outside interests, and the fact that German parties could always secure foreign support. It was the impact of international complications on the process of German political evolution that, from reign to reign, impeded the stabilization of the monarchy; and never was this clearer than during the thirty-three years when Louis of Bavaria occupied the German throne. It was at this period that the existing tendencies within Germany to transfer the real seat of power from king to princes were decisively reinforced; as Louis' reign progressed, it was the estate of princes and not the crown which emerged, at the Diets of Rhens (1338) and Frankfurt (1344), as guardian of German interests. The attempt to strengthen the position of the monarchy by new accretions of territorial power had gradually, from the time of Henry VII, given way to a dynastic policy in the interests of the dynasty temporarily in possession of the throne; thus Louis of Bavaria's acquisition of the march of Brandenburg in 1324 and his attempt to secure the Tyrol in 1341 were both undertaken with a view to Wittelsbach interests. Where territorial aggrandizement had at first been pursued in order to strengthen the monarchy, the crown was now coveted primarily because it gave opportunity for dynastic aggrandizement. Thus the interests of kings and princes, formerly opposed, became identical; all sought for territorial power, and the king, shorn of effective royal authority, adopted the outlook of the estate of princes, of which he was himself a member. By 1349 the tendencies making for a reaffirmation of royal power and a revival of the monarchy were definitely checked. Largely through the action of those European powers whose interests would have suffered through the consolidation of Germany

under effective monarchical government, the principle of elective
monarchy was established and Germany passed under the control
of the estate of princes.

This state of affairs was implicitly accepted by Charles IV (1347-
1378). Secure in his hereditary lands of Bohemia, to which he
devoted his most assiduous attention, he sought to bring about a
pacification in Germany by recognizing the position of the princes,
in particular by agreements with the Habsburgs and the Wittelsbachs. In this policy of pacification he was aided by the course of the
Anglo-French war, by the English victories at Crécy (1346) and
Poitiers (1356), which at long last freed Germany from French
pressure; by simultaneous pacts with France and England he sought
to retain his freedom of action. The English victories also facilitated his relations with the papacy, which might in other circumstances have led to conflict; but Innocent VI (1352-1362) was in
no position to renew the policy of Clement VI or John XXII, and
when Charles crossed the Alps in 1354 to secure his coronation in
Rome, it was with the pope's approval. The coronation of 1355
was a significant event, in so far as it marked the burying of the
imperial question which, without ever reaching solution, had agi-
tated Europe for a century. Owing to the disasters of the Hundred
Years War, French plans for the empire ceased to count, while
Naples sank into anarchy after the death of Robert in 1343 and
was unable to intervene. But Charles had no intention of using
this momentarily favourable situation to return to the policy of
his grandfather, Henry VII. With a sober grasp of realities, he
turned down the importunities of Petrarch, who urged him to pursue
an active Italian policy, and accepted all the conditions laid down
by the pope. Already in 1346 he had agreed to hand over Ferrara to
the papacy and had acknowledged the independence of Provence,
Forcalquier and Piedmont; he had promised to respect the domains
of the church in Italy, never to enter any land pertaining to the
church without permission from the Holy See, only to enter Rome
on the day fixed for his coronation and to leave again the same
day. These promises, which implied complete exclusion from the
affairs of Italy, were duly kept; and thus the separation of Germany
and Italy, the dissolution of the empire, was completed in fact. It
was a compromise solution. The complications involved in earlier
schemes for radical settlement had been too great, the dangers of

substituting another power for Germany too manifest; but by excluding Germany in fact, while leaving the imperial title in German hands, the papacy obtained the solution which best suited its interests. For Charles IV, on the other hand, it was sufficient to secure the imperial title. His real interest was in Germany, and once he was crowned emperor he could turn to the reform of the German constitution, and in particular to the liberation of the German monarchy from the dependence on the papacy which had for so long restricted its freedom of action, without the risk of incurring the complications which had marred the reign of his predecessor, Louis of Bavaria.

Charles IV's coronation in Rome on April 5th, 1355, was therefore essentially a preliminary to a German settlement. He arrived back in Germany in July, and without delay summoned a Reichstag to meet at Nürnberg, before which he laid his proposals for stabilizing the constitutional position in Germany. These proposals were debated by the assembled estates, and early in 1356 the results were published in the famous Golden Bull. Charles' first object was to break the bonds by which Germany had so long been subjected to the papacy. Realizing that the intervention of the papacy in the election and confirmation of the German king was the prime cause of dissension in Germany, Charles reaffirmed for all time the decisions of the Diet of 1338. The right of the seven electors to choose the German king was reasserted, and it was agreed that the candidate receiving a majority of votes should be regarded as unanimously elected; in this way the pope's claim to examine rival candidates was circumvented. It was further stipulated that the prince elected was entitled to exercise full royal rights from the moment of election; the papal pretension to approve and confirm the election was passed over in silence. A clause instituting the duke of Saxony and the Count-Palatine as regents during a vacancy of the throne excluded the pope's claim to act as vicar. Finally to prevent contested elections, which might reopen the door to papal intervention, precise rules were formulated to prevent the division of electoral territories and therewith the multiplication of electoral votes. The net result was that, profiting by the easing of international tension, Charles IV succeeded in excluding papal pretensions without a frontal attack on the papacy, simply by a definition of procedure which left no room for the pope. Innocent VI was hostile, but in no position to protest, and the papacy had no choice save to accept the *fait accompli*. The provisions of the Golden Bull were completely successful; there were no more disputed elections and no more papal interventions. The intervention which had begun in 1076, was by a deft exploitation of favourable circumstances brought to an end: Germany, breaking loose at long last from Italy, had therewith shaken off papal pressure, and was free to go its own way.

If it had been possible to achieve this result during the generation which followed the death of Frederick II, the subsequent course of events might have been very different; left to itself, Germany had still at the end of the thirteenth century a good chance of working out its own salvation. But by the time of Charles IV the preconditions had changed. Every change of dynasty had weakened the position of the monarchy, and Charles IV only secured unity in face of the papacy by adopting the line of policy set out by the electors under Baldwin of Luxemburg in 1338, and by according full recognition to the prerogatives of the princes. In terms reminiscent of Frederick II, he spoke of the seven electors as the seven luminaries, the *candelabra lucentia* illuminating the realm. Hence the exclusion of papal influence in 1356, instead of strengthening the internal position of the monarchy, resulted in the consolidation of the rights of the electors and of princes, such as the duke of Austria, who without being electors had already established their territorial power. The Golden Bull fixed and legalized the *status quo*. The prohibition of partitions of electoral territory established the electorates as fixed elements in German political life; kings might change, the crown pass from dynasty to dynasty, but the electors remained, the enduring factors whom no king henceforward, without tearing up the constitution and revolutionizing the legal order, could displace. At the same time the confirmation of rights of coinage and of the monopoly of gold, silver and other metals within their territories gave the electors a semi-regal position, which was enhanced by the application to offences against their persons of the penalties of *lèse-majesté*. The princes were, Charles wrote, 'a part of our body'; they were 'the solid foundations and the immovable pillars of the empire', and as such were called upon to participate in imperial government. Already under Rudolf I the principle had been established that no transfer of crown lands was valid without their consent, and this intervention was soon extended widely in practice. The substance of government was in their hands; and the king was in practice little more than the mouthpiece and instrument of their policy. Charles IV showed in two ways that he recognized and accepted this position. In the first place, like Frederick II in 1232, he sacrificed the towns which had been the mainstay of the monarchy down to the end of Louis of Bavaria's reign; in the second place he exerted himself in the Golden Bull to secure for his hereditary lands of Bohemia all possible advantages. In Bohemia he was king, but in Germany he was only head of a confederation, of which the real rulers were the princes.

The Golden Bull thus established, after a long period of transition, a federal framework for German political life, in which the princes were the dominant power. It is sometimes asked whether this was an innovation or merely a confirmation of the *status quo*. The answer is that the Golden Bull sanctioned developments which rested on long precedent, but which until that date had never definitely secured acceptance as a recognized scheme of government. It marked the cessation of the attempt to maintain an independent position for the monarchy. Henceforward the principalities were firmly anchored in the constitution, and there could be no attempt to revive the monarchy at the expense of the princes. The cause of this surrender was, beyond doubt, the long struggle which had wearied and worn down the monarchy in Louis of Bavaria's reign. Charles IV came to the throne determined above all else to restore the peace and order which was Germany's prime need; hence he was willing, after the upheavals and uncertainties of the previous reign, to accept a compromise. Unable to stand out simultaneously against the princes and the pope, he came to terms with the former in order to free Germany from the incubus of papal interference. The triumph of the princes, the final establishment of the principle of elective monarchy and the promulgation of a federal constitution, although springing from seeds long planted in Germany, were therefore in the last analysis the result of the discords fostered by foreign powers and by the papacy in league with foreign powers; it was because Germany by 1349 was worn out by the long struggle, that the overpowering need for peace triumphed so far over other considerations that in 1356 the monarchy, taking the line of least resistance, finally accepted the new order. Within measure Charles

IV was successful in the immediate objects which he set himself in the Golden Bull; but the price paid was great. The monarchy was henceforward a nullity and German unity a mere façade. Charles himself in the Golden Bull emphasized 'the variety of customs, ways of life and language, of the various nations' included in the empire, and insisted on the need for 'laws and a method of government that take all this variety into account'. He may have been right; but the result was that Germany advanced towards modern times divided and disunited, under the control of princes whose dynastic interests were no substitute for a German policy and whose rivalries prevented the maintenance of German interests. After 1356 German energies, which as late as 1338 had still responded to the national call, were diverted from the Reich to the principalities; Germany faded into the background and the German territorial states advanced to the front of the stage.

CHAPTER 12

THE CONSOLIDATION OF THE PRINCIPALITIES
(1356-1519)

I

THE Golden Bull of 1356 had a twofold significance. Not only did it, as we have seen, establish a fixed constitutional relationship between the emperor and the princes, which was to endure with only unimportant modifications until the dissolution of the first empire in 1806; it also provided a constitutional basis for the efforts of the princes to consolidate their territories into sovereign states. Although the enactments of the Golden Bull applied strictly only to the seven electoral princes, many of its stipulations were in fact widely accepted as a pattern by other princes endeavouring to build up their power. This applied to its rules on primogeniture and the indivisibility of principalities, which were almost immediately taken over by non-electoral dynasties: in Württemberg, for example, in 1361, in Lippe in 1368, in Baden in 1380. Similarly the privileges *de non evocando* and *de non appellando*, preventing recourse from electoral courts to the imperial *Hofgericht*, which were granted to all electoral princes in the Golden Bull, were soon extended to other princes as well. Of wider significance were the clauses of the Golden Bull prohibiting leagues and confederations between towns and also among the nobility, its attacks on feuds, private war and self-help, which were henceforward regarded as criminal offences, and particularly the enunciation of the principle that offences against electoral princes were acts of treason and would be proceeded against in accordance with the Roman law of treason. None of these clauses or stipulations could in effect be confined exclusively to the electoral princes, whose position in relation to their subjects was in fact no different from that of the other princes of Germany; and the effects of the Golden Bull were therefore widely felt. Almost every clause implied an enhancement of princely authority, a new conception of the relations between subject and State, the State being — in the very nature of the situation with which the Golden Bull dealt — not the Empire as a whole, but the princely territories of which the empire was composed.

The Golden Bull, therefore, marked the beginning of a political renaissance within Germany, a renaissance which brought about a strengthening of the territorial principalities resulting, after generations of strife, in their consolidation into sovereign states similar in form (though never equivalent in strength) to the sovereign states ot western Europe. This consolidation was given full legal recognition in 1648 in the Peace of Westphalia, in the French draft of which the rights of the princes were expressly described as souverainité;[1] but long before 1648 it had existed in fact. The consolidation of princely power took place in the main in the fifteenth century, and was firmly established by the time of the emperors Maximilian I (1493-1519) and Charles V (1519-1556).

Thus we may describe the period 1356-1519 as the period in which the princes, having shaken off in practice the superior control of the emperor and reduced the empire to a mere confederation or agglomeration of principalities, set about the task of asserting their authority over their subjects, destroying the privileges of the feudal classes and the towns, rounding off and consolidating their territorial possessions, creating for themselves the prerogatives and resources of monarchs, and establishing within their lands the same sort of authority as Henry VII established for the Tudor dynasty in England. It was a slow and painful task, performed piecemeal and with many reverses, for the anarchy produced in England by the Wars of the Roses was short-lived and limited by comparison with the state of Germany in the fourteenth and fifteenth centuries. By the end of the fourteenth century all forms of public authority, princely as well as imperial, had sunk so low that an immediate recovery was out of the question. Moreover, as princely authority declined, other political forces rose in its place: cities and leagues of cities, feudal confederations, and — representative of all the forces opposed to the princes — organized 'estates' comprising knights, cities and often prelates banded together in defence of their privileges. Thus two principles of government stood face to face, the one represented by the princes, the other by the 'estates', and open conflict was unavoidable.[2]

[1] Translated, in the final version of the treaty, by the words ius territorii et superioritatis.
[2] With the break-up of Germany into a multitude of principalities the history of German internal development passes from the whole to the parts, and each separate principality requires individual treatment. In the words of Haller (Epochs of German History, 62), 'the

II

Until the end of the fourteenth century, and in many parts of Germany until the middle of the fifteenth century, it seemed as though princely authority, assailed in its turn by the disruptive forces of feudalism, would go the same way as the authority of the emperor. It was not as though the princes, after 1250, succeeded directly to the inheritance of the Hohenstaufen. On the contrary, their strivings for independence from the monarchy had weakened the whole structure of government, broken up its monarchical framework, severed the old political bonds, and left a void which only new political and administrative developments could fill. There is no doubt that the first generation of princes realized its opportunity and — probably consciously adapting the political traditions applied by Frederick II in Sicily and Italy — introduced new and appropriate administrative practices in order to establish their local sovereignty. Recovery of fiefs, distrust and suppression of the feudal nobility,[1] reliance instead on dependable and removable *ministeriales*, the creation of new administrative units in place of hereditary offices, and the erection of castles to dominate their lands, were typical features of the policy of all the great princes of the thirteenth century. Among them we may note Frederick II (1230-1246) and Albrecht I (1282-1308) in Austria, Meinhard II (1258-1295) in the Tyrol, Ludwig II (1253-1294) — one of the most notable princes in the whole history of the house of Wittelsbach — in Bavaria, John I and

history of Germany from the thirteenth to the fifteenth century has no unity. What looks like unity if one confines oneself to the history of the kings, is illusory. The history of the kings is but a part and not always the most important part of the whole. The history of the various provinces is one of innumerable threads which cross and tangle and not seldom get tied up into veritable Gordian knots'. The basis of all further knowledge is, therefore, for this period the history of individual districts, provinces, counties and principalities, whose development has been studied in innumerable monographs. Nevertheless it would be erroneous to suppose that this work is incapable of synthesis, or that it is impossible to discern the general lines of internal and constitutional development common to all the German states. What follows is an outline of the salient developments based primarily on the following authorities: G. von Below, *Territorium und Stadt* (1923), G. von Below, *Vom Mittelalter zur Neuzeit* (1924), H. Spangenberg, *Vom Lehnstaat zum Ständestaat* (1912), O. Gierke, *Das deutsche Genossenschaftsrecht* (1868 sqq.), K. Burdach, *Vom Mittelalter zur Reformation* (1894), W. Andreas, *Deutschland vor der Reformation.* Cf. in addition the summaries in Schröder's *Rechtsgeschichte* and Meister's and Hartung's *Verfassungsgeschichte*; also F. Keutgen, *Der deutsche Staat des Mittelalters* (1918).

[1] Thus of Duke Frederick II of Austria it was said: 'Satagebat etiam nobiles et meliores terrae suae opprimere et ignobiles exaltare' (*Mon. Germ. hist., Scriptores*, XVII, 392).

Otto III who between them made Brandenburg into the most powerful state of northern Germany, Frederick I in Saxony. All these
princes and others showed remarkable energy and ability in consolidating their position and particularly in overcoming the disruptive forces of feudalism. But their success was only temporary.
From the end of the thirteenth century a new phase of internal
disruption began.

Many factors contributed to the weakening of authority and the
growth of territorial divisions which now took place. In the first
place, political conditions in Germany between 1250 and 1356 prevented the princes from concentrating for long on strengthening
their hold over their lands. So long as there was the possibility of a
revival of the power of the monarchy, particularly under the two
Habsburg rulers, Rudolf I and Albrecht I, the political situation was
their first concern. In the same way the Interregnum between 1250
and 1272 and the subsequent periods of internal strife and civil war
under the Emperor Ludwig of Bavaria (1314-1347) naturally saw the
princes intent on fishing in troubled waters and exploiting the situation to their own advantage; Habsburgs, Wittelsbachs and Luxemburgers all sought to succeed to the inheritance of the Hohenstaufen.
But in order to make the most of their opportunities they needed the
military and financial support of their subjects, and these they could
only obtain at a price. Already during the Great Interregnum of
1250-1272 the nobility of Austria and Styria had shown that they
were masters of the situation by accepting a new territorial prince
only after he had recognized and confirmed their privileges. So long
as the princes were struggling for political power against each other
and against the emperor, they could not take a firm stand against
their subjects. Furthermore, they had no generally accepted legal title
to the rights which they were attempting to assume. The position of
the prince, the *dominus terrae*, was built largely on usurpation, often
on sheer force, and his attempts to subordinate counts, the free
nobility and cities and towns to his will were revolutionary acts
implying a breach with the established order. Although we must
beware of idealizing the attitude of the nobility and cities, who after
1250 came forward as upholders of the empire and claimed to be
immediate subjects of the emperor in order to escape 'mediatization'
under the princes, it is nevertheless true that 'the good old right' was
on their side. So long as the empire existed or there was any pros-

pect of a return, even approximately, to the situation obtaining under Frederick II, the counts could with reason hope to remain the local representatives of imperial authority and the cities hope to retain the status of *Reichsstädte*, owing allegiance only to the emperor. It was natural for them to resist subjection to the princes, whose power was *de facto*, and who threatened to cut down their privileges and reduce them to a subordinate position.

Fundamentally more important, on the other hand, was the steady shift in social forces, the rise of new classes seeking after political power. This applied in the first place to the cities or urban communities, whose strength lay partly in their control of ready money, partly in their efficient administration, which gradually replaced that of the lords whose officers were driven out and supplanted by city officials, appointed by the common council (*Stadtrat*). Administrative autonomy and ample means were the keys to the towns' successes, which enabled them in course of time to extend their boundaries over the neighbouring countryside, buying up manors and estates and thus encroaching beyond their walls until in many cases they developed into petty states ready to break free from princely jurisdiction and even from the territorial unity of the principality. In the countryside, the princes had to face a similar rise in the status and independence of the knightly class. The old nobility, attacked from all sides by the princes, had lost influence in the course of the thirteenth century, but in its place the ministerial class rose to new power and from being the willing instrument of the rising princes became the most radical opponent of princely authority.

It was the rise of the *ministeriales*, the transformation of the ministerial class, which above all else brought to nothing the attempts of the princes to consolidate their territorial power in the thirteenth century. We have seen how the dependent *ministeriales* had been the backbone of the rising principalities in the twelfth and thirteenth centuries; but the very freedom with which they were used by the princes, the multiplicity of offices, fiefs, lands and rights which were handed over to them to administer, led to a steady rise in their social status. When princes relied on *ministeriales* and cold-shouldered their free vassals, the latter's only hope of sharing in the advantages of the *ministeriales* was to go over to the ministerial class. This occured on a major scale, and the result was that the differentiating features distinguishing the free nobility and the ministerial classes disappeared.[1] With the extinction of the old free nobility the *ministeriales* became the aristocracy of Germany. They changed their name, becoming Ritter or knights, *milites* instead of *ministeriales*.[2] And with the change of name went a change of status. The old *Dienstrecht* or *Hofrecht*, servile in origin, which had regulated their position, disappeared and their obligations were instead governed by feudal law. This meant a greater freedom, and all the advantages accruing from a place in the feudal hierarchy including the right to enfeoff vassals of their own, to hold courts, and even in certain districts — for example, Mecklenburg, Holstein and the march of Brandenburg — to tax their dependants.

Thus the rise of the *ministeriales*, which in its early stages was sponsored by the princes, finally came to endanger the cohesion of the German territories. Proceeding in exactly the same way as the princes themselves, who had made of feudalism an instrument for weakening the crown and securing their own rise to power, the knightly class within the territorial states set out to undermine the strict feudal rules governing felony, escheat, division and alienation of fiefs, to shake off personal obligations, and to stabilize and consolidate their own hold over their fiefs and offices. Thus a second wave of feudalism, no less serious in its consequences than the first, swept over Germany. Just as the early feudal lordships had broken into the county organization, disrupting the old scheme of government, so in the fourteenth century new lordships arose within the boundaries of the territorial states, which destroyed any hope of territorial cohesion. The towns, on the one hand, with their growing franchises, and on the other hand the manorial lordships of the new knightly class broke down the unity of the local administrative districts and whittled away the direct administrative authority of the princes. In north and eastern Germany in particular the authority of the prince was by the end of the fourteenth century confined almost exclusively to his own demesne lands; outside the demesne all forms

[1] Apart from large-scale transfers to the ministerial class many free noble families simply died out. In part this may have been due to casualties in the crusades; cf. Spangenberg, op. cit., 17-18. In Bavaria the whole of the old aristocracy perished without heirs in the course of the thirteenth century, cf. Spindler, *Die Anfänge des bayerischen Landesfürstentums* (1937), 12. The position in Austria was similar; cf. Dopsch, *Verf.-u. Wirtschaftsgesch.*, 83.

[2] Cf. von Below, *Territorium und Stadt*, 193: 'In the meantime the *ministeriales* (Dienstmannen) had undergone a change in the nomenclature of their class. From the fourteenth century onwards the expression "Dienstmann" disappears and is replaced by the more honourable title "Dienstherr". In the fifteenth century the first half of this title is omitted and the former "Dienstmannen" start to call themselves "Herren" (lords).'

Y

of public authority were in the hands of the aristocracy and urban communities.

Two further developments added to the confusion and played into the hands of the estates. The one was the chronic need of the princes for money, which in a period of rapid economic change the old sources of revenue no longer supplied. The other was the fact that the princes, as a body, shared the feudal outlook of their dependants and regarded their territories as private properties. The idea of the state as an indivisible unity, independent of the actual wielder of authority, died with the Hohenstaufen, and had not yet come to life within the principalities. The principalities which had still until the middle of the thirteenth century represented fiefs of the empire, which could not be disposed of without imperial assent, were treated after the collapse of imperial authority as the private properties of their owners, divided among the sons of the deceased prince, mortgaged, farmed out, alienated. Particularly iniquitous was the practice of sub-division to suit dynastic interests, and the family quarrels and wars of succession and inheritance which arose from it. Its consequences were multifarious, but among the many three stand out. First, the population, treated as chattels, lost all sense of identity with the state, and felt that their interests were at loggerheads with those of the ruling dynasty. Secondly, there came about a wasteful multiplication of princely courts and households, which were a burden on the economic resources of the people, and which added to the financial difficulties of the princes. Finally, the constant sub-division of princely territories reduced the principalities to insignificant proportions and prevented the consolidation of states capable of healthy and vigorous political life. Where, in the thirteenth century, it had for a moment looked as though the nucleus of a considerable state was beginning to crystallize, with its territory more or less rounded off and its borders defined, the fourteenth century saw a relapse and the emergence of the notorious German *Kleinstaaterei*. No example is more typical than Bavaria which, following the division into Upper and Lower Bavaria in 1255, suffered for two centuries from the conflicts within its ruling dynasty. In particular the death of the Emperor Ludwig of Bavaria in 1347 ushered in a period of internal strife and division, which left ineradicable marks. Already in 1349 the duchy, which had been reunited in 1340, was divided in three parts; in 1353 Lower Bavaria was re-divided. In

1392 the same fate overtook Upper Bavaria, reducing what had once been a great duchy into four petty principalities: Munich and Ingolstadt, Landshut and Straubing.

The territorial divisions, reducing the power of the princely dynasties and involving them in internecine struggles, played directly into the hands of the estates, which, in disputes over succession and similar contingencies, stood out as representatives of the interests of the land against the petty self-interest of dynastic policy. Thus as early as 1324 the dukes of Lower Bavaria, involved in serious family conflicts, were forced to promise, at the instance of knights and cities, to act in unison, to keep the land undivided, to lay their disputes before a committee of fifteen councillors, to enter into no new alliances without the assent of the council, similarly to alienate no properties, and finally not to appoint a new council without the assent of the existing one. The Bishop of Liége bound himself in 1316 to rule according to the 'sens du pays', and to this effect was compelled in 1343 to permit the constitution of a tribunal of twenty-two councillors, appointed for life, to watch over the episcopal officials and preserve good government.

But it was the chronic need of the princes for money which was the surest foundation of the power of the estates. From the middle of the thirteenth century knights and cities had resisted the princes' claim to be entitled to raise general taxes at will, and striven to limit taxation to the old-established occasions — the ransom of the lord from captivity, for example, the knighting of the sons and the marriage of daughters. But these regular aids, fixed at standard rates, no longer sufficed with the decline in the value of money and the increase in expenditure which accompanied the rise of princely power, and by the end of the thirteenth century few princes could manage on their normal income. Hence force of circumstance compelled them to give up their claims to impose general taxes in return for single payments. Already in 1276, for example, the princes Henry and John of Werle agreed to forgo all future taxes in return for a single payment to liquidate their debts; and similar agreements with their subjects were made by the counts of Schwerin in 1279 and Duke John of Saxony-Lauenburg in 1280. From Brabant (1292), Brandenburg (1280), Magdeburg (1292) and Silesia we have records of similar arrangements, limiting the rights of taxation of the princes to the recognized cases, and even then in some cases handing over to commissions of knights the decision on the amount to be paid.

The most significant feature of this struggle over taxation was the impetus it gave to common action by the estates. Impelled by their needs, the princes were not only forced to negotiate with the estates, but also to make concessions to them, and to accept the principle that they should remain in existence in order to watch over the performance of the terms of agreement. Thus the estates gradually won a firm place among the institutions of government. We can see this process at work in Bavaria, for example, early in the fourteenth century. After demanding special aids to clear off their debts in 1295, 1304 and 1309, the dukes of Lower Bavaria again found themselves with an empty treasury in 1311, and once again sought to impose an exceptionally heavy tax on all the inhabitants of their land without exception. In this situation all the estates of Lower Bavaria, clergy, nobility and cities, leagued together and obtained from the duke the first general privilege, granting rights of justice to all nobles and urban communities paying the tax and freedom of testamentary disposition to the clergy. More important than this recognition of the principle of *quid pro quo*, however, was the fact that the duke recognized the legality of the league which the nobility formed as protection against high-handed actions by the duke or his officers, and expressly conferred on the confederates the right to resist his authority, if he attempted to undermine their rights. Similar concessions were wrung from Duke Rudolf of Upper Bavaria in 1302; here again the legality of the confederation formed to resist further ducal extortions was explicitly recognized. In particular the estates used their power to ensure that the taxes they had conceded were used for the purposes stipulated, and not dissipated for the general upkeep of the princes' court, appointing to this end commissioners to control expenditure.[1] But the control which they won through exploitation of the princes' financial needs was not confined simply to checking taxation. In Brunswick-Lüneburg, for example, after a period of heavy taxation, the Estates assembled in 1392 and forced on the dukes what amounted to a general capitulation. First the prince had to agree to recognize a perpetual and hereditary con-

---

[1] 'None of the money shall pass into the hands of the prince or his officials', stated the *Rechtsbuch* of the Duchy of Berg in the fourteenth century; cf. G. von Below, *Landständ. Verfassung*, II, 7.

federation of prelates, knights and citizens. Then he had to permit
a committee of eight knights and eight citizens to be set up to see
that the agreement was observed and to adjudicate all complaints of
its breach. This committee was empowered to impose taxes and,
if necessary, military service on all members of the confederation. It
was not answerable to anyone, specifically not to the duke, for its
acts. On the other hand, it was empowered to proceed against
the duke or his servants if they failed to observe the agreement
or to punish non-observers. In the event of a complaint against
the duke himself, he must either make good his infraction or
appear before the committee at Hannover. If he failed to do
this, the committee was entitled to confiscate ducal rents and
revenues up to a sum of 50,000 marks. Finally, if all else failed,
the estates were duly empowered to take up arms in defence of
their rights.

Against dependence on the estates such as was implicit in the
Brunswick treaty of 1392, the princes struggled with varying success.
A few, like the house of Wettin in Meissen and Thuringia, which
derived exceptional wealth from the rich mining industry located
within its territories, managed to hold their own. But most dynasties,
thrown back on more dubious expedients, struggled in vain. Particularly dangerous was the common practice of farming and mort-
gaging properties, demesnes and offices against a cash-loan. On the
one hand, the mortgagees were as often as not the administrators of
the estate or office in question, whose local position was thus
strengthened. On the other hand, the expedient reduced the princes'
income (since rents and profits, and often ultimately the property
itself, went into the pocket of the mortgagees), only temporarily
staved off disaster, and ultimately made the princes' position unten-
able. When Frederick of Hohenzollern was appointed elector of
Brandenburg in 1415, he found the princely estate practically denuded
of its goods and rights and all the castles, with the sole exception of
Spandau, in the possession of his subjects. Much the same position
had been reached half a century earlier in the Tyrol and in Brunswick-
Lüneburg. In fact, by the end of the fourteenth century in many
German lands the position was such that further recourse to mortgage
and farming was scarcely possible.

It was, therefore, at this period and in these circumstances that the
estates rose to the height of their power. In particular, the fourteenth

century saw the fullest expression of the independence of the towns. In north Germany the Hanseatic League pursued its own interests without reference to the territorial princes to whom the member-cities were theoretically subject; for example, the cities of east Prussia took part in the Danish wars of 1362 and 1363, although the Teutonic Order was at peace with Denmark. More generally indeed, the Hanseatic League showed no respect for territorial boundaries; already in 1293 the two Mecklenburg towns of Rostock and Wismar had joined with Lübeck and the Pomeranian towns of Greifswald and Stralsund to form one extra-territorial association. In the south there were similar unions of town communities to resist encroachments by the princes, most famous of all the Swabian-Rhenish League of 1381. Nor was this spirit of resistance the prerogative of the towns. A similar movement united the knightly class in all parts of Germany from Alsace to East Prussia for the defence of their class-interests. In Austria, Brandenburg, Bavaria, Franconia, and Württemberg, knightly leagues stood out, in the second half of the fourteenth century, in opposition to the princes, but also for the defence of knightly interests against the towns, just as the towns in certain cases were as much hostile to the nobility as to the princes.

On the whole, however, the common tendency was for cities and country aristocracy to unite in opposition to the encroachments of the princes; and somewhat later they were joined by the clergy, represented by the prelates who, from the time of the Great Schism (1378-1417), were forced to take new steps to safeguard ecclesiastical liberties against encroachment. This they did by joining forces with the towns and knights. The very fact that, after the publication of the Golden Bull in 1356, a new absolutist spirit began slowly to permeate princely policy, was without doubt a factor in bringing about union between the estates, which saw the need for common action against a common danger. Hence, from about the middle of the fourteenth century, joint assemblies of towns and knights in face of princely attempts to extort new taxes, depreciate the currency or override privileges, became ever more frequent. In the duchy of Lower Bavaria knights and cities joined together in 1347 to form the confederation of Landshut for the mutual protection of their rights and privileges. In the county of Mark they united in the same year in protest against a division of the land. In the case of Jülich the appearance of the towns at meetings of the estates is first mentioned in 1347, in the case of Berg in 1355. In Brandenburg representatives of the towns took part in the assembly at Berlin in 1345, which met in opposition to a proposal to interfere with the currency. The clergy and cities of Brunswick-Lüneburg united in 1355 in defence of their liberties. In the Tyrol the towns took part from 1362 in the general discussion of the affairs of the land. In Austria, on the other hand, they did not put in a regular appearance until after the end of the fourteenth century; but the representatives of twenty cities and market-towns participated with twenty-four prelates and eighty knights in the league formed in 1406 to settle the succession-disputes which were destroying peace and prosperity. In Upper and Lower Bavaria conventions of all three estates — towns, knights and clergy — were formed in 1394 and 1395, and soon acquired major influence in Bavarian affairs, particularly in settling the ever-recurring divisions of the duchy between members of the ruling house.

By the end of the fourteenth century, therefore, the estates had acquired a definite place in German institutions. Through periodic meetings and the appointment of permanent committees to watch over their interests, they had become a power in the land with which the princes had to negotiate and bargain. They had to be conciliated and placated, if only because in large measure they were in control of the sinews of government. If the cities refused to open their purses, the princes were immediately faced by financial difficulties, while without the backing of the knights they could not defend their territories. This situation was further aggravated because, exploiting their advantages, the knights and cities had succeeded in inserting themselves, as intermediary authorities, between the prince and his subjects. Except on his own demesnes, the prince could in general only contact the common people either through the town authorities or through the manorial lords, clerical and lay; in particular it was only through and with the co-operation of the intermediary powers that he could obtain payments and services. As the economic power of the towns and the social importance of the knights increased, the princes therefore fell more and more into dependence on their good will. They became the dominating power in the land, controlling the bulk of the population. For certain periods and in certain districts, some princes managed to trade on the disunity of the estates, and also on their tendency to fall apart, once they had gained their immediate objects.[1] But as the estates gradually coalesced into permanent assemblies, while at the same time the practice of mortgage weakened the princes' independent financial position, such possibilities became increasingly infrequent. By the end of the fourteenth century, the estates were a power in the land at least equal in stature to the prince and his administration, and frequently exercising greater authority with more ample means. Government which, in the thirteenth century, had passed from emperor to princes, was now divided between princes and estates. Against the prince the estates claimed to represent the land and the interests of the land: they were an independent power, strongly buttressed by rights of property and ample credit, asserting their right to control the government of the principalities.

III

The rise of the estates introduced what is known as the period of 'dualism' in German history, with estates and princes facing each other, often in open hostility, as two independent powers in the land. The princes, immersed in dynastic strife and engrossed by dynastic interests, had abdicated any pretension to personify the interests of their territories or to stand forth as protagonists of the public weal. Everywhere there was a sharp cleavage between land and ruler. The ruler was not part of the state: when he wanted to justify his actions, he protested that he had his own and his land's interests at heart, and there was no pretence that the two were identical. The inhabitants — or at least those with political rights — acted in two capacities: on the one hand they were members of the community of the land, whose interests were represented by the estates, on the other they were subjects owing obedience and fealty to the ruler.

This dualism found day-to-day expression in many aspects of public life. It was seen, in the first place, in the recognition accorded by the princes to associations — sometimes of cities, sometimes of knights, sometimes of all estates — formed expressly to defend the

---

[1] There was, in fact, a temporary retrogression in the activity of the estates in the first half of the fourteenth century, once they had secured their immediate ends in the struggle over taxation, limiting the prince's right to raise taxes to certain specified cases and preventing the establishment of a general power of taxation. Cf. Spangenberg, op. cit., 56 sqq.

subjects' rights and privileges against the ruler. It was seen in the acceptance by the princes of a limited form of allegiance, in which the subjects only undertook fealty and obedience on certain specified conditions and for so long as those conditions were fulfilled. But its most characteristic expression was the 'right of resistance' (*Widerstandsrecht*), the right to take up arms against a prince who overrode established rights or liberties. The very existence of this right presupposed that there was no final and impartial authority or tribunal in the land, and revealed most graphically the parlous state of affairs resulting in Germany from the collapse of imperial author- ity and the imperial judicature. The prince was a party in his own case; the emperor was a nullity, without the power (even if he had the will) to intervene; therefore the estates considered themselves justified in taking up arms in their own defence. When in 1416 the knights of Bavaria formed a league in defence of the 'good old law' against 'our gracious lord or any other within or without the land', when they elected a leader to adjudge complaints of members, to seek remedy from the ruler and, if he refused to act, to use force in order to restore the injured party to his rights, they were in fact — whatever the theory may have been — setting up a state within a state, an *imperium in imperio*. When the margraves of Brandenburg in 1280 made a treaty with 'the *ministeriales*, knights, vassals and other subjects' of their land, expressly surrendering any right to levy extraordinary taxes, and when in the same treaty they explicitly recognized the right of 'all vassals and towns' to unite in resistance, if they failed to keep their oath, they were — whatever they may have thought — raising up a power in the land which was their equal. A situation in which the subjects were ever ready and were often legally empowered to offer resistance at the least sign of inter- ference with their privileges, was tantamount to a state of latent civil war.

This situation might not have been so disastrous in its consequences if the estates had shown any constructive ability. Taking all in all, that was not the case. Certain positive achievements may without doubt be credited to them; but they were largely unconscious and unexpected results of their activities. As we have seen, they provided some counter-balance to the petty self-interest of dynastic policy, and their opposition to the alienation and sub-division of territories was an important factor. Furthermore, their increasingly frequent

meetings in defence of their liberties gradually awoke some consciousness of local solidarity, which was a necessary precondition to any
consolidation of the principalities. The autonomous towns were also
responsible for remarkable progress in administrative technique —
up to that time, one of the weakest sides of German government —
particularly in financial administration, which provided a model and
an incentive for the principalities in later centuries and was of general
importance in the history of German government.[1] Finally, whatever their motives, it is undeniable that the estates, through their
defence of ancient custom and established law, and by enunciating
the principle that each man should have his rights and the judgement
of his equals, helped to preserve the rule of law; indeed, their insistence on the law of the land and the judgement of peers has been
described as 'the *habeas corpus* act of the German principalities'.[2]

Nevertheless the attitude of the estates was fundamentally
negative. Their aim was not to promote the welfare of the land or to
acquire general political functions, but rather to cut down the powers
of government and extend class privileges. Similarly, in the struggle
over taxation, through which the Estates rose to power, it was not
the right of assent which was at issue. The estates were not struggling
to secure the constitutional right of assent to taxation; their aim was
to get rid of taxation altogether, or (if that proved impossible,
as was in fact the case) to limit it to a few carefully specified
contingencies.

This attitude was as much common to towns and urban-leagues
as to associations of knights. There has in the past been some
tendency to credit the German towns, as opposed to knights and
princes, with a more exalted sense of German unity and wider
political aims. In this posterity has paid a tribute to the great German
urban confederations, the Rhenish League of 1254, the Swabian

---

[1] 'The cities not merely created organs of their own in place of the prince's officials, but
also developed a large-scale administrative activity. In Germany the mediaeval city was the
forerunner of the modern state ... It was in the cities that public authority first undertook
the solution of the great tasks which are the very essence of modern government. In practically every aspect the history of German administrative law leads back to the institutions and
principles of the fourteenth and fifteenth centuries. The cities developed roads, building, fire
and sanitary services, issued comprehensive sumptuary laws and undertook a thorough reform
of the currency; significant also was their provision for the needy, the sick and for education'
(G. von Below, *Vom Mittelalter zur Neuzeit*, 53; cf. also von Below, 'Die städtische Verwaltung
des Mittelalters als Vorbild der späteren territorialen Verwaltung', *Hist. Zeitschr.*, LXXV, and
F. Rörig, *Bürgertum und Staat in der älteren deutschen Geschichte*, 19).

[2] Von Below, *Territorium u. Stadt*, 269, in a sober, fair-minded assessment of the contribution of the estates to German history.

League of 1376, and above all the Hanseatic League which dominated the northern seas from Kampen on the Zuider Zee to Reval on
the Gulf of Finland. But the economic achievements of the Hanse
should not be allowed to blind us to its political limitations, particularly to the internal dissensions which only too often crippled its
activities. Nor should we exaggerate the breadth of outlook of the
Rhenish and Swabian cities. From 1256 to the end of the fourteenth
century they lost no opportunity of proclaiming their devotion to
the interests of the empire; and it is true that they supported Albrecht
I (1298-1308) against the electoral princes of the Rhineland, and
Ludwig of Bavaria against the papal party led by the ecclesiastical
princes. But their support of the empire was for the most part an
expression of their hostility to the princes, their claim to be immediate
subjects of the empire a means of escaping incorporation into the
territory of a neighbouring prince. Their interest was to maintain
their independence, and when they proclaimed their desire to have
the emperor as lord, this often meant, by the fourteenth century,
little more than a desire to have no effective lord at all. The independence of the towns may have enriched German life, as in a
sense all free associations enrich life; but their policy meant a further
multiplication of petty autonomies in a land already in fragments, it
increased the number of small communities pursuing selfish ends,
added to internal divisions and strife, and impaired any chance of
united political action. The greater the number of sectional interests,
the larger the number of communities to be conciliated and parties
to be won over, the smaller was the hope of securing a sound and
workable constitution. In this respect, the towns were neither worse
nor better than the other estates of Germany in the fourteenth
century; indeed, we can say that, from the time of the Emperor
Frederick II onwards, the emperors had failed the towns, and not
vice versa; that the very community of interests between the monarchy
and the cities provided the former with a substantial foundation for
royal government, which it failed to use. But after the death of
Louis of Bavaria in 1347 even this argument lost force: not only was
the empire manifestly too weak ever again to make use of the
opportunities which Frederick II had let slip, but Charles IV was
clearly bent on coming to terms once and for all time with the
princes. In these circumstances the cities' loyalty to the empire was
evidently only a cloak for their hostility to the princes. It was not a

constructive policy with positive objectives, looking towards a restoration of political stability, nor did it express a political programme; on the contrary, it was an expression of particularism no less narrow than the particularism of the princes.

The lack of a constructive policy on the part of any of the estates, coupled with the impotence of princely government, led German political life into a cul-de-sac. Without doubt the multiplicity of communal organizations and associations which social, political and economic conditions in the fourteenth century produced, might on one condition have made a remarkable contribution to the enrichment of German life — if, namely, the many communities, urban and rural, had taken their place within a single political structure and worked together for common ends. The collapse of effective imperial government and the failure, due to social discords, to find a substitute, left this condition unfulfilled. There was intense life and activity in fourteenth-century Germany; but it was like the undisciplined growth in a garden when the hand of the gardener has been removed and the weeds are getting the upper hand; there were many fine blooms, but their development was marred by the lack of space, and on the whole the rank growths tended to crowd out the finer plants. Thus, in spite of the appearance of much that was new and valuable in itself — in spite, in particular, of the admirable achievement of the civic communities — the general picture was one of growing confusion, increasing disorder and rampant particularism.

As the century progressed, it was not only a case of opposition between the estates and the princes, but also of dissension between and within the estates themselves. Economic changes accentuated the contrast and increased the hostility between towns and knights. From the end of the thirteenth century Germany became a country studded with towns, an industrial and trading country in which money accumulated in the hands of the townsfolk, while the mass of the nobles grew poorer and poorer. They had no significant share in the profits of commerce and industry, while the fixed incomes they derived from their estates decreased in value as a result of depreciations in the currency. Yet at the same time, as a result of the higher standards set by the towns, their standard of living was rising, their needs greater. The inevitable result was increased exploitation of the peasantry, whose fixed tenure was replaced by short-term leases at variable rates. Thus, although the peasants now began to obtain not only personal freedom, but also freedom from the economic controls of manorial agriculture and the power to farm their lands in accordance with their own ideas, these advantages were offset by the fact that they no longer had any land of their own but must rent it from some large proprietor on increasingly onerous terms, and were subject to eviction at short notice. Thus the scene was set for the peasants' revolts which began in the second half of the fifteenth century and culminated in the great peasants' war which was the social and economic concomitant of the Reformation.

Similar dissensions, also economic in origin, were experienced within the towns. Not only was there increasingly bitter strife between the urban patriciate and the craftsmen, who felt with some justice that their interests were given too little consideration in city affairs, but at the same time the growth of the population resulted in a restrictive policy and the deliberate creation of barriers to cut down the influx of immigrants from the countryside. In some degree this was a consequence of the victory of the crafts in their struggle with the patriciate; for a restrictive policy was more common among handworkers, who were already, owing to growing competition, finding it less easy to rise from apprenticeship to the full status of master craftsmen, than among the patriciate whose predominantly commercial interests inclined them to a more liberal economic outlook. In any case, the result was increased tension between towns and countryside, a new spirit of resistance by the latter to urban exploitation, and attempts by the nobility to break down the urban monopolies.

In many parts of Germany the increased hostility between towns and countryside, and the growing impoverishment of the nobility, brought about conditions of open warfare. It was not only that the nobility sought a share of urban prosperity by levying tolls at every bottleneck on the roads; many openly took to banditry as a profession. The famous Götz von Berlichingen who, oppressed by economic misfortunes, made common cause with the rebel peasants at the time of the Reformation, had many predecessors in the latter years of the fourteenth century; one of the last of the Landenburg family, for example, which had once owned broad acres in what is now the eastern part of the canton of Zürich, finished as a robber baron, pursued and executed by the town of Zürich early in the fifteenth century. Nor, with self-help legalized as a political weapon, were such developments unexpected. Yet more characteristic, and fundamentally more serious, than individual acts of violence, was the growth of organized leagues in open opposition to each other. Against the League of Swabian cities, with its eighty-nine members, there arose in 1379 a number of confederations of knights: in Hesse the Company of Horners, in Westphalia the Falconers, in Franconia the League of St. George, in south Germany the League of St. William, and (most famous of all) the 'League of the Growling Lion' — so called from the arms borne by the knights and squires on their shields — which sprang up in the lands between Rhine, Lahn and Main during the same year. No· different in character were the 'Stellmeiser' in the march of Brandenburg, who violently opposed Frederick I of Hohenzollern until 1414, the Company of 'Schlegler' or 'Martinsvögel' which carried on a bloody war with Eberhard of Württemberg after 1367, or the 'Elephant League' formed in the Tyrol in 1406. In vain voluntary associations were formed for the maintenance of peace: their lasting effects were negligible, and it has been truly said that 'never was there less peace in the land than at the period when in all parts of the Reich the estates united to form peace leagues'.[1]

The end of the fourteenth century therefore saw Germany a prey to growing disorders, social and political, against which the flourishing town life provided no effective check. The complexity of individual rights and privileges, the increasing differentiation of social classes, the opposition between princes and estates, friction between agriculture and the town crafts, between commerce and industry, involved the people as a whole in endless strife. The worst sufferers were the country folk, who faced not only a decline in rural economy accentuated by the ravages of private feuds, but also the inflictions of hunger and pestilence. Hundreds of German villages were laid waste, and even to-day only their names remain as a reminder that they once housed a flourishing population. Unrest, lawlessness, violence, insecurity were the keynotes of an age in which only those were safe who were strong enough to protect themselves. It was a state of affairs common to the whole of western

[1] Spangenberg, *Vom Lehnstaat zum Ständestaat*, 92. For a summary of the history of the *Landfrieden* in this period, cf. Schröder, *Rechtsgesch.* (1889), 537 sqq., 617 sqq., and Loserth, *Gesch. d. späteren Mittelalters* (1903), 303 sqq., 422 sqq.

Europe at that date, as much a sign of the times in England and France during the Hundred Years War as in the empire; but owing to the unhealthy development of the German political system, the lack of an effective central government and the unbridled conflicts of equal powers, it was in Germany that the confusion, lawlessness, unrest and social turmoil which everywhere marked the passing of the Middle Ages, reached their peak.

IV

As the social and political controversies and conflicts of the fourteenth century reached their climax, the insecurity of existence and the general sense of decay and decline created a new consciousness that such conditions were insufferable, that a way out must be found, but that it could only be found if law and order were restored through the creation of an effective civil authority which would really rule, would protect the weak, resolve the conflicts between towns and countryside, control class struggles and restore peace and security for persons, property and the communications on which social life depended. This consciousness is apparent throughout the so-called *Reformation of the Emperor Sigismund*, a pamphlet with a marked social bias written by an unknown author in the third decade of the fifteenth century.[1] It was borne home by the disastrous consequences resulting from the antagonism of rulers and estates in the lands of the Teutonic Order: the rout of the Teutonic Knights by the united forces of Poland and Lithuania at the famous battle of Tannenberg (1410), the unwillingness of the Prussian towns and nobility to co-operate to retrieve the defeat, their exploitation of the difficulties of the Order in order to increase their liberties, and finally — after decades of bickering, haggling and dissension — their decision in 1454 to make common cause with the Polish king,

[1] Its demands included suppression of the regalian rights, landed property and rents of the clergy, abolition of serfdom, equality of income for craftsmen in the same profession, freedom of movement throughout the Reich. Tolls were to be raised to maintain bridges and roads; otherwise they were to be suppressed as 'usury'. Coin was to be stamped on one side with the arms of the Reich, on the other with those of the lord with rights of mintage, in order to keep a check on lords depreciating the currency. The pamphlet was no less forthright in its condemnation of the raising of the cost of living by middlemen. Speculation in ordinary foodstuffs was a sin; the solution was for the higher authorities to impose a controlled price. No man was to carry on more than one trade. The acquisition of citizenship should be made more easy, the craft monopolies and the crafts themselves abolished. Cf. Loserth, op. cit., 509.

resulting in the capitulation of the Order in 1466 and the cession of Prussia to Poland.

A return to more regular conditions, a restoration of peace and order, was a social, economic and political necessity. It could be secured only through the rise of a power capable of holding the balance between the opposing social and political elements whose factions were rending the land. An important body of opinion, headed by the distinguished Cardinal Nicholas of Cusa and including leading scholars from the new German universities,[1] still looked to a revival of imperial power as the ideal solution.[2] But by the time of the last two Luxemburg kings, Wenzel (1378-1400) and Sigismund (1410-1437), such a solution was more a pious hope — 'the romantic imperialism of the Humanists'[3] — than a project of practical politics. After the settlement between the imperial government and the princes under Charles IV, the former no longer had any means of independent action, while the princes had no hesitation in exploiting the difficulties and failures of Wenzel and Sigismund in the Hussite wars in Bohemia in order to gain control over imperial government in excess even of that accorded to them under Charles IV. Assembling at Bingen in January 1424, the electoral princes constituted themselves into a permanent body, standing between the ruler and the government and claiming to watch over his performance of his ministry.

In these circumstances any hopes of effective imperial intervention were likely to be delusive. The princes, on the other hand, were suffering from the effects of their own disastrous policy, in particular their inability to free themselves from the narrow feudal preconceptions of their class and the grossly materialistic belief that the territories over which they ruled were feudal properties which they were entitled to exploit at will. The very inability of the princes to rise to higher ideals, to realize the potentialities of their position,

[1] The first German university was that at Prague, founded on the model of Paris by Charles IV in 1348. It was followed by Vienna (1365), Heidelberg (1386), Cologne (1389); thereafter in quick succession by Erfurt, Leipzig, Rostock, Freiburg, Greifswald, Ingolstadt, Tübingen and Wittenberg. The rapid spread of German universities — encouraged by the schism which made it temporarily impossible for Germans to study in Paris — was an important factor in restoring a sense of national unity and cohesion.

[2] 'A mortal disease has befallen the German *Reich*,' wrote Nicholas of Cusa in his *Concordantia Catholica* (1433); 'if it is not speedily treated, death will inexorably ensue. Men will seek for the realm of Germany and will not find it; and in time strangers will seize our habitations and divide them among themselves. So we shall be subjected to another nation.'

[3] Cf. Andreas, *Deutschland vor der Reformation*, 220

justified the opposition and strengthened the power of the estate. Until the princes discarded their feudal outlook, until they ceased to regard themselves as owners of a private property and instead asserted the full rights of sovereign authority, thereby taking their place at the head of the community of the land, the prospect of any improvement in the situation was small. Once, however, they began to act as sovereign powers, conscious of their rights and responsibilities and guided by clear political ideas and objectives, there was every possibility of restoring order, of subordinating conflicting forces to a common objective, and thus of escaping from the confusion which reigned at the end of the fourteenth century.

This essential step forward was taken in the fifteenth century. It was, of course, a slow process. The princes had so impaired their position by alienations, gifts, mortgages and sheer dissipation of resources, that rapid progress was out of the question; the established privileges of the estates barred the way to any scheme of systematic reorganization. Yet decade by decade, particularly in the second half of the century, progress was registered, and by the end of the fifteenth century the internal situation in Germany was very different from that at the beginning. The revival of princely authority not only provided a necessary counter-balance to the power and divergent interests of the estates, but also created the conditions for the establishment of a balanced, constitutional form of government. So long as the princes were weak and without any consciousness of their mission, the estates had the upper hand; as they gradually recovered power and purpose, a new balance was achieved, in which prince and estates each played their part, thus restoring unity and cohesion within the principalities.

The prerequisite for these developments was a new outlook, a new conception of their rights and duties and of the character of the State, on the part of the princes. As we have seen,[1] such a change of outlook was already implicit in the Golden Bull of 1356; indeed Charles IV himself, like his contemporary Rudolf IV (1356-1365) in Austria, provided in his Bohemian administration a forceful example of a modern centralized government with orderly finances and an effective legal system. His model, without doubt, was the France of Philip the Fair; and it is probable that the new ideas of government, of the secular state, and of the rights of the princes penetrated into

[1] Above, p. 321.

z

Germany from France — like so many other French influences —
through the Luxemburg dynasty, in particular through Charles IV.
This is true particularly of Roman law, which had played a major
role in forming the conceptions of Philip the Fair's jurists, and was
no less weighty an influence in the minds of the emperor Charles IV
and his chancellor, Johann of Neumarkt. With its principles of
equality beneath the law, the unity of the State and strong central
authority, its prohibition of unauthorized associations, and its
essential hostility to institutions like the feud, legalized self-help or
the right of resistance, Roman law was not only a practical instrument in the hands of the princes, but also a creative force compelling
men to re-examine the foundations of authority and reconstruct their
political ideology. In place of local custom and class privileges, it
offered the inestimable benefit of a *ius certum*, a complete, unitary,
written code; in place of feudal political conceptions, such as the
alienability and divisibility of public rights and offices, it set forth the
principles of the inalienability of all public rights, the indivisible
authority of the State, and the sovereign will of the prince.

Inspired by ideas such as these — which, like the parallel influence
of Aristotelian philosophy, found wide currency in the universities
of the fourteenth century — a new spirit gradually infused the minds
of the German princes. With the help of Roman law, they set about
rebuilding what feudalism had destroyed, reviving the idea of the
sovereign State which had perished in the welter of particularist
interests. What was important was the spirit and will and personality
of the men involved, without which a political renaissance would
have been unthinkable; but certain changes in external circumstances
and new means of action were contributory factors. Among the
latter was gunpowder, 'the medicine which revived peace and law-
fulness'[1] by transferring the advantage from defence to attack and
thus breaking the stubborn resistance of the lords in their castles.
The Hussite wars (1419-1436) marked the death of chivalry; the
increasing use of cannon, of foot-troops and of mercenaries
ended the military predominance of the knighthood. The defeat of
the 'Stellmeiser' in Brandenburg by Frederick I of Hohenzollern in
1414 spelt the doom of the feudal castle and of aristocratic independence, whilst the *Landfrieden* which Frederick promulgated in the

---

[1] O. von Zallinger, 'Der Kampf um den Landfrieden in Deutschland während des Mittelalters', *Mitteilungen d. Instituts f. Österreich. Geschichtsforschung*, Erg. Bd., IV (1893), 458.

same year signified an end in that province of feuds which were thenceforward punishable as criminal offences.

The first step was to combat the most chronic excesses, feud and self-help, and to enforce peace and authority. The next step was to challenge the independence of cities, estates and associations, and to force them to recognize the superior authority of the territorial government. The defeat of the commune of Berlin by Frederick II of Brandenburg in 1442 was a first milestone along this road; a second was the subjection of Mainz in 1462. The Berliners were forced to surrender their liberties, to hand over their courts and to accept the elector's confirmation of the city council; at the same time all leagues of cities in the Mark were forbidden, save with the prince's consent. In particular, associations with cities outside the frontiers of the principality were prohibited; hence after 1442 the towns of the north had to withdraw from the Hanseatic League. This policy of enforcing control of all associations and attacking any formed without superior consent soon became a general feature of policy. The Elector of Trier, petitioning emperor and pope in 1456 to annul an association of the estates of his territory because it was in conflict with his own sovereign rights, the emperor's majesty and the pope's honour, was expressing the common attitude of contemporary princes; so also the Master of the Teutonic Order, when he condemned leagues of the Prussian estates as *conspirationes*. In asserting control over the clergy, the princes were immeasurably aided by the difficulties facing the papacy as a result of the schism and the Conciliar movement. To make sure of the support of the territorial princes, the popes hastened to grant them comprehensive privileges, which gave them virtual control over episcopal and other ecclesiastical appointments, enabled them to exploit Church property for their own purposes, and allowed them to establish their authority in Church affairs. Such privileges were conferred on Brandenburg and Austria in 1446 and 1447; but even a minor prince like the Duke of Cleves, ably exploiting the conflicting claims of the two rival popes, Felix (1439-1449) and Eugenius IV (1431-1447), so strengthened his position that it was commonly said that 'the Duke of Cleves is pope in his own territories'.

The key to the whole problem lay, however, in finance. The pacification of the land, the new measures of government the princes were striving to carry into effect, all cost money; the growing courts and households, the salaries of trained councillors and jurists, mercenary armies and cannon, all denoted new expense. Yet in most principalities at the beginning of the fifteenth century income was no longer sufficient even to balance current expenditure, and in many parts — particularly in north and east Germany — treasuries were exhausted at the very moment when the scope, and therefore the cost, of administration was increasing. Merely to try to gather together the remains of old imposts, to raise the rate of existing aids, or to win back one by one old sources of revenue long alienated or expropriated, was no longer a feasible policy. What was requisite was a break with the past and its out-lived traditions of levies in kind, commuted services, tolls, fees and *regalia*, and instead the opening-up of new sources of income.

Hence the struggle in the fifteenth century between the princes and the independent estates and communities focused on finance. The new needs and the changed attitude of the governments, which came more and more to the fore during the fifteenth century, led almost of necessity to new methods of taxation. The old lengthy procedure of complicated negotiations with single groups, single cities and even individual members of the nobility, usually involving a series of concessions and privileges, was no longer adequate, apart from reductions due to the expenses and difficulties of collection; furthermore, the exemptions which the nobility had largely succeeded in securing for themselves and their dependants, meant that a large section of the population escaped general taxation, that the peasantry contributed less to the princes' treasury than to the coffers of their immediate lords. There was no idea of an equal repartition of obligations; indeed, there was little idea at all of any general obligation to contribute to the cost of government, so long as government was regarded as a property or investment, like a private business. When, in 1472, Albrecht Achilles of Brandenburg announced that it was the duty of the estates to assume liability for the honourable debts of his predecessors, he was enunciating a new principle: he was pointing out the existence of a public or national debt, distinct from the indebtedness of the prince, and insisting on the responsibility of all members of the community, prince, estates and people, for the liabilities of the State.

To translate this principle into practice, a number of fundamental changes were necessary. In the first place, it was necessary to create a properly constituted body, representative of the whole community, with which the princes (as the heads of the executive government) could negotiate over finance and taxation. More fundamental still, it was necessary to inculcate a sense of territorial unity, so that all groups and communities accepted their share of responsibility for furnishing the needs of government instead of regarding their obligations as confined to their own local requirements. Throughout mediaeval Europe it was a difficult problem to persuade provincial estates or local communities to take a wider view of their responsibilities than that fixed by their immediate horizon; but nowhere was this problem more serious than in Germany, where constant territorial divisions, irrational and haphazard, had destroyed any sense of cohesion, and where in any case the principalities represented fortuitous agglomerations of territories — often scattered parcels and enclaves lacking even in common boundaries — joined together (or separated under different rulers) by the chances of dynastic policy, with little stability and no reference to the needs or interests of the inhabitants. In such circumstances, there could be no easy recognition of common interests or common citizenship of one state. On the contrary, the provincial estates which had grown up in the fourteenth and early fifteenth centuries as spontaneous associations for the defence of local privileges, strongly resisted all attempts to break down provincial particularism and subordinate their local rights to the interests of the whole community; they were violently opposed to any attempt to submerge their identity within the framework of a wider organization, a *Landtag* or States-General representing the whole land.

That this problem was surmounted was due above all else to the will and personality of a series of princes who, imbued with new ideas of government, deliberately set themselves the task of turning their scattered, broken territories into consolidated territorial states. Among the most notable were Albrecht Achilles of Brandenburg (1471-1486), promulgator of the famous Hohenzollern family law of 1473 confining the right to the electoral dignity exclusively to the eldest son; Henry the Rich of Lower Bavaria who restored the finances of his land and thus laid the foundation for the constructive work of his successor, Ludwig (1450-1479); Matthias Corvinus, king of Hungary (1458-1490), who, as ruler of Silesia after 1469, was the creator of a Silesian constitution; Frederick the

Victorious of the Palatinate (1449-1476), who sought to re-unite the principality which had been split into four parts in 1410; Albrecht the Wise of Upper Bavaria (1467-1508), a true forerunner of the enlightened absolutism of the eighteenth century; or finally, Duke Magnus of Mecklenburg (1477-1503) who, in the words of an orator at his funeral, cured the ills of his land with fire and iron.

In all important features, the work of these princes had much in common. All realized that the root of the evil was disunity within the ruling family; none more so than the Bavarian, Albrecht IV, who as early as 1485 nominated the Duke of Lower Bavaria as his successor in the event of his death without heirs of his body (thus passing over his own brothers), 'in order that the honour and dignity of the excellent dynasty and principality of Bavaria may increase, to which end there is nothing more suited than for the same principality to pass under the sway of one single prince'. Acceptance of the principles of primogeniture, of a regular law of succession, and of territorial unity strengthened the power of the princes more than all their campaigns against aristocratic particularism: against a dynasty united in itself the estates, whose victories had been the fruit of dynastic disputes, were ultimately powerless. Temporary successes they might have, like the League of Straubing knights who stood out for ten consecutive years against Albrecht IV of Bavaria's attempts to levy taxes on their peasant dependants and forced him to confirm their privileges in 1493; but in the end the disunity among the estates, their inability to hold firm except in face of a simultaneous threat to all their interests, yielded before the new tenacity of the princes and the stolid realism of their policy.

That policy — however it varied from region to region and whatever the varying degrees of opposition to be overcome — was predicated upon a few basic principles. First there was the categoric denial of the assumed right of the estates to meet together, without summons from above, whenever they thought an injury done to their rights. Instead the princes insisted on their own exclusive right to convene the estates. In this way the periodic meetings of the estates were transformed from conventions springing from opposition to the prince's authority into instruments for securing assent to princely policy. Above all, the States-General was used as an instrument for obtaining the taxes necessary to carry out measures of administrative reform. In order to make grants of taxation by the estates binding, however, two further changes were necessary: the introduction of the majority principle and of the representative principle. It had to be accepted that the decision of the majority was binding, that individuals and communities could not contract out by absence or non-agreement, and also that the States-General was entitled to speak for the whole land (thus overriding the provincial estates). This latter principle, however, had a further significance: it meant that there was at last one body representative of the whole land, thus implying a breach with the characteristic mediaeval divisions and sub-divisions. The States-General were an instrument for welding together the haphazard conglomerations of domains, fiefs, counties and lordships, which were the legacy of the Middle Ages, and for restoring political unity; by forcing the separate estates to accept their position as members of one body politic, the princes created in Germany the unity of the territorial state.

This momentous process, which marked the change from mediaeval to modern political conditions in Germany, just as surely as the reigns of Edward IV and the first two Tudors marked the change from mediaeval to modern in England, can only be briefly illustrated. The opposition of the princes to spontaneous assemblies has already been noted. 'The right to convene the *Landtag* does not pertain to the estates', wrote Albrecht Achilles of Brandenburg in 1472; on the contrary, it was his prerogative which he could use 'as other princes of the Reich use it in their lands'. Ludwig of Bavaria (1450–1479) refused a petition from his estates demanding annual assemblies: it was his right, he said, to convene the estates 'when and so often as he saw fit'. In this attitude, the princes were expressing their new consciousness of their sovereignty. As Matthias Corvinus declared to a Silesian assembly in 1474, 'he was king and lord; what he with his councillors held to be best, it was for them as dutiful subjects to perform'. When representatives of the Bavarian nobility arrived in Munich in 1488 armed with no less than fourteen privileges exempting them from taxation, they were opposed on behalf of Duke Albrecht IV by a learned councillor, who contested the validity of their charters, because earlier dukes had granted them without the emperor's assent, and claimed that the levying of taxes was an inalienable right of the duke flowing directly from his sovereignty. His sovereignty was such, Albrecht asserted, that he had power over the bodies and possessions of his subjects.

Principles such as these were not established without opposition. When Duke Magnus of Mecklenburg sought in 1480 to impose a general tax on his lands, the two important maritime cities of Wismar and Rostock refused to pay on the grounds of exemptions accorded to them and of an agreement they had reached undertaking that neither would pay any further taxes to the prince. Moreover, this attitude was maintained by Rostock in spite of the fact that the city had participated in the assembly which assented to the tax, and in 1482 the duke had for the time being to recognize Rostock's exemption. When the question again arose in 1484, even a formal complaint from the united estates of Mecklenburg, pointing out that Rostock was ignoring agreements made by the whole land, was without effect. The duke returned to the charge in 1489, declaring that 'all good men and subjects, clergy and laity, in our lands' had promised a tax, and that Rostock could not be excepted; but only internal conflicts within the city brought a solution, forcing the citizens to give way in 1491 after eleven years of resistance. Even in 1500 and 1501, however, it was thought necessary to dispatch a special ducal letter, pointing out that Rostock, 'like all our prelates, men and cities', was bound to pay its contribution. Similar difficulties were met by the Bavarian dukes in their dealings with the nobility of the district of Straubing. As early as 1457 the knights, summoned to a meeting of the States-General at Munich, protested that they were not bound to appear outside their own district, and their protest was repeated in 1463. In 1466 they went a step further and formed a league (the 'Böckler') to support their claims, and when Albrecht IV sought to override the privileges of the provincial estates and raise taxes from all his subjects, a still more comprehensive league ('the Knights of the Lion') was formed which forced the duke to give way in 1493.

In the end, however, the princes won through. In Bavaria, it was the reunion of the duchy in 1505, after two and a half centuries of division and sub-division, which provided the prerequisite for Albrecht IV's success, reducing the Straubing opposition party to a small fraction in Bavaria as a whole. In Lower Bavaria the estates had met with some regularity since 1449 on the duke's summons to grant taxes. In Upper Bavaria, Albrecht — gradually overcoming the particularism of the Straubing faction — had assembled the States-General in 1485, 1493 and 1500. From 1505 these separate bodies were replaced by States-General representing the whole of Bavaria, which met annually until Albrecht's death in 1508. In Mecklenburg, a similar change was brought about by Duke Magnus: the tax of 1480 was granted in traditional fashion separately by each province of the land, that of 1489, on the contrary, was granted for the whole principality by the States-General. In Brandenburg Albrecht Achilles summoned the estates of the Altmark to Berlin in 1473 to account for their refusal to pay, and curtly ordered them as a small minority to accept the decision of the majority, i.e. of the States-General representing the whole territory. Between 1474 and his death in 1490 Matthias Corvinus, overriding the rights of the Silesian aristocracy to tax their own localities, imposed nine general taxes, calling together the States-General almost annually to give their assent.

These regular meetings of States-General for the purpose of taxation marked a turning-point in the history of the German principalities. Single communities and provincial estates might hold out, hoping to preserve their privileges and exemptions; but in the end they had to comply, if they did not wish to run the risk of losing the right to participate in the levying and administration of taxes. Hence, once general taxes conceded by meetings of the States-General were introduced, the practice tended quickly to become general. As we have seen, it began in Silesia in 1474 and soon became established; in Pomerania and Mecklenburg the first general tax was in 1484, in the county of Mark in 1486, in Hesse after the reunion of all Hessian territories by Landgrave William II in 1504. Elsewhere the precedent was established earlier: in Austria in 1402, in the prince-bishopric of Magdeburg in 1400, in Osnabrück in 1425, in the electorate of Saxony in 1438, in Jülich in 1447, in Württemberg and the Tyrol during the first half of the fifteenth century. By the end of the fifteenth century, there were few principalities where the *Landtag*, the States-General, created by the princes as an organ for obtaining taxes, had not become a permanent institution for the representation of the land and its inhabitants.

With the establishment of the States-General on a permanent footing, two major results were achieved. First, the principalities were established with all finality as the fundamental political units in Germany; the territorial states became the framework within which the life and activities of the German people were organized. Secondly, the anarchy which seemed to be descending on Germany at the close of the fourteenth century was overcome. In the States-General the political forces which had risen spontaneously but without any constructive policy for the defence of the economically and socially privileged classes against the petty, self-interested materialism of the princes of the fourteenth century, were given purpose and function. However imperfectly, they were made representative of the land, and spoke for the whole land, not for sectional interests. In the States-General and through the States-General a consciousness of the commonweal became possible; it incorporated as an institution the interests of the whole land, where the earlier provincial estates had incorporated only the sectional interests of narrow communities, often violently opposed among themselves. Thus, the supersession of provincial by territorial estates, by general *Landtage*, was important because it widened political horizons. The provincial estates necessarily tended to perpetuate the excessive sub-divisions of the German principalities; the *Landtage*, effacing provincial distinctions, helped to establish and consolidate the new states, which were coming into being by the efforts of the princes to reunite their territories. Moreover, the existence of *Landtage* was an essential factor in overcoming, or (more properly) in 'constitutionalizing', the opposition between princes and estates which had reduced German political life to anarchy. Particularly in regard to the fundamental question of taxation, the emergence of States-General established a constitutional means of raising taxation, thus ending the ceaseless haggling and negotiation with a multiplicity of separate interests which for generations had wasted the energies of the princes, given rise to perpetual conflict, and prevented the smooth running of government. With a clearly established procedure for raising taxes, with the acknowledgement of the representative and majority principles and gradual acceptance of the duty to contribute to common needs, the princes had at length facilities for securing financial stability sufficient for them to develop their administrative machinery and put into execution the tasks of modern government.

In this they were aided by the States-General which (not unlike the English parliament) utilized meetings which were primarily financial in origin, to ventilate grievances and seek reform. Meetings of the *Landtage* became the scene of a reforming activity which 'modernized' the political structure of the principalities; and in the formulation and execution of administrative and other reforms rulers and estates began to co-operate as never before. Nevertheless the 'dualism' which we saw was characteristic of fourteenth-century Germany, was not eradicated: its historical roots were too strong for that, the action of free associations too firmly embedded in German political life. But it was 'canalized' or diverted into new and useful channels. Incorporated in the *Landtage*, the estates were able to provide a counterpoise to the independent power of the princes, thus establishing in Germany the elements of a balanced constitution. But in two significant ways this new 'dualism' at the beginning of the sixteenth century differed from that of the fourteenth century. In the first place, the States-General, of which the free, corporate associations of estates and communities were the forerunners, differed from the latter in having a positive function; their activities were constructive, not — like the old leagues and associations — destructive of ordered political life. In the second place, estates and princes no longer faced each other as mutually hostile powers. With the rebirth of the idea of the State as such, the needs of the whole community provided a standard for measuring both the justification of demands made by the princes and the duty of the estates to meet those demands. Above prince and estates there now arose the State, the interests of which were not necessarily identical either with those of the prince or with those of the chosen representatives. In other words, the progress of political thinking and of political practice, and still more the overruling need to escape from the anarchy of the waning Middle Ages, had brought to life a third entity, which provided a new link between prince and estates: over princes and estates, bridging the old 'dualism', stood the State which comprised both.

If the fifteenth century thus solved the problems left by the fourteenth century by creating a new balance — and, indeed, a basis for co-operation — between princes and estates, between authority and free associations, this success was due in all essentials to the princes. The practice of free, spontaneous association played an important part in the development of the social life of the German people; but in itself it was incapable of creating a general consciousness of political unity based on a feeling of common responsibility for rights and duties. It was the princes who restored calm to the land by assuming responsibility for the maintenance of public peace. It was the princes who created the *Landtage* or States-General, forcing the old existing associations into a constitutional mould. It was, taking all in all, the princes who visualized the needs of the situation, and proved capable of constructive political calculation. It was because the princes put their own house in order that they were in a position to strike a balance with the free estates and the economically powerful cities. It was the princes who attacked the spirit of local particularism, who called in Roman law and Roman lawyers against the stagnant force of inherited custom. It was the princes who, forcing representatives from estates from all parts of their lands to meet regularly together, inculcated a consciousness of common interests and solidarity. It was they who welded such powerful bonds between territories connected only by dynastic ties that they were capable even of outlasting the dynasties themselves. The princes who, in the half century between 1450 and 1500, raised Germany out of its inherited anarchy, laid down the fundamental lines which the constitutional structure of Germany followed from that time forward down to the twentieth century. 'The ending of the old regime in 1806 strengthened the territorial state; the founding of the new in 1870 left it untouched; the revolution of 1918 failed to displace it.'[1] Therein lies the importance in German history of the period between the thirteenth and the fifteenth centuries. It is a period without obvious unity, filled with restless but apparently purposeless activity; there were no outstanding personalities like Frederick I or Frederick II of Hohenstaufen and few notable events. Yet below the surface a pattern gradually becomes clear; and this pattern, once the mould had set, was stamped on German life for centuries to come. With the consolidation of the principalities, which was assured by the end of the fifteenth century, developments reaching back to the Interregnum of 1250-1272 and beyond found their completion, and German history was set finally and irrevocably on a new course. The victory of the princes over the empire was registered for all time in the Golden Bull of 1356; the victory of the princes over the forces of dissolution springing from below was registered with the emergence by the reign of Maximilian I (1493-1519) of the sovereign territorial states.

[1] Haller, *Epochs of German History*, 63.

PART FIVE

THE EMPIRE, THE PRINCIPALITIES AND THE PEOPLE
(1519-1939)

CHAPTER 13

THE ECLIPSE OF THE EMPIRE: THE PRINCES, THE EMPIRE AND THE PEOPLE FROM THE REFORMATION TO THE NINETEENTH CENTURY
(1519-1806)

I

COMPARED with the developments traced in the preceding chapter, which had in them the seeds of the future, the history of the empire in the fifteenth century, down to the accession of Maximilian I in 1493, is a pitiful tale of dissension, debility and disintegration. As the power of the princes in their territories was consolidated, that of the king correspondingly declined. During the fifty years following the death of the Emperor Sigismund in 1437 the monarchy fell into an insignificance unparalleled since the Interregnum. Already in 1424 the electoral princes had sought to establish themselves as a permanent supervisory body controlling the exercise of the emperor's powers; in 1438, after the death of the last Luxemburg monarch, they utilized the change of dynasty to impose stringent conditions on the newly elected emperor, Albrecht II. In these circumstances it is no wonder that cautious princes, weighing the burdens of office against the meagre material advantages, were prone to decline the offer of the imperial throne.[1] Carrying with it neither domains nor income, the disendowed empire was too onerous a commitment for the minor princes of Germany and fell almost of course to a ruler whose non-German lands enabled him to bear its burden.[2]

Those who took the royal and imperial title did so primarily with a view to furthering their own dynastic interests or the interests of their hereditary lands. This was true of Charles IV, whose candidature in opposition to Louis of Bavaria in 1346 was inspired by fear of

---

[1] Of landgrave Ludwig of Hesse, who refused candidature after the death of Albrecht II in 1439, it was said: 'maluit parvo imperio a parentibus sibi relicto utiliter praeesse quam magnum accipiens dissipare.'

[2] A modern writer has likened the emperor to 'the incumbent of a living which was too poorly paid to be held by anyone without private means'.

losing the Tyrol, and who never ceased throughout the thirty years of his reign to pursue the interests of the Luxemburg dynasty and the Bohemian crown. Charles' outstanding acquisition was the province of Brandenburg; but scarcely less important gains were Silesia and the march of Lausitz, and in the south the frontiers of Bohemia were pushed forward almost to the gates of Nürnberg by the annexation of the lands of the Palatinate along the Bohemian borders. All these, for Charles, were additions not to his imperial domain but to the Bohemian kingdom, just as his succession treaty with Austria and the betrothal of his younger son, Sigismund, to the heiress of the king of Hungary and Poland were planned with an eye to Bohemian interests and policy. Far from identifying Bohemia with the Reich, Charles sought to increase the independence of his kingdom, which he hoped to make the nucleus of a predominantly Slav empire reaching from the Elbe to the Lower Danube and east to the Vistula: to emphasize Bohemian independence, the subordination of the church of Prague to the archbishopric of Mainz was abolished in 1344, and a new archbishopric created which was given the prerogative of consecrating and crowning the Bohemian king.

In so far as the only practical basis of the German kingship in this era was the territorial power of the ruling sovereign, Charles IV's Bohemian policy served Germany well, and the words of Adalbert of Prague, in his funeral oration after Charles' death, fairly sum up the achievements of the reign: 'so held he his power in Bohemia and the empire', said the archbishop, 'that neither the empire lacked order nor Bohemia lacked care, and the men of the empire were content and the men of Bohemia found no cause for complaint'. It was otherwise under Charles' sons, Wenzel (1378-1400) and Sigismund (1410-1437). So long as dynastic policy prospered, it helped to stabilize the monarchy; but after Charles' death in 1378 all the difficulties inherent in a complicated, ambitious dynastic policy began to be felt. In 1382 the question of the Hungarian and Polish succession arose, involving the house of Luxemburg in continued warfare. More important, Bohemia itself became the scene of reaction and civil war. In the first place, the aristocracy sought to recover the predominance lost under Charles, and to prevent a further strengthening of the monarchy in league with the towns and the lesser nobility. Secondly, the deliberate emphasis on Bohemian nationalism, which ran consistently through Charles' policy, provoked an anti-German reaction, which took violently nationalist shape when the Hussite movement added religious to political animosity. These complications, threatening to unseat the dynasty in its hereditary lands, absorbed the energies of Wenzel and Sigismund, and Germany was inevitably neglected. We have seen already how the emperor, embroiled in the Hussite wars, declined to intervene in the struggle between the Teutonic Order and Poland.[1] The German lands of the dynasty also suffered from the absence of the ruler; in particular the aristocracy got the upper hand in Brandenburg, and the work of the Ascanian dynasty was undone.[2] Among the causes leading to Wenzel's deposition in 1400 none was weightier than the king's continued residence in Bohemia outside the borders of the German kingdom. Already in 1395, when Wenzel in spite of all complaints had already absented himself from Germany for seven years, the question of deposition was ventilated; and the nomination of Sigismund as imperial vicar the following year did nothing to lessen discontent, since he was fully occupied with the Hungarian question. But the unhappy interlude of Rupert's reign (1400-1410) proved for all time the impotence of a king without broad domains of his own, and particularly the weakness of a king from western Germany in face of the princes of the north and east; and on Rupert's death the electors, almost of necessity,[3] turned again to the house of Luxemburg and elected Sigismund (1410-1437). In practice, no other course was feasible; but the result was that, for still another generation, Germany was neglected while the king strove to restore his position within Bohemia.

The change of dynasty after the death of Sigismund in 1437 brought no immediate improvement. Albrecht of Habsburg (1438-1439), the husband of Sigismund's only daughter, Elizabeth, succeeded as the heir of the house of Luxemburg; but he was also heir to all the complications the Bohemian inheritance carried with

[1] Above, p. 255.
[2] On the early history of Brandenburg, cf. above, p. 279. The decline of the march began after the extinction of the Ascanian dynasty in 1319, when Louis of Bavaria sought to obtain the province for the Wittelsbachs. The subsequent contests for possession and the concessions made to secure support inevitably played into the hands of the aristocracy, whose power reached its peak under Sigismund's absentee rule.
[3] The throne was offered to Henry IV of England — a belated flicker of a policy we have already witnessed in the thirteenth century, and another example of the necessity of finding a foreign monarch to bear the burden — but he declined the offer.

AA

it. Moreover, Habsburg power was at a low ebb. The rule of primogeniture, which from the time of Rudolf I had secured the Habsburgs pre-eminence among the princes of Germany, had lapsed in 1379 and thenceforward there were two Habsburg lines, the one ruling Austria proper, the latter (which was soon subdivided) in control of the minor Habsburg territories. These divisions and the consequent family strife and discord were accentuated by Albrecht's early death, and persisted through the long reign of his successor, Frederick III (1440-1493). The effects of these discords within Austria were such as we are already familiar with in other princely territories: civil war led by opposing branches of the ruling dynasty, leagues of recalcitrant knights, the rise of provincial estates and the predominance of particularist interests. But the fact that Frederick was not only ruler of Austria but also king of Germany implicated the whole Reich in his problems. Scarcely able to maintain himself in his hereditary lands, Frederick was still less able to safeguard the interests and frontiers of Germany. Hence his reign, like that of Sigismund before him, was characterized by growing restrictions on royal power and influence within, and by manifest weakness on all the frontiers.

Within Germany the first half of the fifteenth century was notable for the withdrawal of the monarchy from the colonial lands of the north. The Wittelsbachs and the early Luxemburgs, with a quick eye for the seat of political power, had sought an entry into the north, particularly the march of Brandenburg, hoping thereby to consolidate their position and secure a broader and more lasting foundation for the monarchy. Under Sigismund this policy — which still, until the end of the fourteenth century, carried with it some hope of greater political stability and even ultimately of a restoration of royal power — was abandoned. Engrossed in the problems of Bohemia and Hungary, in dire need of money and allies, and in despair of governing the land, which had become more of a liability than an asset, Sigismund made Frederick of Hohenzollern, burgrave of Nürnberg, his lieutenant in the march of Brandenburg and later, in 1415, created him Elector in reward for his services. More immediately important was his decision in 1423 to confer the electorate and duchy of Saxony, vacant through the extinction of the house of Saxe-Wittenberg, on his staunchest ally in the Hussite wars, Frederick of Meissen. It was more than two

centuries before Brandenburg, under the Great Elector (1640-1688),
began to recover from late-mediaeval anarchy; but the junction of
Meissen, with its flourishing mining industries the most prosperous
principality of mediaeval Germany, and the electorate of Saxony
created a powerful state which, in the early sixteenth century, was to
assume the leadership of the Protestant north against the Habsburgs.
The immediate result of Sigismund's actions, however, was that
the north was left to go its own way, and in fact (though not in
theory) the cleavage between north and south, which had been
resisted throughout the middle ages, was consummated. Only
time and events could determine whether this cleavage was to be
permanent; but with the imperial title vested, from the election of
Albrecht II in 1438 to the end of the old Reich in 1806, in the Habsburg dynasty, every year that passed tended to drive home its
implications and render it more durable.

What men saw and felt in the fifteenth century, however, was not
the breach in German unity — which, in fact, it took centuries to
consummate — but the weakness which overtook German policy on
all its frontiers. Large portions of the borderlands were either
drifting away from the Reich or linked by only the loosest of bonds.
By the Peace of Thorn (1466) the Teutonic Order, weakened and
despoiled, became a vassal of Poland. In the north-west Holstein
was associated by personal union with Denmark, and moved in a
Danish orbit. On the eastern frontier, the agreement of 1436 by
which Sigismund finally secured recognition in Bohemia, left that
country virtually independent under nominal German overlordship;
and even this precarious settlement failed to last. In 1458, native
rulers were elected both in Bohemia and in Hungary, and Frederick
III was not long in granting them formal recognition. Thus the
union of Austria, Bohemia and Hungary, which had cost the Habsburgs so much effort, was destroyed. Disintegration went a step
further when, in 1468, Matthias Corvinus of Hungary set out to
conquer Bohemia, while Poland also fished in troubled waters. The
upshot on the death of the Bohemian king, George Podiebrad, in
1471 was a partition for the benefit of Poland and Hungary; the
Polish prince received Bohemia itself, while the neighbouring
provinces of Moravia, Silesia and Lausitz were incorporated in
Hungary. Frederick III meanwhile stood aside helpless, his own
Austrian lands threatened by Matthias, who conquered and occupied

Vienna in 1485. Nor, if such was the situation in the east, was the position in the west any healthier. As early as 1415 the Swiss of the 'Eight Ancient Cantons', who (profiting from internal dissensions within the house of Habsburg) had already conquered most of the Habsburg lands south of the Rhine, obtained full internal autonomy from Sigismund; as the fifteenth century proceeded successful wars with the dukes of Burgundy and Savoy increased their power, and from 1495 they assumed an attitude of independence which, stalwartly maintained, was formally recognized in 1648. At the same time the power of Burgundy was steadily rising to its culmination under Charles the Bold (1467-1477). After the union of Brabant with Flanders and Burgundy in 1430, the Burgundian dynasty, seeking to strengthen the land-bridge between the Netherlands and Burgundy proper, reached out more and more after imperial lands: Hainault was annexed in 1433, Luxemburg in 1451, then the diocese of Liége and Guelders. In 1469 duke Sigismund of Habsburg handed over Upper Alsace for a money payment; in 1473 the duke of Lorraine was forced to allow the Burgundians to occupy all strongholds throughout his land. Finally in 1474 Charles the Bold sought to annex the electorate of Cologne. Meanwhile France, although threatened as much as the empire by the rise of Burgundian power, was striking out on its own; the end of the Hundred Years War with England left it free to resume the Capetian policy of eastward expansion, and in 1444 a French army appeared in Lorraine and Alsace, took up winter quarters, demanded the submission of Metz and Strassburg, and launched an attack on Basel.

Such, in summary retrospect, was the position on Germany's frontiers on the eve of the reign of Maximilian I (1493-1519). On the one side, Cologne and Strassburg were in danger; on the other Vienna. The princes, intent on their own tasks, were indifferent. Frederick II of Brandenburg alone had any perception of the situation. Seeking to establish his dynasty along the shores of the Baltic, he offered to expel the Danes from German soil if the emperor would grant him Holstein; but Vienna's answer was a curt rebuff. As for the emperor Frederick III, he had neither the will nor the means to cope with the situation. In the east he watched uneasily the rise of Matthias Corvinus of Hungary, consoling himself with the fact that Matthias was childless and that by an Austro-Hungarian treaty of 1463, if either house were to die out, the other was to succeed to its inheritance. In the west, similar calculations governed his relations with Burgundy: Charles the Bold had only one daughter, and Frederick's plan was to secure the Burgundian inheritance by a marriage between her and his own son, Maximilian. There is no sign in these dynastic schemes of any attempt either to calculate realistically the prospects of putting them into effect if the opportunity materialized, or to weigh the cost of straining to incorporate so many heterogeneous territories. In the east, the whole scheme came to nothing by a Hungarian refusal, on the death of Matthias in 1490, to honour the agreement of 1463 – a refusal which neither Frederick nor Maximilian had the means to challenge. In the west it was otherwise. After Charles the Bold's defeat and death at the hands of the Swiss in 1477, the Netherlands diet, in order to protect the country from France, which was determined to lay hands on Charles' inheritance, gave the heiress of Burgundy in marriage to Maximilian.

The Burgundian marriage of 1477 was a turning-point in Habsburg history. It brought back Austria, which was tending more and more to be absorbed in the parochial affairs of south-east Europe, into the main stream of European politics, raised it to a first place among the powers, and gave it a direct interest in western Europe which lasted down to Napoleonic times. For Germany also its consequences were momentous. In the first place, it tied the empire, in Habsburg hands since 1438, irrevocably to Austria. The house of Habsburg was now incomparably stronger than any other German princely family; but it needed the imperial dignity, for only as the reigning imperial house could it knit together and maintain hold over its far-flung territorial possessions stretching from the Lower Rhine and the Scheldt to the Upper Rhine, to the eastern Alps and along the Danube. It could not afford to see another dynasty in possession of the imperial title; for, however weak in itself, such a dynasty would, in alliance with France, constitute a threat to Austrian interests. This was the second direct consequence of the marriage of 1477. France could not be expected to give up the hope of recovering those French lands alienated by the Burgundian dynasty; and with Burgundy, therefore, Austria inherited the perennial hostility of France. This represented almost a revolution in European politics, for in earlier times, as we have seen,[1]

[1] Above, pp. 294-296.

Austria had usually been found aligned with France for the exploitation of western Germany. Now, in defence of its own interests, it was forced to accept the guardianship of the west against French encroachments; but this threw those states in Germany which were opposed to Habsburg predominance into the arms of France. Hence, through the Franco-Austrian opposition over Burgundy, the empire was involved in foreign complications on a scale hitherto unknown. And yet it was not involved on its own account. For the Habsburgs, Germany was a secondary possession, important only as a connecting link between the dispersed Habsburg territories and as a field on which to assemble forces for war against France. There was no longer any imperial policy except in the sense of Habsburg policy; and Habsburg policy was at best only partially in line with German interests. Thus, in the struggles for predominance which filled the European scene after 1494, Germany sank more and more into the condition of a subordinate factor, a field for annexations and compensations fought over by other states.

That such was the case was amply borne out by the history of the years 1493-1519. Maximilian had been elected King of the Romans in 1486, during his father's lifetime, in the hope that, with the Burgundian inheritance behind him, he would be able to restore peace and union to the empire. The inglorious history of the previous half-century had produced, in reaction, a profound movement of German nationalism without parallel since the Diet of Rhens in 1338. It was now that the saga of the emperor Frederick Barbarossa, slumbering on the Kyffhäuser waiting to restore the empire to its old glory, took hold over popular imagination; a number of pseudo-Fredericks appeared and secured a following. A new, more coherent expression of national consciousness found vent in the work of Humanists like Sebastian Brant and Jacob Wimpfeling, who in his *Epitome Rerum Germanicarum* appealed to Germany's past. The Humanists, well aware of the egoism of the princes, looked to Maximilian to restore inner order and external unity. Superficially, he seemed to have the means and — compared with Frederick — the will. He had started well, reuniting all the Habsburg lands in 1490, and recovering the lost districts of Austria from Hungary; hence he had in his hereditary lands the necessary material basis for the exercise of royal power. Among contemporaries there appears to have been no realization that the very extent and diversity of these territories, without any internal bonds of union, were as much a source of weakness as of strength, and in any event a source of constant preoccupation. From the beginning of his reign Maximilian spent his time defending Habsburg dynastic interests and possessions, particularly his Burgundian kingdom, from France. Burgundy was the corner-stone of his policy. Because of Burgundy, he accepted existing conditions in the east, knowing full well that France would exploit any entanglement with Poland or Hungary or Bohemia to seize his Burgundian lands. Because of Burgundy, he went to war with the French in Italy, fearful of any extension of French power. The succession in 1516 to the Spanish throne of his grandson, Charles — ruler of the Netherlands since 1506 — opened up still greater prospects of Habsburg dynastic aggrandizement; but it also added new complications. It made the imperial title still more necessary as a unifying bond between the Habsburg dominions; but it neither served nor was compatible with German interests. Maximilian did not hesitate, when it served his purpose, to claim that his policy was directed to assuring Germany its proper place among nations and protecting its ancient rights against foreigners; but it is difficult for the scrupulous historian to find in it anything but the dynastic interests of the Habsburg house. More than once he frankly stated that it did not suit his purpose for his hereditary lands to be reckoned in the German Reich.[1] His attempts to drag Germany into his wars with France met stubborn opposition alike from princes and towns, for neither of which was the possession of Milan or Picardy a vital interest.[2]

Thus Maximilian's reign brought to the surface the conflict between Habsburg dynastic policy and German interests, which henceforward was endemic in German history. The hopes of a national policy, in defence of the threatened frontiers, with which the reign opened, proved illusory. Through Burgundy, Austria was already caught up in the whirlpool of European policy; this was even more apparent after Maximilian was succeeded by Charles V in 1519. Inevitably this situation was reflected in German internal affairs. For Maximilian, Germany was primarily a source of supply, to which he looked for the financing of his wars; but it never appears to have entered his calculations that the surest way of securing German

---

[1] Andreas, *Deutschland vor der Reformation*, 241.
[2] Cf. Haller, *France and Germany* (1932), 23.

financial and political support was to identify his interests with those of the Reich by co-operating in a long-needed measure of internal reform. It was Machiavelli who said that the disproportion between Germany's natural powers and its political capacities was the result of its defective constitution; and for many years before Maximilian's accession the need for constitutional reform was widely ventilated. From 1485 it was the leading issue in the Reichstag; thereafter the question never ceased to occupy men's minds throughout the quarter-century preceding the Reformation. The soul of the movement for reform was Berthold of Henneberg, elector of Mainz, whose plans had at least the merit of taking full account of the existing conditions; by and large his proposals amounted to a scheme for the constitution of a federal state, in which the administration was to be taken out of the hands of the monarchy and placed in those of an imperial council of seventeen members, of which the president alone would be the emperor's nominee. Such a scheme of government was in line with the course of historical development since the Golden Bull; indeed, if there is any truth in the dictum that the Golden Bull 'legalized anarchy',[1] it may be said that Berthold's plan was to overcome the anarchy by completing the structure legalized in 1356 through the addition of the necessary organs of co-ordination and executive power which the emperor no longer effectively possessed outside his hereditary lands. To the reconstituted government it was proposed to give adequate means of action by reforming the judicature, the imperial finances and the army.

The project of 'Reichsreform', which was fully debated in the Reichstag of 1495, where it won the support of practically every prince and estate, has been much criticized. It was, it has been said,[2] an attempt to carry further the 'diminution of the central power through permanent institutions'; in the eyes of the princes it was simply 'the means of assuring and enlarging their own share in the government of the realm'. But we do not need to overrate the altruism of the princes to see that there was more to it than this. The movement which bore the project forward drew its force from circles far wider than the prince's courts; it reflected the genuine aspirations of the German people. Moreover, permanent institutions far from diminishing the effete central power which had already sunk to its lowest point during the long reign of Frederick III, provided

---

[1] Bryce, *Holy Roman Empire* (ed. 1928), 246.   [2] Cf. Haller, *Epochs of German History*, 110-111.

the only hope of more effective government beyond the narrow limits of the princely territories. The creation, in 1500 and 1512, of ten provincial districts (*Kreise*) comprising each a number of separate principalities, was, despite its limited objects, a step towards greater territorial cohesion, just as the proposal at the Reichstag of 1522-1523 to raise a general imperial customs duty (*Reichsgrenzzoll*) implied recognition of the empire as a single economic unit. All this went beyond the immediate dynastic interests of the princes, as fundamentally did the plans for the reconstruction of imperial taxation. A conflict of interests there was over the methods and form of taxation, one party favouring a poll-tax (*gemeiner Pfennig*), the other the levying of contributions by the individual cities and principalities, each of which was left free to decide how it would collect and pay its contribution; but the very fact that they were willing to put imperial finances on a stable foundation showed that the princes still accepted, and were prepared to make tangible concessions on behalf of, a form of federal state which transcended the boundaries and immediate interests of their principalities.

In view of these considerations it is difficult to stand aside and view the struggle over 'Reichsreform' as simply the expression of the conflicting interests of princes, autonomous cities and emperor, in which all parties were equally intent on self-aggrandizement. On the contrary, the attempt at reform was serious; and although, in view of the complicated state of political organization in Germany, many difficulties were clearly to be anticipated in putting it into effect, the responsibility for the failure to give it a trial rests with Maximilian and his successor, Charles V. Their obtuseness and intransigence threw away the last chance of restoring to Germany a real measure of unity. When Charles V, opening his first diet at Worms in January 1521, stated that 'the empire from of old has had not many masters, but one, and it is our intention to be that one', and when he added that he was not to be treated as of less account than his predecessors, but of more, seeing that he was more powerful than they had been, he was accusing himself of crass historical romanticism or outlining a policy of compulsion, or both. In either case, he was deliberately setting himself against the whole trend of historical development since the days of Charles IV,[1] and—at the very moment

---

[1] That the Habsburgs were perfectly conscious of this is indicated by Maximilian's verdict on Charles IV: 'Carolo quarto pestilentior pestis nunquam alias contigit Germaniae.'

when he needed German support against France — announcing a trial of strength with the princes. It is still often argued that such a trial of strength was, in 1519, far from a hopeless proposition; that the Habsburgs still had the possibility, in view of their wide territories, of enforcing throughout Germany an absolutist régime.[1] Such an argument ignores the external complications, particularly the inevitability of French interference, just as it underrates the progress of the principalities towards consolidation during the latter half of the fifteenth century; still more it forgets that, although the emperor might defeat the German princes by force of Habsburg arms, it was another question to maintain and consolidate his predominance. In 1547 Charles V won complete victory over the German opposition; his position, resting on the arms of his Spanish soldiery, could not have been stronger. But his success lasted only until 1552, and was followed by a collapse so rapid that in 1555 Charles had to acknowledge defeat in the Peace of Augsburg.

The events of 1547-1555 are the best proof that the way to German unity did not lie through armed force, and that any revival of the empire must take account of irrevocable historical developments. That Maximilian and Charles ignored this fact was due not only to intransigence and obtuseness, but also to the conflict of Habsburg and German interests. They could not afford to accede to any project of reform because they did not intend to rule and act as German emperors, and a government directed and controlled by a council (*Reichsregiment*) representing the German estates might well be expected, particularly in foreign affairs, to oppose the employment of German resources for the execution of Habsburg dynastic interests and to insist on a German policy. Here, rather than in the constitutional field, was where the fundamental antagonism lay. Hence the Habsburgs were, from the beginning, determined opponents of the reform movement, who skilfully exploited and accentuated the divergent interests of the different estates so as to bring all projects to nothing; and any concessions won from them were the result either of financial embarrassment or of foreign complications. Even projects, like the plan for an imperial customs system, which might have been thought to their advantage, were dismissed, while such

---

[1] Andreas, op. cit., 264: 'Als dieser (Maximilian) die Augen schloss, war es noch nicht ausgemacht, ob den Reichsständen fürderhin oder dem Kaisertum die volle Ueberlegenheit zufallen werde.'

concessions as were made under the pressure of external events were temporary manœuvres to which neither Maximilian nor Charles had any intention of according permanent validity. Thus the 'Reichsregiment' set up in 1500 for a period of six years, with competence over all internal and external affairs of the empire, was abolished by Maximilian in 1502, and that established by Charles V in 1521, with powers only during the emperor's absence, scarcely lasted until 1530. The proposal of 1495 for annual meetings of a full *Reichstag*, comprising all estates, was never put into effect. After 1530, under the pressure of the Reformation and the overt hostility between the emperor and the Protestant princes, there was neither interest in nor were conditions favourable to peaceful reform: the last opportunity to maintain the unity of Germany by constitutional changes appropriate to the existing political structure had passed, unused and beyond recall.

II

The result of the manœuvres of Maximilian and Charles V was that the constitutional problem, as Germany made the transition from mediaeval to modern times, was left unsolved. But the political movement which found expression in the projects of reform was not assuaged. The very negotiations between the emperor and the estates, protracted, complicated and sometimes excited, produced a state of heightened tension and expectancy. The princes, far from resigning themselves to their lack of success under Maximilian, were only the more determined to secure reform from Charles; hence their decision in 1519 to make the election dependent on the acceptance of a 'capitulation' — the first of a series of 'electoral capitulations' which lasted as long as the old empire — which was neither more nor less than a solemn treaty between the emperor-elect and the electoral princes, covering the whole ambit of imperial government and including an undertaking to set up a 'Reichsregiment' composed of representatives of the estates. But the issue of constitutional reform was only a focus for the sense of frustration and discontent with existing conditions which ran much deeper through the whole of German society. The whole nation, wearied of the disunity, incompetence and lack of governance which were the mark of the preceding century, was in a state of political crisis, which was fanned by the work of propagandists and satirists who, in widely-read verse, attacked Rome and the great prelates, the higher social classes and the corruption of the bourgeoisie by money. Nowhere is the common feeling more graphically portrayed than in the works of Dürer, who gave permanent expression to the sense of insecurity, distress and even desperation which ran throughout Germany. Ulrich von Hutten, in the *Epistolae obscurorum virorum*, published in 1514, raised hostility to Rome to a new peak of violence, and bitterly reproached all classes within Germany with betrayal of their country for their own selfish interests. But it was hostility to Rome which aroused and united national consciousness. It was an extraordinary thing, in this age of territorial division, how wide and popular was the support for the *Gravamina nationis Germanicae*, which formulated the complaints of the German nation against Rome. The Humanists had given new life to the words *Germani* and *Germania*, and to the idea of common nationality which they embodied; Maximilian took it up on the political plane and added the words 'of the German Nation' (*Nationis Teutonicae*) to the old title 'Sacred Roman Empire' (*sacrum imperium Romanum*), thus seeking to give his imperial dignity a national flavour. But, after the disappointments on the political plane, the frustrated hopes of constitutional reform, it was in the religious reformation that the new spirit of German nationalism found expression.

The age produced, in Luther, a figure who transcended his generation; but Luther was fortunate in finding the times propitious. That the Reformation occurred when and where it did was no accident of history; Luther's challenge in the famous Wittenberg 'theses' of 1517 was transformed in a trice from an academic controversy into a burning popular issue because it found an echo in the revolutionary movement fomenting in Germany. The *Gravamina* of 1518 showed that Luther had at his back the whole German people, in spite of the territorial fragmentation of Germany. His challenge to Rome appealed to the national consciousness, disappointed and frustrated by the years of haggling and bargaining over 'Reichsreform'. His belief that the essence of religion lay in an inner experience was in the German tradition of Meister Eckardt, Dietrich of Strassburg and Thomas à Kempis — a mystical tradition in no way purely German, but especially rife in Germany from the fourteenth century onwards because nowhere else were political and social conditions such that the only freedom left to the common man was the inner freedom of the spirit. Believing that the essence of religion lay in spiritual experience, Luther sought to unite the German emperor, princes, clergy and people against the stifling juridical system administered from Rome; he opposed the spiritual Church to the 'human' institutions of the papacy, councils, episcopate and canon law. His appeal was to the 'German nation', to the 'Christian nobility of the German nation'. He planned, of course, to reform the universal Church; but the resistance of Rome threw him back increasingly on German support and gave his propaganda a peculiarly German flavour. 'It is for you Germans', he wrote in 1531, 'that I seek salvation and sanctity.'

The response swept the whole country. A generation later, writing in 1557-1559, the Venetian ambassadors reported that nine-tenths of Germany was Protestant and that it was only a question of time before the whole country would belong to the new faith. But the effects of the movement, corresponding to the forces behind it, extended far beyond the sphere of religion. Luther's appeal, reaching across the outward barriers of territorial particularism, put fresh life into the disjointed body of Germany. His translation of the Bible gave common currency to the new form of the German language, which — springing up in the colonial east, where settlers from all parts of Germany were mingled — had slowly found its way into the chanceries of Vienna and Saxony and Brandenburg, at the same period as a common tongue was gaining ascendency in England over the provincial dialects. Through Luther's Bible, with its vigorous, positive vocabulary, the bond of common language, replacing provincial dialects, became a factor of unity in Germany; the same result was achieved by his treatises addressed to the people in their thousands which (like the subsequent controversial writings of his partisans and adversaries) propagated far and wide a speech common to all Germans. In his manifesto of 1520 'To the Christian nobility of the German nation on the improvement of the Christian condition' he drew up a programme of religious reform applicable to the whole of Germany and called upon the princes of the empire — 'the Christian nobility' — to put it into effect. But his teachings, with their appeal to first principles and their incitement to question the established order, were immediately applied to social and economic, as well as to religious affairs. The hope of immediate, radical

change, cutting short the interminable controversy between the
emperor and the estates, which Lutheranism aroused, found its
earliest expression in a rising among the smaller knights — a class
whose economic depression we have already noted[1] — which took
place in 1522-1523. A few months later, in 1524, the Peasants' War
broke out in south-west Germany, only to be crushed under the
superior military power of the nobility.

Thus the early decades of the sixteenth century witnessed in
Germany a revolutionary ferment which, in reaction against the
decline of the empire in the last two or three generations, was
strongly national in character. In appealing to the German nation,
Luther was at least in part in revolt against the particularism of the
princes, the pretensions of the nobility and the egoism of the townsfolk and peasantry. Humanists like Hutten, because they were
nationalists, were initially faithful — often to the point of illusory
romanticism — to the empire. But the emperor, who had failed to
grasp the fleeting chance of constitutional reform, turned his back
on the opportunity of placing himself at the head of the national
movement. That such an opportunity was there to be taken is
beyond doubt; but once again, deeper than any individual repugnance to the new doctrines or personal loyalty to Rome, the conflict
of German and Habsburg interests was the stumbling-block.
Charles V, the King of Spain, whose real power derived from his
non-German lands,[2] could not afford to compromise his position
outside Germany by placing himself at the head of a German movement directed against Rome. He was a Habsburg first, King of
Spain next, and only at long last the German emperor. Hence,
although committed to the principles of Church reform and steeped
in the conciliar traditions of the fifteenth century, Charles determined from the first to suppress the reform movement, such hesitation and delay as there was being due solely to foreign complications.

The movement which had within it, even at that late date, the
seeds of German unity, thus became the cause of dissension, war and
division. The political history of the German reformation is so
familiar that only the salient points need mention: the Edict of
Worms in 1521, placing Luther under the imperial ban; the approval,

---

[1] Above, pp. 336-337.
[2] His minister, Granvella, informed the Diet of Speyer that 'the emperor has, for the support of his dignity, not a hazel-nut's worth of profit from the empire'.

under imperial pressure, of the edict of 1521 by a majority at the Diet
of Speyer in 1529 and the resultant protest by a number of the most
influential members; the failure of the Diet of Augsburg in 1530 to
restore unity and the formation of the Protestant League; the outbreak of civil war in 1546 (after a long delay due to the appearance
of the Turkish armies before Vienna and war with France) and Charles' ephemeral victory in 1547; the revolt of the Protestants under
Maurice of Saxony in 1552, followed in 1555 by the Peace of Augsburg. As early as 1521 and 1522 the practical measures of reform
which Luther had demanded in his appeal to the Christian nobility
— the sequestration of Church property, the overthrow of Church
authorities, the abolition of celibacy, etc. — had everywhere begun,
and in 1526 the Diet of Speyer charged every estate in the empire to
conduct itself in the ecclesiastical issue according to the dictates of its
own conscience, thus deliberately turning over the decision of the
religious question to each province and territory separately. This
decision, resisted for so long by Charles, was accepted as the basis of
the compromise of 1555: except for the heads of ecclesiastical states,
who were not permitted to change to the reformed faith, each prince
was given the right to decide the religion of his principality, and with
the organization of the two parties into two bodies in the imperial
Diet an uneasy equilibrium was reached, which lasted — due in part
to the decline of Habsburg fortunes and their constant difficulties in
the east — into the seventeenth century. Nevertheless the progress of
Protestantism continued, especially in north Germany, where no
Catholic dynasty remained, and where one bishopric after another
was absorbed until by 1577 only Hildesheim was left. Simultaneously the Catholic counter-reformation began. In 1573 the prince-
abbot of Dernbach forced the Protestant knights of his domains to
return to the Catholic faith; in 1574 the archbishop of Mainz followed his example. A decade later the same issue arose at Cologne;
and the intervention of Spanish troops secured the Westphalian
bishoprics for Catholicism. When, in 1608, duke Maximilian of
Bavaria, the acknowledged Catholic leader, annexed the town of
Donauwörth and forced it to accept the Catholic faith, the whole
issue once more became perilous. Under the leadership of the
Palatinate, the Evangelical Union was formed for the defence of
the religious peace; Bavaria replied in 1609 with the creation of the
Catholic League. All that was wanting was Habsburg intervention.

The emperor Matthias (1612-1619) clung to a policy of mediation, but already by 1617 he had been ousted for all practical purposes by his cousin, Ferdinand of Styria, and when in 1619 Ferdinand was elected emperor the immediate outbreak of civil war could be foreseen.

Once again only a recapitulation of a bare outline of events between 1618 and 1648 is necessary. The struggle opened with revolt in Bohemia, where the counter-reformation simultaneously violated religious feeling and ancient privileges, and the uprising soon spread to Austria. It became a German issue when, in 1619, the Elector Palatine, the leader of the Protestant faction, decided to accept the Bohemian crown at the hands of the rebels. After his annihilating defeat at the battle of the White Mountain, near Prague, in 1620, the war was carried into Germany; Bavaria, which had given Ferdinand the active support of the Catholic League, wanted 'compensation' in the form of the lands of the Upper Palatinate and the electoral dignity; the Spaniards wanted Alsace and the Rhenish Palatinate. From the Palatinate, where Catholic arms were successful, the war was carried into north Germany, and the peace of Lübeck (1629) constituted the high water mark of Ferdinand's power. But the appearance of Spanish Catholicism on the shores of the Baltic constituted a threat to Protestant Sweden, whose whole position rested on the control of the Baltic seas, just as the Spaniards in the Rhineland were a direct threat to France. The invasion of Germany by Gustavus Adolphus of Sweden in 1630 marked the turn of the tide; his alliance with France in 1631 was another milestone in the decline of Habsburg fortunes; and when finally, after Gustavus' death in 1632, France took up arms in 1635, the issue was sealed. Militarily, the Habsburgs were defeated by 1646; but the war dragged on another two years, until it was brought to a close by the Peace of Westphalia.

The treaties of 1648 closed the epoch which began in 1519. Every hope and project inspiring the wave of revolutionary ardour which swept Germany at the beginning of the sixteenth century, had been disappointed. A movement which began as a reaction against foreign intervention, and the internal weakness which permitted foreign intervention, resulted in its last phases in foreign intervention on a scale hitherto unknown. Instead of a restoration, on new and more solid foundations, of a common political and administrative organization for the whole of Germany – an organization which, while taking account of the consolidation of the principalities, would have permitted common action on a federal basis in common problems – the peace of 1648 consecrated the sovereignty of the principalities; after 1648 the subordination of the principalities within the empire was a form of words without political significance, the empire a shadow without substance, beyond all hope of resurrection or reform. A religious movement which, for a short generation, seemed to offer a new bond of unity to the German peoples, where political bonds had failed, was transformed instead, through the opposition of the Habsburgs, into a new cause of division; particularly during the Thirty Years War the breach between Lutherans and Calvinists opened nearly as wide as the chasm between Catholics and Protestants. Confessional dualism allied itself with territorial fragmentation, and the spiritual exaltation which had found expression in the Reformation faded into apathy or turned away into channels remote from politics. Finally Germany suffered the ravages of civil war and the miseries of a Franco-Spanish war fought with unbelievable brutality on German soil.[1] The Thirty Years War decimated the population,[2] depressed the peasants and ruined the towns, and thus changed the whole social and economic substructure of German political life. In this, it only carried a stage further the consequences of the religious wars of the sixteenth century, which had been in large measure consolidated during the uneasy peace between 1555 and 1618; but, taking the period 1519-1648 as a whole, the result was a transformation of German society. The weakening of all classes in town and country, which was the inevitable consequence of generations of strife, the effect of war on commerce, industry and agriculture, brought about, with the religious changes, a further rise in the power of the princes, which ushered in the period of princely absolutism.

---

[1] They are powerfully described in Grimmelshausen's famous novel, *Simplicissimus* (Engl. translation, 1912).

[2] It has been estimated that the number of Germans fell by half or two-thirds, or from more than 16,000,000 to less than 6,000,000. The credibility of the latter figure was accepted by von Inama-Sternegg ('Die volkswirthschaftlichen Folgen des Dreissigjährigen Kriegs', *Hist. Taschenbuch*, 1864), whose work is the basis of the statements of most subsequent writers; but the unreliability of the data for all such estimates should not be forgotten.

III

We saw, at the end of the last chapter, how by the close of the fifteenth century a new stability and balance had been struck within the territorial states of Germany; we saw, in particular, the beginnings of a fruitful co-operation between princes and estates, which boded well for a healthy development of political life and institutions on a basis of progressive 'constitutionalism'.[1] This promise of healthy constitutional development within the territorial states, off-setting in some degree the ills of the imperial constitution, withered away in the storms which accompanied and followed the Reformation.

In the first place, the Reformation itself upset the balance by creating new sources of princely authority. Historians are in the main agreed that Luther himself had no intention of subordinating the Church to the secular power; he was no Erastian, and wanted an independent Church. But the circumstances under, and the methods by which the Reformation was carried out, forced his hand. The unswerving opposition of Charles V compelled him to seek the help of the princes — Frederick the Wise of Saxony to the fore — and, as we have observed, the practical measures of reform in 1521-1522 were carried out by the princes on their own initiative. Frightened by the social unrest of the Peasants' Wars, which was an unwanted consequence of his preaching, Luther sided wholeheartedly with the princes in their suppression, and thus placed himself even more closely under their influence. Moreover, his doctrinal position was not altogether unequivocal: preaching an invisible and purely spiritual Church, in radical opposition to the juridical institutions of Rome, he was led to concede that the state is the form in which, under God's will, the world exists, and that, since ecclesiastical institutions were but the work of man, with no authority in divine law, the state had full right to shape them and make them its own. Thus in the end, partly under duress, partly through the ambiguity of his position, he left to the prince authority over persons, consistories, parishes, pastors, over ecclesiastical properties and even over the forms of religious service and dogma. In brief, the prince became the *summus episcopus* of his territorial Church, and enlisted its resources in support of his territorial power. It was the princes who

[1] Above, p. 350.

decided such matters as the Confession of Augsburg or the Articles of Smalkald. They took advantage of the political conflicts aroused by the Reformation to bind the new churches to the secular power and make of them the most solid supports of their sovereignty.

This early victory of the princes, which at one stroke created a completely new source of power, as effective in their hands as was the English church in the hands of the Tudors, was consolidated at the end of the century, when the dangers of the Counter-Reformation forced the Protestants to accept a new degree of discipline and subordination. Under the influence of Melanchthon, the fervent spirit of primitive Lutheranism was whittled away; the Formula of Concord of 1577, defining the orthodox Lutheran faith and reducing it to a system, introduced a period of stagnation, in which the reformed faith stood on the defensive. This attitude, imposed by the struggle with the Counter-Reformation, was encouraged by the princes, who had adopted Lutheranism for their own profit, and who, regarding their ecclesiastical supremacy as a branch of their secular and territorial power, naturally favoured the development of rigorous orthodoxy, of uniformity and of discipline. Thus was bred the dull, conservative Lutheranism of the seventeenth century, which allied itself with the territorial powers, and established a rigorous disciplinary system subordinating every individual to a state in which the civil and ecclesiastical authorities reigned in concert. Incorporated in the principalities, Lutheranism became hostile to the idea of national unity, which inspired the early popular and democratic phase of the Reformation: the territorial churches became pillars supporting princely power. Nor was the position in Catholic Germany different. In order to make headway, the Counter-Reformation needed the coercive power of the princes, who thus became the determining factor in ecclesiastical affairs, because without them Catholicism would have been quite unable to maintain itself.

The evolution of Lutheranism towards a system of territorial churches, the subordination of religion to the dictates of the princes, also had a stifling effect on political activity. The Reformation had brought a breath of fresh air into Germany. As all churches, Lutheran, Calvinist and Catholic, in their struggle for power developed rigid canons of orthodoxy, this was lost. The whole weight of the organized churches, including their influence over education and morality, was thrown into the scales on the side of government: they were content to preach the duty of obedience to divinely-appointed authority, inculcating the narrow doctrine that man serves God best by gaining a living for his family, performing his everyday duties and conforming with the authority of the State. Thus, between a family life inspired by an old-fashioned patriarchalism and a State not so much patriarchal as despotic, there was — apart from associations of no political significance — no approved outlet for the energies of the individual, particularly of the middle classes; there was no opportunity for broad political activity, such as might develop the political education of the citizens.[1]

These developments, which exercised durable influence on the mentality of the middle classes, leading inevitably to both religious and political indifferentism, occurred at a time when, on the political plane, the middle classes were fighting a losing battle. The subordination of the towns to the princes began, we saw,[2] in the fifteenth century. Their economic decline occurred in the main in the sixteenth century. In part it was a corollary of the rise of Polish and Russian power on the Baltic, depriving the German merchants of their eastern markets;[3] in part it was due to the competition of English, Flemish and Scandinavian merchants, supported by their governments.[4] The consequence was a rapid deterioration in the position of the Hanseatic League, which was in full decay by the end of the sixteenth century, and in 1630 only the three cities of Lübeck, Hamburg and Bremen were represented at the Hanseatic diet. The decline of the cities of the south occurred somewhat later: a turning-point was reached when the great Augsburg banking house of Fugger — a house which gave its name to a whole period of history — went under as a result of the repudiation of the Spanish debt in 1627. Both in north and south, the Thirty Years War completed the ruin of the towns, particularly of the imperial cities which could not claim the protection of a territorial prince. Internally, the decline of trade both before and during the wars encouraged the rise of restrictions and monopolies, through which the more powerful elements sought

[1] The significance of the changes in the character of Lutheranism is emphasized particularly by E. Vermeil, *Germany's Three Reichs* (1944), on whose conclusions the above paragraphs are largely based.
[2] Above, p. 343.
[3] Ivan III closed the German merchants' gild at Novgorod in 1494.
[4] It is characteristic of Habsburg policy that they favoured their dominions in the Netherands at the expense of the German merchants.

to engross what commerce remained. The result was a spirit of petty egoism, and a general stagnation, which was the counterpart to the political indifferentism and weakness already noted.

The collapse of German commerce under the strain of state-fostered foreign competition and civil war weakened the towns in their relations with the princes and simultaneously deranged the whole balance between princes and estates, since the towns on account of their financial resources had, at the end of the fifteenth century, played a leading part in the activities of the States-General. In the territorial states, only very few cities — Rostock and Wismar, Stralsund and Greifswald are examples — succeeded in maintaining any real measure of independence; the rest sank into direct subordination to the general territorial administration, and lost their autonomy except occasionally for petty matters of police. The magistrates, although still mostly chosen by the citizens or a section of the town, were appointed by the territorial authority, and their activities were so circumscribed by the organs of the central administration that they ceased in practice to be representatives of the community they governed and acted rather as indirectly appointed officials of the State. The only exceptions were in territories where the estates succeeded in maintaining their hold; here the interests of the cities were in some measure secured by their participation in activities of the States-General. But in lands like Austria, or Prussia, or Bavaria, where the princes broke the power of the estates, the cities sank rapidly to the level of mere units or districts in the general scheme of territorial administration.

The decline of the towns was thus one aspect of the wider struggle between the princes and the estates, which broke out almost inevitably as a result of the increase in the power of the princes after the Reformation. Once they had bound the territorial churches to the secular power, the princes sought to drive home their advantage by attacking the nobility and the towns and freeing themselves from dependence on the States-General. In the main this occurred in the seventeenth century, for the most part after the settlement of 1648 — the decline of the Bavarian *Landtag* in the sixteenth century was exceptional — and it was a process which affected Catholic and Protestant states equally. Indeed, the forces of the Counter-Reformation were a powerful instrument for the suppression of the estates and their independence; they were used ruthlessly throughout the

Austrian dominions, particularly in Austria itself, where the Catholic rulers broke the backbone of the *Landtag* by persecuting and driving out the Protestant nobility, its most trusty members, at a time when the population of Austria was still almost totally Protestant in faith. A similar policy was pursued in Bohemia, Moravia and Silesia, and outside Austrian territory in Bavaria. Thus a practical example was given of the political value of the victory won by the princes at the Peace of Augsburg in 1555: the famous principle *cuius regio eius religio* was not merely a means of securing religious uniformity, but also an instrument for creating a régime of absolutism.

The uneasy peace of the period between 1555 and 1618 was used by the princes to consolidate their position, and in particular to reorganize and modernize their administrative machinery, which was notoriously retrograde by comparison with England and France. It was at this time that institutions more complex than a single un-differentiated household administration were generally introduced;[1] separate 'colleges' of privy councillors with distinct spheres of action, which were the forerunners of the later ministries, now made their appearance, including consistorial courts controlling all matters of religion. It was at this time that offices like the chancery were de-tached from the royal court and took up permanent residence in a fixed place. But above all this was the period of the rise of a profes-sional bureaucracy, which became the backbone of princely govern-ment, freeing it from dependence on the estates. It was because of the progress of administrative machinery that the princes were able so easily to absorb the autonomous régimes of the towns, and it was with the support of the new bureaucracy, which had every interest in the dissolution of the old aristocratic and oligarchic society, that they broke the power of the States-General.

The struggle between the princes and the estates was fought out over the issue of taxation. In this fundamental question, as we have seen,[2] a solution had been reached by the beginning of the sixteenth century, by which time in practically every territory the prince had secured the right to levy extraordinary taxes with the assent of the States-General, which were thereby accorded a recognized place in German political institutions. Particularly important, from the

[1] Cf. Andreas, *Deutschland vor der Reformation*, 258-265; there is also a useful essay in Below's *Territorium u. Stadt.* — Most princes imitated Austrian institutions, which were reorganized under Maximilian I and Ferdinand I on Burgundian and French models.
[2] Above, p. 349.

point of view of the estates, was the control exercised by the States-General over the taxes which it granted. The prince, through his officials, collected and administered the ordinary revenues; but the taxes granted by the estates remained from beginning to end under their control. They passed into the *Landeskasse*, a treasury distinct from the prince's exchequer, were administered by officers responsible to the estates, and a strict watch was maintained to ensure that they were used only for the purposes for which they were granted. In this respect the German States-General had initially even more effective control than the English parliament; there were here all the germs of a sound constitutional development. But the changed situation after the Reformation and after the Thirty Years War, in particular the waning of the middle-classes, brought all such development to a standstill. At the very period when in England the Civil Wars and the Whig Revolution assured the predominance of the mercantile classes, in Germany the princes freed themselves from the financial and therewith from all other control by the estates. As we have noted, the process began in the sixteenth century in Bavaria, where dukes William and Ludwig, who ruled jointly after 1514, raised three general taxes without seeking the assent of the estates, and by 1577 the decay had proceeded so far that the Bavarian estates, realizing their own powerlessness, themselves requested that their assemblies should be discontinued. In Prussia, where the position of the estates had been materially strengthened during the period of Polish overlordship, when the Polish crown deliberately lent them its support as a counterpoise to the dukes, the struggle was longer and harder. The nobility stood out for the 'policy of the Fatherland' — i.e. local East Prussian interests — in opposition to the 'despotism of the Mark of Brandenburg', and it was only during the reign of the Great Elector (1640-1688) that their opposition was broken. When in 1653 the nobility accepted an offer of increased rights over the peasantry on their estates, and in exchange granted the Elector the taxes he demanded for a period of six years, a turning-point was reached. After the six-year period was ended, the Elector demanded the permanent concession of a regular yearly contribution, and when this was secured in 1662, there was no longer any question of an effective right of assent or dissent by the estates.

These are examples of a process completed almost everywhere in Germany during the generation following the Peace of 1648, if not before. How far the process had gone is illustrated by the fact that in 1670 an attempt was made to introduce an imperial edict of general application throughout the empire, annulling the right of assent to taxation vested in the States-General of the various territories. This attempt to secure an overriding legal ruling was unsuccessful, but as a compromise a general order to all subjects was issued, setting forth their duty to contribute 'in accordance with custom and the princes' needs'. Thus it was established that the princes were within their rights in levying taxes at the rate which had become customary since the introduction of taxation with the assent of the States-General at the end of the fifteenth century. In addition, the princes shook off control by introducing new forms of taxation which lay outside the normal sphere of control of the States-General. It was a more difficult matter to get rid of the separate financial administration of the *Landeskasse*, which remained in existence in Brandenburg-Prussia, Austria and Bavaria, long after the estates had lost their right of assent to taxation; but with the elimination of the estates' control the difference between the two *Kassen* was gradually reduced to one of historical origin, and the two took their place side by side as two branches of a single administration. In Prussia financial dualism was for all practical purposes eliminated by Frederick William I in 1713.

With the termination of the estates' participation in taxation and the emergence of an unlimited princely right to levy taxes, the foundations of the power of the *Landtage* collapsed. Thereafter few princes experienced difficulty in consolidating an absolutist régime. In the course of the seventeenth century full assemblies of the estates were mostly replaced by committees, which were easily subjected to the ruler's will, and which (like the French *parlement* two centuries earlier) became little more than formal meetings for registering the sovereign's decisions. Only in Saxony, Brunswick, Hesse, Württemberg and Mecklenburg did the estates succeed in retaining their status, clinging to their inherited rights and privileges with dogged tenacity; but even here they rarely played any active part in public life. Elsewhere they fell into powerlessness, particularly in the three major states, Austria, Prussia and Bavaria, and the organs of absolute government were constructed without their assent or consultation. At most they were left with certain customary rights, which became increasingly insignificant as new forms and methods of government arose; taxation and legislation became prerogative of the ruler, and supported by a bureaucratic system often built up on the French model and by a mercenary army, the princes emerged from the ruin of the Thirty Years War as absolute rulers.

IV

The new absolutism received its consecration in the peace of Westphalia. The accretion of power which came to the princes as a result of the ruin of their subjects during the Thirty Years War profoundly modified their relations with the empire, particularly as the Emperor Ferdinand III appeared at the settlement as the defeated party. Their victory over their subjects set them on the road to absolute sovereignty, and made it natural for them to claim sovereignty in the international sphere. Even before the beginning of the war in 1618 a number of the more important states — Hesse, Saxony, Brandenburg and, in particular, the Palatinate — had maintained ambassadors at foreign courts, working side by side with, and as often as not in opposition to, the imperial ambassadors. They had not hesitated to enter into foreign alliances without imperial assent. Hence by 1648 they were already acting as independent powers in European politics, and this independence was increased when in the subsequent fifty years more and more imperial territories fell under princes who were independent kings in virtue of possessions lying outside the boundaries of the empire. This was true, in the first place, of Austria which, linked with the Habsburg possessions in Hungary, the Netherlands and Italy, was much more a European power than a German state. It was true of Saxony which, once the leading Protestant state of Germany, saw its elector become a Catholic in order to compass the Polish crown. The elector of Hanover ascended the English throne in 1714. One group of northern provinces was under the king of Sweden, another under the king of Denmark. Even the elector of Brandenburg when, in 1701, he was raised to the royal dignity, took his title from his Prussian lands, which — after existing under Polish overlordship from 1466 to 1657 — were no longer accounted, as in the middle ages, a province of the empire.

This extensive association of German with non-German lands meant in practice a disruption of the territorial unity of Germany, scarcely less final than the annexation of the west German province of Alsace by France which occurred simultaneously. After 1648 the empire had, properly speaking, no history of its own; the territories went their own way without any reference to the destiny of Germany as a whole. In the peace of Westphalia the princes secured all the essentials and most of the trappings of sovereignty; thereafter every prince was emperor in his lands.[1] All the powers they had acquired as a result of the Reformation and of the Thirty Years War were confirmed in the treaty of peace, in particular their authority in matters of religion and their right to form alliances. Any direct interference by the emperor with administration, either in particular regions or throughout the empire, was henceforth out of the question. Even in petty matters like the post, which was an imperial monopoly, or the granting of patents of nobility, the princes were jealous of the emperor's rights, and sought (mostly with success) to bring them into their own hands. It was characteristic, again, of the new state of affairs that the Diet of the Empire, although it had long ceased to be an effective organ of government, was in 1663 transformed into a permanent congress of ambassadors, sitting at Regensburg; here again the change emphasized the independence of the princes. It was, however, in the international sphere that the disruption of the empire was most clearly seen. At the Congress of Utrecht in 1713, for example, only envoys of the several states, not of the empire, were present, while in the following year, when peace was concluded with France, two separate treaties were promulgated at an interval of six months: the treaty of Rastatt for the emperor, and the Treaty of Baden for the princes. Even the pretence of maintaining the formal unity of the empire had been dropped.

The sovereign rights accorded to the princes in the peace of Westphalia were in theory limited by the rights of the empire. They were supposed to observe the laws of the empire and only deviate from them in cases where imperial law laid no claim to general binding force. They were under the obligation to participate in imperial wars, and were not permitted to remain neutral. Any treaties or alliances they entered into were limited by the stipulation that they must not be directed against the peace of either empire or emperor. These limitations were all so many empty words. In the War of the Spanish Succession, Bavaria did not hesitate to take up arms on the

[1] Hence the maxim: 'quilibet status tantum potest in suo territorio, quantum imperator in imperio.'

side of France. In the War of the Austrian Succession, the empire as a body took no part. In the Seven Years War Prussia successfully defied the whole might of the empire. In the Wars of the French Revolution, Prussia withdrew independently into neutrality in 1795, Austria in 1797, although so far as the empire as a whole was concerned the war was not concluded until the Peace of Lunéville in 1801. Independent action in the pursuit of independent interests was thus the rule: long before the demise of the empire was publicly announced in 1806, it had ceased to exist. After 1648 it was no longer an empire at all, and scarcely even a federation: it had no common treasury, no efficient common tribunals and no means of coercing a refractory member. The seventeenth-century jurist who described it as an irregular body — 'irregulare aliquod corpus et monstro simile' — was making a plain statement of fact. It was neither a limited monarchy, as imperialist writers vainly sought to prove, nor a federal state, since effective means of federal action were lacking, particularly in the sphere of war and foreign relations. A federal constitution might still have been created in the days of Maximilian I, but everything that had happened between 1520 and 1648 had made a federal solution more remote.

There was not even sufficient identity of interests to constitute a basis for a federation of sovereign states. After the Thirty Years War the cleavage of interests between the Protestant north and the Catholic south was a dominant theme, and the confessional division was organized in such a way as to permit either party, Catholic or Protestant, to paralyse any attempt at action by the Diet. Intent on their own aggrandizement and on the exploitation of their own sovereign powers, not even the greatest of the princes had any vision of German unity or any consciousness of overriding German nationality. After 1648 the empire was a meaningless historical survival, Germany a geographical expression: the reality was embedded in the principalities, whose only ambition was to develop into sovereign monarchies.

V

The full recognition of the sovereignty of the princes, Catholic and Protestant alike, which was contained in the peace of Westphalia affected not only the relations of the princes with the emperor, but also the relations of the empire with foreign powers. The princes might be sovereigns in their own lands, unimpeded either by the emperor above or by the estates below, but — excluding Austria — none, not even Brandenburg-Prussia, was more than a second-rate power, and none was strong enough to adopt an attitude of independence in foreign affairs. In this respect the treaties of 1648, although only registering the completion of a process which was centuries old, marked a fatal decline in Germany's standing in Europe. Austria after 1648, and particularly in the eighteenth century, concentrated its attention increasingly on its interests in Eastern Europe, turning its back on Germany, and the princes were left to fend for themselves. The result showed how illusory their sovereign independence was, when they came face to face with a great power imbued with strong political traditions. France had had its clients among the German princes since the days of Philip Augustus at the end of the twelfth century; but never was French intervention in German politics so open, so continual and so consistent as after 1648. Broken, divided, economically weak, and lacking any sense of national unity, Germany became virtually a French protectorate: even in the imperial diet at Regensburg the dominant voice was that of the French ambassador.

The peace treaties of 1648 themselves gave a formal sanction to French interference at the conclusion of a war in which Austria was defeated by French and Swedish arms. Opposition to Austria threw one party among the princes into the arms of France, and identified their interests with French interests. As far back as 1552 Mauric of Saxony and his Protestant confederates had allied with France, and agreed to the French annexation of Metz, Toul and Verdun, in order to shake off 'the bestial Spanish servitude'; thereafter France was rarely without an organized party in Germany. In 1629 Richelieu drew up the famous memorial, demonstrating the necessity for French intervention in German affairs, which embodied the permanent guiding principles of French policy,[1] and a few months later, in association with Sweden, put them into effect. A weak and disunited Germany was a French interest — was, indeed, perhaps France's major interest in Europe — and it was with this interest to

[1] 'I shall play the part which Richelieu assigned to France', Napoleon remarked to a Prussian negotiator. — The first, introductory volume of Sorel's *L'Europe et la révolution française* provides a brilliant sketch of the coherence of French policy through the centuries.

the fore that its representatives went to the peace conference in 1648. After 1629 the Thirty Years War had been a war between the Bourbons and the Habsburgs fought out on German soil, but in the treaties of 1648 it was represented as a struggle for the rights and liberties of the German princes against attempts at their suppression by the emperor, in which the French king appeared as the protector of German liberties. The fact that the king of France was a party to the treaty made him a guarantor of the constitution which it regulated, and his guardianship became a pretext for a general supervision of German domestic politics. A similar rôle was assigned to Sweden in the north; but the decline of Swedish power, culminating in the defeat of Poltava in 1709, left France alone in the field. The territorial settlement of 1648 was exactly suited to French interests: a Germany divided into 234 territorial units, all claiming sovereign independence and at loggerheads among themselves, had no hope of escaping French tutelage. With good reason a French diplomat later described the peace of Westphalia as 'one of the finest jewels in the French crown'.[1]

Thus the scene was set for Louis XIV, who systematically exploited German internal divisions as a means of securing both the territorial aggrandizement of France at the expense of Germany, and his own predominance in Europe. At the first imperial election under the new régime, in 1658, France solemnly warned the electors that their freedom was passing from them and that the imperial crown was becoming hereditary in one family, and offered to subsidize the elector of Bavaria, if he would become emperor. A considerable party was even in favour of conferring the imperial crown on Louis himself. When, in the end, the Austrian Leopold I was elected France immediately confronted him with an organized opposition party. Led by the archbishop of Mainz, a number of princes formed the Rhenish League, under French direction, for protection against possible encroachments by Austria. Thus Louis XIV set himself up as protector of the states of south and south-western Germany, and from 1679 his domination over Germany was complete. This period saw the French annexation of Strassburg (1681), and the notorious 'reunions', which consolidated French power in Alsace, assured French control of the left bank of the Rhine for a long stretch from

[1] Sorel, op. cit., I, 401. Sorel himself described the treaties characteristically as 'la grande œuvre européenne de l'ancienne France' (op. cit. I, 270).

the Swiss frontier northwards, and left the imperial territories of Burgundy to the south and Lorraine to the north at the mercy of France. The latter, after being more than once under French occupation, was finally annexed, with the county of Bar, in 1766, when it had been under continuous French occupation since 1735; the free county of Burgundy was ceded to France at the peace of Rastatt in 1714.

It was no accident that the period immediately following the peace of Westphalia witnessed the most serious territorial losses ever suffered by Germany. Inability to defend the frontiers was the inevitable consequence of the total breakdown of internal cohesion. Only the princes immediately concerned by the French 'rectifications' in Alsace and elsewhere were prepared to fight; the others saw only an opportunity for an 'arrangement' to their own advantage. Austria deliberately sacrificed Alsace in order to gain a free hand in Hungary; Brandenburg under the Great Elector, a pensioner of France, deliberately obstructed the formation of an anti-French alliance, when the unprovoked French occupation of Strassburg in 1681 aroused — for almost the last time in the history of the old empire — a wave of resentment and national feeling. It was the opposition of a great European coalition, headed by Great Britain, and not of the German princes, which put a halt to French expansion in the Wars of the Palatinate (1688-1697) and of the Spanish Succession (1701-1714). Only their fear of French hegemony postponed the annexation of the left bank of the Rhine from the age of Louis XIV to that of Napoleon. If the integrity of Germany was maintained, it was because it was in the interests of the powers to prevent the absorption piecemeal of German territory by one of their number; the empire was preserved after 1648 because the great powers could not agree on the division of the spoils.

After 1648 Germany ceased to be a factor in European politics. Only Austria and (after 1740) Prussia counted for anything, and because of their rivalry they tended to cancel each other out. When Frederick the Great in 1756 threw over the traditional Prussian friendship with France in favour of an alliance with England, it was simply the sign for the cementing of a Franco-Austrian alliance. Whatever the constellation of forces, French preponderance over Germany was assured. With France in possession of Alsace and of Strassburg — 'a door through which she can invade German soil as often as she wishes'[1] — western Germany lay exposed and defence-less under the threat of French domination and eventual French conquest, subject without notice to French interference. Because it was a cardinal point of French policy to keep Germany weak and disunited, the long subjection, moral as well as political, of Germany to France was a major cause of German backwardness. A century later, on the eve of the French Revolution, an official of the French foreign ministry described Germany as a bulwark of France which it was an essential French interest to keep in its present state of dis-unity.[2] Like the papacy in the days of Gregory VII and Innocent III, only with a more ruthless logic, France allied with and fostered German particularism in order to further its own political designs. When Napoleon announced that the annihilation of German nationality was an essential feature of his policy, he was only reducing to a phrase what had been the essence of French policy since Riche-lieu. To annex the German territories on the left bank of the Rhine, to dominate the rest by exploiting their divisions, to prevent the growth of common German interests and impede the resurgence of German nationalism, all this was traditional in French policy; but never was it more easily or more successfully encompassed than during the centuries when the principalities, having broken loose and secured sovereignty, assumed control of German destinies. Their concentration on their own interests, their forgetfulness of their common German inheritance, created the atmosphere most congenial to French intrigue: in a welter of petty and divergent interests the princes, for a consideration, gladly signed the death-warrant of Germany.

VI

The decay of any sense of common German nationality was a measure of the havoc wrought in Germany by the Wars of Religion and the ordeal of the Thirty Years War. Earlier a spirit of national-ism had flourished despite (and, indeed, in reaction to) political

---

[1] When the question of recovering Strassburg after the French occupation of 1681 was under debate, the commander of the imperial army, Margrave Ludwig Wilhelm of Baden-Baden, said: 'For Germany the possession of this city means simply a lasting pledge of peace. For France it is a door constantly open for war, through which she can invade German soil as often as she wishes.' Louis XIV's view was substantially the same: Alsace was, he said, 'a passage for our troops to Germany'. Cf. Sorel, op. cit., I, 283-284.

[2] Haller, *France and Germany*, 99.

impotence and fragmentation. After 1648 it perished with the dismemberment of the empire. A last flicker was aroused by the predatory schemes of Louis XIV; but it was soon spent, and its political effect was nil. Art and literature both bore witness to the exhaustion of the German spirit, which found its last refuge in the music of Buxtehude (1637-1707) and Bach (1685-1750). Except for music, where the reverberations of the Reformation still found an echo, the progress of territorialism substituted for the strongly personal and popular art of the Reformation a courtly and aristocratic art aloof from the people and servilely imitative of France and Italy. In this it faithfully reflected political conditions. Nothing more clearly illustrates the extent of the decline which overtook Germany in the seventeenth century than the disappearance of the ideals and impulses which had inspired the generation of 1500-1525.

The disappearance of any sense of common German nationality, which was the mark of the century following the peace of Westphalia was in part the result of sheer physical exhaustion. The desolation of the Thirty Years War left the country incapable of any great corporate effort, concerned almost exclusively with recovery from material devastation. But it was also the result of the triumph of the princes, which the treaties of 1648 had registered. With the ruin of the peasantry and the middle classes government in the German principalities lost all popular associations and all capacity to appeal to popular loyalty; the petty absolutisms of Germany neither possessed nor sought any foundation or support in the people. This was a cardinal fact in German history throughout this period. The absolutism established by the princes after 1648 had, of course, certain advantages to confer; but divorced as it was from the people, it had neither the power to take root nor the resources to grow and mature. A strong autocratic régime was, all in all, a benefit in the years immediately following the Thirty Years War, when the restoration of peace, order and stable government was a first necessity, and no less valuable was the work of the princes in bringing up to date the organs of administration, without which no régime could begin to cope with the intricate problems of modern government. In restoring an ordered administration after a generation of civil war the princes performed a necessary task. But the benefits conferred were meagre when set against the cost; the triumph of the princes was paid for by the German people.

When the principalities rose to power in the thirteenth century it looked as though they would triumph because they, rather than the empire, were capable of absorbing and giving expression to all the vital elements in German life; when they re-arose at the end of the fifteenth century, it was because the princes had found a means of harnessing to their governments the strong currents of political life which emerged in the fourteenth century. Nothing of the sort could be said of the absolutisms which came into existence after 1648. After the ruin of the middle classes there was no vigorous third estate capable either of controlling or of stimulating government. Not all the princes of the new dispensation were tyrants or despots, but all the governments had this in common, that they served no purpose except their own existence. After 1648 government was an 'end in itself'. It exploited the people, because exploitation was its object; it maintained a routine; it revolved on its own axis; but it made no progress, because it had no objectives outside itself towards which to progress; its ideal was a static society, self-sufficient and quiescent. The result of the long process of German territorial development was thus petrifaction: Germany existed but it did not live.

Every change which we have traced in the history of Germany between 1520 and 1648 played its part in confining German political life within the rigid framework of a petrifying territorial absolutism. In the first place, the two hundred odd states which emerged as the ill-assorted, inconsequential units of German political life after the upheavals of the Thirty Years War, were too small to flourish or to achieve a real measure of self-sufficiency except by a conservatism which closed the door on all that was progressive. Their boundaries, still broken by enclaves and determined by the whims of dynastic accident, corresponded to no reality. They were artificial creations, which were unable to stand on their own feet, and only existed as clients of France or of the opponents of France. The princes who ruled them had no object except to continue to rule, unless it were to make their rule more profitable by adding more acres and more bodies to contribute to taxation. With rare exceptions they still acted largely as landed proprietors, who farmed their patrimony to raise an income to support their households, courts and palaces. Thus the resources of the land, dissipated in small fractions, were wasted on the upkeep of a senseless multiplicity of court establish-

cc

ments which served no useful purpose. When we view palaces like the Zwinger in Dresden or Bruchsal, the residence after 1722 of the prince-bishops of Speyer, with their colonnades and wings and orangeries and pavilions, our admiration should be tempered by the knowledge that they were bought by the sweat of an oppressed peasantry, by the acceptance of subsidies from France, and by the sale of mercenaries to the great powers.[1] It should be tempered also by the knowledge that the object of these establishments was to create an impression of solidity, permanence and magnificence, which was the very opposite of the truth, with the object of magnifying the distance between prince and subjects and holding the latter in political subjection; the prince-bishop of Speyer, in his regal splendour at Bruchsal, did not hesitate to notify his people that 'the commanding will of his majesty is none other than the commanding will of God himself'.

These petty absolutisms, whose sole object was self-glorification, rested on the twin pillars of the administration and the army, with moral support from the church. The Thirty Years War had created a soldiery which the princes took care to retain on a permanent footing after peace was restored. Thus the standing army made its first appearance in Germany as a basis and support for local absolutism; in international politics the independent value of the petty armies of the German princes was negligible, but they were useful for securing stability and obedience at home. Hence all liquid capital available, when the voracious needs of princely pomp had been satisfied, was applied to building up armies and bureaucracies. It was to finance the administration and the military system that more and more rigorous taxation was imposed after 1650, because the administration and the army were the instruments through which the princes reduced their subjects to tutelage. The multiplication of bureaucracies was a mark of the times. It was the natural consequence of territorial fragmentation and patriarchal despotism, and it

[1] Cf. Rörig, *Ursachen u. Auswirkungen des deutschen Partikularismus* (1937), 28-29: 'The lunatic sums which Karl-Eugen of Württemberg frivolled away on Italian opera, French ballet, etc., led not only to taxation bordering on forced loans, but also to the provision of 6,000 soldiers (in return for corresponding subsidies) to the French for their war against Frederick the Great of Prussia. But the best proposition for princes with easy consciences occurred after 1775, when England was in need of soldiers for the American war. The landgrave of Hesse-Kassel did the best business at this period, because the relatively orderly state of his military arrangements enabled him to deliver better troops than competitors like the elector of Bavaria or Karl-Eugen of Württemberg. Of 19,400 Hessians supplied to the British government 13,900 returned in 1784; casualties numbered 7,500.'

provided an occupation for the middle classes, which had lost their natural outlet with the decay of commerce. Urban life now revolved round the busy wheels of administration: as the old towns of Germany went down, new towns like Weimar or Karlsruhe, Mannheim or Erlangen, arose whose *raison d'être* was the princely residence to which they were attached and the bureaucracies they housed. For all their beauty they were parasites, draining the country and contributing nothing to its economic resources. Likewise the effects on German middle-class society of its absorption into a bureaucracy inspired by no ideal of public service, were deplorable. The multitude of officials regarded their employment as a particular favour, demanding in return the most absolute subservience to their princely employer. They were in most cases chosen on principle from other territories, so as not to be contaminated by sympathy with the people it was their duty to exploit. And finally their energies were frivolled away in an endlessly repeated administrative routine, in which each territory aped its neighbour: over two hundred states each with its customs system and customs officials, each with its chancery, each with its organization of direct and indirect taxation! The mere cost of this multiplication was sufficient to prevent any recovery of prosperity, to absorb the surpluses which should have gone into commerce and industry, to tie Germany to an obsolescent social and economic system in which agriculture was predominant.

Germany needed a period of peace and stability after the desolation and ravages of the Thirty Years War; but the absolutist régime robbed the country of the benefits of peace and stability. The innumerable territorial barriers alone were a fatal obstacle to commerce. The upkeep of the lavish establishments of the ruling dynasties was a dead weight crushing all productive sections of the population. The very stagnation which the régime produced tended to perpetuate absolutism. Lack of opportunity drove the best elements to seek their fortunes abroad. It was not only that government was divorced from the people; more important was the fact that there were not, as in France or in England, flourishing economic interests which demanded a voice in government. When German territorialism set obstacles in the path of the rise of the middle class, it created a situation which fundamentally differentiated Germany from the west. The cardinal vice of the absolutist régime was that it allowed the middle class to survive only as the salaried pensioner of government. In part, this was deliberate policy, as the sustained attacks on the estates imply. In part, it was the inescapable result of the political condition under which absolutism rose to power. The mercantilism of the age was not foreign to Germany; there were princes enough who saw the advantage of pursuing a definite economic policy and stimulating economic life; but the units were in general too small and artificial, the bounds within which they worked too narrow, for mercantilism to register any notable success. Except for provinces like Meissen, with its rich mineral deposits, commerce and industry in Germany, ruined in the Thirty Years War, continued to be fragile growths, even where most carefully tended, and the middle classes remained economically and politically weak.

Through absolutism, therefore, Germany was riveted to an agrarian régime, which was harsh and oppressive. Almost the sole productive element in the population was the peasantry, which for that very reason was mercilessly exploited by princes whose expenditure, modelled on the standards of Versailles, created an insatiable demand for revenue. It would be hard to say which was the more characteristic feature of the régime, the decay of the bourgeoisie or the deterioration in the position of the peasantry. In west and south-west Germany, the classical land of the petty principality, where prince and landlord were often one, the depression of the peasantry had begun early, the prince using his public powers to reinforce his hold, as landlord, over the peasant population; while the very fact that most landlords were *rentiers*, who had no interest in the working of the land but only in the rents they got out of it, exposed the tenantry to the worst excesses of rack-renting. It was conditions such as these which provoked the Peasants' Wars of 1524-1525, and it was for this reason that the risings occurred almost exclusively in south-west Germany: their failure and the vicious reaction which followed caused further deterioration. But it was in the states of north and north-east Germany, whose very existence was due to the labours of a prosperous free peasantry, that the most sweeping changes occurred. Here again the beginnings reach back to the end of the middle ages, to the century between 1350 and 1450, when the weakening of government and the alienation of rights and properties by impecunious princes played into the hands of the nobility, who took over by grant or usurpation rights of justice and taxation and the public services which the peasants had owed to the government. Thus they asserted rights over the peasants which they had not possessed in the early days of colonization, and the descendants of the early peasant colonists lost the privileges which had attracted their forefathers to the east, particularly the privilege of direct connexion with government cutting out all intermediate authorities. Thereafter many factors contributed to widen the cleft between the nobility and the peasantry and to bring the latter, shorn of their free status, into subjection to the former. The secularization of Church lands, which fell (as in England) in large part into the hands of the aristocracy, was a major factor in raising the east German Junkers head and shoulders above their peasant neighbours, and in helping them to consolidate their scattered holdings into great estates.[1] In those parts of the Reich which fell temporarily under Polish rule, like Prussia, the peasants were ruined, for Polish law encouraged simultaneously both the most extreme forms of serfdom and the most arrant excesses of aristocratic privilege.[2] Another factor affecting the peasants was the struggle between the princes and the estates, for it was often precisely by compensating the nobility at the expense of the peasants, by recognizing the subjection of the peasantry to the nobility and conferring extensive new rights on the latter, that the princes obtained acquiescence in the destruction of the powers of the *Landtag*.[3] Nor should it be forgotten that the *Landtage*, representing the interests of the privileged classes, were themselves instruments for attacking the rights of the peasantry, and that where the *Landtag* retained its privileges (for example, in Mecklenburg) the depression of the peasantry proceeded most systematically. It was, however, not until the Thirty Years War ruined agriculture that the peasants of north and north-east Germany were finally crushed. They had neither the resources nor the capital for recovery, and after the conclusion of the wars in 1648 the nobility won all along the line.

---

[1] The position in the middle ages was very different; cf. above, pp. 276-278. By contrast von Below (*Territorium u. Stadt*, 48) points to Bavaria, where there was no secularization of Church lands and where consequently the scattered holdings of the peasants were a material obstacle to the consolidation of aristocratic estates.

[2] Cf. Treitschke, *Origins*, 150. The expectation of despotic privileges on the Polish model was one of the inducements held out to the Prussian estates to persuade them to desert the Teutonic Order; ibid., 131-132.

[3] For an example of this process at a turning-point in Brandenburg-Prussian history, cf. above, p. 379.

The second half of the seventeenth century saw an extraordinary increase in the number of big noble estates, and the reduction of the peasantry to a state of abject servility.

This was the period when, throughout the north and north-east, peasants were ejected from their holdings to permit the consolidation of demesne farms, when compulsory services (often unlimited in custom or practice) were introduced to compensate for the shortage of labour following the drop in population during the Thirty Years War, when the peasants were reduced to the status of bondmen tied to the glebe. What had begun in consequence of the Thirty Years War was accentuated by the Northern War (1700-1721) and by the Seven Years War (1756-1763). Frederick the Great in Prussia and Joseph II in Austria made some attempt to protect the peasants, if only to ensure that they were not too oppressed to shoulder the burden of taxation or to serve as soldiers; but their policy remained exceptional. Elsewhere, government gave the nobility a free hand, unwilling to arouse the hostility of the only element strong enough to oppose it, and desirous of providing for the class on which it still relied for leadership in war. Thus arose the Junker caste and the *Rittergut* of the German east. Dispossessing or depressing the status of the peasant owners, the nobility carved out a place for themselves under the aegis of absolutism by consolidating vast estates on which they practised large-scale agriculture; they created a new feudalism more rigorous and repressive than mediaeval Germany had ever known; lording it over a ruined peasantry, they became a dominant power in the land.

The final achievement of the period of absolutism was thus the creation of an agricultural proletariat. Except on the crown demesnes of Brandenburg-Prussia, the peasants were chattels, attached to the estate on which they were born, with no hope of improving either their economic lot or their personal status. Improvements in agricultural technique in the second half of the eighteenth century, although restoring agrarian prosperity, brought them no benefits; indeed, in so far as they contributed to the rise of large-scale capitalist agriculture, they added new hardships to old, in the form of enclosures and loss of commons. The peasants counted for nothing in the State, but on them fell its burdens; while the nobility were exempt from direct taxation, the peasants were left with little more than a third of the money they earned. Impoverishment and stagnation were the result. The nobility made agriculture a paying concern by the merciless extortion of heavy predial services, and thus assured their own position; but for Germany as a whole there was no escape from retrogression. The interests which dominated the principalities were too narrow and too harshly predatory to permit of progress. The rigid class structure, and the lack of intermediate gradations between the privileged few and the disfranchised masses, petrified the social structure. The aristocracy, after its retirement to its estates, where in feudal aloofness it exercised all the attributes of government, thought only of maintaining its privileges by raising barriers against all parvenus; anxiously scrutinizing pedigrees and arranging marriages, it formed itself into a closed caste. At certain princely courts and residences a breath of 'enlightenment' was in the air, but in the country — where, in a patrimonial agrarian society, economic and political power lay — a rigorous, stifling conservatism was the rule. A flourishing middle class, with commercial ties extending far and wide, might have transcended the political fragmentation of Germany; but no breadth of vision was to be expected of the dominant agrarian aristocracy in a country cut into more than two hundred segments.

Thus for a century and more after 1648 Germany stagnated. Petty dynasties, class-bound nobilities and corrupt oligarchies, all guided by narrow motives of self-interest, exercised a harsh and oppressive domination over a peasantry and a middle class both ruined by the Thirty Years War. Initiative and freedom were stifled in the strait-waistcoat of a rigidly stratified society. The only opportunity afforded to the middle class was in the service of the princes; and the only bourgeois element which found any scope within the system was therefore a class-conscious body of civil servants, lawyers, university teachers and professional placemen, who glorified the system which assured their existence. For all others, the very structure of Germany was an incitement to live apart from the bureaucratic machinery through which a petty state bore down on the individual. Associations which might have invigorated social or political life were stifled and discouraged; the legal system with its strong flavour of Roman jurisprudence frowned on them as survivals from a barbarous age, the princes opposed any organization standing between them and the direct exploitation of their subjects. Political life was dead, its place taken by the mechanical clockwork of administration. The narrow ambit of the principalities stultified political activity, while the classes which earlier had looked to wider political horizons beyond the frontiers of the principalities had withered and enervated. Never was the divorce between government and the life of the people so complete. The system with its narrow, dominating aristocratic caste and its repressive feudalism is often thought of and described as an outgrowth of the middle ages, the survival of an out-of-date system accounted for by the retrograde character of German political development. This is at best only partly true. The characteristic features of absolutism, the exacting administration, the dependence on a standing army, the oppressive bondage of the peasantry, even the arrogant isolation of the aristocracy, were all products of the seventeenth and eighteenth centuries, which cannot be paralleled in the middle ages. Mediaeval German society had been marked by the fluidity and inherent vigour of social classes, the rise and fall of social groups; it had allowed ample play, particularly in the fourteenth century, to free, spontaneous associations which enriched the texture of economic, social and political life; it had drawn its strength from a stalwart, energetic peasantry; it had suffered more from looseness of organization than from rigidity, but had derived the incidental benefits of a loose political structure in the form of vigorous local and regional activities. Far from being incorporated in the principalities, this regional life and local solidarity was stamped out under the dead weight of uniform administrative practices by governments which arbitrarily destroyed older provincial unities at the behest of dynastic interests. The rigidity and stagnation which set in after 1648, the dissociation of the people from the governments set over them, were not the result of the perpetuation of mediaeval conditions, but the symptom of their death. What was tragic in German history, however, was that with the end of mediaeval society nothing living and progressive was found to take its place. The germs of a new society had been there for all to see as late as the reign of Maximilian I (1493-1519). But they were crushed out of existence by the events of the next century and a half, by the entanglements of Habsburg policy, by foreign intervention in German affairs, by religious disunity, and by the long desolation of savage wars. The result was the establishment of the petrifying régime of petty absolutism, which brought neither comfort for the present nor hope for the future.

VII

The historian's only interest in this stultifying ossification lies in the process by which it was brought to an end, and in its durable effects on the people who underwent it. What the latter were, may (after the foregoing description of the absolutist régime) be summarized under five headings: the fortification of the privileges of a narrow aristocratic caste, more enduringly entrenched even than the absolutist régime itself; the degradation of the agricultural population; the obstacles placed in the way of the liberation and political education of the middle classes; the establishment of the bureaucracy and the army — the officer was simply an official of another order — as the backbone of government; and finally the rigorous stratification of society with each group or class allotted a predetermined place and no scope for individual talent or initiative to overstep the predetermined class divisions. All these characteristics, the results of a century and a half of petty despotism, outlasted the régime under which they were born; they were its lasting consequences, and even in the nineteenth and twentieth centuries they could not be ignored. The absolutist régime itself was more fragile. The political structure of Germany after 1648 was, we have seen, intimately dependent on the European system with which it was integrated. The German *status quo* was ultimately a by-product of the European *status quo*; lacking inherent stability, it had no chance of survival once the European balance of power underwent violent change. The German principalities were simply counters in the game of European politics, too weak in construction to resist outside pressure. Hence, when the end came, it came quickly. Two factors brought about the downfall of the régime of 1648: first, the rise of Prussia, the emergence from the federal body of a state capable (as was proved in the Seven Years War) of standing firm on its own feet, and secondly the upheavals of the years 1789-1815. In the midst of the latter, unmourned and almost unheeded in the revolutions of the Napoleonic period, the old empire, a meaningless survival, finally passed away.

The rise of Brandenburg-Prussia from the ranks of a second-class German territory began when, after the ruin of the Palatinate in the Thirty Years War, it succeeded to the primacy among the German Protestant states. Its early territorial history is a story of tenacity, and the political testaments written by the heads of the house of

Hohenzollern for their successors show how meticulously opportunities were foreseen and watched;[1] but the main feature of Hohenzollern policy is a clear, calculating realization that for a German
principality to prosper its governing principle must be to exploit the
divisions among the great powers. Between Russia, Sweden and
Poland, with France in the background, Hohenzollern policy
steered a devious but gradually successful course. The peace of
Westphalia brought Brandenburg the eastern half of Pomerania,
as well as the bishoprics of Magdeburg, Halberstadt, Minden and
Kammin; in 1657 Prussia (which had been in the hands of the
electors of Brandenburg since 1618) was freed from Polish suzerainty; in 1721 at the end of the Northern Wars, the more important
part of western Pomerania, including Stettin, was added at the
expense of Sweden. In the west the Cleves duchies had been acquired
by inheritance in 1614. Thus the scattered Hohenzollern territories,
reaching across north Germany from the Dutch to the Polish
frontiers, fell into three main blocks: the Mark itself with the con-
tiguous Pomeranian lands, the east Prussian duchy, and the smaller
and less consolidated but richer possessions towards the Rhine.
Even minor acquisitions outside these blocks had their importance:
Minden, for example, was a bridge over the Weser and one of the
main points on the great road from east to west connecting Berlin
with the Lower Rhine, Magdeburg was one of the most important
crossings over the Elbe. By the end of the seventeenth century
something like the framework of a kingdom was coming into being.

Nevertheless the progress of territorial growth must not be exaggerated. Down to 1700 Brandenburg-Prussia was outstripped by
Bavaria, down to the middle of the eighteenth century by Saxony,
in wealth and population. What distinguished the history of Prussia
from that of the other second-class German states in the generations
following the peace of Westphalia was less its territorial history
which revealed no clear signs of future greatness until Frederick the
Great launched his momentous attack on Austria in 1740, than the
subordination of all inhabitants, from the king downwards, to the
service of the State. This was, in part, a consequence of the wide
dispersal of Hohenzollern territory which — contrasted with
Saxony or Bavaria — required special measures to safeguard the

[1] They were collected and published in two volumes in 1919-1920 by G. Küntzel and
M. Hass, *Die politischen Testamente der Hohenzollern.*

scattered fragments, and obtain even a minimum of cohesion. It was also a result of a clear understanding that, to secure any measure of respect and consideration from the greater powers which dominated German politics, a strong military organization was requisite. Provided that the rulers of the Prussian state had the requisite will and traditions and tenacity, the exigencies of their frontiers and the imperative demands of Prussia's critical position in central Europe,

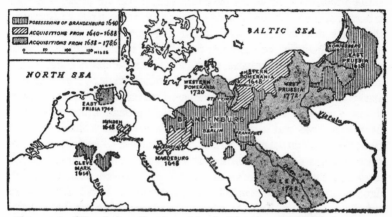

The growth of Brandenburg-Prussia to the end of the reign of Frederick the Great

directly threatened by major powers like Russia and Sweden and Austria, were a powerful incentive to constructive statesmanship. In the three great rulers who formed Prussia, the Great Elector (1640-1688), Frederick William I (1713-1740) and Frederick the Great (1740-1786), leaders were found who impressed a tradition in keeping with Prussia's geographical and political circumstances.

The detailed story of the reforms and reorganization carried out by the Prussian rulers of the eighteenth century, described again and again by historians seeking the key to the modern history of Germany, can be passed over. It was less in its methods than in its energy and purposefulness that the house of Hohenzollern differed from the other dynasties of Germany. In Prussia, as in the rest of Germany, the administration and the army were fundamental. In the scattered territories stretching from the Rhine to the Vistula, there was no unity of common tradition; there was not, until the end of the eighteenth century, the unity of a common body of law;

still less was there any common representative body; the one unity was that of a common administration and a Prussian army. But the Prussian army, unlike the armies of most other states of the period, was not simply a mercenary army. Because of the high cost of recruiting abroad, Frederick William I began to adopt the plan of raising his troops from his own population. By the end of his reign half of his army of 80,000 men was recruited at home; proportionate to the population on which he could call, it was far larger — as well as better drilled and disciplined — than any other army in Europe.[1] Moreover it was maintained, unlike the mercenary armies of the other principalities, which were paid for by foreign subsidies, from the resources of the Prussian state. Frederick William I left, at the end of his reign, a war treasure of six million thalers, equivalent to nearly one and a half years' revenues; Frederick the Great, in spite of his wars, left a treasure of fifty million thalers, amounting to more than two and a quarter years of a revenue which was itself triple the amount that his father had collected. The frugality, the rigorous checks on expenditure, and the careful management which produced this result, were the mark of Prussian administration. Here again there is a marked contrast with the lavish expenditure and the overgrown bureaucracy of the average princely household; practising a severe economy both at court and in the cost of the public administration, the Prussian monarchy disciplined itself to sacrifice the revenues of the crown to the overriding requirements of the state. Brandenburg-Prussia, not the Hohenzollern dynasty, came first: 'I am the Finance Minister and the Field-Marshal of the King of Prussia', said Frederick William I.

It was this sense of subordination to a higher duty, of responsibility to a higher power, which distinguished the Prussian state from the rest of eighteenth-century Germany. The famous doctrine that the prince is the servant of the State was a peculiarly Prussian doctrine. Its kings conscripted the lives of their peasants and the services of their nobles, but they also conscripted themselves. Whatever view we may hold of the ideal of the Fatherland, there can be no doubt

[1] The army of Frederick William I stood at 80,000 when the population of his territories was only some 2,000,000; it was 1 in 25 of the population when the army of France was about 1 in 150. By 1789 the regular army of Prussia was 162,000 men, rising in time of war to 250,000, compared with the French army of 173,000, which could be increased in war to 211,000 or (including the militia) to 287,000. At this date the population of Prussia was less than one-third that of France. Cf. E. Barker, *The Development of Public Services in Western Europe, 1660-1930* (1944), 42-43.

whatever that it represented a revolutionary advance over the practice and theory of the other German states, petrifying in obedience
to the personal will and arbitrary whims of minor potentates.
Whilst they languished under an old-fashioned and wasteful mis-
government, Prussia set the example of an administration which,
while rigorously frugal, strove to develop the resources of the land,
of a highly-disciplined army, and of a tradition of service which in
some degree took the place of free political activity as a source of
cohesion. As a tradition it could only be maintained by the forceful
personality of the ruler, and it therefore quickly withered when,
after Frederick the Great's death, control passed into the hands of a
decadent court.

Nevertheless it remains true that the people of Prussia, under the
constant pressure of royal precept and royal example, alone among
the people of eighteenth-century Germany felt any sense of identity
with the government set above them. It was a stern relationship,
based on duty and obedience, on austerity and work; its substance
was the obligation of every individual, low and exalted, rich and
poor, to serve the State with body and soul in life and death. But,
in contrast with the aimlessness and arbitrariness of political life elsewhere, even this rigorous doctrine of self-abnegation caught hold,
and its sterling value was proved in the Seven Years War when the
indomitable resistance put up by Frederick the Great in face of an
overwhelming odds was made possible by the solid support and
sacrifices of the Prussian people.

The rise of Prussia to the rank of a great power modified the
whole European constellation, and laid the foundation for the
reconstruction of Germany after the French Revolution and the
Napoleonic Wars had overthrown the old order and brought
about a basic territorial simplification. Its emergence as a European
power would have been impossible without the work of internal
consolidation to which Frederick William I and Frederick the Great
directed their energies, the latter particularly in the decade 1745-
1755, following the Treaty of Dresden, and after the conclusion of
the Seven Years War when a vast programme of reform was
inaugurated to heal the wounds the State had suffered in the struggle.
But the driving force behind this consolidation was the unity of the
people round the crown under the pressure of war and resistance to
external threats. The wars with Austria between 1740 and 1763

at once completed the development of the Prussian state and signalled its arrival in the ranks of the great powers. The Treaty of Huburtusburg, signed on February 15th, 1763, demonstrated that the empire no longer contained one great power only, but two; and of these two Prussia was essentially the German power. Austria was more and more involved in eastern Europe and Italy (in 1736 it had bartered away Lorraine for Tuscany), and had been ready in the Seven Years War to abandon its Belgian provinces to France and East Prussia to Russia in return for support against Prussia. With the loss of Silesia it surrendered to Prussia the predominating position in Germany, and the changed relations of the two powers were seen when, in 1785, Frederick grouped round him the electors of Mainz, Hannover and Saxony and a host of minor states in a League of Princes for defence against the emperor, Joseph II, who was seeking to restore Austrian power and prestige in Germany. The League of Princes was no attempt at a reorganization of the decrepit imperial constitution; its object was simply to maintain the *status quo*, and on this score it was severely criticized by contemporaries;[1] but it certainly reflected and marked the complete redistribution of power within Germany which followed the victory of Prussia in the Seven Years War.

With its powerful standing army and its remarkable financial strength, Prussia after 1763 was well able to stand on its own feet. But it was in no position to assume the leadership of Germany or to free Germany from foreign tutelage. The equilibrium between Austria and Prussia in the second half of the eighteenth century enhanced rather than diminished the influence of foreign powers in German affairs, in the first place that of Russia under Catherine II, who assumed the rôle of arbiter between the two German powers, in the second place the all-pervading influence of France. It was only with the greatest effort that Frederick, in the last years of his reign, contrived to maintain the position he had won for himself and for Prussia, particularly when in 1781 Austria and Russia drew together.

[1] Thus Johannes von Müller, in *Deutschlands Erwartungen vom Fürstenbunde*: 'If the German Union serves for nothing better than to maintain the *status quo*, it is against the eternal order of God, by which neither the physical nor the moral world remains for a moment in the *status quo*, but all is life and motion and progress. To exist without law or justice, without security from arbitrary imposts, doubtful whether we can preserve from day to day our children, our honour, our liberties, our rights, our lives, helpless before superior force, without a beneficial connexion between our states, without a national spirit at all, this is the *status quo* of our nation. And it is this that the Union is meant to maintain.'

It was fear of Russia and open jealousy and distrust between Austria and Prussia which led to the three partitions of Poland in 1772, 1792 and 1795. These partitions (and the acquisition of the margraviate of Ansbach and Bayreuth in 1791) materially added to the territories under Prussian rule; but, apart from the acquisition of West Prussia in 1772 — a territory still essentially German in spite of three centuries of Polish misrule — they were a source of weakness and administrative difficulties, rather than of strength. From the point of view of Prussian interests, the partition of Poland was an ill-conceived policy, which brought nothing but misfortune in its train; but its explanation lies less in the pursuit of Prussian interests than in the tension between the three eastern powers. Each feared the aggrandizement of the other; each was determined, in the spirit of the age, to secure 'compensations'; and the two German powers in particular, beneath a cloak of agreement and co-operation, were divided by a fundamental opposition so deep-rooted as to preclude even the idea of combining, with or without Poland, against Russia or in defence of German interests. Neither Prussian policy nor Austrian policy was a German policy; and their crippling hostility, in which each neutralized the other, left the German territories outside the Prussian and Austrian borders a prey to foreign intrigue and foreign intervention. While Frederick William II of Prussia concentrated his efforts on protecting his Polish acquisitions, fearful lest Austria should come to a secret understanding with Russia to rob him of his spoils, a regenerate France, inspired by the fresh vigour of 1789, marched into western Germany, intent on securing at long last the 'natural' frontiers which, since the days of Philip the Fair five centuries earlier, had been the ambition of French policy. France's frontiers, declared Danton at the beginning of 1793, have been fixed by nature on the Rhine: 'it is there that our boundaries are fated to be placed, and no power on earth shall keep us from our goal'.

The resurgence of France, the hostility between Austria and Prussia, and the oblivion of both the great German powers to German interests, combined within little more than a decade to bring about the complete and final collapse of the old order in Germany. After the partition of Poland, in which Austria and Prussia had co-operated with Russia, both turned without hesitation or scruple to a partition of Germany in co-operation with France.

Like every earlier protagonist of French expansion since the first beginnings of French chauvinism, Napoleon found willing accomplices within Germany itself. As early as 1793 Frederick William II withdrew his troops from the west, announcing that thenceforward he intended to devote himself exclusively to the interests of Prussia, and in 1795 he made peace with France by the treaty of Basel. From that moment Prussia abandoned all opposition to the annexation by France of the left bank of the Rhine, merely stipulating that the French should assist her to obtain appropriate compensation in Germany for the Prussian territories lost on the Lower Rhine. Austria resisted more resolutely, taking up arms in 1799 and 1805; but from the time of the peace of Campo Formio in 1797, she also, like Prussia, was ready to adopt a policy of 'compensations',[1] and in the peace of Lunéville (1801) that ominous principle was enshrined.

The deals which followed brought the territorial system of 1648 crashing down. A resolution of the diet on February 25th, 1803, began by suppressing the ecclesiastical principalities, and soon the imperial towns and other small territories suffered the same fate of mediatization. It was the beginning of a far-reaching simplification of German political geography, which laid the foundation for subsequent developments in the nineteenth century. The map of Germany was redrawn, and forty territories took the place of two hundred and thirty-four. The secularization of the ecclesiastical principalities was particularly ominous; for the ecclesiastical princes were the chief supporters of the old order, the most loyal adherents of the empire. In their place arose a small number of medium states — Bavaria and Baden, Württemberg, Nassau and Hesse — which owed their position to Napoleon, and were devoted clients of France. Already in 1804 and 1805, sensing that the old order was past, the emperor Francis II began to style himself 'Hereditary Emperor of Austria'. The real emperor was Napoleon, who had adopted the imperial title in 1804, thus at long last realizing the old French dream of succeeding to the inheritance of Charlemagne. His plan for Germany was masterly in its simplicity: to destroy the empire, to make Prussia and Austria neutralize each other, and to create a screen of small states, dependent on France, strong enough to defend themselves against Austria or Prussia, but not sufficiently

[1] She 'indemnified herself with Salzburg and the Inn country for the fact that the German empire lost the Rhineland' (Haller, *France and Germany*, 94).

strong to pursue a policy of their own. This plan became practical politics in 1806. Bavaria, Württemberg, Baden and several other states, to the number of sixteen in all, repudiated the laws of the empire and announced their secession and the formation of a Confederation of the Rhine under French protection.[1] Simultaneously the French envoy announced to the imperial Diet at Regensburg that Napoleon had consented to become protector of the confederate princes, and no longer recognized the existence of the empire. The constitution of the Confederation of the Rhine took place on July 12th: less than a month later, on August 6th, 1806, Francis II formally abdicated the imperial crown, laying aside the imperial government and freeing all subjects of the empire – in particular the officials and the members of the imperial judiciary – from their oaths and obligations. Thus perished the first empire after almost eight and a half centuries of existence. Politically, it left no gap, for it had been a nullity since 1648; but with it went the last exiguous bond between the German peoples, the one remaining symbol of German unity. The dissolution of the unity for which the Ottonian dynasty had struggled in times long past – a unity secured in the wake of their triumphs in Italy and the east – was now complete: territorialism and particularism, in league with France, had won the long battle which the princes began when, in league with the papacy, they took up arms against the Emperor Henry IV in 1076.

---

[1] After the defeat of Prussia in the war of 1806 and the Peace of Tilsit (1807) all the German states with the exception of Austria and Prussia became members of the Confederation.

CHAPTER 14

THE EMPIRE AND THE PEOPLE IN MODERN GERMANY
(1806-1939)

I

IN 1806 all that remained of the German nation, sacrificed to the exigencies of princely politics, were the tenuous bonds of common kinship, the consciousness of a common past and of achievements won in common, unity of language and—despite the deep-cutting differences of confession—unity of culture, reinforced by an extraordinary unanimity of spirit and of thought. These were not political factors and they had no place in the calculations of politicians and statesmen, except as dangerous manifestations to be circumvented. Among the men in power even the German language was in decay: Frederick William II of Prussia could only express himself haltingly in German, and even the patriot Stein habitually used French in conversing with his family. Nor was the unanimity of thought and spirit identified with any of the existing German states; for artificial creations of Napoleonic policy, like Baden or Hesse, that goes without saying, but even Prussia, whose extraordinary achievements and indomitable spirit in the Seven Years War had won admiration far and wide, forfeited its hold over popular imagination in later decades, as Prussian policy proved unable to rise above a narrow, shameless particularism.[1] Stein's famous manifesto of 1812 expressed better than all else the mood of Germany in the decade between the fall of the old order in 1806 and the establishment of a new order in 1815: 'I have only one Fatherland', he proclaimed, 'and that is Germany . . . To Germany alone, and not to any one part of it, I am devoted with all my soul. At this turning-point in history the dynasties are for me a matter of the completest indifference. It is my wish that Germany shall be great and strong, in order to recover and maintain its independence and its nationality in its position between Russia and France: that is the interest of the nation and of the whole of Europe . . . My creed is unity.'

[1] Cf. the criticism above, p. 402, n. 1. Nowhere in Germany was there less interest in the problems and traditions of the Reich than in Prussia; cf. A. Berney, 'Reichstradition und Nationalstaatsgedanke (1789-1815)', *Hist. Zeitschr.*, CXL (1929), 62.

The rebirth of this spirit of German nationalism, which had been strangled by the principalities, was the result of the French Revolution and of the Napoleonic domination of Germany. The revolution of 1789, freeing France from the shackles of the *ancien régime* and producing a mighty resurgence, filled Germany with a consciousness of her existing impotence; the system of princely absolutism was seen for what it was, a crippling handicap holding down the German people. But it was the Napoleonic régime which turned this new sense of hope and exaltation into nationalist channels. When the first French troops entered the Rhinelands in 1792, they were welcomed as liberators and 'neo-Frankish brothers'; everywhere there was the belief that, under the banner of 'Liberty, Equality, Fraternity', a new era of brotherhood was dawning. Disillusion soon followed.[1] When Napoleon reverted to a policy of balance of power, of compacts and arrangements with princes at the expense of peoples, it became evident that the brief initial cosmopolitanism of the men of eighty-nine had been suppressed. When, after the peace of Lunéville, he developed his plans for Germany to the full, no one could fail to see that he was putting into effect, with an inexorable logic of his own, the time-honoured policy of the French monarchy, the nationalist schemes of Philip the Fair, of Richelieu and of Louis XIV. Until 1806, as a result of the Prussian policy of compromise and a strict attention to Prussian interests, northern Germany had escaped the menace of war, and it could be argued that the struggle was simply a phase in the age-long contest between Austria and France, between Habsburg and Bourbon, and that the humbling of Austria and the elimination of the Empire was a benefit for Germany. But the Franco-Prussian war of 1806, the catastrophic Prussian defeat at Jena, and the destruction of the Prussian state by the Treaty of Tilsit in 1807, changed all this. Western Germany on the right bank of the Rhine became French, partly by annexation and partly through the creation of vassal states, such as the Kingdom of Westphalia and the Grand Duchy of Berg, and French was introduced as the official language from Westphalia to Hamburg.

These were the circumstances which provoked the rebirth of

---

[1] Already before the end of 1792 the conduct of Custine at Frankfurt caused hostile reactions. 'These republicans', it was said, 'are the brothers of the soldiers of Louis XIV, the ravagers of the Palatinate; Custine is a bandit. The philosophers at Paris charged him to make war on the palaces; instead he makes it on wine-cellars, granaries and cash-boxes.' Cf. E. Bourgeois, *Manuel historique de politique étrangere*, II (1920), 78.

German nationalism. The progress of the reaction can be observed in the German armies which were compelled, in pursuit of alleged dynastic interests, to fight on the side of France.[1] The humiliation and sense of impotence inspired by the political bargaining and the cynical accommodations of 1806 were immediately expressed by Heinrich Luden when, in his *Observations on the Confederation of the Rhine* (1808), he wrote that 'the most vital elements in my mind and heart lie buried beneath the ruins of the German nation'. Almost simultaneously, in the winter of 1807-1808, Fichte delivered the course of lectures, afterwards published as *Addresses to the German Nation*, which were expressly directed to 'the German people in general, setting aside and disregarding all those divisions and distinctions between different sections of one nation caused by the unhappy events of past centuries', with the purpose of arousing 'in the minds and hearts of Germans throughout the country a spirit of determined activity'. Even earlier Schiller, who had once counted himself fortunate in losing his country and gaining the world in exchange, published *William Tell* (1804) and the ode *Deütsche Grösse* (1801), the former a symbol of Germany's destiny and both the result of Napoleonic oppression. The same national inspiration lay behind Herder's ode *Germanien*, published after his death in 1803. Of more decisive practical importance was the reaction in Prussia after the catastrophe of 1806, culminating in the programme of administrative, social and military reform, including abolition of peasant serfdom, concession of local administrative autonomy and freedom of enterprise, associated for ever with the names of Scharnhorst, Stein and Hardenberg. Scharnhorst set out to turn the Prussian army into a national army, the embodiment of 'all the moral and physical energies of the nation'. Hardenberg and Stein realized that it was impossible to raise Prussia from the rut into which it had fallen without politically modernizing the state, or to win the support of a population devoted to the patriotic cause and ready for heavy sacrifices without giving them an interest in public affairs.

Yet these reforms, indispensable to the resurrection of Prussia, were resisted tenaciously by the ruling class, headed by Frederick William III himself. Like the emperor Maximilian I three hundred

---

[1] For Bavaria, for example, cf. K. Uebe, *Der Stimmungsumschwung in der bayerischen Armee gegenüber den Franzosen, 1806-1812* (1939).

years before him, he had no idea of putting himself at the head of a national movement; like Maximilian, he took refuge in a policy of procrastination and obstruction. The War of Liberation, which flamed up in 1813, was a national and popular movement, into which Frederick William III was unwillingly dragged. The alliance with Russia was forced on him against his will, after General Yorck had concluded the convention of Tauroggen on his own responsibility. The famous proclamation 'To My People', fore-shadowing the reconstitution of a German Empire by the united action of princes and people, was extorted from him with difficulty. Nor, if the prince who had most to gain by a bold assumption of leadership was hesitant and reluctant to the last, were the other German rulers less timid and aloof. The Austrian emperor was even more conscious than Frederick William III of the dangerous implications of a popular movement sweeping Germany, while the king of Württemberg, who had basked so long in Napoleon's favour, did not hesitate to express his indignation at the 'ridiculous notion' of trying to make a 'so-called national unit' out of the multi-farious German peoples. Even in the year 1813 — often described as an *annus mirabilis* of German history — when the spirit of national devotion and sacrifice reached heights unparalleled for centuries, the cleft carved by history between the nation and the principalities, between the princes and the people, gaped wide.

It is thus not surprising that the War of Liberation ended without any solution of the German problem. Germany was liberated from French rule and domination; but it was not liberated from the heritage of its own past. It was an ominous foreshadowing of the shape of things to come when Frederick William III's call to his people, issued at Kalisch on March 25th, 1813, was followed before the end of the same year by treaties guaranteeing full sovereignty to Bavaria and Württemberg. A few months later, in the Treaty of Paris (1814), the powers laid down that Germany should be formed into a federation of independent sovereign states, and a year later this principle, decided over the heads of the people, was embodied in the final act of the Congress of Vienna. Apart from changes of detail, the territorial system created by Napoleon in 1806 was accepted as the basis of the new order — a system which, as has been seen, was designed in the interests of French policy to consecrate for ever the sovereignty of the principalities and the territorial divisions of Germany. But these principalities, hitherto united only in and through the Napoleonic Empire, of which all but Austria and Prussia were satellites, were now united 'for the maintenance of external and internal security' in the Germanic Confederation. This confederation was, however, a union not of the German people, but of the German states. The federal diet was a meeting of representatives of the governments, and all attempts to secure representation for the people were a failure. As far as the statesmen who produced the settlement were concerned, the national movement which culminated in the War of Liberation might never have occurred. For them the people were still simply the population, to be disposed of in the interests and for the benefit of their lords. How little they had learnt or forgotten was demonstrated by the territorial settlement of the Saar question in the first Peace of Paris: as a whole the Saar was left in French hands, but it was decided to separate a total of 69,000 'souls', divided with minute exactitude into five portions of 13,800 each, as 'compensation' for the princely houses of Mecklenburg-Strelitz, Pappenheim, Saxe-Coburg, Hessen-Homburg and Oldenburg. Such was the recognition which the German people received for its share in the overthrow of Napoleon.

As in earlier centuries, the fate of Germany was settled, its frontiers drawn, by the princes in league with foreign powers. In this respect also the system of 1815 was a direct continuation of the old system. Like the settlement of 1648 the German settlement of 1815 was part of a European settlement: it was drawn up partly in the interests of the German princes, largely in the interests of the great powers, and not at all in the interests of the German people. Thus it was the English desire for a strong barrier against French aggression, reinforced by the necessity for finding territorial compensations to offset the Russian absorption of nearly the whole of Poland, which led to the acquisition by Prussia of a major accretion of territory on the Rhine – a cardinal change in the political geography of the Prussian state and in the direction of Prussian policy without which its rise to predominance between 1815 and 1871 would scarcely have been thinkable. The fall of Napoleon, the defeat of France, brought about a change of masters, but not a change in the system by which the political organization of Germany was made to subserve the interests of the powers. If England, in the person of Castlereagh, set up Prussia as watchdog on the Rhine,

Austria, which was now only in small degree a German state, was interested in the maintenance of the Napoleonic states of south Germany both as a barrier against France and as potential allies against Prussia. Every interest was heard and respected except the interest of the German people. Even the centuries' old plea for a common coinage and for the abolition of barriers to trade and communications — pleas which had been loud as far back as the reform movement of the fifteenth century — were ignored: nothing, in the view of the Congress of Vienna, must stand in the way of the full sovereign prerogatives of the individual German states.

Such, then, was the state of Germany on the threshold of the nineteenth century. The particularism which reached its culmination in 1806 was consecrated and legitimized in 1815; it had carried all before it, and the particular interests of Prussia and Bavaria, of Saxony and Württemberg and the rest, had written the name of Germany off the political map of Europe. On the other hand, none of these states, not even Prussia, had succeeded in taking over, even within the limits of its own territorial boundaries, the loyalties which had formerly animated the Reich. Many were recent Napoleonic creations, but even those which had existed since 1648 had failed to establish that identity of government and people, of state and folk, which gives endurance and stability to political society. They were still, at the end as at the beginning, the arbitrary product of accidental contingencies, superimposed on the population regardless of race, geography or history; they were able to interfere with the economic and social life of the people — and had, in fact, cruelly impeded its healthy development — but they were unable to gather the life of the people round them, to make themselves the centres of popular life and activity, expressing the common interests of their inhabitants. They had, for more than a century after 1648, undermined the sense of common German nationality which had been vigorous as late as the sixteenth century, but they had failed to set anything else in its place. And even that piece of destruction, which for long seemed permanent, proved transitory. The generation between 1790 and 1815 witnessed a revival of the German national spirit so strong that neither the settlement of 1815 nor the repressive régime which followed, was able to expunge it. Furthermore, this nationalism, born of the rancour engendered by French rule and French political domination and inspired by the consciousness of a

great German past, transcended the accredited system of particularist sovereignties, and looked beyond the existing states, none of
which fulfilled its aspirations, to a new Germany representative of
the German people.[1]

II

The settlement of 1815 set the stage for the political struggles of
the nineteenth century. Already in 1815 a clear-sighted observer,
surveying the balance established between Austria and Prussia,
remarked that the 'settlement must inevitably lead to a struggle for
supremacy in Germany'; but the fundamental issue at stake was less
the struggle for supremacy between Austria and Prussia than that
between the principles of unity and particularism. What Prussia
set out under Bismarck to overcome in the wars of 1866 and 1870
was the particularism enshrined in the Peace of Vienna; and its blows
were directed at Austria, and then at France, as the two mainstays of
German particularism, the two powers which had organized German territorial disunity in their own interests and to further their
own ends. But Prussian policy under Bismarck was designed to
further Prussian, not German, interests and to safeguard Prussia's
position as a great power; and it was only Bismarck's success that
gave general credence to the theory that Prussian self-preservation
and the cause of German unity were identical.[2] The Austro-
Prussian antithesis was long dormant, strictly subordinated both by

[1] This spirit was well expressed in a letter addressed in 1813 to the future historian, Johann
Friedrich Böhmer, by his father in an attempt to dissuade Böhmer from volunteering for
service against the French. 'Unhappily', he wrote, 'those fighting for the great patriotic
cause are not so much Germans as Bavarians, Württemberger, Hessians, Saxons, Nassauer,
Würzburger and even subjects of the petty state of Ysenburg. What our fortunes are under
so many paltry sovereigns bitter experience has taught us. In this respect, it seems to me that
enough is being done for the German princes, but nothing for the people. It is my heartfelt
conviction that the latter can only achieve happiness and well-being, if Germany constitutes
one great Reich . . . To this end no sacrifices would be too great, but so far this objective has
not been set before us' (Berney, op. cit., 67).

[2] Bismarck himself in his later life and writings propagated the theory that he had planned
from the beginning to unite Germany, and the official historians of the Hohenzollern Empire,
in particular Treitschke and Sybel, set themselves the task of proving that Prussia had always
been the nucleus of a united Germany and had aimed at unification consistently since 1815.
Already before 1918, however, German historians (e.g. Friedrich Meinecke and Erich
Brandenburg) had discredited the forced interpretations of Treitschke (*Deutsche Geschichte im
19. Jahrhundert*, Engl. trans. 1915-1919) and Sybel (*Die Begründung des deutschen Reiches*, Engl.
trans. 1890-1891), and after 1918 a more critical attitude towards their views, hitherto long
predominant, became general.

Metternich and by Frederick William III to princely solidarity against popular unrest and radical and nationalist agitation; but even when it emerged into the open, far from expressing in practical terms the problem of unity or particularism, the struggle between Austria and Prussia cut across that issue. At the time of the War of Liberation Fichte had sought to identify the cause of Prussia and German unity, but in the generation down to 1848 the overwhelming majority in the politically articulate classes looked to Austria, rather than Prussia, to provide the nucleus of a united German state. On the other hand, the strength of Austria's position in the day-to-day manœuvres of German politics lay in the support of the rulers of the small and medium states, who feared Prussian hegemony, and hoped with Austrian support to resist the movement for unification of which they would necessarily be the first victims. Hence the adherents of Austria comprised irreconcilable elements: conservatives intent only on maintaining the old order, and liberals bent on its destruction. And similar divergencies divided the adherents of Prussia; for where Fichte had envisaged the absorption of Prussia into Germany, a second school of thought (of which Niebuhr was protagonist) postulated the absorption of Germany into Prussia, a solution abhorrent to most liberals. Finally, there was a cleavage between liberalism and nationalism, in so far as many middle-class liberals, satisfied with conditions in the smaller states of southern and western Germany, which had undergone a process of administrative reform under French rule, were opposed to any change which, by destroying the identity of the principalities, might undermine the constitutional régime they enjoyed.

These extreme divergencies of aim exerted decisive influence after 1815. It was because of the disunity and still more the incompatibility of the various groups opposed to the Vienna settlement that the question of national unity was, under the influence of Metternich, so easily dismissed from the field of practical politics. There was no natural alignment between the movement for German unification and existing political forces, and so the movement could not make use of existing political combinations to help it forward. Nor could it, like the radical movement in nineteenth-century England, make use of rapid social and economic change. Germany in 1815 was still almost entirely an agricultural country with old-established handicrafts, such as the weaving of Silesia and the cutlery of Solingen, but without flourishing industries or a prosperous manufacturing class; and although in the next thirty years there was a rise in population amounting to no less than 38 per cent, the proportions of town and country dwellers remained virtually unchanged.[1] Few towns had recovered from the effects of the Thirty Years War and the stagnation of the eighteenth century, and at the beginning of the nineteenth century the total population of all the free cities and university towns of Germany was scarcely the equivalent of the population of Paris. Hence neither industrial capitalists nor industrial workers existed as a serious political force, and the towns were still, as in the eighteenth century, dominated by a professional and bureaucratic middle-class, which had little to gain by radical political change. These factors go far to explain the failure of the revolution of 1848-1849; but what is more remarkable is the persistence in such circumstances of a current of radical and national feeling strong enough, once the European situation was favourable, to kindle the sparks of revolution. As soon as the outbreak of revolution in France created the necessary external conditions, a spontaneous uprising against which the princely governments were helpless, took place simultaneously throughout the thirty-nine German states; and in this movement the old problem of national unity and particularism quickly came to the fore. It came to the fore inevitably because ever since the time of Stein it had been manifest that abrogation of the rights of the princes, and of the privileges of the aristocracy which were vested in the principalities, was the first necessary step towards securing the welfare of the German people: no reform was possible, no extension of civil rights, without a thorough revision of the federal system which, from the time of the Carlsbad Decrees (1819), had consistently been applied for the repression of civic liberties.

The attitude of disparagement and contempt once adopted by historians towards the revolution of 1848 — an attitude derived from implicit acceptance of Bismarck's famous judgement: 'The great questions of the day will be settled not by resolutions and majorities — that was the mistake of 1848 and 1849 — but by blood and iron' —

[1] Excluding the Austrian lands, population rose from 24,500,000 in 1816 to 34,000,000 in 1846. But whereas in Prussia 73.5 per cent of the population was classed as rural in 1816, no less than 72 per cent was similarly classified in 1846, and the rural population was still 71.5 per cent of the whole as late as 1852; cf. J. H. Clapham, *The Economic Development of France and Germany, 1815-1914* (1921), 82 sqq.

has given way to a more realistic appraisal of the facts, in which the positive achievements of the movement, and not merely its failure, receive due emphasis.[1] No historian is likely to underrate the failure of the liberals who controlled the Frankfurt parliament to attempt a transformation of 'real power-relations', to offer a social programme such as made the French revolutionary changes of 1789–1793 irrevocable. They strained too anxiously after legality, had too implicit a faith in constitutional schemes unaccompanied by changes in the seat of political power necessary to make them effective; they feared popular upheaval and hoped rather by the creation of a complicated machinery of checks and balances to reform the old order. With no independent power of their own, they were unable to oppose reaction, and as soon as the Prussian armies had reasserted control in Berlin, the fate of the movement was in the hands of the king of Prussia. With Prussian co-operation German unity was possible; without it there was no means of compelling the princes to accept the Frankfurt constitution. By 1849 this hard fact was understood, and a deputation was sent to offer the German crown (Austria excluded) to Frederick William IV. Frederick William's refusal to 'pick up a crown from the gutter' set the seal of defeat on the movement. A radical minority sought, too late, to stir up popular support, but Prussian arms easily suppressed popular risings in Saxony, the Bavarian Palatinate and Baden; and these risings, in any case, failed to secure the support of the liberal majority. On May 28th, 1849, sixty-five members quitted the Frankfurt assembly in a body, declaring that they were not prepared to foster civil war, and would therefore transfer the work of constitutional reform to the governments of the individual states, leaving the national cause to develop of itself. This was abdication, for the prospect of voluntary reforms within the principalities was negligible. The reformers had paid the penalty for their refusal to enlist popular support, to seize the 'victorious moment', and to stimulate a genuine social revolution. And yet it may be doubted, having regard to the backwardness of German social and economic development in 1848, whether a genuine attempt to 'go with the masses' offered any real prospect of success; in which case the failure of the Frankfurt parliament was due rather to circumstances beyond its control than to the deficiencies of

---

[1] Cf. the useful summary by J. A. Hawgood, 'The Frankfurt Parliament of 1848-1849', in *History*, XVII (1932).

its members and the dilatoriness of its procedure.[1] Economic and political conditions, very different from those in France and England, were scarcely favourable to an assertion of middle-class, still less of working-class power. The important fact about the revolution was therefore the very fact of revolution, of a true popular upheaval sweeping the whole of Germany. The movement of 1848-1849 proved with all finality that the issue of German unity was alive and could not be shelved. Despite all manœuvres under Austrian influence after 1850 to set the clock back, despite the restoration of the old Confederation in its old form, there was in fact no going back on the substantial results of 1848. The ideas and projects of 1848 dominated the mind of the next generation. How firm a hold they had taken was immediately evident when, in 1849, immediately after the triumph of conservative reaction in Prussia, Frederick William IV's minister, Radowitz, took up the ideas of the Frankfurt Assembly and, adapting them to Prussian interests, sought on the basis of the Frankfurt constitution to create a new federation embodying the essential points sought a few weeks earlier by the Frankfurt parliament when it offered the German crown to the king of Prussia. Radowitz's scheme, opposed by Austria and Russia, was no more successful than the Frankfurt programme; but its adoption was an important indication that the ideas of 1848-1849 had come to stay, and it is significant that Bismarck later approved Radowitz's policy and believed the opportunity favourable to Prussia. What Radowitz failed to do in 1850, Bismarck achieved in 1867; it was no accident that his North German Constitution of 1867 was in numerous places reminiscent of that of 1849. His debt to the work of 1848-1849, which cleared the road for Prussian action, was greater than he would have liked to admit. Nor, on the other hand, were the 'Fundamental Rights of the German People' — the *Grundrechte* formulated in 1848 — so ineffectual as has been supposed. It was easy for the Federal Diet in 1851 to decree them out of existence; but they remained as a practical statement of radical aims, and no sober minister could doubt the necessity of taking them into account. Here again Bismarck, most realistic and most far-seeing statesman of his age, paid an unconscious tribute to the work of

---

[1] So much may be said in criticism of Marx and Engels, *Revolution and Counter-Revolution in Germany* (1852) and of the Marxian arguments in Lassalle's *Ueber Verfassungswesen*; otherwise these are still the best analyses of the events of 1848.

1848-1849; he did not make the mistake of underestimating the strength of German liberalism. On the contrary, his very efforts to preserve the predominance of the Junker aristocracy in Prussia, and in particular the methods by which he pursued this inflexible objective, revealed his awareness of the seriousness of the inroads which the revolution of 1848-1849 had made upon the Junker position. On the surface, all was as before; but the revolution had failed primarily because it could not rely on the support of any existing political force, and if such support were forthcoming he well knew that it would be fatal both to Prussia's position in Germany and to the survival in Prussia of the military monarchy and of the Junker caste. When after 1861, Austria under Schmerling, the leader of the Austrian party at Frankfurt in 1848, reverted to a liberal policy, and began to press for a reform of the German confederation, and when in 1863 the Austrian emperor actually summoned all the German sovereigns to a congress at Frankfurt to establish a strengthened federal authority, the only way out for Prussia was war, and Bismarck spent the next three years in diplomatic and military preparation for the decisive struggle with Austria which broke out in 1866.

Bismarck thus realized that, despite the setback of 1848-1849, German liberalism and nationalism supported by Austria were still a serious threat to Prussian particularism and Prussian aristocratic privilege. To maintain the prerogatives of the Junker class a conservative alliance between Austria and Prussia against liberalism was necessary, such as had existed before 1848; against an alliance between Austria and the German nationalist movement, on the other hand, Prussia could only hold its own by enlisting the support of the whole Prussian people, and this implied a surrender to liberalism which would cut the roots of Junker power. In these circumstances Bismarck sought for long to obtain a conservative alliance with Austria; but it was a sign of his superb realism that, when this failed, he grasped the necessity for compromise on one score or the other with the forces of 1848. Inevitably it was the movement for national unity with which he came to terms. Liberalism was fatal to the social order for which Bismarck stood; but nationalism, carefully handled, could be made to subserve the purposes of Prussia. Thus Bismarck defeated the forces of 1848 by a policy of *divide et impera*. He separated German national aspirations from the liberal background which, from 1813 to 1848 and in centuries past, had given them meaning. Nationalism had grown strong as an instrument of liberal reform, as an essential means of breaking the stranglehold of particularist interests over the German people; Bismarck's achievement — an achievement which served only the purposes of the Prussian Junker class — was to make it an end in itself and turn it against its liberal past. In Bismarck's system nationalism, long the concomitant of liberalism, was deliberately fostered as an antidote to liberal and radical demands; he offered the German people unity, but at the expense of the radical reform which alone made unity worth while.

Bismarck's accession to power in 1862 was therefore a turning-point in the history of nineteenth-century Germany; his forceful personality, and still more his strategic mastery and firm grasp of political reality, brought into play a totally new approach to the age-old problem of German unity. The German leaders in 1848 had sought liberal reform and national unity, the latter primarily as a means to self-government; Bismarck was not interested in self-government and his approach was therefore different. The basis of his work was the revolutionary ferment of 1848-1849, firstly because the revolution had made the question of unity an issue which could not be shelved, and secondly because the projects of Schmerling, to which Bismarck's policy was a hostile reply, were an adaptation of the projects of the Frankfurt parliamentarians. But his methods were new and the foundations on which he built were utterly different. It was not simply that he, unlike the men of 1848, understood the virtues of 'blood and iron' and the futility of 'resolutions and majorities'; rather the contrast was that, pursuing objectives radically different from those of Bismarck, the leaders of the movement of 1848-1849 were not, whereas Bismarck was, prepared to make 'blood and iron' the basis of policy. Bismarck's aim — once he had given up hope of a renewed 'Holy Alliance' with Austria — was to achieve German unity without revolution so as to fend off the social consequences of successful revolution. For this task a firm grasp of the grim realities of power-politics, which the leaders in 1848 had disastrously neglected, was essential both in internal and in foreign relations. In 1848 revolution in Paris and Vienna had momentarily obviated the risk of foreign interference in Germany, and it was one of the tragedies of the failure that the politicians at Frankfurt were incapable of exploiting this unique opportunity to settle Germany's problems without foreign intervention; for in more normal circumstances not only France and Austria but Russia also had a direct interest in maintaining German backwardness and disunity. Hence there was small prospect except in times of revolution – and revolution was the last thing Bismarck wanted – of establishing German unity unless a favourable constellation of forces in Europe had previously been secured. For this reason Bismarck's energies were largely devoted to foreign affairs. The detail of this work must be ignored, although its importance was great. Its keystone was the convention of 1863 with Russia, which freed Bismarck's hands against Austria; while later the Czar acquiesced in Prussian plans in order, with Prussian support, to recover control over the Black Sea which Russia had lost after the Crimean War. Further stages were the exploitation of differences over Italy to divide Austria and France, and of French projects for the annexation of Belgium to divide France and England. Thus the possibility of the formation of a conservative *bloc* was obviated. Bismarck was fortunate also in having an unwitting accomplice in Louis Napoleon, whose inept and puerile diplomacy played into the Prussian minister's hands.[1] Without doubt, Bismarck's skilful manipulation of the European balance of power was the very foundation of Prussia's military successes against Austria in 1866 and against France in 1870; and these military successes were indispensable steps in the creation of German unity. Louis Napoleon had been prepared, for a moment, to support the formation of a major north German state around Prussia, provided France obtained 'compensations'; but this was a personal policy, for which he failed to secure French support, and in any case it did not extend to a union between Prussia and the German states south of the Main. The exclusion of Austria from Germany, and therewith the end of the crippling Austro-Prussian dualism which reached back to 1763, was a first-step; but German unity could not be secured without the defeat of France, the age-old protagonist of German particularism, and this fact fatally influenced the course of German unification. Prussia alone was powerful enough to unite Germany notwithstanding French opposition; and it was therefore no accident that the defeat of France and the

[1] For the detail of European diplomacy between 1862 and 1870, which cannot be considered here, cf. A. Debidour, *Histoire diplomatique de l'Europe*, II (1891), 248-401, and R.H. Lord, *The Origins of the War of 1870* (1924).

birth of a united Germany went together, and that the second German Empire was proclaimed by the victor at Versailles on January 18th, 1871, sixty-five years after the dissolution of the old Empire at the hands of Napoleon Bonaparte.

Many years before 1871 the Prussian militarist, Clausewitz, had ventured the opinion that there was 'only one way for Germany to attain political unity, and that is by the sword: one of the states must bring all others into subjection'. The wars of 1866 and 1870 seemed to prove him right. In many respects it is true that Germany was a Prussian conquest won at the expense of Austria and France. In 1866 German opinion as a whole was on the side of Austria, and even in Prussia, particularly in the Rhinelands, there was resistance to the war, including demonstrations in Berlin. In the Federal Diet all states not absolutely dominated by Prussian guns voted in condemnation of Prussia; and although this vote expressed primarily the opinion of the princes, it also represented liberal middle-class sentiment, which was alienated by Bismarck's unconstitutional government. There is therefore much truth in the view that Germany was 'conquered, not united'. And yet this is not the whole truth. Many long-standing factors worked in Prussia's favour, and it has been said with some justification that 'Germany was practically united before Bismarck began to work at all'.[1] Avoiding the mistakes of 1848-1849, Bismarck built his policy on the firm foundation of existing tendencies, making the most of the factors favourable to the Prussian cause. First among these was the fact that Austria was on the defensive, seeking to check Prussian ambitions, but unwilling herself to shoulder the burdens and responsibilities of German affairs; she was not a competitor herself for the German crown, which Francis I had refused in 1815, but only an opponent determined that the throne the Habsburgs had vacated in 1806 should remain vacant. Secondly, there was the territorial redistribution of Prussian power in the 1815 settlement: stretching from the Rhine to the Vistula, with considerable accretions of territory and a reformed and reinvigorated administration, she was in a position for the first time to close the gap between east and west and dominate the whole of the north German plain. But neither of these advantages was so important as the advent of the industrial revolution, which gave Germany both an overriding practical motive and the means for

[1] W. O. Henderson, 'The Zollverein', *History*, XIX (1934), 18.

unification, which had earlier been wanting. The *Zollverein* of 1834, the modelling of a unifying railway system and the German industrial revolution which began after 1850, were milestones along the road to the Bismarckian Empire of 1871 [1] They enhanced the sense of German unity, and both in that respect and as practical instruments of policy they were adroitly used by Prussia, which was fortunate in possessing the great coalfields of the Ruhr. When after 1850 these deposits were seriously exploited, they provided the foundation for an iron and steel industry which soon challenged the old-established industry of Bohemia. The result was that Prussia made rapid strides forward, quickly out-distancing Austria, which still remained predominantly rural in structure. Moreover, the prosperity between 1850 and 1871 greatly favoured Bismarck's policy. Just as in England after the Great Exhibition of 1851 the working-class movement entered on a generation of apathy, so in Germany the dawning of an age of plenty took the sting out of radical agitation; it seemed in both countries as though well-being and liberalism would be achieved by the blind working of beneficent economic forces, broadening from precedent to precedent, and that the radicalism of 1830-1848 had been no less misguided than unsuccessful. Thus a favourable economic environment made it more easy for Bismarck to dissociate nationalism from liberalism; the economic advantages of unification became more evident at the very moment when the benefits of prosperity made radical reform less urgent. This was an important point. Bismarck knew full well that, in opposition to Austria and France, German unity would have to be conquered; but in relation to the German people he wanted more than the victory of a conqueror, for only so could victory be made permanent. He realized as fully as the men of 1848-1849 the gulf between the national aspirations of 1790-1815 and the reality of the 1815 régime, and he spared no effort to enlist the disappointed hopes of the German people on the side of Prussia. That he succeeded was

[1] The British expert, Dr. John Bowring, who visited Germany on behalf of the Foreign Office in 1840, reported that 'the general feeling in Germany towards the *Zollverein* is that it is the first step towards what is called the Germanization of the people. It has broken down some of the strongest holds of alienation and hostility. By a community of interests on commercial and trading questions it has prepared the way for a political nationality – it has subdued much local feeling and habit and replaced them by a wider and stronger element of German nationality'. For railway development cf. Clapham, op. cit., 130 sqq. As early as 1828 Goethe wrote: 'I have no misgivings about the union of Germany; our good roads and future railways will do their share.'

due not least of all to the brief phase of prosperity during which his main work was accomplished. National unity without liberal reform would have satisfied no party before 1849, and it was no satisfaction to the German people later after the slump of 1873; but Bismarck had the advantage of circumstances and the skill to use his advantage. When, in 1866, after his victory over Austria, the Prussian parliament indemnified him by 230 votes to 75 for the unconstitutional collection of taxes without parliamentary assent since 1862, it was his first victory over liberalism, the first proof that — for a moment — national unity was rated higher than the benefits of self-government. This victory was driven home in the war with France. Exploiting the follies of Louis Napoleon, Bismarck united the German people, conscious of centuries of French aggression and countless humiliations, under Prussian leadership against France. He acted in the nick of time. Two years later, in 1873, the onset of economic depression again made social and economic problems more acute than national unity; but in the meantime the new order, of which the North German Confederation of 1867 had created the framework, was anchored fast in the constitution of 1871. That constitution set the seal on Bismarck's work.

The establishment of German unity, implicit in the sweeping revolutionary movement of 1848 and thereafter overpoweringly fostered by rapid economic change, was inevitable. What Bismarck did was to determine the particular form which it took, and the particular moment at which it occurred. His masterly diplomacy defeated the inveterate hostility of France, which might otherwise have postponed a decision for decades, and secured with a minimum of upheaval a result which might otherwise have necessitated European war and even revolution. His manipulation of the unitary forces within Germany, on the other hand, ensured that Germany should be united under Prussia. But for Bismarck the unification of Germany might have taken a radically different course. Hostility towards Prussia and fear of Prussian hegemony had been lively in 1848; and it was due to Bismarck alone, aided by social and economic developments which he put to good use, that after 1866 this hostility was overcome. The new Reich of 1871 — whatever the theory — was in practice a Prussian Reich, shaped to accord with Prussian interests, constructed in conformity with Prussian traditions, ruled by the dynasty of Hohenzollern, and dominated by the Prussian

Junker class. We may admire the steadfast logic with which Bismarck pursued his objects to the very end, the skill with which he triumphed over obstacles which had defeated generations of German statesmen, until the German nation — which in 1806 had been visible only in a transcendental unity of language and of culture — was united in a single political body; but the fact remains that the curse of German particularism was expunged only by the triumph of the most successful of German particularisms, which had no intention of disowning its own particular origins and traditions.

This was made evident by the constitution drawn up for the new Empire by Bismarck in 1871. It is usual, in analysing the constitution of 1871, to emphasize its federal character, pointing out that it betrays in every paragraph the conflicts of a thousand years of German history.[1] But the reality was otherwise. The federal rights retained by the states south of the Main, Bavaria in particular, were illusory, and such compromise as Bismarck sanctioned stopped short at a point which debarred them from an effective voice in imperial affairs. In the Federal Council, or Bundesrat, composed of representatives of the constituent states, Prussia had sufficient votes to veto constitutional change, but more important was the fact that the chancellor was under no necessity of consulting the council on any question of major political importance: during the crisis preceding the outbreak of war in 1914, for example, neither the Bundesrat nor the Reichstag was consulted, and on August 4th both the German people and the federal states were confronted with a *fait accompli*. The abrogation of particularism would, indeed, have been unexceptionable if it had meant the transfer of political power, in the spirit of 1848, from the princes to the people. But such was not the case.[2] There was no mention in the new constitution of the 'Fundamental Rights of the German People', on which the Frankfurt parliament of 1848-1849 had spent so much time and toil. The system contrived in 1871 included a Reichstag elected by universal and equal franchise; but its powers were limited. It could debate but not initiate legislation; it could in theory control expenditure, but

[1] Cf. Bryce, *Holy Roman Empire* (ed. 1910), 476 sqq.; A. L. Lowell, *Governments and Parties in Continental Europe*, I (1896), 232 sqq.; F. A. Ogg, *The Governments of Europe* (1919), 202 sqq.; H. Finer, *The Theory and Practice of Modern Government*, I (1932), 258 sqq.; J. A Hawgood, *Modern Constitutions since 1789* (1939), 238 sqq.
[2] The position was tersely summarized by Laband (*Das Staatsrecht des deutschen Reiches*, I, 91) when he described the Empire as 'composed not of 56,000,000 but of 25 members', i.e. the twenty-five member-states of the confederation; cf. Ogg, op. cit., 204.

it had no power of voting or refusing to vote taxes — the only effective means of exercising its theoretical control — since the imperial revenue was provided partly from permanent fixed duties, partly by *pro rata* contributions from the individual federal states. In Prussia, however, which had by far the largest population and therefore the heaviest responsibility in imperial finance, representation in the Diet was determined not, as in the Reichstag, by an equal franchise, but by the notorious three-class electoral system, which ensured permanent Junker domination.[1] Finally, the Reichstag had no control over the executive ministers, who were responsible only to the Prussian king who was also German emperor; it might vote against the chancellor, but only loss of the emperor's confidence, not an adverse vote, entailed his resignation. The German labour leader, Wilhelm Liebknecht, was therefore not wide of the mark in dubbing the Reichstag 'the fig-leaf of absolutism'; the system of government established in 1871 was, in fact, a veiled form of monarchical absolutism vested in the king of Prussia. But beneath this monarchical exterior, decked out with the trappings of representative democracy and federal balance, was the hard reality of the Junker class which — far more effectively than the Hohenzollern monarchy — exercised political influence through the Prussian Diet, wielded economic power through its control of the soil, and dominated imperial policy through its grip over the army and the bureaucracy. The real power of the state was wielded by the Prussian aristocracy: through Bismarck it became the dominant force not only in Prussian but also in German life. The constitution of 1871, fending off the realities of popular self-government, ensured both the preponderance of the Junkers in Prussia and the preponderance of Prussia in the Reich.

III

Bismarck's successes transcended but did not solve the great problems ventilated in 1848. With something of the skill of a gamester he had finessed the strong cards in his opponents' hands, bluffed his way against the insistent demand for radical reform, and saddled Germany with a constitution deliberately designed to

[1] In the elections for the Prussian Diet in 1908 no less than 600,000 votes were required to secure the return of six Social Democrat deputies, but 418,000 votes were sufficient to gain 212 Conservative seats.

conserve the military caste without which it was impossible in his view to keep the new Reich in being. It was a momentous fact that, due to Bismarck, Germany passed over into the new age of industrial and capitalist imperialism, which opened after 1871, shackled by its past as embodied in the new constitution. In the first place, the settlement of 1871, although it marked the end of the worst excesses of German particularism, in particular its nefarious tendency to ally with foreign powers,[1] failed to eradicate particularist tendencies; rather these took on a new lease of life in a new constitutional form, securing a measure of genuine popular support hitherto unknown as the expression of the resistance of the people in the more liberal regions, in Westphalia and Baden and Bavaria, to the Prussian spirit which henceforward dominated the government of the Reich. But more important still was the fact that Bismarck's constitution left intact and even consecrated the vested interests which had grown up with and profited from particularism; indeed, their conservation was the price inexorably extorted by Bismarck for the merging of Germany into one national state. Although Germany in 1871 secured unity, it was not a unity expressed in self-government by the German people; the new state was designed not to represent the will of the German people but to maintain, as in generations past, the subjection of the people to the will of a privileged minority.

It was another question whether Bismarck's settlement of 1871 would stand fast as a barrier against the insistent demand for improved working-conditions, the sweeping away of class prerogatives and the introduction of self-government. Bismarck had hoped that it would mark a halting-place, introducing a phase of quiet consolidation; but in fact the new uniformity of administration, the abrogation of internal tariff barriers and the removal of trade restrictions, which followed on unification, inaugurated a period of rapid development in all facets of German life which could not be confined within the rigid structure of the new Empire. In the economic sphere, in particular, the progress of industrialization

[1] After 1871 there was no revival of the connexion between German particularism and foreign states, which had been so dangerous a factor in German politics in earlier generations; nor was there, either in 1918 or in 1945 any spontaneous movement of separatism. The 'autonomous Government' set up in the Rhine-Palatinate after 1918 by 'an insignificant group of renegades' owed its existence entirely to French intrigue, and collapsed as soon as France — under British pressure — withdrew its support; cf. W. O. Henderson, *History*, XXVI (1941), 63.

was stupendous; and the rapid growth of an industrial working-class resulted, as always, in a parallel increase in the political consciousness of the masses. Bismarck's work, far from ending the German revolution, as he intended, released forces beyond his control. The balance he had contrived worked satisfactorily so long as the favourable economic environment in which the new Reich was born persisted. But the slump of 1873 was a first warning of the precariousness of the balance; and within a few months, as is well known, Bismarck himself lost faith in the stability of his system and began the feverish but hopeless task of erecting new props to hold it up. In the first place, he sought to broaden the basis of the system by admitting the upper middle classes, in particular the great industrialists, to the inner circle of privilege. The alliance of 1867 with the National Liberals was cemented by the economic depression, which made the industrialists willing to pay the necessary price for governmental support; the instrument used was the Protective Tariff of 1879, in exchange for which the most powerful and influential section of the liberal party entered the government *bloc*. The agrarian tariffs introduced simultaneously won over the smaller farmers and the peasantry, hitherto — in opposition to the Junker landowners — steadfastly liberal. Thus Bismarck contrived to carry on and with the support of a parliamentary majority to launch an attack on the working classes, which — in consequence of the abdication of the liberals — constituted the only force in Germany with a practical and vital interest in the attainment of democracy. It was a two-sided attack. In the first place the Social Democratic party, only founded in 1875, and the free Trade Union movement, only legalized in 1869, were outlawed by anti-Socialist legislation in 1878; the party organization was proscribed, its newspapers suppressed and hundreds of leading members thrown into prison. In the second place, Bismarck sought to take the sting out of labour agitation by the introduction of extensive schemes of social security; between 1883 and 1889 compulsory insurance for workers against sickness, accident, old age, etc., was introduced in the hope of bribing the working classes into quiescence. Neither repression nor cajolery was a success. Organized labour realized that it owed the benefits of Bismarck's social legislation ultimately to the Social Democrat party and its political pressure; and the party continued to grow. Even at the Reichstag elections of 1884, in the heat of the conflict, the Social

Democrats increased their vote. The elections of 1890 proved the bankruptcy of Bismarck's system. Twelve years of persecution resulted in a doubling of the Social Democrat vote, which rose to one and a half millions, and an increase in the number of labour members from twelve to thirty-five. Trades Union membership increased similarly from around 50,000 in 1877 to 278,000 in 1891. The election of 1890 was almost a landslide. The right-wing coalition dropped from 220 to 135; the opposition rose from 141 to 207. Bismarck had exhausted all expedients and knew one remedy alone: to abrogate the constitution, to limit the franchise and to drive the Social Democrats completely out of existence. It was a counsel of desperation, involving serious danger of revolution and civil war, and the new emperor, William II, who had succeeded to the throne in 1888, was not prepared to imperil his dynasty in such a gamble. In March 1890, Bismarck was dismissed.

The fall of Bismarck revealed with dramatic abruptness the rising social tension within the Reich; it showed that the forces and ideals of 1848 could not so easily be circumvented as Bismarck had once believed. But it was after Bismarck's fall, during the four years of the 'New Course' between 1890 and 1894, that the intensity of social antagonisms and the inherent instability of the Bismarckian Reich became fully manifest. William II — optimistically underestimating the strength of the opposition — hoped, by sacrificing Bismarck, to conciliate the German people without genuine concessions to radicalism. But Caprivi, who followed Bismarck as chancellor, was a man of undoubted good will, genuinely desirous of following a more liberal course. In foreign affairs he refused to renew the alliance with Russia, which for many was the symbol of Germany's alignment with the forces of reaction, and sought instead to reach understanding with France and England. In the same spirit he set up in the eastern provinces of Prussia an administration which was favourable to the Polish element in the population, thereby offending both the Czar and the Prussian Junker class, and modified Bismarck's protective system in the interests of the industrial workers, hoping as a result of good relations with England and France to import foodstuffs from abroad instead of subsidizing German agriculture. The corollary of this liberal economic policy and of co-operation with western European liberalism was liberalism at home. In the first place, Caprivi refused to renew Bismarck's anti-socialist laws, with the result that the Social Democrat vote again increased in 1892. Secondly, he proposed to reduce military service from three to two years, and cut the period of the army grant from seven to five years — a token of his rejection of the militarism of 'blood and iron'. Finally by resigning the Prussian premiership he severed the connexion of the Reich government and Prussia which had been the basis of Bismarck's system, with the intention of reducing Prussia to an equality with the other states and eliminating the Prussian predominance in Germany by which the whole organization of German political life had been perverted. Without doubt Caprivi's progressive policy offered the only prospect of a peaceful evolution of German political life. But it immediately awakened the violent opposition of all classes and factions which had seen in Bismarck's policy a guarantee of their interests; and the constitution of 1871, so long as it remained in force, assured their preponderance in the state. The opposition centred round the question of Prussia. Caprivi's liberalism, his refusal to continue the attack on Social Democracy and his commercial policy, were repugnant to the powerful industrialists; but it was the agrarian interests east of the Elbe which he really injured. In 1894 he came into open conflict with the prime minister of Prussia, who had the solid backing of the Junker class. The only effective remedy would have been far-reaching constitutional change, above all else the transformation of Prussia into a democratic state by the abolition of the iniquitous three-class franchise; but such a course which would have implied revolutionary upheaval, was impossible against the emperor — of whom the chancellor was, according to the constitution of 1871, the servant — and Caprivi never contemplated it. Yet under the constitution of 1871 it was impossible to rule against Prussian opposition, and the breach with Prussia therefore meant stalemate. At the end of 1894 Caprivi passed into oblivion.

If the fall of Bismarck in 1890 was due fundamentally to the strength of German radicalism, over which he had attempted to ride roughshod, the fall of Caprivi in 1894 was due to the strength of German reaction. Taken together, the two events were a revelation of the deadlock in which Germany had been placed by the settlement of 1871. So long as the growing popular forces were excluded from government, there could be no stability for the Reich. But so long as political and social power remained in the hands of the old order, there was no hope of peaceful evolution; for the privileged classes resisted any alteration of the constitution of 1871, which was their charter of privileges, for fear that the flood-waters of radicalism, bursting through the breach, would tear down the whole dam. Moreover, Bismarck's tactical success in 1879 in winning over the liberal industrialists, heightened the tension; for it meant that the liberal middle classes which elsewhere — for example, in England — were driven by their impelling interests to assume leadership in the fight for political democracy, in Germany sided with the forces of reaction. Unlike the British labour movement, which, after the period of Chartism, never had to fight for political democracy, but simply stepped into the liberal inheritance, the German labour movement had to concentrate all its energies on the struggle for democracy; and this struggle was a fight not within but against the existing constitution, which was deliberately designed to place power in the hands of a privileged minority. By allying with heavy industry, Bismarck increased a hundredfold the powers of resistance of this minority. Alone, the Junkers could scarcely have held out more than a few years longer; in alliance with the industrialists their power was practically unchallengeable. And yet in another sense Bismarck's tactical success resulted inevitably in a weakening of Junker predominance. In the coalition with the rising industrialists who controlled the sinews of economic power, the needy Junker landlords could not hope to hold their own; they retained their social prerogatives and their control of the army, but as well-paid servants of the capitalist classes, into whose hands after 1879 the effective government of the Reich passed by rapid stages. After 1890, still more after 1894, German policy was the policy of the industrial and commercial capitalists who exploited their position in the coalition to use the coercive power of government to hold the working-classes in check, to destroy competition and to secure markets abroad. In this way Germany was launched along the road of capitalist imperialism. Much against his will, Bismarck was forced between 1884 and 1890 to join with Great Britain and France in the scramble for territories in Africa[1] — a development

---

[1] He resisted the pressure of commercial and financial interests from 1876 to 1884, saying that 'for Germany to acquire colonies would be like a poverty-stricken Polish nobleman providing himself with silks and sables when he needed shirts'. In fact the colonies acquired were useless for emigration and their exploitation was expensive and uneconomical; as late as 1914 the area of 1,026,220 square miles acquired by Germany (as against 4,754,000 square miles

which contributed, a decade later, to the demand for a great navy
and from 1900 to the naval competition with Great Britain. Still
more important, however, was the pressure of the industrialists on
the government to find an outlet for the products of heavy industry.
The result was the beginning of a phase of economic warfare which,
in conflict with rival imperialisms, culminated in the outbreak of
European war in 1914.

The development of the European crisis from 1894 to 1914 is a
process which we can do no more than illustrate.[1] In Germany, as
elsewhere, it was quickened by the simultaneous growth of internal
tension; indeed, it is scarcely an exaggeration to state that it was
largely accidental whether the attempt to save the old order would
take the form of a frontal attack on the forces of democracy at home
or of a successful war which, by opening new markets and destroying foreign competition, would reaffirm the stability of the existing
system in the face of internal unrest. All parties in all countries were
aware that internal and foreign affairs were but two aspects of one
and the same problem; hence in all countries organized labour was
before 1914 the protagonist of pacifism and internationalism against
the self-styled 'national' parties. But of no organized party in
Europe was this more true than of the German Social Democrats,
for the simple reason that in no country west of the Vistula had the
working classes more to lose from a successful imperialist war.
After the fall of Caprivi in 1894 the foundation of brute force on
which Junker-industrialist power rested, and the impossibility of
compromise were manifest, and it was evident that only a social
revolution could shake the existing system. But, as Engels pointed

acquired by England and 3,583,580 square miles acquired by France at the same period) contained only about 5,000 permanent German inhabitants. As the Social Democrats never ceased
to point out, the only people who benefited from the colonies were the capitalists; but the
large profits which the trading companies made were paid for many times over by the
German tax-payers, who had to foot the bill for the subsidies by which the colonies were kept
going. Cf. W. O. Henderson, 'The German Colonial Empire, 1884-1918', History, XX (1935).
151-158.
[1] There are good, trustworthy accounts in J. A. Spender, Fifty Years of Europe (1933), E.
Brandenburg, From Bismarck to the World War (1930), A. F. Pribram, England and the International Policy of the European Great Powers, 1871-1914 (1931), G. Lowes Dickinson, The
International Anarchy, 1904-1914 (1937), S. B. Fay, The Origins of the World War (1929).
Particularly valuable are the various writings of G. P. Gooch; his History of Modern Europe, 1878-
1919 (1923), suffers from having been written before many of the documentary sources had
been published, but it has been supplemented and revised in a number of volumes of important
essays (Before the War, Recent Revelations of European Diplomacy, 1930, etc.), which are marked
by exceptional sobriety of judgement; cf. especially the essay on 'Franco-German Relations,
1871-1914', Studies in Diplomacy and Statecraft (1942), 1-59.

out in 1895, the development of military technique – in particular the invention of the machine-gun – had destroyed all prospect of successful revolutionary upheaval against loyal troops. Hence the only hope of introducing democracy lay in the shattering of the existing system by its own inherent contradictions. These contradictions were more developed in Germany than elsewhere, except perhaps in Russia. The privileges enjoyed by the Junkers were of a type which had been swept away in France in 1789 and had scarcely existed in England even before the seventeenth-century revolution. The power of the industrialists, on the other hand, was built on unstable foundations; for German heavy industry, because it arrived late on the scene, was a top-heavy structure, extremely sensitive to economic trends and unable to maintain itself without lavish government support. So long as capitalist expansion was maintained and economic prosperity grew, it was possible to placate the working-classes and to circumvent political demands by concessions to popular interests, in particular by concessions to the trades unions on questions of hours and wages. But, on the one hand, such a policy only postponed the day of reckoning, for organized labour was not weaned from radicalism by such methods – on the contrary, the Social Democratic party continued to grow, rising by 1903 to 3,000,000 out of a total of 9,000,000 voters. On the other hand, the knowledge that they were swimming against a flood, which would burst its banks at the first moment the wheels of the capitalist machine slowed down, drove the parties in possession to adopt ever more violent methods of maintaining expansion, leading to conflict and acute tension in the field of foreign politics. Even this tension, however, served its purpose in so far as it could be used to divert the attention of the German people from the enemy at home to the enemy abroad. Hence, in line with parallel interests in England and France, German industrialists and conservatives began to organize and finance 'patriotic' societies – the Pan-German League, the Colonial Society, the Navy League – in order both to create a fictitious 'national' solidarity against the foe without and to justify ever-expanding armaments programmes, without which industry could no longer pay its way. Between 1909 and 1914 the cost of British armaments increased by more than 30 per cent, of Russian armaments by 53 per cent, of German armaments by 69 per cent, while the cost of French armaments soared to no less than 86 per cent above the earlier figure. The 'defence' expenditure of the six European great powers, which in 1883 had totalled £140,000,000, reached in 1913 the figure of £404,000,000.

After the fall of Caprivi in 1894 all the tendencies outlined above — in particular the tendency to turn to foreign adventure as a distraction from the insoluble problems of internal politics — gained the upper hand. The tension was such that no statesman could control it, and in fact no statesman made the attempt; they were satisfied if only they could open valves to let off some of the pressure. In these circumstances policy gave place to an endless series of expedients and manœuvres, lacking either principle or coherence, with no object except to maintain as long as possible the actual distribution of power and postpone the dissolution of the existing régime. On the one side, it was essential, if necessary by renewed concessions, to keep the support of the Junkers and industrialists who had demonstrated in their victory over Caprivi the impossibility, under the existing system, of governing without their support. On the other side, since it was clear that the forces in possession would tolerate no step towards self-government, the German people had somehow to be reconciled to the autocratic régime. It was an impossible task, but it was the task assigned — after the brief interlude of Hohenlohe, whose policy amounted only to undoing what Caprivi had done — to Eulenburg and Bülow, who became secretary of state in 1897 and chancellor in 1901. To follow the detail of their policy, or that of Bülow's successor, Bethmann-Hollweg, who became chancellor in 1909, is neither possible nor necessary, for the die was already cast in 1894. The bankruptcy of imperial policy thereafter was implicit in Eulenburg's own definition of his aims: 'to satisfy Germany without injuring the Emperor'. Since the satisfaction which Germany desired was the transformation of imperial autocracy into popular self-government and the destruction of the privileges of the Junker class on which the emperor's power rested, this was a policy of reconciling irreconcilables. In fact, the attempt at reconciliation was only superficial. All the substantial concessions went to the Junkers and industrialists — to the former tax rebates and credits and the new tariff of 1902, to the latter the naval programme of 1900 and the consequent government contracts — and to Bülow was left the task of fobbing off the people by a demonstrative foreign policy, designed to secure

THE EMPIRE, THE PRINCIPALITIES AND THE PEOPLE   433

solidarity and submission with the cry: 'the fatherland in danger'. But Bülow's foreign policy, the ineptitude of which is proverbial,[1] failed in its purpose. The Morocco crisis of 1905-1906 was followed immediately by a defeat of the military estimates in the Reichstag; the famous incident of the Kaiser's *Daily Telegraph* interview in 1908, in which he painted a totally false picture of the strength of anti-British sentiment in Germany, provoked such a storm that William II had to announce that, in future, he would cease meddling in foreign affairs, and 'respect his constitutional obligations'. But the culmination was reached when, after the second Morocco crisis in 1911, the general elections of 1912 resulted in an outstanding victory for the Social Democrats — the party which throughout had steadfastly refused to vote for the army and navy estimates — which with 4,250,000 votes became the largest single party in the Reichstag. More important, perhaps, was the fact that the middle-class parties at last made up their minds to co-operate with the Social Democrats. The crisis was brought to a head in the following year by the famous Zabern affair, in which the whole country united in protest against Prussian militarism. When the commander of the garrison in this petty Alsatian town arrested and imprisoned some of the inhabitants in defiance of the law, his exhibition of military arrogance stirred all Germany. The chancellor, Bethmann-Hollweg, although convinced that the military were in the wrong, attempted to defend them in the Reichstag. When he was defeated by a vote of 293 to 54, the fig-leaf attached by Bismarck fell off and the naked-ness of the power on which government depended, was exposed. Bethmann remained chancellor, the military commander at Zabern was even acquitted by court-martial; but the sole reason was because under the existing constitution there was no means of giving effect to the will of the German people. The Zabern affair, following on the Social Democratic victory in 1912, left no doubt of the serious-ness of the crisis within Germany; the long-postponed day of judgement was near.

It is important not to underrate the connexion between the Social Democratic victory in 1912, the Zabern crisis in 1913 and the out-break of European war in 1914. The sweeping tide of Social Demo-cracy, the growing revolt against internal conditions, profoundly

---

[1] Cf. Haller, *France and Germany* (1932), 252, 255, 259, 263, summarizing the views of his earlier work, *Die Aera Bülow* (1922).

alarmed the ruling classes in Germany; and there is little room for
doubt that one reason why, in the words of a competent French
authority, 'the German military aristocracy decided in July 1914
to run the risk of a great European war' was 'a growing sense of dis-
comfort under the increasing pressure of Social Democracy, and a
surmise that a bold attempt to give a set-back to Socialism, by asserting themselves once more as the party of war and victory, might
prove the wisest course'.[1] Such a calculation – no doubt less
conscious than implicitly fostered by the threatening atmosphere –
was, of course, not operative by itself; it has to be considered in
connexion with the international situation, and with the desire of the
German militarists to forestall Franco-Russian preparations for war,
which (as was well known among the European cabinets) were timed
to mature in 1915.[2] In international affairs the decisive factor was
the situation in the Balkans, where Russia, 'having stolen a march
on Austria through the success of the Balkan League',[3] had changed
the balance of power, and was preparing, after the conclusion of the
Second Balkan war in 1913, further alterations in her own favour.
Such changes, aimed directly at Austria, were an indirect blow at
Germany, which, as the German foreign secretary pointed out in
an able exposition of the German point of view written in July 1914,[4]
could not passively watch 'the establishment of absolute Russian
hegemony in the Balkans'. Nevertheless the growing tension in
south-east Europe, and the Russian threat to German political and
commercial interests in this area, is not alone a sufficient explanation
of the drift towards war, and its outbreak in August 1914. During
the Balkan wars in 1912-1913 Germany had exercised a strong restrain-
ing influence over Austria under considerable provocation, although
militarily Austro-German prospects were good; in 1905-1906 at the
time of the first Morocco crisis, and in 1908 during the crisis over

---

[1] Cf. E. Halévy, *The World Crisis of 1914-1918* (1930), 11. – This attitude was not, of course,
confined to Germany; for England cf. Halévy, *History of the English People 1895-1914*, I, 259,
and E. Wingfield-Stratford, *The Victorian Aftermath*, 310 ('if the war peril from Germany
delayed much longer to materialize, it seemed quite on the cards that it might be forestalled by
revolution. As the Edwardian passes into the Georgian age ... class rises against class ...
faction against faction – it is a question whether international will not be anticipated by civil
war').

[2] Cf. the report of the conversation of the Serbian minister in London with the French
ambassador in December 1911, printed in Lowes Dickinson, op. cit., 214.

[3] R. C. K. Ensor, *England, 1870-1914* (1936), 573; cf. ibid., 463 sqq.

[4] *Die deutschen Dokumente zum Kriegsausbruch* (ed. in collaboration with K. Kautsky by
Graf Max Montgelas and Prof. W. Schücking) I (1919), 99-101 (no. 72); cf. Lowes Dickinson,
op. cit., 413-415.

Bosnia-Herzegovina, when Russia was suffering from revolution and defeat at the hands of Japan, the prospects of the central powers were brighter still. If the German imperial government which, for all its threats, had no serious intention of provoking war during these earlier crises, was prepared in 1914 to risk a general conflagration, it was not least of all because the internal situation was by this time such that it could not afford even the appearance of a diplomatic setback, which would have condemned it in the eyes of its 'nationalist' supporters and strengthened the opposition. What impelled it along the road of greater risks after 1912 was the situation at home. Bethmann had, after the Social Democrat victory, undertaken to reform the Prussian franchise— the bone of internal discord — but only with the idea of gaining time. In these circumstances any further failure was bound to have disastrous repercussions, and it is significant that in the important dispatch referred to above, the German foreign secretary urged the necessity of supporting Austria against Russia 'both for internal and external reasons'. Even in 1914, of course, there was no deliberate intention of provoking European war. Gambling in part on the equivocal attitude of Great Britain, the German government hoped — as all imperialisms hope in such circumstances — for a diplomatic success to justify it in the eyes of the people. It is no part of our task to explain why this was impossible; one factor was without doubt the intense naval rivalry with Great Britain, which cemented the alliance between England, France and Russia. The outcome was that during July 1914, Europe — betrayed by contrary councils and conflicting interests in all the European capitals — broke up into two armed camps and drifted into war.

All historians who have examined the evidence in detail are agreed that responsibility for the outbreak of war in 1914 cannot be placed exclusively on the shoulders of any one government; there was none which was not willing at that stage to use war in the last resort as an instrument of national policy. We have done no more than consider one or two of the factors which affected the calculation of the German government; to trace the development of the crisis in its European ramifications, it would be necessary to do likewise for the other governments involved, which were all beset in greater or lesser degree by the same problems as the ministers of William II. It must also be observed that the factors at play were in their very nature factors influencing the governments and not the peoples; just as the British government desisted from taking parliament into its confidence until August 3rd, by which time the die was cast, so the German government, as has already been noted,[1] sedulously avoided consulting either the Bundesrat or the Reichstag. The result was that war was sprung upon an opinion unprepared, after many false alarms, for the reality of war; and in all countries the people, succumbing to nationalist propaganda, rallied to the nationalist cause against the foe without. In Germany this volte-face was facilitated by the fact that the war was represented as a struggle for the defence of civilization against Czarist despotism, against 'the dark Asiatic power' which (as Marx had said) lay 'in the background as a last resource against the advancing tide of working-class democracy'. In the Social Democrat declaration of August 4th, 1914, announcing the party's majority decision to vote for the war credits, the emphasis lay on the danger of 'a victory of Russian despotism which has soiled itself with the blood of the best of its own people'; compared with the barbarism of Russian Czardom, Hohenzollern absolutism was, for the German worker, the lesser evil. It was a difficult decision — far more difficult than that facing the democratic forces in England and France which had at any rate a clear-cut issue between parliamentary and absolutist imperialism — and it is not easy, reviewing the circumstances, to condemn it out of hand. Nevertheless it ultimately split the Social Democratic party. More important, the German workers' recovery from the initial war fever was rapid; they soon realized that a victory for Hohenzollern imperialism would be scarcely less disastrous for them than defeat by France and Russia. Hence, in spite of ruthless repression, the anti-war movement gained ground more quickly in Germany than elsewhere. Already in March 1915, more than a quarter of the Social Democrats in the Reichstag refused to vote for the war credits, and a few weeks later, in June 1915, an open letter signed by nearly a thousand well-known members of the Social Democratic party denounced the war policy of the majority. At the same period, Karl Liebknecht issued his famous leaflet with the title: 'The Main Enemy Stands at Home'. A year later, on June 17th, 1916, the labour representation in the Prussian diet put forward a motion which, after indicting the German Government, went on to declare:

[1] Above, p. 423.

We do not see our well-being in the creation of an imperialist Greater Germany, or of a Mitteleuropa, but in mutual political and economic relations between the nations, fostered by the extension of democracy, the abolition of secret diplomacy and by agreements aiming at the abolition of customs barriers. As international Social Democrats, faithful to our principles, we will never take responsibility for the infringement of the political and economic independence of other nations or for their oppression. For we feel the sufferings of the workers of the countries confronting us to-day as enemies as deeply as we feel the sufferings of our own people. . . . The common people of no country have willed the war. . . . If the governments of the belligerent countries still refuse to make peace, they act in antagonism to the great masses of the population who long to return to peaceful work. . . . We demand that the German government, before all other governments, should take the first step and should relinquish their plans of conquest, thus paving the way for peace. The war and its course have stigmatized the imperialist system of force before the eyes of the world. Peace and civilisation cannot be secured by the force of bayonets, by conquest and oppression, but only by the solidarity of the workers of all countries.

This was the authentic voice of the German people; and the fact that it was raised in 1916, more than a year before the entry of the United States into the war, at a time when Germany's armies stood firm in France and Russia, is itself sufficient to disprove the ill-considered assertion that the growing demonstrations against the policy of the German government were simply manifestations of war-weariness and defeatism. In face of the coercive machinery of the state and the massive force of official propaganda, such protests were, of course, long ineffective; but three events gave them political weight. The first was the Russian revolution in March 1917, which gave new confidence to the workers in all countries, in particular in Germany. The second was the peace of Brest-Litovsk, imposed on Russia by the German High Command, which by opening the eyes of the German people to the unrepentant imperialism of their government, created a revolutionary atmosphere throughout the country. The third was President Wilson's enunciation, on January 7th, 1918, of the 'Fourteen Points', which—for those who were not aware that they constituted for England and France only (in the words of Wilson's confidant, Colonel House) 'an

admirable tool of propaganda' – appeared to offer a substantial basis
for a just peace. These events stimulated the German people to
proceed from protests and manifestos to action. In April 1917, a
great strike involving two hundred thousand workers took place
in Berlin and Leipzig, the main demands of the strikers being the
introduction of a democratic régime and immediate peace negotiations on the basis of 'no annexations'. More serious and more widespread were the munition workers' strikes in January 1918 – a
direct reply of the German people to the insolence and intransigence of the German negotiators at Brest-Litovsk – which occurred
at the very moment when Ludendorff was preparing his last gigantic
thrust against France, the famous spring offensive of 1918 designed
to secure a final German victory. The strikes were suppressed by
force; but they constituted none the less a clear manifestation of the
spirit of the German people, which at this critical period ignored the
appeals of the government to give all their strength for the last
decisive blow, and sought instead a peace of reconciliation on the
basis of the Fourteen Points. To the enduring credit of the German
people, the final overthrow of Hohenzollern imperialism was in no
small measure the result of the distrust and overt opposition maintained by German labour organizations.[1] The failure of Ludendorff's
spring offensive created the conditions for a renewal of the German
opposition, quelled in January 1918; and the German High Command, aware of the imminence of revolution, hastened to conclude
an armistice while the army was still intact. This decision was made
more urgent by the collapse of Bulgaria in September 1918, and the
crumbling of the Austrian front; complete military defeat, although
not yet a fact, was within sight and Ludendorff knew that a defensive
war – which, in the judgement of the French experts, was still
militarily possible – could not be fought in view of the revolutionary spirit in Germany. It was a typical decision that he determined
to make peace with the Entente before the army disintegrated, and
thus to conserve the armed forces as a political factor for use in
Germany. At the end of September the High Command abdicated

[1] Thus H. W. V. Temperley, *History of the Peace Conference* I (1920), 213; cf. also General
Smuts' view (in his pamphlet, *The League of Nations*, 14): 'The German battlefront collapsed
the more readily before Foch because the scandalous Brest-Litovsk Treaty had thoroughly
disillusioned and demoralized the German people.' How enduring was the impression created
in Germany by Brest-Litovsk is indicated by Hitler's confession (recorded by Fraser, *Germany
between Two Wars*, 42) that his attempts, at a later date, to stir up popular resentment against
the Versailles Treaty were met by the cry: 'And Brest-Litovsk?'

the dictatorial powers which it had exercised since 1916 and a constitutional government was set up under Prince Max of Baden with the avowed object of securing peace on the basis of the Fourteen Points; on November 11th, 1918, an armistice was concluded.

Only military defeat, neutralizing the armed power on which government rested, could destroy the rigid system of class domination and Prussian hegemony which Bismarck had fastened on the body of Germany in 1871. At no time between 1871 and 1918 was revolution within the bounds of practical politics; and internal revolution was the only alternative to military defeat as a means of getting rid of the system. Peaceful evolution under a parliamentary régime, which in England offered the people a constitutional means of making their aspirations heard and their interests felt, was excluded by the very character of the German constitution of 1871 which was designed, under the simulacrum of parliamentary government, to prevent peaceful evolution; this was evident — although many contemporary observers, particularly in England, failed to perceive it — in every crisis from 1894 to 1913. Undoubtedly the Bismarckian Reich, although eventually it rested on bare force, corresponded to and satisfied the interests of certain important groups in Germany; apart from the Junkers, to perpetuate whose power it was contrived, it furthered the interests of the powerful industrial and commercial classes, and could usually count after 1890 on the support of the Catholic Centre Party and the equivalent party in Bavaria, which regarded it as a bulwark against social changes anathematized by the church. It was a rallying-point for all who had something to lose by popular government working for the interests of the people. More ominous for the future was the fact that an element in the labour and trades union movement, observing the indisputable improvement of wages and working conditions under the stimulus of capitalist expansion, was prepared to compromise with the existing system, in the belief that it could, by steady pressure, gradually be transformed into a political and social democracy. But such views, scarcely even warranted under English political conditions, were a delusion in imperialist Germany; and they were consistently rejected by the majority of Social Democrats. It was possible to maintain — as one of the minority wrote during the war years — that 'the ruin of German industry would be the ruin of the German working-class'; but the working-classes themselves, as they demonstrated in the political strikes which began in 1916, believed on the contrary that a victory for German imperialism and for German capitalism would be as crushing a defeat for them as for the workers in the enemy lands; it would rivet more firmly the privileges of the self-styled 'nationalist' classes and give a new lease of life to the constitution which in practice disfranchised the workers. Hence from 1917 onwards the anti-war movement grew. After the issue of the Fourteen Points defeat was not regarded with fear; for Wilson's declaration contained the promise of a saner international order, in which the German people, with the promise of democracy and self-determination, could take its place. The end of the war thus seemed to betoken the dawn of a new era under a republican government, expressing the will and promoting the interests of the German people; the defeat of Prussian militarism and of all that went with it seemed for the first time to offer the German people the opportunity of moulding its own destiny.

IV

The hopes and expectations roused in 1918 by the defeat of Hohenzollern militarism were doomed to disappointment; the opportunity to remodel German society and German political life in a new international framework was missed. Three main factors explain the failure. First, the army, the unswerving guardian of the old order, although defeated on the field of battle, remained in existence, a potent reactionary factor in German politics. Secondly, the German people was not left free to reshape German society on democratic lines; instead it was subjected to Allied pressure and, at many important points, to Allied veto, and the creation of an efficient government capable of expressing the will of the German people was subordinated to the national interests of the victorious Entente. Thirdly, the German leaders who emerged after the flight of William II on November 9th, 1918, proved totally incapable of rising to the magnitude of the tasks facing them; instead of placing themselves at the head of the revolutionary forces which the military failure had released, and carrying through a total reorganization of German society, they sought to steer a cautious middle course and let slip the opportunity for fundamental change which alone could have assured the prevalence of the strong democratic forces in Germany.

Nothing was clearer, after the experiences of the period 1871-1918, than the fact that without a real shift in economic and social power, transferring political initiative from the Junkers and capitalist interests to the people, the introduction of a lasting democratic régime was impossible. The revolution which began on November 3rd, 1918, with the naval mutiny at Kiel and spread rapidly through the whole country between November 6th and 9th, opened up the immediate prospect of fundamental change; for it was a spontaneous movement directed by workers' and soldiers' councils elected everywhere in workshops, mines, docks and barracks, and this movement, at its first congress in December 1918, formulated demands which included the socialization of key industries and, pending its replacement by a people's militia, a purge of the army. If put into effect, this programme would, without doubt, have brought about the fundamental shift in economic and political power which was the essential pre-condition for the success of the whole revolutionary movement. But it was not put into effect. Gröner, who had replaced Ludendorff on October 26th as quartermaster-general, informed the government that he and the entire High Command would resign immediately, if the workers' proposals were put into effect; and before this ultimatum the government, although it was a Social Democratic government nominated by the workers' and soldiers' councils, capitulated. Instead of proceeding to the immediate socialization of industry at the moment when the workers' councils were in effective control of the workshops, it set up a 'Socialization Commission' with employers' and workers' representatives, which naturally failed to reach agreement and soon faded ineffectually out of existence. Instead of partitioning the great estates east of the Elbe, it appointed another commission to study the problem. Instead of convoking immediately a national assembly, it decided to hold elections on January 19th, 1919, and refused to take any decisive steps until the new assembly's authorization had been secured. Thus, through the anxious, cautious constitutionalism of the Social Democrat leaders, Ebert and Scheidemann, none of the three fundamental reforms — democratization of the army, public control of heavy industry, redistribution of landed property — was secured; and the reason was that to secure them it would have been necessary to rely on extra-parliamentary means and have recourse to popular pressure. Such a policy was alien to the whole character of the Social Democratic leadership, which had for decades past known no higher aim than the attainment of parliamentary democracy and the representation in parliament of working-class interests. No minister had the courage to accept the responsibility of using the power actually in his possession in order to change the internal balance of power or to secure control of its mainsprings. Hence the constituent assembly which met at Weimar to draft a new constitution in the spring of 1919 succeeded only in grafting mechanical devices, such as proportional representation, parliamentary sovereignty and the referendum, on to the existing body politic; but under this liberal cloak the old economic and political forces of the Hohenzollern Empire continued to exist undisturbed. The Weimar Constitution established the external forms of political liberty, but without the changes in social and economic power which alone could give them vitality.

This initial failure, from which recovery in fact proved impossible, was not, of course, the result of a deliberate betrayal of the revolution by the Social Democrat leaders. It was due to the limitations of the men themselves, and it was due in part at least to external circumstances, before which they capitulated. They were afraid lest economic experiment might produce chaos, and expose Germany to the famine and misery from which Russia was then suffering. They were afraid lest social change, easily denounced as 'Bolshevism', might lead to Allied intervention. These fears were not unjustified. All the Entente powers were preoccupied with the dangers of 'Bolshevism' and particularly afraid of 'Bolshevik revolution' in Germany,[1] and were prepared to co-operate with the German army to preserve 'order' in Germany, just as they co-operated with it in the Baltic states and the Ukraine against the Russian revolution. Thus the German revolution was from the very beginning frustrated by the hostility of the victorious powers, and there is no reason to believe that they would have shrunk from the use of force and the

[1] 'Russia', said R. S. Baker, a member of the American delegation at the peace conference in Paris, 'played a more vital part at Paris than Prussia. Without ever being represented at Paris at all, the Bolsheviki and Bolshevism were powerful elements at every turn' (*Woodrow Wilson and World Settlement*, II, 64). How deep-seated fear of Bolshevism was, is revealed in a striking memorandum drawn up by Lloyd George, ibid. III, 449-457. 'As long as order was maintained in Germany', said Lloyd George, 'a breakwater would exist between the countries of the Allies and the waters of revolution beyond. But once that breakwater was swept away, he could not speak for France, and he trembled for his own country.'

terrible weapon of blockade, as occurred in the case of Hungary, had it proved necessary to oppose fundamental social change. In these circumstances a policy of radical social and economic reform undoubtedly entailed serious risks, and could not have been carried through without heavy sacrifices on the part of the German people, for which the rulers were unwilling to take responsibility. The failure of the Social Democrat leaders — and, indeed, of the Allied powers — was the failure to realize that these risks were no less serious than the dangers of doing nothing, which gave reaction the chance of recovery. Instead they concentrated their efforts, partly to keep Allied confidence, partly to prove their ability to govern, on the maintenance of law and order. Because they feared that their removal would have disturbed the smooth running of the public services, they left the officials of the old imperial bureaucracy in office; because they feared that his dismissal would complicate demobilization and worsen relations with the victorious Entente, they retained Hindenburg, and with him the core of the old army. Worse still, the preoccupation of the government with law and order brought it into conflict with the very forces whose spontaneous action had brought about the November revolution of 1918. This conflict came to a head in January 1919, when the Social Democrat defence minister, Gustav Noske, called in the notorious Free Corps to crush the left-wing labour movement in Berlin, and followed up this success by a series of punitive expeditions extending from Bremen to Munich. The civil war which raged for the first three months of 1919 sealed the fate of the German republic; the victory of Ebert and Noske was hailed as a victory for the middle-class republic and democracy over Bolshevism, but in reality it was a victory for the Free Corps, for the anti-democratic forces which had come to the rescue of the republic to prevent social change, but which only tolerated the republican government temporarily as the lesser evil. On the other hand, it created a breach between the right and left wings of the German labour movement so deep that it could never again be bridged; and this breach permanently crippled the powers of resistance of the democratic forces when reaction had sufficiently recovered to raise its head. The attitude of the people to the republican government was aptly described as early as June 1919, by one of the more foresighted Social Democrat ministers, Rudolf Wissel; 'in spite of the Revolution', he said, the hopes of the people have been disappointed. The government has not lived up to the expectations of the people. We have, indeed, constructed a formal political democracy, but fundamentally we have done no more than continue the programme initiated by the imperial government of Prince Max of Baden. We drew up the constitution without real participation by the people. We failed to satisfy the masses, because we had no proper programme.

Essentially, we have governed in the old ways, and there has been little sign of a new spirit informing the old procedure. We have not been able to influence the course of the Revolution in such a way that Germany is swayed by a new inspiration. The essential character of German civilization and social life is little altered, and that little not always for the better. The people believes that the achievements of the Revolution are of a merely negative character, that the only change is in the set of persons exercising military and bureaucratic authority, and that the present principles of government do not differ in essentials from those of the old régime ... It is my belief that the verdict of history on the national assembly and on us, the members of the government, will be hard and bitter.[1]

The attitude of profound disillusion with the Republic reflected in Wissel's speech of June 14th, 1919, was confirmed by the terms of the peace settlement, which was signed a few days later, on June 28th. It is no part of our business to enter into the unending controversy which, ever since 1919, has centred round the Treaty of Versailles, its relation to Wilson's Fourteen Points and to the fundamental principle of 'self-determination' on which they were based.[2] It is enough to note that certain facts impressed themselves on Germans of all parties. First, the settlement was 'dictated', i.e. contrary to previous international practice the French representative, Clemenceau, prevented verbal negotiations. Secondly, in spite of Allied lip-service to the principles of 'self-determination' wide areas were detached from Germany without plebiscite,[3] the *Anschluss* of Germany and Austria was vetoed by France, and over three and a

---

[1] A. Rosenberg, *Gesch. d. deutschen Republik* (1935), 105.
[2] There is a careful summary, free from propagandist bias, by Henderson, 'The Peace Settlement, 1919', in *History*, XXVI (1941), 60–69; the historian will be well advised to consult this survey, and the literature there referred to, rather than unreliable propaganda published more recently.
[3] Cf. Henderson, op. cit., 65–66: 'In the east Germany lost nine-tenths of Posen and two-thirds of West Prussia without a plebiscite'. In 'Upper Silesia', which 'had been under German rule in one form or another for six centuries', although 'nearly sixty per cent of those who went to the polls voted for Germany', 'the new frontier gave the Poles five-sixths of the industrial area and eighty per cent of the coal-bearing region'.

half million Germans, who actively sought incorporation in the new Austrian republic, were compelled against their will to remain in the new Czechoslovak state. Thirdly, despite the assurance of 'a free, open-minded and absolutely impartial adjustment of all colonial claims', Germany was deprived of all her colonies without a formal hearing. Fourthly, the German representatives were compelled — in contradiction to Wilson's promise of December 4th, 1917, that 'no people shall be ... punished because the responsible rulers of a single country have themselves done deep and abominable wrong' — to sign a statement that Germany, along with the other defeated powers, 'accepted the responsibility' for causing all the loss and damage brought about by a war 'imposed upon' the world 'by the aggression of Germany and her allies'. Fifthly, on the basis of this clause 'reparations' amounting to 132 milliard gold marks were demanded, i.e. twenty-two times the amount demanded of Russia by the German imperial government in the notorious treaty of Brest-Litovsk.[1] Juridically, it is possible to justify most, if not all, of these terms as part of a settlement imposed by a conqueror on a vanquished enemy; but they were a serious blow to the forces of German democracy which, confident in the promises of Wilson and Lloyd George,[2] sincerely believed that Germany, once it had overthrown the Hohenzollerns and broken, under a democratic régime, with the traditions of Hohenzollern imperialism, could count on terms such as would enable the republic to take its place in the comity of nations. Instead it was saddled with 'guilt' for the policy of William II, in which it had no share and which it had rejected. The inexpediency of this policy, the moving spirit behind which was France, was recognized at the time by both Wilson and Lloyd George;[3] but, with their hands tied by secret treaties con-

---

[1] This is described by Fraser, *Germany between Two Wars* (1941), 61, as 'a big advance in leniency towards the defeated side'.

[2] For example, Lloyd George's speech of January 5th, 1918, to a congress of Trade Union delegates, summed up in a Labour party manifesto in the following terms: 'it reveals a government and a people seeking no selfish and predatory aims of any kind, pursuing with one mind one unchanging purpose: to obtain justice for others so that we thereby secure for ourselves a lasting peace. We desire neither to destroy Germany nor diminish her boundaries; we seek neither to exalt ourselves nor to enlarge our Empire'.

[3] In the memorandum referred to above, p. 442, n. 1, for example, Lloyd George wrote: 'You may strip Germany of her colonies, reduce her armaments to a mere police force and her navy to that of a fifth-rate power; all the same in the end if she feels that she has been unjustly treated in the peace of 1919 she will find means of exacting retribution from her conquerors ... I would, therefore, put it in the forefront of the peace that ... we will ... do everything possible to enable the German people to get upon their legs again.'

cluded during the war, neither was able to put up a firm opposition to the policy of France, as enunciated by Clemenceau, and which once again, as so often in the past, was not easy to reconcile with lasting European settlement. French demands for the annexation of the Saar and the separation of the Rhineland from Germany were successfully resisted; but French policy created ineradicable suspicions and there were few Germans — or, for the matter of that, few Americans or Englishmen — who did not believe that the principle of national 'self-determination', as applied in the case of Poland and Czechoslovakia, had been used as a cloak for a French attempt to raise clients in the east, whose political function was to aid France in perpetuating Germany's defeat. Such a view was unjust to Wilson and Lloyd George; but it reflected the policy of Poincaré and Clemenceau.[1] The pursuit of unrepentant power-politics at a moment when, in Europe and America, a new generation, reacting against pre-war imperialism, was prepared to renounce power-politics as an instrument of national interests, destroyed the hopes of 1919. In Germany the effects of this policy were disastrous. The treatment of the new German republic as a weak and defeated power equated the republic and weakness and thereby strengthened immeasurably the hand of all reactionary forces within Germany opposed to the republican régime. 'The outcome', as a leading English historian has said, 'has been the Germany of Hitler that we know.'[2]

To follow in detail the well-known story of the years from 1919 to 1933, from Versailles to Hitler, is not necessary, for in all essentials, due to the folly of the Allies and the failures of the German democratic leaders, the die was, as early as 1919, already cast. From the start, the Weimar republic failed to arouse the enthusiasm or anchor the loyalties of the great majority of Germans. On the right, the

[1] In the words of Lloyd George, 'the dead hand of Poincaré lay heavy on Europe'; cf. G. P. Gooch, 'British Foreign Policy 1919-1938', *Studies in Diplomacy and Statecraft* (1942), 175.

[2] Cf. G. M. Trevelyan, *British History in the Nineteenth Century and After* (1937), 483-485: 'The great error of the Treaty was the harsh treatment of the new German Republic. It should have been the first object of England and France to enable it to survive as a peaceful democracy. But the German nation was humiliated by the dictation of terms on the hardships of which she was not even permitted to plead before the victors; she was kept disarmed while other nations (though not England) remained armed to the teeth; she was forbidden to unite with Austria; she was excluded from the League of Nations; in the matter of reparations she was treated in a manner so fantastic as to help to ruin her without benefiting her creditors ... France could not change or forget. She not only refused to disarm, but continued for years to harass the German Republic, thus preparing the way for its transformation into the Nazi régime ... The outcome has been the Germany of Hitler that we know.'

nationalist sections, which still exerted immense pressure, regarded it as a transitory stage on the road towards the reassertion both of their old preponderance at home and of German military power in Europe. On the left, the bulk of the German people regarded it as an equally transitory stage towards a form of political organization which really reflected popular aspirations. What backing it had came from the middle classes; but owing to the unbalanced development of German society from the time of the Thirty Years War onwards, the middle classes were too weak and politically too unreliable to carry alone the burden of government, and if they had to choose between the left, with the threat of real social change, and the reactionary groups of the right, they preferred co-operation with the latter. This weakness played into the hands of the right wing sections, which soon established themselves in a position of control, enabling them to use the constitutional machinery of government for their own ends. It played into the hands of the Reichswehr which, in 1923, forced the working-class governments of Saxony and Thuringia to resign. Still more ominous, it played into the hands of the industrialists, who after November 1922, loosed the horrors of inflation on Germany in order, while freeing themselves from internal indebtedness, to destroy the resources of organized labour. With the appointment of Wilhelm Cuno, director-general of the Hamburg-Amerika line, as prime minister in 1923, the undisguised rule of large-scale capital began;[1] the attack on the Eight Hour Day and the refusal to meet expenditure by direct taxation revealed that the notorious Hugo Stinnes and Fritz Thyssen were in the saddle. Heavy industry prospered as never before, while the nation was starving and the state facing bankruptcy; from 1920 to 1924 the power of capital increased immensely, and its hold was consolidated after 1924 in the course of reconstruction and rationalization and the progress of industrial monopoly.[2]

These tendencies were concealed but in no way reversed by the period of relative prosperity between 1924 and 1929. The fact that business, supported by foreign loans, was again back to normal brought a gradual slackening of tension, particularly in the indus-

[1] Rosenberg, op. cit., 95. Fraser, op. cit., 88, describes the economic policy of the Cuno government as 'an integral part of the great conspiracy against the German people'.

[2] The two most powerful German trusts were formed during this period, the I. G. Farbenindustrie (i.e. the German Dye Trust) in 1925, and the Vereinigte Stahlwerke (United Steel Works) in 1926.

trial field, and it seemed as though democracy were at last functioning properly and booking results in the form of improved housing conditions and similar social benefits. But the effect of such social services, however welcome in themselves, on German economic structure was nil, and under the surface the old balance of power persisted. The election of Hindenburg to the presidency in 1925 was an index of the true situation; it revealed in a flash how far removed from power the democratic and progressive forces were in the mid-twenties. Although 'the great majority of Germans' wanted to 'settle down to a life of peace and international co-operation',[1] the power of heavy industry, which ultimately could only keep going on the basis of a great armaments programme, continued to expand. The desire of the German people for a continuation of peace and democratic government was expressed in the elections of 1928, when the Social Democratic vote, which had slumped in 1921 and 1923, rose to over nine millions, and the two working-class parties, the Social Democrats and the Communists, together secured over 42 per cent of the seats in the Reichstag. But this swing in the voting, unaccompanied by any move to break the economic and social power of the industrial and landed classes, did not imply a fundamental strengthening of democratic government. It only needed a break in prosperity to bring back into the open the antagonism between the army and the great industrial monopolies on the one hand, and the people on the other. This came in 1929. Already by February 1929, the total number of unemployed had passed the three million mark. In October 1929, there followed the Wall Street crash. Short-term loans — fifty per cent of the loans to Germany totalling twenty milliard marks were short-term, unconsolidated loans — were recalled; German industry, dependent on foreign markets because low wages and drastic inequalities of income prevented the creation of a great domestic market, slumped rapidly; and unemployment increased apace. By January 1933,

[1] Thus Lindsay, *Germany between Two Wars*, 77–78. Elsewhere he concedes that there is 'every reason to believe that the war aspirations of the men behind the scenes were not shared by the German people. In 1926 a member of the Reichstag, Philipp Scheidemann, had discovered the arrangements in force for building aeroplanes and training crews in Russia. This revelation caused an immense sensation in Germany, and the reaction of the ordinary German was thoroughly hostile. Two years later, when the question of building a new battle-cruiser came up before the Reichstag, the proposal, though entirely in conformity with the Treaty of Versailles, was violently opposed by the left-wing parties and was only in the end forced through with the utmost difficulty'. But 'the constitutional government of Germany was not strong enough to enforce a policy of peace upon the fanatics behind the scenes' (ibid., 84).

official unemployment figures passed the six million mark, but the actual number of unemployed rose to between eight and nine millions.

V

The crisis which set in during 1929 brought about the death of the German republic. Having failed to enlist the support of the working-classes, the republic was dependent upon the middle-class vote of the centre parties. But the middle classes, the small property owners and shopkeepers, who had already been hit by the inflation, collapsed before the slump of 1929-1933; the rapid decline in the workers' purchasing power ruined millions of small shopkeepers, tradesmen, artisans, black-coated workers and peasants, and these elements — which had, as a class, nothing to hope from a working-class movement — turned to Hitler and the specious promises of National Socialism. The National Socialist vote, which had rallied only 800,000 supporters in 1923, rose in September 1930, to almost 6,500,000, and the National Socialists emerged from insignificance to the position of second strongest party in the Reichstag. Two years later, in July 1932, the vote for Hitler more than doubled, rising to 13,700,000 out of a total electorate of some 45,000,000 — the highest vote ever obtained by National Socialism in a free election. This success, born of the crisis, was secured at the expense of the middle and upper class parties; as indicated in the table over-leaf,[1] the working-class electorate — in spite of the miseries of poverty and unemployment — tenaciously resisted the blandish-ments of Hitler's demagogy, and the working-class vote, cast in favour of Social Democracy and Communism, stood firm through-out, just as the Catholic vote stood firm. The split in the left-wing forces, and in particular the purblind policy of the Communist leaders, unhappily facilitated the rise of National Socialism; but the real strength of Hitlerism lay in the support of the privileged classes, of the industrial 'kings', the Junkers and the army, with the conniv-ance of parallel interests in England and France. At no stage from the onset of the crisis in 1929 until 1933 had Hitler any hope of succeeding to power, even by unconstitutional means, without the

[1] Quoted from E. Anderson, *Hammer or Anvil. The Story of the German working-class move-ment* (1945), 141, whose careful analyses may be consulted for further detail.

backing of capitalist and reactionary interests. Before the inaugura-
tion of the Hitler terror National Socialism never obtained the support of more than one-third of the German people; and in the last
six months of 1932 National Socialist strength actually decreased by
2,000,000 votes. When on January 30th, 1933, Hitler was made

VOTES (IN MILLIONS) AT GENERAL ELECTIONS, 1924–1932

Parties	1924	1928	1930	July 1932	Nov. 1932
Working-class parties (Social Democrats and Communists)	10.5	12.3	13.0	13.1	13.1
Middle-class parties (excluding Centre party)	13.2	12.9	10.3	4.0	5.3
Catholic Centre Party	4.1	3.7	4.1	4.5	4.2
National Socialists	0.9	0.8	6.4	13.7	11.7

chancellor, it was not through the support of, but rather as the
result of a conspiracy against the German people: his rise to power
was the work of Hindenburg representing the army, of Papen
representing the aristocracy, of Hugenberg, the press-lord, and of
Thyssen representing the industrialists of the Ruhr. It was this un-
holy alliance which led the German people to ruin and Europe to war.

The alliance with National Socialism, contrived by Hugenberg as
early as 1929 and formally concluded by Papen at the beginning of
1933, was only the last step in a campaign against the democratic
republic and the German people waged by the 'national' interests
ever since the onset of the economic crisis in 1929. For these interests
the depression was a welcome opportunity – 'this', one industrialist
declared, 'is the crisis we need!' – to break for ever the power of the
German people to guide their own destinies, and in particular to
destroy organized labour. As in the inflation they had attacked the
Eight Hour Day, so in 1930 they immediately launched an attack

on the unemployment fund, while resisting the Social Democratic attempt to impose direct taxes. The resignation of the Social Democrat ministers and the appointment of Brüning as chancellor in March 1930, marked their success, and the end of democratic government in Germany. Thenceforward government was in the hands of a narrow clique, which, supported by the army and the executive under Hindenburg, dispensed with constitutional forms and ruled by emergency decrees. These decrees were directed ruthlessly against the working classes: indirect taxation was increased, new capitation taxes were introduced, bearing as heavily on the poor as on the rich, food prices were forced up in the interests of the agriculturists by heavy import duties. At the same time a devastating policy of deflation was introduced to support German export industries, and huge sums were paid out as subsidies to the bankrupt Junker agriculturists east of the Elbe. It was class rule on a huge scale, unashamedly pursuing class interests at the expense of the people; its naked use of force was seen when on July 20th, 1932, Papen ousted the constitutional labour government of Prussia and entrusted executive power to General von Rundstedt. But it was class rule on a narrow foundation. The working-class parties, as has been seen, remained firm, holding the allegiance of their traditional supporters to the last; but the 'nationalist' parties underwent a disastrous decline. The scandals of the *Osthilfe*, the endless government subsidies to its Junker supporters, could not be hushed up; the demand for a re-distribution of the land in eastern Germany for the benefit of the people could not be quelled. On the other hand, there were limits, even in Germany in 1933, to an unconcealed dictatorship based on the armed forces. For landowners and industrialists alike the sharp decline in the National Socialist vote in November 1932, and the signs of a swing to the extreme left, were ominous trends, alarming indications that the day of reckoning was at hand. Their alliance with Hitler was the sequel. It was an alliance reluctantly entered into; but, their own supporters having disintegrated, it was necessary as a device to throw a cloak of popular support over the dictatorship which, under a rotting veil, they had exercised ever since the Social Democrats were forced out of office in March 1930.

The calculations of the 'national' industrial and Junker interests miscarried. When on January 30th, 1933, Hindenburg and Papen called in Hitler, hoping thereby to stabilize their own hold over

Germany, they gave themselves and Germany a new master, implacable and ruthless. They thought they had secured an instrument for the enslavement of the German people; but although Hitler ruthlessly destroyed German labour, he was no instrument of the reactionaries and the industrial capitalists. Through a deliberate policy of brute repression and armed might he manœuvred the National Socialist party — still a minority party, supported by less than 44 per cent of the electorate, even after the burning of the Reichstag and the proscription and persecution of the Communists[1] — into a position of unassailable preponderance; but his dominion was not based on brute force alone. The régime of regimentation, the extirpation of working-class leaders, the abolition of rights of assembly and discussion and the suppression of freedom of speech and of the press, played their part, preventing any organization of the workers as a political and social force and leaving the individual helpless in face of the machinery of party and state; but at the same time Hitler took positive steps to win majority support for National Socialism. He promised more than any other party offered; and for a time, from 1933 to 1938, he seemed to keep his promises. He promised work, and in fact he conquered unemployment, though only through a vast rearmament programme. He promised peace — 'National Socialist Germany', he said in 1935, 'desires peace from its deepest inner creed and conviction' — and at the same time a righting of the injustices done at Versailles; and in annulling the demilitarization of the Rhineland in 1936, and in securing the *Anschluss* with Austria in 1938 and the incorporation, six months later, of the Sudeten Germans into the Reich without war, he seemed to have kept his promise. His success was the more impressive because, as late as 1931, French opposition had prevented the union of Germany and Austria, with the result that after 1936 many in Germany who had sponsored peaceful negotiation were forced to admit that in a world dominated by power politics armed force had achieved incisive results beyond the capacity of the peaceful policy of the republic.

[1] At the elections held on March 5th, 1933, in spite of intimidation and terror, the National Socialists won only 288 seats out of 647, as compared with 120 for the Social Democrats, 81 for the Communists, 73 for the Catholic Centre, and 52 for the German Nationalists. The Social Democrats lost only one seat, the Communists (already declared illegal and rounded up into concentration camps) only nineteen; the Catholic Centre even won three new seats. It was only through the adhesion of the right-wing Nationalists and by declaring the Communist vote illegal, that the National Socialists, even after five weeks of repression, could claim an absolute majority.

Yet, in fact, Hitler's successes in foreign policy were due less to German rearmament, the deficiencies and limitations of which were known in competent military circles, than to the tacit alliance of powerful reactionary elements in England and France, which, though loath to see a reassertion of German equality, were still more unwilling to check it by military alliance with Soviet Russia or to run the risk of social revolution as a result of Hitler's fall. Just as, at home, Hitler commended himself to the right wing 'nationalist' parties by his attack on labour, so abroad he was hailed as the saviour of Europe from Communism; when, in 1938 his policy seemed to be leading directly to war with Czechoslovakia, which in the opinion of the High Command would have been 'catastrophic' for Germany, it was the intervention of the English premier, Chamberlain, which saved him from deposition by the German army.[1] But if Hitler secured the support of German and European reaction, he did not make the mistake of identifying himself with the reactionary cause. His party was, in theory, a 'socialist' party, and had in its early days undoubtedly incorporated genuine socialist elements; and even after the 'blood bath' of June 30th, 1934, when the section in the party which hoped for social revolution was eliminated, National Socialist propaganda took care to pay court to what Hitler described as 'the anti-capitalist longing of the masses'. In fact, none of the 'socialist' demands which figured in the official National Socialist programme was ever put into effect; but the importance of Hitler's 'social demagogy' should not for that reason be underrated.[2] Above

[1] The facts about the preparations to get rid of Hitler, timed to take effect on September 14th-15th, 1938, are well attested. The official deposition of Generaloberst Halder, Chief of the German General Staff from 1938 to 1942, a full and reliable report of which appeared in the *Daily Worker* of September 12th, 1945, has been corroborated from a number of independent sources; cf. H. B. Gisevius, *Bis zum bitteren Ende* (1946), A. W. Dulles, *Germany's Underground* (1947), H. R. Trevor-Roper, *The Last Days of Hitler* (1947). A. W. Dulles, who as head of the United States intelligence service in Switzerland had unusual facilities for securing and checking information, states that Halder's predecessor in office, Generaloberst Beck, made contact with the British authorities and urged Chamberlain to take a firm stand against Hitler, at the same time laying plans to seize Hitler's person, if he persisted in his programme of aggression. Chamberlain's capitulation, enabling Hitler, in the words of *The Times* (March 15th, 1946), to 'pose before the German people as the peacemaker' at the very moment when his bellicose policy and fear of war had weakened German support and so created the necessary preconditions for successful action by the German general staff, cut the ground away from under the feet of the resistance; as Trevor-Roper writes (p. 8), it 'knocked the weapons from their hands as they were preparing to strike'.
[2] The 'Twenty-Five Points' of 1920, in which the programme of the National Socialist party was enunciated, are printed in Oakeshott, *The Social and Political Doctrines of Contemporary Europe* (1939), 190 sqq. They include abolition of unearned income and 'emancipation from the slavery of interest charges' (§ 11), confiscation of war profits (§ 12), nationalization

all else it gave foundation to his claim to stand for the interests of the whole German people, and thus differentiated his policy from that of the old 'nationalist' parties, whose pursuit of class interests was barefaced. Even in this last phase, therefore, the long-standing conflict between the interests and aims of the ruling classes and the interests of the German people, deftly exploited by Nazi propaganda, played its part. The long-felt desire for a Germany of the German people, the hope which had arisen and been dashed in 1848 and again in 1918, was taken up and exploited by the leaders of the revolution of 1933. Hitler — claiming, like Napoleon, to represent better than any assembly the will of the people — denounced democratic and parliamentary government as merely a cloak for the pursuit of sectional interests at the expense of the people; and of parliamentary government as it functioned in Germany between 1918 and 1933 this denunciation was not untrue. The insistence of National Socialist philosophy and propaganda on the 'folk' was not, as is often assumed, designed simply as part of a theory of racial superiority; its essential purpose at home was to emphasize the popular foundations of National Socialist rule, and writers of the period between 1933 and 1939 never tired of praising the National Socialist achievement in identifying 'folk' and 'state'. After generations in which the German people had been held at arm's length and divorced from politics, Hitler claimed to have consummated the unity of state and folk, of government and governed.

The claim was false. In the present state of knowledge we do not know, and — due to deliberate Nazi falsification — we probably never shall know, how implicitly the German people accepted Hitler's professions; but it is certain that any trust placed by Germany in Hitler was betrayed. He worked for war, although (as he rightly said) 'if leaders and rulers only desire peace, the people have never wanted war'. He promised the destruction of 'interest slavery' and liberation from 'monopoly capitalism'; but he destroyed the defences built up by the German working classes against the evils of German industrialism and betrayed the German people into the hands of the very industrial and agrarian interests from which he claimed to have rescued them. His government was based not, as he

of trusts (§ 13), introduction of profit sharing (§ 14), 'communalization' of the big departmental stores (§ 16), a programme of agrarian reform including 'confiscation without compensation' of land for communal purposes (§ 17); cf. also §§ 15, 18 (death penalty for usury and profiteering), 20, 21.

represented, on popular mandate, but on an alliance with financial and military interests which differed only from earlier alliances in so far as the National Socialist party and not the interests concerned retained the upper hand. He feared the people, as much as the forces of German reaction feared the people, and therefore he stifled every free expression of popular will, because, like the 'national' interests, he recognized the deep cleft between his own objectives and the aspirations of the German people. When National Socialist policy unleashed war on September 1st, 1939, the attitude of the German people was, in the words of a competent American observer, 'the most striking demonstration against war I have ever seen';[1] but an expression of the views and will of the German people was even more impossible in 1939 than it had been under Hohenzollern imperialism. For Hitler the German people was, as he said, 'a flock of sheep', fit only for obedience, which had to be dragooned into the 'nationalist' path. From 1933 to 1939 he pursued this dragooning with a skill which it would be a fatal error to underestimate and with effects the durability of which time alone can prove or disprove; by repressing opposition, by perverting education, by exploiting genuine grievances and by conferring limited benefits, he fastened on Germany a régime hostile to all the German people had striven after, ever since, between 1815 and 1848, that same people first asserted the right to control its own destinies. This fundamental right, denied for long centuries before 1848, was never securely grasped at any stage between 1848 and 1939; the opposing interests consecrated by history, were too strongly entrenched. But the problem still remains, the enduring legacy of German history, to build a Germany of the German people, representing not the will of a predatory minority, but the sober interests and aspirations of the German-speaking millions in the historic German lands between France and the Slavonic east.

---

[1] W. L. Shirer, *Berlin Diary* (1941), 119. This and other eye-witness reports are collected by Anderson, op. cit., 183. Cf. also *The Problem of Germany* (Royal Institute of International Affairs, 1943) 26.

CONCLUSION

GERMANY YESTERDAY, TO-DAY AND TO-MORROW

WE stand at the end of a thousand years of history and the German dilemma still remains, the great unsolved problem in the heritage of western Europe. The story of England and France is different. They have their problems, problems of adjustment to a twentieth-century environment, for there is no finality or stability in the process of history; but it is adjustment in a framework of continuity, which even the greatest upheavals, such as the revolution of 1789, accentuated and consolidated far more than they disturbed. German history, on the contrary, is a story of discontinuity, of development cut short, of incompleteness and retardation; the consolidation of the early monarchy was cut short in 1076, the establishment of national unity was fatally checked after 1250, the growth of representative estates withered after the Reformation, the expansion of the middle classes was halted as a result of the Thirty Years War, the settlement of 1815 prolonged particularism, the growth of self-government was stunted by the constitution of 1871, the transfer of social and economic power was sidetracked in 1918 and 1919. These are the dates and facts which stand out as we survey the long course of German history; they are the salient features emerging as the historical background of the German problem. The essential requirement of the present is to diagnose this problem, to examine its symptoms and uncover its causes, to disentangle it from the transient and inessential complications with which, in the process of time, it has been bound up. Accurate diagnosis is the first step towards cure, and accurate diagnosis of the causes of maladies in the body politic is an essential function of the historian.

It is true that history can only contribute within limits to the solution of political problems; economic and geo-political factors, inexorably moulding the framework of human activity, will always rightly claim prior consideration. But statesmen will at their peril ignore (or misinterpret) the historical and human background against which these factors play out their role, and the living consciousness of the past which interacts with them and which influences, sometimes decisively, men's reactions to the stark economic facts and the economic dilemmas with which they have to cope. A historical approach to the present is not the only approach; but it is a necessary approach. Herein lies the justification for a lengthy and, in places, a detailed book. It would be easy to pick out shortly the phases and turning-points in German history, and to show how stage by stage in a long process of evolution Germany gradually drew apart in political development from France and England, the monarchies of western Europe. But that is not enough. It is necessary to know not only what happened, but why and how it happened; for the particular road traversed is as important, in the impression it leaves on the mind of the traveller, as the destination finally reached, and the way we arrive at a particular end often no less revealing than the end towards which we progress. When we turn to Germany to-day it is essential to be aware of the past in all its complexity, for the past as it lives on in human consciousness is an integral part of the present: it is the hard core of the German problem.

The German problem, as it faces the world to-day on the morrow of the defeat of National Socialism, is not the problem of National Socialism. National Socialism, with its hateful racial doctrines and its schemes of world-domination, emerged in the aftermath of the war of 1914-1918 as the creed of a fanatical minority; it became an effective political movement as a result of the economic crisis of 1929-1933, which led millions of Germans to welcome or accept a desperate remedy which only a few years earlier they had rejected out of hand. Its roots, like those of the parallel movements which swept Europe, and many countries outside the European continent, between 1919 and 1939, spring essentially from the chaotic conditions of modern society, and there is general agreement that the only certain way of preventing its resurgence is to take steps to prevent the recurrence of the conditions which nurtured it. That is a question of contemporary social organization which, although it comprises Germany and cannot be completed without the reorganization of Germany, does not concern us directly here.[1] The roots

---

[1] It is therefore out of the question to examine the vast literature, polemical and much of it ephemeral, concerned with the political consequences of German National Socialism and European (or international) Fascism; probably the best and most philosophical treatment is in H. J. Laski, *Reflections on the Revolution of Our Time* (1943); cf. particularly cap. 3 (pp. 86-127) on 'The Meaning Of Fascism'.

of National Socialism lie in the present; the roots of the German problem lie far back in the past. What confuses the issue is that the National Socialists, with the deliberate aim of securing the widest possible measure of popular support in Germany, took over and incorporated into their political programme the major problems which were the legacy of German history; they were revolutionaries in arms against a disjointed society, but they claimed also to be the true heirs of Germany's past. It is too obvious to need proof that the movement of reaction, between 1919 and 1939, against liberal capitalist society was an international movement, transcending national boundaries, perhaps the universal 'outcome of capitalism in decay';[1] but each national variation of the movement had its own distinctive characteristics conditioned by the social anatomy of the country in which it appeared, by the soil from which it sprang and by the environment in which it came to fruition. What characterizes National Socialism is the skill with which its exponents appropriated and identified the National Socialist movement with the deep, underlying currents of German history; their specific doctrines were combined, in their programme, with aspirations accepted by millions of Germans who were not National Socialists.[2] They offered a solution — specious but boldly enunciated — not only of the immediate evil of unemployment, but also of the two great unsolved problems which stood out as the enduring legacy of Germany's past: the problem of German unity and the problem of creating political institutions representative of the German people. These problems, which existed long before the birth of National Socialism and cannot be disposed of merely by the destruction of National Socialism, stood in the very forefront of the National Socialist programme of 1920. The first two articles of the 'Twenty-Five Points', with their demand for 'the union of all Germans on the basis of the right of national self-determination' and 'juridical equality for the German people in its dealings with other nations', expressed in form

[1] Laski, op. cit., 95.
[2] In the Twenty-Five Points embodying the National Socialist programme of 1920 (Oakeshott, op. cit., 190-193) only §§ 4, 5, 6, 8, 10, 18, 19, 20, 23, 24 (i.e. two-fifths of the whole) reflect specific doctrines of National Socialist philosophy, and in §§ 5, 8, 10, 20, 24, this is expressed in an innocuous form. The first article, with its demand for 'the union of all Germans to form one Great Germany' has been proved by later events to have a specifically National Socialist content, but it had of course also a legitimate and normal meaning, and it is important to distinguish between the normal sense of the words and their perversion by National Socialism after it had arrived in power.

nothing new, nothing revolutionary and nothing specifically National Socialist, for no one outside the narrow circle of the party leadership had, before 1938, any suspicion of the sinister meaning and secret purposes with which National Socialism imbued the right of self-determination. The numerous clauses committing the party to radical social and economic change – although, as we have seen, they had no reflection in National Socialist practice – set forth only what was generally regarded as necessary to secure the transfer of political power from the privileged classes to the people; and when National Socialism undertook 'to defend the people as a whole against the individual, when and wherever the interests of the individual are out of harmony with the common weal', and proclaimed that in the National Socialist state there was 'no difference, still less opposition, between the state as a separate legal structure and the totality of citizens',[1] it was only claiming to make itself the executor of necessary reforms in a state in which political power was still engrossed by an unrepresentative minority. In all these points the National Socialists appropriated demands which antedated National Socialism, and by weaving them into the National Socialist programme, confused the historical aspirations of the German people with the special tenets of the National Socialist creed. But the two are distinct, historically and as a matter of practical politics. The demand for the protection of the 'people as a whole' from exploitation by private interests is legitimate, and is not identical with the subordination of the individual to the vilest forms of state-tyranny, to which end it was perverted by National Socialism; the demand for 'juridical equality' is legitimate and is not in itself merely a first stage towards hegemony, even if this is what National Socialism made of it; the demand for national unity on the basis of self-determination is legitimate and is not identical with the ruthless exploitation of minority grievances, real and alleged, for the subjection of alien races, although it was used in this way by National Socialist politicians. *Abusus non tollit usum.* The aspirations which, manipulated by Hitler, became the instruments of an intolerable system of power-politics, are not for that reason illegitimate aspirations, and the fact that they were exploited by National Socialism does not condemn them out of hand. They were a part of the National Socialist programme, because they were deliberately

[1] Cf. Oakeshott, op. cit., 227.

inserted into that programme to give it a semblance of popularity which the fanatical creed of National Socialism could not alone secure; but they are not an integral part of it. They have their own causes and origins, reaching deep into German history; and the danger is that, through their factitious association with National Socialism, they will be treated as an integral part of National Socialism and not receive the separate consideration and independent handling which they require. National Socialism must be suppressed and eradicated; but the problem of Germany must be cured, if there is to be lasting settlement in Europe.

What, then, disentangled from its associations, since 1933, with National Socialism, is the German problem? In its essence it is an historical problem. It is the problem of a nation whose historical development has been retarded or arrested in two fundamental ways. Its progress towards national unity — the unity which in England and France has been an accepted heritage since the middle ages — was postponed until 1871; and even after 1871 it has never been secure against the machinations of French policy, which refused to accept the restitution to Germany of Alsace-Lorraine and never finally renounced the age-old ambition of the Rhine frontier, bridgeheads across the Rhine, the Saar valley and the dismemberment of Germany. Its progress towards representative institutions was blocked until 1918; and even after 1918 such institutions were never safe against the machinations of the minority possessing social and economic power. Here in the unsolved problems of unity and democracy, which run like red threads through German history, is the substantial legacy of Germany's past to Germany's present, and we cannot expunge this legacy by ignoring its existence; whilst if we treat the aspirations of the German people to unity and democracy as no more than off-shoots of National Socialism and seek to drive them out of existence by repression, we run the risk of fostering the survival of the National Socialist spirit in Germany, in exactly the same way as in 1918 failure to distinguish between Hohenzollern imperialism and the will of the German people expressed through the Republic helped to preserve the spirit of German nationalism. National Socialism itself is no longer a danger; but it can be transformed into a danger even at this stage if, through the failure of European statesmen to satisfy the deep aspirations of the German people, it is again allowed to identify

itself with the two great currents of German history. The key to
lasting settlement lies in completing, not in thwarting, German
aspirations to unity and democracy; and these twin aspirations, linked
since 1848, cannot hopefully be separated. Democracy, as the
history of Germany between 1815 and 1871 went to show, cannot
prosper without unity; and unity without democracy, as was proved
between 1871 and 1918, is no guarantee of European peace. If
Germany is to cease to be a danger-spot in Europe, it can only be
through the creation of a united, democratic Germany within its
historic boundaries; the forces at play are too deep-rooted and too
vital for any other solution to endure. The present cannot with
impunity turn its back on a thousand years of history; and statesmen
who attempt to build a settlement at variance with historical realities
doom themselves to appear, in the ceaseless annals of Clio, as myopic
dwarfs constructing with Lilliputian hammers a matchwood dam
against an irresistible stream.

The German problem confronting Europe to-day has been
analysed too exclusively in the light of the present and of the
immediate past; its origins have been traced to Hitler's seizure of
power in 1933, to the Versailles settlement of 1919, to the Franco-
Prussian war of 1870. But we shall never understand its essentials
unless we lengthen our perspective and realize how deep its roots go.
French memories of invasion reach back to 1870; but German
memories of unprovoked French aggression reach back to the
thirteenth century. One turning-point was 1648 and the creation in
the Peace of Westphalia of a European system designed to consecrate
German division and political impotence; for it was ultimately a
consequence of the system consolidated in 1648 that the problem of
German unity, when it came to a head in the nineteenth century,
became at once a European problem, and that the unification of
Germany took place under the aegis of Prussia, the only German
power capable of carrying through unification against foreign
opposition and despite the threat of foreign intervention. The
'Prussian solution' of the German problem was implicit in the
European situation. But it was helped also by the internal development of Germany, by the territorial fragmentation which became
irrevocable between 1356 and 1648; for this meant that unity, when
it came, was not a unification of the German people, but 'the
triumph of the most successful of German particularisms', asserting

its predominance over the rest of Germany.[1] In this respect, analysis
of the German problem of to-day takes us back, through the
generations, to the far-off days at the end of the eleventh century
when the old German monarchy, in the person of Henry IV,
suffered defeat at the hands of German particularism in alliance with
the papacy of Gregory VII. In the middle ages the only effective
guardian of the common heritage was a powerful monarchy,
capable of suppressing sectional interests; and the lasting result of
the events of 1076-1106 was that Germany, unlike England and
France, forewent the benefits of effective monarchical government
and after 1250 fell under the dominion of a princely aristocracy
which, powerfully aided by foreign intervention, strengthened its
hold in the centuries that followed. Princely particularism, the
unlimited sovereignty of the princes, was, as Bismarck said, 'a
revolutionary acquisition won at the expense of the nation'. By
stifling the development of the middle classes and accumulating
social and economic privileges in the hands of the few, it prevented
the peaceful evolution of German life into democratic forms
capable of expressing the will of the German people. The great
question of the nineteenth and twentieth centuries was to determine whether, in face of the rising demand for popular self-government in accordance with popular interests, the predominance of the
privileged classes was to be maintained and the destinies of the
German people subjected to the will of a narrow unrepresentative
minority. The outcome is all too well known. Through Bismarck's tactical skill, through the caution and timidity of the
leaders of 1918, and finally through the alliance of reaction and
privilege with Hitlerism, the popular forces suffered defeat. They
were defeated also because in 1918 the dominant forces in Europe
feared social revolution, which alone could have assured the victory
of German democracy, and because the victorious Entente, instead
of supporting the German revolt against Hohenzollern imperialism,
used its victory to pursue national policies, thus provoking a
counter-wave of nationalism in Germany which played into the
hands of the German 'national' parties, the inveterate enemies of the
republic, of peace and of democracy.[2] Thus 'the Allies', as a leading

[1] Cf. above, p. 423.
[2] Cf. W. N. Medlicott, *British Foreign Policy since Versailles* (1940), 299: 'The Versailles
settlement and the dark years that followed it called into being the irreconcilable right-wing
groups and ruined the chance of a general acceptance of Weimar Republicanism'.

British authority has said, 'after winning the war lost the peace'; by failing to use the victory of 1918 with reasonable intelligence, they made inevitable another catastrophe.[1]

The question in 1946 is whether the victorious powers will repeat the mistakes of 1919. The way to a lasting settlement is pointed unmistakably by sober historical analysis: it is to complete, in a framework of German unity, the process of democratization checked in 1918 and 1919, and this can be done in favourable conditions since there is, this time, no German army in existence to serve as a bulwark of reaction, while throughout Europe there is no disposition on the part of the ruling majorities to deny the need for radical social change. This is a policy of eliminating the factors which, through the ages, have retarded German development, and thus of preparing the way for Germany, purged of National Socialism, to take its place as an equal partner in Europe; it is a policy of stilling what has been called 'the sleepless antagonism between the beneficiaries and the victims of the *status quo*'.[2] But there is an alternative solution, a policy which, equating Germany with the German government and postulating the 'war guilt' of the German people, proposes to prevent its resurgence by a peace of desolation such as Rome imposed on Carthage, by territorial cessions, fragmentation and 'pastoralization'.[3] It is a policy which, as every reader of the foregoing story will perceive, implies the reversal by force of a long and powerful process of historical development, and is based upon the unwarrantable assumption that the German states – 'fortuitous agglomerations of territory', 'superimposed on the population regardless of race, geography or history'[4] – represent stable elements in German life. It goes without saying that such a solution, resurrecting the 'fantastic map of German particularism',[5] can only be imposed from outside, and postulates the ability of the victorious powers to erect new and, this time, unbreakable barriers to hold back the forces of German unity and German democracy. It is a

[1] G. P. Gooch, 'British Foreign Policy, 1919-1939', *Studies in Diplomacy and Statecraft* (1942), 224.

[2] Gooch, op. cit., 192.

[3] It is set out in detail in the notorious 'Morgenthau plan'; cf. H. Morgenthau, Jr., *Germany is our problem* (1945). The economic consequences of such a policy do not fall within the province of this book; but cf. E. H. Carr, *Conditions of Peace* (1942), 222 sqq., and the brief cogent argument in *Europe and Germany: To-day and To-morrow* (1945).

[4] Cf. above, pp. 345, 411.

[5] Cf. above, p. 147.

solution which, if undertaken, will last as long as the victorious powers unite to impose it, but no longer; at the first divergence of interests among the conquerors it will crumble. No one, within Germany or without, doubts that Germany's victims in the war of 1939-1945, France to the fore, have a just claim to security; but it is another question whether security lies this way. The French statesmen of the eighteenth century who repudiated the dangerous traditions of Philip the Fair and Richelieu, who counselled moderation and a renunciation of conquests at the expense of Germany realizing the risk for France of rousing an implacable German determination to recover the lost provinces, were wise in their own day and have much of lasting importance to teach European statesmen of the present.[1] 'One of the chief lessons of history', it has rightly been said, 'is the resilience of nations.' To-day, with Germany weak and broken, there is nothing to prevent the establishment, on the basis of military occupation, of a federal régime in a truncated Reich; but in what fatal resurgence of German power may it not end? The words uttered by Lloyd George in 1919 remain as true to-day as then:

> It is comparatively easy to patch up a peace which will last for thirty years. What is difficult is to draw up a peace which will not provoke a fresh struggle when those who have had practical experience of what war means have passed away ... You may strip Germany of her colonies, reduce her armaments to a mere police force and her navy to that of a fifth-rate power; all the same in the end if she feels that she has been unjustly treated ... she will find means of exacting retribution from her conquerors.

The truth of Lloyd George's prediction, uncompromisingly vindicated in 1939, should serve as a warning against any settlement which ignores the fundamental problems and the sweeping currents of history, and relies instead, as its instrument, on naked force and what a distinguished French historian once denounced as a *com-*

---

[1] The eighteenth-century reaction against the tradition of French encroachment on Germany is well described by Sorel, *L'Europe et la Révolution française* I, 311 sqq. Among those who doubted the wisdom of territorial annexations were d'Argenson (p. 313), Mirabeau (p. 318), Talleyrand (p. 317), and Vergennes, whose views, set out in a memoir of 1777, are summarized by Sorel (p. 314) as follows:' Les pays du Rhin sont très tentants; ils se prêtent d'une merveilleuse façon à l'arrondissement de la France; mais il faut réfléchir aux conséquences de l'annexation: le préjudice qui en résulterait dépasserait beaucoup l'étendue des bénéfices. La France demeurerait sans politique dans une Europe livrée à l'anarchie.'

munauté de convoitises. When in 1940 the British Labour Party proclaimed its belief that 'history teaches that any attempt to keep Germany an outcast after the war, or to deprive her of such security as her neighbours rightly claim for themselves, will fail', it was only repeating Lloyd George's warning in other words. When it went on to urge that 'the most far-sighted and least dangerous policy is to seek to win the co-operation, as an equal partner, of a Germany governed by a political system whose aims and needs run parallel with ours', it was setting out the framework of an alternative policy in which 'the just and real interests of all peoples will be respected, including those of the German people'. After the bitter experiences of National Socialism, such a policy requires courage and statesmanship of a high order; for the cruelty and oppression of the German conquerors in the Slav countries, their massacres and rapacity, have produced in the twentieth century a reaction no less formidable than that which occurred in the tenth century,[1] arousing passions which make far-sighted statesmanship difficult. Nevertheless the policy outlined in 1940 remains the only realistic policy. It is realistic because it does not forget the seventeen million votes cast against Hitler at the last free election in 1932; it is realistic because it takes account of the German liberal and working-class movements, the first victims of Hitlerism, which suffered from 1933 the martyrdom inflicted after 1939 on the other peoples of Europe; it is realistic because it comprehends that social and economic conditions are the determining factors in human society, and that social and economic conditions, as moulded by centuries of history, consistently thwarted the free expression of the will of the German people; it is realistic because it sees behind the façade of National Socialism, the product of a dozen years, the German people which has endured and laboured for a millennium, often oppressed and wretched, but contributing by its labours to the spread and flowering of European civilization. And yet its supreme realism lies elsewhere. It lies, firstly, in the fact that it is a policy which marches with history and renounces the vain attempt to reverse history's march. And it is realistic, finally and above all else, because it is a policy of conciliation, and only a conciliation of all peoples, including the German people, carries with it any assurance for the future. The problem of Germany can only be solved in the framework of a solution of the

[1] Cf. above, p. 42.

European problem; it is not a separate problem and has never, in the whole course of Germany's history, been a separate problem. What is at stake is not the fate of Germany alone, but the fate of Europe; for there can be no lasting settlement in Europe without a settlement of the German question which, removing the age-old bars to German unity and German democracy, permits the German people to take its place as an equal partner in the comity of European nations. The alternative, as Wilson foretold on his way to the peace conference in 1919, is 'another break-up of the world, and when such a break-up comes it will not be a war but a cataclysm'.

INDEX

INDEX

INDEX